Wesley's Notes on the Bible
The New Testament
By John Wesley
Edited by Anthony Uyl

Woodstock, Ontario, 2017

Wesley's Notes on the Bible - The New Testament

Wesley's Notes on the Bible - The New Testament
By John Wesley (1703-1791)
Edited by Anthony Uyl

The text of Wesley's Notes on the Bible - The New Testament is all in the Public Domain. This edition is published by Devoted Publishing a division of 2165467 Ontario Inc.

**What kind of philosophies do you have?
Let us know!**

Contact us at: devotedpub@hotmail.com
Visit our shop on Facebook: @DevotedPublishing

Published in Woodstock, Ontario, Canada 2017

For bulk educational rates, please contact us at the above email address.

ISBN: 978-1-77356-066-3

Table of Contents

PREFACE 4
NOTES ON THE GOSPEL ACCORDING TO ST. MATTHEW 6
NOTES ON THE GOSPEL ACCORDING TO ST. MARK 49
NOTES ON THE GOSPEL ACCORDING TO ST. LUKE 63
NOTES ON THE GOSPEL ACCORDING TO ST. JOHN 91
NOTES ON THE ACTS OF THE APOSTLES 120
NOTES ON ST PAUL'S EPISTLE TO THE ROMANS 157
NOTES ON ST. PAUL'S FIRST EPISTLE TO THE CORINTHIANS 185
NOTES ON ST. PAUL'S SECOND EPISTLE TO THE CORINTHIANS 207
NOTES ON ST. PAUL'S EPISTLE TO THE GALATIANS 219
NOTES ON ST. PAUL'S EPISTLE TO THE EPHESIANS 228
NOTES ON ST. PAUL'S EPISTLE TO THE PHILIPPIANS 238
NOTES ON ST. PAUL'S EPISTLE TO THE COLOSSIANS 244
NOTES ON ST. PAUL'S FIRST EPISTLE TO THE THESSALONIANS 249
NOTES ON ST. PAUL'S SECOND EPISTLE TO THE THESSALONIANS 253
NOTES ON ST. PAUL'S FIRST EPISTLE TO TIMOTHY 256
NOTES ON ST. PAUL'S SECOND EPISTLE TO TIMOTHY 263
NOTES ON ST. PAUL'S EPISTLE TO TITUS 267
NOTES ON ST. PAUL'S EPISTLE TO PHILEMON 270
NOTES ON THE EPISTLE TO THE HEBREWS 271
NOTES ON THE GENERAL EPISTLE OF ST. JAMES 289
NOTES ON THE FIRST EPISTLE GENERAL OF ST. PETER 295
NOTES ON THE SECOND EPISTLE GENERAL OF ST. PETER 302
NOTES ON THE FIRST EPISTLE OF ST. JOHN 307
NOTES ON THE SECOND EPISTLE OF ST. JOHN 315
NOTES ON THE THIRD EPISTLE OF ST. JOHN 316
NOTES ON THE GENERAL EPISTLE OF ST. JUDE 317
NOTES ON THE REVELATION OF JOHN 320

John Wesley

PREFACE

1. For many years I have had a desire of setting down and laying together, what has occurred to my mind, either in reading, thinking, or conversation, which might assist serious persons, who have not the advantage of learning, in understanding the New Testament. But I have been continually deterred from attempting any thing of this kind, by a deep sense of my own inability: of my want, not only of learning for such a work, but much more, of experience and wisdom. This has often occasioned my laying aside the thought. And when, by much importunity, I have been prevailed upon to resume it, still I determined to delay it as long as possible, that (if it should please God) I might finish my work and my life together.

2. But having lately had a loud call from God to arise and go hence, I am convinced that if I attempt any thing of this kind at all, I must not delay any longer. My day is far spent, and (even in a natural way) the shadows of the evening come on apace. And I am the rather induced to do what little I can in this way, because I can do nothing else: being prevented, by my present weakness, from either travelling or preaching. But, blessed be God, I can still read, and write, and think. O that it may be to his glory!

3. It will be easily discerned, even from what I have said already, and much more from the notes themselves, that they were not principally designed for men of learning; who are provided with many other helps: and much less for men of long and deep experience in the ways and word of God. I desire to sit at their feet, and to learn of them. But I write chiefly for plain unlettered men, who understand only their mother tongue, and yet reverence and love the word of God, and have a desire to save their souls.

4. In order to assist these in such a measure as I am able, I design first to set down the text itself, for the most part, in the common English translation, which is, in general, (so far as I can judge) abundantly the best that I have seen. Yet I do not say it is incapable of being brought, in several places, nearer to the original. Neither will I affirm, that the Greek copies from which this translation was made, are always the most correct. And therefore I shall take the liberty, as occasion may require, to make here and there a small alteration.

5. I am very sensible this will be liable to objections: nay, to objections of quite opposite kinds. Some will probably think, the text is altered too much; and others, that it is altered too little. To the former I would observe, that I never knowingly, so much as in one place, altered it for altering sake: but there, and there only, where first, the sense was made better, stronger, clearer, or more consistent with the context: secondly, where the sense being equally good, the phrase was better or nearer the original. To the latter, who think the alterations too few, and that the translation might have been nearer still, I answer, this is true: I acknowledge it might. But what valuable end would it have answered, to multiply such trivial alterations as add neither clearness nor strength to the text? This I could not prevail upon myself to do: so much the less because there is, to my apprehension, I know not what, peculiarly solemn and venerable in the old language of our translation. And suppose this a mistaken apprehension, and an instance of human infirmity; yet, is it not an excusable infirmity, to be unwilling to part with what we have been long accustomed to; and to love the very words by which God has often conveyed strength or comfort to our souls!

6. I have endeavoured to make the notes as short as possible that the comment may not obscure or swallow up the text: and as plain as possible, in pursuance of my main design, to assist the unlearned reader: for this reason I have studiously avoided, not only all curious and critical inquiries, and all use of the learned languages, but all such methods of reasoning and modes of expression as people in common life are unacquainted with: for the same reason, as I rather endeavour to obviate than to propose and answer questions, so I purposely decline going deep into many difficulties, lest I should leave the ordinary reader behind me.

7. I once designed to write down barely what occurred, to my own mind, consulting none but the inspired writers. But no sooner was I acquainted with that great light of the Christian world, (lately gone to his reward,) Bengelius, than I entirely changed my design, being thoroughly convinced it might be of more service to the cause of religion, were I barely to translate his Gnomon Novi Testamenti, than to write many volumes upon it. Many of his excellent notes I have therefore translated. Many more I have abridged, omitting that part which was purely critical, and giving the substance of the rest. Those

various readings likewise, which he has showed to have a vast majority of ancient copies and translations on their side, I have without scruple incorporated with the text; which, after his manner, I have divided all along (though not omitting the common division into chapters and verses, which is of use on various accounts) according to the matter it contains, making a larger or smaller pause, just as the sense requires. And even this is such a help in many places, as one who has not tried it can scarcely conceive.

8. I am likewise indebted for some useful observations to Dr. Heylin's Theological Lectures: and for many more to Dr. Guyse, and to the Family Expositor of the late pious and learned Dr. Doddridge. It was a doubt with me for some time, whether I should not subjoin to every note I received from them the name of the author from whom it was taken; especially considering I had transcribed some, and abridged many more, almost in the words of the author. But upon further consideration, I resolved to name none, that nothing might divert the mind of the reader from keeping close to the point in view, and receiving what was spoken only according to its own intrinsic value.

9. I cannot flatter myself so far (to use the words of one of the above-named writers) as to imagine that I have fallen into no mistakes in a work of so great difficulty. But my own conscience acquits me of having designedly misrepresented any single passage of Scripture, or of having written one line with a purpose of inflaming the hearts of Christians against each other. God forbid that I should make the words of the most gentle and benevolent Jesus a vehicle to convey such poison. Would to God that all the party names, and unscriptural phrases and forms, which have divided the Christian world, were forgot: and that we might all agree to sit down together, as humble, loving disciples, at the feet of our common Master, to hear his word, to imbibe his Spirit, and to transcribe his life in our own!

10. Concerning the Scriptures in general, it may be observed, the word of the living God, which directed the first patriarchs also, was, in the time of Moses, committed to writing. To this were added, in several succeeding generations, the inspired writings of the other prophets. Afterward, what the Son of God preached, and the Holy Ghost spake by the apostles, the apostles and evangelists wrote. - This is what we now style the Holy Scripture: this is that word of God which remaineth forever: of which, though heaven and earth pass away, one jot or tittle shall not pass away. The Scripture therefore of the Old and New Testament is a most solid and precious system of Divine truth. Every part thereof is worthy of God; and all together are one entire body, wherein is no defect, no excess. It is the fountain of heavenly wisdom, which they who are able to taste, prefer to all writings of men, however wise, or learned, or holy.

11. An exact knowledge of the truth was accompanied in the inspired writers with an exactly regular series of arguments, a precise expression of their meaning, and a genuine vigour of suitable affections. The chain of argument in each book is briefly exhibited in the table prefixed to it, which contains also the sum thereof, and may be of more use than prefixing the argument to each chapter; the division of the New Testament into chapters having been made in the dark ages, and very incorrectly; often separating things that are closely joined, and joining those that are entirely distinct from each other.

12. In the language of the sacred writings, we may observe the utmost depth, together with the utmost ease. All the elegancies of human composures sink into nothing before it: God speaks not as man, but as God. His thoughts are very deep: and thence his words are of inexhaustible virtue. And the language of his messengers also is exact in the highest degree: for the words which were given them accurately answered the impression made upon their minds: and hence Luther says, "Divinity is nothing but a grammar of the language of the Holy Ghost." To understand this thoroughly, we should observe the emphasis which lies on every word; the holy affections expressed thereby, and the tempers shown by every writer. But how little are these, the latter especially, regarded? Though they are wonderfully diffused through the whole New Testament, and are in truth a continued commendation of him who acts, or speaks, or writes.

13. The New Testament is all those sacred writings in which the New Testament or covenant is described. The former part of this contains the writings of the evangelists and apostles: the latter, the Revelation of Jesus Christ. In the former is, first, the history of Jesus Christ, from his coming in the flesh to his ascension into heaven; then the institution and history of the Christian Church, from the time of his ascension. The Revelation delivers what is to be, with regard to Christ, the Church, and the universe, till the consummation of all things. BRISTOL HOT-WELLS, January 4, 1754.

NOTES ON THE GOSPEL ACCORDING TO ST. MATTHEW

THE Gospel (that is, good tidings) means a book containing the good tidings of our salvation by Jesus Christ. St. Mark in his Gospel presupposes that of St. Matthew, and supplies what is omitted therein. St. Luke supplies what is omitted by both the former: St. John what is omitted by all the three. St. Matthew particularly points out the fulfilling of the prophecies for the conviction of the Jews. St. Mark wrote a short compendium, and yet added many remarkable circumstances omitted by St. Matthew, particularly with regard to the apostles, immediately after they were called. St. Luke treated principally of the office of Christ, and mostly in a historical manner. St. John refuted those who denied his Godhead: each choosing to treat more largely on those things, which most suited the time when, and the persons to whom, he wrote.

The Gospel according to St. Matthew contains,

I. The birth of Christ, and what presently followed it
    a. His genealogy Chap i. 1-17
    b. His birth 18-25
    c. The coming of the wise men ii, 1-12
    d. His flight into Egypt, and return 13-23

II. The introduction
    a. John the Baptist iii, 1-12
    b. The baptism of Christ 13-17
    c. His temptation and victory iv, 1-11

III. The actions and words by which Jesus proved he was the Christ
    a. At Capernaum 12-16

Where we may observe
    1. His preaching 17
    2. Calling Andrew and Peter, James and John 18-22
    3. Preaching and healing, 23-25
    4. Sermon on the mount v, vi, vii
    5. Healing the leper viii, 1-4
    6. The centurion's servant 5-13
    7. Peter's mother-in-law 14-15
    8. Many that were sick 16-17
        b. In his journey (wherein he admonished two that offered to follow him) over the sea. Here we may observe
    1. His dominion over the winds and seas 18-27
    2. The devils passing from the men into the swine 28-34
        c. At Capernaum again Here, ix,
1. He cures the paralytic 1-8
2. Calls Matthew, and defends his conversing with publicans and sinners 9-13
3. Answers concerning fasting 14-17
4. Raises Jairus's daughter (after curing the issue of blood). 18-26
5. Gives sight to two blind men 27-31
6. Dispossesses the demoniac 32-34
7. Goes through the cities, and directs to pray for labourers. 35-38
8. Sends and instructs labourers, and preaches himself. x, 1; xi, 1
9. Answers the message of John 2-6
10. Commends John, reproves the unbelieving cities, invites the weary 7-30
11. Defends the disciples' plucking the corn Chap. xii, 1-8

12. Heals the withered hand 9-13
13. Retires from the Pharisees lying in wait 14-21
14. Cures the demoniac, while the people wonder, and the Pharisees blaspheming, are refuted 22-37
15. Reproves them that require a sign 38-45
16. Declares who are his relations, and 46-50
17. Teaches by parables xiii, 1-52
    d. At Nazareth 53-58
    e. In other places

1. Herod having killed John, doubts concerning Jesus. Jesus retiring, is sought for by the people xiv, 1-13
2. He heals the sick, and feeds five thousand 14-21
3. His voyage and miracles in the land of Gennesaret 22-36
4. Unwashen hands xv, 1-20
5. The woman of Canaan 21-28
6. Many sick healed 29-31
7. Four thousand fed 32-38
8. Those who require a sign reproved xv, 39; xvi, 1-4
9. The leaven of the Pharisees 5-12

IV. Predictions of his death and resurrection
    a. The first prediction
1. Preparation for it by a confirmation that he is the Christ. 13-20
2. The prediction itself, and reproof of Peter 21-28
    b. The second prediction
1. The transfiguration, and silence enjoined xvii, 1-13
2. The lunatic healed 14-21
3. The prediction itself 22-23
4. The tribute paid 24-27
5. Who is greatest in Christ's kingdom xviii, 1-20
6. The duty of forgiving our brother 21-35
    c. The third prediction
1. Jesus departs out of Galilee xix, 1-2
2 Of divorce and celibacy 3-12
3. His tenderness to little children 13-15
4. The rich man drawing back, and hence 16-22 Of the salvation of the rich 23-26 Of the reward of following Christ 27-30 Of the last and the first xx, 1-16
5. The prediction itself 17-19
6. The request of James and John; humility enjoined 20-28
7. The two blind men cured 29-34

V. Transactions at Jerusalem before his passion
    a. Sunday His royal entry into Jerusalem xxi, 1-11 His purging the temple 12-17
    b. Monday The barren fig tree 18-22
    c. Tuesday, transactions In the temple
1. The chief priests and elders confuted By a question concerning John's baptism 23-27 By the parables Of the two sons 28-32 Of the vineyard 33-44
2. Seek to lay hands on him 45-46
3. The parable of the marriage feast xxii, 1-14
4. He is questioned, concerning paying tribute 15-22 The resurrection 23-33 The great commandment 34-40
5. Christ's question concerning David's Lord 41-46 Caution concerning the scribes and Pharisees xxiii, 1-12 Severe reproof of them 13-36 and of Jerusalem 37-39 Out of the temple:
1. His discourse of the destruction of Jerusalem, and the end of the world Chap. xxiv, 1-51
2. The ten virgins, the talents; the last judgment . xxv, 1-46

VI. His passion and resurrection
    A. His passion, death, and burial xxvi, 1-2
        a. Wednesday His prediction xxvi, 1-2 The consultation of the chief priests and elders 3-5 Judas bargains to betray him 6-16
        b. Thursday

1. In the day time The passover prepared 17-19
2. In the evening The traitor discovered 20-25 The Lord's Supper 26-29
3. In the night

1. Jesus foretells the cowardice of the apostles 33-35
2. Is in agony 36-46
3. Is apprehended, reproves Peter and the multitude; is forsaken of all 47-56
4. Is led to Caiaphas, falsely accused, owns himself the Son of God, is condemned, derided 57-68
5. Peter denies him and weeps 69-75
   c. Friday
1. The height of his passion In the morning
1. Jesus is delivered to Pilate xxvii, 1-2
2. The death of Judas 3-10
3. Jesus's kingdom and silence 11-14
4. Pilate, though warned by his wife, condemns him 15-26
5. He is mocked and led forth 27-32 The third hour The vinegar and gall: the crucifixion; his garments divided; the inscription on the cross; the two robbers; blasphemies 33-44 From the sixth to the ninth hour The darkness, his last agony 45-49
2. His death 50 The veil rent, and a great earthquake 51-53 The centurion wonders; the women behold 54-56
3. His burial 57-61
d. Saturday The sepulchre secured 62-66
B. His resurrection
1. Testified to the women by an angel xxviii, 1-8 By our Lord himself 9-10
2. Denied by his adversaries 11-15
1. Proved to his apostles 16-20

ST. MATTHEW

I

1. The book of the generation of Jesus Christ -- that is, strictly speaking, the account of his birth and genealogy. This title therefore properly relates to the verses that immediately follow: but as it sometimes signifies the history of a person, in that sense it may belong to the whole book. If there were any difficulties in this genealogy, or that given by St. Luke, which could not easily be removed, they would rather affect the Jewish tables, than the credit of the evangelists: for they act only as historians setting down these genealogies, as they stood in those public and allowed records. Therefore they were to take them as they found them. Nor was it needful they should correct the mistakes, if there were any. For these accounts sufficiently answer the end for which they are recited. They unquestionably prove the grand point in view, that Jesus was of the family from which the promised seed was to come. And they had more weight with the Jews for this purpose, than if alterations had been made by inspiration itself. For such alterations would have occasioned endless disputes between them and the disciples of our Lord. The son of David, the son of Abraham - He is so called, because to these he was more peculiarly promised; and of these it was often foretold the Messiah should spring. Luke iii, 31.

3. Of Thamar - St. Matthew adds the names of those women also, that were remarkable in the sacred history.

4. Naasson -- who was prince of the tribe of Judah, when the Israelites entered into Canaan.

5. Obed begat Jesse -- the providence of God was peculiarly shown in this, that Salmon, Boaz, and Obed, must each of them have been near a hundred years old, at the birth of his son here recorded.

6. David the king -- particularly mentioned under this character, because his throne is given to the Messiah.

8. Jehoram begat Uzziah - Jehoahaz, Joash, and Amaziah coming between. So that he begat him mediately, as Christ is mediately the son of David and of Abraham. So the progeny of Hezekiah, after many generations, are called the sons that should issue from him, which he should beget, Isaiah xxxix, 7.

11. Josiah begat Jeconiah -- mediately, Jehoiakim coming between. And his brethren - That is, his uncles. The Jews term all kinsmen brethren. About the time they were carried away -- which was a little after the birth of Jeconiah.

16. The husband of Mary - Jesus was generally believed to be the son of Joseph. It was needful for all who believed this, to know, that Joseph was sprung from David. Otherwise they would not allow Jesus to be the Christ. Jesus, who is called Christ - The name Jesus respects chiefly the promise of blessing made to Abraham: the name Christ, the promise of the Messiah's kingdom, which was made to

David. It may be further observed, that the word Christ in Greek, and Messiah in Hebrews, signify anointed, and imply the prophetic, priestly, and royal characters, which were to meet in the Messiah. Among the Jews, anointing was the ceremony whereby prophets, priests, and kings were initiated into those offices. And if we look into ourselves, we shall find a want of Christ in all these respects. We are by nature at a distance from God, alienated from him, and incapable of a free access to him. Hence we want a mediator, an intercessor, in a word, a Christ, in his priestly office. This regards our state with respect to God. And with respect to ourselves, we find a total darkness, blindness, ignorance of God, and the things of God. Now here we want Christ in his prophetic office, to enlighten our minds, and teach us the whole will of God. We find also within us a strange misrule of appetites and passions. For these we want Christ in his royal character, to reign in our hearts, and subdue all things to himself.

17. So all the generations -- observe, in order to complete the three fourteens, David ends the first fourteen, and begins the second (which reaches to the captivity) and Jesus ends the third fourteen. When we survey such a series of generations, it is a natural and obvious reflection, how like the leaves of a tree one passeth away, and another cometh! Yet the earth still abideth. And with it the goodness of the Lord which runs from generation to generation, the common hope of parents and children. Of those who formerly lived upon earth, and perhaps made the most conspicuous figure, how many are there whose names are perished with them? How many, of whom only the names are remaining? Thus are we likewise passing away! And thus shall we shortly be forgotten! Happy are we, if, while we are forgotten by men, we are remembered by God! If our names, lost on earth, are at length found written in the book of life!

19. A just man -- a strict observer of the law: therefore not thinking it right to keep her.

21. Jesus - That is, a Saviour. It is the same name with Joshua (who was a type of him) which properly signifies, The Lord, Salvation. His people - Israel. And all the Israel of God.

23. They shall call his name Emmanuel -- to be called, only means, according to the Hebrews manner of speaking, that the person spoken of shall really and effectually be what he is called, and actually fulfil that title. Thus, Unto us a child is born - and his name shall be called Wonderful, Counsellor, the Mighty God, the Prince of Peace -- that is, he shall be all these, though not so much nominally, as really, and in effect. And thus was he called Emmanuel; which was no common name of Christ, but points out his nature and office; as he is God incarnate, and dwells by his Spirit in the hearts of his people. It is observable, the words in Isaiah are, Thou (namely, his mother) shalt call; but here, They - that is, all his people, shall call - shall acknowledge him to be Emmanuel, God with us. Which being interpreted -- this is a clear proof that St. Matthew wrote his Gospel in Greek, and not in Hebrew. Isaiah vii, 14.

25. He knew her not, till after she had brought forth. It cannot be inferred from hence, that he knew her afterward: no more than it can be inferred from that expression, 2 Sam. vi, 23, Michal had no child till the day of her death, that she had children afterward. Nor do the words that follow, the first-born son, alter the case. For there are abundance of places, wherein the term first born is used, though there were no subsequent children. Luke ii, 7.

II

1. Bethlehem of Judea - There was another Bethlehem in the tribe of Zebulon. In the days of Herod - commonly called Herod the Great, born at Ascalon. The scepter was now on the point of departing from Judah. Among his sons were Archelaus, mentioned ver. 22; Herod Antipas, mentioned chap. xiv, and Philip, mentioned Luke iii, 19. Herod Agrippa, mentioned Acts xii, 1; &c., was his grandson. Wise men - The first fruits of the Gentiles. Probably they were Gentile philosophers, who, through the Divine assistance, had improved their knowledge of nature, as a means of leading to the knowledge of the one true God. Nor is it unreasonable to suppose, that God had favoured them with some extraordinary Revelations of himself, as he did Melchisedec, Job, and several others, who were not of the family of Abraham; to which he never intended absolutely to confine his favours. The title given them in the original was anciently given to all philosophers, or men of learning; those particularly who were curious in examining the works of nature, and observing the motions of the heavenly bodies. From the east - So Arabia is frequently called in Scripture. It lay to the east of Judea, and was famous for gold, frankincense, and myrrh. We have seen his star - Undoubtedly they had before heard Balaam's prophecy. And probably when they saw this unusual star, it was revealed to them that this prophecy was fulfilled. In the east - That is, while we were in the east.

2. To do him homage - To pay him that honour, by bowing to the earth before him, which the eastern nations used to pay to their monarchs.

4. The chief priests - That is, not only the high priest and his deputy, with those who formerly had born that office: but also the chief man in each of those twenty-four courses, into which the body of priests were divided, 1 Chron. xxiv, 6-19. The scribes were those whose peculiar business it was to explain the Scriptures to the people. They were the public preachers, or expounders of the law of Moses.

Wesley's Notes on the Bible - The New Testament

Whence the chief of them were called doctors of the law.

6. Thou art in nowise the least among the princes of Judah - That is, among the cities belonging to the princes or heads of thousands in Judah. When this and several other quotations from the Old Testament are compared with the original, it plainly appears, the apostles did not always think it necessary exactly to transcribe the passages they cited, but contented themselves with giving the general sense, though with some diversity of language. The words of Micah, which we render, Though thou be little, may be rendered, Art thou little? And then the difference which seems to be here between the prophet and the evangelist vanishes away. Micah v, 2.

8. And if ye find him, bring me word - Probably Herod did not believe he was born; otherwise would not so suspicious a prince have tried to make sure work at once?

10. Seeing the star - Standing over where the child was.

11. They presented to him gifts - It was customary to offer some present to any eminent person whom they visited. And so it is, as travelers observe, in the eastern countries to this day. Gold, frankincense, and myrrh - Probably these were the best things their country afforded; and the presents ordinarily made to great persons. This was a most seasonable, providential assistance for a long and expensive journey into Egypt, a country where they were entirely strangers, and were to stay for a considerable time.

15. That it might be fulfilled - That is, whereby was fulfilled. The original word frequently signifies, not the design of an action, but barely the consequence or event of it. Which was spoken of the Lord by the prophet - on another occasion: Out of Egypt have I called my Son - which was now fulfilled as it were anew; Christ being in a far higher sense the Son of God than Israel, of whom the words were originally spoken. Hosea xi, 1.

16. Then Herod, seeing that he was deluded by the wise men - So did his pride teach him to regard this action, as if it were intended to expose him to the derision of his subjects. Sending forth - a party of soldiers: In all the confines thereof - In all the neighbouring places, of which Rama was one.

17. Then was fulfilled - A passage of Scripture, whether prophetic, historical, or poetical, is in the language of the New Testament fulfilled, when an event happens to which it may with great propriety be accommodated.

18. Rachel weeping for her children - The Benjamites, who inhabited Rama, sprung from her. She was buried near this place; and is here beautifully represented risen, as it were out of her grave, and bewailing her lost children. Because they are not - that is, are dead. The preservation of Jesus from this destruction, may be considered as a figure of God's care over his children in their greatest danger. God does not often, as he easily could, cut off their persecutors at a stroke. But he provides a hiding place for his people, and by methods not less effectual, though less pompous, preserves them from being swept away, even when the enemy comes in like a flood. Jer. xxxi, 15.

22. He was afraid to go thither - into Judea; and so turned aside into the region of Galilee - a part of the land of Israel not under the jurisdiction of Archelaus.

23. He came and dwelt in Nazareth - (where he had dwelt before he went to Bethlehem) a place contemptible to a proverb. So that hereby was fulfilled what has been spoken in effect by several of the prophets, (though by none of them in express words,) He shall be called a Nazarene - that is, he shall be despised and rejected, shall be a mark of public contempt and reproach.

III

1. In those days - that is, while Jesus dwelt there. In the wilderness of Judea - This was a wilderness properly so called, a wild, barren, desolate place as was that also where our Lord was tempted. But, generally speaking, a wilderness in the New Testament means only a common, or less cultivated place, in opposition to pasture and arable land. Mark i, 1; Luke iii, 1.

2. The kingdom of heaven, and the kingdom of God, are but two phrases for the same thing. They mean, not barely a future happy state, in heaven, but a state to be enjoyed on earth: the proper disposition for the glory of heaven, rather than the possession of it. Is at hand - As if he had said, God is about to erect that kingdom, spoken of by Daniel, Dan. ii, 44; vii, 13, 14; the kingdom of the God of heaven. It properly signifies here, the Gospel dispensation, in which subjects were to be gathered to God by his Son, and a society to be formed, which was to subsist first on earth, and afterward with God in glory. In some places of Scripture, the phrase more particularly denotes the state of it on earth: in, others, it signifies only the state of glory: but it generally includes both. The Jews understood it of a temporal kingdom, the seat of which they supposed would be Jerusalem; and the expected sovereign of this kingdom they learned from Daniel to call the Son of man. Both John the Baptist and Christ took up that phrase, the kingdom of heaven, as they found it, and gradually taught the Jews (though greatly unwilling to learn) to understand it right. The very demand of repentance, as previous to it, showed it was a spiritual kingdom, and that no wicked man, how politic, brave, or learned soever, could possibly be a subject of it.

John Wesley

3. The way of the Lord - Of Christ. Make his paths straight - By removing every thing which might prove a hindrance to his gracious appearance. Isaiah xl, 3.

4. John had his raiment of camel's hair - Coarse and rough, suiting his character and doctrine. A leathern girdle - Like Elijah, in whose spirit and power he came. His food was locusts and wild honey - Locusts are ranked among clean meats, Lev. xi, 22. But these were not always to be had. So in default of those, he fed on wild honey.

6. Confessing their sins - Of their own accord; freely and openly. Such prodigious numbers could hardly be baptized by immerging their whole bodies under water: nor can we think they were provided with change of raiment for it, which was scarcely practicable for such vast multitudes. And yet they could not be immerged naked with modesty, nor in their wearing apparel with safety. It seems, therefore, that they stood in ranks on the edge of the river, and that John, passing along before them, cast water on their heads or faces, by which means he might baptize many thousands in a day. And this way most naturally signified Christ's baptizing them with the Holy Ghost and with fire, which John spoke of, as prefigured by his baptizing with water, and which was eminently fulfilled, when the Holy Ghost sat upon the disciples in the appearance of tongues, or flames of fire.

7. The Pharisees were a very ancient sect among the Jews. They took their name from a Hebrew word, which signifies to separate, because they separated themselves from all other men. They were outwardly strict observers of the law, fasted often, made long prayers, rigorously kept the Sabbath, and paid all tithe, even of mint, anise, and cummin. Hence they were in high esteem among the people. But inwardly, they were full of pride and hypocrisy. The Sadducees were another sect among the Jews, only not so considerable as the Pharisees. They denied the existence of angels, and the immortality of the soul, and by consequence the resurrection of the dead. Ye brood of vipers - In like manner, the crafty Herod is styled a fox, and persons of insidious, ravenous, profane, or sensual dispositions, are named respectively by him who saw their hearts, serpents, dogs, wolves, and swine; terms which are not the random language of passion, but a judicious designation of the persons meant by them. For it was fitting such men should be marked out, either for a caution to others, or a warning to themselves.

8. Repentance is of two sorts; that which is termed legal, and that which is styled evangelical repentance. The former (which is the same that is spoken of here) is a thorough conviction of sin. The latter is a change of heart (and consequently of life) from all sin to all holiness.

9. And say not confidently - The word in the original, vulgarly rendered, Think not, seems here, and in many places, not to diminish, but rather add to the force of the word with which it is joined. We have Abraham to our father - It is almost incredible, how great the presumption of the Jews was on this their relation to Abraham. One of their famous sayings was, "Abraham sits near the gates of hell, and suffers no Israelite to go down into it." I say unto you - This preface always denotes the importance of what follows. Of these stones - Probably pointing to those which lay before them.

10. But the axe also already lieth - That is, there is no room for such idle pretenses. Speedy execution is determined against all that do not repent. The comparison seems to be taken from a woodman that has laid down his axe to put off his coat, and then immediately goes to work to cut down the tree. This refers to the wrath to come in verse 7. Is hewn down - Instantly, without farther delay.

11. He shall baptize you with the Holy Ghost and with fire - He shall fill you with the Holy Ghost, inflaming your hearts with that fire of love, which many waters cannot quench. And this was done, even with a visible appearance as of fire, on the day of pentecost.

12. Whose fan - That is, the word of the Gospel. His floor - That is, his Church, which is now covered with a mixture of wheat and chaff. He will gather the wheat into the garner - Will lay up those who are truly good in heaven.

13. Mark i, 9; Luke iii, 21

15. It becometh us to fulfil all righteousness - It becometh every messenger of God to observe all his righteous ordinances. But the particular meaning of our Lord seems to be, that it becometh us to do (me to receive baptism, and you to administer it) in order to fulfil, that is, that I may fully perform every part of the righteous law of God, and the commission he hath given me.

16. And Jesus being baptized - Let our Lord's submitting to baptism teach us a holy exactness in the observance of those institutions which owe their obligation merely to a Divine command. Surely thus it becometh all his followers to fulfil all righteousness. Jesus had no sin to wash away. And yet he was baptized. And God owned his ordinance, so as to make it the season of pouring forth the Holy Spirit upon him. And where can we expect this sacred effusion, but in an humble attendance on Divine appointments? Lo, the heavens were opened, and he saw the Spirit of God - St. Luke adds, in a bodily form - Probably in a glorious appearance of fire, perhaps in the shape of a dove, descending with a hovering motion, till it rested upon him. This was a visible token of those secret operations of the blessed Spirit, by which he was anointed in a peculiar manner; and abundantly fitted for his public work.

17. And lo, a voice - We have here a glorious manifestation of the ever - blessed Trinity: the Father speaking from heaven, the Son spoken to, the Holy Ghost descending upon him. In whom I

delight - What an encomium is this! How poor to this are all other kinds of praise! To be the pleasure, the delight of God, this is praise indeed: this is true glory: this is the highest, the brightest light, that virtue can appear in.

IV

1. Then - After this glorious evidence of his Father's love, he was completely armed for the combat. Thus after the clearest light and the strongest consolation, let us expect the sharpest temptations. By the Spirit - Probably through a strong inward impulse. Mark i, 12; Luke iv, 1.

2. Having fasted - Whereby doubtless he received more abundant spiritual strength from God. Forty days and forty nights - As did Moses, the giver of the law, and Elijah, the great restorer of it. He was afterward hungry - And so prepared for the first temptation.

3. Coming to him - In a visible form; probably in a human shape, as one that desired to inquire further into the evidences of his being the Messiah.

4. It is written - Thus Christ answered, and thus we may answer all the suggestions of the devil. By every word that proceedeth out of the mouth of God - That is, by whatever God commands to sustain him. Therefore it is not needful I should work a miracle to procure bread, without any intimation of my Father's will. Deut. viii, 3.

5. The holy city - So Jerusalem was commonly called, being the place God had peculiarly chosen for himself. On the battlement of the temple - Probably over the king's gallery, which was of such a prodigious height, that no one could look down from the top of it without making himself giddy.

6. In their hands - That is, with great care. Psalm xci, 11, 12.

7. Thou shalt not tempt the Lord thy God - By requiring farther evidence of what he hath already made sufficiently plain. Deut. vi, 16.

8. Showeth him all the kingdoms of the world - In a kind of visionary representation.

9. If thou wilt fall down and worship me - Here Satan clearly shows who he was. Accordingly Christ answering this suggestion, calls him by his own name, which he had not done before.

10. Get thee hence, Satan - Not, get thee behind me, that is, into thy proper place; as he said on a quite different occasion to Peter, speaking what was not expedient. Deut. vi, 13.

11. Angels came and waited upon him - Both to supply him with food, and to congratulate his victory.

12. He retired into Galilee - This journey was not immediately after his temptation. He first went from Judea into Galilee, John i, 43; ii, 1. Then into Judea again, and celebrated the passover at Jerusalem, John ii, 13. He baptized in Judea while John was baptizing at Enon, John iii, 22, 23. All this time John was at liberty, John iii, 24. But the Pharisees being offended, John iv, 1; and John put in prison, he then took this journey into Galilee. Mark i, 14.

13. Leaving Nazareth - Namely, when they had wholly rejected his word, and even attempted to kill him, Luke iv, 29.

15. Galilee of the Gentiles - That part of Galilee which lay beyond Jordan was so called, because it was in a great measure inhabited by Gentiles, that is, heathens. Isaiah ix, 1, 2.

16. Here is a beautiful gradation, first, they walked, then they sat in darkness, and lastly, in the region of the shadow of death.

17. From that time Jesus began to preach - He had preached before, both to Jews and Samaritans, John iv, 41, 45. But from this time begin his solemn stated preaching. Repent, for the kingdom of heaven is at hand - Although it is the peculiar business of Christ to establish the kingdom of heaven in the hearts of men, yet it is observable, he begins his preaching in the same words with John the Baptist: because the repentance which John taught still was, and ever will be, the necessary preparation for that inward kingdom. But that phrase is not only used with regard to individuals in whom it is to be established, but also with regard to the Christian Church, the whole body of believers. In the former sense it is opposed to repentance; in the latter the Mosaic dispensation.

18. Mark i, 16; Luke v, 1.

23. The Gospel of the kingdom - The Gospel, that is, the joyous message, is the proper name of our religion: as will be amply verified in all who earnestly and perseveringly embrace it.

24. Through all Syria - The whole province, of which the Jewish country was only a small part. And demoniacs - Men possessed with devils: and lunatics, and paralytics - Men ill of the palsy, whose cases were of all others most deplorable and most helpless.

25. Decapolis - A tract of land on the east side of the sea of Galilee, in which were ten cities near each other.

John Wesley

V

1. And seeing the multitudes - At some distance, as they were coming to him from every quarter. He went up into the mountain - Which was near: where there was room for them all. His disciples - not only his twelve disciples, but all who desired to learn of him.

2. And he opened his mouth - A phrase which always denotes a set and solemn discourse; and taught them - To bless men; to make men happy, was the great business for which our Lord came into the world. And accordingly he here pronounces eight blessings together, annexing them to so many steps in Christianity. Knowing that happiness is our common aim, and that an innate instinct continually urges us to the pursuit of it, he in the kindest manner applies to that instinct, and directs it to its proper object. Though all men desire, yet few attain, happiness, because they seek it where it is not to be found. Our Lord therefore begins his Divine institution, which is the complete art of happiness, by laying down before all that have ears to hear, the true and only true method of acquiring it. Observe the benevolent condescension of our Lord. He seems, as it were, to lay aside his supreme authority as our legislator, that he may the better act the part of: our friend and saviour. Instead of using the lofty style, in positive commands, he, in a more gentle and engaging way, insinuates his will and our duty, by pronouncing those happy who comply with it.

3. Happy are the poor - In the following discourse there is,

1. A sweet invitation to true holiness and happiness, ver. 3-12.

2. A persuasive to impart it to others, ver. 13-16.

3. A description of true Christian holiness, ver. 17; chap.vii, 12. (in which it is easy to observe, the latter part exactly answers the former.)

4. The conclusion: giving a sure mark of the true way, warning against false prophets, exhorting to follow after holiness. The poor in spirit - They who are unfeignedly penitent, they who are truly convinced of sin; who see and feel the state they are in by nature, being deeply sensible of their sinfulness, guiltiness, helplessness. For theirs is the kingdom of heaven - The present inward kingdom: righteousness, and peace, and joy in the Holy Ghost, as well as the eternal kingdom, if they endure to the end. Luke vi, 20.

4. They that mourn - Either for their own sins, or for other men's, and are steadily and habitually serious. They shall be comforted - More solidly and deeply even in this world, and eternally in heaven.

5. Happy are the meek - They that hold all their passions and affections evenly balanced. They shall inherit the earth - They shall have all things really necessary for life and godliness. They shall enjoy whatever portion God hath given them here, and shall hereafter possess the new earth, wherein dwelleth righteousness.

6. They that hunger and thirst after righteousness - After the holiness here described. They shall be satisfied with it.

7. The merciful - The tender-hearted: they who love all men as themselves: They shall obtain mercy - Whatever mercy therefore we desire from God, the same let us show to our brethren. He will repay us a thousand fold, the love we bear to any for his sake.

8. The pure in heart - The sanctified: they who love God with all their hearts. They shall see God - In all things here; hereafter in glory.

9. The peace makers - They that out of love to God and man do all possible good to all men. Peace in the Scripture sense implies all blessings temporal and eternal. They shall be called the children of God - Shall be acknowledged such by God and man. One would imagine a person of this amiable temper and behaviour would be the darling of mankind. But our Lord well knew it would not be so, as long as Satan was the prince of this world. He therefore warns them before of the treatment all were to expect, who were determined thus to tread in his steps, by immediately subjoining, Happy are they who are persecuted for righteousness' sake. Through this whole discourse we cannot but observe the most exact method which can possibly be conceived. Every paragraph, every sentence, is closely connected both with that which precedes, and that which follows it. And is not this the pattern for every Christian preacher? If any then are able to follow it without any premeditation, well: if not, let them not dare to preach without it. No rhapsody, no incoherency, whether the things spoken be true or false, comes of the Spirit of Christ.

10. For righteousness' sake - That is, because they have, or follow after, the righteousness here described. He that is truly a righteous man, he that mourns, and he that is pure in heart, yea, all that will live godly in Christ Jesus, shall suffer persecution, 2 Tim. iii, 12. The world will always say, Away with such fellows from the earth. They are made to reprove our thoughts. They are grievous to us even to behold. Their lives are not like other men's; their ways are of another fashion.

11. Revile - When present: say all evil - When you are absent.

12. Your reward - Even over and above the happiness that naturally and directly results from holiness.

13. Ye - Not the apostles, not ministers only; but all ye who are thus holy, are the salt of the earth -

Are to season others. Mark ix, 50; Luke xiv, 34.

14. *Ye are the light of the world* - If ye are thus holy, you can no more be hid than the sun in the firmament: no more than a city on a mountain - Probably pointing to that on the brow of the opposite hill.

15. Nay, the very design of God in giving you this light was, that it might shine. Mark iv, 21; Luke viii, 16; xi, 33.

16. *That they may see* - and *glorify* - That is, that seeing your good works, they may be moved to love and serve God likewise.

17. *Think not* - Do not imagine, fear, hope, that *I am come* - Like your teachers, to destroy the law or the prophets. *I am not come to destroy* - The moral law, but *to fulfil* - To establish, illustrate, and explain its highest meaning, both by my life and doctrine.

18. *Till all things shall be effected* - Which it either requires or foretells. For the law has its effect, when the rewards are given, and the punishments annexed to it inflicted, as well as when its precepts are obeyed. Luke xvi, 17; xxi, 33.

19. *One of the least* - So accounted by men; *and shall teach* - Either by word or example; *shall be the least* - That is, shall have no part therein.

20. *The righteousness of the scribes and Pharisees* - Described in the sequel of this discourse.

21. *Ye have heard* - From the scribes reciting the law; *Thou shalt do no murder* - And they interpreted this, as all the other commandments, barely of the outward act. *The judgement* - The Jews had in every city a court of twenty-three men, who could sentence a criminal to be strangled. But the sanhedrim only (the great council which sat at Jerusalem, consisting of seventy-two men,) could sentence to the more terrible death of stoning. That was called the judgment, this the council. Exod. xx, 13.

22. *But I say unto you* - Which of the prophets ever spake thus? Their language is, Thus saith the Lord. Who hath authority to use this language, but the one lawgiver, who is able to save and to destroy. *Whosoever is angry with his brother* - Some copies add, *without a cause* - But this is utterly foreign to the whole scope and tenor of our Lord's discourse. If he had only forbidden the being angry *without a cause*, there was no manner of need of that solemn declaration, I say unto you; for the scribes and Pharisees themselves said as much as this. Even they taught, men ought not to be angry without a cause. So that this righteousness does not exceed theirs. But Christ teaches, that we ought not, for any cause, to be so angry as to call any man Raca, or fool. We ought not, for any cause, to be angry at the person of the sinner, but at his sins only. Happy world, were this plain and necessary distinction thoroughly understood, remembered, practised! *Raca* means, a silly man, a trifler. *Whosoever shall say, Thou fool* - Shall revile, or seriously reproach any man. Our Lord specified three degrees of murder, each liable to a sorer punishment than the other: not indeed from men, but from God. *Hell fire* - In the valley of Hinnom (whence the word in the original is taken) the children were used to be burnt alive to Moloch. It was afterward made a receptacle for the filth of the city, where continual fires were kept to consume it. And it is probable, if any criminals were burnt alive, it was in this accursed and horrible place. Therefore both as to its former and latter state, it was a fit emblem of hell. It must here signify a degree of future punishment, as much more dreadful than those incurred in the two former cases, as burning alive is more dreadful than either strangling or stoning.

23. *Thy brother hath aught against thee* - On any of the preceding accounts: for any unkind thought or word: any that did not spring from love.

24. *Leaving thy gift, go* - For neither thy gift nor thy prayer will atone for thy want of love: but this will make them both an abomination before God.

25. *Agree with thine adversary* - With any against whom thou hast thus offended: *while thou art in the way* - Instantly, on the spot; before you part. *Lest the adversary deliver thee to the judge* - Lest he commit his cause to God. Luke xii, 58.

26. *Till thou hast paid the last farthing* - That is, for ever, since thou canst never do this. What has been hitherto said refers to meekness: what follows, to purity of heart.

27. *Thou shalt not commit adultery* - And this, as well as the sixth commandment, the scribes and Pharisees interpreted barely of the outward act. Exod. xx, 14.

29, 30. *If a person as dear as a right eye, or as useful as a right hand, cause thee thus to offend, though but in heart*. Perhaps here may be an instance of a kind of transposition which is frequently found in the sacred writings: so that the 29th verse may refer to 27, 28; and the 30th to ver. 21, 22. As if he had said, Part with any thing, however dear to you, or otherwise useful, if you cannot avoid sin while you keep it. Even cut off your right hand, if you are of so passionate a temper, that you cannot otherwise be restrained from hurting your brother. Pull out your eyes, if you can no otherwise be restrained from lusting after women. Chap. xviii, 8; Mark ix, 43.

31. *Let him give her a writing of divorce* - Which the scribes and Pharisees allowed men to do on any trifling occasion. Deut. xxiv, 1; Matt. xix, 7; Mark x, 2; Luke xvi, 18.

32. *Causeth her to commit adultery* - If she marry again.

33. Our Lord here refers to the promise made to the pure in heart of seeing God in all things, and points out a false doctrine of the scribes, which arose from their not thus seeing God. What he forbids is, the swearing at all, 1, by any creature, 2, in our ordinary conversation: both of which the scribes and Pharisees taught to be perfectly innocent. Exod. xx, 7.

36. For thou canst not make one hair white or black - Whereby it appears, that this also is not thine but God's.

37. Let your conversation be yea, yea; nay, nay - That is, in your common discourse, barely affirm or deny.

38. Ye have heard - Our Lord proceeds to enforce such meekness and love on those who are persecuted for righteousness' sake (which he pursues to the end of the chapter) as were utterly unknown to the scribes and Pharisees. It hath been said - In the law, as a direction to Judges, in ease of violent and barbarous assaults. An eye for an eye, and a tooth for a tooth - And this has been interpreted, as encouraging bitter and rigorous revenge. Deut. xix, 21.

39. But I say unto you, that ye resist not the evil man - Thus; the Greek word translated resist signifies standing in battle array, striving for victory. If a man smite thee on the right cheek - Return not evil for evil: yea, turn to him the other - Rather than revenge thyself.

40, 41. Where the damage is not great, choose rather to suffer it, though possibly it may on that account be repeated, than to demand an eye for an eye, to enter into a rigorous prosecution of the offender. The meaning of the whole passage seems to be, rather than return evil for evil, when the wrong is purely personal, submit to one bodily wrong after another, give up one part of your goods after another, submit to one instance of compulsion after another. That the words are not literally to be understood, appears from the behaviour of our Lord himself, John xviii, 22,

42. Thus much for your behaviour toward the violent. As for those who use milder methods, Give to him that asketh thee - Give and lend to any so far, (but no further, for God never contradicts himself) as is consistent with thy engagements to thy creditors, thy family, and the household of faith. Luke vi, 30.

43. Thou shalt love thy neighbour; And hate thy enemy - God spoke the former part; the scribes added the latter. Lev. xix, 18.

44. Bless them that curse you - Speak all the good you can to and of them, who speak all evil to and of you. Repay love in thought, word, and deed, to those who hate you, and show it both in word and deed. Luke vi, 27, 35.

45. That ye may be the children - That is, that ye may continue and appear such before men and angels. For he maketh his sun to rise - He gives them such blessings as they will receive at his hands. Spiritual blessings they will not receive.

46. The publicans - were officers of the revenue, farmers, or receivers of the public money: men employed by the Romans to gather the taxes and customs, which they exacted of the nations they had conquered. These were generally odious for their extortion and oppression, and were reckoned by the Jews as the very scum of the earth.

47. And if ye salute your friends only - Our Lord probably glances at those prejudices, which different sects had against each other, and intimates, that he would not have his followers imbibe that narrow spirit. Would to God this had been more attended to among the unhappy divisions and subdivisions, into which his Church has been crumbled! And that we might at least advance so far, as cordially to embrace our brethren in Christ, of whatever party or denomination they are!

48. Therefore ye shall be perfect; as your Father who is in heaven is perfect - So the original runs, referring to all that holiness which is described in the foregoing verses, which our Lord in the beginning of the chapter recommends as happiness, and in the close of it as perfection. And how wise and gracious is this, to sum up, and, as it were, seal all his commandments with a promise! Even the proper promise of the Gospel! That he will put those laws in our minds, and write them in our hearts! He well knew how ready our unbelief would be to cry out, this is impossible! And therefore stakes upon it all the power, truth, and faithfulness of him to whom all things are possible.

VI

1. In the foregoing chapter our Lord particularly described the nature of inward holiness. In this he describes that purity of intention without which none of our outward actions are holy. This chapter contains four parts,
    1. The right intention and manner of giving alms, ver. 1-4.
    2. The right intention, manner, form, and prerequisites of prayer, ver. 5-15.
    3. The right intention, and manner of fasting, ver. 16-18.
    4. The necessity of a pure intention in all things, unmixed either with the desire of riches, or worldly care, and fear of want, ver. 19-34. This verse is a general caution against vain glory, in any of our good works: All these are here summed up together, in the comprehensive word righteousness. This

Wesley's Notes on the Bible - The New Testament

general caution our Lord applies in the sequel to the three principal branches of it, relating to our neighbour, ver. 2-iv, to God, ver. 5, vi, and to ourselves, ver. 16-18. To be seen - Barely the being seen, while we are doing any of these things, is a circumstance purely indifferent. But the doing them with this view, to be seen and admired, this is what our Lord condemns.

2. As the hypocrites do - Many of the scribes and Pharisees did this, under a pretense of calling the poor together. They have their reward - All they will have; for they shall have none from God.

3. Let not thy left hand know what thy right hand doth - A proverbial expression for doing a thing secretly. Do it as secretly as is consistent,

1. With the doing it at all.
2. With the doing it in the most effectual manner.

5. The synagogues - These were properly the places where the people assembled for public prayer, and hearing the Scriptures read and expounded. They were in every city from the time of the Babylonish captivity, and had service in them thrice a day on three days in the week. In every synagogue was a council of grave and wise persons, over whom was a president, called the ruler of the synagogue. But the word here, as well as in many other texts, signifies any place of public concourse.

6. Enter into thy closet - That is, do it with as much secrecy as thou canst.

7. Use not vain repetitions - To repeat any words without meaning them, is certainly a vain repetition. Therefore we should be extremely careful in all our prayers to mean what we say; and to say only what we mean from the bottom of our hearts. The vain and heathenish repetitions which we are here warned against, are most dangerous, and yet very common; which is a principal cause why so many, who still profess religion, are a disgrace to it. Indeed all the words in the world are not equivalent to one holy desire. And the very best prayers are but vain repetitions, if they are not the language of the heart.

8. Your Father knoweth what things ye have need of - We do not pray to inform God of our wants. Omniscient as he is, he cannot be informed of any thing which he knew not before: and he is always willing to relieve them. The chief thing wanting is, a fit disposition on our part to receive his grace and blessing. Consequently, one great office of prayer is, to produce such a disposition in us: to exercise our dependence on God; to increase our desire of the things we ask for; to us so sensible of our wants, that we may never cease wrestling till we have prevailed for the blessing.

9. Thus therefore pray ye - He who best knew what we ought to pray for, and how we ought to pray, what matter of desire, what manner of address would most please himself, would best become us, has here dictated to us a most perfect and universal form of prayer, comprehending all our real wants, expressing all our lawful desires; a complete directory and full exercise of all our devotions. Thus - For these things; sometimes in these words, at least in this manner, short, close, full. This prayer consists of three parts, the preface, the petitions, and the conclusion. The preface, Our Father, who art in heaven, lays a general foundation for prayer, comprising what we must first know of God, before we can pray in confidence of being heard. It likewise points out to us our that faith, humility, love, of God and man, with which we are to approach God in prayer.

10. Our Father - Who art good and gracious to all, our Creator, our Preserver; the Father of our Lord, and of us in him, thy children by adoption and grace: not my Father only, who now cry unto thee, but the Father of the universe, of angels and men: who art in heaven - Beholding all things, both in heaven and earth; knowing every creature, and all the works of every creature, and every possible event from everlasting to everlasting: the almighty Lord and Ruler of all, superintending and disposing all things; in heaven - Eminently there, but not there alone, seeing thou fillest heaven and earth. II.

1. Hallowed be thy name - Mayest thou, O Father, be truly known by all intelligent beings, and with affections suitable to that knowledge: mayest thou be duly honoured, loved, feared, by all in heaven and in earth, by all angels and all men.

2. Thy kingdom come - May thy kingdom of grace come quickly, and swallow up all the kingdoms of the earth: may all mankind, receiving thee, O Christ, for their king, truly believing in thy name, be filled with righteousness, and peace, and joy; with holiness and happiness, till they are removed hence into thy kingdom of glory, to reign with thee forever and ever.

3. Thy will be done on earth, as it is in heaven - May all the inhabitants of the earth do thy will as willingly as the holy angels: may these do it continually even as they, without any interruption of their willing service; yea, and perfectly as they: mayest thou, O Spirit of grace, through the blood of the everlasting covenant, make them perfect in every good work to do thy will, and work in them all that is well pleasing in thy sight.

4. Give us - O Father (for we claim nothing of right, but only of thy free mercy) this day - (for we take no thought for the morrow) our daily bread - All things needful for our souls and bodies: not only the meat that perisheth, but the sacramental bread, and thy grace, the food which endureth to everlasting life.

5. And forgive us our debts, as we also forgive our debtors - Give us, O Lord, redemption in thy blood, even the forgiveness of sins: as thou enablest us freely and fully to forgive every man, so do thou

forgive all our trespasses.

6. And lead us not into temptation, but deliver us from evil - Whenever we are tempted, O thou that helpest our infirmities, suffer us not to enter into temptation; to be overcome or suffer loss thereby; but make a way for us to escape, so that we may be more than conquerors, through thy love, over sin and all the consequences of it. Now the principal desire of a Christian's heart being the glory of God, (ver. 9, 10,) and all he wants for himself or his brethren being the daily bread of soul and body, (or the support of life, animal and spiritual,) pardon of sin, and deliverance from the power of it and of the devil, (ver. 11, 12, 13,) there is nothing beside that a Christian can wish for; therefore this prayer comprehends all his desires. Eternal life is the certain consequence, or rather completion of holiness.

III. For thine is the kingdom - The sovereign right of all things that are or ever were created: The power - the executive power, whereby thou governest all things in thy everlasting kingdom: And the glory - The praise due from every creature, for thy power, and all thy wondrous works, and the mightiness of thy kingdom, which endureth through all ages, even forever and ever. It is observable, that though the doxology, as well as the petitions of this prayer, is threefold, and is directed to the Father, Son, and Holy Ghost distinctly, yet is the whole fully applicable both to every person, and to the ever - blessed and undivided trinity. Luke xi, 2.

14. Mark xi, 25.

16. When ye fast? - Our Lord does not enjoin either fasting, alms- deeds, or prayer: all these being duties which were before fully established in the Church of God. Disfigure - By the dust and ashes which they put upon their heads, as was usual at the times of solemn humiliation.

17. Anoint thy head - So the Jews frequently did. Dress thyself as usual.

19. Lay not up for yourselves - Our Lord here makes a transition from religious to common actions, and warns us of another snare, the love of money, as inconsistent with purity of intention as the love of praise. Where rust and moth consume - Where all things are perishable and transient. He may likewise have a further view in these words, even to guard us against making any thing on earth our treasure. For then a thing properly becomes our treasure, when we set our affections upon it. Luke xii, 33.

21. Luke xi, 34.

22. The eye is the lamp of the body - And what the eye is to the body, the intention is to the soul. We may observe with what exact propriety our Lord places purity of intention between worldly desires and worldly cares, either of which directly tend to destroy. If thine eye be single - Singly fixed on God and heaven, thy whole soul will be full of holiness and happiness. If thine eye be evil - Not single, aiming at any thing else.

24. Mammon - Riches, money; any thing loved or sought, without reference to God. Luke xvi, 13.

25. And if you serve God, you need be careful for nothing. Therefore take no thought - That is, be not anxiously careful. Beware of worldly cares; for these are as inconsistent with the true service of God as worldly desires. Is not the life more than meat? - And if God give the greater gift, will he deny the smaller? Luke xii, 22.

27. And which of you - If you are ever so careful, can even add a moment to your own life thereby? This seems to be far the most easy and natural sense of the words.

29. Solomon in all his glory was not arrayed like one of these - Not in garments of so pure a white. The eastern monarchs were often clothed in white robes.

30. The grass of the field - is a general expression, including both herbs and flowers. Into the still - This is the natural sense of the passage. For it can hardly be supposed that grass or flowers should be thrown into the oven the day after they were cut down. Neither is it the custom in the hottest countries, where they dry fastest, to heat ovens with them. If God so clothe - The word properly implies, the putting on a complete dress, that surrounds the body on all sides; and beautifully expresses that external membrane, which (like the skin in a human body) at once adorns the tender fabric of the vegetable, and guards it from the injuries of the weather. Every microscope in which a flower is viewed gives a lively comment on this text.

31. Therefore take not thought - How kind are these precepts! The substance of which is only this, Do thyself no harm! Let us not be so ungrateful to him, nor so injurious to ourselves, as to harass and oppress our minds with that burden of anxiety, which he has so graciously taken off. Every verse speaks at once to the understanding, and to the heart. We will not therefore indulge these unnecessary, these useless, these mischievous cares. We will not borrow the anxieties and distresses of the morrow, to aggravate those of the present day. Rather we will cheerfully repose ourselves on that heavenly Father, who knows we have need of these things; who has given us the life, which is more than meat, and the body, which is more than raiment. And thus instructed in the philosophy of our heavenly Master, we will learn a lesson of faith and cheer. fulness from every bird of the air, and every flower of the field.

33. Seek the kingdom of God and his righteousness - Singly aim at this, that God, reigning in your heart, may fill it with the righteousness above described. And indeed whosoever seeks this first, will soon come to seek this only.

34. *The morrow shall take thought for itself* - That is, be careful for the morrow when it comes. *The evil thereof* - Speaking after the manner of men. But all trouble is, upon the whole, a real good. It is good physic which God dispenses daily to his children, according to the need and the strength of each.

VII

Our Lord now proceeds to warn us against the chief hindrances of holiness. And how wisely does he begin with judging? wherein all young converts are so apt to spend that zeal which is given them for better purposes.

1. *Judge not* - any man without full, clear, certain knowledge, without absolute necessity, without tender love. Luke vi, 37.

2. *With what measure ye mete, it shall be measured to you* - Awful words! So we may, as it were, choose for ourselves, whether God shall be severe or merciful to us. God and man will favour the candid and benevolent: but they must expect judgment without mercy, who have showed no mercy.

3. In particular, why do you open your eyes to any fault of your brother, while you yourself are guilty of a much greater? *The mote* - The word properly signifies a splinter or shiver of wood. This and a beam, its opposite, were proverbially used by the Jews, to denote, the one, small infirmities, the other, gross, palpable faults. Luke vi, 41.

4. *How sayest thou* - With what face?

5. *Thou hypocrite* - It is mere hypocrisy to pretend zeal for the amendment of others while we have none for our own. *Then* - When that which obstructed thy sight is removed.

6. Here is another instance of that transposition, where of the two things proposed, the latter is first treated of. *Give not* - *to dogs* - lest turning they rend you: *Cast not* - *to swine* - lest they trample them under foot. Yet even then, when the beam is cast out of thine own eye, *Give not* - That is, talk not of the deep things of God to those whom you know to be wallowing in sin. neither declare the great things God hath done for your soul to the profane, furious, persecuting wretches. Talk not of perfection, for instance, to the former; not of your experience to the latter. But our Lord does in nowise forbid us to reprove, as occasion is, both the one and the other.

7. *But ask* - Pray for them, as well as for yourselves: in this there can be no such danger. *Seek* - Add your own diligent endeavours to your asking: and *knock* - Persevere importunately in that diligence. Luke xi, 9.

8. *For every one that asketh receiveth* - Provided he ask aright, and ask what is agreeable to God's will.

11. *To them that ask him* - But on this condition, that ye follow the example of his goodness, by doing to all as ye would they should do to you. *For this is the law and the prophets* - This is the sum of all, exactly answering Chap. v, 17. The whole is comprised in one word, Imitate the God of love. Thus far proceeds the doctrinal part of the sermon. In the next verse begins the exhortation to practice it.

12. Luke vi, 31.

13. *The strait gate* - The holiness described in the foregoing chapters. And this is the narrow way. *Wide is the gate, and many there are that go in through it* - They need not seek for this; they come to it of course. *Many go in through it, because strait is the other gate* - Therefore they do not care for it; they like a wider gate. Luke xiii, 24.

15. *Beware of false prophets* - Who in their preaching describe a broad way to heaven: it is their prophesying, their teaching the broad way, rather than their walking in it themselves, that is here chiefly spoken of. All those are false prophets, who teach any other way than that our Lord hath here marked out. *In sheep's clothing* - With outside religion and fair professions of love: *Wolves* - Not feeding, but destroying souls.

16. *By their fruits ye shall know them* - A short, plain, easy rule, whereby to know true from false prophets: and one that may be applied by people of the weakest capacity, who are not accustomed to deep reasoning. True prophets convert sinners to God, or at least confirm and strengthen those that are converted. False prophets do not. They also are false prophets, who though speaking the very truth, yet are not sent by the Spirit of God, but come in their own name, to declare it: their grand mark is, "Not turning men from the power of Satan to God." Luke vi, 43, 44.

18. *A good tree cannot bring forth evil fruit, neither a corrupt tree good fruit* - But it is certain, the goodness or badness here mentioned respects the doctrine, rather than the personal character. For a bad man preaching the good doctrine here delivered, is sometimes an instrument of converting sinners to God. Yet I do not aver, that all are true prophets who speak the truth, and thereby convert sinners. I only affirm, that none are such who do not.

19. *Every tree that bringeth not forth good fruit is hewn down and cast into the fire* - How dreadful then is the condition of that teacher who hath brought no sinners to God!

21. *Not every one* - That is, no one that saith, Lord, Lord - That makes a mere profession of me and my religion, *shall enter* - Whatever their false teachers may assure them to the contrary: He that

doth the will of my Father - as I have now declared it. Observe: every thing short of this is only saying, Lord, Lord. Luke vi, 46.

22. We have prophesied - We have declared the mysteries of thy kingdom, wrote books; preached excellent sermons: In thy name done many wonderful works - So that even the working of miracles is no proof that a man has saving faith.

23. I never knew you - There never was a time that I approved of you: so that as many souls as they had saved, they were themselves never saved from their sins. Lord, is it my case? Luke xiii, 27.

24. Luke vi, 47.

29. He taught them - The multitudes, as one having authority - With a dignity and majesty peculiar to himself as the great Lawgiver, and with the demonstration and power of the Spirit: and not as the scribes - Who only expounded the law of another; and that in a lifeless, ineffectual manner.

VIII

2. A leper came - Leprosies in those countries were seldom curable by natural means, any more than palsies or lunacy. Probably this leper, though he might not mix with the people, had heard our Lord at a distance. Mark i, 40; Luke v, 12.

4. See thou tell no man - Perhaps our Lord only meant here, Not till thou hast showed thyself to the priest-who was appointed to inquire into the case of leprosy. But many others he commanded, absolutely, to tell none of the miracles he had wrought upon them. And this he seems to have done, chiefly for one or more of these reasons:

1. To prevent the multitude from thronging him, in the manner related Mark i, 45.

2. To fulfil the prophecy, Isaiah xlii, 1, that he would not be vain or ostentatious. This reason St. Matthew assigns, chap. xii, 17, &c.

3. To avoid the being taken by force and made a king, John vi, 15. And,

4. That he might not enrage the chief priests, scribes, and Pharisees, who were the most bitter against him, any more than was unavoidable, Matt. xvi, 20, 21. For a testimony - That I am the Messiah; to them - The priests, who otherwise might have pleaded want of evidence. Lev. xiv, 2.

5. There came to him a centurion - A captain of a hundred Roman soldiers. Probably he came a little way toward him, and then went back. He thought himself not worthy to come in person, and therefore spoke the words that follow by his messengers. As it is not unusual in all languages, so in the Hebrew it is peculiarly frequent, to ascribe to a person himself the thing which is done, and the words which are spoken by his order. And accordingly St. Matthew relates as said by the centurion himself, what others said by order from him. An instance of the same kind we have in the case of Zebedee's children. From St. Matthew xx, 20, we learn it was their mother that spoke those words, which, Mark x, 35, 37, themselves are said to speak; because she was only their mouth. Yet from ver. 13, Go thy way home, it appears he at length came in person, probably on hearing that Jesus was nearer to his house than he apprehended when he sent the second message by his friends. Luke vii, 1.

8. The centurion answered - By his second messengers.

9. For I am a man under authority - I am only an inferior officer: and what I command, is done even in my absence: how much more what thou commandest, who art Lord of all!

10. I have not found so great faith, no, not in Israel - For the centurion was not an Israelite.

11. Many from the farthest parts of the earth shall embrace the terms and enjoy the rewards of the Gospel covenant established with Abraham. But the Jews, who have the first title to them, shall be shut out from the feast; from grace here, and hereafter from glory. Luke xiii, 29.

12. The outer darkness - Our Lord here alludes to the custom the ancients had of making their feast in the night time. Probably while he was speaking this, the centurion came in person. Matt. xiii, 42, 50; xxii, 13; xxiv, 51; xxv, 30.

14. Peter's wife's mother - St. Peter was then a young man, as were all the apostles. Mark i, 29; Luke iv, 38.

16. Mark i, 32; Luke iv, 40.

17. Whereby was fulfilled what was spoken by the Prophet Isaiah - He spoke it in a more exalted sense. The evangelist here only alludes to those words, as being capable of this lower meaning also. Such instances are frequent in the sacred writings, and are elegancies rather than imperfections. He fulfilled these words in the highest sense, by bearing our sins in his own body on the tree: in a lower sense, by sympathizing with us in our sorrows, and healing us of the diseases which were the fruit of sin. Isaiah liii, 4.

18. He commanded to go to the other side - That both himself and the people might have a little rest.

19. Luke ix, 57.

20. The Son of man - The expression is borrowed from Dan. vii, 13, and is the appellation which Christ generally gives himself: which he seems to do out of humility, as having some relation to his

mean appearance in this world. Hath not where to lay his head - Therefore do not follow me from any view of temporal advantage.

21. Another said - I will follow thee without any such view; but I must mind my business first. It is not certain that his father was already dead. Perhaps his son desired to stay with him, being very old, till his death.

22. But Jesus said - When God calls, leave the business of the world to them who are dead to God.

23. Mark iv, 35; Luke viii, 22.

24. The ship was covered - So man's extremity is God's opportunity.

26. Why are ye fearful - Then he rebuked the winds - First, he composed their spirits, and then the sea.

28. The country of the Gergesenes - Or of the Gadarenes - Gergesa and Gadara were towns near each other. Hence the country between them took its name, sometimes from the one, sometimes from the other. There met him two demoniacs - St. Mark and St. Luke mention only one, who was probably the fiercer of the two, and the person who spoke to our Lord first. But this is no way inconsistent with the account which St. Matthew gives. The tombs - Doubtless those malevolent spirits love such tokens of death and destruction. Tombs were usually in those days in desert places, at a distance from towns, and were often made in the sides of caves, in the rocks and mountains. No one could pass - Safely. Mark v, 1; Luke viii, 26.

29. What have we to do with thee - This is a Hebrew phrase, which signifies, Why do you concern yourself about us? 2 Sam. xvi, 10. Before the time - The great day.

30. There was a herd of many swine - Which it was not lawful for the Jews to keep. Therefore our Lord both justly and mercifully permitted them to be destroyed.

31. He said, Go - A word of permission only, not command.

34. They besought him to depart out of their coasts - They loved their swine so much better than their souls! How many are of the same mind!

IX

1. His own city - Capernaum, chap. iv, 13; Mark v, 18; Luke viii, 37.

2. Seeing their faith - Both that of the paralytic, and of them that brought him. Son - A title of tenderness and condescension. Mark ii, 3; Luke v, 18.

3. This man blasphemeth - Attributing to himself a power (that of forgiving sins) which belongs to God only.

5. Which is easier - Do not both of them argue a Divine power? Therefore if I can heal his disease, I can forgive his sins: especially as his disease is the consequence of his sins. Therefore these must be taken away, if that is.

6. On earth - Even in my state of humiliation.

8. So what was to the scribes an occasion of blaspheming, was to the people an incitement to praise God.

9. He saw a man named Matthew - Modestly so called by himself. The other evangelists call him by his more honourable name, Levi. Sitting - In the very height of his business, at the receipt of custom - The custom house, or place where the customs were received. Mark ii, 14; Luke v, 27.

10. As Jesus sat at table in the house - Of Matthew, who having invited many of his old companions, made him a feast, Mark ii, 15; and that a great one, though he does not himself mention it. The publicans, or collectors of the taxes which the Jews paid the Romans, were infamous for their illegal exactions: Sinners - Open, notorious, sinners.

11. The Pharisees said to his disciples, Why eateth your Master? - Thus they commonly ask our Lord, Why do thy disciples this? And his disciples, Why doth your Master?

13. Go ye and learn - Ye that take upon you to teach others. I will have mercy and not sacrifice - That is, I will have mercy rather than sacrifice. I love acts of mercy better than sacrifice itself. Hosea vi, 6.

14. Then - While he was at table. Mark ii, 18; Luke v, 33.

15. The children of the bride chamber - The companions of the bridegroom. Mourn - Mourning and fasting usually go together. As if he had said, While I am with them, it is a festival time, a season of rejoicing, not mourning. But after I am gone, all my disciples likewise shall be in fastings often.

16. This is one reason, - It is not a proper time for them to fast. Another is, they are not ripe for it. New cloth - The words in the original properly signify cloth that hath not passed through the fuller's hands, and which is consequently much harsher than what has been washed and worn; and therefore yielding less than that, will tear away the edges to which it is sewed.

17. New - Fermenting wine will soon burst those bottles, the leather of which is almost worn out. The word properly means vessels made of goats' skins, wherein they formerly put wine, (and do in some countries to this day) to convey it from place to place. Put new wine into new bottles - Give harsh

doctrines to such as have strength to receive them.

18. Just dead - He had left her at the point of death, Mark v, 23. Probably a messenger had now informed him she was dead. Mark v, 22; Luke viii, 41.

20. Coming behind - Out of bashfulness and humility.

22. Take courage - Probably she was struck with fear, when he turned and looked upon her, Mark v, 33; Luke viii, 47; lest she should have offended him, by touching his garment privately; and the more so, because she was unclean according to the law, Lev. xv, 25.

23. The minstrels - The musicians. The original word means flute players. Musical instruments were used by the Jews as well as the heathens, in their Lamentations for the dead, to soothe the melancholy of surviving friends, by soft and solemn notes. And there were persons who made it their business to perform this, while others sung to their music. Flutes were used especially on the death of children; louder instruments on the death of grown persons.

24. Withdraw - There is no need of you now; for the maid is not dead - Her life is not at an end; but sleepeth - This is only a temporary suspension of sense and motion, which should rather be termed sleep than death.

25. The maid arose - Christ raised three dead persons to life; this child, the widow's son, and Lazarus: one newly departed, another on the bier, the third smelling in the grave: to show us that no degree of death is so desperate as to be past his help.

32. Luke xi, 14.

33. Even in Israel - Where so many wonders have been seen.

36. Because they were faint - In soul rather than in body. As sheep having no shepherd - And yet they had many teachers; they had scribes in every city. But they had none who cared for their souls, and none that were able, if they had been willing, to have wrought any deliverance. They had no pastors after God's own heart.

37. The harvest truly is great - When Christ came into the world, it was properly the time of harvest; till then it was the seed time only. But the labourers are few - Those whom God sends; who are holy, and convert sinners. Of others there are many. Luke x, 2.

38. The Lord of the harvest - Whose peculiar work and office it is, and who alone is able to do it: that he would thrust forth - for it is an employ not pleasing to flesh and blood; so full of reproach, labour, danger, temptation of every kind, that nature may well be averse to it. Those who never felt this, never yet knew what it is to be labourers in Christ's harvest. He sends them forth, when he calls them by his Spirit, furnishes them with grace and gifts for the work, and makes a way for them to be employed therein.

X

1. His twelve disciples - Hence it appears that he had already chosen out of his disciples, those whom he afterward termed apostles. The number seems to have relation to the twelve patriarchs, and the twelve tribes of Israel. Mark iii, 14; vi, 7; Luke vi, 13; ix, 1.

2. The first, Simon - The first who was called to a constant attendance on Christ; although Andrew had seen him before Simon. Acts i, 13.

3. Lebbeus - Commonly called Judas, the brother of James.

4. Iscariot - So called from Iscarioth, (the place of his birth,) a town of the tribe of Ephraim, near the city of Samaria.

5. These twelve Jesus sent forth - Herein exercising his supreme authority, as God over all. None but God can give men authority to preach his word. Go not - Their commission was thus confined now, because the calling of the Gentiles was deferred till after the more plentiful effusion of the Holy Ghost on the day of pentecost. Enter not - Not to preach; but they might to buy what they wanted, John iv, 9.

8. Cast out devils - It is a great relief to the spirits of an infidel, sinking under a dread, that possibly the Gospel may be true, to find it observed by a learned brother, that the diseases therein ascribed to the operation of the devil have the very same symptoms with the natural diseases of lunacy, epilepsy, or convulsions; whence he readily and very willingly concludes, that the devil had no hand in them. But it were well to stop and consider a little. Suppose God should suffer an evil spirit to usurp the same power over a man's body, as the man himself has naturally; and suppose him actually to exercise that power; could we conclude the devil had no hand therein, because his body was bent in the very same manner wherein the man himself might have bent it naturally? And suppose God gives an evil spirit a greater power, to effect immediately the organ of the nerves in the brain, by irritating them to produce violent motions, or so relaxing them that they can produce little or no motion; still the symptoms will be those of over tense nerves, as in madness, epilepsies, convulsions; or of relaxed nerves, as in paralytic cases. But could we conclude thence that the devil had no hand in them? Will any man affirm that God cannot or will not, on any occasion whatever, give such a power to an evil spirit? Or that effects, the like of which may be produced by natural causes, cannot possibly be produced by

preternatural? If this be possible, then he who affirms it was so, in any particular case, cannot be justly charged with falsehood, merely for affirming the reality of a possible thing. Yet in this manner are the evangelists treated by those unhappy men, who above all things dread the truth of the Gospel, because, if it is true, they are of all men the most miserable. Freely ye have received - All things; in particular the power of working miracles; freely give - Exert that power wherever you come. Mark vi, 7; Luke ix, 2.

9. Provide not - The stress seems to lie on this word: they might use what they had ready; but they might not stay a moment to provide any thing more, neither take any thought about it. Nor indeed were they to take any thing with them, more than was strictly necessary.

1. Lest it should retard them.
2. Because they were to learn hereby to trust to God in all future exigencies.

10. Neither scrip - That is, a wallet, or bag to hold provisions: Nor yet a staff - We read, Mark vi, 8, Take nothing, save a staff only. He that had one might take it; they that had none, might not provide any. For the workman is worthy of his maintenance - The word includes all that is mentioned in the 9th and 10th verses; all that they were forbidden to provide for themselves, so far as it was needful for them. Luke x, 7.

11. Inquire who is worthy - That you should abide with him: who is disposed to receive the Gospel. There abide - In that house, till ye leave the town. Mark vi, 10; Luke ix, 4.

12. Salute it - In the usual Jewish form, "Peace (that is, all blessings) be to this house."

13. If the house be worthy - of it, God shall give them the peace you wish them. If not, he shall give you what they refuse. The same will be the case, when we pray for them that are not worthy.

14. Shake off the dust from your feet - The Jews thought the land of Israel so peculiarly holy, that when they came home from any heathen country, they stopped at the borders and shook or wiped off the dust of it from their feet, that the holy land might not be polluted with it. Therefore the action here enjoined was a lively intimation, that those Jews who had rejected the Gospel were holy no longer, but were on a level with heathens and idolaters.

16. Luke x, 3.

17. But think not that all your innocence and all your wisdom will screen you from persecution. They will scourge you in their synagogues - In these the Jews held their courts of judicature, about both civil and ecclesiastical affairs. Matt. xxiv, 9.

19. Take no thought - Neither at this time, on any sudden call, need we be careful how or what to answer. Luke xii, 11.

21. Luke xxi, 16.

22. Of all men - That know not God. Matt. xxiv, 13.

23. Ye shall not have gone over the cities of Israel - Make what haste ye will; till the Son of man be come - To destroy their temple and nation.

24. Luke vi, 30; John xv, 20.

25. How much more - This cannot refer to the quantity of reproach and persecution: (for in this the servant cannot be above his Lord:) but only to the certainty of it. Matt. xii, 24.

26. Therefore fear them not - For ye have only the same usage with your Lord. There is nothing covered - So that however they may slander you now, your innocence will at length appear. Mark iv, 22; Luke viii, 17; xii, 2.

27. Even what I now tell you secretly is not to be kept secret long, but declared publicly. Therefore, What ye hear in the ear, publish on the house-top - Two customs of the Jews seem to be alluded to here. Their doctors used to whisper in the ear of their disciples what they were to pronounce aloud to others. And as their houses were low and flat roofed, they sometimes preached to the people from thence. Luke xii, 3.

28. And be not afraid - of any thing which ye may suffer for proclaiming it. Be afraid of him who is able to destroy both body and soul in hell - It is remarkable, that our Lord commands those who love God, still to fear him, even on this account, under this notion.

29, 30. The particular providence of God is another reason for your not fearing man. For this extends to the very smallest things. And if he has such care over the most inconsiderable creatures, how much more will he take care of you, (provided you confess him before men, before powerful enemies of the truth,) and that not only in this life, but in the other also?

32. Whosoever shall confess me - Publicly acknowledge me for the promised Messiah. But this confession implies the receiving his whole doctrine, Mark viii, 38, and obeying all his commandments. Luke ix, 26.

33, 34. Whosoever shall deny me before men - To which ye will be strongly tempted. For Think not that I am come - That is, think not that universal peace will be the immediate consequence of my coming. Just the contrary. Both public and private divisions will follow, wheresoever my Gospel comes with power. Ye - this is not the design, though it be the event of his coming, through the opposition of devils and men.

36. And the foes of a man - That loves and follows me. Micah vii, 6.

37. He that loveth father or mother more than me - He that is not ready to give up all these, when they stand in competition with his duty.

38. He that taketh not his cross - That is, whatever pain or inconvenience cannot be avoided, but by doing some evil, or omitting some good. Matt. xvi, 24; Luke xiv, 27.

39. He that findeth his life shall lose it - He that saves his life by denying me, shall lose it eternally; and he that loseth his life by confessing me, shall save it eternally. And as you shall be thus rewarded, so in proportion shall they who entertain you for my sake. Matt. xvi, 25; John xii, 25.

40. Matt. xviii, 5; Luke x, 16; John xiii, 20.

41. He that entertaineth a prophet - That is, a preacher of the Gospel: In the name of a prophet - That is, because he is such, shall share in his reward.

42. One of these little ones - The very least Christian. Mark ix, 41.

XI

1. In their cities - The other cities of Israel.

2. He sent two of his disciples - Not because he doubted himself; but to confirm their faith. Luke vii, 18.

3. He that is to come - The Messiah.

4. Go and tell John the things that ye hear and see - Which are a stronger proof of my being the Messiah, than any bare assertion can be.

5. The poor have the Gospel preached to them - The greatest mercy of all. Isaiah xxix, 18; xxxv, 5.

6. Happy is he who shall not be offended at me - Notwithstanding all these proofs that I am the Messiah.

7. As they departed, he said concerning John - Of whom probably he would not have said so much when they were present. A reed shaken by the wind? - No; nothing could ever shake John in the testimony he gave to the truth. The expression is proverbial.

8. A man clothed in soft, delicate raiment - An effeminate courtier, accustomed to fawning and flattery? You may expect to find persons of such a character in palaces; not in a wilderness.

9. More than a prophet - For the prophets only pointed me out afar off; but John was my immediate forerunner.

10. Mal. iii, 1.

11. But he that is least in the kingdom of heaven, is greater than he - Which an ancient author explains thus: - "One perfect in the law, as John was, is inferior to one who is baptized into the death of Christ. For this is the kingdom of heaven, even to be buried with Christ, and to be raised up together with him. John was greater than all who had been then born of women, but he was cut off before the kingdom of heaven was given." [He seems to mean, that righteousness, peace, and joy, which constitute the present inward kingdom of heaven.] "He was blameless as to that righteousness which is by the law; but he fell short of those who are perfected by the spirit of life which is in Christ. Whosoever, therefore, is least in the kingdom of heaven, by Christian regeneration, is greater than any who has attained only the righteousness of the law, because the law maketh nothing perfect." It may farther mean, the least true Christian believer has a more perfect knowledge of Jesus Christ, of his redemption and kingdom, than John the Baptist had, who died before the full manifestation of the Gospel.

12. And from the days of John - That is, from the time that John had fulfilled his ministry, men rush into my kingdom with a violence like that of those who are taking a city by storm.

13. For all the prophets and the law prophesied until John - For all that is written in the law and the prophets only foretold as distant what is now fulfilled. In John the old dispensation expired, and the new began. Luke xvi, 16.

14. Mal. iv, 5.

15. He that hath ears to hear, let him hear - A kind of proverbial expression; requiring the deepest attention to what is spoken.

16. This generation - That is, the men of this age. They are like those froward children of whom their fellows complain, that they will be pleased no way.

18. John came neither eating nor drinking - In a rigorous austere way, like Elijah. And they say, He hath a devil - Is melancholy, from the influence of an evil spirit.

19. The Son of man came eating and drinking - Conversing in a free, familiar way. Wisdom is justified by her children - That is, my wisdom herein is acknowledged by those who are truly wise.

20. Then began he to upbraid the cities - It is observable he had never upbraided them before. Indeed at first they received him with all gladness, Capernaum in particular.

21. Woe to thee, Chorazin - That is, miserable art thou. For these are not curses or imprecations, as has been commonly supposed; but a solemn, compassionate declaration of the misery they were bringing on themselves. Chorazin and Bethsaida were cities of Galilee, standing by the lake Gennesareth. Tyre and Sidon were cities of Phenicia, lying on the sea shore. The inhabitants of them

were heathens. Luke x, 13.

22, 24. *Moreover I say unto you* - Beside the general denunciation of woee to those stubborn unbelievers, the degree of their misery will be greater than even that of Tyre and Sidon, yea, of Sodom.

23. *Thou Capernaum, who hast been exalted to heaven* - That is, highly honoured by my presence and miracles.

25. *Jesus answering* - This word does not always imply, that something had been spoken, to which an answer is now made. It often means no more than the speaking in reference to some action or circumstance preceding. The following words Christ speaks in reference to the case of the cities above mentioned: *I thank thee* - That is, I acknowledge and joyfully adore the justice and mercy of thy dispensations: *Because thou hast hid* - That is, because thou hast suffered these things to be hid from men, who are in other respects wise and prudent, while thou hast discovered them to those of the weakest understanding, to them who are only wise to Godward. Luke x, 21.

27. *All things are delivered to me* - Our Lord, here addressing himself to his disciples, shows why men, wise in other things, do not know this: namely, because none can know it by natural reason: none but those to whom he revealeth it.

28. *Come to me* - Here he shows to whom he is pleased to reveal these things to the weary and heavy laden; *ye that labour* - After rest in God: and *are heavy laden* - With the guilt and power of sin: and *I will give you rest* - I alone (for none else can) will freely give you (what ye cannot purchase) rest from the guilt of sin by justification, and from the power of sin by sanctification.

29. *Take my yoke upon you* - Believe in me: receive me as your prophet, priest, and king. *For I am meek and lowly in heart* - Meek toward all men, lowly toward God: *and ye shall find rest* - Whoever therefore does not find rest of soul, is not meek and lowly. The fault is not in the yoke of Christ: but in thee, who hast not taken it upon thee. Nor is it possible for any one to be discontented, but through want of meekness or lowliness.

30. *For my yoke is easy* - Or rather gracious, sweet, benign, delightful: *and my burden* - Contrary to those of men, is ease, liberty, and honour.

XII

1. *His disciples plucked the ears of corn, and ate* - Just what sufficed for present necessity: dried corn was a common food among the Jews. Mark ii, 23; Luke vi, 1.

3. *Have ye not read what David did* - And necessity was a sufficient plea for his transgressing the law in a higher instance.

4. *He entered into the house of God* - Into the tabernacle. The temple was not yet built. *The show bread* - So they called the bread which the priest, who served that week, put every Sabbath day on the golden table that was in the holy place, before the Lord. The loaves were twelve in number, and represented the twelve tribes of Israel: when the new were brought, the stale were taken away, but were to be eaten by the priests only. 1 Sam. xxi, 6.

5. *The priests in the temple profane the Sabbath* - That is, do their ordinary work on this, as on a common day, cleansing all things, and preparing the sacrifices. *A greater than the temple* - If therefore the Sabbath must give way to the temple, much more must it give way to me.

7. *I will have mercy and not sacrifice* - That is, when they interfere with each other, I always prefer acts of mercy, before matters of positive institution: yea, before all ceremonial institutions whatever; because these being only means of religion, are suspended of course, if circumstances occur, wherein they clash with love, which is the end of it. Matt. ix, 13.

8. *For the Son of man* - Therefore they are guiltless, were it only on this account, that they act by my authority, and attend on me in my ministry, as the priests attended on God in the temple: *is Lord even of the Sabbath* - This certainly implies, that the Sabbath was an institution of great and distinguished importance; it may perhaps also refer to that signal act of authority which Christ afterward exerted over it, in changing it from the seventh to the first day of the week. If we suppose here is a transposition of the 7th and 8th verses, then the 8th verse is a proof of the 6th. Matt. xii, 7, 8, 6.

9. Mark iii, 1; Luke vi, 6.

12. *It is lawful to do good on the Sabbath day* - To save a beast, much more a man.

18. *He shall show judgment to the heathens* - That is, he shall publish the merciful Gospel to them also: the Hebrew word signifies either mercy or justice. Isaiah xlii, 1, &c.

19. *He shall not strive, nor clamour; neither shall any man hear his voice in the streets* - That is, he shall not be contentious, noisy, or ostentatious: but gentle, quiet, and lowly. We may observe each word rises above the other, expressing a still higher degree of humility and gentleness.

20. *A bruised reed* - A convinced sinner: one that is bruised with the weight of sin: *smoking flax* - One that has the least good desire, the faintest spark of grace: *till he send forth judgment unto victory* - That is, till he make righteousness completely victorious over all its enemies.

21. *In his name* - That is, in him.

22. A demoniac, blind and dumb - Many undoubtedly supposed these defects to be merely natural. But the Spirit of God saw otherwise, and gives the true account both of the disorder and the cure. How many disorders, seemingly natural, may even now be owing to the same cause? Luke xi, 14.

23. Is not this the son of David - That is, the Messiah.

24. Mark iii, 22.

25. Jesus knowing their thoughts - It seems they had as yet only said it in their hearts.

26. How shall his kingdom be established - Does not that subtle spirit know this is not the way to establish his kingdom?

27. By whom do your children - That is, disciples, cast them out - It seems, some of them really did this; although the sons of Sceva could not. Therefore shall they be your judge - Ask them, if Satan will cast out Satan: let even them be Judge in this matter. And they shall convict you of obstinacy and partiality, who impute that in me to Beelzebub, which in them you impute to God. Beside, how can I rob him of his subjects, till I have conquered him? The kingdom of God is come upon you - Unawares; before you expected: so the word implies.

29. How can one enter into the strong one's house, unless he first bind the strong one - So Christ coming into the world, which was then eminently the strong one's, Satan's house, first bound him, and then took his spoils.

30. He that is not with me is against me - For there are no him; either a loyal subject or a rebel. And there are none upon earth, who neither promote nor obstruct his kingdom. For he that does not gather souls to God, scatters them from him.

31. The blasphemy against the Spirit - How much stir has been made about this? How many sermons, yea, volumes, have been written concerning it? And yet there is nothing plainer in all the Bible. It is neither more nor less than the ascribing those miracles to the power of the devil, which Christ wrought by the power of the Holy Ghost. Mark iii, 28; Luke xii, 10.

32. Whosoever speaketh against the Son of man - In any other respects: It shall be forgiven him - Upon his true repentance: But whosoever speaketh thus against the Holy Ghost, it shall not be forgiven, neither in this world nor in the world to come - This was a proverbial expression among the Jews, for a thing that would never be done. It here means farther, He shall not escape the punishment of it, either in this world, or in the world to come. The judgment of God shall overtake him, both here and hereafter.

33. Either make the tree good and its fruit good: or make the tree corrupt and its fruit corrupt - That is, you must allow, they are both good, or both bad.- For if the fruit is good, so is the tree; if the fruit is evil, so is the tree also. For the tree is known by its fruit - As if he had said, Ye may therefore know me by my fruits. By my converting sinners to God, you may know that God hath sent me. Matt. vii, 16; Luke vi, 43.

34. In another kind likewise, the tree is known by its fruit - Namely, the heart by the conversation.

36. Ye may perhaps think, God does not so much regard your words. But I say to you - That not for blasphemous and profane words only, but for every idle word which men shall speak - For want of seriousness or caution; for every discourse which is not conducive to the glory of God, they shall give account in the day of judgment.

37. For by thy words (as well as thy tempers and works) thou shalt then be either acquitted or condemned. - Your words as well as actions shall be produced in evidence for or against you, to prove whether you was a true believer or not. And according to that evidence you will either be acquitted or condemned in the great day.

38. We would see a sign - Else we will not believe this. Matt. xvi, 1; Luke xi, 16, 29.

39. An adulterous generation - Whose heart wanders from God, though they profess him to be their husband. Such adulterers are all those who love the world, and all who seek the friendship of it. Seeketh a sign - After all they have had already, which were abundantly sufficient to convince them, had not their hearts been estranged from God, and consequently averse to the truth. The sign of Jonah - Who was herein a type of Christ.

40. Three days and three nights - It was customary with the eastern nations to reckon any part of a natural day of twenty-four hours, for the whole day. Accordingly they used to say a thing was done after three or seven days, if it was done on the third or seventh day, from that which was last mentioned. Instances of this may be seen, 1 Kings xx, 29; and in many other places. And as the Hebrews had no word to express a natural day, they used night and day, or day and night for it. So that to say a thing happened after three days and three nights, was with them the very same, as to say, it happened after three days, or on the third day. See Esther iv, 16; v, 1; Gen. vii, 4, 12; Exod. xxiv, 18; xxxiv, 28. Jonah ii, 1.

42. She came from the uttermost parts of the earth - That part of Arabia from which she came was the uttermost part of the earth that way, being bounded by the sea. 1 Kings x, 7.

43. But how dreadful will be the consequence of their rejecting me? When the unclean spirit goeth out - Not willingly, but being compelled by one that is stronger than he. He walketh - Wanders up and down; through dry places - Barren, dreary, desolate; or places not yet watered with the Gospel: Seeking

rest, and findeth none - How can he, while he carries with him his own hell? And is it not the case of his children too? Reader, is it thy case? Luke xi, 24.

44. Whence he came out - He speaks as if he had come out of his own accord: See his pride! He findeth it empty - of God, of Christ, of his Spirit: Swept - from love, lowliness, meekness, and all the fruits of the Spirit: And garnished - With levity and security: so that there is nothing to keep him out, and much to invite him in.

45. Seven other spirits - That is, a great many; a certain number being put for an uncertain: More wicked than himself - Whence it appears, that there are degrees of wickedness among the devils themselves: They enter in and dwell - For ever in him who is forsaken of God. So shall it be to this wicked generation - Yea, and to apostates in all ages.

46. His brethren -- his kinsmen: they were the sons of Mary, the wife of Cleopas, or Alpheus, his mother's sister; and came now seeking to take him, as one beside himself, Mark iii, 21. Mark iii, 31; Luke viii, 19.

48. And he answering, said - Our Lord's knowing why they came, sufficiently justifies his seeming disregard of them.

49, 50. See the highest severity, and the highest goodness! Severity to his natural, goodness to his spiritual relations! In a manner disclaiming the former, who opposed the will of his heavenly Father, and owning the latter, who obeyed it.

XIII

1. Mark iv, 1; Luke viii, 4.

2. He went into the vessel - Which constantly waited upon him, while he was on the sea coast.

3. In parables - The word is here taken in its proper sense, for apt similes or comparisons. This way of speaking, extremely common in the eastern countries, drew and fixed the attention of many, and occasioned the truths delivered to sink the deeper into humble and serious hearers. At the same time, by an awful mixture of justice and mercy, it hid them from the proud and careless. In this chapter our Lord delivers seven parables; directing the four former (as being of general concern) to all the people; the three latter to his disciples. Behold the sower - How exquisitely proper is this parable to be an introduction to all the rest! In this our Lord answers a very obvious and a very important question. The same sower, Christ, and the same preachers sent by him, always sow the same seed: why has it not always the same effect? He that hath ears to hear, let him hear!

4. And while he sowed, some seeds fell by the highway side, and the birds came and devoured them - It is observable, that our Lord points out the grand hindrances of our bearing fruit, in the same order as they occur. The first danger is, that the birds will devour the seed. If it escape this, there is then another danger, namely, lest it be scorched, and wither away. It is long after this that the thorns spring up and choke the good seed. A vast majority of those who hear the word of God, receive the seed as by the highway side. Of those who do not lose it by the birds, yet many receive it as on stony places. Many of them who receive it in a better soil, yet suffer the thorns to grow up, and choke it: so that few even of these endure to the end, and bear fruit unto perfection: yet in all these cases, it is not the will of God that hinders, but their own voluntary perverseness.

8. Good ground - Soft, not like that by the highway side; deep, not like the stony ground; purged, not full of thorns.

11. To you, who have, it is given to know the mysteries of the kingdom of heaven - The deep things which flesh and blood cannot reveal, pertaining to the inward, present kingdom of heaven. But to them who have not, it is not given - Therefore speak I in parables, that ye may understand, while they do not understand.

12. Whosoever hath - That is, improves what he hath, uses the grace given according to the design of the giver; to him shall be given - More and more, in proportion to that improvement. But whosoever hath not - Improves it not, from him shall be taken even what he hath - Here is the grand rule of God's dealing with the children of men: a rule fixed as the pillars of heaven. This is the key to all his providential dispensations; as will appear to men and angels in that day. Matt. xxv, 29; Mark iv, 25; Luke viii, 18; xix, 26.

13. Therefore I speak to them in parables, because seeing, they see not - In pursuance of this general rule, I do not give more knowledge to this people, be. cause they use not that which they have already: having all the means of seeing, hearing, and understanding, they use none of them: they do not effectually see, or hear, or understand any thing.

14. Hearing ye will hear, but in nowise understand - That is, Ye will surely hear. All possible means will be given you: yet they will profit you nothing; because your heart is sensual, stupid, and insensible; your spiritual senses are shut up; yea, you have closed your eyes against the light; as being unwilling to understand the things of God, and afraid, not desirous that he should heal you. Isaiah vi, 9; John xii, 40; Acts xxviii, 26.

John Wesley

16. But blessed are your eyes - For you both see and understand. You know how to prize the light which is given you. Luke x, 23.

19. When any one heareth the word, and considereth it not - The first and most general cause of unfruitfulness. The wicked one cometh - Either inwardly; filling the mind with thoughts of other things; or by his agent. Such are all they that introduce other subjects, when men should be considering what they have heard.

20. The seed sown on stony places, therefore sprang up soon, because it did not sink deep, ver. 5. He receiveth it with joy - Perhaps with transport, with ecstasy: struck with the beauty of truth, and drawn by the preventing grace of God.

21. Yet hath he not root in himself - No deep work of grace: no change in the ground of his heart. Nay, he has no deep conviction; and without this, good desires soon wither away. He is offended - He finds a thousand plausible pretenses for leaving so narrow and rugged a way.

22. He that received the seed among the thorns, is he that heareth the word and considereth it - In spite of Satan and his agents: yea, hath root in himself is deeply convinced, and in a great measure inwardly changed; so that he will not draw back, even when tribulation or persecution ariseth. And yet even in him, together with the good seed, the thorns spring up, ver. 7. (perhaps unperceived at first) till they gradually choke it, destroy all its life and power, and it becometh unfruitful. Cares are thorns to the poor: wealth to the rich; the desire of other things to all. The deceitfulness of riches - Deceitful indeed! for they smile, and betray: kiss, and smite into hell. They put out the eyes, harden the heart, steal away all the life of God; fill the soul with pride, anger, love of the world; make men enemies to the whole cross of Christ! And all the while are eagerly desired, and vehemently pursued, even by those who believe there is a God!

23. Some a hundred fold, some sixty, some thirty - That is, in various proportions; some abundantly more than others.

24. He proposed another parable - in which he farther explains the case of unfruitful hearers. The kingdom of heaven (as has been observed before) sometimes signifies eternal glory: sometimes the way to it, inward religion; sometimes, as here, the Gospel dispensation: the phrase is likewise used for a person or thing relating to any one of those: so in this place it means, Christ preaching the Gospel, who is like a man sowing good seed - The expression, is like, both here and in several other places, only means, that the thing spoken of may be illustrated by the following similitude. Who sowed good seed in his field - God sowed nothing but good in his whole creation. Christ sowed only the good seed of truth in his Church.

25. But while men slept - They ought to have watched: the Lord of the field sleepeth not. His enemy came and sowed darnel - This is very like wheat, and commonly grows among wheat rather than among other grain: but tares or vetches are of the pulse kind, and bear no resemblance to wheat.

26. When the blade was sprung up, then appeared the darnel - It was not discerned before: it seldom appears, as soon as the good seed is sown: all at first appears to be peace, and love, and joy.

27. Didst not thou sow good seed in thy field? Whence then hath it darnel? - Not from the parent of good. Even the heathen could say, "No evil can from thee proceed: 'Tis only suffer'd, not decreed: As darkness is not from the sun, Nor mount the shades, till he is gone."

28. He said, An enemy hath done this - A plain answer to the great question concerning the origin of evil. God made men (as he did angels) intelligent creatures, and consequently free either to choose good or evil: but he implanted no evil in the human soul: An enemy (with man's concurrence) hath done this. Darnel, in the Church, is properly outside Christians, such as have the form of godliness, without the power. Open sinners, such as have neither the form nor the power, are not so properly darnel, as thistles and brambles: these ought to be rooted up without delay, and not suffered in the Christian community. Whereas should fallible men attempt to gather up the darnel, they would often root up the wheat with them.

31. He proposed to them another parable - The former parables relate chiefly to unfruitful hearers; these that follow, to those who bear good fruit. The kingdom of heaven - Both the Gospel dispensation, and the inward kingdom. Mark iv, 30; Luke xiii, 18.

32. The least - That is, one of the least: a way of speaking extremely common among the Jews. It becometh a tree - In those countries it grows exceeding large and high. So will the Christian doctrine spread in the world, and the life of Christ in the soul.

33. Three measures - This was the quantity which they usually baked at once: till the whole was leavened - Thus will the Gospel leaven the world and grace the Christian. Luke xiii, 20.

34. Without a parable spake he not unto them - That is, not at that time; at other times he did.

35. Psalm lxxviii, 2.

38. The good seed are the children of the kingdom - That is, the children of God, the righteous.

41. They shall gather all things that offend - Whatever had hindered or grieved the children of God; whatever things or persons had hindered the good seed which Christ had sown from taking root or bearing fruit. The Greek word is, All scandals.

44. The three following parables are proposed, not to the multitude, but peculiarly to the apostles: the two former of them relate to those who receive the Gospel; the third, both to those who receive, and those who preach it. The kingdom of heaven is like treasure hid in a field - The kingdom of God within us is a treasure indeed, but a treasure hid from the world, and from the most wise and prudent in it. He that finds this treasure, (perhaps when he thought it far from him,) hides it deep in his heart, and gives up all other happiness for it.

45. The kingdom of heaven - That is, one who earnestly seeks for it: in verse 47 it means, the Gospel preached, which is like a net gathering of every kind: just so the Gospel, wherever it is preached, gathers at first both good and bad, who are for a season full of approbation and warm with good desires. But Christian discipline, and strong, close exhortation, begin that separation in this world, which shall be accomplished by the angels of God in the world to come.

52. Every scribe instructed unto the kingdom of heaven - That is, every duly prepared preacher of the Gospel has a treasure of Divine knowledge, out of which he is able to bring forth all sorts of instructions. The word treasure signifies any collection of things whatsoever, and the places where such collections are kept.

53. He departed thence - He crossed the lake from Capernaum: and came once more into his own country - Nazareth: but with no better success than he had had there before.

54. Whence hath HE - Many texts are not understood, for want of knowing the proper emphasis; and others are utterly misunderstood, by placing the emphasis wrong. To prevent this in some measure, the emphatical words are here printed in capital letters. Mark vi, 1; Luke iv, 16, 22.

55. The carpenter's son - The Greek, word means, one that works either in wood, iron, or stone. His brethren -- our kinsmen. They were the sons of Mary, sister to the virgin, and wife of Cleophas or Alpheus. James - Styled by St. Paul also, the Lord's brother, Gal. i, 19. Simon - Surnamed the Canaanite.

57. They were offended at him - They looked on him as a mean, ignoble man, not worthy to be regarded. John iv, 44; Luke vii, 23.

58. He wrought not many mighty works, because of their unbelief - And the reason why many mighty works are not wrought now, is not, that the faith is not everywhere planted; but, that unbelief every where prevails.

XIV

1. At that time - When our Lord had spent about a year in his public ministry. Tetrarch - King of a fourth part of his father's dominions. Mark vi, 14.

2. He is risen from the dead - Herod was a Sadducee: and the Sadducees denied the resurrection of the dead. But Sadduceeism staggers when conscience awakes.

3. His brother Philip's wife - Who was still alive. Mark vi, 17.

4. It is not lawful for thee to have her - It was not lawful indeed for either of them to have her. For her father Aristobulus was their own brother. John's words were rough, like his raiment. He would not break the force of truth by using soft words, even to a king.

5. He would have put him to death - In his fit of passion; but he was then restrained by fear of the multitude; and afterward by the reverence he bore him.

6. The daughter of Herodias - Afterward infamous for a life suitable to this beginning.

8. Being before instructed by her mother - Both as to the matter and manner of her petition: She said, Give me here - Fearing if he had time to consider, he would not do it: John the Baptist's head in a charger - A large dish or bowl.

9. And the king was sorry - Knowing that John was a good man. Yet for the oath's sake - So he murdered an innocent man from mere tenderness of conscience.

10. And he sent and beheaded John in the prison, and his head was given to the damsel - How mysterious is the providence, which left the life of so holy a man in such infamous hands! which permitted it to be sacrificed to the malice of an abandoned harlot, the petulancy of a vain girl, and the rashness of a foolish, perhaps drunken prince, who made a prophet's head the reward of a dance! But we are sure the Almighty will repay his servants in another world for whatever they suffer in this.

13. Jesus withdrew into a desert place -
1. To avoid Herod:
2. Because of the multitude pressing upon him, Mark vi, xxxii, and
3. To talk with his disciples, newly returned from their progress, Luke ix, x, apart - From all but his disciples. John vi, 1.

15. The time is now past - The usual meal time. Mark vi, 35; Luke ix, 12.

22. He constrained his disciples - Who were unwilling to leave him. Mark vi, 45; John vi, 15.

24. In the evening - Learned men say the Jews reckoned two evenings; the first beginning at three in the afternoon, the second, at sunset. If so, the latter is meant here.

25. The fourth watch - The Jews (as well as the Romans) usually divided the night into four watches, of three hours each. The first watch began at six, the second at nine, the third at twelve, the fourth at three in the morning. If it be thou - It is the same as, Since it is thou. The particle if frequently bears this meaning, both in ours and in all languages. So it means, John xiii, 14, 17. St. Peter was in no doubt, or he would not have quitted the ship.

30. He was afraid - Though he had been used to the sea, and was a skilful swimmer. But so it frequently is. When grace begins to act, the natural courage and strength are withdrawn.

33. Thou art the Son of God - They mean, the Messiah.

35. Mark vi, 45.

XV

1. Mark vii, 1.

2. The elders - The chief doctors or, teachers among the Jews.

3. They wash not their hands when they eat bread - Food in general is termed bread in Hebrew; so that to eat bread is the same as to make a meal.

4. honour thy father and mother - Which implies all such relief as they stand in need of. Exod. xx, 12; xxi, 17.

5. It is a gift by whatsoever thou mightest have been profited by me - That is, I have given, or at least, purpose to give to the treasury of the temple, what you might otherwise have had from me.

7. Well did Isaiah prophesy of you, saying - That is, the description which Isaiah gave of your fathers, is exactly applicable to you. The words therefore which were a description of them, are a prophecy with regard to you.

8. Their heart is far from me - And without this all outward worship is mere mockery of God. Isaiah xxix, 13.

9. Teaching the commandments of men - As equal with, nay, superior to, those of God. What can be a more heinous sin?

13. Every plant - That is, every doctrine.

14. Let them alone - If they are indeed blind leaders of the blind; let them alone: concern not yourselves about them: a plain direction how to behave with regard to all such. Luke vi, 39.

17. Are ye also yet without understanding - How fair and candid are the sacred historians? Never concealing or excusing their own blemishes.

19. First evil thoughts - then murders - and the rest. Railings - The Greek word includes all reviling, backbiting, and evil speaking.

21. Mark vii, 24.

22. A woman of Canaan - Canaan was also called Syrophenicia, as lying between Syria properly so called, and Phenicia, by the sea side. Cried to him - From afar, Thou Son of David - So she had some knowledge of the promised Messiah.

23. He answered her not a word - He sometimes tries our faith in like manner.

24. I am not sent - Not primarily; not yet.

25. Then came she - Into the house where he now was.

28. Thy faith - Thy reliance on the power and goodness of God.

29. The sea of Galilee - The Jews gave the name of seas to all large lakes. This was a hundred furlongs long, and forty broad. It was called also, the sea of Tiberias. It lay on the borders of Galilee, and the city of Tiberias stood on its western shore. It was likewise styled the lake of Gennesareth: perhaps a corruption of Cinnereth, the name by which it was anciently called, Num. xxxiv, 11. Mark vii, 31.

32. They continue with me now three days - It was now the third day since they came. Mark viii, 1.

36. He gave thanks, or blessed the food - That is, he praised God for it, and prayed for a blessing upon it.

XVI

1. A sign from heaven - Such they imagined Satan could not counterfeit. Mark viii, 11; Matt. xii, 38.

2. Luke xii, 54.

3. The signs of the times - The signs which evidently show, that this is the time of the Messiah.

4. A wicked and adulterous generation - Ye would seek no further sign, did not your wickedness, your love of the world, which is spiritual adultery, blind your understanding.

5. Mark viii, 14.

6. Beware of the leaven of the Pharisees - That is, of their false doctrine: this is elegantly so called;

for it spreads in the soul, or the Church, as leaven does in meal. Luke xii, 1.

7. They reasoned among themselves - What must we do then for bread, since we have taken no bread with us?

8. Why reason ye - Why are you troubled about this? Am I not able, if need so require, to supply you by a word?

11. How do ye not understand - Beside, do you not understand, that I did not mean bread, by the leaven of the Pharisees and Sadducees?

13. And Jesus coming - There was a large interval of time between what has been related, and what follows. The passages that follow were but a short time before our Lord suffered. Mark viii, 27; Luke ix, 18.

14. Jeremiah, or one of the prophets - There was at that time a current tradition among the Jews, that either Jeremiah, or some other of the ancient prophets would rise again before the Messiah came.

16. Peter - Who was generally the most forward to speak.

17. Flesh and blood - That is, thy own reason, or any natural power whatsoever.

18. On this rock - Alluding to his name, which signifies a rock, namely, the faith which thou hast now professed; I will build my Church - But perhaps when our Lord uttered these words, he pointed to himself, in like manner as when he said, Destroy this temple, John ii, 19; meaning the temple of his body. And it is certain, that as he is spoken of in Scripture, as the only foundation of the Church, so this is that which the apostles and evangelists laid in their preaching. It is in respect of laying this, that the names of the twelve apostles (not of St. Peter only) were equally inscribed on the twelve foundations of the city of God, Rev. xxi, 14. The gates of hell - As gates and walls were the strength of cities, and as courts of judicature were held in their gates, this phrase properly signifies the power and policy of Satan and his instruments. Shall not prevail against it - Not against the Church universal, so as to destroy it. And they never did. There hath been a small remnant in all ages.

19. I will give thee the keys of the kingdom of heaven - Indeed not to him alone, (for they were equally given to all the apostles at the same time, John xx, 21, 22, 23;) but to him were first given the keys both of doctrine and discipline. He first, after our Lord's resurrection, exercised the apostleship, Acts i, 15. And he first by preaching opened the kingdom of heaven, both to the Jews, Acts ii, , and to the Gentiles, Acts x, . Under the term of binding and loosing are contained all those acts of discipline which Peter and his brethren performed as apostles: and undoubtedly what they thus performed on earth, God confirmed in heaven. Matt. xviii, 18.

20. Then charged he his disciples to tell no one that he was the Christ. Jesus himself had not said it expressly even to his apostles, but left them to infer it from his doctrine and miracles. Neither was it proper the apostles should say this openly, before that grand proof of it, his resurrection. If they had, they who believed them would the more earnestly have sought to take and make him a king: and they who did not believe them would the more vehemently have rejected and opposed such a Messiah.

21. From that time Jesus began to tell his disciples, that he must suffer many things - Perhaps this expression, began, always implied his entering on a set and solemn discourse. Hitherto he had mainly taught them only one point, That he was the Christ. From this time he taught them another, That Christ must through sufferings and death enter into his glory. From the elders - The most honourable and experienced men; the chief priests - Accounted the most religious; and the scribes - The most learned body of men in the nation. Would not one have expected, that these should have been the very first to receive him? But not many wise, not many noble were called. favour thyself - The advice of the world, the flesh, and the devil, to every one of our Lord's followers. Mark viii, 31; Luke ix, 22.

23. Get thee behind me - Out of my sight. It is not improbable, Peter might step before him, to stop him. Satan - Our Lord is not recorded to have given so sharp a reproof to any other of his apostles on any occasion. He saw it was needful for the pride of Peter's heart, puffed up with the commendation lately given him. Perhaps the term Satan may not barely mean, Thou art my enemy, while thou fanciest thyself most my friend; but also, Thou art acting the very part of Satan, both by endeavouring to hinder the redemption of mankind, and by giving me the most deadly advice that can ever spring from the pit of hell. Thou savourest not - Dost not relish or desire. We may learn from hence,

1. That whosoever says to us in such a case, favour thyself, is acting the part of the devil:
2. That the proper answer to such an adviser is, Get thee behind me:
3. That otherwise he will be an offense to us, an occasion of our stumbling, if not falling:
4. That this advice always proceeds from the not relishing the things of God, but the things of men. Yea, so far is this advice, favour thyself, from being fit for a Christian either to give or take, that if any man will come after Christ, his very first step is to deny, or renounce himself: in the room of his own will, to substitute the will of God, as his one principle of action.

24. If any man be willing to come after me - None is forced; but if any will be a Christian, it must be on these terms, Let him deny himself, and take up his cross - A rule that can never be too much observed: let him in all things deny his own will, however pleasing, and do the will of God, however painful. Should we not consider all crosses, all things grievous to flesh and blood, as what they really

are, as opportunities of embracing God's will at the expense of our own? And consequently as so many steps by which we may advance toward perfection? We should make a swift progress in the spiritual life, if we were faithful in this practice. Crosses are so frequent, that whoever makes advantage of them, will soon be a great gainer. Great crosses are occasions of great improvement: and the little ones, which come daily, and even hourly, make up in number what they want in weight. We may in these daily and hourly crosses make effectual oblations of our will to God; which oblations, so frequently repeated, will soon amount to a great sum. Let us remember then (what can never be sufficiently inculcated) that God is the author of all events: that none is so small or inconsiderable, as to escape his notice and direction. Every event therefore declares to us the will of God, to which thus declared we should heartily submit. We should renounce our own to embrace it; we should approve and choose what his choice warrants as best for us. Herein should we exercise ourselves continually; this should be our practice all the day long. We should in humility accept the little crosses that are dispensed to us, as those that best suit our weakness. Let us bear these little things, at least for God's sake, and prefer his will to our own in matters of so small importance. And his goodness will accept these mean oblations; for he despiseth not the day of small things. Matt. x, 38.

25. Whosoever will save his life - At the expense of his conscience: whosoever, in the very highest instance, that of life itself, will not renounce himself, shall be lost eternally. But can any man hope he should be able thus to renounce himself, if he cannot do it in the smallest instances? And whosoever will lose his life shall find it - What he loses on earth he shall find in heaven. Matt. x, 39; Mark viii, 35; Luke ix, 24; xvii, 33; John xii, 25.

27. For the Son of man shall come - For there is no way to escape the righteous judgment of God.

28. And as an emblem of this, there are some here who shall live to see the Messiah coming to set up his mediatorial kingdom, with great power and glory, by the increase of his Church, and the destruction of the temple, city, and polity of the Jews.

XVII

1. A high mountain - Probably Mount Tabor. Mark ix, 2; Luke ix, 28.

2. And was transfigured - Or transformed. The indwelling Deity darted out its rays through the veil of the flesh; and that with such transcendent splendour, that he no longer bore the form of a servant. His face shone with Divine majesty, like the sun in its strength; and all his body was so irradiated by it, that his clothes could not conceal its glory, but became white and glittering as the very light, with which he covered himself as with a garment.

3. There appeared Moses and Elijah - Here for the full confirmation of their faith in Jesus, Moses, the giver of the law, Elijah, the most zealous of all the prophets, and God speaking from heaven, all bore witness to him.

4. Let us make three tents - The words of rapturous surprise. He says three, not six: because the apostles desired to be with their Master.

5. Hear ye him - As superior even to Moses and the prophets. See Deut. xviii, 17.

7. Be not afraid - And doubtless the same moment he gave them courage and strength.

9. Tell the vision to no man - Not to the rest of the disciples, lest they should be grieved and discouraged because they were not admitted to the sight: nor to any other persons, lest it should enrage some the more, and his approaching sufferings shall make others disbelieve it; till the Son of man be risen again - Till the resurrection should make it credible, and confirm their testimony about it.

10. Why then say the scribes, that Elijah must come first - Before the Messiah? If no man is to know of his coming? Should we not rather tell every man, that he is come, and that we have seen him, witnessing to thee as the Messiah?

11. Regulate all things - In order to the coming of Christ.

12. Elijah is come already - And yet when the Jews asked John, Art thou Elijah? He said, I am not, John i, 21. His meaning was, I am not Elijah the Tishbite, come again into the world. But he was the person of whom Malachi prophesied under that name.

14. Mark ix, 14; Luke xi, 37.

15. He is lunatic - This word might with great propriety he used, though the case was mostly preternatural; as the evil spirit would undoubtedly take advantage of the influence which the changes of the moon have on the brain and nerves.

17. O unbelieving and perverse generation - Our Lord speaks principally this to his disciples. How long shall I be with you? - Before you steadfastly believe?

20. Because of your unbelief - Because in this particular they had not faith. If ye have faith as a grain of mustard seed - That is, the least measure of it. But it is certain, the faith which is here spoken of does not always imply saving faith. Many have had it who thereby cast out devils, and yet will at last have their portion with them. It is only a supernatural persuasion given a man, that God will work thus by him at that hour. Now, though I have all this faith so as to remove mountains, yet if I have not the

faith which worketh by love, I am nothing. To remove mountains was a proverbial phrase among the Jews, and is still retained in their writings, to express a thing which is very difficult, and to appearance impossible. Matt. xxi, 21; Luke xvii, 6.

21. This kind of devils - goeth not out but by prayer and fasting - What a testimony is here of the efficacy of fasting, when added to fervent prayer! Some kinds of devils the apostles had cast out before this, without fasting.

22. Mark ix, 30; Luke ix, 44.

24. When they were come to Capernaum - Where our Lord now dwelt. This was the reason why they stayed till he came thither, to ask him for the tribute. Doth not your Master pay tribute? - This was a tribute or payment of a peculiar kind, being half a shekel, (that is, about fifteen pence,) which every master of a family used to pay yearly to the service of the temple, to buy salt, and little things not otherwise provided for. It seems to have been a voluntary thing, which custom rather than any law had established.

25. Jesus prevented him - Just when St. Peter was going to ask him for it. Of their own sons, or of strangers? - That is, such as are not of their own family.

26. Then are the sons free - The sense is, This is paid for the use of the house of God. But I am the Son of God. Therefore I am free from any obligation of paying this to my own Father.

27. Yet that, we may not offend them - Even those unjust, unreasonable men, who claim what they have no manner of right to: do not contest it with them, but rather yield to their demand, than violate peace or love. O what would not one of a loving spirit do for peace! Any thing which is not expressly forbidden in the word of God. A piece of money - The original word is a stater, which was in value two shillings and sixpence: just the sum that was wanted. Give for me and thee - Peter had a family of his own: the other apostles were the family of Jesus. How illustrious a degree of knowledge and power did our Lord here discover! Knowledge, penetrating into this animal, though beneath the waters; and power, in directing this very fish to Peter's hook, though he himself was at a distance! How must this have encouraged both him and his brethren in a firm dependence on Divine Providence.

XVIII

1. Who is the greatest in the kingdom of heaven? - Which of us shall be thy prime minister? They still dreamed of a temporal kingdom.

2. And Jesus calling to him a little child - This is supposed to have been the great Ignatius, whom Trajan, the wise, the good Emperor Trajan, condemned to be cast to the wild beasts at Rome! Mark ix, 36; Luke ix, 47.

3. Except ye be converted - The first step toward entering into the kingdom of grace, is to become as little children: lowly in heart, knowing yourselves utterly ignorant and helpless, and hanging wholly on your Father who is in heaven, for a supply of all your wants. We may further assert, (though it is doubtful whether this text implies so much,) except ye be turned from darkness to light, and from the power of Satan to God:, except ye be entirely, inwardly changed, renewed in the image of God, ye cannot enter into the kingdom of glory. Thus must every man be converted in this life, or he can never enter into life eternal. Ye shall in no wise enter - So far from being great in it. Matt. xix, 14.

5, 6. And all who are in this sense little children are unspeakably dear to me. Therefore help them all you can, as if it were myself in person, and see that ye offend them not; that is, that ye turn them not out of the right way, neither hinder them in it. Matt. x, 40; Luke x, 16; John xiii, 20.

7. Woe to the world because of offenses - That is, unspeakable misery will be in the world through them; for it must needs be that offenses come - Such is the nature of things, and such the weakness, folly, and wickedness of mankind, that it cannot be but they will come; but wo to that man - That is, miserable is that man, by whom the offense cometh. Offenses are, all things whereby any one is turned out of, or hindered in the way of God.

8, 9. If thy hand, foot, eye, cause thee to offend - If the most dear enjoyment, the most beloved and useful person, turn thee out of, or hinder thee in the way Is not this a hard saying? Yes; if thou take counsel with flesh and blood. Matt. v, 29; Mark ix, 43.

10. See that ye despise not one of these little ones - As if they were beneath your notice. Be careful to receive and not to offend, the very weakest believer in Christ: for as inconsiderable as some of these may appear to thee, the very angels of God have a peculiar charge over them: even those of the highest order, who continually appear at the throne of the Most High. To behold the face of God seems to signify the waiting near his throne; and to be an allusion to the office of chief ministers in earthly courts, who daily converse with their princes.

11. Another, and yet a stronger reason for your not despising them is, that I myself came into the world to save them. Luke xix, 10.

12. Luke xv, 4.

14. So it is not the will of your Father - Neither doth my Father despise the least of them. Observe

the gradation. The angels, the Son, the Father.

15. But how can we avoid giving offense to some? or being offended at others! Especially suppose they are quite in the wrong? Suppose they commit a known sin? Our Lord here teaches us how: he lays down a sure method of avoiding all offenses. Whosoever closely observes this threefold rule, will seldom offend others, and never be offended himself. If any do any thing amiss, of which thou art an eye or ear witness, thus saith the Lord, If thy brother - Any who is a member of the same religious community: Sin against thee,

1. Go and reprove him alone - If it may be in person; if that cannot so well be done, by thy messenger; or in writing. Observe, our Lord gives no liberty to omit this; or to exchange it for either of the following steps. If this do not succeed,

2. Take with thee one or two more - Men whom he esteems or loves, who may then confirm and enforce what thou sayest; and afterward, if need require, bear witness of what was spoken. If even this does not succeed, then, and not before,

3. Tell it to the elders of the Church - Lay the whole matter open before those who watch over yours and his soul. If all this avail not, have no farther intercourse with him, only such as thou hast with heathens. Can any thing be plainer? Christ does here as expressly command all Christians who see a brother do evil, to take this way, not another, and to take these steps, in this order, as he does to honour their father and mother. But if so, in what land do the Christians live? If we proceed from the private carriage of man to man, to proceedings of a more public nature, in what Christian nation are Church censures conformed to this rule? Is this the form in which ecclesiastical judgments appear, in the popish, or even the Protestant world? Are these the methods used even by those who boast the most loudly of the authority of Christ to confirm their sentences? Let us earnestly pray, that this dishonour to the Christian name may be wiped away, and that common humanity may not, with such solemn mockery, be destroyed in the name of the Lord! Let him be to thee as the heathen - To whom thou still owest earnest good will, and all the offices of humanity. Luke xvii, 3.

18. Whatsoever ye shall bind on earth - By excommunication, pronounced in the spirit and power of Christ. Whatsoever ye shall loose - By absolution from that sentence. In the primitive Church, absolution meant no more than a discharge from Church censure. Again I say - And not only your intercession for the penitent, but all your united prayers, shall be heard. How great then is the power of joint prayer! If two of you - Suppose a man and his wife. Matt. xvi, 19.

20. Where two or three are gathered together in my name - That is, to worship me. I am in the midst of them - By my Spirit, to quicken their prayers, guide their counsels, and answer their petitions.

22. Till seventy times seven - That is, as often as there is occasion. A certain number is put for an uncertain.

23. Therefore - In this respect.

24. One was brought who owed him ten thousand talents - According to the usual computation, if these were talents of gold, this would amount to seventy-two millions sterling. If they were talents of silver, it must have been four millions, four hundred thousand pounds. Hereby our Lord intimates the vast number and weight of our offenses against God, and our utter incapacity of making him any satisfaction.

25. As he had not to pay, his Lord commanded him to be sold - Such was the power which creditors anciently had over their insolvent debtors in several countries.

30. Went with him before a magistrate, and cast him into prison, protesting he should lie there, till he should pay the whole debt.

34. His Lord delivered him to the tormentors - Imprisonment is a much severer punishment in the eastern countries than in ours. State criminals, especially when condemned to it, are not only confined to a very mean and scanty allowance, but are frequently loaded with clogs or heavy yokes, so that they can neither lie nor sit at ease: and by frequent scourgings and sometimes rackings are brought to an untimely end. Till he should pay all that was due to him - That is, without all hope of release, for this he could never do. How observable is this whole account; as well as the great inference our Lord draws from it:

1. The debtor was freely and fully forgiven;

2. He wilfully and grievously offended;

3. His pardon was retracted, the whole debt required, and the offender delivered to the tormentors forever. And shall we still say, but when we are once freely and fully forgiven, our pardon can never be retracted? Verily, verily, I say unto you, So likewise will my heavenly Father do to you, if ye from your hearts forgive not every one his brother their trespasses.

Wesley's Notes on the Bible - The New Testament
XIX

1. He departed - and from that time walked no more in Galilee. Mark x, 1.

2. Multitudes followed him, and he healed them there - That is, wheresoever they followed him.

3. The Pharisees came tempting him - Trying to make him contradict Moses. For every cause - That is, for any thing which he dislikes in her. This the scribes allowed.

4. He said, Have ye not read - So instead of contradicting him, our Lord confutes them by the very words of Moses. He who made them, made them male and female from the beginning - At least from the beginning of the Mosaic creation. And where do we read of any other? Does it not follow, that God's making Eve was part of his original design, and not a consequence of Adam's beginning to fall? By making them one man and one woman, he condemned polygamy: by making them one flesh, he condemned divorce.

5. And said - By the mouth of Adam, who uttered the words. Gen. ii, 24.

7. Why did Moses command - Christ replies, Moses permitted (not commanded) it, because of the hardness of your hearts - Because neither your fathers nor you could bear the more excellent way. Deut. xxiv, 1; Matt. v, 31; Mark x, 2; Luke xvi, 18.

9. And I say to you - I revoke that indulgence from this day, so that from henceforth, Whosoever, &c.

11. But he said to them - This is not universally true; it does not hold, with regard to all men, but with regard to those only to whom is given this excellent gift of God. Now this is given to three sorts of persons to some by natural constitution, without their choice: to others by violence, against their choice; and to others by grace with their choice: who steadily withstand their natural inclinations, that they may wait upon God without distraction.

12. There are eunuchs who have made themselves eunuchs for the kingdom of heaven's sake - Happy they! who have abstained from marriage (though without condemning or despising it) that they might walk more closely with God! He that is able to receive it, let him receive it - This gracious command (for such it is unquestionably, since to say, such a man may live single, is saying nothing. Who ever doubted this?) is not designed for all men: but only for those few who are able to receive it. O let these receive it joyfully!

13. That he should lay his hands on them - This was a rite which was very early used, in praying for a blessing on young persons. See Gen. xlviii, 14, 20. The disciples rebuked them - That is, them that brought them: probably thinking such an employ beneath the dignity of their Master. Mark x, 13; Luke xviii, 15.

14. Of such is the kingdom of heaven - Little children, either in a natural or spiritual sense, have a right to enter into my kingdom. Matt. xviii, 3.

16. And behold one came - Many of the poor had followed him from the beginning. One rich man came at last. Mark x, 17; Luke xviii, 18.

17. Why callest thou me good - Whom thou supposest to be only a man. There is none good - Supremely, originally, essentially, but God. If thou wilt enter into life, keep the commandments - From a principle of loving faith. Believe, and thence love and obey. And this undoubtedly is the way to eternal life. Our Lord therefore does not answer ironically, which had been utterly beneath his character, but gives a plain, direct, serious answer to a serious question.

19. Exod. xx, 12. &c.

20. The young man saith, All these have I kept from my childhood - So he imagined; and perhaps he had, as to the letter; but not as to the spirit, which our Lord immediately shows.

21. If thou desirest to be perfect - That is, to be a real Christian: Sell what thou hast - He who reads the heart saw his bosom sin was love of the world; and knew he could not be saved from this, but by literally renouncing it. To him therefore he gave this particular direction, which he never designed for a general rule. For him that was necessary to salvation: to us it is not. To sell all was an absolute duty to him; to many of us it would be an absolute sin. The young man went away - Not being willing to have salvation at so high a price.

24. It is easier for a camel to go through the eye of a needle, (a proverbial expression,) than for a rich man to go through the strait gate: that is, humanly speaking, it is an absolute impossibility. Rich man! tremble! feel this impossibility; else thou art lost forever!

25. His disciples were amazed, saying, Who then can be saved? - If rich men, with all their advantages, cannot? Who? A poor man; a peasant; a beggar: ten thousand of them, sooner than one that is rich.

26. Jesus looking upon them - To compose their hurried spirits. O what a speaking look was there! Said to them - With the utmost sweetness: With men this is impossible - It is observable, he does not retract what he had said: no, nor soften it in the least degree, but rather strengthens it, by representing the salvation of a rich man as the utmost effort of Omnipotence.

28. In the renovation - In the final renovation of all things: Ye shall sit - In the beginning of the

judgment they shall stand, 2 Cor. v, 10. Then being absolved, they shall sit with the Judge, 1 Cor. vi, ii, On twelve thrones - So our Lord promised, without expressing any condition: yet as absolute as the words are, it is certain there is a condition implied, as in many scriptures, where none is expressed. In consequence of this, those twelve did not sit on those twelve thrones: for the throne of Judas another took, so that he never sat thereon.

29. And every one - In every age and country; not you my apostles only; That hath forsaken houses, or brethren, or wife, or children - Either by giving any of them up, when they could not be retained with a clear conscience or by willingly refraining from acquiring them: Shall receive a hundred-fold - In value, though not in kind, even in the present world.

30. But many first - Many of those who were first called, shall be last - Shall have the lowest reward: those who came after them being preferred before them: and yet possibly both the first and the last may be saved, though with different degrees of glory. Matt. xx, 16; Mark x, 31; Luke xiii, 30.

XX

1. That some of those who were first called may yet be last, our Lord confirms by the following parable: of which the primary scope is, to show, That many of the Jews would be rejected, and many of the Gentiles accepted; the secondary, That of the Gentiles, many who were first converted would be last and lowest in the kingdom of glory; and many of those who were last converted would be first, and highest therein. The kingdom of heaven is like - That is, the manner of God's proceeding in his kingdom resembles that of a householder. In the morning - At six, called by the Roman and Jews, the first hour. From thence reckoning on to the evening, they called nine, the third hour; twelve, the sixth; three in the afternoon, the ninth; and five, the eleventh. To hire labourers into his vineyard - All who profess to be Christians are in this sense labourers, and are supposed during their life to be working in God's vineyard.

2. The Roman penny was about seven pence halfpenny. [About thirteen and three quarter cents, American.] This was then the usual price of a day's labour.

6. About the eleventh hour - That is, very late; long after the rest were called.

8. In the evening - Of life; or of the world.

9. Who were hired about the eleventh hour - Either the Gentiles, who were called long after the Jews into the vineyard of the Church of Christ; or those in every age who did not hear, or at least understand the Gospel call, till their day of life was drawing to a period. Some circumstances of the parable seem best to suit the former, some the latter of these senses.

10. The first supposed they should have received more - Probably the first here may mean the Jews, who supposed they should always be preferred before the Gentiles.

12. Thou hast made them equal to us - So St. Peter expressly, Acts xv, 9. God-hath put no difference between us (Jews) and them, (Gentiles,) purifying their hearts by faith. And those who were equally holy here, whenever they were called, will be equally happy hereafter.

14. It is my will to give to this last called among the heathens even as to the first called among the Jews: yea, and to the late converted publicans and sinners, even as to those who, were called long before.

15. Is it not lawful for me to do what I will with my own? - Yea, doubtless, to give either to Jew or Gentile a reward infinitely greater than he deserves. But can it be inferred from hence, that it is lawful, or possible, for the merciful Father of spirits to "Consign an unborn soul to hell? Or damn him from his mother's womb?" Is thine eye evil because I am good - Art thou envious, because I am gracious? Here is an evident reference to that malignant aspect, which is generally the attendant of a selfish and envious temper.

16. So the last shall be first, and the first last - Not only with regard to the Jews and Gentiles, but in a thousand other instances. For many are called - All who hear the Gospel; but few chosen - Only those who obey it. Matt. xix, 30; xxii, 14.

17. Mark x, 32; Luke xviii, 31.

20. Then came to him the mother of Zebedee's children - Considering what he had been just speaking, was ever any thing more unreasonable? Perhaps Zebedee himself was dead, or was not a follower of Christ. Mark x, 35.

21. In thy kingdom - Still they expected a temporal kingdom.

22. Ye know not what is implied in being advanced in my kingdom, and necessarily prerequired thereto. All who share in my kingdom must first share in my sufferings. Are you able and willing to do this? Both these expressions, The cup, the baptism, are to be understood of his sufferings and death. The like expressions are common among the Jews.

23. But to sit on my right hand - Christ applies to the glories of heaven, what his disciples were so stupid as to understand of the glories of earth. But he does not deny that this is his to give. It is his to give in the strictest propriety, both as God, and as the Son of man. He only asserts, that he gives it to

none but those for whom it is originally prepared; namely, those who endure to the end in the faith that worketh by love.

25. Ye know that the princes of the Gentiles Lord it over them - And hence you imagine, the chief in my kingdom will do as they: but it will be quite otherwise.

26. Your minister - That is, your servant. Matt. xxiii, 11.

29. Mark x, 46; Luke xviii, 35.

30. Behold two blind men cried out - St. Mark and St. Luke mention only one of them, blind Bartimeus. He was far the more eminent of the two, and, as it seems, spoke for both.

31. The multitude charged them to hold their peace - And so they will all who begin to cry after the Son of David. But let those who feel their need of him cry the more; otherwise they will come short of a cure.

XXI

1. Mark xi, 1; Luke xix, 29; John xii, 12.

5. The daughter of Sion - That is, the inhabitants of Jerusalem: the first words of the passage are cited from Isaiah lxii, 11; the rest from Zech. ix, 9. The ancient Jewish doctors were wont to apply these prophecies to the Messiah. On an ass - The Prince of Peace did not take a horse, a warlike animal. But he will ride on that by and by, Rev. xix, 11. In the patriarchal ages, illustrious persons thought it no disgrace to make use of this animal: but it by no means appears, that this opinion prevailed, or this custom continued, till the reign of Tiberias. Was it a mean attitude wherein our Lord then appeared? Mean even to contempt! I grant it: I glory in it: it is for the comfort of my soul for the honour of his humility, and for the utter confusion of all worldly pomp and grandeur.

7. They set him thereon - That is, on the clothes.

8. A great multitude spread their garments in the way - A custom which was usual at the creation of a king, 2 Kings ix, 13.

9. The multitudes cried, saying - Probably from a Divine impulse; for certainly most of them understood not the words they uttered. Hoseanna - (Lord save us) was a solemn word in frequent use among the Jews. The meaning is, "We sing hosanna to the Son of David. Blessed is he, the Messiah, of the Lord. Save. Thou that art in the highest heavens." Our Lord restrained all public tokens of honour from the people till now, lest the envy of his enemies should interrupt his preaching before the time. But this reason now ceasing, he suffered their acclamations, that they might be a public testimony against their wickedness, who in four or five days after cried out, Crucify him, crucify him. The expressions recorded by the other evangelists are somewhat different from these: but all of them were undoubtedly used by some or others of the multitude.

11. This is Jesus from Nazareth - What a stumbling block was this! if he was of Nazareth, he could not be the Messiah. But they who earnestly desired to know the truth would not stumble threat: for upon inquiry (which such would not fail to make) they would find, he was not of Nazareth, but Bethlehem.

12. He cast out all that sold and bought - Doves and oxen for sacrifice. He had cast them out three years before, John ii, 14; bidding them not make that house a house of merchandise. Upon the repetition of the offense, he used sharper words. In the temple - That is, in the outer court of it, where the Gentiles used to worship. The money changers - The exchangers of foreign money into current coin, which those who came from distant parts might want to offer for the service of the temple. Mark xi, 11, 15; Luke xix, 45.

13. A den of thieves - A proverbial expression, for a harbour of wicked men. Isaiah lvi, 7; Jer. vii, 11.

16. Psalm viii, 2.

17. Mark xi, 11, 12.

20. The disciples seeing it - As they went by, the next day.

21. Jesus answering, said, If ye have faith - Whence we may learn, that one great end of our Lord in this miracle was to confirm and increase their faith: another was, to warn them against unfruitfulness. Matt. xvii, 20.

23. When he was come into the temple, the chief priests came - Who thought he violated their right: and the elders of the people - Probably, members of the sanhedrim, to whom that title most properly belonged: which is the more probable, as they were the persons under whose cognizance the late action of Christ, in purging the temple, would naturally fall. These, with the chief priests, seem purposely to have appeared in a considerable company, to give the more weight to what they said, and if need were, to bear a united testimony against him. As he was teaching - Which also they supposed he had no authority to do, being neither priest, nor Levite, nor scribe. Some of the priests (though not as priests) and all the scribes were authorized teachers. By what authority dost thou these things - Publicly teach the people! And drive out those who had our commission to traffic in the outer court? Luke xx, 1;

Mark xi, 27.

24. I will ask you one thing - Who have asked me many: The baptism, that is, the whole ministry of John, was it from heaven or from men? - By what authority did he act and teach? Did man or God give him that authority? Was it not God? But if so, the consequence was clear. For John testified that Jesus was the Christ.

25. Why did ye not believe him - Testifying this.

27. Neither tell I you - Not again, in express terms: he had often told them before, and they would not believe him.

30. He answered, I go, sir: but went not - Just so did the scribes and Pharisees: they professed the greatest readiness and zeal in the service of God: but it was bare profession, contradicted by all their actions.

32. John came in a way of righteousness - Walking in it, as well as teaching it. The publicans and harlots - The most notorious sinners were reformed, though at first they said, I will not. And ye seeing the amazing change which was wrought in them, though at first ye said, I go, sir, repented not afterward - Were no more convinced than before. O how is this scripture fulfilled at this day!

33. A certain householder planted a vineyard - God planted the Church in Canaan; and hedged it round about - First with the law, then with his peculiar providence: and digged a wine press - Perhaps it may mean Jerusalem: and built a tower - The temple: and went into a far country - That is, left the keepers of his vineyard, in some measure, to behave as they should see good. Mark xii, 1; Luke xx, 9.

34. He sent his servants - His extraordinary messengers, the prophets: to the husbandmen - The ordinary preachers or ministers of the Jews.

41. They say - Perhaps some of the by-standers, not the chief priests or Pharisees; who, as St. Luke relates, said, God forbid, Luke xx, 16.

42. The builders - The scribes and priests, whose office it was to build up the Church. Is become the head of the corner - Or the chief corner stone: he is become the foundation of the Church, on which the whole building rests, and is the principal corner stone, for uniting the Gentiles to it, as the chief corner stone of a house supports and links its two sides together. Psalm cxviii, 22.

43. Therefore - Because ye reject this corner stone. The kingdom of God - That is, the Gospel.

44. Whosoever shall fall on this stone shall be broken - Stumblers at Christ shall even then receive much hurt. He is said to fall on this stone, who hears the Gospel and does not believe. But on whomsoever it shall fall - In vengeance, it will utterly destroy him. It will fall on every unbeliever, when Christ cometh in the clouds of heaven. Luke xx, 18.

XXII

1. Jesus answering, spake - That is, spake with reference to what had just past.

2. A king, who made a marriage feast for his son - So did God, when he brought his first - begotten into the world.

3. Them that were invited - Namely, the Jews.

4. Fatlings - Fatted beasts and fowls.

5. One to his farm, another to his merchandise - One must mind what he has; another, gain what he wants. How many perish by misusing lawful things!

7. The king sending forth his troops - The Roman armies employed of God for that purpose. Destroyed those murderers - Primarily the Jews.

8. Go into the highways - The word properly signifies, the by- ways, or turnings of the road.

10. They gathered all - By preaching everywhere.

11. The guest - The members of the visible Church.

12. A wedding garment - The righteousness of Christ, first imputed, then implanted. It may easily be observed, this has no relation to the Lord's Supper, but to God's proceeding at the last day.

14. Many are called; few chosen - Many hear; few believe. Yea, many are members of the visible, but few of the invisible Church. Matt. xx, 16.

15. Mark xii, 13; Luke xx, 20.

16. The Herodians were a set of men peculiarly attached to Herod, and consequently zealous for the interest of the Roman government, which was the main support of the dignity and royalty of his family. Thou regardest not the person of men - Thou favourest no man for his riches or greatness.

17. Is it lawful to give tribute to Caesar? - If he had said, Yes, the Pharisees would have accused him to the people, as a betrayer of the liberties of his country. If he had said, No, the Herodians would have accused him to the Roman governor.

18. Ye hypocrites - Pretending a scruple of conscience.

20. The tribute money - A Roman coin, stamped with the head of Caesar, which was usually paid in tribute.

21. They say to him, Caesar's - Plainly acknowledging, by their having received his coin, that they

were under his government. And indeed this is a standing rule. The current coin of every nation shows who is the supreme governor of it. Render therefore, ye Pharisees, to Caesar the things which ye yourselves acknowledge to be Ciaesar's: and, ye Herodians, while ye are zealous for Caesar, see that ye render to God the things that are God's.

23. Mark xii, 18.

24. Deut. xxv, 5.

25. Now there were with us seven brethren -- this story seems to have been a kind of common-place objection, which no doubt they brought upon all occasions.

29. Ye err, not knowing the Scriptures - Which plainly assert a resurrection. Nor the power of God - Which is well able to effect it. How many errors flow from the same source?

30. They are as the angels - Incorruptible and immortal. So is the power of God shown in them! So little need had they of marriage!

31. Have ye not read - The Sadducees had a peculiar value for the books of Moses. Out of these therefore our Lord argues with them.

32. I am the God of Abraham - The argument runs thus: God is not the God of the dead, but of the living: (for that expression, Thy God, implies both benefit from God to man, and duty from man to God) but he is the God of Abraham, Isaac, and Jacob: therefore, Abraham, Isaac, and Jacob are not dead, but living. Therefore, the soul does not die with the body. So indeed the Sadducees supposed, and it was on this ground that they denied the resurrection. Exod. iii, 6.

33. At his doctrine - At the clearness and solidity of his answers.

34. Mark xii, 28; Luke x, 25.

35. A scribe asking him a question, trying him - Not, as it seems, with any ill design: but barely to make a further trial of that wisdom, which he had shown in silencing the Sadducees.

37. Deut. vi, 5.

39. Lev. xix, 18.

42. Luke xx, 41.

43. How doth David then by the Spirit - By inspiration, call him Lord? If he be merely the son (or descendant) of David? If he be, as you suppose, a mere man, the son of a man?

44. The Lord said to my Lord - This his dominion, to which David himself was subject, shows both the heavenly majesty of the king, and the nature of his kingdom. Sit thou on my right hand - That is, remain in the highest authority and power. Psalm cx, 1.

46. Neither durst any question him any more - Not by way of ensnaring or tempting him.

XXIII

1. Then - Leaving all converse with his adversaries, whom he now left to the hardness of their hearts.

2. The scribes sit in the chair of Moses - That is, read and expound the law of Moses, and are their appointed teachers.

3. All things therefore - Which they read out of the law, and enforce therefrom.

4. Luke xi, 46.

5. Their phylacteries - The Jews, understanding those words literally, It shall be as a token upon thy hand, and as frontlets between thine eyes, Exod. xiii, 16. And thou shalt bind these words for a sign upon thine hand, and they shall be as frontlets between thine eyes, Deut. vi, 8; used to wear little scrolls of paper or parchment, bound on their wrist and foreheads, on which several texts of Scripture were writ. These they supposed, as a kind of charm, would preserve them from danger. And hence they seem to have been called phylacteries, or preservatives. The fringes of their garments - Which God had enjoined them to wear, to remind them of doing all the commandments, Num. xv, 38. These, as well as their phylacteries, the Pharisees affected to wear broader and larger than other men. Mark xii, 38.

8, 9, 10. The Jewish rabbis were also called father and master, by their several disciples, whom they required,

1. To believe implicitly what they affirmed, without asking any further reason;

2. To obey implicitly what they enjoined, without seeking further authority. Our Lord, therefore, by forbidding us either to give or receive the title of rabbi, master, or father, forbids us either to receive any such reverence, or to pay any such to any but God.

11. Matt. xx, 26.

12. Whosoever shall exalt himself shall be humbled, and he that shall humble himself shall be exalted - It is observable that no one sentence of our Lord's is so often repeated as this: it occurs, with scarce any variation, at least ten times in the evangelists. Luke xiv, 11; xviii, 14.

13. Woe to you - Our Lord pronounced eight blessings upon the mount: he pronounces eight woes here; not as imprecations, but solemn, compassionate declarations of the misery, which these stubborn sinners were bringing upon themselves. Ye go not in - For ye are not poor in spirit; and ye hinder those

that would be so.

14. Mark xii, 40; Luke xx, 47.

16. Woe to you, ye blind guides - Before he had styled them hypocrites, from their personal character: now he gives them another title, respecting their influence upon others. Both these appellations are severely put together in the 23rd and 25th verses; and this severity rises to the height in the 33rd verse. The gold of the temple - The treasure kept there. He is bound - To keep his oath.

20. He that sweareth by the altar, sweareth by it, and by all things thereon - Not only by the gift, but by the holy fire, and the sacrifice; and above all, by that God to whom they belong; inasmuch as every oath by a creature is an implicit appeal to God.

23. Judgment - That is, justice: Faith - The word here means fidelity.

24. Ye blind guides, who teach others to do as you do yourselves, to strain out a gnat - From the liquor they are going to drink! and swallow a camel - It is strange, that glaring false print, strain at a gnat, which quite alters the sense, should run through all the editions of our English Bibles.

25. Full of rapine and intemperance - The censure is double (taking intemperance in the vulgar sense.) These miserable men procured unjustly what they used intemperately. No wonder tables so furnished prove a snare, as many find by sad experience. Thus luxury punishes fraud while it feeds disease with the fruits of injustice. But intemperance in the full sense takes in not only all kinds of outward intemperance, particularly in eating and drinking, but all intemperate or immoderate desires, whether of honour, gain, or sensual pleasure.

26. Ye build the tombs of the prophets - And that is all, for ye neither observe their sayings, nor imitate their actions.

30. We would not have been partakers - So ye make fair professions, as did your fathers.

31. Wherefore ye testify against yourselves - By your smooth words as well as devilish actions: that ye are the genuine sons of them who killed the prophets of their own times, while they professed the utmost veneration for those of past ages. From the 3rd to the 30th is exposed every thing that commonly passes in the world for religion, whereby the pretenders to it keep both themselves and others from entering into the kingdom of God; from attaining, or even seeking after those tempers, in which alone true Christianity consists. As,

1. Punctuality in attending on public and private prayer, ver. 4-14. Matt. xxiii, 4-14

2. Zeal to make proselytes to our opinion or communion, though they have less of the spirit of religion than before, ver. 15.

3. A superstitious reverence for consecrated places or things, without any for Him to whom they are consecrated, ver. 16-22.

4. A scrupulous exactness in little observances, though with the neglect of justice, mercy, and faith, ver. 23, 24.

5. A nice cautiousness to cleanse the outward behaviour, but without any regard to inward purity, ver. 25, 26.

6. A specious face of virtue and piety, covering the deepest hypocrisy and villany, ver. 27, 28.

7. A professed veneration for all good men, except those among whom they live.

32. Fill ye up - A word of permission, not of command: as if he had said, I contend with you no longer: I leave you to yourselves: you have conquered: now ye may follow the devices of your own hearts. The measure of your fathers - Wickedness: ye may now be as wicked as they.

33. Ye serpents - Our Lord having now lost all hope of reclaiming these, speaks so as to affright others from the like sins.

34. Wherefore - That it may appear you are the true children of those murderers, and have a right to have their iniquities visited on you: Behold, I send - Is not this speaking as one having authority? Prophets - Men with supernatural credentials: Wise men - Such as have both natural abilities and experience; and scribes - Men of learning: but all will not avail. Luke xi, 49.

35. That upon you may come - The consequence of which will be, that upon you will come the vengeance of all the righteous blood shed on the earth - Zechariah the son of Barachiah - Termed Jehoiada, 2 Chron. xxiv, 20, where the story is related: Ye slew - Ye make that murder also of your fathers your own, by imitating it: Between the temple - That is, the inner temple, and the altar - Which stood in the outer court. Our Lord seems to refer to this instance, rather than any other, because he was the last of the prophets on record that were slain by the Jews for reproving their wickedness: and because God's requiring this blood as well as that of Abel, is particularly taken notice of in Scripture.

37. Luke xiii, 34.

38. Behold your house - The temple, which is now your house, not God's: Is left unto you - Our Lord spake this as he was going out of it for the last time: Desolate - Forsaken of God and his Christ, and sentenced to utter destruction.

39. Ye - Jews in general; men of Jerusalem in particular: shall not see me from this time - Which includes the short space till his death, till, after a long interval of desolation and misery, ye say, Blessed is he that cometh in the name of the Lord - Ye receive me with joyful and thankful hearts. This also

shall be accomplished in its season.

XXIV

1. Mark xiii, 1; Luke xxi, 5.

2. There shall not be left one stone upon another - This was most punctually fulfilled; for after the temple was burnt, Titus, the Roman general, ordered the very foundations of it to be dug up; after which the ground on which it stood was ploughed up by Turnus Rufus.

3. As he sat on the Mount of Olives - Whence they had a full view of the temple. When shall these things be? And what shall be the sign of thy coming, and of the end of the world? - The disciples inquire confusedly
1. Concerning the time of the destruction of the temple;
2. Concerning the signs of Christ's coming, and of the end of the world, as if they imagined these two were the same thing. Our Lord answers distinctly concerning
   1. The destruction of the temple and city, with the signs preceding, ver. 4, &c., 15, &c.
   2. His own coming, and the end of the world, with the signs thereof, ver. 29-31.
   3. The time of the destruction of the temple, ver. 32, &c.
   4. The time of the end of the world, ver. 36.

4. Take heed that no man deceive you - The caution is more particularly designed for the succeeding Christians, whom the apostles then represented. The first sign of my coming is, the rise of false prophets. But it is highly probable, many of these things refer to more important events, which are yet to come.

5. Many shall come in my name - First, false Christs, next, false prophets, Matt. xxiv, 11. At length, both together, ver. 24. And indeed never did so many impostors appear in the world as a few years before the destruction of Jerusalem; undoubtedly because that was the time wherein the Jews in general expected the Messiah.

6. Wars - Near: Rumours of wars - At a distance. All these things must come to pass - As a foundation for lasting tranquillity. But the end - Concerning which ye inquire, is not yet - So far from it, that this is but the beginning sorrows.

9. Then shall they deliver you up to affliction - As if ye were the cause of all these evils. And ye shall be hated of all nations - Even of those who tolerate all other sects and parties; but in no nation will the children of the devil tolerate the children of God. Matt. x, 17.

10. Then shall many be offended - So as utterly to make shipwreck of faith and a pure conscience. But hold ye fast faith, ver. 11. in spite of false prophets: love, even when iniquity and offenses abound, ver. 12. And hope, unto the end, ver. 13. He that does so, shall be snatched out of the burning. The love of many will wax cold - The generality of those who love God will (like the Church at Ephesus, Rev. ii, 4,) leave their first love.

13. Matt. x, 22; Mark xiii, 13; Luke xxi, 17.

14. This Gospel shall be preached in all the world - Not universally: this is not done yet: but in general through the several parts of the world, and not only in Judea And this was done by St. Paul and the other apostles, before Jerusalem was destroyed. And then shall the end come - Of the city and temple. Josephus's History of the Jewish War is the best commentary on this chapter. it is a wonderful instance of God's providence, that he, an eye witness, and one who lived and died a Jew, should, especially in so extraordinary a manner, be preserved, to transmit to us a collection of important facts, which so exactly illustrate this glorious prophecy, in almost every circumstance. Mark xiii, 10.

15. When ye see the abomination of desolation - Daniel's term is, The abomination that maketh desolate, Dan. xi, 31; that is, the standards of the desolating legions, on which they bear the abominable images of their idols: Standing in the holy place - Not only the temple and the mountain on which it stood, but the whole city of Jerusalem, and several furlongs of land round about it, were accounted holy; particularly the mount on which our Lord now sat, and on which the Roman afterward planted their ensigns. He that readeth let him understand - Whoever reads that prophecy of Daniel, let him deeply consider it. Mark xiii, 14; Luke xxi, 20; Dan. ix, 27.

16. Then let them who are in Judea flee to the mountains - So the Christians did, and were preserved. It is remarkable that after the Roman under Cestus Gallus made their first advances toward Jerusalem, they suddenly withdrew again, in a most unexpected and indeed impolitic manner. This the Christians took as a signal to retire, which they did, some to Pella, and others to Mount Libanus.

17. Let not him that is on the house top come down to take any thing out of his house - It may be remembered that their stairs used to be on the outside of their houses.

19. Woe to them that are with child, and to them that give suck - Because they cannot so readily make their escape.

20. Pray ye that your flight be not in the winter - They did so; and their flight was in the spring. Neither on the Sabbath - Being on many accounts inconvenient; beside that many would have scrupled

to travel far on that day. For the Jews thought it unlawful to walk above two thousand paces (two miles) on the Sabbath day.

21. Then shall be great tribulation - Have not many things spoken in the chapter, as well as in Mark xiii, , Luke xxi, . a farther and much more extensive meaning than has been yet fulfilled?

22. And unless those days were shortened - By the taking of Jerusalem sooner than could be expected: No flesh would be saved - The whole nation would be destroyed. But for the elect's sake - That is, for the sake of the Christians.

23. Mark xiii, 21; Luke xvii, 23.

24. They would deceive, if possible, the very elect - But it is not possible that God should suffer the body of Christians to be thus deceived.

27. For as the lightning goeth forth - For the next coming of Christ will be as quick as lightning; so that there will not be time for any such previous warning.

28. For wheresoever the carcass is, there will the eagles he gathered together - Our Lord gives this, as a farther reason, why they should not hearken to any pretended deliverer. As if he had said, Expect not any deliverer of the Jewish nation; for it is devoted to destruction. It is already before God a dead carcass, which the Roman eagles will soon devour. Luke xvii, 37.

29. Immediately after the tribulation of those days - Here our Lord begins to speak of his last coming. But he speaks not so much in the language of man as of God, with whom a thousand years are as one day, one moment. Many of the primitive Christians not observing this, thought he would come immediately, in the common sense of the word: a mistake which St. Paul labours to remove, in his Second Epistle to the Thessalonians. The powers of the heavens - Probably the influences of the heavenly bodies. Mark xiii, 24; Luke xxi, 25.

30. Then shall appear the sign of the Son of man in heaven - It seems a little before he himself descends. The sun, moon, and stars being extinguished, (probably not those of our system only) the sign of the Son of man (perhaps the cross) will appear in the glory of the Lord.

31. They shall gather together his elect - That is, all that have endured to the end in the faith which worketh by love.

32. Learn a parable - Our Lord having spoke of the signs preceding the two grand events, concerning which the apostles had inquired, begins here to speak of the time of them. And to the question proposed, ver. 3, concerning the time of the destruction of Jerusalem, he answers ver. 34. Concerning the time of the end of the world, he answers chap. xxiv, 36. Mark xiii, 28; Luke xxi, 29.

34. This generation of men now living shall not pass till all these things be done - The expression implies, that great part of that generation would be passed away, but not the whole. Just so it was. For the city and temple were destroyed thirty-nine or forty years after.

36. But of that day - The day of judgment; Knoweth no man - Not while our Lord was on earth. Yet it might be afterward revealed to St. John consistently with this.

37. Luke xvii, 26.

40. One is taken - Into God's immediate protection: and one is left - To share the common calamities. Our Lord speaks as having the whole transaction present before his eyes.

41. Two women shall be grinding - Which was then a common employment of women.

42. Ye know not what hour your Lord cometh - Either to require your soul of you, or to avenge himself of this nation. Mark xiii, 33; Luke xii, 35; xxi, 34.

45. Who then is the faithful and wise servant - Which of you aspires after this character? Wise - Every moment retaining the clearest conviction, that all he now has is only intrusted to him as a steward: Faithful - Thinking, speaking, and acting continually, in a manner suitable to that conviction.

48. But if that evil servant - Now evil, having put away faith and a good conscience.

51. And allot him his portion with the hypocrites - The worst of sinners, as upright and sincere as he was once. If ministers are the persons here primarily intended, there is a peculiar propriety in the expression. For no hypocrisy can be baser, than to call ourselves ministers of Christ, while we are the slaves of avarice, ambition, or sensuality. Wherever such are found, may God reform them by his grace, or disarm them of that power and influence, which they continually abuse to his dishonour, and to their own aggravated damnation!

XXV

This chapter contains the last public discourse which our Lord uttered before he was offered up. He had before frequently declared what would be the portion of all the workers of iniquity. But what will become of those who do no harm? Honest, inoffensive, good sort of people? We have here a clear and full answer to this important question.

1. Then shall the kingdom of heaven - That is, the candidates for it, be like ten virgins - The bridemaids on the wedding night were wont to go to the house where the bride was, with burning lamps or torches in their hands, to wait for the bride groom's coming. When he drew near, they went to meet

him with their lamps, and to conduct him to the bride.

3. *The foolish took no oil with them* - No more than kept them burning just for the present. None to supply their future want, to recruit their lamp's decay. The lamp is faith. A lamp and oil with it, is faith working by love.

4. *The wise took oil in their vessels* - Love in their hearts. And they daily sought a fresh supply of spiritual strength, till their faith was made perfect.

5. *While the bridegroom delayed* - That is, before they were called to attend him, they all slumbered and slept - Were easy and quiet, the wise enjoying a true, the foolish a false peace.

6. *At midnight* - In an hour quite unthought of.

7. *They trimmed their lamps* - They examined themselves and prepared to meet their God.

8. *Give us of your oil, for our lamps are gone out* - Our faith is dead. What a time to discover this! Whether it mean the time of death, or of judgment. Unto which of the saints wilt thou then turn? Who can help thee at such a season?

9. *But the wise answered, Lest there be not enough for us and you!* - Beginning the sentence with a beautiful abruptness; such as showed their surprise at the state of those poor wretches, who had so long received them, as well as their own souls. Lest there be not enough - It is sure there is not; for no man has more than holiness enough for himself. *Go ye rather to them that sell* - Without money and without price: that is, to God, to Christ. *And buy* - If ye can. O no! The time is past and returns no more!

13. *Watch therefore* - He that watches has not only a burning lamp, but likewise oil in his vessel. And even when he sleepeth, his heart waketh. He is quiet; but not secure.

14. Our Lord proceeds by a parable still plainer (if that can be) to declare the final reward of a harmless man. May God give all such in this their day, ears to hear and hearts to understand it! *The kingdom of heaven* - That is, the King of heaven, Christ. Mark xiii, 34; Luke xix, 12.

15. *To one he gave five talents, to another two, and to another one* - And who knows whether (all circumstances considered) there be a greater disproportion than this, in the talents of those who have received the most, and those who have received the fewest? *According to his own ability* - The words may be translated more literally, according to his own mighty power. *And immediately took his journey* - To heaven.

18. *He that had received one* - Made his having fewer talents than others a pretense for not improving any. *Went and hid his master's money* - Reader, art thou doing the same? Art thou hiding the talent God hath lent thee?

24. *I knew thou art a hard man* - No. Thou knowest him not. He never knew God, who thinks him a hard master. *Reaping where thou hast not sown* - That is, requiring more of us than thou hast given us power to perform. So does every obstinate sinner, in one kind or other, lay the blame of his own sins on God.

25. *And I was afraid* - Lest if I had improved my talent, I should have had the more to answer for. So from this fear, one will not learn to read, another will not hear sermons!

26. *Thou knewest* - That I require impossibilities! This is not an allowing, but a strong denial of the charge.

27. *Thou oughtest therefore* - On that very account, on thy own supposition, to have improved my talent, as far as was possible.

29. *To every one that hath shall be given* - So close does God keep to this stated rule, from the beginning to the end of the world. Matt. xiii, 12.

30. *Cast ye the unprofitable servant into the outer darkness* - For what? what had he done? It is true he had not done good. But neither is he charged with doing any harm. Why, for this reason, for barely doing no harm, he is consigned to outer darkness. He is pronounced a wicked, because he was a slothful, an unprofitable servant. So mere harmlessness, on which many build their hope of salvation, was the cause of his damnation! *There shall be the weeping* - Of the careless thoughtless sinner; and the gnashing of teeth - Of the proud and stubborn. The same great truth, that there is no such thing as negative goodness, is in this chapter shown three times:

1. In the parable of the virgins;
2. In the still plainer parable of the servants, who had received the talents; and
3. In a direct unparabolical declaration of the manner wherein our Lord will proceed at the last day. The several parts of each of these exactly answers each other, only each rises above the preceding.

31. *When the Son of man shall come in his glory, and all the holy angels with him* - With what majesty and grandeur does our Lord here speak of himself Giving us one of the noblest instances of the true sublime. Indeed not many descriptions in the sacred writings themselves seem to equal this. Methinks we can hardly read it without imagining ourselves before the awful tribunal it describes.

34. *Inherit the kingdom* - Purchased by my blood, for all who have believed in me with the faith which wrought by love. *Prepared for you* - On purpose for you. May it not be probably inferred from hence, that man was not created merely to fill up the places of the fallen angels?

35. *I was hungry, and ye gave me meat; I was thirsty, and ye gave me drink* - All these works of

outward mercy suppose faith and love, and must needs he accompanied with works of spiritual mercy. But works of this kind the Judge could not mention in the same manner. He could not say, I was in error, and ye recalled me to the truth; I was in sin, and ye brought me to repentance. In prison - Prisoners need to be visited above all others, as they are commonly solitary and forsaken by the rest of the world.

37. Then shall the righteous answer - It cannot be, that either the righteous or the wicked should answer in these very words. What we learn herefrom is, that neither of them have the same estimation of their own works as the Judge hath.

40. Inasmuch as ye did it to one of the least of these my brethren, ye did it to me - What encouragement is here to assist the household of faith? But let us likewise remember to do good to all men.

41. Depart into the everlasting fire, which was prepared for the devil and his angels - Not originally for you: you are intruders into everlasting fire.

44. Then will they answer - So the endeavour to justify themselves, will remain with the wicked even to that day!

46. And these shall go away into everlasting punishment, but the righteous into life everlasting - Either therefore the punishment is strictly eternal, or the reward is not: the very same expression being applied to the former as to the latter. The Judge will speak first to the righteous, in the audience of the wicked. The wicked shall then go away into everlasting fire, in the view of the righteous. Thus the damned shall see nothing of the everlasting life; but the just will see the punishment of the ungodly. It is not only particularly observable here

1. That the punishment lasts as long as the reward; but,
2. That this punishment is so far from ceasing at the end of the world, that it does not begin till then.

XXVI

1. When Jesus had finished all these discourses - When he had spoken all he had to speak. Till then he would not enter upon his passion: then he would delay it no longer. Mark xiv, 1; Luke xxii, 1.

2. After two days is the Passover - The manner wherein this was celebrated gives much light to several circumstances that follow. The master of the family began the feast with a cup of wine, which having solemnly blessed, he divided among the guests, Luke xxii, 17. Then the supper began with the unleavened bread and bitter herbs; which when they had all tasted, one of the young persons present, according to Exod. xii, 26, asked the reason of the solemnity. This introduced the showing forth, or declaration of it: in allusion to which we read of showing forth the Lord's death, 1 Cor. xi, 26. Then the master rose up and took another cup, before the lamb was tasted. After supper, he took a thin loaf or cake, which he broke and divided to all at the table, and likewise the cup, usually called the cup of thanksgiving, of which he drank first, and then all the guests. It was this bread and this cup which our Lord consecrated to be a standing memorial of his death.

3. The chief priests and the scribes and the elders of the people - (Heads of families.) These together constituted the sanhedrim, or great council, which had the supreme authority, both in civil and ecclesiastical affairs.

5. But they said, Not at the feast - This was the result of human wisdom. But when Judas came they changed their purpose. So the counsel of God took place, and the true paschal Lamb was offered up on the great day of the paschal solemnity.

6. Mark xiv, 3.

8. His disciples seeing it, had indignation, saying - It seems several of them were angry, and spoke, though none so warmly as Judas Iscariot.

11. Ye have the poor always with you - Such is the wise and gracious providence of God, that we may have always opportunities of relieving their wants, and so laying up for ourselves treasures in heaven.

12. She hath done it for my burial - As it were for the embalming of my body. Indeed this was not her design: but our Lord puts this construction upon it, to confirm thereby what he had before said to his disciples, concerning his approaching death.

13. This Gospel - That is, this part of the Gospel history.

14. Mark xiv, 10; Luke xxii, 3.

15. They bargained with him for thirty pieces of silver - (About three pounds fifteen shillings sterling; or sixteen dollars sixty- seven cents) the price of a slave, Exod. xxi, 32.

17. On the first day of unleavened bread - Being Thursday, the fourteenth day of the first month, Exod. xii, 6, 15. Mark xiv, 12 Luke xxii, 7

18. The Master saith, My time is at hand - That is, the time of my suffering.

20. Mark xiv, 17; Luke xxii, 14.

Wesley's Notes on the Bible - The New Testament

23. He that dippeth his hand with me in the dish - Which it seems Judas was doing at that very time. This dish was a vessel full of vinegar, wherein they dipped their bitter herbs.

24. The Son of man goeth through sufferings to glory, as it is written of him - Yet this is no excuse for him that betrayeth him: miserable will that man be: it had been good for that man if he had not been born - May not the same be said of every man that finally perishes? But who can reconcile this, if it were true of Judas alone, with the doctrine of universal salvation?

25. Thou hast said - That is, it is as thou hast said.

26. Jesus took the bread - the bread or cake, which the master of the family used to divide among them, after they had eaten the passover. The custom our Lord now transferred to a nobler use. This bread is, that is, signifies or represents my body, according to the style of the sacred writers. Thus Gen. xl, 12, The three branches are three days. Thus Gal. iv, 24, St. Paul speaking of Sarah and Hagar, says, These are the two covenants. Thus in the grand type of our Lord, Exod. xii, 11, God says of the paschal lamb, This is the Lord's passover. Now Christ substituting the holy communion for the passover, follows the style of the Old Testament, and uses the same expressions the Jews were wont to use in celebrating the passover.

27. And he took the cup - Called by the Jews the cup of thanksgiving; which the master of the family used likewise to give to each after supper.

28. This is the sign of my blood, whereby the new testament or covenant is confirmed. Which is shed for many - As many as spring from Adam.

29. I will not drink henceforth of this fruit of the vine, till I drink it new with you in my Father's kingdom - That is, I shall taste no more wine, till I drink wine of quite another kind in the glorious kingdom of my Father. And of this you shall also partake with me.

30. And when they had sung the hymn - Which was constantly sung at the close of the passover. It consisteth of six psalms, from the 113th to the 118th. The Mount of Olives - Was over against the temple, about two miles from Jerusalem. Mark xiv, 26; Luke xxii, 39; John xviii, 1.

31. All ye will be offended at me - Something will happen to me, which will occasion your falling into sin by forsaking me. Zech. xiii, 7.

32. But notwithstanding this, after I am risen I will go before you (as a shepherd before his sheep) into Galilee. Though you forsake me, I will not for this forsake you.

34. Before cock crowing thou wilt deny me thrice - That is, before three in the morning, the usual time of cock crowing: although one cock was heard to crow once, after Peter's first denial of his Lord.

35. In like manner also said all the disciples - But such was the tenderness of our Lord, that he would not aggravate their sin by making any reply.

36. Then cometh Jesus to a place called Gethsemane - That is, the valley of fatness. The garden probably had its name from its soil and situation, laying in some little valley between two of those many hills, the range of which constitutes the Mount of Olives. Mark xiv, 32; Luke xxii, 40.

37. And taking with him Peter and the two sons of Zebedee - To be witnesses of all; he began to be sorrowful and in deep anguish - Probably from feeling the arrows of the Almighty stick fast in his soul, while God laid on him the iniquities of us all. Who can tell what painful and dreadful sensations were then impressed on him by the immediate hand of God? The former word in the original properly signifies, to be penetrated with the most exquisite sorrow; the latter to be quite depressed, and almost overwhelmed with the load.

39. And going a little farther - About a stone's cast, Luke xxii, 41 - So that the apostles could both see and hear him still. If it be possible, let this cup pass from me - And it did pass from him quickly. When he cried unto God with strong cries and tears, he was heard in that which he feared. God did take away the terror and severity of that inward conflict.

41. The spirit - Your spirit: ye yourselves. The flesh - Your nature. How gentle a rebuke was this, and how kind an apology! especially at a time when our Lord's own mind was so weighed down with sorrow.

45. Sleep on now, if you can, and take your rest - For any farther service you can be of to me.

47. Mark xiv, 43; Luke xxii, 47; John xviii, 2.

50. The heroic behaviour of the blessed Jesus, in the whole period of his sufferings, will be observed by every attentive eye, and felt by every pious heart: although the sacred historians, according to their usual but wonderful simplicity, make no encomiums upon it. With what composure does he go forth to meet the traitor! With what calmness receive that malignant kiss! With what dignity does he deliver himself into the hands of his enemies! Yet plainly showing his superiority over them, and even then leading as it were captivity captive!

51. And one of them striking the servant of the high priest - Probably the person that seized Jesus first; Cut off his ear - Aiming, it seems, to cleave his head, but that by a secret providence interposing, he declined the blow. Mark xiv, 47; Luke xxii, 49; John xviii, 10.

52. All they that take the sword - Without God's giving it them: without sufficient authority.

53. He will presently give me more than twelve legions of angels - The least of whom, it is

probable, could overturn the earth and destroy all the inhabitants of it.

55. Mark xiv, 48; Luke xxii, 52

57. They led him away to Caiaphas - From the house of Annas, the father-in-law of Caiaphas, to whom they had carried him first. Mark xiv, 53; Luke xxii, 54; John xviii, 12.

58. But Peter followed him afar off - Variously agitated by conflicting passions; love constrained him to follow his Master; fear made him follow afar off. And going in, sat with the servants - Unfit companions as the event showed.

60. Yet found they none - On whose evidence they could condemn him to die. At last came two false witnesses - Such they were, although part of what they said was true; because our Lord did not speak some of those words at all; nor any of them in this sense.

64. Hereafter shall ye see the Son of man - He speaks in the third person, modestly, and yet plainly; Sitting on the right hand of power - That is, the right hand of God: And coming upon the clouds of heaven - As he is represented by Daniel, Dan. vii, 13, 14. Our Lord looked very unlike that person now! But nothing could be more awful, more majestic and becoming, than such an admonition in such circumstances!

65. Then the high priest rent his clothes - Though the high priest was forbidden to rend his clothes (that is, his upper garment) in some cases where others were allowed to do it, Lev. xxi, 10; yet in case of blasphemy or any public calamity, it was thought allowable. Caiaphas hereby expressed, in the most artful manner, his horror at hearing such grievous blasphemy.

67. Then - After he had declared he was the Son of God, the sanhedrim doubtless ordered him to be carried out, while they were consulting what to do. And then it was that the soldiers who kept him began these insults upon him.

72. He denied with an oath - To which possibly he was not unaccustomed, before our Lord called him.

73. Surely thou art also one of them, for thy speech discovereth thee - Malchus might have brought a stronger proof than this. But such is the overruling providence of God, that the world, in the height of their zeal, commonly catch hold of the very weakest of all arguments against the children of God.

74. Then began he to curse and to swear - Having now quite lost the reins, the government of himself.

XXVII

1. In the morning - As the sanhedrim used to meet in one of the courts of the temple, which was never opened in the night, they were forced to stay till the morning before they could proceed regularly, in the resolution they had taken to put him to death. Mark xv, 1; Luke xxii, 66; xxiii, 1; John xviii, 28.

2. Having bound him - They had bound him when he was first apprehended. But they did it now afresh, to secure him from any danger of an escape, as he passed through the streets of Jerusalem.

3. Then Judas seeing that he was condemned - Which probably he thought Christ would have prevented by a miracle.

4. They said, what is that to us? - How easily could they digest innocent blood! And yet they had a conscience! It is not lawful (say they) to put it into the treasury - But very lawful to slay the innocent!

5. In that part of the temple where the sanhedrim met.

7. They bought with them the potter's field - Well known, it seems, by that name. This was a small price for a field so near Jerusalem. But the earth had probably been digged for potters' vessels, so that it was now neither fit for tillage nor pasture, and consequently of small value. Foreigners - Heathens especially, of whom there were then great numbers in Jerusalem.

9. Then was fulfilled - What was figuratively represented of old, was now really accomplished. What was spoken by the prophet - The word Jeremy, which was added to the text in latter copies, and thence received into many translations, is evidently a mistake: for he who spoke what St. Matthew here cites (or rather paraphrases) was not Jeremy, but Zechariah. Zech. xi, 12.

10. As the Lord commanded me - To write, to record.

11. Art thou the king of the Jews? - Jesus before Caiaphas avows himself to be the Christ, before Pilate to be a king; clearly showing thereby, that his answering no more, was not owing to any fear.

15. At every feast - Every year, at the feast of the passover. Mark xv, 6; Luke xxiii, 17; John xviii, 39.

18. He knew that for envy they had delivered him - As well as from malice and revenge; they envied him, because the people magnified him.

22. They all say, Let him be crucified - The punishment which Barabbas had deserved: and this probably made them think of it. But in their malice they forgot with how dangerous a precedent they furnished the Roman governor. And indeed within the compass of a few years it turned dreadfully upon themselves.

Wesley's Notes on the Bible - The New Testament

24. Then Pilate took water and washed his hands - This was a custom frequently used among the heathens as well as among the Jews, in token of innocency.

25. His blood be on us and on our children - As this imprecation was dread. fully answered in the ruin so quickly brought on the Jewish nation, and the calamities which have ever since pursued that wretched people, so it was peculiarly fulfilled by Titus the Roman general, on the Jews whom he took during the siege of Jerusalem. So many, after having been scourged in a terrible manner, were crucified all round the city, that in a while there was not room near the wall for the crosses to stand by each other. Probably this befell some of those who now joined in this cry, as it certainly did many of their children: the very finger of God thus pointing out their crime in crucifying his Son.

26. He delivered him to be crucified - The person crucified was nailed to the cross as it lay on the ground, through each hand extended to the utmost stretch, and through both the feet together. Then the cross was raised up, and the foot of it thrust with a violent shock into a hole in the ground prepared for it. This shock disjointed the body, whose whole weight hung upon the nails, till the persons expired through mere dint of pain. This kind of death was used only by the Romans, and by them inflicted only on slaves and the vilest criminals.

27. The whole troop - or cohort. This was a body of foot commanded by the governor, which was appointed to prevent disorders and tumults, especially on solemn occasions. Mark xv, 16 John xix, 2.

28. They put on him a scarlet robe - Such as kings and generals wore; probably an old tattered one.

32. Him they compelled to bear his cross - He bore it himself, till he sunk under it, John xix, 17.

33. A place called Golgotha, that is, the place of a skull - Golgotha in Syriac signifies a skull or head: it was probably called so from this time; being an eminence upon Mount Calvary, not far from the king's gardens. Mark xv, 22; Luke xxiii, 33; John xix, 17

34. They gave him vinegar mingled with gall - Out of derision: which, however nauseous, he received and tasted of. St. Mark mentions also a different mixture which was given him, Wine mingled with myrrh: such as it was customary to give to dying criminals, to make them less sensible of their sufferings: but this our Lord refused to taste, determining to bear the full force of his pains.

35. They parted his garments - This was the custom of the Romams. The soldiers performed the office of executioners, and divided among them the spoils of the criminals. My vesture - That is, my inner garment. Psalm xxii, 18.

38. Mark xv, 27; Luke xxiii, 32.

44. Mark xv, 32; Luke xxiii, 33.

45. From the sixth hour, there was darkness over all the earth unto the ninth hour - Insomuch, that even a heathen philosopher seeing it, and knowing it could not be a natural eclipse, because it was at the time of the full moon, and continued three hours together, cried out, "Either the God of nature suffers, or the frame of the world is dissolved." By this darkness God testified his abhorrence of the wickedness which was then committing. It likewise intimated Christ's sore conflicts with the Divine justice, and with all the powers of darkness.

46. About the ninth hour, Jesus cried with a loud voice - Our Lord's great agony probably continued these three whole hours, at the conclusion of which be thus cried out, while he suffered from God himself what was unutterable. My God, my God, why hast thou forsaken me? - Our Lord hereby at once expresses his trust in God, and a most distressing sense of his letting loose the powers of darkness upon him, withdrawing the comfortable discoveries of his presence, and filling his soul with a terrible sense of the wrath due to the sins which he was bearing. Psalm xxii, 1.

48. One taking a sponge, filled it with vinegar - Vinegar and water was the usual drink of the Roman soldiers. It does not appear, that this was given him in derision, but rather with a friendly design, that he might not die before Elijah came. John xix, 28.

50. After he had cried with a loud voice - To show that his life was still whole in him. He dismissed his spirit - So the original expression may be literally translated: an expression admirably suited to our Lord's words, John x, xviii, No man taketh my life from me, but I lay it down of myself. He died by a voluntary act of his own, and in a way peculiar to himself. He alone of all men that ever were, could have continued alive even in the greatest tortures, as long as he pleased, or have retired from the body whenever he had thought fit. And how does it illustrate that love which he manifested in his death? Insomuch as he did not use his power to quit his body, as soon as it was fastened to the cross, leaving only an insensible corpse, to the cruelty of his murderers: but continued his abode in it, with a steady resolution, as long as it was proper. He then retired from it, with a majesty and dignity never known or to be known in any other death: dying, if one may so express it, like the Prince of life.

51. Immediately upon his death, while the sun was still darkened, the veil of the temple, which separated the holy of holies from the court of the priests, though made of the richest and strongest tapestry, was rent in two from the top to the bottom: so that while the priest was ministering at the golden altar (it being the time of the sacrifice) the sacred oracle, by an invisible power was laid open to full view: God thereby signifying the speedy removal of the veil of the Jewish ceremonies the casting down the partition wall, so that the Jews and Gentiles were now admitted to equal privileges, and the

opening a way through the veil of his flesh for all believers into the most holy place. And the earth was shaken - There was a general earthquake through the whole globe, though chiefly near Jerusalem: God testifying thereby his wrath against the Jewish nation, for the horrid impiety they were committing.

52. Some of the tombs were shattered and laid open by the earthquake, and while they continued unclosed (and they must have stood open all the Sabbath, seeing the law would not allow any attempt to close them) many bodies of holy men were raised, (perhaps Simeon, Zacharias, John the Baptist, and others who had believed in Christ, and were known to many in Jerusalem,) And coming out of the tombs after his resurrection, went into the holy city (Jerusalem) and appeared to many - Who had probably known them before: God hereby signifying, that Christ had conquered death, and would raise all his saints in due season.

54. The centurion - The officer who commanded the guard; and they that were with him feared, saying, Truly this was the Son of God - Referring to the words of the chief priests and scribes, chap. xxvii, xliii, He said, I am the Son of God.

56. James - The less: he was so called, to distinguish him from the other James, the brother of John; probably because he was less in stature.

57. When the evening was come - That is, after three o'clock; the time from three to six they termed the evening. Mark xv, 42; Luke xxiii, 50; John xix, 38.

62. On the morrow, the day that followed the day of the preparation - The day of preparation was the day before the Sabbath, whereon they were to prepare for the celebration of it. The next day then was the Sabbath according to the Jews. But the evangelist seems to express it by this circumlocution, to show the Jewish Sabbath was then abolished.

63. That impostor said, while he was yet alive, After three days I will rise again - We do not find that he had ever said this to them, unless when he spoke of the temple of his body, John ii, 19, 21. And if they here refer to what he then said, how perverse and iniquitous was their construction on these words, when he was on his trial before the council? Chap. xxvi, 61. Then they seemed not to understand them!

65. Ye have a guard - Of your own, in the tower of Antonia, which was stationed there for the service of the temple.

66. They went and secured the sepulchre, sealing the stone, and setting a guard - They set Pilate's signet, or the public seal of the sanhedrim upon a fastening which they had put on the stone. And all this uncommon caution was overruled by the providence of God, to give the strongest proofs of Christ's ensuing resurrection; since there could be no room for the least suspicion of deceit, when it should be found, that his body was raised out of a new tomb, where there was no other corpse, and this tomb hewn out of a rock, the mouth of which was secured by a great stone, under a seal, and a guard of soldiers.

XXVIII

1. Mark xvi, 1; Luke xxiv, 1; John xx, 1

2. An angel of the Lord had rolled away the stone and sat upon it - St. Luke and St. John speak of two angels that appeared: but it seems as if only one of them had appeared sitting on the stone without the sepulchre, and then going into it, was seen with another angel, sitting, one where the head, the other where the feet of the body had lain.

6. Come, see the place where the Lord lay - Probably in speaking he rose up, and going before the women into the sepulchre, said, Come, see the place. This clearly reconciles what St. John relates, John xx, 12, this being one of the two angels there mentioned.

7. There shall ye see him - In his solemn appearance to them all together. But their gracious Lord would not be absent so long: he appeared to them several times before then. Lo, I have told you - A solemn confirmation of what he had said.

9. Hail - The word in its primary sense means, "Rejoice:" in its secondary and more usual meaning, "Happiness attend you."

10. Go tell my brethren -- I still own them as such, though they so lately disowned and forsook me.

13. Say, his disciples came by night, and stole him while we slept - Is it possible, that any man of sense should digest this poor, shallow inconsistency? If ye were awake, why did you let the disciples steal him? If asleep, how do you know they did?

16. To the mountain where Jesus had appointed them - This was probably Mount Tabor, where, (it is commonly supposed) he had been before transfigured. It seems to have been here also, that he appeared to above five hundred brethren at once.

18. All power is given to me - Even as man. As God, he had all power from eternity.

19. Disciple all nations - Make them my disciples. This includes the whole design of Christ's commission. Baptizing and teaching are the two great branches of that general design. And these were to be determined by the circumstances of things; which made it necessary in baptizing adult Jews or

heathens, to teach them before they were baptized; in discipling their children, to baptize them before they were taught; as the Jewish children in all ages were first circumcised, and after taught to do all God had commanded them. Mark xvi, 15.

John Wesley

NOTES ON THE GOSPEL ACCORDING TO ST. MARK

THIS CONTAINS,

I. The beginning of the Gospel,
       a. John prepares the way Chap. i, 1-8
       b. Baptizes Jesus, who is proclaimed the Son of God 9-11
       c. Tempted of Satan, served by angels 12, 13

II. The Gospel itself,
    A. In Galilee: where we may observe three periods,
       a. After John was cast into prison, In general,
  1. The place and matter of his preaching, 14, 15
  2. The calling of several of the apostles 16-20 In particular,
  1. Actions not censured by his adversaries
  1. He teaches with authority 21, 22
  2. Cures the demoniac 23-28
  3. Heals many sick 29-34
  4. Prays 35
  5. Teaches everywhere 36-39
  6. Cleanses the leper 40-45
  2. Actions censured by them, Here occur,
  1. The paralytic forgiven and healed ii, 1-12
  2. The call of Levi, and eating with publicans and sinners. 13-17
  3. The question concerning fasting answered 18-22
  4. The ears of corn plucked 23-28
  5. The withered hand restored: Snares laid iii, 1-6
  3. Our Lord's retirement,
  1. At the sea 7-12
  2. In the mountain, where the apostles are called 13-19
  3. In the house, where after refuting the blasphemy of the Pharisees, he shows who are his mother and his brethren. 20-35
  4. In the ship; various parables iv, 1-34
  5. On the sea, and beyond it 35-41 v, 1-20
  6. On this side the sea: Again: Jairus, and the woman with the flux of blood 21-43
  7. At Nazareth: His countrymen offended vi, 1-6
  8. The apostles sent forth 7-13
       b. After John was put to death,
  1. Herod's hearing of Jesus, and judgment of him 14-29
  2. Christ's retiring with his apostles, now returned 30-32
  3. The earnestness of the people; Christ's compassion; five thousand fed 33-44
  4. His walking on the sea 45-52
  5. He heals many in the land of Gennesaret 53-56
  6. And teaches what defiles a man vii, 1-23
  7. A devil cast out in the coasts of Tyre and Sidon 24-30
  8. At the sea of Galilee, the deaf and dumb healed; four thousand fed 31-37 viii, 1-9
  9. He comes into the parts of Dalmanutha, and answers concerning the sign from heaven Chap. viii, 10-13
    10. In the ship, he warns them of evil leaven 14-21
    11. At Bethsaida, heals the sick 22-26
       c. After he was acknowledged to be the Son of God,
  1. Peter confessing him, he enjoins his disciples silence; foretells his passion; reproves Peter; exhorts to follow him 21 ix, 1
  2. Is transfigured: casts out a devil; foretells his passion. 2-32

3. Reproves and instructs his disciples 33-50
B. In Judea,
    a. In the borders x, 1
1. He treats of divorce 2-12
2. Of little children 13-16
3. Of entering into life, and of the danger of riches 17-31
    b. In his way to the city,
1. He foretells his passion a third time 32-34
2. Answers James and John, and instructs them all 35-45
3. At Jericho, gives sight to Bartimeus 46-52
4. At Jerusalem xi, 1
    a. His royal entry' 2-11
    b. The day after, the fig tree cursed 12-14 the temple purged 15- 19
    c. The day after that,
1. Near the fig tree, he shows the power of faith 20-26
2. In the temple,
1. His authority vindicated 27-33
2. The parable of the wicked husbandmen xii, 1-12
3. Of paying tribute to Caesar 13-17
4. Of the resurrection 18-27
5. Of the great commandment 28-34
6. Of David's Lord 35-37
7. He warns the people of the scribes 38-40
8. Commends the poor widow 41-44
3. On Mount Olivet, he foretells the destruction of the city and temple, and the end of the world xiii, 1-37
    d. Two days before the passover; his enemies bargain with Judas. xiv. 1-11
    e. On the first day of unleavened bread,
1. The passover prepared 12-16
2. The Lord's Supper instituted 17-25
3. After the hymn, the offense of the disciples and Peter's denial foretold 26-31
4. In Gethsemane, Jesus prays; wakes his disciples 32-42 is betrayed; taken; forsaken of all 43-52
5. In the high priest's palace, He is condemned to death 53-65 Denied by Peter 66-72
    f. Friday, What was done,
1. In Pilate's palace xv, 1-20
2. In the way 21
3. At Golgotha 22
1. The wine and myrrh offered 23
2. The crucifixion; his garments parted 24, 25
3. The title 26
4. The two malefactors 27, 28
5. Revilings 29-32
6. The darkness; the cry of Jesus; the scoff; the vinegar; his death; the veil rent 33-38
7. The saying of the centurion; the women looking on 39-41
4. In the evening, the burial 42-47
    g. Sunday, Our Lord's resurrection declared,
1. By an angel Chap. xvi, 1-8
2. By himself, To Mary Magdalene 9-11 To two going into the country 12, 13 To the eleven sitting at meat 14

III. The Gospel,
    1. Committed by Christ to apostles after his resurrection. 15-18
    2. Confirmed after his ascension 19, 20

MARK

I

1. *The beginning of the Gospel of Jesus Christ* - The evangelist speaks with strict propriety: for the beginning of the Gospel is in the account of John the Baptist, contained in the first paragraph; the Gospel itself in the rest of the book. Matt. iii, 1; Luke iii, 1

2. *Mal.* iii, 1

3. Isaiah xl, 3.

4. Preaching the baptism of repentance - That is, preaching repentance, and baptizing as a sign and means of it.

7. The latchet of whose shoes I am not worthy to unloose - That is, to do him the very meanest service.

9. Matt. iii, 13; Luke iii, 21.

12. And immediately the Spirit thrusteth him out into the wilderness - So in all the children of God, extraordinary manifestations of his favour are wont to be followed by extraordinary temptations. Matt. iv, 1; Luke iv, 1.

13. And he was there forty days, tempted by Satan - Invisibly. After this followed the temptation by him in a visible shape, related by St. Matthew. And he was with the wild beasts - Though they had no power to hurt him. St. Mark not only gives us a compendium of St. Matthew's Gospel, but likewise several valuable particulars, which the other evangelists have omitted.

14. Matt. iv, 12.

15. The time is fulfilled - The time of my kingdom, foretold by Daniel, expected by you, is fully come.

16. Matt. iv, 18; Luke v, 1.

18. Straightway leaving their nets, they followed him - From this time they forsook their employ, and constantly attended him. Happy they who follow Christ at the first call!

21. Luke iv, 31.

26. A loud noise - For he was forbidden to speak. Christ would neither suffer those evil spirits to speak in opposition, nor yet in favour of him. He needed not their testimony, nor would encourage it, lest any should infer that he acted in concert with them.

29. Matt. viii, 14; Luke iv, 38.

32. When the sun was set - And, consequently, the Sabbath was ended, which they reckoned from sunset to sunset.

33. And the whole city was gathered together at the door - O what a fair prospect was here! Who could then have imagined that all these blossoms would die away without fruit?

34. He suffered not the devils to say that they knew him - That is, according to Dr. Mead's hypothesis, (that the Scriptural demoniacs were only diseased persons) He suffered not the diseases to say that they knew him!

35. Rising a great while before day - So did he labour for us, both day and night. Luke iv, 42.

40. Matt. viii, 2; Luke v, 12.

44. See thou say nothing to any man - But our blessed Lord gives no such charge to us. If he has made us clean from our leprosy of sin, we are not commanded to conceal it. On the contrary, it is our duty to publish it abroad, both for the honour of our Benefactor, and that others who are sick of sin may be encouraged to ask and hope for the same benefit. But go, show thyself to the priest, and offer for thy cleansing what Moses commanded for a testimony to them - The priests seeing him, pronouncing him clean, Lev. xiii, 17, 23, 28, 37, and accordingly allowing him to offer as Moses commanded, Lev. xiv, 2, 7, was such a proof against them, that they durst never say the leper was not cleansed; which out of envy or malice against our saviour they might have been ready to say, upon his presenting himself to be viewed, according to the law, if by the cleansed person's talking much about his cure, the account of it had reached their ears before he came in person. This is one great reason why our Lord commanded this man to say nothing.

45. So that Jesus could no more openly enter into the city - It was also to prevent this inconvenience that our Lord had enjoined him silence.

II

1. And again - After having been in desert places for some time, he returned privately to the city. In the house - In Peter's house.

2. And immediately many were gathered together - Hitherto continued the general impression on their hearts. Hitherto, even at Capernaum, all who heard received the word with joy.

3. Matt. ix, 2; Luke v, 18.

4. They uncovered the roof - Or, took up the covering, the lattice or trap door, which was on all their houses, (being flat roofed.) And finding it not wide enough, broke the passage wider, to let down the couch.

6. But certain of the scribes - See whence the first offense cometh! As yet not one of the plain unlettered people were offended. They all rejoiced in the light, till these men of learning came, to put darkness for light, and light for darkness. Woe to all such blind guides! Good had it been for these if they had never been born. O God, let me never offend one of thy simple ones! Sooner let my tongue cleave to the roof of my mouth!

12. They were all amazed - Even the scribes themselves for a time.

13. All the multitude came to him - Namely, by the sea side. And he as readily taught them there as if they had been in a synagogue.

14. Matt. ix, 9; Luke v, 27.

15. Many publicans and notorious sinners sat with Jesus - Some of them doubtless invited by Matthew, moved with compassion for his old companions in sin. But the next words, For there were many, and they followed him, seem to imply, that the greater part, encouraged by his gracious words and the tenderness of his behaviour, and impatient to hear more, stayed for no invitation, but pressed in after him, and kept as close to him as they could.

16. And the scribes and Pharisees said - So now the wise men being joined by the saints of the world, went a little further in raising prejudices against our Lord. In his answer he uses as yet no harshness, but only calm, dispassionate reasoning.

17. I came not to call the righteous - Therefore if these were righteous I should not call them. But now, they are the very persons I came to save.

18. Matt. ix, 14; Luke v, 33.

23. Matt. xii, 1; Luke vi, 1.

26. In the days of Abiathar the high priest - Abimelech, the father of Abiathar, was high priest then; Abiathar himself not till some time after. This phrase therefore only means, In the time of Abiathar, who was afterward the high priest. 1 Sam. xxi, 6.

27. The Sabbath was made for man - And therefore must give way to man's necessity.

28. Moreover the Son of man is Lord even of the Sabbath - Being the supreme Lawgiver, he hath power to dispense with his own laws; and with this in particular.

III

He entered again into the synagogue - At Capernaum on the same day. Matt. xii, 9; Luke vi, 6.

2. And they - The scribes and Pharisees, watched him, that they might accuse him - Pride, anger, and shame, after being so often put to silence, began now to ripen into malice.

4. Is it lawful to save life or to kill? - Which he knew they were seeking occasion to do. But they held their peace - Being confounded, though not convinced.

5. Looking round upon them with anger, being grieved - Angry at the sin, grieved at the sinner; the true standard of Christian anger. But who can separate anger at sin from anger at the sinner? None but a true believer in Christ.

6. The Pharisees going out - Probably leaving the scribes to watch him still: took counsel with the Herodians - as bitter as they usually were against each other.

8. From Idumea - The natives of which had now professed the Jewish religion above a hundred and fifty years. They about Tyre and Sidon - The Israelites who lived in those coasts.

10. Plagues or scourges (so the Greek word properly means) seem to be those very painful or afflictive disorders which were frequently sent, or at least permitted of God, as a scourge or punishment of sin.

12. He charged them not to make him known - It was not the time: nor were they fit preachers.

13. He calleth whom he would - With regard to the eternal states of men, God always acts as just and merciful. But with regard to numberless other things, he seems to us to act as a mere sovereign. Luke vi, 12

14. Matt. x, 2; Luke vi, 13; Acts i, 13.

16. He surnamed them sons of thunder - Both with respect to the warmth and impetuosity of their spirit, their fervent manner of preaching, and the power of their word.

20. To eat bread - That is, to take any subsistence.

21. His relations - His mother and his brethren, ver. 31. But it was some time before they could come near him.

22. The scribes and Pharisees, Matt. xii, 22; who had come down from Jerusalem - Purposely on the devil's errand. And not without success. For the common people now began to drink in the poison, from these learned, good, honourable men! He hath Beelzebub - at command, is in league with him: And by the prince of the devils casteth he out devils - How easily may a man of learning elude the strongest proof of a work of God! How readily can he account for every incident without ever taking God into the question. Matt. xii, 24; Luke xi, 15.

28. Matt. xii, 31; Luke xii, 10.

30. Because they said, He hath an unclean spirit - Is it not astonishing, that men who have ever read these words, should doubt, what is the blasphemy against the Holy Ghost? Can any words declare more plainly, that it is "the ascribing those miracles to the power of the devil which Christ wrought by the power of the Holy Ghost?"

31. Then come his brethren and his mother - Having at length made their way through the crowd,

so as to come to the door. His brethren are here named first, as being first and most earnest in the design of taking him: for neither did these of his brethren believe on him. They sent to him, calling him - They sent one into the house, who called him aloud, by name. Matt. xii, 46; Luke viii, 19.

34. Looking round on them who sat about him - With the utmost sweetness; He said, Behold my mother and my brethren -- in this preference of his true disciples even to the Virgin Mary, considered merely as his mother after the flesh, he not only shows his high and tender affection for them, but seems designedly to guard against those excessive and idolatrous honours, which he foresaw would in after ages be paid to her.

IV

1. Matt. xiii, 1; Luke viii, 4.

2. He taught them many things by parables - After the usual manner of the eastern nations, to make his instructions more agreeable to them, and to impress them the more upon attentive hearers. A parable signifies not only a simile or comparison, and sometimes a proverb, but any kind of instructive speech, wherein spiritual things are explained and illustrated by natural, Prov. i, 6. To understand a proverb and the interpretation - The proverb is the literal sense, the interpretation is the spiritual resting in the literal sense killeth, but the spiritual giveth life.

3. Hearken - This word he probably spoke with a loud voice, to stop the noise and hurry of the people.

10. When he was alone - That is, retired apart from the multitude.

11. To them that are without - So the Jews termed the heathens: so our Lord terms all obstinate unbelievers: for they shall not enter into his kingdom: they shall abide in outer darkness.

12. So that seeing they see and do not perceive - They would not see before now they could not, God having given them up to the blindness which they had chosen.

13. Know ye not this parable? - Which is as it were the foundation of all those that I shall speak hereafter; and is so easy to be understood?

19. The desire of other things choke the word - A deep and important truth! The desire of any thing, otherwise than as it leads to happiness in God, directly tends to barrenness of soul. Entering in - Where they were not before. Let him therefore who has received and retained the word, see that no other desire then enter in, such as perhaps till then he never knew. It becometh unfruitful - After the fruit had grown almost to perfection.

21. And he said, Is a candle - As if he had said, I explain these things to you, I give you this light, not to conceal, but to impart it to others. And if I conceal any thing from you now, it is only that it may be more effectually manifested hereafter. Matt. v, 15; Luke xvi, 16; xi, 33.

22. Matt. x, 26; Luke viii, 17.

24. Take heed what ye hear - That is, attend to what you hear, that it may have its due influence upon you. With what measure you mete - That is, according to the improvement you make of what you have heard, still further assistance shall be given. And to you that hear - That is, with improvement.

25. He that hath - That improves whatever he has received, to the good of others, as well as of his own soul. Matt. xiii, 12; Luke viii, 18.

26. So is the kingdom of God - The inward kingdom is like seed which a man casts into the ground - This a preacher of the Gospel casts into the heart. And he sleeps and rises night and day - That is, he has it continually in his thoughts. Meantime it springs and grows up he knows not how - Even he that sowed it cannot explain how it grows. For as the earth by a curious kind of mechanism, which the greatest philosophers cannot comprehend, does as it were spontaneously bring forth first the blade, then the ear, then the full corn in the ear: so the soul, in an inexplicable manner, brings forth, first weak graces, then stronger, then full holiness: and all this of itself, as a machine, whose spring of motion is within itself. Yet observe the amazing exactness of the comparison. The earth brings forth no corn (as the soul no holiness) without both the care and toil of man, and the benign influence of heaven.

29. He putteth in the sickle - God cutteth down and gathereth the corn into his garner.

30. Matt. xiii, 31; Luke xiii, 18.

33. He spake the word as they were able to hear it - Adapting it to the capacity of his hearers; and speaking as plain as he could without offending them. A rule never to be forgotten by those who instruct others.

35. Matt. viii, 23; Luke viii, 22.

36. They take him as he was in the vessel - They carried him immediately in the same vessel from which he had been preaching to the people.

38. On the pillow - So we translate it, for want of a proper English expression, for that particular part of the vessel near the rudder, on which he lay.

39. Peace - Cease thy tossing: Be still - Cease thy roaring; literally, Be thou gagged.

Wesley's Notes on the Bible - The New Testament

V

1. Matt. viii, 28; Luke viii, 26.
2. There met him a man with an unclean spirit - St. Matthew mentions two. Probably this, so particularly spoken of here, was the most remarkably fierce and ungovernable.
9. My name is Legion! for we are many - But all these seem to have been under one commander, who accordingly speaks all along, both for them and himself.
15. And they were afraid - It is not improbable they might otherwise have offered some rudeness, if not violence.
18. Matt. ix, 1; Luke viii, 37;
19. Tell them how great things the Lord hath done for thee - This was peculiarly needful there, where Christ did not go in person.
20. He published in Decapolis - Not only at home, but in all that country where Jesus himself did not come.
21. Luke viii, 40.
22. One of the rulers of the synagogue - To regulate the affairs of every synagogue, there was a council of grave men. Over these was a president, who was termed the ruler of the synagogue. Sometimes there was no more than one ruler in a synagogue. Matt. ix, 18; Luke viii, 41.
25. Matt. ix, 20; Luke viii, 43.
37. John, the brother of James - When St. Mark wrote, not long after our Lord's ascension, the memory of St. James, lately beheaded, was so fresh, that his name was more known than that of John himself.
40. Them that were with him - Peter, James, and John.
43. He charged them that no man should know it - That he might avoid every appearance of vain glory, might prevent too great a concourse of people, and might not further enrage the scribes and Pharisees against him; the time for his death, and for the full manifestation of his glory, being not yet come. He commanded something should be given her to eat - So that when either natural or spiritual life is restored, even by immediate miracle, all proper means are to be used in order to preserve it.

VI

1. Matt. xiii, 54; Luke iv, 16.
3. Is not this the carpenter? - There can be no doubt, but in his youth he wrought with his supposed father Joseph.
5. He could do no miracle there - Not consistently with his wisdom and goodness. It being inconsistent with his wisdom to work them there, where it could not promote his great end; and with his goodness, seeing he well knew his countrymen would reject whatever evidence could be given them. And therefore to have given them more evidence, would only have increased their damnation.
6. He marvelled - As man. As he was God, nothing was strange to him.
7. Matt. x, 1; Luke ix, 1.
8. He commanded them to take nothing for their journey - That they might be always unincumbered, free, ready for motion. Save a staff only - He that had one might take it; but he that had not was not to provide one, Matt. x, 9. Luke ix, 3.
9. Be shod with sandals - As you usually are. Sandals were pieces of strong leather or wood, tied under the sole of the foot by thongs, something resembling modern clogs. The shoes which they are in St. Matthew forbidden to take, were a kind of short boots, reaching a little above the mid-leg, which were then commonly used in journeys. Our Lord intended by this mission to initiate them into their apostolic work. And it was doubtless an encouragement to them all their life after, to recollect the care which God took of them, when they had left all they had, and went out quite unfurnished for such an expedition. In this view our Lord himself leads them to consider it, Luke xxii, xxxv, When I sent you forth without purse or scrip, lacked ye any thing?
10. Matt. x, 11; Luke ix, 4.
12. Luke ix, 6.
13. They anointed with oil many that were sick - Which St. James gives as a general direction, James v, 14, 15, adding those peremptory words, And the Lord shall heal him - He shall be restored to health: not by the natural efficacy of the oil, but by the supernatural blessing of God. And it seems this was the great standing means of healing, desperate diseases in the Christian Church, long before extreme unction was used or heard of, which bears scarce any resemblance to it; the former being used only as a means of health; the latter only when life is despaired of.
14. Matt. xiv, 1; Luke ix, 7.
15. A prophet, as one of the prophets - Not inferior to one of the ancient prophets.
16. But Herod hearing thereof - Of their various judgments concerning him, still said, It is John.

20. And preserved him - Against all the malice and contrivances of Herodias. And when he heard him - Probably sending for him, at times, during his imprisonment, which continued a year and a half. He heard him gladly - Delusive joy! While Herodias lay in his bosom.

21. A convenient day - Convenient for her purpose. His lords, captains, and principal men of Galilee - The great men of the court, the army, and the province.

23. To the half of my kingdom - A proverbial expression.

26. Yet for his oath's sake, and for the sake of his guests - Herod's honour was like the conscience of the chief priests, Matt. xxvii, 6. To shed innocent blood wounded neither one nor the other.

30. Luke ix, 10.

31. Matt. xiv, 13; John vi, 1.

32. They departed - Across a creek or corner of the lake.

34. Coming out - of the vessel.

40. They sat down in ranks - The word properly signifies a parterre or bed in a garden; by a metaphor, a company of men ranged in order, by hundreds and by fifties - That is, fifty in rank, and a hundred in file. So a hundred multiplied by fifty, make just five thousand.

43. Full of the fragments - of the bread.

45. He constrained his disciples - Who did not care to go without him. Matt. xiv, 22.

46. Matt. xiv, 23; John vi, 15.

48. And he saw them - For the darkness could veil nothing from him. And would have passed by them - That is, walked, as if he was passing by.

52. Their heart was hardened - And yet they were not reprobates. It means only, they were slow and dull of apprehension.

53. Matt. xiv, 34; John vi, 21.

VII

1. Coming from Jerusalem - Probably on purpose to find occasion against him. Matt. xv, 1.

4. Washing of cups and pots and brazen vessels and couches - The Greek word (baptisms) means indifferently either washing or sprinkling. The cups, pots, and vessels were washed; the couches sprinkled.

5. The tradition of the elders - The rule delivered down from your forefathers.

6. Isaiah xxix, 13.

10. Exod. xx, 12; Exod. xxi, 17.

15. There is nothing entering into a man from without which can defile him - Though it is very true, a man may bring guilt, which is moral defilement, upon himself by eating what hurts his health, or by excess either in meat or drink yet even here the pollution arises from the wickedness of the heart, and is just proportionable to it. And this is all that our Lord asserts.

19. Purging all meats - Probably the seat was usually placed over running water.

22. Wickedness - The word means ill natured, cruelty, inhumanity, and all malevolent affections. Foolishness - Directly contrary to sobriety of thought and discourse: all kind of wild imaginations and extravagant passions.

24. Matt. xv, 21.

26. The woman was a Greek (that is, a Gentile, not a Jew) a Syrophenician or Canaanite. Canaan was also called Syrophenicia, as lying between Syria, properly so called, and Phenicia.

31. Matt. xv, 29.

33. He put his fingers into his ears - Perhaps intending to teach us, that we are not to prescribe to him (as they who brought this man attempted to do) but to expect his blessing by whatsoever means he pleases: even though there should be no proportion or resemblance between the means used, and the benefit to be conveyed thereby.

34. Ephphatha - This was a word of SOVEREIGN AUTHORITY, not an address to God for power to heal: such an address was needless; for Christ had a perpetual fund of power residing in himself, to work all miracles whenever he pleased, even to the raising the dead, John v, 21, 26.

36. Them - The blind man and those that brought him.

VIII

1. Matt. xv, 32.

8. So they did eat - This miracle was intended to demonstrate, that Christ was the true bread which cometh down from heaven; for he who was almighty to create bread without means to support natural life, could not want power to create bread without means to support spiritual life. And this heavenly bread we stand so much in need of every moment, that we ought to be always praying, Lord, evermore give us this bread.

Wesley's Notes on the Bible - The New Testament

11. Tempting him - That is, trying to ensnare him. Matt. xvi, 1.

12. Matt. xvi, 4.

15. Beware of the leaven of the Pharisees and of Herod, or of the Sadducees; two opposite extremes.

17, 18. Our Lord here affirms of all the apostles, (for the question is equivalent to an affirmation,) That their hearts were hardened; that having eyes they saw not, having ears they heard not; that they did not consider, neither understand: the very same expressions that occur in the thirteenth of Matthew. And yet it is certain they were not judicially hardened. Therefore all these strong expressions do not necessarily import any thing more than the present want of spiritual understanding.

23. He led him out of the town - It was in just displeasure against the inhabitants of Bethsaida for their obstinate infidelity, that our Lord would work no more miracles among them, nor even suffer the person he had cured, either to go into the town, or to tell it to any therein.

24. I see men as trees walking - He distinguished men from trees only by their motion.

27. Matt. xvi, 13; Luke ix, 18.

30. He enjoined them silence for the present,
1. That he might not encourage the people to set him up for a temporal king;
2. That he might not provoke the scribes and Pharisees to destroy him before the time and,
3. That he might not forestall the bright evidence which was to be given of his Divine character after his resurrection.

31. Matt. xvi, 21; Luke ix, 22.

32. He spake that saying openly - Or in express terms. Till now he had only intimated it to them. And Peter taking hold of him - Perhaps by the arms or clothes.

33. Looking on his disciples - That they might the more observe what he said to Peter.

34. And when he called the people - To hear a truth of the last importance, and one that equally concerned them all. Let him deny himself - His own will, in all things small and great, however pleasing, and that continually: And take up his cross - Embrace the will of God, however painful, daily, hourly, continually. Thus only can he follow me in holiness to glory.

35. Matt. xvi, 25; Luke ix, 24; Luke xvii, 33; John xii, 25.

38. Whosoever shall be ashamed of me and of my words - That is, avowing whatever I have said (particularly of self denial and the daily cross) both by word and action. Matt. x, 32; Luke ix, 26; Luke xii, 8.

IX

1. Till they see the kingdom of God coming with power - So it began to do at the day of pentecost, when three thousand were converted to God at once.

2. By themselves - That is, separate from the multitude: Apart - From the other apostles: and was transfigured - The Greek word seems to refer to the form of God, and the form of a servant, {mentioned by St. Paul, Phil. ii, 6, 7} and may intimate, that the Divine rays, which the indwelling God let out on this occasion, made the glorious change from one of these forms into the other. Matt. xvii, 1; Luke ix, 28.

3. White as snow, such as no fuller can whiten - Such as could not be equalled either by nature or art.

4. Elijah - Whom they expected: Moses, whom they did not.

7. There came a (bright, luminous) cloud, overshadowing them - This seems to have been such a cloud of glory as accompanied Israel in the wilderness, which, as the Jewish writers observe, departed at the death of Moses. But it now appeared again, in honour of our Lord, as the great Prophet of the Church, who was prefigured by Moses. Hear ye him - Even preferably to Moses and Elijah.

12. Elijah verily coming first restoreth all things: and how it is written - That is, And he told them how it is written - As if he had said, Elijah's coming is not inconsistent with my suffering. He is come: yet I shall suffer. The first part of the verse answers their question concerning Elijah; the second refutes their error concerning the Messiah's continuing forever.

14. Matt. xvii, 14; Luke ix, 37.

15. All the multitude seeing him were greatly amazed - At his coming so suddenly, so seasonably, so unexpectedly: perhaps also at some unusual rays of majesty and glory, which yet remained on his countenance.

17. And one of the multitude answering - The scribes gave no answer to our Lord's question. They did not care to repeat what they had said to his disciples. A dumb spirit - A spirit that takes his speech from him.

20. When he saw him - When the child saw Christ; when his deliverance was at hand. Immediately the spirit tore him - Made his last grand effort to destroy him. Is it not generally so, before Satan is cast out of a soul, of which he has long had possession?

22. If thou canst do any thing - In so desperate a case: Have compassion on us - Me as well as him.

23. If thou canst believe - As if he had said, The thing does not turn on my power, but on thy faith. I can do all things: canst thou believe?

24. Help thou mine unbelief - Although my faith be so small, that it might rather be termed unbelief, yet help me.

25. Thou deaf and dumb spirit - So termed, because he made the child so. When Jesus spake, the devil heard, though the child could not. I command thee - I myself now; not my disciples.

26. Having rent him sore - So does even the body sometimes suffer, when God comes to deliver the soul from Satan.

30. They passed through Galilee - Though not through the cities, but by them, in the most private ways. He was not willing that any should know it: for he taught his disciples - He wanted to be alone with them some time, in order to instruct them fully concerning his sufferings. The Son of man is delivered - It is as sure as if it were done already. Matt. xvii, 22; Luke ix, 44.

32. They understood not the word - They did not understand how to reconcile the death of our saviour (nor consequently his resurrection, which supposed his death) with their notions of his temporal kingdom.

33. Luke ix, 46.

34. Who should be greatest - Prime minister in his kingdom.

35. Let him be the least of all - Let him abase himself the most.

36. Matt. xviii, 2; Luke ix, 47.

37. One such little child - Either in years or in heart.

38. And John answered him - As if he had said, But ought we to receive those who follow not us? Master, we saw one casting out devils in thy name - Probably this was one of John the Baptist's disciples, who believed in Jesus, though he did not yet associate with our Lord's disciples. And we forbad him, because he followeth not us - How often is the same temper found in us? How readily do we also lust to envy? But how does that spirit become a disciple, much more a minister of the benevolent Jesus! St. Paul had learnt a better temper, when he rejoiced that Christ was preached, even by those who were his personal enemies. But to confine religion to them that follow us, is a narrowness of spirit which we should avoid and abhor. Luke ix, 49.

39. Jesus said - Christ here gives us a lovely example of candour and moderation. He was willing to put the best construction on doubtful cases, and to treat as friends those who were not avowed enemies. Perhaps in this instance it was a means of conquering the remainder of prejudice, and perfecting what was wanting in the faith and obedience of these persons. Forbid him not - Neither directly nor indirectly discourage or hinder any man who brings sinners from the power of Satan to God, because he followeth not us, in opinions, modes of worship, or any thing else which does not affect the essence of religion.

40. For he that is not against you, is for you - Our Lord had formerly said, he that is not with me, is against me: thereby admonishing his hearers, that the war between him and Satan admitted of no neutrality, and that those who were indifferent to him now, would finally be treated as enemies. But here in another view, he uses a very different proverb; directing his followers to judge of men's characters in the most candid manner; and charitably to hope that those who did not oppose his cause wished well to it. Upon the whole, we are to be rigorous in judging ourselves, and candid in judging each other.

41. For whosoever shall give you a cup - Having answered St. John, our Lord here resumes the discourse which was broken off at the 37th verse. Mark ix, 37. Matt. x, 42.

42. On the contrary, whosoever shall offend the very least Christian. Matt. xviii, 6; Luke xvii, 1.

43. And if a person cause thee to offend - (The discourse passes from the case of offending, to that of being offended) if one who is as useful or dear to thee as a hand or eye, hinder or slacken thee in the ways of God, renounce all intercourse with him. This primarily relates to persons, secondarily to things. Matt. v, 29; Matt. xviii, 8.

44. Where their worm - That gnaweth the soul, (pride, self will, desire, malice, envy, shame, sorrow, despair) dieth not - No more than the soul itself: and the fire (either material, or infinitely worse!) that tormenteth the body, is not quenched forever. Isaiah lxvi, 24.

49. Everyone - Who does not cut off the offending member, and consequently is cast into hell, shall be, as it were, salted with fire, preserved, not consumed thereby whereas every acceptable sacrifice shall be salted with another kind of salt, even that of Divine grace, which purifies the soul, (though frequently with pain) and preserves it from corruption.

50. Such salt is good indeed; highly beneficial to the world, in respect of which I have termed you the salt of the earth. But if the salt which should season others, have lost its own saltness, wherewith will ye season it? - Beware of this; see that ye retain your savour; and as a proof of it, have peace one with another. More largely this obscure text might be paraphrased thus:- As every burnt offering was

salted with salt, in order to its being cast into the fire of the altar, so every one who will not part with his hand or eye, shall fall a sacrifice to Divine justice, and be cast into hell fire, which will not consume, but preserve him from a cessation of being. And on the other hand, every one, who, denying himself and taking up his cross, offers up himself as a living sacrifice to God, shall be seasoned with grace, which like salt will make him savoury, and preserve him from destruction forever. As salt is good for preserving meats, and making them savoury, so it is good that ye be seasoned with grace, for the purifying your hearts and lives, and for spreading the savour of my knowledge, both in your own souls, and wherever ye go. But as salt if it loses its saltness is fit for nothing, so ye, if ye lose your faith and love, are fit for nothing but to be utterly destroyed. See therefore that grace abide in you, and that ye no more contend, Who shall be greatest. Matt. v, 13; Luke xiv, 34.

X

1. He cometh thence - From Galilee. Matt. xix, 1.
2. Matt. v, 31; Matt. xix, 7; Luke xvi, 18.
4. Deut. xxiv, 1.
6. From the beginning of the creation - Therefore Moses in the first of Genesis gives us an account of things from the beginning of the creation. Does it not clearly follow, that there was no creation previous to that which Moses describes? God made them male and female - Therefore Adam did not at first contain both sexes in himself: but God made Adam, when first created, male only; and Eve female only. And this man and woman he joined together, in a state of innocence, as husband and wife.
7. Gen. ii, 24.
11, 12. All polygamy is here totally condemned.
13. Matt. xix, 13.
14. Jesus seeing it was much displeased - At their blaming those who were not blame worthy: and endeavouring to hinder the children from receiving a blessing. Of such is the kingdom of God - The members of the kingdom which I am come to set up in the world are such as these, as well as grown persons, of a child-like temper.
15. Whosoever shall not receive the kingdom of God as a little child - As totally disclaiming all worthiness and fitness, as if he were but a week old.
17. Matt. xix, 16; Luke xviii, 18.
20. He answering, said to him, Master - He stands reproved now, and drops the epithet good.
21. Jesus looking upon him - And looking into his heart, loved him - Doubtless for the dawnings of good which he saw in him: and said to him - Out of tender love, One thing thou lackest - The love of God, without which all religion is a dead carcass. In order to this, throw away what is to thee the grand hindrance of it. Give up thy great idol, riches. Go, sell whatsoever thou hast.
24. Jesus saith to them, Children - See how he softens the harsh truth, by the manner of delivering it! And yet without retracting or abating one tittle: How hard is it for them that trust in riches - Either for defense, or happiness, or deliverance from the thousand dangers that life is continually exposed to. That these cannot enter into God's glorious kingdom, is clear and undeniable: but it is easier for a camel to go through a needle's eye, than for a man to have riches, and not trust in them. Therefore, it is easier for a camel to go through the eye of a needle, than for a rich man to enter the kingdom.
28. Lo, we have left all - Though the young man would not.
30. He shall receive a hundred fold, houses, etc. - Not in the same kind: for it will generally be with persecutions: but in value: a hundred fold more happiness than any or all of these did or could afford. But let it be observed, none is entitled to this happiness, but he that will accept it with persecutions.
32. They were in the way to Jerusalem, and Jesus went before them: and they were amazed - At his courage and intrepidity, considering the treatment which he had himself told them he should meet with there: and as they followed, they were afraid - Both for him and themselves: nevertheless he judged it best to prepare them, by telling them more particularly what was to ensue. Matt. xx, 17; Luke xviii, 31.
35. Saying - By their mother. It was she, not they that uttered the words. Matt. xx, 20.
38. Ye know not what ye ask - Ye know not that ye ask for sufferings, which must needs pave the way to glory. The cup - Of inward; the baptism - Of outward sufferings. Our Lord was filled with sufferings within, and covered with them without.
40. Save to them for whom it is prepared - Them who by patient continuance in well doing, seek for glory, and honour, and immortality. For these only eternal life is prepared. To these, only he will give it in that day; and to every man his own reward, according to his own labour.
45. A ransom for many - Even for as many souls as needed such a ransom, 2 Cor. v, 15.
46. Matt. xx, 29; Luke xviii, 35.
50. Casting away his garment - Through joy and eagerness.

XI

1. To Bethphage and Bethany, at the Mount of Olives - The limits of Bethany reached to the Mount of Olives, and joined to those of Bethphage. Bethphage was part of the suburbs of Jerusalem, and reached from the Mount of Olives to the walls of the city. Our Lord was now come to the place where the boundaries of Bethany and Bethphage met. Matt. xxi, 1; Luke xix, 29; John xii, 12.

11. Matt. xxi, 10, 17.

12. Matt. xxi, 18.

13. For it was not a season of figs - It was net (as we say) a good year for figs; at least not for that early sort, which alone was ripe so soon in the spring. If we render the words, It was not the season of figs, that is, the time of gathering them in, it may mean, The season was not yet: and so (inclosing the words in a parenthesis, And coming to it, he found nothing but leaves) it may refer to the former part of the sentence, and may be considered as the reason of Christ's going to see whether there were any figs on this tree. Some who also read that clause in a parenthesis, translate the following words, for where he was, it was the season of figs. And it is certain, this meaning of the words suits best with the great design of the parable, which was to reprove the Jewish Church for its unfruitfulness at that very season, when fruit might best be expected from them.

15. Matt. xxi, 12; Luke xix, 45.

16. He suffered not that any should carry a vessel through the temple - So strong notions had our Lord, of even relative holiness! And of the regard due to those places (as well as times) that are peculiarly dedicated to God.

17. Isaiah lvi, 7; Jer. vii, 11.

18. They feared him - That is, they were afraid to take him by violence, lest it should raise a tumult; because all the people were astonished at his teaching - Both at the excellence of his discourse, and at the majesty and authority with which he taught.

20. Matt. xxi, 20.

22. Have faith in God - And who could find fault, if the Creator and Proprietor of all things were to destroy, by a single word of his mouth, a thousand of his inanimate creatures, were it only to imprint this important lesson more deeply on one immortal spirit?

25. When ye stand praying - Standing was their usual posture when they prayed. Forgive - And on this condition, ye shall have whatever you ask, without wrath or doubting. Matt. vi, 14.

27. Matt. xxi, 23; Luke xx, 1.

XII

1. Matt. xxi, 43; Luke xx, 9.

10. Psalm cxviii, 22.

12. They feared the multitude - How wonderful is the providence of God, using all things for the good of his children! Generally the multitude is restrained from tearing them in pieces only by the fear of their rulers. And here the rulers themselves are restrained, through fear of the multitude!

13. Matt. xxii, 15; Luke xx, 20.

17. They marvelled at him - At the wisdom of his answer.

18. Matt. xxi, 23; Luke xx, 27.

19. Deut. xxv, 5.

25. When they rise from the dead, neither men marry nor women are given in marriage.

26. Exod. iii, 6.

27. He is not the God of the dead, but the God of the living - That is, (if the argument be proposed at length,) since the character of his being the God of any persons, plainly intimates a relation to them, not as dead, but as living; and since he cannot be said to be at present their God at all, if they are utterly dead; nor to be the God of human persons, such as Abraham, Isaac, and Jacob, consisting of souls and bodies, if their bodies were to abide in everlasting death; there must needs be a future state of blessedness, and a resurrection of the body to share with the soul in it.

28. Which is the first commandment? - The principal, and most necessary to be observed. Matt. xxii, 34; Luke x, 25.

29. The Lord our God is one Lord - This is the foundation of the first commandment, yea, of all the commandments. The Lord our God, the Lord, the God of all men, is one God, essentially, though three persons. From this unity of God it follows, that we owe all our love to him alone. Deut. vi, 4.

30. With all thy strength - That is, the whole strength and capacity of thy understanding, will, and affections.

31. The second is like unto it - Of a like comprehensive nature: comprising our whole duty to man. There is no other moral, much less ceremonial commandment, greater than these. Lev. xix, 18.

33. To love him with all the heart - To love and serve him, with all the united powers of the soul in

their utmost vigour; and to love his neighbour as himself - To maintain the same equitable and charitable temper and behaviour toward all men, as we, in like circumstances, would wish for from them toward ourselves, is a more necessary and important duty, than the offering the most noble and costly sacrifices.

34. Jesus said to him, Thou art not far from the kingdom of God - Reader, art not thou? then go on: be a real Christian: else it had been better for thee to have been afar off.

35. Matt. xxii, 41; Luke xx, 41.

36. Psalm cx, 1.

38. Beware of the scribes - There was an absolute necessity for these repeated cautions. For, considering their inveterate prejudices against Christ, it could never be supposed the common people would receive the Gospel till these incorrigible blasphemers of it were brought to just disgrace. Yet he delayed speaking in this manner till a little before his passion, as knowing what effect it would quickly produce. Nor is this any precedent for us: we are not invested with the same authority. Matt. xxiii, 5; Luke xx, 46.

41. He beheld how people cast money into the treasury - This treasury received the voluntary contributions of the worshippers who came up to the feast; which were given to buy wood for the altar, and other necessaries not provided for in any other way. Luke xxi, 1.

43. I say to you, that this poor widow hath cast in more than they all - See what judgement is cast on the most specious, outward actions by the Judge of all! And how acceptable to him is the smallest, which springs from self-denying love!

XIII

1. Matt. xxiv, 1; Luke xxi, 5.

4. Two questions are here asked; the one concerning the destruction of Jerusalem: the other concerning the end of the world.

9. Luke xxi, 12.

10. Matt. xxiv, 14.

11. The Holy Ghost will help you. But do not depend upon any other help For all the nearest ties will be broken.

14. Where it ought not - That place being set apart for sacred use. Matt. xxiv, 15; Luke xxi, 20; Dan. ix, 27.

19. In those days shall be affliction, such as was not from the beginning of the creation - May it not be doubted, whether this be yet fully accomplished? Is not much of this affliction still to come?

20. The elect - The Christians: whom he hath chosen - That is, hath taken out of, or separated from, the world, through sanctification of the Spirit and belief of the truth. He hath shortened - That is, will surely shorten.

21. Matt. xxiv, 23.

24. But in those days - Which immediately precede the end of the world: after that tribulation - Above described.

28. Matt. xxiv, 32; Luke xxi, 28.

29. He is nigh - The Son of man.

30. All these things - Relating to the temple and the city.

32. Of that day - The day of judgment is often in the Scriptures emphatically called that day. Neither the Son - Not as man: as man he was no more omniscient than omnipresent. But as God he knows all the circumstances of it.

33. Matt. xxiv, 42; Luke xxi, 34.

34. The Son of man is as a man taking a far journey - Being about to leave this world and go to the Father, he appoints the services that are to be performed by all his servants, in their several stations. This seems chiefly to respect ministers at the day of judgment: but it may be applied to all men, and to the time of death. Matt. xxv, 14; Luke xix, 12.

XIV

1. Matt. xxvi, 1; Luke xxii, 1.

3. Matt. xxvi, 6.

4. Some had indignation - Being incited thereto by Judas: and said - Probably to the women.

10. Judas went to the chief priests - Immediately after this reproof, having anger now added to his covetousness. Matt. xxvi, 14; Luke xxii, 3.

12. Matt. xxvi, 17; Luke xxii, 7.

13. Go into the city, and there shall meet you a man - It was highly seasonable for our Lord to give them this additional proof both of his knowing all things, and of his influence over the minds of men.

15. Furnished - The word properly means, spread with carpets.

17. Matt. xxvi, 20; Luke xxii, 14.

24. This is my blood of the New Testament - That is, this I appoint to be a perpetual sign and memorial of my blood, as shed for establishing the new covenant, that all who shall believe in me may receive all its gracious promises.

25. I will drink no more of the fruit of the vine, till I drink it new in the kingdom of God - That is, I shall drink no more before I die: the next wine I drink will not be earthly, but heavenly.

26. Matt. xxvi, 30; Luke xxii, 39; John xviii, 1.

27. This night - The Jews in reckoning their days began with the evening, according to the Mosaic computation, which called the evening and the morning the first day, Gen. i, 5. And so that which after sunset is here called this night is, ver. 30, called today. The expression there is peculiarly significant. Verily I say to thee, that thou thyself, confident as thou art, today, even within four and twenty hours; yea, this night, or ever the sun be risen, nay, before the cock crow twice, before three in the morning, wilt deny me thrice. Our Lord doubtless spoke so determinately, as knowing a cock would crow once before the usual time of cock crowing. By chap. xiii, 35, it appears, that the third watch of the night, ending at three in the morning, was commonly styled the cock crowing. Zech. xiii, 7.

32. Matt. xxvi, 36.

33. Sore amazed - The original word imports the most shocking amazement, mingled with grief: and that word in the next verse which we render sorrowful intimates, that he was surrounded with sorrow on every side, breaking in upon him with such violence, as was ready to separate his soul from his body.

36. Abba, Father - St. Mark seems to add the word Father, by way of explication.

37. Saith to Peter - The zealous, the confident Peter.

43. Matt. xxvi, 47; Luke xxii, 47; John xviii, 2.

44. Whomsoever I shall kiss - Probably our Lord, in great condescension, had used (according to the Jewish custom) to permit his disciples to do this, after they had been some time absent.

47. Matt. xxvi, 51; Luke xxii, 49; John xviii, 10.

51. A young man - It does not appear, that he was one of Christ's disciples. Probably hearing an unusual noise, he started up out of his bed, not far from the garden, and ran out with only the sheet about him, to see what was the matter. And the young men laid hold on him - Who was only suspected to be Christ's disciple: but could not touch them who really were so.

53. Matt. xxvi, 57; Luke xxii, 54; John xviii, 12.

55. All the council sought for witness and found none - What an amazing proof of the overruling providence of God, considering both their authority, and the rewards they could offer, that no two consistent witnesses could be procured, to charge him with any gross crime. Matt. xxvi, 59.

56. Their evidences were not sufficient - The Greek words literally rendered are, Were not equal: not equal to the charge of a capital crime: it is the same word in the 59th verse.

58. We heard him say - It is observable, that the words which they thus misrepresented, were spoken by Christ at least three years before, John ii, 19. Their going back so far to find matter for the charge, was a glorious, though silent attestation of the unexceptionable manner wherein he had behaved, through the whole course of his public ministry.

61. Matt. xxvi, 63; Luke xxii, 67.

66. Matt. xxvi, 69; Luke xxii, 56; John xviii, 25.

72. And he covered his head - Which was a usual custom with mourners, and was fitly expressive both of grief and shame.

XV

1. Matt. xxvii, 1, 2; Luke xxii, 66; Luke xxiii, 1; John xviii, 28.

3. Matt. xxvii, 12.

7. Insurrection - A crime which the Roman governors, and Pilate in particular, were more especially concerned and careful to punish.

9. Will ye that I release to you the king of the Jews - Which does this wretched man discover most? Want of justice, or courage, or common sense? The poor coward sacrifices justice to popular clamour, and enrages those whom he seeks to appease, by so unseasonably repeating that title, The king of the Jews, which he could not but know was so highly offensive to them.

16. Praetorium - The inner hall, where the praetor, a Roman magistrate, used to give judgment. But St. John calls the whole palace by this name. Matt. xxvii, 27; John xix, 2.

17. Purple - As royal robes were usually purple and scarlet, St. Mark and John term this a purple robe, St. Matthew a scarlet one. The Tyrian purple is said not to have been very different from scarlet.

20. Matt. xxvii, 31; John xix, 16.

21. The father of Alexander and Rufus - These were afterward two eminent Christians, and must

have been well known when St. Mark wrote.

22. Matt. xxvii, 33; Luke xxiii, 33; John xix, 17.

24, 25. St. Mark seems to intimate, that they first nailed him to the cross, then parted his garments, and afterward reared up the cross.

28. Isaiah liii, 12.

29. Matt. xxvii, 39.

33. Matt. xxvii, 45; Luke xxiii, 44.

34. My God, my God, why hast thou forsaken me - Thereby claiming God as his God; and yet lamenting his Father's withdrawing the tokens of his love, and treating him as an enemy, while he bare our sins.

37. Matt. xxvii, 50; Luke xxiii, 46; John xix, 30.

41. Who served him - Provided him with necessaries.

42. Because it was the day before the Sabbath - And the bodies might not hang on the Sabbath day: therefore they were in haste to have them taken down.

43. honourable - A man of character and reputation: A counsellor - A member of the sanhedrim. Who waited for the kingdom of God - Who expected to see it set up on earth. Matt. xxvii, 57; Luke xxiii, 50; John xix, 38.

46. He rolled a stone - By his servants. It was too large for him to roll himself.

XVI

1. Matt. xxviii, 1; Luke xxiv, 1; John xx, 1.

2. At the rising of the sun - They set out while it was yet dark, and came within sight of the sepulchre, for the first time, just as it grew light enough to discern that the stone was rolled away, Matt. xxviii, 1; Luke xxiv, 1; John xx, 1. But by the time Mary had called Peter and John, and they had viewed the sepulchre, the sun was rising.

3. Who shall roll us away the stone - This seems to have been the only difficulty they apprehended. So they knew nothing of Pilate's having sealed the stone, and placed a guard of soldiers there.

7. And Peter - Though he so oft denied his Lord. What amazing goodness was this!

9. John xx, 11.

10. Luke xxiv, 9; John xx, 18.

12. Luke xxiv, 13.

13. Neither believed they them - They were moved a little by the testimony of these, added to that of St. Peter, Luke xxiv, 34; but they did not yet fully believe it.

14. Luke xxiv, 36; John xx, 19.

15. Go ye into all the world, and preach the Gospel to every creature - Our Lord speaks without any limitation or restriction. If therefore every creature in every age hath not heard it, either those who should have preached, or those who should have heard it, or both, made void the counsel of God herein. Matt. xxviii, 19.

16. And is baptized - In token thereof. Everyone that believed was baptized. But he that believeth not - Whether baptized or unbaptized, shall perish everlastingly.

17. And these signs shall follow them that believe - An eminent author sub-joins, "That believe with that very faith mentioned in the preceding verse." (Though it is certain that a man may work miracles, and not have saving faith, Matt. vii, 22, 23.) "It was not one faith by which St. Paul was saved, another by which he wrought miracles. Even at this day in every believer faith has a latent miraculous power; (every effect of prayer being really miraculous;) although in many, both because of their own littleness of faith, and because the world is unworthy, that power is not exerted. Miracles, in the beginning, were helps to faith; now also they are the object of it. At Leonberg, in the memory of our fathers, a cripple that could hardly move with crutches, while the dean was preaching on this very text, was in a moment made whole." Shall follow - The word and faith must go before. In my name - By my authority committed to them. Raising the dead is not mentioned. So our Lord performed even more than he promised.

18. If they drink any deadly thing - But not by their own choice. God never calls us to try any such experiments.

19. The Lord - How seasonable is he called by this title! After he had spoken to them - For forty days. Luke xxiv, 50.

20. They preached everywhere - At the time St. Mark wrote, the apostles had already gone into all the known world, Rom. x, 18; and each of them was there known where he preached: the name of Christ only was known throughout the world.

John Wesley

NOTES ON THE GOSPEL ACCORDING TO ST. LUKE

HEREIN WE MAY OBSERVE,

I. The beginning: and therein.
    1. The conception of John Chap. i, 5-25
    2. The conception of Christ 26-56
    3. The birth and circumcision of John; the hymn of Zacharias; the youth of John 57-80
    4. Christ's birth ii, 1-20 Christ's circumcision and name 21 Presentation in the temple 22-38
Country and growth 39, 40

II. The middle, when he was twelve years old and upward 41-52

III. The course of the history.
    A. The introduction, wherein are described John the Baptist; Christ's baptism, and temptation iii, iv, 1-13
    B. The acceptable year in Galilee,
        a. Proposed at Nazareth 14-30
        b. Actually exhibited,

I. At Capernaum and near it; here we may observe,
    1. Actions not censured, while Jesus
    1. Teaches with authority 31, 32
    2. Casts out a devil 33-37
    3. Heals many sick 38-41
    4. Teaches everywhere 42-44
    5. Calls Peter; then James and John Chap. v, 1-11
    6. Cleanses the leper 12-16
    2. Actions censured, more and more severally, here occur,
    1. The healing the paralytic 17-26
    2. The calling of Levi; eating with publicans and sinners. 27-32
    3. The question concerning fasting 33-39
    4. The plucking the ears of corn vi, 1-5
    5. The withered hand restored; snares laid 6-11
    3. Actions having various effects on various persons,
    1. Upon the apostles 12-16
    2. Upon other hearers 17-40
    3. Upon the centurion vii, 1-10
    4. Upon the disciples of John,
The occasion: the young man raised 11-17
The message and answer 18-23
The reproof of them that believed not John 24-35
    5. Upon Simon and the penitent sinner 36-50
    6. Upon the woman who ministered to him viii, 1-3
    7. Upon the people 4-18 Upon his mother and brethren 19-21

II. On the sea, and 22-26 Beyond it 27-39

III. On this side again.
    1. Jairus and the flux of blood 40-55
    2. The apostles sent ix, 1-6
    3. Herod's doubting 7-9
    4. The relation of the apostles 10
    5. The earnestness of the people; our Lord's benignity; five thousand fed 11-17

C. The preparation for his passion,
    a. A recapitulation of the doctrine concerning his person: his passion foretold 18-27
    b. His transfiguration; the lunatic healed; his passion again foretold; humility enjoined 28-50
    c. His last journey to Jerusalem, which we may divide into eighteen intervals,
1. The inhospitable Samaritans born with 51-57
2. In the way, improper followers repelled, Proper ones pressed forward 58-62
3. Afterward the seventy sent; and received again x, 1-24
And the scribe taught to love his neighbour, by the example of the good Samaritan 25-37
4. In Bethany, Mary preferred before Martha 38-42
5. In a certain place the disciples taught to pray xi, 1-13
A devil cast out, and the action defended 14-26
The acclamation of the woman corrected 27, 28
Those who desire a sign reproved 29-36
6. In a certain house, the scribes and Pharisees censured. 37-54
7. Our Lord's discourse to his disciples xii, 1-12
To one that interrupts him 13-21
To his disciples again 22-40
To Peter 41-53
To the people 54-59
8. The necessity of repentance shown xiii, 1-9
A woman healed on the Sabbath 10-21
9. The fewness of them that are saved 22-30
10. Herod termed a fox: Jerusalem reproved 31-35
11. In the Pharisee's house, he cures the dropsy on the Sabbath; and xiv, 1-6
Teaches humility 7-11
Hoseapitality 12-14
The nature of the great supper 15-24
The necessity of self denial 25-35
12. Joy over repenting sinners defended, and xv, 1-10
Illustrated by the story of the prodigal son 11-32
The unjust steward, wise in his generation xvi, 1-13
The Pharisees reproved; and warned by the story of 14-18 the rich man and Lazarus 19-31
Cautions against scandals xvii, 1-4
The faith of the apostles increased 5-10
13. In the confines of Samaria and Galilee he heals ten lepers. 11-19
14. Answers the question concerning the time when the kingdom of God should come 20-37
Commends constant prayer xviii, 1-8
Recommends humility by the story of the Pharisee and publican 9-14
15. Blesses little children 15-17
Answers the rich young man 18-27
And Peter, asking what he should have 28-30
16. Foretells his passion a third time 31-34
17. Near Jericho, cures a blind man 35-42
18. In Jericho, brings salvation to Zacchaeus xix, 1-10 Answers touching the sudden appearance of his kingdom. 11-28
    D. Transactions at Jerusalem,
        a. The four first days of the great week,
1. His royal entry 29-44
2. The abuse of the temple corrected 45, 46
Its use restored, and 47, 48
Vindicated xx, 1-8
3. His discourses in the temple,
1. The parable of the husbandmen 9-19
2. The answer concerning paying tribute 20-26
And the resurrection 27-40
3. The question concerning the Son of David 41-44
4. The disciples admonished 45-47
5. The poor widow's offering commended xxi, 1-4
4. His prediction of the end of the temple, the city, and the world 5-38
5. Judas's agreement with the chief priests xxii, 1-6

John Wesley

    b. Thursday,
1. Peter and John prepare the passover 7-13
2. The Lord's Supper: discourse after it 14-23
3. The dispute, which of them was greatest 24-30
4. Peter, and the other apostles warned 31-38
5. On the Mount of Olives,
1. Jesus prays; is in an agony; strengthened by an angel; wakes his disciples 39-46
2. Is betrayed; unseasonably defended 47-53
3. Carried to the high priest's house 54
Denied by Peter 55-62
Mocked 63-65
    c. Friday,
1. His passion and death: transactions,
1. In the council 66-71
2. With Pilate xxiii, 1-5
3. With Herod 6-12
4. With Pilate again 13-25
5. In the way 26-32
6. At Golgotha, where,
The crucifixion itself, and Jesus's prayer 33, 34
His garments parted 34
Scoffs: the inscription on the cross 35-39
The penitent thief 40-43
The prodigies, and the death of Jesus 44-46
The beholders of it 47-49
2. His burial 50-53
    d. Friday evening and Saturday 54-56
    e. His resurrection made known,
1. To the women Chap. xxiv, 1-12
2. To the two going into the country, and to Peter 13-35
3. To the other apostles 36-45
f. The instructions given his apostles: his ascension 46-53

THE GOSPEL OF LUKE

I

1, 2. **This short, weighty, artless, candid dedication, belongs to the Acts, as well as the Gospel of St. Luke. Many have undertaken** - He does not mean St. Matthew or Mark; and St. John did not write so early. For these were eye witnesses themselves and ministers of the word.

3. **To write in order** - St. Luke describes in order of time; first, The Acts of Christ; his conception, birth, childhood, baptism, miracles, preaching, passion, resurrection, ascension: then, The Acts of the Apostles. But in many smaller circumstances he does not observe the order of time. **Most excellent Theophilus** - This was the appellation usually given to Roman governors. Theophilus (as the ancients inform us) was a person of eminent quality at Alexandria. In Acts i, 1, St. Luke does not give him that title. He was then probably a private man. After the preface St. Luke gives us the history of Christ, from his coming into the world to his ascension into heaven.

5. **The course of Abia** - The priests were divided into twenty-four courses, of which that of Abia was the eighth, 1 Ch xxiv, 10. Each course ministered in its turn, for seven days, from Sabbath to Sabbath. And each priest of the course or set in waiting, had his part in the temple service assigned him by lot.

6. **Walking in all the moral commandments, and ceremonial ordinances, blameless** - How admirable a character! May our behaviour be thus unblamable, and our obedience thus sincere and universal!

10. **The people were praying without, at the time of the incense** - So the pious Jews constantly did. And this was the foundation of that elegant figure, by which prayer is in Scripture so often compared to incense. Perhaps one reason of ordaining incense might be, to intimate the acceptableness of the prayer that accompanied it; as well as to remind the worshippers of that sacrifice of a sweet-smelling savour, which was once to be offered to God for them, and of that incense, which is continually offered with the prayers of the saints, upon the golden altar that is before the throne, Rev. viii, 3, 4.

12. **Zacharias was troubled** - Although he was accustomed to converse with God, yet we see he was thrown into a great consternation, at the appearance of his angelical messenger, nature not being

able to sustain the sight. Is it not then an instance of the goodness is well as of the wisdom of God, that the services, which these heavenly spirits render us, are generally invisible?

13. Thy prayer is heard - Let us observe with pleasure, that the prayers of pious worshippers come up with acceptance before God; to whom no costly perfume is so sweet, as the fragrancy of an upright heart. An answer of peace was here returned, when the case seemed to be most helpless. Let us wait patiently for the Lord, and leave to his own wisdom the time and manner wherein he will appear for us. Thou shalt call his name John - John signifies the grace or favour of Jehovah. A name well suiting the person, who was afterward so highly in favour with God, and endued with abundance of grace; and who opened a way to the most glorious dispensation of grace in the Messiah's kingdom. And so Zacharias's former prayers for a child, and the prayer which he, as the representative of the people, was probably offering at this very time, for the appearing of the Messiah, were remarkably answered in the birth of his forerunner.

15. He shall be great before the Lord - God the Father: of the Holy Ghost and the Son of God mention is made immediately after. And shall drink neither wine nor strong drink - Shall be exemplary for abstemiousness and self-denial; and so much the more filled with the Holy Ghost.

16. And many of the children of Israel shall he turn - None therefore need be ashamed of "preaching like John the Baptist." To the Lord their God - To Christ.

17. He shall go before him, Christ, in the power and spirit of Elijah - With the same integrity, courage, austerity, and fervour, and the same power attending his word: to turn the hearts of the fathers to the children - To reconcile those that are at variance, to put an end to the most bitter quarrels, such as are very frequently those between the nearest relations: and the hearts of the disobedient to the wisdom of the just - And the most obstinate sinners to true wisdom, which is only found among them that are righteous before God.

18. Zacharias said, Whereby shall I know this? - In how different a spirit did the blessed virgin say, How shall this be? Zacharias disbelieved the fact: Mary had no doubt of the thing; but only inquired concerning the manner of it.

19. I am Gabriel, that stand in the presence of God - Seven angels thus stand before God, Rev. vii, 2; who seem the highest of all. There seems to be a remarkable gradation in the words, enhancing the guilt of Zacharias's unbelief. As if he had said, I am Gabriel, a holy angel of God: yea, one of the highest order. Not only so, but am now peculiarly sent from God; and that with a message to thee in particular. Nay, and to show thee glad tidings, such as ought to be received with the greatest joy and readiness.

20. Thou shalt be dumb - The Greek word signifies deaf, as well as dumb: and it seems plain, that he was as unable to hear, as he was to speak; for his friends were obliged to make signs to him, that he might understand them, ver. 62.

21. The people were waiting - For him to come and dismiss them (as usual) with the blessing.

24. Hid herself - She retired from company, that she might have the more leisure to rejoice and bless God for his wonderful mercy.

25. He looked upon me to take away my reproach - Barrenness was a great reproach among the Jews. Because fruitfulness was promised to the righteous.

26. In the sixth month - After Elisabeth had conceived.

27. Espoused - It was customary among the Jews, for persons that married to contract before witnesses some time before. And as Christ was to be born of a pure virgin, so the wisdom of God ordered it to be of one espoused, that to prevent reproach he might have a reputed father, according to the flesh.

28. Hail, thou highly favoured; the Lord is with thee; blessed art thou among women - Hail is the salutation used by our Lord to the women after his resurrection: thou art highly favoured, or hast found favour with God, ver. 30, is no more than was said of Noah, Moses, and David. The Lord is with thee, was said to Gideon, Judg. vi, 12; and blessed shall she be above women, of Jael, Judg. v, 24. This salutation gives no room for any pretense of paying adoration to the virgin; as having no appearance of a prayer, or of worship offered to her.

32. He shall be called the Son of the Highest - In this respect also: and that in a more eminent sense than any, either man or angel, can be called so. The Lord shall give him the throne of his father David - That is, the spiritual kingdom, of which David's was a type.

33. He shall reign over the house of Jacob - In which all true believers are included.

35. The Holy Ghost shall come upon thee, and the power of the Highest shall overshadow thee - The power of God was put forth by the Holy Ghost, as the immediate Divine agent in this work: and so he exerted the power of the Highest as his own power, who together with the Father and the Son is the most high God. Therefore also - Not only as he is God from eternity, but on this account likewise he shall be called the Son of God.

36. And behold, thy cousin Elisabeth - Though Elisabeth was of the house of Aaron, and Mary of the house of David, by the fathers side, they might be related by their mothers. For the law only forbad

heiresses marrying into another tribe. And so other persons continually intermarried; particularly the families of David and of Levi.

38. And Mary said, Behold the handmaid of the Lord - It is not improbable, that this time of the virgin's humble faith, consent, and expectation, might be the very time of her conceiving.

39. A city of Judah - Probably Hebron, which was situated in the hill country of Judea, and belonged to the house of Aaron.

41. When Elisabeth heard the salutation of Mary - The discourse with which she saluted her, giving an account of what the angel had said, the joy of her soul so affected her body, that the very child in her womb was moved in an uncommon manner, as if it leaped for joy.

45. Happy is she that believed - Probably she had in her mind the unbelief of Zacharias.

46. And Mary said - Under a prophetic impulse, several things, which perhaps she herself did not then fully understand.

47. My spirit hath rejoiced in God my saviour - She seems to turn her thoughts here to Christ himself, who was to be born of her, as the angel had told her, he should be the Son of the Highest, whose name should be Jesus, the saviour. And she rejoiced in hope of salvation through faith in him, which is a blessing common to all true believers, more than in being his mother after the flesh, which was an honour peculiar to her. And certainly she had the same reason to rejoice in God her saviour hat we have: because he had regarded the low estate of his handmaid, in like manner as he regarded our low estate; and vouchsafed to come and save her and us, when we were reduced to the lowest estate of sin and misery.

51. He hath wrought strength with his arm - That is, he hath shown the exceeding greatness of his power. She speaks prophetically of those things as already done, which God was about to do by the Messiah. He hath scattered the proud - Visible and invisible.

52. He hath put down the mighty - Both angels and men.

54. He hath helped his servant Israel - By sending the Messiah.

55. To his seed - His spiritual seed: all true believers.

56. Mary returned to her own house - And thence soon after to Bethlehem.

60. His mother said - Doubtless by Revelation, or a particular impulse from God.

66. The hand of the Lord - The peculiar power and blessing of God.

67. And Zacharias prophesied - Of things immediately to follow. But it is observable, he speaks of Christ chiefly; of John only, as it were, incidentally.

69. A horn - Signifies honour, plenty, and strength. A horn of salvation - That is, a glorious and mighty saviour.

70. His prophets, who have been since the world began - For there were prophets from the very beginning.

74. To serve him without fear - Without any slavish fear. Here is the substance of the great promise. That we shall be always holy, always happy: that being delivered from Satan and sin, from every uneasy and unholy temper, we shall joyfully love and serve God, in every thought, word, and work.

76. And thou, child - He now speaks to John; yet not as a parent, but as a prophet.

77. To give knowledge of salvation by the remission of sins - The knowledge of the remission of our sins being the grand instrument of present and eternal salvation, Heb. viii, 11, 12. But the immediate sense of the words seems to be, to preach to them the Gospel doctrine of salvation by the remission of their sins.

78. The day spring - Or the rising sun; that is, Christ.

II

1. That all the world should be enrolled - That all the inhabitants, male and female, of every town in the Roman empire, with their families and estates, should be registered.

2. When Cyrenius was governor of Syria - When Publius Sulpicius Quirinus governed the province of Syria, in which Judea was then included.

6. And while they were there, the days were fulfilled that she should be delivered - Mary seems not to have known that the child must have been born in Bethlehem, agreeably to the prophecy. But the providence of God took care for it.

7. She laid him in the manger - Perhaps it might rather be translated in the stall. They were lodged in the ox stall, fitted up on occasion of the great concourse, for poor guests. There was no room for them in the inn - Now also, there is seldom room for Christ in an inn. Matt. i, 25

11. To you - Shepherds; Israel; mankind.

14. Glory be to God in the highest; on earth peace; good will toward men - The shouts of the multitude are generally broken into short sentences. This rejoicing acclamation strongly represents the piety and benevolence of these heavenly spirits: as if they had said, Glory be to God in the highest

heavens: let all the angelic legions resound his praises. For with the Redeemer's birth, peace, and all kind of happiness, come down to dwell on earth: yea, the overflowings of Divine good will and favour are now exercised toward men.

20. For all the things that they had heard - From Mary; as it was told them - By the angels.

21. To circumcise the child - That he might visibly be made under the law by a sacred rite, which obliged him to keep the whole law; as also that he might be owned to be the seed of Abraham, and might put an honour on the solemn dedication of children to God.

22. The days - The forty days prescribed, Lev. xii, 2, 4.

23. Exod. xiii, 2.

24. A pair of turtle doves, or two young pigeons - This offering sufficed for the poor. Lev. xii, 8.

25. The consolation of Israel - A common phrase for the Messiah, who was to be the everlasting consolation of the Israel of God. The Holy Ghost was upon him - That is, he was a prophet.

27. By the Spirit - By a particular Revelation or impulse from him.

30. Thy salvation - Thy Christ, thy saviour.

32. And the glory of thy people Israel - For after the Gentiles are enlightened, all Israel shall be saved.

33. Joseph and his mother marvelled at those things which were spoken - For they did not thoroughly understand them.

34. Simeon blessed them - Joseph and Mary. This child is set for the fall and rising again of many - That is, he will be a savour of death to some, to unbelievers: a savour of life to others, to believers: and for a sign which shall be spoken against - A sign from God, yet rejected of men: but the time for declaring this at large was not yet come: that the thoughts of many hearts may be revealed - The event will be, that by means of that contradiction, the inmost thoughts of many, whether good or bad, will be made manifest.

35. A sword shall pierce through thy own soul - So it did, when he suffered: particularly at his crucifixion.

37. Fourscore and four years - These were the years of her life, not her widowhood only. Who departed not from the temple - Who attended there at all the stated hours of prayer. But served God with fastings and prayers - Even at that age. Night and day - That is, spending therein a considerable part of the night, as well as of the day.

38. To all that were waiting for redemption - The scepter now appeared to be departing from Judah, though it was not actually gone: Daniel's weeks were plainly near their period. And the revival of the spirit of prophecy, together with the memorable occurrences relating to the birth of John the Baptist, and of Jesus, could not but encourage and quicken the expectation of pious persons at this time. Let the example of these aged saints animate those, whose hoary heads, like theirs, are a crown of glory, being found in the way of righteousness. Let those venerable lips, so soon to be silent in the grave, be now employed in the praises of their Redeemer. Let them labour to leave those behind, to whom Christ will be as precious as he has been to them; and who will be waiting for God's salvation, when they are gone to enjoy it.

40. And the child grew - In bodily strength and stature; and waxed strong in spirit - The powers of his human mind daily improved; filled with wisdom - By the light of the indwelling Spirit, which gradually opened itself in his soul; and the grace of God was upon him - That is, the peculiar favour of God rested upon him, even as man.

43. The child Jesus - St. Luke describes in order Jesus the fruit of the womb, chap. i, 42; an infant, chap. ii, 12; a little child, ver. 40; a child here, and afterward a man. So our Lord passed through and sanctified every stage of human life. Old age only did not become him.

44. Supposing him to have been in the company - As the men and women usually travelled in distinct companies.

46. After three days - The first day was spent in their journey, the second, in their return to Jerusalem: and the third, in searching for him there: they found him in the temple - In an apartment of it: sitting in the midst of the doctors - Not one word is said of his disputing with them, but only of his asking and answering questions, which was a very usual thing in these assemblies, and indeed the very end of them. And if he was, with others, at the feet of these teachers (where learners generally sat) he might be said to be in the midst of them, as they sat on benches of a semicircular form, raised above their hearers and disciples.

49. Why sought ye me? - He does not blame them for losing, but for thinking it needful to seek him: and intimates, that he could not be lost, nor found any where, but doing the will of a higher parent.

50. It is observable that Joseph is not mentioned after this time; whence it is probable, he did not live long after.

52. Jesus increased in wisdom - As to his human nature, and in favour with God - In proportion to that increase. It plainly follows, that though a man were pure, even as Christ was pure, still he would have room to increase in holiness, and in consequence thereof to increase in the favour, as well as in the

love of God.

III

1. The fifteenth year of Tiberius - Reckoning from the time when Angustus made him his colleague in the empire. Herod being tetrarch of Galilee - The dominions of Herod the Great were, after his death, divided into four parts or tetrarchies. This Herod his son was tetrarch of Galilee, reigning over that fourth part of his dominions. His brother reigned over two other fourth parts, the region of Iturea, and that of Trachonitis (that tract of land on the other side Jordan, which had formerly belonged to the tribe of Manasseh.) And Lysanias (probably descended from a prince of that name, who was some years before governor of that country) was tetrarch of the remaining part of Abilene, which was a large city of Syria, whose territories reached to Lebanon and Damascus, and contained great numbers of Jews. Matt. iii, 1; Mark i, 1.

2. Annas being high priest, and Caiaphas - There could be but one high priest, strictly speaking, at once. Annas was the high priest at that time, and Caiaphas his sagan or deputy.

4. Isaiah xl, 3.

5. Every valley shall be filled, &c. - That is, every hindrance shall be removed.

6. The salvation of God - The saviour, the Messiah.

8. Say not within yourselves, We have Abraham to our father - That is, trust not in your being members of the visible Church, or in any external privileges whatsoever: for God now requires a change of heart; and that without delay.

10. He answereth - It is not properly John, but the Holy Ghost, who teaches us in the following answers, how to come ourselves, and how to instruct other penitent sinners to come to Christ, that he may give them rest. The sum of all this is, Cease to do evil, learn to do well. These are the fruits worthy of repentance.

20. He shut up John - This circumstance, though it happened after, is here mentioned before our Lord's baptism, that his history (that of John being concluded) may then follow without any interruption.

21. Jesus praying, the heaven was opened - It is observable, that the three voices from heaven, see chap. ix, 29, 35; John xii, 28; by which the Father bore witness to Christ, were pronounced either while he was praying, or quickly after it. Matt. iii, 13; Mark i, 9.

23. And Jesus was - John's beginning was computed by the years of princes: our saviour's by the years of his own life, as a more august era. About thirty years of age - He did not now enter upon his thirtieth year (as the common translation would induce one to think) but he now entered on his public ministry: being of such an age as the Mosaic law required. Our great Master attained not, as it seems, to the conclusion of his thirty-fourth year. Yet what glorious achievements did he accomplish within those narrow limits of time! Happy that servant, who, with any proportionable zeal, despatches the great business of life; and so much the more happy, if his sun go down at noon. For the space that is taken from the labours of time, shall be added to the rewards of eternity. The son of Heli - That is, the son-in-law: for Heli was the father of Mary. So St. Matthew writes the genealogy of Joseph, descended from David by Solomon; St. Luke that of Mary, descended from David by Nathan. In the genealogy of Joseph (recited by St. Matthew) that of Mary is implied, the Jews being accustomed to marry into their own families.

38. Adam the son of God - That is, whatever the sons of Adam receive from their human parents, Adam received immediately from God, except sin and misery.

IV

1. The wilderness - Supposed by some to have been in Judea; by others to have been that great desert of Horeb or Sinai, where the children of Israel were tried for forty years, and Moses and Elijah fasted forty days. Matt. iv, 1; Mark i, 12.

4. Deut. viii, 3.

6. I give it to whomsoever I will - Not so, Satan. It is God, not thou, that putteth down one, and setteth up another: although sometimes Satan, by God's permission, may occasion great revolutions in the world.

8. Deut. vi, 13.

10. Psalm xci, 11.

12. Deut. vi, 16.

13. A convenient season - In the garden of Gethsemane, chap. xxii, 53.

14. Jesus returned in the power of the Spirit - Being more abundantly strengthened after his conflict.

15. Being glorified of all - So God usually gives strong cordials after strong temptations. But

Wesley's Notes on the Bible - The New Testament

neither their approbation continued long, nor the outward calm which he now enjoyed.

16. He stood up - Showing thereby that he had a desire to read the Scripture to the congregation: on which the book was given to him. It was the Jewish custom to read standing, but to preach sitting. Matt. xiii, 54; Mark vi, 1.

17. He found - It seems, opening upon it, by the particular providence of God.

18. He hath anointed me - With the Spirit. He hath by the power of his Spirit which dwelleth in me, set me apart for these offices. To preach the Gospel to the poor - Literally and spiritually. How is the doctrine of the ever-blessed trinity interwoven, even in those scriptures where one would least expect it? How clear a declaration of the great Three-One is there in those very words, The Spirit - of the Lord is upon me! To proclaim deliverance to the captives, and recovery of sight to the blind, to set at liberty them that are bruised - Here is a beautiful gradation, in comparing the spiritual state of men to the miserable state of those captives, who are not only cast into prison, but, like Zedekiah, had their eyes put out, and were laden and bruised with chains of iron. Isaiah lxi, 1.

19. The acceptable year - Plainly alluding to the year of jubilee, when all, both debtors and servants, were set free.

21. Today is this scripture fulfilled in your ears - By what you hear me speak.

22. The gracious words which proceeded out of his mouth - A person of spiritual discernment may find in all the discourses of our Lord a peculiar sweetness, gravity, and becomingness, such as is not to be found in the same degree, not even in those of the apostles.

23. Ye will surely say - That is, your approbation now outweighs your prejudices. But it will not be so long. You will soon ask, why my love does not begin at home? Why I do not work miracles here, rather than at Capernaum? It is because of your unbelief. Nor is it any new thing for me to be despised in my own country. So were both Elijah and Elisha, and thereby driven to work miracles among heathens, rather than in Israel.

24. No prophet is acceptable in his own country - That is, in his own neighbourhood. It generally holds, that a teacher sent from God is not so acceptable to his neighbours as he is to strangers. The meanness of his family, or lowness of his circumstances, bring his office into contempt: nor can they suffer that he, who was before equal with, or below themselves, should now bear a superior character.

25. When the heaven was shut up three years and six months - Such a proof had they that God had sent him. In 1 Kings xviii, 1, it is said, The word of the Lord came to Elijah in the third year: namely, reckoning not from the beginning of the drought, but from the time when he began to sojourn with the widow of Sarepta. A year of drought had preceded this, while he dwelt at the brook Cherith. So that the whole time of the drought was (as St. James likewise observes) three years and six months. 1 Kings xvii, 19; xviii, 44.

27. 2 Kings v, 14.

28. And all in the synagogue were filled with fury - Perceiving the purport of his discourse, namely, that the blessing which they despised, would be offered to, and accepted by, the Gentiles. So changeable are the hearts of wicked men! So little are their starts of love to be depended on! So unable are they to bear the close application, even of a discourse which they most admire!

30. Passing through the midst of them - Perhaps invisibly; or perhaps they were overawed; so that though they saw, they could not touch him.

31. He came down to Capernaum - And dwelt there, entirely quitting his abode at Nazareth. Mark i, 21.

34. What have we to do with thee - Thy present business is with men, not with devils. I know thee who thou art - But surely he did not know a little before, that he was God over all, blessed forever; or he would not have dared to tell him, All this power is delivered to me, and I give it to whomsoever I will. The Holy One of God - Either this confession was extorted from him by terror, (for the devils believe and tremble,) or he made it with a design to render the character of Christ suspected. Possibly it was from hence the Pharisees took occasion to say, He casteth out devils by the prince of the devils.

38. Matt. viii, 14; Mark i, 29.

40. When the sun was set - And consequently the Sabbath ended, which they reckoned from sunset to sunset. Matt. viii, 16; Mark i, 32.

42. Mark i, 35.

V

1. Matt. iv, 18; Mark i, 16.

6. Their net brake - Began to tear.

8. Depart from me, for I am a sinful man - And therefore not worthy to be in thy presence.

11. They forsook all and followed him - They had followed him before, John i, 43, but not so as to forsake all. Till now, they wrought at their ordinary calling.

12. Matt. viii, 2; Mark i, 40.

14. Lev. xiv, 2.

16. He withdrew - The expression in the original implies, that he did so frequently.

17. Sitting by - As being more honourable than the bulk of the congregation, who stood. And the power of the Lord was present to heal them - To heal the sickness of their souls, as well as all bodily diseases.

18. Matt. ix, 2; Mark ii, 3.

19. Not being able to bring him in through the multitude, they went round about by a back passage, and going up the stairs on the outside, they came upon the flat-roofed house, and let him down through the trap door, such as was on the top of most of the Jewish houses: doubtless, with such circumspection as the circumstances plainly required.

26. We have seen strange things today - Sins forgiven, miracles wrought.

27. Matt. ix, 9; Mark ii, 14.

28. Leaving all - His business and gain.

29. And Levi made him a great entertainment - It was necessarily great, because of the great number of guests.

33. Make prayers - Long and solemn. Matt. ix, 14; Mark ii, 18.

34. Can ye make - That is, is it proper to make men fast and mourn, during a festival solemnity?

36. He spake also a parable - Taken from clothes and wine; therefore peculiarly proper at a feast.

39. And no man having drunk old wine - And beside, men are not wont to be immediately freed from old prejudices.

VI

1. The first Sabbath - So the Jews reckoned their Sabbaths, from the passover to pentecost; the first, second, third, and so on, till the seventh Sabbath (after the second day.) This immediately preceded pentecost, which was the fiftieth day after the second day of unleavened bread. Matt. xii, 1; Mark ii, 23.

2. Why do ye - St. Matthew and Mark represent the Pharisees as proposing the question to our Lord himself. It was afterward, probably, they proposed it to his disciples.

4. 1 Sam. xxi, 6.

6. Matt. xii, 9; Mark iii, 1.

9. To save life or to kill - He just then probably saw the design to kill him rising in their hearts.

12. In the prayer of God - The phrase is singular and emphatical, to imply an extraordinary and sublime devotion. Mark iii, 13.

13. Matt. x, 2; Mark iii, 14; Acts i, 13.

15. Simon called Zelotes - Full of zeal; otherwise called Simon the Canaanite.

17. On a plain - At the foot of the mountain.

20. In the following verses our Lord, in the audience of his newly- chosen disciples, and of the multitude, repeats, standing on the plain, many remarkable passages of the sermon he had before delivered, sitting on the mount. He here again pronounces the poor and the hungry, the mourners, and the persecuted, happy; and represents as miserable those who are rich, and full, and joyous, and applauded: because generally prosperity is a sweet poison, and affliction a healing, though bitter medicine. Let the thought reconcile us to adversity, and awaken our caution when the world smiles upon us; when a plentiful table is spread before us, and our cup is running over; when our spirits are gay; and we hear (what nature loves) our own praise from men. Happy are ye poor - The word seems here to be taken literally: ye who have left all for me. Matt. v, 3.

24. Miserable are ye rich - If ye have received or sought your consolation or happiness therein.

25. Full - Of meat and drink, and worldly goods. That laugh - That are of a light trifling spirit.

26. Woe to you when all men shall speak well of you - But who will believe this?

27. But I say to you that hear - Hitherto our Lord had spoken only to particular sorts of persons: now he begins speaking to all in general. Matt. v, 44.

29. To him that smiteth thee on the cheek - Taketh away thy cloak - These seem to be proverbial expressions, to signify an invasion of the tenderest points of honour and property. Offer the other - Forbid not thy coat - That is, rather yield to his repeating the affront or injury, than gratify resentment in righting your self; in any method not becoming Christian love. Matt. v, 39.

30. Give to every one - Friend or enemy, what thou canst spare, and he really wants: and of him that taketh away thy goods - By borrowing, if he be insolvent, ask them not again. Matt. v, 42.

31. Matt. vii, 12.

32. It is greatly observable, our Lord has so little regard for one of the highest instances of natural virtue, namely, the returning love for love, that he does not account it even to deserve thanks. For even sinners, saith he, do the same: men who do not regard God at all. Therefore he may do this, who has not taken one step in Christianity.

37. Matt. vii, 1.

38. Into your bosom - Alluding to the mantles the Jews wore, into which a large quantity of corn

might be received. With the same measure that ye mete with, it shall be measured to you again - Amazing goodness! So we are permitted even to carve for ourselves! We ourselves are, as it were, to tell God how much mercy he shall show us! And can we be content with less than the very largest measure? Give then to man, what thou designest to receive of God.

39. He spake a parable - Our Lord sometimes used parables when he knew plain and open declarations would too much inflame the passions of his hearers. It is for this reason he uses this parable, Can the blind lead the blind? - Can the scribes teach this way, which they know not themselves? Will not they and their scholars perish together? Can they make their disciples any better than themselves? But as for those who will be my disciples, they shall be all taught of God; who will enable them to come to the measure of the stature of the fulness of their Master. Be not ye like their disciples, censuring others, and not amending yourselves. Matt. xv, 14.

40. Matt. x, 24; John xv, 20.
41. Matt. vii, 3.
46. And why call ye me Lord, Lord - What will fair professions avail, without a life answerable thereto? Matt. vii, 21.
47. Matt. vii, 24.

VII

1. Matt. viii, 5.
3. Hearing of Jesus - Of his miracles, and of his arrival at Capernaum.
18. Matt. xi, 2.
22. To the poor the Gospel is preached - Which is the greatest mercy, and the greatest miracle of all.
24. When the messengers were departed - He did not speak the following things in the hearing of John's disciples, lest he should seem to flatter John, or to compliment him into an adherence to his former testimony. To avoid all suspicion of this kind, he deferred his commendation of him, till the messengers were gone; and then delivered it to the people, to prevent all imaginations, as if John were wavering in his judgment, and had sent the two disciples for his own, rather than their satisfaction.
27. Mal. iii, 1.
28. There is not a greater prophet than John - A greater teacher. But he that is least in the kingdom of God - The least teacher whom I send forth.
29. And all the people - Our Lord continues his discourse: justified God - Owned his wisdom and mercy in thus calling them to repentance, and preparing them for Him that was to come.
30. But the Pharisees and scribes - The good, learned, honourable men: made void the counsel, the gracious design, of God toward them - They disappointed all these methods of his love, and would receive no benefit from them.
32. They are like children sitting in the market place - So froward and perverse, that no contrivance can be found to please them. It is plain our Lord means, that they were like the children complained of, not like those that made the complaint.
34. But wisdom is justified by all her children - The children of wisdom are those who are truly wise unto salvation. The wisdom of God in all these dispensations, these various methods of calling sinners to repentance, is owned and heartily approved by all these.
36. And one of the Pharisees asked him to eat with him - Let the candour with which our Lord accepted this invitation, and his gentleness and prudence at this ensnaring entertainment, teach us to mingle the wisdom of the serpent, with the innocence and sweetness of the dove. Let us neither absolutely refuse all favours, nor resent all neglects, from those whose friendship is at best very doubtful, and their intimacy by no means safe.
37. A woman - Not the same with Mary of Bethany, who anointed him six days before his last passover.
40. And Jesus said, Simon, I have somewhat to say to thee - So tender and courteous an address does our Lord use even to a proud, censorious Pharisee!
43. Which of them will love him most? - Neither of them will love him at all, before he has forgiven them. An insolvent debtor, till he is forgiven, does not love, but fly his creditor.
44. Thou gavest me no water - It was customary with the Jews to show respect and kindness to their welcome guests, by saluting them with a kiss, by washing their feet, and anointing their heads with oil, or some fine ointment.
47. Those many sins of hers are forgiven; therefore she loveth much - The fruit of her having had much forgiven. It should carefully be observed here, that her love is mentioned as the effect and evidence, not the cause of her pardon. She knew that much had been forgiven her, and therefore she loved much.
50. Thy faith hath saved thee - Not thy love. Love is salvation.

VIII

2. Mary Magdalene - Or Mary of Magdala, a town in Galilee: probably the person mentioned in the last chapter.

4. Matt. xiii, 1; Mark iv, 1.

15. Who - keep it - Not like the highway side: And bring forth fruit - Not like the thorny ground: With perseverance - Not like the stony.

16. No man having lighted a candle - As if he had said, And let your good fruit appear openly. Matt. v, 15; Mark iv, 21; Chap. xi, 33.

17. For nothing is hid - Strive not to conceal it at all; for you can conceal nothing long. Matt. x, 26; Mark iv, 22; Chap. xii, 2.

18. The word commonly translated seemeth, wherever it occurs, does not weaken, but greatly strengthens the sense. Matt. xiii, 12; Mark iv, 25; Luke xix, 26.

19. Matt. xii, 46; Mark iii, 31.

22. Matt. viii, 23; Mark iv, 35.

26. Matt. viii, 28; Mark v, 1.

29. For many times it had caught him - Therefore our compassionate Lord made the more haste to cast him out.

31. The abyss - That is, the bottomless pit.

32. To enter into the swine - Not that they were any easier in the swine than out of them. Had it been so, they would not so soon have dislodged themselves, by destroying the herd.

37. Matt. ix, 1; Mark v, 18.

40. Mark v, 21.

52. She is not dead but sleepeth - Her soul is not separated finally from the body; and this short separation is rather to be called sleep than death.

IX

1. Matt. x, 1; Mark vi, 7.

4. There abide and thence depart - That is, stay in that house till ye leave the city.

7. It was said by some - And soon after by Herod himself. Matt. xiv, 1; Mark vi, 14.

8. That Elijah had appeared - He could not rise again, because he did not die.

10. Mark vi, 30.

12. Matt. xiv, 15; Mark vi, 35; John vi, 3.

18. Apart - From the multitude. And he asked them - When he had done praying, during which they probably stayed at a distance. Matt. xiv, 13; Mark viii, 27.

22. Saying - Ye must prepare for a scene far different from this.

23. Let him deny himself, and take up his cross - The necessity of this duty has been shown in many places: the extent of it is specified here, daily - Therefore that day is lost wherein no cross is taken up.

24. Matt. xvi, 25; Mark viii, 35; John xii, 25.

28. Matt. xvii, 1; Mark ix, 2.

31. In glory - Like Christ with whom they talked.

32. They saw his glory - The very same expression in which it is described by St. John, John i, 14; and by St. Peter, 2 Pet. i, 16.

34. A cloud came and overshadowed them all. And they, the apostles, feared, while they (Moses and Elijah) entered into the cloud, which took them away.

37. Matt. xvii, 14; Mark ix, 14.

44. Let these sayings sink down into your ears - That is, consider them deeply. In joy remember the cross. So wisely does our Lord balance praise with sufferings. Matt. xvii, 22; Mark ix, 31.

46. And there arose a reasoning among them - This kind of reasoning always arose at the most improper times that could be imagined.

47. Matt. xviii, 2; Mark ix, 37.

48. And said to them - If ye would be truly great, humble yourselves to the meanest offices. He that is least in his own eyes shall be great indeed.

49. Mark ix, 38.

51. The days are fulfilled that he should be received up - That is, the time of his passion was now at hand. St. Luke looks through this, to the glory which was to follow. He steadfastly set his face - Without fear of his enemies, or shame of the cross, Heb. xii, 2.

52. He sent messengers to make ready - A lodging and needful entertainment for him and those with him.

53. His face was as though he would go to Jerusalem - It plainly appeared, he was going to

worship at the temple, and thereby, in effect, to condemn the Samaritan worship at Mount Gerizim.

54. As Elisha did - At or near this very place, which might put it into the minds of the apostles to make the motion now, rather than at any other time or place, where Christ had received the like affront.

55. Ye know not what manner of spirit - The spirit of Christianity is. It is not a spirit of wrath and vengeance, but of peace, and gentleness, and love.

57. Matt. viii, 19.

58. But Jesus said to him - First understand the terms: consider on what conditions thou art to follow me.

61. Suffer me first to bid them farewell that are in my house - As Elisha did after Elijah had called him from the plough, 1 Kings xix, 19; to which our Lord's answer seems to allude.

62. Is fit for the kingdom of God - Either to propagate or to receive it.

X

2. Pray ye the Lord of the harvest, that he would thrust forth labourers - For God alone can do this: he alone can qualify and commission men for this work. Matt. ix, 37.

3. Matt. x, 16.

4. Salute no man by the way - The salutations usual among the Jews took up much time. But these had so much work to do in so short a space, that they had not a moment to spare.

6. A son of peace - That is, one worthy of it.

7. Matt. x, 11.

11. The kingdom of God is at hand - Though ye will not receive it.

13. Woe to thee, Chorazin - The same declaration Christ had made some time before. By repeating it now, he warns the seventy not to lose time by going to those cities. Matt. xi, 21.

16. Matt. x, 40; John xiii, 20.

18. I beheld Satan - That is, when ye went forth, I saw the kingdom of Satan, which was highly exalted, swiftly and suddenly cast down.

19. I give you power - That is, I continue it to you: and nothing shall hurt you - Neither the power, nor the subtilty of Satan.

20. Rejoice not so much that the devils are subject to you, as that your names are written in heaven - Reader, so is thine, if thou art a true, believer. God grant it may never be blotted out!

21. Lord of heaven and earth - In both of which thy kingdom stands, and that of Satan is destroyed. That thou hast hid these things - He rejoiced not in the destruction of the wise and prudent, but in the display of the riches of God's grace to others, in such a manner as reserves to Him the entire glory of our salvation, and hides pride from man. Matt. xi, 25.

22. Who the Son is - Essentially one with the Father: who the Father is - How great, how wise, how good!

23. Matt. xiii, 16.

25. Matt. xxii, 35; Mark xii, 28.

27. Thou shalt love the Lord thy God - That is, thou shalt unite all the faculties of thy soul to render him the most intelligent and sincere, the most affectionate and resolute service. We may safely rest in this general sense of these important words, if we are not able to fix the particular meaning of every single word. If we desire to do this, perhaps the heart, which is a general expression, may be explained by the three following, With all thy soul, with the warmest affection, with all thy strength, the most vigourous efforts of thy will, and with all thy mind or understanding, in the most wise and reasonable manner thou canst; thy understanding guiding thy will and affections. Deut. vi, 5; Lev. xix, 18.

28. Thou hast answered right; this do, and thou shalt live - Here is no irony, but a deep and weighty truth. He, and he alone, shall live forever, who thus loves God and his neighbour in the present life.

29. To justify himself - That is, to show he had done this. Lev. xviii, 5.

30. From Jerusalem to Jericho - The road from Jerusalem to Jericho (about eighteen miles from it) lay through desert and rocky places: so many robberies and murders were committed therein, that it was called the bloody way. Jericho was situated in the valley: hence the phrase of going down to it. About twelve thousand priests and Levites dwelt there, who all attended the service of the temple.

31. The common translation is, by chance - Which is full of gross improprieties. For if we speak strictly, there is no such thing in the universe as either chance or fortune. A certain priest came down that way, and passed by on the other side - And both he and the Levite no doubt could find an excuse for passing over on the other side, and might perhaps gravely thank God for their own deliverance, while they left their brother bleeding to death. Is it not an emblem of many living characters, perhaps of some who bear the sacred office? O house of Levi and of Aaron, is not the day coming, when the virtues of heathens and Samaritans will rise up in judgment against you?

33. But a certain Samaritan came where he was - It was admirably well judged to represent the distress on the side of the Jew, and the mercy on that of the Samaritan. For the case being thus proposed, self interest would make the very scribe sensible, how amiable such a conduct was, and would lay him open to our Lord's inference. Had it been put the other way, prejudice might more easily have interposed, before the heart could have been affected.

34. Pouring in oil and wine - Which when well beaten together are one of the best balsams that can be applied to a fresh wound.

36. Which of these was the neighbour to him that fell among the robbers - Which acted the part of a neighbour?

37. And he said, He that showed mercy on him - He could not for shame say otherwise, though he thereby condemned himself and overthrew his own false notion of the neighbour to whom our love is due. Go and do thou in like manner - Let us go and do likewise, regarding every man as our neighbour who needs our assistance. Let us renounce that bigotry and party zeal which would contract our hearts into an insensibility for all the human race, but a small number whose sentiments and practices are so much our own, that our love to them is but self love reflected. With an honest openness of mind let us always remember that kindred between man and man, and cultivate that happy instinct whereby, in the original constitution of our nature, God has strongly bound us to each other.

40. Martha was encumbered - The Greek word properly signifies to be drawn different ways at the same time, and admirably expresses the situation of a mind, surrounded (as Martha's then was) with so many objects of care, that it hardly knows which to attend to first.

41. Martha, Martha - There is a peculiar spirit and tenderness in the repetition of the word: thou art careful, inwardly, and hurried, outwardly.

42. Mary hath chosen the good part - To save her soul. Reader, hast thou?

XI

1. Lord, teach us to pray, as John also taught his disciples - The Jewish masters used to give their followers some short form of prayer, as a peculiar badge of their relation to them. This it is probable John the Baptist had done. And in this sense it seems to be that the disciples now asked Jesus, to teach them to pray. Accordingly he here repeats that form, which he had before given them in his sermon on the mount, and likewise enlarges on the same head, though still speaking the same things in substance. And this prayer uttered from the heart, and in its true and full meaning, is indeed the badge of a real Christian: for is not he such whose first and most ardent desire is the glory of God, and the happiness of man by the coming of his kingdom? Who asks for no more of this world than his daily bread, longing meantime for the bread that came down from heaven? And whose only desires for himself are forgiveness of sins, (as he heartily forgives others,) and sanctification.

2. When ye pray, say - And what he said to them is undoubtedly said to us also. We are therefore here directed, not only to imitate this in all our prayers, but to use this very form of prayer. Matt. vi, 9.

4. Forgive us; for we forgive them - Not once, but continually. This does not denote the meritorious cause of our pardon; but the removal of that hindrance which otherwise would render it impossible.

5. At midnight - The most unseasonable time: but no time is unseasonable with God, either for hearing or answering prayer.

9. Matt. vii, 7.

13. How much more shall your heavenly Father - How beautiful is the gradation! A friend: a father: God! Give the Holy Spirit - The best of gifts, and that which includes every good gift.

14. It was dumb - That is, it made the man so. Matt. xii, 22.

15. But some said, He casteth out devils by Beelzebub - These he answers, ver. 17. Others, to try whether it were so or no, sought a sign from heaven. These he reproves in ver. 29 and following verses. Beelzebub signifies the Lord of flies, a title which the heathens gave to Jupiter, whom they accounted the chief of their gods, and yet supposed him to be employed in driving away flies from their temple and sacrifices. The Philistines worshipped a deity under this name, as the God of Ekron: from hence the Jews took the name, and applied it to the chief of the devils. Mark iii, 22.

16. Matt. xii, 38.

17. A house - That is, a family.

20. If I cast out devils by the finger of God - That is, by a power manifestly Divine. Perhaps the expression intimates farther, that it was done without any labour: then the kingdom of God is come upon you - Unawares, unexpected: so the Greek word implies.

21. The strong one armed - The devil, strong in himself, and armed with the pride, obstinacy, and security of him in whom he dwells.

26. The last state of that man becometh worse than the first - Whoever reads the sad account Josephus gives of the temple and conduct of the Jews, after the ascension of Christ and before their final

destruction by the Romans, must acknowledge that no emblem could have been more proper to describe them. Their characters were the vilest that can be conceived, and they pressed on to their own ruin, as if they had been possessed by legions of devils, and wrought up to the last degree of madness. But this also is fulfilled in all who totally and finally apostatize from true faith.

27. Blessed is the womb that bare thee, and the paps which thou hast sucked! - How natural was the thought for a woman! And how gently does our Lord reprove her!

28. Yea, rather blessed are they that hear the word of God and keep it - For if even she that bare him had not done this, she would have forfeited all her blessedness.

29. It seeketh - The original word implies seeking more, or over and above what one has already.

32. They repented at the preaching of Jonah - But it was only for a season. Afterward they relapsed into wickedness, till (after about forty years) they were destroyed. It is remarkable, that in this also the comparison held. God reprieved the Jews for about forty years; but they still advanced in wickedness, till having filled up their measure, they were destroyed with an utter destruction.

33. The meaning is, God gives you this Gospel light, that you may repent. Let your eye be singly fixed on him, aim only at pleasing God; and while you do this, your whole soul will be full of wisdom, holiness, and happiness. Matt. v, 15; Mark iv, 21; Luke viii, 16.

34. But when thine eye is evil - When thou aimest at any thing else, thou wilt be full of folly, sin, and misery. On the contrary, Matt. vi, 22.

36. If thy whole body be full of light - If thou art filled with holy wisdom, having no part dark, giving way to no sin or folly, then that heavenly principle will, like the clear flame of a lamp in a room that was dark before, shed its light into all thy powers and faculties.

39. Now ye Pharisees - Probably many of them were present at the Pharisee's house. Matt. xxiii, 25.

41. Give what is in them - The vessels which ye clean, in alms, and all things are clean to you. As if he had said, By acts directly contrary to rapine and wickedness, show that your hearts are cleansed, and these outward washings are needless.

42. Woe to you - That is, miserable are you. In the same manner is the phrase to be understood throughout the chapter.

44. For ye are as graves which appear not - Probably in speaking this our Lord fixed his eyes on the scribes. As graves which appear not, being overgrown with grass, so that men are not aware, till they stumble upon them, and either hurt themselves, or at least are defiled by touching them. On another occasion Christ compared them to whited sepulchres, fair without, but foul within; Matt. xxiii, 27.

45. One of the lawyers - That is scribes; expounders of the law.

48. Whom they killed, ye build their sepulchres - Just like them pretending great reverence for the ancient prophets, while ye destroy those whom God sends to yourselves. Ye therefore bear witness by this deep hypocrisy that ye are of the very same spirit with them.

49. The wisdom of God, agreeably to this, hath said - In many places of Scripture, though not in these very words, I will send them prophets - Chiefly under the Old Testament: and apostles - Under the New. Matt. xxiii, 34.

50. The blood of all shall be required of this generation - That is, shall be visibly and terribly punished upon it.

51. And so it was within forty years, in a most astonishing manner, by the dreadful destruction of the temple, the city, and the whole nation. Between the temple and the altar - In the court of the temple.

52. Ye have taken away the key of knowledge - Ye have obscured and destroyed the knowledge of the Messiah, which is the key of both the present and the future kingdom of heaven; the kingdom of grace and glory. Ye have not entered in - Into the present kingdom of heaven.

XII

1. He said to his disciples first - But afterward ver. 54 to all the people. Matt. xvi, 6.

3. Matt. x, 27.

4. But I say to you, Fear not - Let not the fear of man make you act the hypocrite, or conceal any thing which I have commissioned you to publish.

5. Fear him who hath power to cast into hell - Even to his peculiar friends, Christ gives this direction. Therefore the fearing of God as having power to cast into hell, is to be pressed even on true believers.

6. Are not five sparrows - But trust as well as fear him.

7. Matt. x, 30.

8. And I say to you - If you avoid all hypocrisy, and openly avow my Gospel: The Son of man shall confess you - before the angels - At the last day. Mark viii, 38; Chap. ix, 26.

10. And whosoever - As if he had said, Yet the denying me in some degree, may, upon true repentance, be forgiven; but if it rise so high as that of the blasphemy against the Holy Ghost, it shall

never be forgiven, neither is there place for repentance. Matt. xii, 31; Mark iii, 28.

11. Take no thought - Be not solicitous about the matter or manner of your defense; nor how to express yourselves. Matt. x, 19; Luke xxi, 12.

14. Who made me a judge? - In worldly things. His kingdom is not of this world.

15. He said to them - Perhaps to the two brothers, and through them to the people. A man's life - That is, the comfort or happiness of it.

17. What shall I do? - The very language of want! Do? Why, lay up treasure in heaven.

20. Thou fool - To think of satisfying thy soul with earthly goods! To depend on living many years! Yea, one day! They - The messengers of death, commissioned by God, require thy soul of thee!

21. Rich toward God - Namely, in faith, and love, and good works.

22. Matt. vi, 25.

25. Which of you can add the least measure - It seems, to add one cubit to a thing (which is the phrase in the original) was a kind of proverbial expression for making the least addition to it.

28. The grass - The Greek word means all sorts of herbs and flowers.

29. Neither be ye of a doubtful mind - The word in the original signifies, any speculations or musings in which the mind fluctuates, or is suspended (like meteors in the air) in an uneasy hesitation.

32. It is your Father's good pleasure to give you the kingdom - How much more food and raiment? And since ye have such an inheritance, regard not your earthly possessions.

33. Sell what ye have - This is a direction, not given to all the multitude: (much less is it a standing rule for all Christians:) neither to the apostles; for they had nothing to sell, having left all before: but to his other disciples, (mentioned chap. xii, 22, and Acts i, 15,) especially to the seventy, that they might be free from all worldly entanglements. Matt. vi, 19.

35. Let your loins be girt - An allusion to the long garments, worn by the eastern nations, which they girded or tucked up about their loins, when they journeyed or were employed in any labour: as also to the lights that servants used to carry at weddings, which were generally in the night.

37. He will come and serve them - The meaning is, he will show them his love, in the most condescending and tender manner.

38. The Jews frequently divided the night into three watches, to which our Lord seems here to allude.

41. Speakest thou this parable to us - Apostles and disciples: Or to all - The people? Does it concern us alone? Or all men?

42. Who is that faithful and wise steward - Our Lord's answer manifestly implies, that he had spoken this parable primarily (though not wholly) to the ministers of his word: Whom his Lord shall make ruler over his household - For his wisdom and faithfulness.

43. Happy is that servant - God himself pronounces him wise, faithful, happy! Yet we see, he might fall from all, and perish forever.

46. The Lord will appoint him his portion - His everlasting portion, with the unfaithful - As faithful as he was once, God himself being the Judge!

47. And that servant who knew his Lord's will shall be beaten with many stripes - And his having much knowledge will increase, not lessen, his punishment.

49. I am come to send fire - To spread the fire of heavenly love over all the earth.

50. But I have a baptism to be baptized with - I must suffer first, before I can set up my kingdom. And how I long to fight my way through all!

51. Suppose ye that I am come to send peace upon earth - That universal peace will be the immediate effect of my coming? Not so, but quite the contrary. Matt. x, 34.

52. There shall be five in one house, three against two, and two against three - There being an irreconcilable enmity between the Spirit of Christ and the spirit of the world.

53. The father against the son - For those who reject me will be implacable toward their very nearest relations who receive me. At this day also is this scripture fulfilled. Now likewise there is no concord between Christ and Belial.

54. And he said to the people also - In the preceding verses he speaks only to his disciples. From the west - In Judea, the west wind, blowing from the sea, usually brought rain: the south wind, blowing from the deserts of Arabia, occasioned sultry heat. Matt. xvi, 2.

56. How do ye not discern this season - Of the Messiah's coming, distinguishable by so many surer signs.

57. Why even of yourselves, without any external sign, judge ye not what is right? - Why do ye not discern and acknowledge the intrinsic excellence of my doctrine?

58. When thou art going - As if he had said, And ye have not a moment to lose. For the executioners of God's vengeance are at hand. And when he hath once delivered you over to them, ye are undone forever. Matt. v, 25.

59. A mite - was about the third part of a farthing sterling.

XIII

1. The Galileans, whose blood Pilate had mingled with their sacrifices - Some of the followers of Judas Gaulonites. They absolutely refused to own the Roman authority. Pilate surrounded and slew them, while they were worshipping in the temple, at a public feast.

3. Ye shall all likewise perish - All ye of Galilee and of Jerusalem shall perish in the very same manner. So the Greek word implies. And so they did. There was a remarkable resemblance between the fate of these Galileans and of the main body of the Jewish nation; the flower of which was slain at Jerusalem by the Roman sword, while they were assembled at one of their great festivals. And many thousands of them perished in the temple itself, and were literally buried under its ruins.

6. A man had a fig tree - Either we may understand God the Father by him that had the vineyard, and Christ by him that kept it: or Christ himself is he that hath it, and his ministers they that keep it. Psalm lxxx, 8. &c.

7. Three years - Christ was then in the third year of his ministry. But it may mean only several years; a certain number being put for an uncertain. Why doth it also cumber the ground? - That is, not only bear no fruit itself, but take up the ground of another tree that would.

11. She was bowed together, and utterly unable to lift up herself - The evil spirit which possessed her afflicted her in this manner. To many doubtless it appeared a natural distemper. Would not a modern physician have termed it a nervous case?

15. Thou hypocrite - For the real motive of his speaking was envy, not (as he pretended) pure zeal for the glory of God.

16. And ought not this woman? - Ought not any human creature, which is so far better than an ox or an ass? Much more, this daughter of Abraham - probably in a spiritual as well as natural sense, to be loosed?

18. Matt. xiii, 31; Mark iv, 30.

20. Matt. xiii, 33.

21. Covered up - So that, for a time, nothing of it appeared.

24. Strive to enter in - Agonize. Strive as in an agony. So the word signifies Otherwise none shall enter in. Barely seeking will not avail. Matt. vii, 13.

25. And even agonizing will not avail, after the door is shut. Agonize, therefore, now by faith, prayer, holiness, patience. And ye begin to stand without - Till then they had not thought of it! O how new will that sense of their misery be? How late? How lasting? I know not whence ye are - I know not, that is, I approve not of your ways.

27. Matt. vii, 23.

28. Matt. viii, 11.

29. They shall sit down in the kingdom of God - Both the kingdom of grace and of glory.

30. But there are last - Many of the Gentiles who were latest called, shall be most highly rewarded; and many of the Jews who were first called, shall have no reward at all. Matt. xix, 30.

31. Herod is minded to kill thee - Possibly they gave him the caution out of good will.

32. And he said, Go and tell that fox - With great propriety so called, for his subtilty and cowardice. The meaning of our Lord's answer is, Notwithstanding all that he can do, I shall for the short time I have left, do the works of him that sent me. When that time is fulfilled, I shall be offered up. Yet not here, but in the bloody city. Behold, I cast out devils - With what majesty does he speak to his enemies! With what tenderness to his friends! The third day I am perfected - On the third day he left Galilee, and set out for Jerusalem, to die there. But let us carefully distinguish between those things wherein Christ is our pattern, and those which were peculiar to his office. His extraordinary office justified him in using that severity of language, when speaking of wicked princes, and corrupt teachers, to which we have no call; and by which we should only bring scandal on religion, and ruin on ourselves, while we irritated rather than convinced or reformed those whom we so indecently rebuked.

33. It cannot be, that a prophet perish out of Jerusalem - Which claims prescription for murdering the messengers of God. Such cruelty and malice cannot be found elsewhere.

34. How often would I have gathered thy children together - Three solemn visits he had made to Jerusalem since his baptism for this very purpose. Matt. xxiii, 37.

35. Your house is left to you desolate - Is now irrecoverably consigned to desolation and destruction: And verily I say to you, after a very short space, ye shall not see me till the time come, when taught by your calamities, ye shall be ready and disposed to say, Blessed is he that cometh in the name of the Lord. It does not imply, that they should then see Jesus at all; but only that they would earnestly wish for the Messiah, and in their extremity be ready to entertain any who should assume that character.

XIV

2. *There was a certain man before him* - It does not appear that he was come thither with any insidious design. Probably he came, hoping for a cure, or perhaps was one of the family.

3. *And Jesus answering, spake* - Answering the thoughts which he saw rising in their hearts.

7. *He spake a parable* - The ensuing discourse is so termed, because several parts are not to be understood literally. The general scope of it is, Not only at a marriage feast, but on every occasion, he that exalteth himself shall be abased, and he that abaseth himself shall be exalted.

11. Matt. xxiii, 12.

12. *Call not thy friends* - That is, I do not bid thee call thy friends or thy neighbours. Our Lord leaves these offices of humanity and courtesy as they were, and teaches a higher duty. But is it not implied herein, that we should be sparing in entertaining those that need it not, in order to assist those that do need, with all that is saved from those needless entertainments? *Lest a recompense be made* - This fear is as much unknown to the world, as even the fear of riches.

14. *One of them that sat at table hearing these things* - And being touched therewith, said, *Happy is he that shall eat bread in the kingdom of God* - Alluding to what had just been spoken. It means, he that shall have a part in the resurrection of the just.

16. *Then said he* - Continuing the allusion. A certain man made a great supper - As if he had said, All men are not sensible of this happiness. Many might have a part in it, and will not.

18. *They all began to make excuse* - One of them pleads only his own will, I go: another, a pretended necessity, I must needs go: the third, impossibility, I cannot come: all of them want the holy hatred mentioned ver. 26. All of them perish by things in themselves lawful. *I must needs go* - The most urgent worldly affairs frequently fall out just at the time when God makes the freest offers of salvation.

21. *The servant came and showed his Lord these things* - So ministers ought to lay before the Lord in prayer the obedience or disobedience of their hearers.

23. *Compel them to come in* - With all the violence of love, and the force of God's word. Such compulsion, and such only, in matters of religion, was used by Christ and his apostles.

24. *For* refers to Go out, ver. 23.

26. *If any man come to me, and hate not his father* - Comparatively to Christ: yea, so as actually to renounce his field, oxen, wife, all things, and act as if he hated them, when they stand in competition with him. Matt. x, 37.

28. *And which of you intending to build a tower* - That is, and whoever of you intends to follow me, let him first seriously weigh these things.

31. *Another king* - Does this mean, the prince of this world? Certainly he has greater numbers on his side. How numerous are his children and servants!

33. *So* - Like this man, who, being afraid to face his enemy, sends to make peace with him, every one who forsaketh not all that he hath -

1. By withdrawing his affections from all the creatures;
2. By enjoying them only in and for God, only in such a measure and manner as leads to him;
3. By hating them all, in the sense above mentioned, *cannot be my disciple* - But will surely desist from building that tower, neither can he persevere in fighting the good fight of faith.

34. *Salt* - Every Christian, but more eminently every minister. Matt. v, 13; Mark ix, 50.

XV

1. *All the publicans* - That is, all who were in that place. It seems our Lord was in some town of Galilee of the Gentiles, from whence he afterward went to Jerusalem, chap. xvii, 11.

3. *He spake* - Three parables of the same import: for the sheep, the piece of silver, and the lost son, all declare (in direct contrariety to the Pharisees and scribes) in what manner God receiveth sinners.

4. *Leave the ninety and nine in the wilderness* - Where they used to feed: all uncultivated ground, like our commons, was by the Jews termed wilderness or desert. *And go after* - In recovering a lost soul, God as it were labours. May we not learn hence, that to let them alone who are in sin, is both unchristian and inhuman! Matt. xviii, 12.

7. *Joy shall be* - Solemn and festal joy, in heaven - First, in our blessed Lord himself, and then among the angels and spirits of just men, perhaps informed thereof by God himself, or by the angels who ministered to them. *Over one sinner* - One gross, open, notorious sinner, *that repenteth* - That is, thoroughly changed in heart and life; *more than over ninety and nine just persons* - Comparatively just, outwardly blameless: *that need not such a repentance* - For they need not, cannot repent of the sins which they never committed. The sum is, as a father peculiarly rejoices when an extravagant child, supposed to be utterly lost, comes to a thorough sense of his duty; or as any other person who has recovered what he had given up for gone, has a more sensible satisfaction in it, than in several other things equally valuable, but not in such danger: so do the angels in heaven peculiarly rejoice in the

conversion of the most abandoned sinners. Yea, and God himself so readily forgives and receives them, that he may be represented as having part in the joy.

12. *Give me the part of goods that falleth to me* - See the root of all sin! A desire of disposing of ourselves; of independency on God!

13. *He took a journey into a far country* - Far from God: God was not in all his thoughts: And *squandered away his substance* - All the grace he had received.

14. *He began to be in want* - All his worldly pleasures failing, he grew conscious of his want of real good.

15. *And he joined himself to a citizen of that country* - Either the devil or one of his children, the genuine citizens of that country which is far from God. *He sent him to feed swine* - He employed him in the base drudgery of sin.

16. *He would fain have filled his belly with the husks* - He would fain have satisfied himself with worldly comforts. Vain, fruitless endeavour!

17. *And coming to himself* - For till then he was beside himself, as all men are, so long as they are without God in the world.

18. *I will arise and go to my father* - How accurately are the first steps of true repentance here pointed out! *Against Heaven* - Against God.

20. *And he arose and came to his father* - The moment he had resolved, he began to execute his resolution. *While he was yet a great way off, his father saw him* - Returning, starved, naked.

22. *But the father said* - Interrupting him before he had finished what he intended to say. So does God frequently cut an earnest confession short by a display of his pardoning love.

23. *Let us be merry* - Both here, and wherever else this word occurs, whether in the Old or New Testament, it implies nothing of levity, but a solid, serious, religious, heartfelt joy: indeed this was the ordinary meaning of the word two hundred years ago, when our translation was made.

25. The elder son seems to represent the Pharisees and scribes, mentioned chap. xv, 2.

27. *Thy father hath killed the fatted calf* - Perhaps he mentions this rather than the robe or ring, as having a nearer connection with the music and dancing.

28. *He was angry, and would not go in* - How natural to us is this kind of resentment!

29. *Lo, so many years do I serve thee* - So he was one of the instances mentioned ver. 7. How admirably therefore does this parable confirm that assertion! *Yet thou never gavest me a kid, that I might make merry with my friends* - Perhaps God does not usually give much joy to those who never felt the sorrows of repentance.

31. *Thou art ever with me, and all that I have is thine* - This suggests a strong reason against murmuring at the indulgence shown to the greatest of sinners. As the father's receiving the younger son did not cause him to disinherit the elder; so God's receiving notorious sinners will be no loss to those who have always served him; neither will he raise these to a state of glory equal to that of those who have always served him, if they have, upon the whole, made a greater progress in inward as well as outward holiness.

32. *This thy brother was dead, and is alive* - A thousand of these delicate touches in the inspired writings escape an inattentive reader. In ver. 30, the elder son had unkindly and indecently said, This thy son. The father in his reply mildly reproves him, and tenderly says, This thy brother - Amazing intimation, that the best of men ought to account the worst sinners their brethren still; and should especially remember this relation, when they show any inclination to return. Our Lord in this whole parable shows, not only that the Jews had no cause to murmur at the reception of the Gentiles, (a point which did not at that time so directly fall under consideration,) but that if the Pharisees were indeed as good as they fancied themselves to be, still they had no reason to murmur at the kind treatment of any sincere penitent. Thus does he condemn them, even on their own principles, and so leaves them without excuse. We have in this parable a lively emblem of the condition and behaviour of sinners in their natural state. Thus, when enriched by the bounty of the great common Father, do they ungratefully run from him, ver. 12. Sensual pleasures are eagerly pursued, till they have squandered away all the grace of God, ver. 13. And while these continue, not a serious thought of God can find a place in their minds. And even when afflictions come upon them, ver. 14, still they will make hard shifts before they will let the grace of God, concurring with his providence, persuade them to think of a return, ver. 15, 16. When they see themselves naked, indigent, and undone, then they recover the exercise of their reason, ver. 17. Then they remember the blessings they have thrown away, and attend to the misery they have incurred. And hereupon they resolve to return to their father, and put the resolution immediately in practice, ver. 18, 19. Behold with wonder and pleasure the gracious reception they find from Divine, injured goodness! When such a prodigal comes to his father, he sees him afar off, ver. 20. He pities, meets, embraces him, and interrupts his acknowledgments with the tokens of his returning favour, ver. 21. He arrays him with the robe of a Redeemer's righteousness, with inward and outward holiness; adorns him with all his sanctifying graces, and honours him with the tokens of adopting love, ver. 22. And all this he does with unutterable delight, in that he who was lost is now found, ver. 23, 24. Let no elder brother

murmur at this indulgence, but rather welcome the prodigal back into the family. And let those who have been thus received, wander no more, but emulate the strictest piety of those who for many years have served their heavenly Father, and not transgressed his commandments.

XVI

And he said also to his disciples - Not only to the scribes and Pharisees to whom he had hitherto been speaking, but to all the younger as well as the elder brethren: to the returning prodigals who were now his disciples. A certain rich man had a steward - Christ here teaches all that are now in favour with God, particularly pardoned penitents, to behave wisely in what is committed to them.

3. To beg I am ashamed - But not ashamed to cheat! This was likewise a sense of honour! "By men called honour, but by angels pride."

4. I know - That is, I am resolved, what to do.

8. And the Lord commended the unjust steward - Namely, in this respect, because he had used timely precaution: so that though the dishonesty of such a servant be detestable, yet his foresight, care, and contrivance, about the interests of this life, deserve our imitation, with regard to the more important affairs of another. The children of this world - Those who seek no other portion than this world: Are wiser - Not absolutely, for they are, one and all, egregious fools; but they are more consistent with themselves; they are truer to their principles; they more steadily pursue their end; they are wiser in their generation - That is, in their own way, than the children of light - The children of God, whose light shines on their hearts.

9. And I say to you - Be good stewards even of the lowest talents wherewith God hath intrusted you. Mammon means riches or money. It is termed the mammon of unrighteousness, because of the manner wherein it is commonly either procured or employed. Make yourselves friends of this, by doing all possible good, particularly to the children of God: that when ye fail, when your flesh and your heart faileth, when this earthly tabernacle is dissolved, those of them who have gone before may receive, may welcome you into the everlasting habitations.

10. And whether ye have more or less, see that ye be faithful as well as wise stewards. He that is faithful in what is meanest of all, worldly substance, is also faithful in things of a higher nature; and he that uses these lowest gifts unfaithfully, is likewise unfaithful in spiritual things.

11. Who will intrust you with the true riches? - How should God intrust you with spiritual and eternal, which alone are true riches?

12. If ye have not been faithful in that which was another's - None of these temporal things are yours: you are only stewards of them, not proprietors: God is the proprietor of all; he lodges them in your hands for a season: but still they are his property. Rich men, understand and consider this. If your steward uses any part of your estate (so called in the language of men) any farther or any otherwise than you direct, he is a knave: he has neither conscience nor honour. Neither have you either one or the other, if you use any part of that estate, which is in truth God's, not yours, any otherwise than he directs. That which is your own - Heaven, which when you have it, will be your own forever.

13. And you cannot be faithful to God, if you trim between God and the world, if you do not serve him alone. Matt. vi, 24.

15. And he said to them, Ye are they who justify yourselves before men - The sense of the whole passage is, that pride, wherewith you justify yourselves, feeds covetousness, derides the Gospel, ver. 14, and destroys the law, ver. 18. All which is illustrated by a terrible example. Ye justify yourselves before men - Ye think yourselves righteous, and persuade others to think you so.

16. The law and the prophets were in force until John: from that time the Gospel takes place; and humble upright men receive it with inexpressible earnestness. Matt. xi, 13.

17. Not that the Gospel at all destroys the law. Matt. v, 18.

18. But ye do; particularly in this notorious instance. Matt. v, 31; xix, 7.

19. There was a certain rich man - Very probably a Pharisee, and one that justified himself before men; a very honest, as well as honourable gentleman: though it was not proper to mention his name on this occasion: who was clothed in purple and fine linen - and doubtless esteemed on this account, (perhaps not only by those who sold it, but by most that knew him,) as encouraging trade, and acting according to his quality: And feasted splendidly every day - And consequently was esteemed yet more, for his generosity and hospitality in keeping so good a table.

20. And there was a certain beggar named Lazarus, (according to the Greek pronunciation) or Eleazer. By his name it may be conjectured, he was of no mean family, though it was thus reduced. There was no reason for our Lord to conceal his name, which probably was then well known. Theophylact observes, from the tradition of the Hebrews, that he lived at Jerusalem. Yea, the dogs also came and licked his sores - It seems this circumstance is recorded to show that all his ulcers lay bare, and were not closed or bound up.

22. And the beggar - Worn out with hunger, and pain, and want of all things, died: and was carried

by angels (amazing change of the scene!) into Abraham's bosom - So the Jews styled paradise; the place where the souls of good men remain from death to the resurrection. The rich man also died, and was buried - Doubtless with pomp enough, though we do not read of his lying in state; that stupid, senseless pageantry, that shocking insult on a poor, putrefying carcass, was reserved for our enlightened age!

23. He seeth Abraham afar off - And yet knew him at that distance: and shall not Abraham's children, when they are together in paradise, know each other!

24. Father Abraham, have mercy on me - It cannot be denied, but here is one precedent in Scripture of praying to departed saints: but who is it that prays, and with what success? Will any, who considers this, be fond of copying after him?

25. But Abraham said, Son - According to the flesh. Is it not worthy of observation, that Abraham will not revile even a damned soul? and shall living men revile one another? Thou in thy lifetime receivedst thy good things - Thou didst choose and accept of worldly things as thy good, thy happiness. And can any be at a loss to know why he was in torments? This damnable idolatry, had there been nothing more, was enough to sink him to the nethermost hell.

26. Beside this there is a great gulf fixed - Reader, to which side of it wilt thou go?

28. Lest they also come into this place - He might justly fear lest their reproaches should add to his own torment.

31. Neither will they be persuaded - Truly to repent: for this implies an entire change of heart: but a thousand apparitions cannot, effect this. God only can, applying his word.

XVII

1. It is impossible but offenses will come - And they ever did and do come chiefly by Pharisees, that is, men who trust in themselves that they are righteous, and despise others. Matt. xviii, 6; Mark ix, 42.

2. Little ones - Weak believers.

3. Take heed to yourselves - That ye neither offend others, nor be offended by others. Matt. xviii, 15.

4. If he sin against thee seven times in a day, and seven times in a day return, saying, I repent - That is, if he give sufficient proof that he does really repent, after having sinned ever so often, receive him just as if he had never sinned against thee. But this forgiveness is due only to real penitents. In a lower sense we are to forgive all, penitent or impenitent; (so as to bear them the sincerest good will, and to do them all the good we can;) and that not seven times only, but seventy times seven.

5. Lord, increase our faith - That we may thus forgive, and may neither offend nor be offended. Matt. xvii, 20.

6. And he said, If ye had faith as a grain of mustard seed - If ye had the least measure of true faith, no instance of duty would be too hard for you. Ye would say to this sycamine tree - This seems to have been a kind of proverbial expression.

7. But which of you - But is it not meet that you should first obey, and then triumph? Though still with a deep sense of your utter unprofitableness.

9. Doth he thank that servant - Does he account himself obliged to him?

10. When ye have done all, say, We are unprofitable servants - For a man cannot profit God. Happy is he who Judges himself an unprofitable servant: miserable is he whom God pronounces such. But though we are unprofitable to him, our serving him is not unprofitable to us. For he is pleased to give by his grace a value to our good works, which in consequence of his promise entitles us to an eternal reward.

20. The kingdom of God cometh not with observation - With such outward pomp as draws the observation of every one.

21. Neither shall they say, Lo here, or lo there - This shall not be the language of those who are, or shall be sent by me, to declare the coming of my kingdom. For behold the kingdom of God is within or among you - Look not for it in distant times or remote places: it is now in the midst of you: it is come: it is present in the soul of every true believer: it is a spiritual kingdom, an internal principle. Wherever it exists, it exists in the heart.

22. Ye shall desire to see one of the days of the Son of man - One day of mercy or one day wherein you might converse with me, as you do now.

23. They shall say, See, Christ is here, or there - Limiting his presence to this or that place. Matt. xxiv, 23.

24. So shall also the Son of man be - So swift, so wide, shall his appearing be: In his day - The last day.

26. The days of the Son of man - Those which immediately follow that which is eminently styled his day. Matt. xxiv, 37.

31. In that day - (Which will be the grand type of the last day) when ye shall see Jerusalem

encompassed with armies.

32. Remember Lot's wife - And escape with all speed, without ever looking behind you. Luke ix, 24; John xii, 25.

33. The sense of this and the following verses is, Yet as great as the danger will be, do not seek to save your life by violating your conscience: if you do, you will surely lose it: whereas if you should lose it for my sake, you shall be paid with life everlasting. But the most probable way of preserving it now, is to be always ready to give it up: a peculiar Providence shall then watch over you, and put a difference between you and other men.

37. Matt. xxiv, 28.

XVIII

1. He spake a parable to them - This and the following parable warn us against two fatal extremes, with regard to prayer: the former against faintness and weariness, the latter against self confidence.

7. And shall not God - The most just Judge, vindicate his own elect - Preserve the Christians from all their adversaries, and in particular save them out of the general destruction, and avenge them of the Jews? Though he bear long with them - Though he does not immediately put an end, either to the wrongs of the wicked, or the sufferings of good men.

8. Yet when the Son of man cometh, will he find faith upon earth - Yet notwithstanding all the instances both of his long suffering and of his justice, whenever he shall remarkably appear, against their enemies in this age or in after ages, how few true believers will be found upon earth!

9. He spake this parable - Not to hypocrites; the Pharisee here mentioned was no hypocrite, no more than an outward adulterer: but he sincerely trusted in himself that he was righteous, and accordingly told God so, in the prayer which none but God heard.

12. I fast twice in the week - So did all the strict Pharisees: every Monday and Thursday. I give tithes of all that I possess - Many of them gave one full tenth of their income in tithes, and another tenth in alms, the sum of this plea is, I do no harm: I use all the means of grace: I do all the good I can.

13. The publican standing afar off - From the holy of holies, would not so much as lift up his eyes to heaven - Touched with shame, which is more ingenuous than fear.

14. This man went down - From the hill on which the temple stood, justified rather than the other - That is, and not the other.

15. Matt. xix, 13; Mark x, 13.

16. Calling them - Those that brought the children: of such is the kingdom of God - Such are subjects of the Messiah's kingdom. And such as these it properly belongs to.

18. Matt. xix, 16; Mark x, 17.

20. Exod. xx, 12, &c.

22. Yet lackest thou one thing - Namely, to love God more than mammon. Our saviour knew his heart, and presently put him upon a trial which laid it open to the ruler himself. And to cure his love of the world, which could not in him be cured otherwise, Christ commanded him to sell all that he had. But he does not command us to do this; but to use all to the glory of God.

31. Matt. xx, 17; Mark x, 32.

34. They understood none of these things - The literal meaning they could not but understand. But as they could not reconcile this to their preconceived opinion of the Messiah, they were utterly at a loss in what parabolical or figurative sense to take what he said concerning his sufferings; having their thoughts still taken up with the temporal kingdom.

35. Matt. xx, 29; Mark x, 46.

XIX

1. He passed through Jericho - So that Zacchaeus must have lived near the end of the town: the tree was in the town itself. And he was rich - These words seem to refer to the discourse in the last chapter, ver. 24, particularly to ver. 27. Zacchiaeus is a proof, that it is possible by the power of God for even a rich man to enter into the kingdom of heaven.

2. The chief of the publicans - What we would term, commissioner of the customs. A very honourable as well as profitable place.

4. And running before - With great earnestness. He climbed up - Notwithstanding his quality: desire conquering honour and shame.

5. Jesus said, Zacchaeus, make haste and come down - What a strange mixture of passions must Zacchaeus have now felt, hearing one speak, as knowing both his name and his heart!

7. They all murmured - All who were near: though most of them rather out of surprise than indignation.

8. And Zacchaeus stood - Showing by his posture, his deliberate, purpose and ready mind, and

said, Behold, Lord, I give - I determine to do it immediately.

9. He also is a son of Abraham - A Jew born, and as such has a right to the first offer of salvation.

10. Matt. xviii, 11.

11. They thought the kingdom of God - A glorious temporal kingdom, would immediately appear.

12. He went into a far country to receive a kingdom - Christ went to heaven, to receive his sovereign power as wan, even all authority in heaven and earth. Matt. xxv, 14; Mark xiii, 34.

13. Trade till I come - To visit the nation, to destroy Jerusalem, to judge the world: or, in a more particular sense, to require thy soul of thee.

14. But his citizens - Such were those of Jerusalem, hated him, and sent an embassy after him - The word seems to imply, their sending ambassadors to a superior court, to enter their protest against his being admitted to the regal power. In such a solemn manner did the Jews protest, as it were, before God, that Christ should not reign over them: this man - So they call him in contempt.

15. When he was returned - In his glory.

23. With interest - Which does not appear to be contrary to any law of God or man. But this is no plea for usury, that is, the taking such interest as implies any degree of oppression or extortion.

25. They said - With admiration, not envy.

26. Matt. xxv, 29; Luke viii, 18.

27. He went before - The foremost of the company, showing his readiness to suffer.

29. He drew nigh to the place where the borders of Bethphage and Bethany met, which was at the foot of the Mount of Olives. Matt. xxi, 1; Mark xi, 1.

37. The whole multitude began to praise God - Speaking at once, as it seems, from a Divine impulse, words which most of them did not understand.

38. Peace in heaven - God being reconciled to man.

39. Rebuke thy disciples - Paying thee this immoderate honour.

40. If these should hold their peace, the stones, which lie before you, would cry out - That is, God would raise up some still more unlikely instruments to declare his praise. For the power of God will not return empty.

42. O that thou hadst known, at least in this thy day - After thou hast neglected so many. Thy day - The day wherein God still offers thee his blessings.

43. Thine enemies shall cast a trench about thee, and compass thee around - All this was exactly performed by Titus, the Roman general.

44. And thy children within thee - All the Jews were at that time gathered together, it being the time of the passover. They shall not leave in thee one stone upon another - Only three towers were left standing for a time, to show the former strength and magnificence of the place. But these likewise were afterward levelled with the ground.

45. Matt. xxi, 12; Mark xi, 11.

46. Isaiah lvi, 7.

XX

1. Matt. xxi, 23; Mark xi, 27.

9. A long time - It was a long time from the entrance of the Israelites into Canaan to the birth of Christ. Matt. xxi, 33; Mark xii, 1.

16. He will destroy these husbandmen - Probably he pointed to the scribes, chief priests, and elders: who allowed, he will miserably destroy those wicked men, Matt. xxi, 41; but could not bear that this should be applied to themselves. They might also mean, God forbid that we should be guilty of such a crime as your parable seems to charge us with, namely, rejecting and killing the heir. Our saviour answers, But yet will ye do it, as is prophesied of you.

17. He looked on them - To sharpen their attention. Psalm cxviii, 22.

18. Matt. xxi, 45.

20. Just men - Men of a tender conscience. To take hold of his discourse - If he answered as they hoped he would. Matt. xxii, 16; Mark xii, 12.

21. Thou speakest - In private, and teachest - In public.

24. Show me a penny - A Roman penny, which was the money that was usually paid on that occasion.

26. They could not take hold of his words before the people - As they did afterward before the sanhedrim, in the absence of the people, chap. xxii, 67.

27. Matt. xxii, 23; Mark xii, 18.

28. Deut. xxv, 5.

34. The children of this world - The inhabitants of earth, marry and are given in marriage - As being all subject to the law of mortality; so that the species is in need of being continually repaired.

35. But they who obtain that world - Which they enter into, before the resurrection of the dead.

36. They are the children of God - In a more eminent sense when they rise again.

37. That the dead are raised, even Moses, as well as the other prophets showed, when he calleth - That is, when he recites the words which God spoke of himself, I am the God of Abraham, &c. It cannot properly be said, that God is the God of any who are totally perished. Exod. iii, 6.

38. He is not a God of the dead, or, there is no God of the dead - That is, tho term God implies such a relation, as cannot possibly subsist between him and the dead; who in the Sadducees' sense are extinguished spirits; who could neither worship him, nor receive good from him. So that all live to him - All who have him for their God, live to and enjoy him. This sentence is not an argument for what went before; but the proposition which was to be proved. And the consequence is apparently just. For as all the faithful are the children of Abraham, and the Divine promise of being a God to him and his seed is entailed upon them, it implies their continued existence and happiness in a future state as much as Abraham's. And as the body is an essential part of man, it implies both his resurrection and theirs; and so overthrows the entire scheme of the Sadducean doctrine.

40. They durst not ask him any question - The Sadducees durst not. One of the scribes did, presently after.

41. Matt. xxii, 41; Mark xii, 35.

42. Psalm cx, 1.

46. Matt. xxiii, 5.

47. Matt. xxiii, 14.

XXI

1. He looked up - From those on whom his eyes were fixed before. Mark xii, 41.

5. Goodly stones - Such as no engines now in use could have brought, or even set upon each other. Some of them (as an eye witness who lately measured them writes) were forty - five cubits long, five high, and six broad; yet brought thither from another country. And gifts - Which persons delivered from imminent dangers had, in accomplishment of their vows, hung on the walls and pillars. The marble of the temple was so white, that it appeared like a mountain of snow at a distance. And the gilding of many parts made it, especially when the sun shone, a most splendid and beautiful spectacle. Matt. xxiv, 1; Mark xiii, 1.

8. I am the Christ; and the time is near - When I will deliver you from all your enemies. They are the words of the seducers.

9. Commotions - Intestine broils; civil wars.

11. Fearful sights and signs from heaven - Of which Josephus gives a circumstantial account.

12. Mark xiii, 9.

13. It shall turn to you for a testimony - Of your having delivered your own souls, and of their being without excuse.

16. Matt. x, 21.

17. Matt. xxiv, 13; Mark xiii, 13.

18. Not a hair of your head - A proverbial expression, shall perish - Without the special providence of God. And then, not before the time, nor without a full reward.

19. In your patience possess ye your souls - Be calm and serene, masters of yourselves, and superior to all irrational and disquieting passions. By keeping the government of your spirits, you will both avoid much misery, and guard the better against all dangers.

21. Let them that are in the midst of it - Where Jerusalem stands (that is, they that are in Jerusalem) depart out of it, before their retreat is cut off by the uniting of the forces near the city, and let not them that are in the adjacent countries by any means enter into it.

22. And things which are written - Particularly in Daniel.

24. They shall fall by the edge of the sword, and shall be led away captive - Eleven hundred thousand perished in the siege of Jerusalem, and above ninety thousand were sold for slaves. So terribly was this prophecy fulfilled! And Jerusalem shall be trodden by the Gentiles - That is, inhabited. So it was indeed. The land was sold, and no Jew suffered even to come within sight of Jerusalem. The very foundations of the city were ploughed up, and a heathen temple built where the temple of God had stood. The times of the Gentiles - That is, the times limited for their treading the city; which shall terminate in the full conversion of the Gentiles.

25. And there shall be - Before the great day, which was typified by the destruction of Jerusalem: signs - Different from those mentioned in ver. 11. Matt. xxiv, 29; Mark xiii, 24.

28. Now when these things - Mentioned ver. 8, 10, &c., begin to come to pass, look up with firm faith, and lift up your heads with joy: for your redemption out of many troubles draweth nigh, by God's destroying your implacable enemies.

29. Behold the fig tree and all the trees - Christ spake this in the spring, just before the passover; when all the trees were budding on the Mount of Olives, where they then were.

30. Ye know of yourselves - Though none teach you.

31. The kingdom of God is nigh - The destruction of the Jewish city, temple, and religion, to make way for the advancement of my kingdom.

32. Till all things be effected - All that has been spoken of the destruction of Jerusalem, to which the question, ver. 7, relates: and which is treated of from ver. 8-24.

34. Take heed, lest at any time your hearts be overloaded with gluttony and drunkenness - And was there need to warn the apostles themselves against such sins as these? Then surely there is reason to warn even strong Christians against the very grossest sins. Neither are we wise, if we think ourselves out of the reach of any sin: and so that day - Of judgment or of death, come upon you, even you that are not of this world-Unawares. Matt. xxiv, 42; Mark xiii, 33; Luke xii, 35.

35. That sit - Careless and at ease.

36. Watch ye therefore - This is the general conclusion of all that precedes. That ye may be counted worthy - This word sometimes signifies an honour conferred on a person, as when the apostles are said to be counted worthy to suffer shame for Christ, Acts v, 41. Sometimes meet or becoming: as when John the Baptist exhorts, to bring fruits worthy of repentance, chap. iii, 8. And so to be counted worthy to escape, is to have the honour of it, and to be fitted or prepared for it. To stand - With joy and triumph: not to fall before him as his enemies.

37. Now by day - In the day time, he was teaching in the temple - This shows how our Lord employed his time after coming to Jerusalem: but it is not said, he was this day in the temple, and next morning the people came. It does not therefore by any means imply, that he came any more after this into the temple.

38. And all the people came early in the morning to hear him - How much happier were his disciples in these early lectures, than the slumbers of the morning could have made them on their beds! Let us not scruple to deny ourselves the indulgence of unnecessary sleep, that we may morning after morning place ourselves at his feet, receiving the instructions of his word, and seeking those of his Spirit.

XXII

1. Matt. xxvi, 1; Mark xiv, 1.

3. Then entered Satan - Who is never wanting to assist those whose heart is bent upon mischief.

4. Captains - Called captains of the temple, ver. 52. They were Jewish officers, who presided over the guards which kept watch every night in the temple.

7. Matt. xxvi, 17; Mark xiv, 12.

14. Matt. xxvi, 20; Mark xiv, 17.

15. With desire have I desired - That is, I have earnestly desired it. He desired it, both for the sake of his disciples, to whom he desired to manifest himself farther, at this solemn parting: and for the sake of his whole Church, that he might institute the grand memorial of his death.

16. For I will not eat thereof any more - That is, it will be the last I shall eat with you before I die. The kingdom of God did not properly commence till his resurrection. Then was fulfilled what was typified by the passover.

17. And he took the cup - That cup which used to be brought at the beginning of the paschal solemnity, and said, Take this and divide it among yourselves; for I will not drink - As if he had said, Do not expect me to drink of it: I will drink no more before I die.

19. And he took bread - Namely, some time after, when supper was ended, wherein they had eaten the paschal lamb. This is my body - As he had just now celebrated the paschal supper, which was called the passover, so in like figurative language, he calls this bread his body. And this circumstance of itself was sufficient to prevent any mistake, as if this bread was his real body, any more than the paschal lamb was really the passover.

20. This cup is the New Testament - Here is an undeniable figure, whereby the cup is put for the wine in the cup. And this is called, The New Testament in Christ's blood, which could not possibly mean, that it was the New Testament itself, but only the seal of it, and the sign of that blood which was shed to confirm it.

21. The hand of him that betrayeth me is with me on the table - It is evident Christ spake these words before he instituted the Lord's Supper: for all the other evangelists mention the sop, immediately after receiving which he went out: John xiii, 30. Nor did he return any more, till he came into the garden to betray his Master. Now this could not be dipped or given, but while the meat was on the table. But this was all removed before that bread and cup were brought.

24. There was also a contention among them - It is highly probable, this was the same dispute which is mentioned by St. Matthew and St. Mark: and consequently, though it is related here, it happened some time before.

25. They that exercise the most arbitrary authority over them, have from their flatterers the vain

title of benefactors.

26. But ye are to be benefactors to mankind, not by governing, but by serving.

27. For - This he proves by his own example. I am in the midst of you - Just now: see with your eyes. I take no state upon me, but sit in the midst, on a level with the lowest of you.

28. Ye have continued with me in my temptations - And all his life was nothing else, particularly from his entering on his public ministry.

29. And I - Will preserve you in all your temptations, till ye enter into the kingdom of glory: appoint to you - By these very words. Not a primacy to one, but a kingdom to every one: on the same terms: as my Father hath appointed to me - Who have fought and conquered.

30. That ye may eat and drink at my table - That is, that ye may enjoy the highest happiness, as guests, not as servants. These expressions seem to be primarily applicable to the twelve apostles, and secondarily, to all Christ's servants and disciples, whose spiritual powers, honours, and delights, are here represented in figurative terms, with respect to their advancement both in the kingdom of grace and of glory.

31. Satan hath desired to have you - My apostles, that he might sift you as wheat - Try you to the uttermost.

32. But I have prayed for thee - Who wilt be in the greatest danger of all: that thy faith fail not - Altogether: and when thou art returned - From thy flight, strengthen thy brethren -- all that are weak in faith; perhaps scandalized at thy fall.

34. It shall not be the time of cock crowing this day - The common time of cock crowing (which is usually about three in the morning) probably did not come till after the cock which Peter heard had crowed twice, if not oftener.

35. When I sent you - lacked ye any thing - Were ye not born above all want and danger?

36. But now - You will be quite in another situation. You will want every thing. He that hath no sword, let him sell his garment and buy one - It is plain, this is not to be taken literally. It only means, This will be a time of extreme danger.

37. The things which are written concerning me have an end - Are now drawing to a period; are upon the point of being accomplished. Isaiah liii, 12.

38. Here are two swords - Many of Galilee carried them when they travelled, to defend themselves against robbers and assassins, who much infested their roads. But did the apostles need to seek such defense? And he said; It is enough - I did not mean literally, that every one of you must have a sword.

39. Matt. xxvi, 30.

40. The place - The garden of Gethsemane.

43. Strengthening him - Lest his body should sink and die before the time.

44. And being in an agony - Probably just now grappling with the powers of darkness: feeling the weight of the wrath of God, and at the same time surrounded with a mighty host of devils, who exercised all their force and malice to persecute and distract his wounded spirit. He prayed more earnestly - Even with stronger cries and tars: and his sweat - As cold as the weather was, was as it were great drops of blood - Which, by the vehement distress of his soul, were forced out of the pores, in so great a quantity as afterward united in large, thick, grumous drops, and even fell to the ground.

48. Betrayest thou the Son of man - He whom thou knowest to be the Son of man, the Christ?

49. Seeing what would follow - That they were just going to seize him. Matt. xxvi, 51; Mark xiv, 47.

51. Suffer me at least to have my hands at liberty thus far, while I do one more act of mercy.

52. Jesus said to the chief priests, and captains, and the elders who were come - And all these came of their own accord: the soldiers and servants were sent.

53. This is your hour - Before which ye could not take me: and the power of darkness - The time when Satan has power.

54. Matt. xxvi, 57; Mark xiv, 53; John xviii, 12.

58. Another man saw him and said - Observe here, in order to reconcile the four evangelists, that divers persons concurred in charging Peter with belonging to Christ.

1. The maid that led him in, afterward seeing him at the fire, first put the question to him, and then positively affirmed, that he was with Christ.

2. Another maid accused him to the standers by, and gave occasion to the man here mentioned, to renew the charge against him, which caused the second denial.

3. Others of the company took notice of his being a Galilean, and were seconded by the kinsman of Malchus, who affirmed he had seen him in the garden. And this drew on the third denial.

59. And about one hour after - So he did not recollect himself in all that time.

63. Matt. xxvi, 67; Mark xiv, 65.

64. And having blindfolded him, they struck him on the face - This is placed by St. Matthew and Mark, after the council's condemning him. Probably he was abused in the same manner, both before and after his condemnation.

Wesley's Notes on the Bible - The New Testament

65. **Many other things blasphemously spake they against him** - The expression is remarkable. They charged him with blasphemy, because he said he was the Son of God: but the evangelist fixes that charge on them, because he really was so.

66. Matt. xxvi, 63; Mark xiv, 61.

70. **They all said, Art thou then the Son of God?** - Both these, the Son of God, and the Son of man, were known titles of the Messiah; the one taken from his Divine, and the other from his human nature.

XXIII

1. Matt. xxvii, 1; Mark xv, 1; John xviii, 28.

4. **Then said Pilate** - After having heard his defense-I find no fault in this man - I do not find that he either asserts or attempts any thing seditious or injurious to Caesar.

5. **He stirreth up the people, beginning from Galilee** - Probably they mentioned Galilee to alarm Pilate, because the Galileans were notorious for sedition and rebellion.

7. **He sent him to Herod** - As his proper judge.

8. **He had been long desirous to see him** - Out of mere curiosity.

9. **He questioned him** - Probably concerning the miracles which were reported to have been wrought by him.

11. **Herod set him at nought** - Probably judging him to be a fool, because he answered nothing. In a splendid robe - In royal apparel; intimating that he feared nothing from this king.

15. **He hath done nothing worthy of death** - According to the judgment of Herod also.

16. **I will therefore chastise him** - Here Pilate began to give ground, which only encouraged them to press on. Matt. xxvii, 15; Mark xv, 6; John xviii, 39.

22. **He said to them the third time, Why, what evil hath he done?** - As Peter, a disciple of Christ, dishonoured him by denying him thrice, so Pilate, a heathen, honoured Christ, by thrice owning him to be innocent.

26. Matt. xxvii, 31; Mark xv, 21; John xix, 16.

30. Hosea x, 8.

31. **If they do these things in the green tree, what shall be done in the dry?** - Our Lord makes use of a proverbial expression, frequent among the Jews, who compare a good man to a green tree, and a bad man to a dead one: as if he had said, If an innocent person suffer thus, what will become of the wicked? Of those who are as ready for destruction as dry wood for the fire?

34. **Then said Jesus** - Our Lord passed most of the time on the cross in silence: yet seven sentences which he spoke thereon are recorded by the four evangelists, though no one evangelist has recorded them all. Hence it appears that the four Gospels are, as it were, four parts, which, joined together, make one symphony. Sometimes one of these only, sometimes two or three, sometimes all sound together. Father - So he speaks both in the beginning and at the end of his sufferings on the cross: Forgive them - How striking is this passage! While they are actually nailing him to the cross, he seems to feel the injury they did to their own souls more than the wounds they gave him; and as it were to forget his own anguish out of a concern for their own salvation. And how eminently was his prayer heard! It procured forgiveness for all that were penitent, and a suspension of vengeance even for the impenitent.

35. **If thou be the Christ;** ver. 37. **If thou be the king** - The priests deride the name of Messiah: the soldiers the name of king.

38. Matt. xxvii, 37; Mark xv, 26; John xix, 19.

39. **And one of the malefactors reviled him** - St. Matthew says, the robbers: St. Mark, they that were crucified with him, reviled him. Either therefore St. Matthew and Mark put the plural for the singular (as the best authors sometimes do) or both reviled him at the first, till one of them felt "the overwhelming power of saving grace."

40. **The other rebuked him** - What a surprising degree was here of repentance, faith, and other graces! And what abundance of good works, in his public confession of his sin, reproof of his fellow criminal, his honourable testimony to Christ, and profession of faith in him, while he was in so disgraceful circumstances as were stumbling even to his disciples! This shows the power of Divine grace. But it encourages none to put off their repentance to the last hour; since, as far as appears, this was the first time this criminal had an opportunity of knowing any thing of Christ, and his conversion was designed to put a peculiar glory on our saviour in his lowest state, while his enemies derided him, and his own disciples either denied or forsook him.

42. **Remember me when thou comest** - From heaven, in thy kingdom - He acknowledges him a king, and such a king, as after he is dead, can profit the dead. The apostles themselves had not then so clear conceptions of the kingdom of Christ.

43. **In paradise** - The place where the souls of the righteous remain from death till the resurrection. As if he had said, I will not only remember thee then, but this very day.

44. **There was darkness over all the earth** - The noon-tide darkness, covering the sun, obscured all

the upper hemisphere. And the lower was equally darkened, the moon being in opposition to the sun, and so receiving no light from it. Matt. xxvii, 45.

45. Mark xv, 38.

46. Father, into thy hands - The Father receives the Spirit of Jesus: Jesus himself the spirits of the faithful.

47. Certainly this was a righteous man - Which implies an approbation of all he had done and taught.

48. All the people - Who had not been actors therein, returned smiting their breasts - In testimony of sorrow.

50. Matt. xxvii, 57; Mark xv, 43; John xix, 38.

XXIV

1. Certain others with them - Who had not come from Galilee. Matt. xxviii, 1; Mark xvi, 1; John xx, 1.

4. Behold two - Angels in the form of men. Mary had seen them a little before. They had disappeared on these women's coming to the sepulchre, but now appeared again. St. Matthew and Mark mention only one of them, appearing like a young man.

6. Remember how he spake to you, saying, The Son of man must be delivered - This is only a repetition of the words which our Lord had spoken to them before his passion But it is observable, he never styles himself the Son of man after his resurrection.

13. Mark xvi, 12.

21. Today is the third day - The day he should have risen again, if at all.

25. O foolish - Not understanding the designs and works of God: And slow of heart - Unready to believe what the prophets have so largely spoken.

26. Ought not Christ - If he would redeem man, and fulfil the prophecies concerning him, to have suffered these things? - These very sufferings which occasion your doubts, are the proofs of his being the Messiah. And to enter into his glory - Which could be done no other way.

28. He made as though he would go farther - Walking forward, as if he was going on; and he would have done it, had they not pressed him to stay.

29. They constrained him - By their importunate entreaties.

30. He took the bread, and blessed, and brake - Just in the same manner as when he instituted his last supper.

31. Their eyes were opened - That is, the supernatural cloud was removed: And he vanished - Went away insensibly.

32. Did not our heart burn within us - Did not we feel an unusual warmth of love! Was not our heart burning, &c.

33. The same hour - Late as it was.

34. The Lord hath appeared to Simon - Before he was seen of the twelve apostles, 1 Cor. xv, 5. He had, in his wonderful condescension and grace, taken an opportunity on the former part of that day (though where, or in what manner, is not recorded) to show himself to Peter, that he might early relieve his distresses and fears, on account of having so shamefully denied his Master.

35. In the breaking of bread - The Lord's Supper.

36. Jesus stood in the midst of them - It was just as easy to his Divine power to open a door undiscernibly, as it was to come in at a door opened by some other hand. Mark xvi, 14, 19; John xx, 19.

40. He showed them his hands and his feet - That they might either see or feel the prints of the nails.

41. While they believed not for joy - They did in some sense believe: otherwise they would not have rejoiced. But their excess of joy prevented a clear, rational belief.

43. He took it and ate before them - Not that he had any need of food; but to give them still further evidence.

44. And he said - On the day of his ascension. In the law, and the prophets, and the Psalms - The prophecies as well as types, relating to the Messiah, are contained either in the books of Moses (usually called the law) in the Psalms, or in the writings of the prophets; little being said directly concerning him in the historical books.

45. Then opened he their understanding, to understand the Scriptures - He had explained them before to the two as they went to Emmaus. But still they understood them not, till he took off the veil from their hearts, by the illumination of his Spirit.

47. Beginning at Jerusalem - This was appointed most graciously and wisely: graciously, as it encouraged the greatest sinners to repent, when they saw that even the murderers of Christ were not excepted from mercy: and wisely, as hereby Christianity was more abundantly attested; the facts being published first on the very spot where they happened.

49. Behold I send the promise - Emphatically so called; the Holy Ghost.

50. He led them out as far as Bethany - Not the town, but the district: to the Mount of Olives, Acts i, 12, which stood within the boundaries of Bethany.

51. And while he was blessing them, he was parted from them - It was much more proper that our Lord should ascend into heaven, than that he should rise from the dead, in the sight of the apostles. For his resurrection was proved when they saw him alive after his passion: but they could not see him in heaven while they continued on earth. Please see Notes at Matt. i, 1

John Wesley

NOTES ON THE GOSPEL ACCORDING TO ST. JOHN

In this book is set down the history of the Son of God dwelling among men; that,

I. Of the first days, where the apostle, premising the sum of the whole Chap. i, 1-14 Mentions the testimony given by John, after the baptism of Christ, and the first calling of some of the apostles. Here is noted what fell out,
    The first day 15-28
    The day after 29-34
    The day after 35-42
    The day after 43-52
    The third day ii, 1-11
    After this 12

II. Of the two years between, spent chiefly in journeys to and from Jerusalem,
    A. The first journey, to the passover 13
        a. Transactions in the city,
1. Zeal for his Father's house 14-22
2. The power and wisdom of Jesus 23-25
3. The instruction of Nicodemus iii, 1-21
        b. His abode in Judea; the rest of John's testimony 22-36
        c. His journey through Samaria (where he confers with the Samaritan woman) into Galilee, where he heals the nobleman's son iv, 1-54
    B. The second journey to the feast of pentecost. Here may be observed transactions,
        a. In the city, relating to the impotent man, healed at the pool of Bethesda v, 1-47
        b. In Galilee, before the second passover and after. Here we may note,
1. His feeding the five thousand vi, 1-14
2. Walking upon the sea 15-21
3. Discourse of himself, as the bread of life 22-59
4. Reproof of those who objected to it 60-65
5. Apostasy of many, and steadiness of the apostles 66-71
6. His continuance in Galilee ` vii, 1
    C. The third journey, to the feast of tabernacles 2-13 Here may be observed transactions,
        a. In the city,
1. In the middle and end of the feast 14-53 viii; Where note,
1. The woman taken in adultery 2-12
2. Christ's preaching and vindicating his doctrine 13-30
3. His confuting the Jews and escape from them 31-59
4. His healing the man born blind ix, 1-7
5. Several discourses on that occasion 8-41
6. Christ the Door and the Shepherd of the sheep, 1-18
7. Different opinions concerning him 19-21
2. At the feast of the dedication. here occur,
1. His disputes with the Jews Chap. x, 22-38
2. His escaping their fury 39
        b. Beyond Jordan 40-42

III. Of the last days, which were,
    A. Before the great week, where we may note,
        a. The two days spent out of Judea, while Lazarus was sick and died xi, 1-6
        b. The journey into Judea; the raising of Lazarus; the advice of Caiaphas; Jesus's abode in Ephraim; the order given by his adversaries 7-57
        c. The sixth day, before the passover; the supper at Bethany; the ointment poured on Jesus xii, 1-11

B. In the great week, wherein was the third passover, occur,
    a. On the three former days, his royal entry into the city; the desire of the Greeks; the obstinacy of the Jews; the testimony given to Jesus from heaven 12-50
    b. On the fourth day, the washing the feet of the disciples; the discovery of the traitor, and his going out by night xiii, 1-30
    c. On the fifth day,
1. His discourse
  1. Before the paschal supper 31, xiv, 1-31
  2. After it xv, and xvi.
2. His prayer xvii, 1-26
3. The beginning of his passion,
  1. In the garden xviii, 1-11
  2. In Caiaphas's house 12-27
    d. On the sixth day,
1. His passion under Pilate,
  1. In the palace of Pilate 28 xix, 1-16
2. On the cross 17-30
2. His death 30-37
3. His burial 38-42
C. After the great week,
    a. On the day of the resurrection xx, 1-25
    b. Eight days after 26-31
    c. After that
1. He appears to his disciples at the sea of Tiberias. xxi, 1-14
2. Orders Peter to feed his sheep and lambs 15-17
3. Foretells the manner of Peter's death, and checks his curiosity about St John 18-23
4. The conclusion 24, 25

THE GOSPEL OF JOHN

I

1. *In the beginning* - (Referring to Gen. i, 1, and Prov. viii, 23.) When all things began to be made by the Word: in the beginning of heaven and earth, and this whole frame of created beings, the Word existed, without any beginning. He was when all things began to be, whatsoever had a beginning. *The Word* - So termed Psalm xxxiii, 6, and frequently by the seventy, and in the Chaldee paraphrase. So that St. John did not borrow this expression from Philo, or any heathen writer. He was not yet named Jesus, or Christ. He is the Word whom the Father begat or spoke from eternity; by whom the Father speaking, maketh all things; who speaketh the Father to us. We have, in the 18th verse, both a real description of the Word, and the reason why he is so called. He is the only begotten Son of the Father, who is in the bosom of the Father, and hath declared him. *And the Word was with God* - Therefore distinct from God the Father. The word rendered with, denotes a perpetual tendency as it were of the Son to the Father, in unity of essence. He was with God alone; because nothing beside God had then any being. *And the Word was God* - Supreme, eternal, independent. There was no creature, in respect of which he could be styled God in a relative sense. Therefore he is styled so in the absolute sense. The Godhead of the Messiah being clearly revealed in the Old Testament, (Jer. xxiii, 7; Hosea i, 6; Psalm xxiii, 1,) the other evangelists aim at this, to prove that Jesus, a true man, was the Messiah. But when, at length, some from hence began to doubt of his Godhead, then St. John expressly asserted it, and wrote in this book as it were a supplement to the Gospels, as in the Revelation to the prophets.

2. *The same was in the beginning with God* - This verse repeats and contracts into one the three points mentioned before. As if he had said, This Word, who was God, was in the beginning, and was with God.

3. *All things beside God were made, and all things which were made, were made by the Word*. In the first and second verse is described the state of things before the creation: verse 3, In the creation: verse 4, In the time of man's innocency: verse 5, In the time of man's corruption.

4. *In him was life* - He was the foundation of life to every living thing, as well as of being to all that is. *And the life was the light of men* - He who is essential life, and the giver of life to all that liveth, was also the light of men; the fountain of wisdom, holiness, and happiness, to man in his original state.

5. *And the light shineth in darkness* - Shines even on fallen man; but *the darkness* - Dark, sinful man, *perceiveth it not*.

6. *There was a man* - The evangelist now proceeds to him who testified of the light, which he had spoken of in the five preceding verses.

7. The same came for (that is, in order to give) a testimony - The evangelist, with the most strong and tender affection, interweaves his own testimony with that of John, by noble digressions, wherein he explains the office of the Baptist; partly premises and partly subjoins a further explication to his short sentences. What St. Matthew, Mark, and Luke term the Gospel, in respect of the promise going before, St. John usually terms the testimony, intimating the certain knowledge of the relator; to testify of the light - Of Christ.

9. Who lighteth every man - By what is vulgarly termed natural conscience, pointing out at least the general lines of good and evil. And this light, if man did not hinder, would shine more and more to the perfect day.

10. He was in the world - Even from the creation.

11. He came - In the fulness of time, to his own - Country, city, temple: And his own - People, received him not.

12. But as many as received him - Jews or Gentiles; that believe on his name - That is, on him. The moment they believe, they are sons; and because they are sons, God sendeth forth the Spirit of his Son into their hearts, crying, Abba, Father.

13. Who were born - Who became the sons of God, not of blood - Not by descent from Abraham, nor by the will of the flesh - By natural generation, nor by the will of man - Adopting them, but of God - By his Spirit.

14. Flesh sometimes signifies corrupt nature; sometimes the body; sometimes, as here, the whole man. We beheld his glory - We his apostles, particularly Peter, James, and John, Luke ix, 32. Grace and truth - We are all by nature liars and children of wrath, to whom both grace and truth are unknown. But we are made partakers of them, when we are accepted through the Beloved. The whole verse might be paraphrased thus: And in order to raise us to this dignity and happiness, the eternal Word, by a most amazing condescension, was made flesh, united himself to our miserable nature, with all its innocent infirmities. And he did not make us a transient visit, but tabernacled among us on earth, displaying his glory in a more eminent manner, than even of old in the tabernacle of Moses. And we who are now recording these things beheld his glory with so strict an attention, that we can testify, it was in every respect such a glory as became the only begotten of the Father. For it shone forth not only in his transfiguration, and in his continual miracles, but in all his tempers, ministrations, and conduct through the whole series of his life. In all he appeared full of grace and truth: he was himself most benevolent and upright; made those ample discoveries of pardon to sinners, which the Mosaic dispensation could not do: and really exhibited the most substantial blessings, whereas that was but a shadow of good things to come.

15. John cried - With joy and confidence; This is he of whom I said - John had said this before our Lord's baptism, although he then knew him not in person: he knew him first at his baptism, and afterward cried, This is he of whom I said. &c. He is preferred before me - in his office: for he was before me - in his nature.

16. And - Here the apostle confirms the Baptist's words: as if he had said, He is indeed preferred before thee: so we have experienced: We all - That believe: have received - All that we enjoy out of his fulness: and in the particular, grace upon grace - One blessing upon another, immeasurable grace and love.

17. The law - Working wrath and containing shadows: was given - No philosopher, poet, or orator, ever chose his words so accurately as St. John. The law, saith he, was given by Moses: grace was by Jesus Christ. Observe the reason for placing each word thus: The law of Moses was not his own. The grace of Christ was. His grace was opposite to the wrath, his truth to the shadowy ceremonies of the law. Jesus - St. John having once mentioned the incarnation (ver. 14,) no more uses that name, the Word, in all his book.

18. No man hath seen God - With bodily eyes: yet believers see him with the eye of faith. Who is in the bosom of the Father - The expression denotes the highest unity, and the most intimate knowledge.

19. The Jews - Probably the great council sent.

20. I am not the Christ - For many supposed he was.

21. Art thou Elijah? - He was not that Elijah (the Tishbite) of whom they spoke. Art thou the prophet - Of whom Moses speaks, Deut. xviii, 15.

23. He said - I am that forerunner of Christ of whom Isaiah speaks. I am the voice - As if he had said, Far from being Christ, or even Elijah, I am nothing but a voice: a sound that so soon as it has expressed the thought of which it is the sign, dies into air, and is known no more. Isaiah xl, 3.

24. They who were sent were of the Pharisees - Who were peculiarly tenacious of old customs, and jealous of any innovation (except those brought in by their own scribes) unless the innovator had unquestionable proofs of Divine authority.

25. They asked him, Why baptizest thou then? - Without any commission from the sanhedrim? And not only heathens (who were always baptized before they were admitted to circumcision) but Jews also?

26. *John answered, I baptize* - To prepare for the Messiah; and indeed to show that Jews, as well as Gentiles, must be proselytes to Christ, and that these as well as those stand in need of being washed from their sins.

28. *Where John was baptizing* - That is, used to baptize.

29. *He seeth Jesus coming and saith, Behold the Lamb* - Innocent; to be offered up; prophesied of by Isaiah, Isaiah liii, 7, typified by the paschal lamb, and by the daily sacrifice: *The Lamb of God* - Whom God gave, approves, accepts of; *who taketh away* - Atoneth for; *the sin* - That is, all the sins: *of the world* - Of all mankind. Sin and the world are of equal extent.

31. *I knew him not* - Till he came to be baptized. How surprising is this; considering how nearly they were related, and how remarkable the conception and birth of both had been. But there was a peculiar providence visible in our saviour's living, from his infancy to his baptism, at Nazareth: John all the time living the life of a hermit in the deserts of Judea, Luke i, 80, ninety or more miles from Nazareth: hereby that acquaintance was prevented which might have made John's testimony of Christ suspected.

34. *I saw it* - That is, the Spirit so descending and abiding on him. *And testified* - From that time.

37. *They followed Jesus* - They walked after him, but had not the courage to speak to him.

41. *He first findeth his own brother Simon* - Probably both of them sought him: *Which is, being interpreted, the Christ* - This the evangelist adds, as likewise those words in ver. 38, that is, being interpreted, Master.

42. *Jesus said, Thou art Simon, the son of Jonah* - As none had told our Lord these names, this could not but strike Peter. *Cephas, which is Peter* - Moaning the same in Syriac which Peter does in Greek, namely, a rock.

45. *Jesus of Nazareth* - So Philip thought, not knowing he was born in Bethlehem. Nathanael was probably the same with Bartholomew, that is, the son of Tholomew. St. Matthew joins Bartholomew with Philip, Matt. x, 3, and St. John places Nathanael in the midst of the apostles, immediately after Thomas, chap. xxi, 2, just as Bartholomew is placed, Acts i, 13.

46. *Can any good thing come out of Nazareth?* - How cautiously should we guard against popular prejudices? When these had once possessed so honest a heart as that of Nathanael, they led him to suspect the blessed Jesus himself for an impostor, because he had been brought up at Nazareth. But his integrity prevailed over that foolish bias, and laid him open to the force of evidence, which a candid inquirer will always be glad to admit, even when it brings the most unexpected discoveries. *Can any good thing* - That is, have we ground from Scripture to expect the Messiah, or any eminent prophet from Nazareth? *Philip saith, Come and see* - The same answer which he had received himself from our Lord the day before.

48. *Under the fig tree I saw thee* - Perhaps at prayer.

49. *Nathanael answered* - Happy are they that are ready to believe, swift to receive the truth and grace of God. *Thou art the Son of God* - So he acknowledges now more than he had heard from Philip: *The Son of God, the king of Israel* - A confession both of the person and office of Christ.

51. *Hereafter ye shall see* - All of these, as well as thou, who believe on me now in my state of humiliation, shall hereafter see me come in my glory, and all the angels of God with me. This seems the most natural sense of the words, though they may also refer to his ascension.

II

1. *And the third day* - After he had said this. *In Cana of Galilee* - There were two other towns of the same name, one in the tribe of Ephraim, the other in Caelosyria.

2. *Jesus and his disciples were invited to the marriage* - Christ does not take away human society, but sanctifies it. Water might have quenched thirst; yet our Lord allows wine; especially at a festival solemnity. Such was his facility in drawing his disciples at first, who were afterward to go through rougher ways.

3. *And wine falling short* - How many days the solemnity had lasted, and on which day our Lord came, or how many disciples might follow him, does not appear. *His mother saith to him, They have not wine* - Either she might mean, supply them by miracle; or, Go away, that others may go also, before the want appears.

4. *Jesus saith to her, Woman* - So our Lord speaks also, chap. xix, 26. It is probable this was the constant appellation which he used to her. He regarded his Father above all, not knowing even his mother after the flesh. *What is it to me and thee?* A mild reproof of her inordinate concern and untimely interposal. *Mine hour is not yet come* - The time of my working this miracle, or of my going away. May we not learn hence, if his mother was rebuked for attempting to direct him in the days of his flesh, how absurd it is to address her as if she had a right to command him, on the throne of his glory? Likewise how indecent it is for us to direct his supreme wisdom, as to the time or manner in which he shall appear for us in any of the exigencies of life!

5. His mother saith to the servants - Gathering from his answer he was about to do something extraordinary.

6. The purifying of the Jews - Who purified themselves by frequent washings particularly before eating.

9. The governor of the feast - The bridegroom generally procured some friend to order all things at the entertainment.

10. And saith - St. John barely relates the words he spoke, which does not imply his approving them. When they have well drunk - does not mean any more than toward the close of the entertainment.

11. And his disciples believed - More steadfastly.

14. Oxen, and sheep, and doves - Used for sacrifice: And the changers of money - Those who changed foreign money for that which was current at Jerusalem, for the convenience of them that came from distant countries.

15. Having made a scourge of rushes - (Which were strewed on the ground,) he drove all out of the temple, (that is, the court of it,) both the sheep and the oxen - Though it does not appear that he struck even them; and much less, any of the men. But a terror from God, it is evident, fell upon them.

17. Psalm lxix, 9.

18. Then answered the Jews - Either some of those whom he had just driven out, or their friends: What sign showest thou? - So they require a miracle, to confirm a miracle!

19. This temple - Doubtless pointing, while he spoke, to his body, the temple and habitation of the Godhead.

20. Forty and six years - Just so many years before the time of this conversation, Herod the Great had begun his most magnificent reparation of the temple, (one part after another,) which he continued all his life, and which was now going on, and was continued thirty-six years longer, till within six or seven years of the destruction of the state, city, and temple by the Romans.

22. They believed the scripture, and the word which Jesus had said - Concerning his resurrection.

23. Many believed - That he was a teacher sent from God.

24. He did not trust himself to them - Let us learn hence not rashly to put ourselves into the power of others. Let us study a wise and happy medium between universal suspiciousness and that easiness which would make us the property of every pretender to kindness and respect.

25. He - To whom all things are naked, knew what was in man - Namely, a desperately deceitful heart.

III

1. A ruler - One of the great council.

2. The same came - Through desire; but by night - Through shame: We know - Even we rulers and Pharisees.

3. Jesus answered - That knowledge will not avail thee unless thou be born again - Otherwise thou canst not see, that is, experience and enjoy, either the inward or the glorious kingdom of God. In this solemn discourse our Lord shows, that no external profession, no ceremonial ordinances or privileges of birth, could entitle any to the blessings of the Messiah's kingdom: that an entire change of heart as well as of life was necessary for that purpose: that this could only be wrought in man by the almighty power of God: that every man born into the world was by nature in a state of sin, condemnation, and misery: that the free mercy of God had given his Son to deliver them from it, and to raise them to a blessed immortality: that all mankind, Gentiles as well as Jews, might share in these benefits, procured by his being lifted up on the cross, and to be received by faith in him: but that if they rejected him, their eternal, aggravated condemnation, would be the certain consequence. Except a man be born again - If our Lord by being born again means only reformation of life, instead of making any new discovery, he has only thrown a great deal of obscurity on what was before plain and obvious.

4. When he is old - As Nicodemus himself was.

5. Except a man be born of water and of the Spirit - Except he experience that great inward change by the Spirit, and be baptized (wherever baptism can be had) as the outward sign and means of it.

6. That which is born of the flesh is flesh - Mere flesh, void of the Spirit, yea, at enmity with it; And that which is born of the Spirit is spirit - Is spiritual, heavenly, divine, like its Author.

7. Ye must be born again - To be born again, is to be inwardly changed from all sinfulness to all holiness. It is fitly so called, because as great a change then passes on the soul as passes on the body when it is born into the world.

8. The wind bloweth - According to its own nature, not thy will, and thou hearest the sound thereof - Thou art sure it doth blow, but canst not explain the particular manner of its acting. So is every one that is born of the Spirit - The fact is plain, the manner of his operations inexplicable.

11. We speak what we know - I and all that believe in me.

12. Earthly things - Things done on earth; such as the new birth, and the present privileges of the

children of God. Heavenly things - Such as the eternity of the Son, and the unity of the Father, Son, and Spirit.

13. For no one - For here you must rely on my single testimony, whereas there you have a cloud of witnesses: Hath gone up to heaven, but he that came down from heaven. Who is in heaven - Therefore he is omnipresent; else he could not be in heaven and on earth at once. This is a plain instance of what is usually termed the communication of properties between the Divine and human nature; whereby what is proper to the Divine nature is spoken concerning the human, and what is proper to the human is, as here, spoken of the Divine.

14. And as Moses - And even this single witness will soon be taken from you; yea, and in a most ignominious manner. Num. xxi, 8, 9.

15. That whosoever - He must be lifted up, that hereby he may purchase salvation for all believers: all those who look to him by faith recover spiritual health, even as all that looked at that serpent recovered bodily health.

16. Yea, and this was the very design of God's love in sending him into the world. Whosoever believeth on him - With that faith which worketh by love, and hold fast the beginning of his confidence steadfast to the end. God so loved the world - That is, all men under heaven; even those that despise his love, and will for that cause finally perish. Otherwise not to believe would be no sin to them. For what should they believe? Ought they to believe that Christ was given for them? Then he was given for them. He gave his only Son - Truly and seriously. And the Son of God gave himself, Gal. iv, 4, truly and seriously.

17. God sent not his Son into the world to condemn the world - Although many accuse him of it.

18. He that believeth on him is not condemned - Is acquitted, is justified before God. The name of the only-begotten Son of God - The name of a person is often put for the person himself. But perhaps it is farther intimated in that expression, that the person spoken of is great and magnificent. And therefore it is generally used to express either God the Father or the Son.

19. This is the condemnation - That is, the cause of it. So God is clear.

21. He that practiceth the truth (that is, true religion) cometh to the light - So even Nicodemus, afterward did. Are wrought in God - That is, in the light, power, and love of God.

22. Jesus went - From the capital city, Jerusalem, into the land of Judea - That is, into the country. There he baptized - Not himself; but his disciples by his order, chap. iv, 2.

23. John also was baptizing - He did not repel them that offered, but he more willingly referred them to Jesus.

25. The Jews - Those men of Judea, who now went to be baptized by Jesus; and John's disciples, who were mostly of Galilee: about purifying - That is, baptism. They disputed, which they should be baptized by.

27. A man can receive nothing - Neither he nor I. Neither could he do this, unless God had sent him: nor can I receive the title of Christ, or any honour comparable to that which he hath received from heaven. They seem to have spoken with jealousy and resentment; John answers with sweet composure of spirit.

29. He that hath the bride is the bridegroom - He whom the bride follows. But all men now come to Jesus. Hence it is plain he is the bridegroom. The friend who heareth him - Talk with the bride; rejoiceth greatly - So far from envying or resenting it.

30. He must increase, but I must decrease - So they who are now, like John, burning and shining lights, must (if not suddenly eclipsed) like him gradually decrease, while others are increasing about them; as they in their turns grew up, amidst the decays of the former generation. Let us know how to set, as well as how to rise; and let it comfort our declining days to trace, in those who are likely to succeed us in our work, the openings of yet greater usefulness.

31. It is not improbable, that what is added, to the end of the chapter, are the words of the evangelist, not the Baptist. He that is of the earth - A mere man; of earthly original, has a spirit and speech answerable to it.

32. No man - None comparatively, exceeding few; receiveth his testimony - With true faith.

33. Hath set to his seal - It was customary among the Jews for the witness to set his seal to the testimony he had given. That God is true - Whose words the Messiah speaks.

34. God giveth not him the Spirit by measure - As he did to the prophets, but immeasurably. Hence he speaketh the words of God in the most perfect manner.

36. He that believeth on the Son hath everlasting life - He hath it already. For he loves God. And love is the essence of heaven. He that obeyeth not - a consequence of not believing.

John Wesley

IV

1. **The Lord knew** - Though none informed him of it.
3. **He left Judea** - To shun the effects of their resentment.
4. **And he must needs go through Samaria** - The road lying directly through it.
5. **Sychar** - Formerly called Sichem or Shechem. **Jacob gave** - On his death bed, Gen. xlviii, 22.
6. **Jesus sat down** - Weary as he was. **It was the sixth hour** - Noon; the heat of the day.
7. **Give me to drink** - In this one conversation he brought her to that knowledge which the apostles were so long in attaining.
8. **For his disciples were gone** - Else he needed not have asked her.
9. **How dost thou** - Her open simplicity appears from her very first words. **The Jews have no dealings** - None by way of friendship. They would receive no kind of favour from them.
10. **If thou hadst known the gift** - The living water; **and who it is** - He who alone is able to give it: **thou wouldst have asked of him** - On those words the stress lies. **Water** - In like manner he draws the allegory from bread, chap. vi, 27, and from light, viii, 12; the first, the most simple, necessary, common, and salutary things in nature. **Living water** - The Spirit and its fruits. But she might the more easily mistake his meaning, because living water was a common phrase among the Jews for spring water.
12. **Our father Jacob** - So they fancied he was; whereas they were, in truth, a mixture of many nations, placed there by the king of Assyria, in the room of the Israelites whom he had carried away captive, 2 Kings xvii, 24. **Who gave us the well** - In Joseph their supposed forefather: and drank thereof - So even he had no better water than this.
14. **Will never thirst** - Will never (provided he continue to drink thereof) be miserable, dissatisfied, without refreshment. If ever that thirst returns, it will be the fault of the man, not the water. **But the water that I shall give him** - The spirit of faith working by love, shall become in him - An inward living principle, **a fountain** - Not barely a well, which is soon exhausted, **springing up into everlasting life** - Which is a confluence, or rather an ocean of streams arising from this fountain.
15. **That I thirst not** - She takes him still in a gross sense.
16. **Jesus saith to her** - He now clears the way that he might give her a better kind of water than she asked for. **Go, call thy husband** - He strikes directly at her bosom sin.
17. **Thou hast well said** - We may observe in all our Lord's discourses the utmost weightiness, and yet the utmost courtesy.
18. **Thou hast had five husbands** - Whether they were all dead or not, her own conscience now awakened would tell her.
19. **Sir, I perceive** - So soon was her heart touched.
20. The instant she perceived this, she proposes what she thought the most important of all questions. **This mountain** - Pointing to Mount Gerizim. Sanballat, by the permission of Alexander the Great, had built a temple upon Mount Gerizim, for Manasseh, who for marrying Sanballat's daughter had been expelled from the priesthood and from Jerusalem, Neh. xiii, 28. This was the place where the Samaritans used to worship in opposition to Jerusalem. And it was so near Sychar, that a man's voice might be heard from the one to the other. **Our fathers worshipped** - This plainly refers to Abraham and Jacob (from whom the Samaritans pretended to deduce their genealogy) who erected altars in this place: Gen. xii, 6, 7, and Gen. xxxiii, 18, 20. And possibly to the whole congregation, who were directed when they came into the land of Canaan to put the blessing upon Mount Gerizim, Deut. xi, 29. **Ye Jews say, In Jerusalem is the place** - Namely, the temple.
21. **Believe me** - Our Lord uses this expression in this manner but once; and that to a Samaritan. To his own people, the Jews, his usual language is, I say unto you. **The hour cometh when ye** - Both Samaritans and Jews, **shall worship neither in this mountain, nor at Jerusalem** - As preferable to any other place. True worship shall be no longer confined to any one place or nation.
22. **Ye worship ye know not what** - Ye Samaritans are ignorant, not only of the place, but of the very object of worship. Indeed, they feared the Lord after a fashion; but at the same time served their own gods, 2 Kings xvii, 33. **Salvation is from the Jews** - So spake all the prophets, that the saviour should arise out of the Jewish nation: and that from thence the knowledge of him should spread to all nations under heaven.
23. **The true worshippers shall worship the Father** - Not here or there only, but at all times and in all places.
24. **God is a Spirit** - Not only remote from the body, and all the properties of it, but likewise full of all spiritual perfections, power, wisdom, love, holiness. And our worship should be suitable to his nature. We should worship him with the truly spiritual worship of faith, love, and holiness, animating all our tempers, thoughts, words, and actions.
25. **The woman saith** - With joy for what she had already learned, and desire of fuller instruction.
26. **Jesus saith** - Hasting to satisfy her desire before his disciples came. **I am He** - Our Lord did not speak this so plainly to the Jews who were so full of the Messiah's temporal kingdom. If he had, many

would doubtless have taken up arms in his favour, and others have accused him to the Roman governor. Yet he did in effect declare the thing, though he denied the particular title. For in a multitude of places he represented himself, both as the Son of man, and as the Son of God: both which expressions were generally understood by the Jews as peculiarly applicable to the Messiah.

27. His disciples marvelled that he talked with a woman - Which the Jewish rabbis reckoned scandalous for a man of distinction to do. They marvelled likewise at his talking with a woman of that nation, which was so peculiarly hateful to the Jews. Yet none said - To the woman, What seekest thou? - Or to Christ, Why talkest thou with her?

28. The woman left her water pot - Forgetting smaller things.

29. A man who told me all things that ever I did - Our Lord had told her but a few things. But his words awakened her conscience, which soon told her all the rest. Is not this the Christ? - She does not doubt of it herself, but incites them to make the inquiry.

31. In the meantime - Before the people came.

34. My meat - That which satisfies the strongest appetite of my soul.

35. The fields are white already - As if he had said, The spiritual harvest is ripe already. The Samaritans, ripe for the Gospel, covered the ground round about them.

36. He that reapeth - Whoever saves souls, receiveth wages - A peculiar blessing to himself, and gathereth fruit - Many souls: that he that soweth - Christ the great sower of the seed, and he that reapeth may rejoice together - In heaven.

37. That saying - A common proverb; One soweth - The prophets and Christ; another reapeth - The apostles and succeeding ministers.

38. I - he Lord of the whole harvest, have sent you - He had employed them already in baptizing, ver. 2.

42. We know that this is the saviour of the world - And not of the Jews only.

43. He went into Galilee - That is, into the country of Galilee: but not to Nazareth. It was at that town only that he had no honour. Therefore he went to other towns.

44. Matt. xiii, 57.

47. To come down - For Cana stood much higher than Capernaum.

48. Unless ye see signs and wonders - Although the Samaritans believed without them.

52. He asked the hour when he amended - The more exactly the works of God are considered, the more faith is increased.

V

1. A feast - Pentecost.

2. There is in Jerusalem - Hence it appears, that St. John wrote his Gospel before Jerusalem was destroyed: it is supposed about thirty years after the ascension. Having five porticos - Built for the use of the sick. Probably the basin had five sides! Bethesda signifies the house of mercy.

4. An angel - Yet many undoubtedly thought the whole thing to be purely natural. At certain times - Perhaps at a certain hour of the day, during this paschal week, went down - The Greek word implies that he had ceased going down, before the time of St. John's writing this. God might design this to raise expectation of the acceptable time approaching, to add a greater lustre to his Son's miracles, and to show that his ancient people were not entirely forgotten of him. The first - Whereas the Son of God healed every day not one only, but whole multitudes that resorted to him.

7. The sick man answered - Giving the reason why he was not made whole, notwithstanding his desire.

14. Sin no more - It seems his former illness was the effect or punishment of sin.

15. The man went and told the Jews, that it was Jesus who had made him whole - One might have expected, that when he had published the name of his benefactor, crowds would have thronged about Jesus, to have heard the words of his mouth, and to have received the blessings of the Gospel. Instead of this, they surround him with a hostile intent: they even conspire against his life, and for an imagined transgression in point of ceremony, would have put out this light of Israel. Let us not wonder then, if our good be evil spoken of: if even candour, benevolence, and usefulness, do not disarm the enmity of those who have been taught to prefer sacrifice to mercy; and who, disrelishing the genuine Gospel, naturally seek to slander and persecute the professors, but especially the defenders of it.

17. My Father worketh until now, and I work - From the creation till now he hath been working without intermission. I do likewise. This is the proposition which is explained ver. 19-30, confirmed and vindicated in ver. 31 and following verses.

18. His own Father - The Greek word means his own Father in such a sense as no creature can speak. Making himself equal with God - It is evident all the hearers so understood him, and that our Lord never contradicted, but confirmed it.

19. The Son can do nothing of himself - This is not his imperfection, but his glory, resulting from

his eternal, intimate, indissoluble unity with the Father. Hence it is absolutely impossible, that the Son should judge, will, testify, or teach any thing without the Father, ver. 30, &c.; chap. vi, 38; chap. vii, 16; or that he should be known or believed on, separately from the Father. And he here defends his doing good every day, without intermission, by the example of his Father, from which he cannot depart: these doth the Son likewise - All these, and only these; seeing he and the Father are one.

20. The Father showeth him all things that himself doth - A proof of the most intimate unity. And he will show him - By doing them. At the same time (not at different times) the Father showeth and doth, and the Son seeth and doth. Greater works - Jesus oftener terms them works, than signs or wonders, because they were not wonders in his eyes. Ye will marvel - So they did, when he raised Lazarus.

21. For - He declares which are those greater works, raising the dead, and judging the world. The power of quickening whom he will follows from the power of judging. These two, quickening and judging, are proposed ver. 21, 22. The acquittal of believers, which presupposes judgment, is treated of ver. 24; the quickening some of the dead, ver. 25; and the general resurrection, ver. 28.

22. For neither doth the Father judge - Not without the Son: but he doth judge by that man whom he hath ordained, Acts xvii, 31.

23. That all men may honour the Son, even as they honour the Father - Either willingly, and so escaping condemnation, by faith: or unwillingly, when feeling the wrath of the Judge. This demonstrates the EQUALITY of the Son with the Father. If our Lord were God only by office or investiture, and not in the unity of the Divine essence, and in all respects equal in Godhead with the Father, he could not be honoured even as, that is, with the same honour that they honoured the Father. He that honoureth not the Son - With the same equal honour, greatly dishonoureth the Father that sent him.

24. And cometh not into condemnation - Unless he make shipwreck of the faith.

25. The dead shall hear the voice of the Son of God - So did Jairus's daughter, the widow's son, Lazarus.

26. He hath given to the Son - By eternal generation, to have life in himself - Absolute, independent.

27. Because he is the Son of man - He is appointed to judge mankind because he was made man.

28. The time is coming - When not two or three, but all shall rise.

29. The resurrection of life - That resurrection which leads to life everlasting.

30. I can do nothing of myself - It is impossible I should do any thing separately from my Father. As I hear - Of the Father, and see, so I judge and do; A because I am essentially united to him. See ver. 19.

31. If I testify of myself - That is, if I alone, (which indeed is impossible,) my testimony is not valid.

32. There is another - The Father, ver. 37, and I know that, even in your judgment, his testimony is beyond exception.

33. He bare testimony - That I am the Christ.

34. But I have no need to receive, &c. But these things - Concerning John, whom ye yourselves reverence, I say, that ye may be saved - So really and seriously did he will their salvation. Yet they were not saved. Most, if not all of them, died in their sins.

35. He was a burning and a shining light - Inwardly burning with love and zeal, outwardly shining in all holiness. And even ye were willing for a season - A short time only.

37. He hath testified of me - Namely at my baptism. I speak not of my supposed father Joseph. Ye are utter strangers to him of whom I speak.

38. Ye have not his word - All who believe have the word of the Father (the same with the word of the Son) abiding in them, that is, deeply ingrafted in their hearts.

39. Search the Scriptures - A plain command to all men. In them ye are assured ye have eternal life - Ye know they show you the way to eternal life. And these very Scriptures testify of me.

40. Yet ye will not come unto me - As they direct you.

41. I receive not honour from men - I need it not. I seek it not from you for my own sake.

42. But I know you - With this ray he pierces the hearts of the hearers. And this doubtless he spake with the tenderest compassion.

43. If another shall come - Any false Christ.

44. While ye receive honour - That is, while ye seek the praise of men rather than the praise of God. At the feast of pentecost, kept in commemoration of the giving the law from Mount Sinai, their sermons used to be full of the praises of the law, and of the people to whom it was given. How mortifying then must the following words of our Lord be to them, while they were thus exulting in Moses and his law!

45. There is one that accuseth you - By his writings.

46. He wrote of me - Everywhere; in all his writings; particularly Deut. xviii, 15, 18.

Wesley's Notes on the Bible - The New Testament

VI

1. After these things - The history of between ten and eleven months is to be supplied here from the other evangelists. Matt. xiv, 13; Mark vi, 32; Luke ix, 10.

3. Jesus went up - Before the people overtook him.

5. Jesus saith to Philip - Perhaps he had the care of providing victuals for the family of the apostles.

15. He retired to the mountain alone - Having ordered his disciples to cross over the lake.

16. Matt. xiv, 22; Mark vi, 45.

22. Who had stood on the other side - They were forced to stay a while, because there were then no other vessels; and they stayed the less unwillingly, because they saw that Jesus was not embarked.

26. Our Lord does not satisfy their curiosity, but corrects the wrong motive they had in seeking him: because ye did eat - Merely for temporal advantage. Hitherto Christ had been gathering hearers: he now begins to try their sincerity, by a figurative discourse concerning his passion, and the fruit of it, to be received by faith.

27. labour not for the meat which perisheth - For bodily food: not for that only not chiefly: not at all, but in subordination to grace, faith, love, the meat which endureth to everlasting life. labour, work for this; foreverlasting life. So our Lord expressly commands, work for life, as well as from life: from a principle of faith and love. Him hath the Father sealed - By this very miracle, as well as by his whole testimony concerning him. See chap. iii, 33. Sealing is a mark of the authenticity of a writing.

28. The works of God - Works pleasing to God.

29. This is the work of God - The work most pleasing to God, and the foundation of all others: that ye believe - He expresses it first properly, afterward figuratively.

30. What sign dost thou? - Amazing, after what they had just seen!

31. Our fathers ate manna - This sign Moses gave them. He gave them bread from heaven - From the lower sublunary heaven; to which Jesus opposes the highest heaven: in which sense he says seven times, ver. 32, 33, 38, 50, 58, 62, that he himself came down from heaven.

32. Moses gave you not bread from heaven - It was not Moses who gave the manna to your fathers; but my Father who now giveth the true bread from heaven. Psalm lxxviii, 24.

33. He that - giveth life to the world - Not (like the manna) to one people only: and that from generation to generation. Our Lord does not yet say, I am that bread; else the Jews would not have given him so respectful an answer, ver. 34.

34. Give us this bread - Meaning it still, in a literal sense: yet they seem now to be not far from believing.

35. I am the bread of life - Having and giving life: he that cometh -he that believeth - Equivalent expressions: shall never hunger, thirst - Shall be satisfied, happy, forever.

36. I have told you - Namely, ver. 26.

37. All that the Father giveth me - All that feel themselves lost, and follow the drawings of the Father, he in a peculiar manner giveth to the Son: will come to me - By faith. And him that thus cometh to me, I will in nowise cast out - I will give him pardon, holiness, and heaven, if he endure to the end - to rejoice in his light.

39. Of all which he hath already given me - See chap. xvii, 6, 12. If they endure to the end. But Judas did not.

40. Here is the sum of the three foregoing verses. This is the will of him that sent me - This is the whole of what I have said: this is the eternal, unchangeable will of God. Everyone who truly believeth, shall have everlasting life. Everyone that seeth and believeth - The Jews saw, and yet believed not. And I will raise him up - As this is the will of him that sent me, I will perform it effectually.

44. Christ having checked their murmuring, continues what he was saying, ver. 40. No man comes to me, unless my Father draw him - No man can believe in Christ, unless God give him power: he draws us first, by good desires. Not by compulsion, not by laying the will under any necessity; but by the strong and sweet, yet still resistible, motions of his heavenly grace.

45. Every man that hath heard - The secret voice of God, he, and he only believeth. Isaiah liv, 13.

46. Not that any one - Must expect him to appear in a visible shape. He who is from or with God - In a more eminent manner than any creature.

50. Not die - Not spiritually; not eternally.

51. If any eat of this bread - That is, believe in me: he shall live forever - In other words, he that believeth to the end shall be saved. My flesh which I will give you - This whole discourse concerning his flesh and blood refers directly to his passion, and but remotely, if at all, to the Lord's Supper.

52. Observe the degrees: the Jews are tried here; the disciples, ver. 60-66, the apostles, ver. 67.

53. Unless ye eat the flesh of the Son of man - Spiritually: unless ye draw continual virtue from him by faith. Eating his flesh is only another expression for believing.

55. Meat - drink indeed - With which the soul of a believer is as truly fed, as his body with meat

and drink.

57. I live by the Father - Being one with him. He shall live by me -Being one with me. Amazing union!

58. This is - That is, I am the bread - Which is not like the manna your fathers ate, who died notwithstanding.

60. This is a hard saying - Hard to the children of the world, but sweet to the children of God. Scarce ever did our Lord speak more sublimely, even to the apostles in private. Who can hear - Endure it?

62. What if ye shall see the Son of man ascend where he was before? - How much more incredible will it then appear to you, that he should give you his flesh to eat?

63. It is the Spirit - The spiritual meaning of these words, by which God giveth life. The flesh - The bare, carnal, literal meaning, profiteth nothing. The words which I have spoken, they are spirit - Are to be taken in a spiritual sense and, when they are so understood, they are life - That is, a means of spiritual life to the hearers.

64. But there are some of you who believe not - And so receive no life by them, because you take them in a gross literal sense. For Jesus knew from the beginning - Of his ministry: who would betray him - Therefore it is plain, God does foresee future contingencies:- "But his foreknowledge causes not the fault, Which had no less proved certain unforeknown."

65. Unless it be given - And it is given to those only who will receive it on God's own terms.

66. From this time many of his disciples went back - So our Lord now began to purge his floor: the proud and careless were driven away, and those remained who were meet for the Master's use.

68. Thou hast the words of eternal life - Thou, and thou alone, speakest the words which show the way to life everlasting.

69. And we - Who have been with thee from the beginning, whatever others do, have known - Are absolutely assured, that thou art the Christ.

70. Jesus answered the - And yet even ye have not all acted suitable to this knowledge. Have I not chosen or elected you twelve? - But they might fall even from that election. Yet one of you - On this gracious warning, Judas ought to have repented; is a devil - Is now influenced by one.

VII

1. After these things Jesus walked in Galilee - That is, continued there, for some months after the second passover. For he would not walk - Continue in Judea; because the Jews - Those of them who did not believe; and in particular the chief priests, scribes, and Pharisees, sought an opportunity to kill him.

2. The feast of tabernacles - The time, manner, and reason of this feast may be seen, Lev. xxiii, 34, &c.

3. His brethren -- so called according to the Jewish way of speaking. They were his cousins, the sons of his mother's sister. Depart hence - From this obscure place.

4. For no man doth any thing - Of this kind, in secret; but rather desireth to be of public use. If thou really dost these things -These miracles which are reported; show thyself to the world - To all men.

6. Jesus saith, Your time is always ready - This or any time will suit you.

7. The world cannot hate you - Because ye are of the world. But me it hateth - And all that bear the same testimony.

10. He also went up to the feast - This was his last journey but one to Jerusalem. The next time he went up he suffered.

11. The Jews - The men of Judea, particularly of Jerusalem.

12. There was much murmuring among the multitude - Much whispering; many private debates with each other, among those who were come from distant parts.

13. However no man spake openly of him - Not in favour of him: for fear of the Jews - Those that were in authority.

14. Now at the middle of the feast - Which lasted eight days. It is probable this was on the Sabbath day. Jesus went up into the temple - Directly, without stopping any where else.

15. How does this man know letters, having never learned? - How come he to be so well acquainted with sacred literature as to be able thus to expound the Scripture, with such propriety and gracefulness, seeing he has never learned this, at any place of education?

16. My doctrine is not mine - Acquired by any labour of learning; but his that sent me - Immediately infused by him.

17. If any man be willing to do his will, he shall know of the doctrine, whether it be of God - This is a universal rule, with regard to all persons and doctrines. He that is thoroughly willing to do it, shall certainly know what the will of God is.

18. There is no unrighteousness in him - No deceit or falsehood.

19. But ye are unrighteous; for ye violate the very law which ye profess so much zeal for.

20. The people answered, Thou hast a devil - A lying spirit. Who seeketh to kill thee? - These, coming from distant parts, probably did not know the design of the priests and rulers.

21. I did - At the pool of Bethesda: one work - Out of many: and ye all marvelled at it - Are amazed, because I did it on the Sabbath day.

22. Moses gave you circumcision - The sense is, because Moses enjoined your circumcision (though indeed it was far more ancient than him) you think it no harm to circumcise a man on the Sabbath: and are ye angry at me (which anger had now continued sixteen months) for doing so much greater a good, for healing a man, body and soul, on the Sabbath?

27. When Christ cometh, none knoweth whence he is - This Jewish tradition was true, with regard to his Divine nature: in that respect none could declare his generation. But it was not true with regard to his human nature, for both his family and the place of his birth were plainly foretold.

28. Then cried Jesus - With a loud and earnest voice. Do ye both know me, and know whence I am? - Ye do indeed know whence I am as a man. But ye know not my Divine nature, nor that I am sent from God.

29. I am from him - By eternal generation: and he hath sent me - His mission follows from his generation. These two points answer those: Do ye know me? Do ye know whence I am?

30. His hour - The time of his suffering.

33. Then said Jesus - Continuing his discourse (from ver. 29) which they had interrupted.

34. Ye shall seek me - Whom ye now despise. These words are, as it were, the text which is commented upon in this and the following chapter. Where I am - Christ's so frequently saying while on earth, where I am, when he spake of his being in heaven, intimates his perpetual presence there in his Divine nature: though his going thither was a future thing, with regard to his human nature.

35. Will he go to the dispersed among the Greeks - The Jews scattered abroad in heathen nations, Greece particularly. Or, Will he teach the Greeks? - The heathens themselves.

37. On the last, the great day of the feast - On this day there was the greatest concourse of people, and they were then wont to fetch water from the fountain of Siloam, which the priests poured out on the great altar, singing one to an other, With joy shall ye draw water from the wells of salvation. On this day likewise they commemorated God's miraculously giving water out of the rock, and offered up solemn prayers for seasonable rains.

38. He that believeth - This answers to let him come to me. And whosoever doth come to him by faith, his inmost soul shall be filled with living water, with abundance of peace, joy, and love, which shall likewise flow from him to others. As the Scripture hath said - Not expressly in any one particular place. But here is a general reference to all those scriptures which speak of the effusion of the Spirit by the Messiah, under the similitude of pouring out water. Zech. xiv, 8.

39. The Holy Ghost was not yet given - That is, those fruits of the Spirit were not yet given even to true believers, in that full measure.

40. The prophet - Whom we expect to be the forerunner of the Messiah.

42. From Bethlehem - And how could they forget that Jesus was born there? Had not Herod given them terrible reason to remember it? Micah v, 2.

48. Hath any of the rulers - Men of rank or eminence, or of the Pharisees - Men of learning or religion, believed on him?

49. But this populace, who know not the law - This ignorant rabble; are accursed - Are by that ignorance exposed to the curse of being thus seduced.

50. Nicodemus, he that came to him by night - Having now a little more courage, being one of them - Being present as a member of the great council, saith to them - Do not we ourselves act as if we knew not the law, if we pass sentence on a man before we hear him?

52. They answered - By personal reflection; the argument they could not answer, and therefore did not attempt it. Art thou also a Galilean? - One of his party? Out of Galilee ariseth no prophet - They could not but know the contrary. They knew Jonah arose out of Gethhepher; and Nahum from another village in Galilee. Yea, and Thisbe, the town of Elijah, the Tishbite, was in Galilee also. They might likewise have known that Jesus was not born in Galilee, but at Bethlehem, even from the public register there, and from the genealogies of the family of David. They were conscious this poor answer would not bear examination, and so took care to prevent a reply.

53. And every man went to his own house - So that short plain question of Nicodemus spoiled all their measures, and broke up the council! A word spoken in season, how good it is! Especially when God gives it his blessing.

VIII

5. *Moses hath commanded us to stone such* - If they spoke accurately, this must have been a woman, who, having been betrothed to a husband, had been guilty of this crime before the marriage was completed; for such only Moses commanded to be stoned. He commanded indeed that other adulteresses should be put to death; but the manner of death was not specified. Deut. xxii, 23.

6. *That they might have to accuse him* - Either of usurping the office of a judge, if he condemned her, or of being an enemy to the law, if he acquitted her. Jesus stooping down, wrote with his finger on the ground - God wrote once in the Old Testament; Christ once in the New: perhaps the words which he afterward spoke, when they continued asking him. By this silent action, he, 1, fixed their wandering, hurrying thoughts, in order to awaken their consciences: and, 2, signified that he was not then come to condemn but to save the world.

7. *He that is without sin* - He that is not guilty: his own conscience being the judge) either of the same sin, or of some nearly resembling it; let him - as a witness, cast the first stone at her.

9. *Beginning at the eldest* - Or the elders. Jesus was left alone -By all those scribes and Pharisees who proposed the question. But many others remained, to whom our Lord directed his discourse presently after.

10. *Hath no man condemned thee?* - Hath no judicial sentence been passed upon thee?

11. *Neither do I condemn thee* - Neither do I take upon me to pass any such sentence. Let this deliverance lead thee to repentance.

12. *He that followeth me shall in nowise walk in darkness* - In ignorance, wickedness, misery: but shall have the light of life -He that closely, humbly, steadily follows me, shall have the Divine light continually shining upon him, diffusing over his soul knowledge, holiness, joy, till he is guided by it to life everlasting.

13. *Thou testifiest of thyself; thy testimony is not valid* - They retort upon our Lord his own words, chap. v, 31; if I testify of myself, my testimony is not valid. He had then added, There is another who testifieth of me. To the same effect he replies here, verse 14, Though I testify of myself, yet my testimony is valid; for I am inseparably united to the Father. I know - And from firm and certain knowledge proceeds the most unexceptionable testimony: whence I came, and whither I go - To these two heads may be referred all the doctrine concerning Christ. The former is treated of verse 16, &c., the latter ver. 21, &c. For I know whence I came - That is, For I came from God, both as God and as man. And I know it, though ye do not.

15. *Ye judge after the flesh* - As the flesh, that is, corrupt nature dictates. I judge no man - Not thus; not now; not at my first coming.

16. *I am not alone* - No more in judging, than in testifying: but I and the Father that sent me - His Father is in him, and he is in the Father, chap. xiv, 10, 11; and so the Father is no more alone without the Son, than the Son is without the Father, Prov. viii, 22, 23, 30. His Father and he are not one and another God, but one God, (though distinct persons,) and so inseparable from each other. And though the Son came from the Father, to assume human nature, and perform his office as the Messiah upon earth, as God is sometimes said to come from heaven, for particular manifestations of himself; yet Christ did not leave the Father, nor the Father leave him, any more than God leaves heaven when he is said to come down to the earth.

17. Deut. xix, 15.

19. *Then said they to him, Where is thy Father? Jesus answered* - Showing the perverseness of their question; and teaching that they ought first to know the Son, if they would know the Father. Where the Father is - he shows, ver. 23. Meantime he plainly intimates that the Father and he were distinct persons, as they were two witnesses; and yet one in essence, as the knowledge of him includes the knowledge of the Father.

23. *Ye are* - Again he passes over their interruption, and proves what he advanced, ver. 21. Of them that are beneath - From the earth. I am of them that are above - Here he directly shows whence he came, even from heaven, and whither he goes.

24. *If ye believe not that I AM* - Here (as in ver. 58) our Lord claims the Divine name, I AM, Exod. iii, 14. But the Jews, as if he had stopped short, and not finished the sentence, answered, Who art thou?

25. *Even what I say to you from the beginning* - The same which I say to you, as it were in one discourse, with one even tenor from the time I first spake to you.

26. *I have many things to say and to judge of you* - I have much to say concerning your inexcusable unbelief: but he that sent me is true - Whether ye believe or no. And I speak the things which I have heard from him - I deliver truly what he hath given me in charge.

27. *They understood not* - That by him that sent him he meant God the Father. Therefore in ver. 28, 29 he speaks plainly of the Father, and again claims the Divine name, I AM.

28. *When ye shall have lifted up* - On the cross, ye shall know - And so many of them did, that I

AM - God over all; and that I do nothing of myself - Being one with the Father.

29. The Father hath not left me alone - Never from the moment I came into the world.

32. The truth - Written in your hearts by the Spirit of God, shall make you free - From guilt, sin, misery, Satan.

33. They - The other Jews that were by, (not those that believed,) as appears by the whole tenor of the conversation. We were never enslaved to any man - A bold, notorious untruth. At that very time they were enslaved to the Romans.

34. Jesus answered - Each branch of their objection, first concerning freedom, then concerning their being Abraham's offspring, ver. 37, &c. He that committeth sin, is, in fact, the slave of sin.

35. And the slave abideth not in the house - All sinners shall be cast out of God's house, as the slave was out of Abraham's: but I, the Son, abide therein forever.

36. If I therefore make you free, ye - shall partake of the same privilege: being made free from all guilt and sin, ye shall abide in the house of God forever.

37. I know that ye are Abraham's offspring - As to the other branch of your objection, I know that, ye are Abraham's offspring, after the flesh; but not in a spiritual sense. Ye are not followers of the faith of Abraham: my word hath no place in your hearts.

41. Ye do the deeds of your father - He is not named yet. But when they presumed to call God their Father, then he is expressly called the devil, ver. 44.

42. I proceeded forth - As God, and come - As Christ.

43. Ye cannot - Such is your stubbornness and pride, hear - Receive, obey my word. Not being desirous to do my will, ye cannot understand my doctrine, chap. vii, 17.

44. He was a murderer - In inclination, from the beginning - Of his becoming a devil; and abode not in the truth - Commencing murderer and liar at the same time. And certainly he was a killer of men (as the Greek word properly signifies) from the beginning of the world: for from the very creation he designed and contrived the ruin of men. When he speaketh a lie, he speaketh of his own - For he is the proper parent, and, as it were, creator of it. See the origin not only of lies, but of evil in general!

45. Because I speak the truth - Which liars hate.

46. Which of you convicteth me of sin? - And is not my life as unreprovable as my doctrine? Does not my whole behaviour confirm the truth of what I teach?

47. He that is of God - That either loves or fears him, heareth - With joy and reverence, God's words - Which I preach.

48. Say we not well - Have we not just cause to say, Thou art, a Samaritan - An enemy to our Church and nation; and hast a devil? -Art possessed by a proud and lying spirit?

49. I honour my Father - I seek his honour only.

50. I seek not my own glory - That is, as I am the Messiah, I consult not my own glory. I need not. For my Father consulteth it, and will pass sentence on you accordingly.

51. If a man keep my word - So will my Father consult my glory. We keep his doctrine by believing, his promises by hoping, his command by obeying. He shall never see death - That is, death eternal. He shall live forever. Hereby he proves that he was no Samaritan; for the Samaritans in general were Sadducees.

54. If I honour myself - Referring to their words, Whom makest thou thyself?

56. He saw it - By faith in types, figures, and promises; as particularly in Melchisedec; in the appearance of Jehovah to him in the plains of Mamre, Gen. xviii, 1; and in the promise that in his seed all the nations of the earth shall be blessed. Possibly he had likewise a peculiar Revelation either of Christ's first or second coming.

57. Thou art not yet fifty years old - At the most. Perhaps the gravity of our Lord's countenance, together with his afflictions and labours, might make him appear older than he really was. Hast thou seen Abraham - Which they justly supposed must have been, if Abraham had seen him.

58. Before Abraham was I AM - Even from everlasting to everlasting. This is a direct answer to the objection of the Jews, and shows how much greater he was than Abraham.

59. Then they took up stones - To stone him as a blasphemer; but Jesus concealed himself - Probably by becoming invisible; and so passed on - With the same ease as if none had been there.

IX

2. Who sinned, this man or his parents, that he was born blind? - That is, was it for his own sins, or the sins of his parents? They suppose (as many of the Jews did, though without any ground from Scripture) that he might have sinned in a pre-existent state, before he came into the world.

3. Jesus answered, Neither hath this man sinned, nor his parents - It was not the manner of our Lord to answer any questions that were of no use, but to gratify an idle curiosity. Therefore he determines nothing concerning this. The scope of his answer is, It was neither for any sins of his own, nor yet of his parents; but that the power of God might be displayed.

4. The night is coming - Christ is the light. When the light is withdrawn night comes, when no man can work - No man can do any thing toward working out his salvation after this life is ended. Yet Christ can work always. But he was not to work upon earth, only during the day, or season which was appointed for him.

5. I am the light of the world - I teach men inwardly by my Spirit, and outwardly by my preaching, what is the will of God; and I show them, by my example, how they must do it.

6. He anointed the eyes of the blind man with the clay - This might almost have blinded a man that had sight. But what could it do toward curing the blind? It reminds us that God is no farther from the event, when he works either with, or without means, and that all the creatures are only that which his almighty operation makes them.

7. Go, wash at the pool of Siloam - Perhaps our Lord intended to make the miracle more taken notice of. For a crowd of people would naturally gather round him to observe the event of so strange a prescription, and it is exceeding probable, the guide who must have led him in traversing a great part of the city, would mention the errand he was going upon, and so call all those who saw him to a greater attention. From the fountain of Siloam, which was without the walls of Jerusalem, a little stream flowed into the city, and was received in a kind of basin, near the temple, and called the pool of Siloam. Which is, by interpretation, Sent - And so was a type of the Messiah, who was sent of God. He went and washed, and came seeing - He believed, and obeyed, and found a blessing. Had he been wise in his own eyes, and reasoned, like Naaman, on the impropriety of the means, he had justly been left in darkness. Lord, may our proud hearts be subdued to the methods of thy recovering grace! May we leave thee to choose how thou wilt bestow favours, which it is our highest interest to receive on any terms.

11. A man called Jesus - He seems to have been before totally ignorant of him.

14. Anointing the eyes - With any kind of medicine on the Sabbath, was particularly forbidden by the tradition of the elders.

16. This man is not of God - Not sent of God. How can a man that is a sinner - That is, one living in wilful sin, do such miracles?

17. What sayest thou of him, for that he hath opened thine eyes? - What inference dost thou draw herefrom?

22. He should be put out of the synagogue - That is be excommunicated.

27. Are ye also - As well as I, at length convinced and willing to be his disciples?

29. We know not whence he is - By what power and authority he does these things.

30. The man answered - Utterly illiterate as he was. And with what strength and clearness of reason! So had God opened the eyes of his understanding, as well as his bodily eyes. Why, herein is a marvelous thing, that ye - The teachers and guides of the people, should not know, that a man who has wrought a miracle, the like of which was never heard of before, must be from heaven, sent by God.

31. We - Even we of the populace, know that God heareth not sinners - Not impenitent sinners, so as to answer their prayers in this manner. The honest courage of this man in adhering to the truth, though he knew the consequence, ver. 22, gives him claim to the title of a confessor.

33. He could do nothing - Of this kind; nothing miraculous.

34. Born in sin - And therefore, they supposed, born blind. They cast him out - Of the synagogue; excommunicated him.

35. Having found him - For he had sought him.

36. Who is he, that I may believe? - This implies some degree of faith already. He was ready to receive whatever Jesus said.

37. Lord, I believe - What an excellent spirit was this man of! Of so deep and strong an understanding; (as he had just shown to the confusion of the Pharisees,) and yet of so teachable a temper!

39. For judgment am I come into the world - That is, the consequence of my coming will be, that by the just judgment of God, while the blind in body and soul receive their sight, they who boast they see, will be given up to still greater blindness than before.

41. If ye had been blind - Invincibly ignorant; if ye had not had so many means of knowing: ye would have had no sin - Comparatively to what ye have now. But now ye say - Ye yourselves acknowledge, Ye see, therefore your sin remaineth - Without excuse, without remedy.

X

1. He that entereth not by the door - By Christ. He is the only lawful entrance. Into the sheepfold - The Church. He is a thief and a robber - In God's account. Such were all those teachers, to whom our Lord had just been speaking.

3. To him the door keeper openeth - Christ is considered as the shepherd, ver. 11. As the door in the first and following verses. And as it is not unworthy of Christ to be styled the door, by which both the sheep and the true pastor enter, so neither is it unworthy of God the Father to be styled the door

keeper. See Acts xiv, 27; Colossians iv, 3; Rev. iii, 8; Acts xvi, 14. And the sheep hear his voice - The circumstances that follow, exactly agree with the customs of the ancient eastern shepherds. They called their sheep by name, went before them and the sheep followed them. So real Christians hear, listen to, understand, and obey the voice of the shepherd whom Christ hath sent. And he counteth them his own, dearer than any friend or brother: calleth, advises, directs each by name, and leadeth them out, in the paths of righteousness, beside the waters of comfort.

4. He goeth before them - In all the ways of God, teaching them in every point, by example as well as by precept; and the sheep follow him - They tread in his steps: for they know his voice - Having the witness in themselves that his words are the wisdom and the power of God. Reader, art thou a shepherd of souls? Then answer to God. Is it thus with thee and thy flock?

5. They will not follow a stranger - One whom Christ hath not sent, who doth not answer the preceding description. Him they will not follow - And who can constrain them to it? But will flee from him - As from the plague. For they know not the voice of strangers - They cannot relish it; it is harsh and grating to them. They find nothing of God therein.

6. They - The Pharisees, to whom our Lord more immediately spake, as appears from the close of the foregoing chapter.

7. I am the door - Christ is both the Door and the Shepherd, and all things.

8. Whosoever are come - Independently of me, assuming any part of my character, pretending, like your elders and rabbis, to a power over the consciences of men, attempting to make laws in the Church, and to teach their own traditions as the way of salvation: all those prophets and expounders of God's word, that enter not by the door of the sheepfold, but run before I have sent them by my Spirit. Our Lord seems in particular to speak of those that had undertaken this office since he began his ministry, are thieves -Stealing temporal profit to themselves, and robbers - Plundering and murdering the sheep.

9. If any one - As a sheep, enter in by me - Through faith, he shall be safe - From the wolf, and from those murdering shepherds. And shall go in and out - Shall continually attend on the shepherds whom I have sent; and shall find pasture - Food for his soul in all circumstances.

10. The thief cometh not but to steal, and to kill, and to destroy - That is, nothing else can be the consequence of a shepherd's coming, who does not enter in by me.

12. But the hireling - It is not the bare receiving hire, which denominates a man a hireling: (for the labourer is worthy of his hire; Jesus Christ himself being the Judge: yea, and the Lord hath ordained, that they who preach the Gospel, should live of the Gospel:) but the loving hire: the loving the hire more than the work: the working for the sake of the hire. He is a hireling, who would not work, were it not for the hire; to whom this is the great (if not only) motive of working. O God! If a man who works only for hire is such a wretch, a mere thief and a robber, what is he who continually takes the hire, and yet does not work at all? The wolf - signifies any enemy who, by force or fraud, attacks the Christian's faith, liberty, or life. So the wolf seizeth and scattereth the flock - He seizeth some, and scattereth the rest; the two ways of hurting the flock of Christ.

13. The hireling fleeth because he is a hireling - Because he loves the hire, not the sheep.

14. I know my sheep - With a tender regard and special care: and am known of mine - With a holy confidence and affection.

15. As the Father knoweth me, and I know the Father - With such a knowledge as implies an inexpressible union: and I lay down my life - Speaking of the present time. For his whole life was only a going unto death.

16. I have also other sheep - Which he foreknew; which are not of this fold - Not of the Jewish Church or nation, but Gentiles. I must bring them likewise - Into my Church, the general assembly of those whose names are written in heaven. And there shall be one flock - (Not one fold, a plain false print) no corrupt or divided flocks remaining. And one shepherd - Who laid down his life for the sheep, and will leave no hireling among them. The unity both of the flock and the shepherd shall be completed in its season. The shepherd shall bring all into one flock: and the whole flock shall hear the one shepherd.

17. I lay down my life that I may take it again - I cheerfully die to expiate the sins of men, to the end I may rise again for their justification.

18. I lay it down of myself - By my own free act and deed. I have power to lay it down, and I have power to take it again - I have an original power and right of myself, both to lay it down as a ransom, and to take it again, after full satisfaction is made, for the sins of the whole world. This commission have I received of my Father - Which I readily execute. He chiefly spoke of the Father, before his suffering: of his own glory, after it. Our Lord's receiving this commission as mediator is not to be considered as the ground of his power to lay down and resume his life. For this he had in himself, as having an original right to dispose thereof, antecedent to the Father's commission. But this commission was the reason why he thus used his power in laying down his life. He did it in obedience to his Father.

21. These are not the words - The word in the original takes in actions too.

22. It was the feast of the dedication - Instituted by Judas Maccabeus, 1 Macc. iv, 59, when he purged and dedicated the altar and temple after they had been polluted. So our Lord observed festivals even of human appointment. Is it not, at least, innocent for us to do the same?

23. In Solomon's portico - Josephus informs us, that when Solomon built the temple, he filled up a part of the adjacent valley, and built a portico over it toward the east. This was a noble structure, supported by a wall four hundred cubits high: and continued even to the time of Albinus and Agrippa, which was several years after the death of Christ.

26. Ye do not believe, because ye are not of my sheep - Because ye do not, will not follow me: because ye are proud, unholy, lovers of praise, lovers of the world, lovers of pleasure, not of God.

27, 28, 29. My sheep hear my voice, and I know them, and they follow me, &c.- Our Lord still alludes to the discourse he had before this festival. As if he had said, My sheep are they who,

1. Hear my voice by faith;
2. Are known (that is, approved) by me, as loving me; and
3. Follow me, keep my commandments, with a believing, loving heart. And to those who,

1. Truly believe (observe three promises annexed to three conditions) I give eternal life. He does not say, I will, but I give. For he that believeth hath everlasting life. Those whom,
2. I know truly to love me, shall never perish, provided they abide in my love.
3. Those who follow me, neither men nor devils can pluck out of my hand. My Father who hath, by an unchangeable decree, given me all that believe, love, and obey, is greater than all in heaven or earth, and none is able to pluck them out of his hand.

30. I and the Father are one - Not by consent of will only, but by unity of power, and consequently of nature. Are - This word confutes Sabellius, proving the plurality of persons: one - This word confutes Arius, proving the unity of nature in God. Never did any prophet before, from the beginning of the world, use any one expression of himself, which could possibly be so interpreted as this and other expressions were, by all that heard our Lord speak. Therefore if he was not God he must have been the vilest of men.

34. Psalm lxxxii, 6.

35. If he (God) called them gods unto whom the word of God came, (that is, to whom God was then speaking,) and the Scripture cannot be broken - That is, nothing which is written therein can be censured or rejected.

36. Say ye of him whom the Father hath sanctified, and sent into the world - This sanctification (whereby he is essentially the Holy One of God) is mentioned as prior to his mission, and together with it implies, Christ was God in the highest sense, infinitely superior to that wherein those Judges were so called.

38. That ye may know and believe - In some a more exact knowledge precedes, in others it follows faith. I am in the Father and the Father in me. I and the Father are one - These two sentences illustrate each other.

40. To the desert place where John baptized, and gave so honourable a testimony of him.

41. John did no miracle - An honour reserved for him, whose forerunner he was.

XI

1. One Lazarus - It is probable, Lazarus was younger than his sisters. Bethany is named, the town of Mary and Martha, and Lazarus is mentioned after them, ver. 5. Ecclesiastical history informs us, that Lazarus was now thirty years old, and that he lived thirty years after Christ's ascension.

2. It was that Mary who afterward anointed, &c. She was more known than her elder sister Martha, and as such is named before her.

4. This sickness is not to death, but for the glory of God - The event of this sickness will not be death, in the usual sense of the word, a final separation of his soul and body; but a manifestation of the glorious power of God.

7. Let us go into Judea - From the country east of Jordan, whither he had retired some time before, when the Jews sought to stone him, chap. x, 39, 40.

9. Are there not twelve hours in the day? - The Jews always divided the space from sunrise to sunset, were the days longer or shorter, into twelve parts: so that the hours of their day were all the year the same in number, though much shorter in winter than in summer. If any man walk in the day he stumbleth not - As if he had said, So there is such a space, a determined time, which God has allotted me. During that time I stumble not, amidst all the snares that are laid for me. Because he seeth the light of this world - And so I see the light of God surrounding me.

10. But if a man walk in the night - If he have not light from God; if his providence does no longer protect him.

11. Our friend Lazarus sleepeth - This he spoke, just when he died. Sleepeth - Such is the death of good men in the language of heaven. But the disciples did not yet understand this language. And the

Wesley's Notes on the Bible - The New Testament

slowness of our understanding makes the Scripture often descend to our barbarous manner of speaking.

16. Thomas in Hebrew, as Didymus in Greek, signifies a twin. With him - With Jesus, whom he supposed the Jews would kill. It seems to be the language of despair.

20. Mary sat in the house - Probably not hearing what was said.

22. Whatsoever thou wilt ask, God will give it thee - So that she already believed he could raise him from the dead.

25. I am the resurrection - Of the dead. And the life - Of the living. He that believeth in me, though he die, yet shall he live - In life everlasting.

32. She fell at his feet - This Martha had not done. So she makes amends for her slowness in coming.

33. He groaned - So he restrained his tears. So he stopped them soon after, ver. 38. He troubled himself - An expression amazingly elegant, and full of the highest propriety. For the affections of Jesus were not properly passions, but voluntary emotions, which were wholly in his own power. And this tender trouble which he now voluntarily sustained, was full of the highest order and reason.

35. Jesus wept - Out of sympathy with those who were in tears all around him, as well as from a deep sense of the misery sin had brought upon human nature.

37. Could not this person have even caused, that this man should not have died? - Yet they never dreamed that he could raise him again! What a strange mixture of faith and unbelief.

38. It was a cave - So Abraham, Isaac, and Jacob, and their wives, except Rachel, were buried in the cave of Machpelah, Gen. xlix, 29-31. These caves were commonly in rocks, which abounded in that country, either hollowed by nature or hewn by art. And the entrance was shut up with a great stone, which sometimes had a monumental inscription.

39. Lord, by this time he stinketh - Thus did reason and faith struggle together.

40. Said I not - It appears by this, that Christ had said more to Martha than is before recorded.

41. Jesus lifted up his eyes - Not as if he applied to his Father for assistance. There is not the least show of this. He wrought the miracle with an air of absolute sovereignty, as the Lord of life and death. But it was as if he had said, I thank thee, that by the disposal of thy providence, thou hast granted my desire, in this remarkable opportunity of exerting my power, and showing forth thy praise.

43. He cried with a loud voice - That all who were present might hear. Lazarus, come forth - Jesus called him out of the tomb as easily as if he had been not only alive, but awake also.

44. And he came forth bound hand and foot with grave clothes - Which were wrapt round each hand and each foot, and his face was wrapt about with a napkin - If the Jews buried as the Egyptians did, the face was not covered with it, but it only went round the forehead, and under the chin; so that he might easily see his way.

45. Many believed on Him - And so the Son of God was glorified, according to what our Lord had said, ver. 4.

46. But some of them went to the Pharisees - What a dreadful confirmation of that weighty truth, If they hear not Moses and the prophets, neither will they be persuaded though one rose from the dead!

47. What do we? - What? Believe. Yea, but death yields to the power of Christ sooner than infidelity.

48. All men will believe - And receive him as the Messiah. And this will give such umbrage to the Roman that they will come and subvert both our place - Temple; and nation - Both our Church and state. Were they really afraid of this? Or was it a fair colour only? Certainly it was no more. For they could not but know, that he that raised the dead was able to conquer the Romans.

49. That year - That memorable year, in which Christ was to die. It was the last and chief of Daniel's seventy weeks, the fortieth year before the destruction of Jerusalem, and was celebrated for various causes, in the Jewish history. Therefore that year is so peculiarly mentioned: Caiaphas was the high priest both before and after it. Ye know nothing - He reproves their slow deliberations in so clear a case.

50. It is expedient that one man should die for the people - So God overruled his tongue, for he spake not of himself, by his own spirit only, but by the spirit of prophecy. And thus he gave unawares as clear a testimony to the priestly, as Pilate did to the kingly office of Christ.

52. But that, he might gather into one - Church, all the children of God that were scattered abroad - Through all ages and nations.

55. Many went up to purify themselves - That they might remove all hindrances to their eating the passover.

XII

1. Six days before the passover - Namely, on the Sabbath: that which was called by the Jews, "The Great Sabbath." This whole week was anciently termed "The great and holy week." Jesus came - From Ephraim, chap. xi, 54.

2. It seems Martha was a person of some figure, from the great respect which was paid to her and her sister, in visits and condolences on Lazarus' death, as well as from the costly ointment mentioned in the next verse. And probably it was at their house our Lord and his disciples lodged, when he returned from Jerusalem to Bethany, every evening of the last week of his life, upon which he was now entered.

3. Then Mary, taking a pound of ointment - There were two persons who poured ointment on Christ. One toward the beginning of his ministry, at or near Nain, Luke vii, 37, &c. The other six days before his last passover, at Bethany; the account of whom is given here, as well as by St. Matthew and Mark.

7. Against the day of my burial - Which now draws nigh.

10. The chief priests consulted, how to kill Lazarus also - Here is the plain reason why the other evangelists, who wrote while Lazarus was living, did not relate his story.

12. The next day - On Sunday. Who were come to the feast - So that this multitude consisted chiefly of Galileans, not men of Jerusalem. Matt. xxi, 8.

13. Psalm cxviii, 26; Mark xi, 8; Luke xix, 36.

15. Fear not - For his meekness forbids fear, as well as the end of his coming. Zech. ix, 9.

16. These things his disciples understood not at first - The design of God's providential dispensations is seldom understood at first. We ought therefore to believe, though we understand not, and to give ourselves up to the Divine disposal. The great work of faith is, to embrace those things which we knew not now, but shall know hereafter. When he had been glorified - At his ascension.

17. When he called Lazarus out of the tomb - How admirably does the apostle express, as well the greatness of the miracle, as the facility with which it was wrought! The easiness of the Scripture style on the most grand occurrences, is more sublime than all the pomp of orators.

18. The multitude went to meet him, because they heard - From those who had seen the miracle. So in a little time both joined together, to go before and to follow him.

20. Certain Greeks - A prelude of the Gentile Church. That these were circumcised does not appear. But they came up on purpose to worship the God of Israel.

21. These came to Philip of Bethsaida in Galilee - Perhaps they used to lodge there, in their journey to Jerusalem. Or they might believe, a Galilean would be more ready to serve them herein, than a Jew. Sir - They spake to him, as to one they were little acquainted with. We would see Jesus - A modest request. They could scarce expect that he would now have time to talk with them.

23. The hour is come that the Son of man should be glorified - With the Father and in the sight of every creature. But he must suffer first.

24. Unless a grain of wheat die - The late resurrection of Lazarus gave our Lord a natural occasion of speaking on this subject. And agreeable to his infinite knowledge, he singles out, from among so many thousands of seeds, almost the only one that dies in the earth: and which therefore was an exceeding proper similitude, peculiarly adapted to the purpose for which he uses it. The like is not to be found in any other grain, except millet, and the large bean.

25. He that loveth his life - More than the will of God; shall lose it eternally: and he that hateth his life - In comparison of the will of God, shall preserve it. Matt. x, 39.

26. Let him follow me - By hating his life: and where I am - In heaven. If any man serve me - Thus, him will the Father honour.

27. Now is my soul troubled - He had various foretastes of his passion. And what shall I say? - Not what shall I choose? For his heart was fixed in choosing the will of his Father: but he laboured for utterance. The two following clauses, Save me from this hour - For this cause I came - Into the world; for the sake of this hour (of suffering) seem to have glanced through his mind in one moment. But human language could not so express it.

28. Father, glorify thy name - Whatever I suffer. Now the trouble was over. I have glorified it - By thy entrance into this hour. And I will glorify it - By thy passing through it.

29. The multitude who stood and heard - A sound, but not the distinct words - In the most glorious Revelations there may remain something obscure, to exercise our faith. Said, It thundered -Thunder did frequently attend a voice from heaven. Perhaps it did so now.

31. Now - This moment. And from this moment Christ thirsted more than ever, till his baptism was accomplished. Is the judgment of this world - That is, now is the judgment given concerning it, whose it shall be. Now shall the prince of this world - Satan, who had gained possession of it by sin and death, be cast out -That is, judged, condemned, cast out of his possession, and out of the bounds of Christ's kingdom.

32. Lifted up from the earth - This is a Hebraism which signifies dying. Death in general is all that

is usually imported. But our Lord made use of this phrase, rather than others that were equivalent, because it so well suited the particular manner of his death. I will draw all men - Gentiles as well as Jews. And those who follow my drawings, Satan shall not be able to keep.

34. How sayest thou, The Son of man must be lifted up? - How can these things be reconciled? Very easily. He first dies, and then abideth forever. Who is this Son of man? - Is he the Christ? Psalm cx, 4.

35. Then Jesus said to them - Not answering them directly, but exhorting them to improve what they had heard already. The light - I am my doctrine.

36. The children of light - The children of God, wise, holy, happy.

37. Though he had done so many miracles before them - So that they could not but see them.

38. The arm of the Lord - The power of God manifested by Christ, in his preaching, miracles, and work of redemption. Isaiah liii, 1.

39. Therefore now they could not believe - That is, by the just judgment of God, for their obstinacy and wilful resistance of the truth, they were at length so left to the hardness of their hearts, that neither the miracles nor doctrines of our Lord could make any impression upon them.

40. Isaiah vi, 10; Matt. xiii, 14; Acts xxviii, 26.

41. When he saw his glory - Christ's, Isaiah vi, 1, &c. And it is there expressly said to be the glory of the Lord, Jehovah, the Supreme God.

44. Jesus said with a loud voice - This which follows to the end of the chapter, is with St. John the epilogue of our Lord's public discourses, and a kind of recapitulation of them. Believeth not on me - Not on me alone, but also on him that sent me: because the Father hath sent the Son, and because he and the Father are one.

45. And he that seeth me - By the eye of faith.

47. I judge him not - Not now: for I am not come to judge the world. See, Christ came to save even them that finally perish! Even these are a part of that world, which he lived and died to save.

50. His commandment - Kept, is life everlasting - That is the way to it, and the beginning of it.

XIII

1. Before the feast - Namely, on Wednesday, in the paschal week. Having loved his own - His apostles, he loved them to the end - Of his life.

2. Having now - Probably now first.

3. Jesus knowing - Though conscious of his own greatness, thus humbled himself.

4. Layeth aside his garments - That part of them which would have hindered him.

5. Into the basin - A large vessel was usually placed for this very purpose, wherever the Jews supped.

7. What I do thou knowest not now; but thou shalt know hereafter - We do not now know perfectly any of his works, either of creation, providence, or grace. It is enough that we can love and obey now, and that we shall know hereafter.

8. If I wash thee not - If thou dost not submit to my will, thou hast no part with me - Thou art not my disciple. In a more general sense it may mean, If I do not wash thee in my blood, and purify thee by my Spirit, thou canst have no communion with me, nor any share in the blessings of my kingdom.

9. Lord, not my feet only - How fain would man be wiser than God! Yet this was well meant, though ignorant earnestness.

10. And so ye, having been already cleansed, need only to wash your feet - That is, to walk holy and undefiled.

14. Ye ought also to wash one another's feet - And why did they not? Why do we not read of any one apostle ever washing the feet of any other? Because they understood the Lord better. They knew he never designed that this should be literally taken. He designed to teach them the great lesson of humble love, as well as to confer inward purity upon them. And hereby he teaches us,

1. In every possible way to assist each other in attaining that purity;

2. To wash each other's feet, by performing all sorts of good offices to each other, even those of the lowest kind, when opportunity serves, and the necessity of any calls for them.

16. The servant is not greater than his Lord - Nor therefore ought to think much of either doing or suffering the same things.

18. I speak not of you all - When I call you happy, I know one of you twelve whom I have chosen, will betray me; whereby that scripture will be fulfilled. Psalm xli, 9.

20. And I put my own honour upon you, my ambassadors. Matt. x, 40.

21. One of you - The speaking thus indefinitely at first was profitable to them all.

23. There was lying in the bosom of Jesus -- that is, sitting next to him at table. This phrase only expresses the then customary posture at meals, where the guests all leaned sidewise on couches. And each was said to lie in the bosom of him who was placed next above him. One of the disciples whom

Jesus loved - St. John avoids with great care the expressly naming himself. Perhaps our Lord now gave him the first proof of his peculiar love, by disclosing this secret to him.

24. Simon Peter - Behind Jesus, who lay between them.

25. Leaning down, and so asking him privately.

26. Jesus answered - In his ear. So careful was he not to offend (if it had been possible) even Judas himself. The sop - Which he took up while he was speaking. He giveth it to Judas - And probably the other disciples thought Judas peculiarly happy! But when even this instance of our Lord's tenderness could not move him, then Satan took full possession.

27. What thou doest, do quickly - This is not a permission, much less a command. It is only as if he had said, If thou art determined to do it, why dost thou delay? Hereby showing Judas, that he could not be hid, and expressing his own readiness to suffer.

28. None knew why he said this - Save John and Judas.

30. He went out - To the chief priests. But he returned afterward, and was with them when they ate the passover, Matt. xxvi, 20, though not at the Lord's Supper.

31. Jesus saith - Namely, the next day; on Thursday, in the morning. Here the scene, as it were, is opened, for the discourse which is continued in the following chapters. Now - While I speak this, the Son of man is glorified - Being fully entered into his glorious work of redemption. This evidently relates to the glory which belongs to his suffering in so holy and victorious a manner.

33. Ye cannot come - Not yet; being not yet ripe for it. John vii, 34.

34. A new commandment - Not new in itself; but new in the school of Christ: for he had never before taught it them expressly. Likewise new, as to the degree of it, as I have loved you.

36. Peter saith, Lord, whither goest thou? - St. Peter seems to have thought, that Christ, being rejected by the Jews, would go to some other part of the earth to erect his throne, where he might reign without disturbance, according to the gross notions he had of Christ's kingdom. Thou canst not follow me now - But Peter would not believe him. And he did follow him, Chap. xviii, 15. But it was afar off. And not without great loss.

38. The cock shall not have crowed - That is, cock crowing shall not be over, till thou hast denied me thrice - His three-fold denial was thrice foretold; first, at the time mentioned here; secondly, at that mentioned by St. Luke; lastly, at that recorded by St. Matthew and Mark.

XIV

1. Let not your heart be troubled - At my departure. Believe - This is the sum of all his discourse, which is urged till they did believe, Chap. xvi, 30. And then our Lord prays and departs.

2. In my Father's house are many mansions - Enough to receive both the holy angels, and your predecessors in the faith, and all that now believe, and a great multitude, which no man can number.

4. The way - Of faith, holiness, sufferings.

5. Thomas saith - Taking him in a gross sense.

6. To the question concerning the way, he answers, I am the way. To the question concerning knowledge, he answers, I am the truth. To the question whither, I am the life. The first is treated of in this verse; the second, ver. 7-17; the third, xiv, 18, &c.

7. Ye have known - Ye have begun to know him.

10. I am in the Father - The words that I speak, &c. - That is, I am one with the Father, in essence, in speaking, and in acting.

11. Believe me - On my own word, because I am God. The works - This respects not merely the miracles themselves, but his sovereign, Godlike way of performing them.

12. Greater works than these shall he do - So one apostle wrought miracles merely by his shadow, Acts v, 15; another by handkerchiefs carried from his body, Acts xix, 12; and all spake with various tongues. But the converting one sinner is a greater work than all these. Because I go to my Father - To send you the Holy Ghost.

15. If ye love me, keep my commandments - Immediately after faith he exhorts to love and good works.

16. And I will ask the Father - The 21st verse, ver. 21, shows the connection between this and the preceding verses. And he will give you another Comforter - The Greek word signifies also an advocate, instructer, or encourager. Another - For Christ himself was one. To remain with you forever - With you, and your followers in faith, to the end of the world.

17. The Spirit of truth - Who has, reveals, testifies, and defends the truth as it is in Jesus. Whom the world - All who do not love or fear God, cannot receive, because it seeth him not - Having no spiritual senses, no internal eye to discern him; nor consequently knoweth him. He shall be in you - As a constant guest. Your bodies and souls shall be temples of the Holy Ghost dwelling in you.

18. I will not leave you orphans - A word that is elegantly applied to those who have lost any dear friend. I come to you - What was certainly and speedily to be, our Lord speaks of as if it were already.

19. **But ye see me** - That is, ye shall certainly see me. **Because I live, ye shall live also** - Because I am the living One in my Divine nature, and shall rise again in my human nature, and live for ever in heaven: therefore ye shall live the life of faith and love on earth, and hereafter the life of glory.

20. **At that day** - When ye see me after my resurrection; but more eminently at the day of pentecost.

21. **He that hath my commandments** - Written in his heart. **I will manifest myself to him** - More abundantly.

23. **Jesus answered** - Because ye love and obey me, and they do not, therefore I will reveal myself to you, and not to them. **My Father will love him** - The more any man loves and obeys, the more God will love him. **And we will come to him, and make our abode with him** - Which implies such a large manifestation of the Divine presence and love, that the former in justification is as nothing in comparison of it.

26. **In my name** - For my sake, in my room, and as my agent. **He will teach you all things** - Necessary for you to know. Here is a clear promise to the apostles, and their successors in the faith, that the Holy Ghost will teach them all that truth which is needful for their salvation.

27. **Peace I leave with you** - Peace in general; peace with God and with your own consciences. **My peace** - In particular; that peace which I enjoy, and which I create, I give - At this instant. **Not as the world giveth** - Unsatisfying unsettled, transient; but filling the soul with constant, even tranquillity. Lord, evermore give us this peace! How serenely may we pass through the most turbulent scenes of life, when all is quiet and harmonious within! Thou hast made peace through the blood of thy cross. May we give all diligence to preserve the inestimable gift inviolate, till it issue in everlasting peace!

28. **God the Father is greater than I** - As he was man. As God, neither is greater nor less than the other.

29. **I have told you** - Of my going and return.

30. **The prince of this world is coming** - To make his grand assault. **But he hath nothing in me** - No right, no claim, or power. There is no guilt in me, to give him power over me; no corruption to take part with his temptation.

31. But I suffer him thus to assault me,

1. Because it is the Father's commission to me, Chap. x, 18.

2. To convince the world of my love to the Father, in being obedient unto death, Phil. ii, 8. **Arise, let us go hence** - Into the city, to the passover. All that has been related from Chap. xii, 31, was done and said on Thursday, without the city. But what follows in the fifteenth, sixteenth, and seventeenth chapters, was said in the city, on the very evening of the passover just before he went over the brook Kedron.

XV

1. **I am the true vine** - So the true bread, Chap. vi, 32; that is, the most excellent.

2. **Everyone that beareth fruit, he purifieth** - by obeying the truth, 1 Pet. i, 22; and by inward or outward sufferings, Heb. xii, 10, 11. So purity and fruitfulness help each other. **That it may bear more fruit** - For this is one of the noblest rewards God can bestow on former acts of obedience, to make us yet more holy, and fit for farther and more eminent service.

3. **Ye are clean** - All of you, to whom I now speak, are purged from the guilt and power of sin; **by the word** - Which, applied by the Spirit, is the grand instrument of purifying the soul.

4. **Abide in me** - Ye who are now pure by living faith, producing all holiness; by which alone ye can be in me.

5. **I am the vine, ye are the branches** - Our Lord in this whole passage speaks of no branches but such as are, or at least were once, united to him by living faith.

6. **If any one abide not in me** - By living faith; not by Church communion only. He may thus abide in Christ, and be withered all the time, and cast into the fire at last. **He is cast out** - Of the vineyard, the invisible Church. Therefore he was in it once.

7. **If ye abide in me, ye shall ask** - Prayers themselves are a fruit of faith, and they produce more fruit.

8. **So shall ye be my disciples** - Worthy of the name. To be a disciple of Christ is both the foundation and height of Christianity.

9. **Abide ye in my love** - Keep your place in my affection. See that ye do not forfeit that invaluable blessing. How needless a caution, if it were impossible for them not to abide therein?

10. **If ye keep my commandments, ye shall abide in my love** - On these terms, and no other, ye shall remain the objects of my special affection.

11. **That my joy might remain in you** - The same joy which I feel in loving the Father, and keeping his commandments.

12. Your joy will be full, if ye so love one another.

13. Greater love - To his friends. He here speaks of them only.

14. Ye are my friends, if ye do whatsoever I command you - On this condition, not otherwise. A thunderbolt for Antinomianism! Who then dares assert that God's love does not at all depend on man's works?

15. All things - Which might be of service to you.

16. Ye - My apostles, have not chosen me, but I have chosen you - As clearly appears from the sacred history: and appointed you, that ye may go and bear fruit - I have chosen and appointed you for this end, that ye may go and convert sinners: and that your fruit may remain - That the fruit of your labours may remain to the end of the world; yea, to eternity; that whatsoever ye shall ask - The consequence of your going and bearing fruit will be, that all your prayers will be heard.

19. Because ye are not of the world, therefore the world hateth you - Because your maxims, tempers, actions, are quite opposite to theirs. For the very same reason must the world in all ages hate those who are not of the world.

20. John xiii, 16; Matt. x, 24; Luke vi, 40.

21. All these things will they do to you, because they know not him that sent me - And in all ages and nations they who know not God will, for this cause, hate and persecute those that do.

22. They had not had sin - Not in this respect.

23. He that hateth me - As every unbeliever doth, For as the love of God is inseparable from faith, so is the hatred of God from unbelief.

25. Psalm lxix, 4.

26. When the Comforter is come, whom I will send from the Father, the Spirit of truth, who proceedeth from the Father, he shall testify of me - The Spirit's coming, and being sent by our Lord from the Father, to testify of him, are personal characters, and plainly distinguish him from the Father and the Son; and his title as the Spirit of truth, together with his proceeding from the Father, can agree to none but a Divine person. And that he proceeds from the Son, as well as from the Father, may be fairly argued from his being called the Spirit of Christ, 1 Pet. i, 11; and from his being here said to be sent by Christ from the Father, as well as sent by the Father in his name.

XVI

2. The time cometh, that whosoever killeth you will think he doth God service - But, blessed be God, the time is so far past, that those who bear the name of Christ do not now generally suppose they do him service by killing each other for a difference in opinion or mode of worship.

3. They have not known the Father nor me - This is the true root of persecution in all its forms.

4. I did not tell you these things at the beginning, because I was with you - To bear the chief shock in my own person, and to screen you from it.

5. None of you asketh me - Now when it is most seasonable. Peter did ask this before, Chap. xiii, 36.

7. It is expedient for you - In respect of the Comforter, ver. 7, &c., and of me, ver. 16, &c., and of the Father, ver. 23, &c.

8. He - Observe his twofold office; toward the world, ver. 8, &c.; toward believers, ver. 12, &c.: will convince - All of the world - Who do not obstinately resist, by your preaching and miracles, of sin, and of righteousness, and of judgment - He who is convinced of sin either accepts the righteousness of Christ, or is judged with Satan. An abundant accomplishment of this we find in the Acts of the Apostles.

9. Of sin - Particularly of unbelief, which is the confluence of all sins, and binds them all down upon us.

10. Of righteousness, because I go to my Father - Which the Spirit will testify, though ye do not then see me. But I could not go to him if I were not righteous.

11. The prince of this world is judged - And in consequence thereof dethroned, deprived of the power he had so long usurped over men. Yet those who reject the deliverance offered them will remain slaves of Satan still.

12. I have yet many things to say - Concerning my passion, death, resurrection, and the consequences of it. These things we have, not in uncertain traditions, but in the Acts, the Epistles, and the Revelation. But ye cannot bear them now - Both because of your littleness of faith, and your immoderate sorrow.

13. When he is come - It is universally allowed that the Father, Son, and Holy Ghost dwell in all believers. And the internal agency of the Holy Ghost is generally admitted. That of the Father and the Son, as represented in this Gospel, deserves our deepest consideration.

15. All things that the Father hath are mine - Could any creature say this?

16. A little while and ye shall not see me - When I am buried: and again, a little while, and ye shall see me - When I am risen: because I go to my Father - I die and rise again, in order to ascend to my Father.

19. Jesus said to them - Preventing their question.

20. Ye will weep and lament - When ye see me dead; but your sorrow will be turned into joy - When ye see me risen.

22. Ye now therefore have sorrow - This gives us no manner of authority to assert all believers must come into a state of darkness. They never need lose either their peace, or love, or the witness that they are the children of God. They never can lose these, but either through sin, or ignorance, or vehement temptation, or bodily disorder.

23. Ye shall not question me about any thing - Which you do not now understand. You will not need to inquire of me; for you will know all things clearly. Whatsoever ye shall ask - Knowledge, love, or any thing else, he will give it - Our Lord here gives us a charte blanche. Believer, write down what thou wilt. He had said, Chap. xiv, 13, I will do it, where the discourse was of glorifying the Father through the Son. Here, speaking of the love of the Father to believers, he saith, He will give it.

24. Hitherto ye have asked nothing in my name - For they had asked him directly for all they wanted.

26. At that day ye shall ask - For true knowledge begets prayer. And I say not that I will pray - This in nowise implies that he will not: it means only, The Father himself now loves you, not only because of my intercession, but also because of the faith and love which he hath wrought in you.

30. Thou knowest all things - Even our hearts. Although no question is asked thee, yet thou answerest the thoughts of every one. By this we believe that thou camest forth from God - They, as it were, echo back the words which he had spoken in ver. 27, implying, We believe in God; we believe also in thee.

XVII

In this chapter our Lord prays,

1. For himself, ver. 1-5. John xvii, 1-5
2. For the apostles, ver. 6-19; John xvii, 6-19 and again, ver. 24- 26. John xvii, 24-26
3. For all believers, ver. 20-23. John xvii, 20-23 And
4. For the world, ver. 21-23. John xvii, 21-23 In his prayer he comprises all he had said from 31, and seals, as it were, all he had hitherto done, beholding things past, present, and to come. This chapter contains the easiest words, and the deepest sense of any in all the Scripture: yet is here no incoherent rhapsody, but the whole is closely and exactly connected.

1. Father - This simplicity of appellation highly became the only- begotten Son of God; to which a believer then makes the nearest approach, when he is fullest of love and humble confidence. The hour is come - The appointed time for it; glorify thy Son - The Son glorified the Father, both before and after his own glorification. When he speaks to the Father he does not style himself the Son of man.

2. As thou hast given him power over all flesh - This answers to glorify thy Son. That he may give eternal life, &c.-This answers to that thy Son may glorify thee. To all whom thou hast given him - To all believers. This is a clear proof that Christ designed his sacrifice should avail for all: yea, that all flesh, every man, should partake of everlasting life. For as the Father had given him power over all flesh, so he gave himself a ransom for all.

3. To know - By loving, holy faith, thee the only true God - The only cause and end of all things; not excluding the Son and the Holy Ghost, no more than the Father is excluded from being Lord, 1 Cor. viii, 6; but the false gods of the heathens; and Jesus Christ - As their prophet, priest, and king: this is life eternal - It is both the way to, and the essence of, everlasting happiness.

4. I have finished the work - Thus have I glorified thee, laying the foundation of thy kingdom on earth.

5. The glory which I had - He does not say received - He always had it, till he emptied himself of it in the days of his flesh.

6. I have manifested thy name - All thy attributes; and in particular thy paternal relation to believers; to the men whom thou hast given me - The apostles, and so ver. 12. They were thine - By creation, and by descent from Abraham. And thou hast given them me - By giving them faith in what I have spoken. So ver. 9.

7. Now they know that all things - Which I have done and spoken, are of thee - And consequently right and true.

8. They have received them - By faith.

9. I pray not for the world - Not in these petitions, which are adapted to the state of believers only. (He prays for the world at ver. 21, 23, that they may believe - That they may know God hath sent him.) This no more proves that our Lord did not pray for the world, both before and afterward, than his praying for the apostles alone, ver. 6-19, proves that he did not pray for them also which shall believe through their word, ver. 20.

10. All things that are mine are thine, and that are thine are mine - These are very high and strong expressions, too grand for any mere creature to use; as implying that all things whatsoever, inclusive of

the Divine nature, perfections, and operations, are the common property of the Father and the Son. And this is the original ground of that peculiar property, which both the Father and the Son have in the persons who were given to Christ as Mediator; according to what is said in the close of the verse, of his being glorified by them; namely, believing in him, and so acknowledging his glory.

11. Keep them through thy name - Thy power, mercy, wisdom, that they may be one - with us and with each other; one body, separate from the world: as we are - By resemblance to us, though not equality.

12. Those whom thou hast given me I have guarded, and none of them is lost, but the son of perdition - So one even of them whom God had given him is lost. So far was even that decree from being unchangeable! That the Scripture might be fulfilled - That is, whereby the Scripture was fulfilled. The son of perdition signifies one that deservedly perishes; as a son of death, 2 Sam. xii, 5; children of hell, Matt. xxiii, 15, and children of wrath, Eph. ii, 3, signify persons justly obnoxious to death, hell, wrath, Psalm cix, 8.

13. In the world - That is, before I leave the world. My joy - The joy I feel at going to the Father.

15. That thou wouldest take them out of the world - Not yet: but that thou wouldest keep them from the evil one - Who reigns therein.

17. Sanctify - Consecrate them by the anointing of thy Spirit to their office, and perfect them in holiness, by means of thy word.

19. I sanctify myself - I devote myself as a victim, to be sacrificed.

20. For them who will believe - In all ages.

21. As thou art in me - This also is to be understood in a way of similitude, and not of sameness or equality. That the world may believe - Here Christ prays for the world. Observe the sum of his whole prayer,

    1. Receive me into thy own and my glory;

    2. Let my apostles share therein;

    3. And all other believers:

    4. And let all the world believe.

22. The glory which thou hast given me, I have given them - The glory of the only begotten shines in all the sons of God. How great is the majesty of Christians.

24. Here he returns to the apostles. I will - He asks, as having a right to be heard, and prays, not as a servant, but a Son: that they may behold my glory - Herein Is the happiness of heaven, 1 John iii, 2.

25. Righteous Father - The admission of believers to God through Christ, flows even from the justice of God.

26. I have declared to them thy name - Thy new, best name of love; that the love wherewith thou hast loved me - That thou and thy love, and I and my love, may be in them - That they may love me with that love.

XVIII

1. A garden - Probably belonging to one of his friends. He might retire to this private place, not only for the advantage of secret devotion, but also that the people might not be alarmed at his apprehension, nor attempt, in the first sallies of their zeal, to rescue him in a tumultuous manner. Kedron was (as the name signifies) a dark shady valley, on the east side of Jerusalem, between the city and the Mount of Olives, through which a little brook ran, which took its name from it. It was this brook, which David, a type of Christ, went over with the people, weeping in his flight from Absalom. Matt. xxvi, 30; Mark xiv, 26; Luke xxii, 39.

2. Mark xiv, 43; Luke xxii, 47.

3. A troop of soldiers - A cohort of Roman foot.

6. As soon as he said, I am he, they went backward and fell to the ground - How amazing is it, that they should renew the assault, after so sensible an experience both of his power and mercy! But probably the priests among them might persuade themselves and their attendants, that this also was done by Beelzebub; and that it was through the providence of God, not the indulgence of Jesus, that they received no further damage.

8. If ye seek me, let these (my disciples) go - It was an eminent instance of his power over the spirits of men, that they so far obeyed this word, as not to seize even Peter, when he had cut off the ear of Malchus.

9. John xvii, 12.

10. Then Simon Peter - No other evangelist names him. Nor could they safely. But St. John, writing after his death, might do it without any such inconvenience.

13. Annas had been high priest before his son-in-law Caiaphas. And though he had for some time resigned that office, yet they paid so much regard to his age and experience, that they brought Christ to Annas first. But we do not read of any thing remarkable which passed at the house of Annas; for, which

reason, his being carried thither is omitted by the other evangelists. Matt. xxvi, 57; Mark xiv, 53; Luke xxii, 54.

17. *Art thou also* - As well as the others, one of this man's disciples - She does not appear to have asked with any design to hurt him.

20. *I spake openly* - As to the manner: continually - As to the time: in the synagogue and temple - As to the place. In secret have I said nothing - No point of doctrine which I have not taught in public.

21. *Why askest thou me* - Whom thou wilt not believe?

22. *Answerest thou the high priest so?* - With so little reverence?

24. *Now Annas had sent him to Caiaphas* - As is implied ver. 13. Bound - Being still bound, ver. 12.

28. *They went not into the palace themselves, lest they should be defiled* - By going into a house which was not purged from leaven, Deut. xvi, 4. Matt. xxvii, 2; Mark xv, 1; Luke xxiii, 1.

31. *It is not lawful for us to put any man to death* - The power of inflicting capital punishment had been taken from them that very year. So the scepter was departed from Judah, and transferred to the Romans.

32. *Signifying what death he should die* - For crucifixion was not a Jewish, but a Roman punishment. So that had he not been condemned by the Roman governor, he could not have been crucified. Chap. iii, 14.

36. *My kingdom is not of this world* - Is not an external, but a spiritual kingdom; that I might not be delivered to the Jews - Which Pilate had already attempted to do, ver. 31, and afterward actually did, chap. xix, 16.

37. *Thou sayest* - The truth. To this end was I born - Speaking of his human origin: his Divine was above Pilate's comprehension. Yet it is intimated in the following words, I came into the world, that I might witness to the truth - Which was both declared to the Jews, and in the process of his passion to the princes of the Gentiles also. Everyone that is of the truth - That is, a lover of it, heareth my voice - A universal maxim. Every sincere lover of truth will hear him, so as to understand and practice what he saith.

38. *What is truth?* - Said Pilate, a courtier; perhaps meaning what signifies truth? Is that a thing worth hazarding your life for? So he left him presently, to plead with the Jews for him, looking upon him as an innocent but weak man.

XIX

1. Matt. xxvii, 26; Mark xv, 15.

7. *By our law he ought to die, because he made himself the Son of God* - Which they understood in the highest sense, and therefore accounted blasphemy.

8. *He was the more afraid* - He seems to have been afraid before of shedding innocent blood.

9. *Whence art thou?* - That is, whose son art thou?

11. *Thou couldst have no power over me* - For I have done nothing to expose me to the power of any magistrate. Therefore he that delivered me to thee, namely, Caiaphas, knowing this, is more blamable than thou.

13. *Pilate sat down on the judgment seat* - Which was then without the palace, in a place called, in Greek, the pavement, on account of a beautiful piece of Mosaic work, with which the floor was adorned: but in Hebrew, Gabbatha - Or the high place, because it stood on an eminence, so that the judge sitting on his throne might be seen and heard by a considerable number of people.

14. *It was the preparation of the passover* - For this reason both the Jews and Pilate were desirous to bring the matter to a conclusion. Every Friday was called the preparation, (namely, for the Sabbath.) And as often as the passover fell on a Friday, that day was called the preparation of the passover.

17. *Bearing his cross* - Not the whole cross, (for that was too large and heavy,) but the transverse beam of it, to which his hands were afterward fastened. This they used to make the person to be executed carry. Matt. xxvii, 31; Mark xv, 20; Luke xxiii, 26.

19. *Jesus of Nazareth, the king of the Jews* - Undoubtedly these were the very words, although the other evangelists do not express them at large.

20. *It was written in Latin* - For the majesty of the Roman empire; in Hebrew - Because it was the language of the nation; and in Greek - For the information of the Hellenists, who spoke that language, and came in great numbers to the feast.

22. *What I have written, I have written* - That shall stand.

23. *The vesture* - The upper garment.

24. *They parted my garments among them* - No circumstance of David's life bore any resemblance to this, or to several other passages in the 22nd Psalm. So that in this scripture, as in some others, the prophet seems to have been thrown into a preternatural ecstasy, wherein, personating the Messiah, he spoke barely what the Spirit dictated, without any regard to himself. Psalm xxii, 18.

25. His mother's sister - But we do not read she had any brother. She was her father's heir, and as such transmitted the right of the kingdom of David to Jesus: Mary, the wife of Cleopas - Called likewise Alpheus, the father, as Mary was the mother of James, and Joses, and Simon, and Judas.

27. Behold thy mother - To whom thou art now to perform the part of a son in my place, a peculiar honour which Christ conferred on him. From that hour - From the time of our Lord's death.

29. A stalk of hyssop - Which in those countries grows exceeding large and strong. Psalm lxix, 21.

30. It is finished - My suffering: the purchase of man's redemption. He delivered up his spirit - To God, Matt. xxvii, 50.

31. Lest the bodies should remain on the cross on the Sabbath - Which they would have accounted a profanation of any Sabbath, but of that in particular. For that Sabbath was a great day - Being not only a Sabbath, but the second day of the feast of unleavened bread (from whence they reckoned the weeks to pentecost:) and also the day for presenting and offering the sheaf of new corn: so that it was a treble solemnity.

34. Forthwith there came out blood and water - It was strange, seeing he was dead, that blood should come out; more strange, that water also; and most strange of all, that both should come out immediately, at one time, and yet distinctly. It was pure and true water, as well as pure and true blood. The asseveration of the beholder and testifier of it, shows both the truth and greatness of the miracle and mystery.

35. His testimony is true - Valid, unexceptionable. And he knoweth - And his conscience beareth him witness, that he testifieth this for no other end, than that ye may believe.

36. A bone of it shall not be broken - This was originally spoken of the paschal lamb, an eminent type of Christ. Exod. xii, 46.

37. They shall look on him whom they have pierced - He was pierced by the soldier's spear. They who have occasioned his sufferings by their sins (and who has not?) shall either look upon him in this world with penitential sorrow: or with terror, when he cometh in the clouds of heaven, Rev. i, 7. Zech. xii, 10.

38. Joseph of Arimathea asked Pilate - And Nicodemus also came - Acknowledging Christ, when even his chosen disciples forsook him. In that extremity Joseph was no longer afraid, Nicodemus no longer ashamed.

41. In the place where he was crucified - There was a garden in the same tract of land: but the cross did not stand in the garden.

42. Because of the preparation - That is, they chose the rather to lay him in that sepulchre which was nigh, because it was the day before the Sabbath, which also was drawing to an end, so that they had no time to carry him far.

XX

1. Matt. xxviii, 1; Mark xvi, 1; Luke xxiv, 1.
3. Peter went out - Of the city.
6. Peter seeth the linen clothes lie - and the napkin folded up - The angels who ministered to him when he rose, undoubtedly folded up the napkin and linen clothes.
8. He saw - That the body was not there, and believed - That they had taken it away as Mary said.
9. For as yet - They had no thought of his rising again.
10. They went home - Not seeing what they could do farther.
11. But Mary stood - With more constancy. Mark xvi, 9.
16. Jesus saith to her, Mary - With his usual voice and accent.
17. Touch me not - Or rather, Do not cling to me (for she held him by the feet,) Matt. xxviii, 9. Detain me not now. You will have other opportunities of conversing with me. For I am not ascended to my Father - I have not yet left the world. But go immediately to my brethren -- thus does he intimate in the strongest manner the forgiveness of their fault, even without ever mentioning it. These exquisite touches, which everywhere abound in the evangelical writings, show how perfectly Christ knew our frame. I ascend - He anticipates it in his thoughts, and so speaks of it as a thing already present. To my Father and your Father, to my God and your God - This uncommon expression shows that the only-begotten Son has all kind of fellowship with God. And a fellowship with God the Father, some way resembling his own, he bestows upon his brethren. Yet he does not say, Our God: for no creature can be raised to an equality with him: but my God and your God: intimating that the Father is his in a singular and incommunicable manner; and ours through him, in such a kind as a creature is capable of.

19. Mark xvi, 14 Luke xxiv, 36.

21. Peace be unto you - This is the foundation of the mission of a true Gospel minister, peace in his own soul, 2 Cor. iv, 1. As the Father hath sent me, so send I you - Christ was the apostle of the Father, Heb. iii, 1. Peter and the rest, the apostles of Christ.

22. He breathed on them - New life and vigour, and saith, as ye receive this breath out of my

mouth, so receive ye the Spirit out of my fulness: the Holy Ghost influencing you in a peculiar manner, to fit you for your great embassy. This was an earnest of pentecost.

23. Whosoever sins ye remit - (According to the tenor of the Gospel, that is, supposing them to repent and believe) they are remitted, and whosoever sins ye retain (supposing them to remain impenitent) they are retained. So far is plain. But here arises a difficulty. Are not the sins of one who truly repents, and unfeignedly believes in Christ, remitted, without sacerdotal absolution? And are not the sins of one who does not repent or believe, retained even with it? What then does this commission imply? Can it imply any more than,

1. A power of declaring with authority the Christian terms of pardon; whose sins are remitted and whose retained? As in our daily form of absolution; and

2. A power of inflicting and remitting ecclesiastical censures? That is, of excluding from, and re-admitting into, a Christian congregation.

26. After eight days - On the next Sunday.

28. And Thomas said, My Lord and my God - The disciples had said, We have seen the Lord. Thomas now not only acknowledges him to be the Lord, as he had done before, and to be risen, as his fellow disciples had affirmed, but also confesses his Godhead, and that more explicitly than any other had yet done. And all this he did without putting his hand upon his side.

30. Jesus wrought many miracles, which are not written in this book - Of St. John, nor indeed of the other evangelists.

31. But these things are written that ye may believe - That ye may be confirmed in believing. Faith cometh sometimes by reading; though ordinarily by hearing.

XXI

2. There were together - At home, in one house.

4. They knew not that it was Jesus - Probably their eyes were holden.

6. They were not able to draw it for the multitude of fishes - This was not only a demonstration of the power of our Lord, but a kind supply for them and their families, and such as might be of service to them, when they waited afterward in Jerusalem. It was likewise an emblem of the great success which should attend them as fishers of men.

7. Peter girt on his upper coat (for he was stript of it before) - Reverencing the presence of his Lord: and threw himself into the sea - To swim to him immediately. The love of Christ draws men through fire and water.

12. Come ye and dine - Our Lord needed not food. And none presumed - To ask a needless question.

14. The third time - That he appeared to so many of the apostles together.

15. Simon, son of Jonah - The appellation Christ had given him, when be made that glorious confession, Matt. xvi, 16, the remembrance of which might make him more deeply sensible of his late denial of him whom he had so confessed. Lovest thou me? - Thrice our Lord asks him, who had denied him thrice: more than these - Thy fellow disciples do? - Peter thought so once, Matt. xxvi, 33, but he now answers only- I love thee, without adding more than these. Thou knowest - He had now learnt by sad experience that Jesus knew his heart. My lambs - The weakest and tenderest of the flock.

17. Because he said the third time - As if he did not believe him.

18. When thou art old - He lived about thirty-six years after this: another shall gird thee - They were tied to the cross till the nails were driven in; and shall carry thee - With the cross: whither thou wouldest not - According to nature; to the place where the cross was set up.

19. By what death he should glorify God - It is not only by acting, but chiefly by suffering, that the saints glorify God. Follow me - Showing hereby likewise what death he should die.

20. Peter turning - As he was walking after Christ. Seeth the disciple whom Jesus loved following him - There is a peculiar spirit and tenderness in this plain passage. Christ orders St. Peter to follow him in token of his readiness to be crucified in his cause. St. John stays not for the call; he rises and follows him too; but says not one word of his own love or zeal. He chose that the action only should speak this; and even when he records the circumstance, he tells us not what that action meant, but with great simplicity relates the fact only. If here and there a generous heart sees and emulates it, be it so; but he is not solicitous that men should admire it. It was addressed to his beloved Master, and it was enough that he understood it.

22. If I will that he tarry - Without dying, till I come - To judgment. Certainly he did tarry, till Christ came to destroy Jerusalem. And who can tell, when or how he died? What is that to thee? - Who art to follow me long before.

23. The brethren -- that is, the Christians. Our Lord himself taught them that appellation, chap. xx, 17. Yet Jesus did not say to him, that he should not die - Not expressly. And St. John himself, at the time of writing his Gospel, seems not to have known clearly, whether he should die or not.

24. This is the disciple who testifieth - Being still alive after he had wrote. And we know that his testimony is true - The Church added these words to St. John's, Gospel, as Tertius did those to St. Paul's Epistle to the Romans, Rom. xvi, 22.

25. If they were to be written particularly - Every fact, and all the circumstances of it. I suppose - This expression, which softens the hyperbole, shows that St. John wrote this verse.

NOTES ON THE ACTS OF THE APOSTLES

THIS book, in which St. Luke records the actions of the apostles, particularly of St. Peter and St. Paul, (whose companion in travel he was,) is as it were the center between the Gospel and the Epistles. It contains, after a very brief re-capitulation of the evangelical history, a continuation of the history of Christ, the event of his predictions, and a kind of supplement to what he had before spoken to his disciples, by the Holy Ghost now given unto them. It contains also the seeds, and first stamina of all those things, which are enlarged upon in the epistles. The Gospels treat of Christ the head. The Acts show that the same things befell his body; which is animated by his Spirit, persecuted by the world, defended and exalted by God. In this book is shown the Christian doctrine, and the method of applying it to Jews, heathens, and believers; that is, to those who are to be converted, and those who are converted: the hindrances of it in particular men, in several kinds of men, in different ranks and nations: the propagation of the Gospel, and that grand revolution among both Jews and heathens: the victory thereof, in spite of all opposition, from all the power, malice, and wisdom of the whole world, spreading from one chamber into temples, houses, streets, markets, fields, inns, prisons, camps, courts, chariots, ships, villages, cities, islands: to Jews, heathens, magistrates, generals, soldiers, eunuchs, captives, slaves, women, children, sailors: to Athens, and at length to Rome.

THE PARTS OF IT ARE SEVEN
1. Pentecost, with its antecedents Chap. i-ii
2. Transactions w/the Jews, in Jerusalem, in all Judea, and in Samaria iii-ix
3. Transactions at Cesarea, and the reception of the Gentiles x-xi
4. The first course of Barnabas and Paul among the Gentiles xiii- xiv
5. The embassy to, and council at Jerusalem: liberty of the Gentiles xv
6. The second course of St. Paul xvi-xix
7. His third, as far as Rom. xix-xxviii

THE ACTS

I

1. *The former treatise* - In that important season which reached from the resurrection of Christ to his ascension, the former treatise ends, and this begins: this describing the Acts of the Holy Ghost, (by the apostles,) as that does the acts of Jesus Christ. *Of all things* - In a summary manner: which Jesus *began to do - until the day* - That is, of all things which Jesus did from the beginning till that day.

2. *After having given commandment* - In the 3rd verse St. Luke expresses in general terms what Christ said to his apostles during those forty days. But in the 4th and following verses he declares what he said on the day of his ascension. He had brought his former account down to that day; and from that day begins the Acts of the Apostles.

3. *Being seen by them forty days* - That is, many times during that space. *And speaking of the things pertaining to the kingdom of God* - Which was the sum of all his discourses with them before his passion also.

4. *Wait for the promise of the Father, which ye have heard from me* - When he was with them a little before, as it is recorded, Luke xxiv, 49.

5. *Ye shall be baptized with the Holy Ghost* - And so are all true believers to the end of the world. But the extraordinary gifts of the Holy Ghost also are here promised.

6. *Dost thou at this time* - At the time thou now speakest of? not many days hence? *restore the kingdom to Israel?* - They still seemed to dream of an outward, temporal kingdom, in which the Jews should have dominion over all nations. It seems they came in a body, having before concerted the design, to ask when this kingdom would come.

7. *The times or the seasons* - Times, in the language of the Scriptures, denote a longer; seasons, a shorter space. *Which the Father hath put in his own power* - To be revealed when and to whom it pleaseth him.

8. *But ye shall receive power - and shall be witnesses to me* - That is, ye shall be empowered to

witness my Gospel, both by your preaching and suffering.

12. A Sabbath-day's journey - The Jews generally fix this to two thousand cubits, which is not a mile.

13. They went up into the upper room - The upper rooms, so frequently mentioned in Scripture, were chambers in the highest part of the house, set apart by the Jews for private prayer. These, on account of their being so retired and convenient, the apostles now used for all the offices of religion. Matt. x, 2; Mark iii, 14; Luke vi, 13.

14. His brethren -- his near kinsmen, who for some time did not believe; it seems not till near his death.

15. The number of persons together - Who were together in the upper room. were a hundred and twenty - But he had undoubtedly many more in other places; of whom more than five hundred saw him at once after his resurrection, 1 Cor. xv, 6.

16. Psalm xli, 9.

18. This man purchased a field with the reward of iniquity - That is, a field was purchased with the reward of his iniquity; though very possibly Judas might design the purchase. And falling down on his face - It seems the rope broke before, or as he died.

19. In their own tongue - This expression, That is, the field of blood, St. Luke seems to have added to the words of St. Peter, for the use of Theophilus and other readers who did not understand Hebrew.

20. His bishopric - That is, his apostleship. Psalm lxix, 25.

21. All the time that the Lord Jesus was going in and out - That is, conversing familiarly: over us - as our Master. Psalm cix, 8.

22. To be a witness with us of his resurrection - And of the circumstances which preceded and followed it.

23. And they appointed two - So far the faithful could go by consulting together, but no further. Therefore here commenced the proper use of the lot, whereby a matter of importance, which cannot be determined by any ordinary method, is committed to the Divine decision.

25. Fell - By his transgression - Some time before his death: to go to his own place - That which his crimes had deserved, and which he had chosen for himself, far from the other apostles, in the region of death.

II

1. At the pentecost of Sinai, in the Old Testament, and the pentecost of Jerusalem, in the New, where the two grand manifestations of God, the legal and the evangelical; the one from the mountain, and the other from heaven; the terrible, and the merciful one. They were all with one accord in one place - So here was a conjunction of company, minds, and place; the whole hundred and twenty being present.

2. And suddenly there came a sound from heaven - So will the Son of man come to judgment. And it filled all the house - That is, all that part of the temple where they were sitting.

3. And there appeared distinct tongues, as of fire - That is, small flames of fire. This is all which the phrase, tongues of fire, means in the language of the seventy. Yet it might intimate God's touching their tongues as it were (together with their hearts) with Divine fire: his giving them such words as were active and penetrating, even as flaming fire.

4. And they began to speak with other tongues - The miracle was not in the ears of the hearers, (as some have unaccountably supposed,) but in the mouth of the speakers. And this family praising God together, with the tongues of all the world, was an earnest that the whole world should in due time praise God in their various tongues. As the Spirit gave them utterance - Moses, the type of the law, was of a slow tongue; but the Gospel speaks with a fiery and flaming one.

5. And there were dwelling in Jerusalem Jews - Gathered from all parts by the peculiar providence of God.

6. The multitude came together, and were confounded - The motions of their minds were swift and various.

9. Judea - The dialect of which greatly differed from that of Galilee. Asia - The country strictly so called.

10. Roman sojourners - Born at Rome, but now living at Jerusalem. These seem to have come to Jerusalem after those who are above mentioned. All of them were partly Jews by birth, and partly proselytes.

11. Cretans - One island seems to be mentioned for all. The wonderful works of God - Probably those which related to the miracles, death, resurrection, and ascension of Christ, together with the effusion of his Spirit, as a fulfilment of his promises, and the glorious dispensations of Gospel grace.

12. They were all amazed - All the devout men.

13. But others mocking - The world begins with mocking, thence proceeds to cavilling, chap. iv, 7; to threats, iv, 17; to imprisoning, chap. v, 18; blows, v, 40; to slaughter, chap. vii, 58. These mockers

appear to have been some of the natives of Judea, and inhabitants of Jerusalem, (who understood only the dialect of the country,) by the apostle's immediately directing his discourse to them in the next verse. They are full of sweet wine - So the Greek word properly signifies. There was no new wine so early in the year as pentecost. Thus natural men are wont to ascribe supernatural things to mere natural causes; and many times as impudently and unskilfully as in the present case.

14. Then Peter standing up - All the gestures, all the words of Peter, show the utmost sobriety; lifted up his voice - With cheerfulness and boldness; and said to them - This discourse has three parts; each of which, ver. 14, 22, 29, begins with the same appellation, men: only to the last part he prefixes with more familiarity the additional word brethren. Men of Judea - That is, ye that are born in Judea. St. Peter spoke in Hebrew, which they all understood.

15. It is but the third hour of the day - That is, nine in the morning. And on the solemn festivals the Jews rarely ate or drank any thing till noon.

16. But this is that which was spoken of by the prophet - But there is another and better way of accounting for this. Joel ii, 28

17. The times of the Messiah are frequently called the last days, the Gospel being the last dispensation of Divine grace. I will pour out of my Spirit - Not on the day of pentecost only, upon all flesh - On persons of every age, sex, and rank. And your young men shall see visions - In young men the outward sense, are most vigourous, and the bodily strength is entire, whereby they are best qualified to sustain the shock which usually attends the visions of God. In old men the internal senses are most vigourous, suited to divine dreams. Not that the old are wholly excluded from the former, nor the young from the latter.

18. And upon my servants - On those who are literally in a state of servitude.

19. And I will show prodigies in heaven above, and signs on earth beneath - Great Revelations of grace are usually attended with great judgments on those who reject it. In heaven - Treated of, ver. 20. On earth - Described in this verse. Such signs were those mentioned, ver. 22, before the passion of Christ; which are so mentioned as to include also those at the very time of the passion and resurrection, at the destruction of Jerusalem, and at the end of the world. Terrible indeed were those prodigies in particular which preceded the destruction of Jerusalem: such as the flaming sword hanging over the city, and the fiery comet pointing down upon it for a year; the light that shone upon the temple and the altar in the night, as if it had been noon-day; the opening of the great and heavy gate of the temple without hands; the voice heard from the most holy place, Let us depart hence; the admonition of Jesus the son of Ananus, crying for seven years together, Woe, woe, woe; the vision of contending armies in the air, and of entrenchments thrown up against a city there represented; the terrible thunders and lightnings, and dreadful earthquakes, which every one considered as portending some great evil: all which, through the singular providence of God, are particularly recorded by Josephus. Blood - War and slaughter. Fire - Burnings of houses and towns, involving all in clouds of smoke.

20. The moon shall be turned into blood - A bloody colour: before the day of the Lord - Eminently the last day; though not excluding any other day or season, wherein the Lord shall manifest his glory, in taking vengeance of his adversaries.

21. But - whosoever shall call on the name of the Lord - This expression implies the whole of religion, and particularly prayer uttered in faith; shall be saved - From all those plagues; from sin and hell.

23. Him, being delivered by the determinate counsel and foreknowledge of God - The apostle here anticipates an objection, Why did God suffer such a person to be so treated? Did he not know what wicked men intended to do? And had he not power to prevent it? Yea. He knew all that those wicked men intended to do. And he had power to blast all their designs in a moment. But he did not exert that power, because he so loved the world! Because it was the determined counsel of his love, to redeem mankind from eternal death, by the death of his only-begotten Son.

24. Having loosed the pains of death - The word properly means, the pains of a woman in travail. As it was not possible that he should be held under it - Because the Scripture must needs be fulfilled.

25. Psalm xvi, 8.

27. Thou wilt not leave my soul in hades - The invisible world. But it does not appear, that ever our Lord went into hell. His soul, when it was separated from the body, did not go thither, but to paradise, Luke xxiii, 43. The meaning is, Thou wilt not leave my soul in its separate state, nor suffer my body to be corrupted.

28. Thou hast made known to me the ways of life - That is, Thou hast raised me from the dead. Thou wilt fill me with joy by thy countenance - When I ascend to thy right hand.

29. The patriarch - A more honourable title than king.

30. Psalm lxxxix, 4, &c.

32. He foreseeing this, spake of the resurrection Of Christ - St. Peter argues thus: It is plain, David did not speak this of himself. Therefore he spake of Christ's rising. But how does that promise of a kingdom imply his resurrection? Because he did not receive it before he died, and because his kingdom

was to endure forever, 2 Sam. vii, 13.

33. Being exalted by the right hand of God - By the right hand; that is, the mighty power of God. Our Lord was exalted at his ascension to God's right hand in heaven.

34. Sit thou on my right hand - In this and the following verse is an allusion to two ancient customs; one, to the highest honour that used to be paid to persons by placing them on the right hand, as Solomon did Bathsheba, when sitting on his throne, 1 Kings ii, 19; and the other, to the custom of conquerors, who used to tread on the necks of their vanquished enemies, as a token of their entire victory and triumph over them.

35. Until I make thine enemies thy footstool - This text is here quoted with the greatest address, as suggesting in the words of David, their great prophetic monarch, how certain their own ruin must be, if they went on to oppose Christ. Psalm cx, 1.

36. Lord - Jesus, after his exaltation, is constantly meant by this word in the New Testament, unless sometimes where it occurs, in a text quoted from the Old Testament.

37. They said to the apostles, Brethren - They did not style them so before.

38. Repent - And hereby return to God: be baptized - Believing in the name of Jesus - And ye shall receive the gift of the Holy Ghost - See the three-one God clearly proved. See chap. xxvi, 20. The gift of the Holy Ghost does not mean in this place the power of speaking with tongues. For the promise of this was not given to all that were afar off, in distant ages and nations. But rather the constant fruits of faith, even righteousness, and peace, and joy in the Holy Ghost. Whomsoever the Lord our God shall call - (Whether they are Jews or Gentiles) by his word and by his Spirit: and who are not disobedient to the heavenly calling. But it is observable St. Peter did not yet understand the very words he spoke.

40. And with many other words did he testify and exhort - In such an accepted time we should add line upon line, and not leave off, till the thing is done. Save yourselves from this perverse generation - Many of whom were probably mocking still.

41. And there were added - To the hundred and twenty.

42. And they continued steadfast - So their daily Church communion consisted in these four particulars:

1. Hearing the word;
2. Having all things common;
3. Receiving the Lord's Supper;
4. Prayer. Ye diffrent sects, who all declare, Lo here is Christ, and Christ is there; Your stronger proofs divinely give, And show me where the Christians live!

43. And fear came upon every soul - Of those who did not join with them: whereby persecution was prevented, till it was needful for them.

45. And sold their possessions - Their lands and houses; and goods - Their movables. And parted them to all as any one had need - To say the Christians did this only till the destruction of Jerusalem, is not true; for many did it long after. Not that there was any positive command for so doing: it needed not; for love constrained them. It was a natural fruit of that love wherewith each member of the community loved every other as his own soul. And if the whole Christian Church had continued in this spirit, this usage must have continued through all ages. To affirm therefore that Christ did not design it should continue, is neither more nor less than to affirm, that Christ did not design this measure of love should continue. I see no proof of this.

46. Continuing daily - breaking the bread - in the Lord's Supper, as did many Churches for some ages. They partook of their food with gladness and singleness of heart - They carried the same happy and holy temper through all their common actions: eating and working with the same spirit wherewith they prayed and received the Lord's Supper.

47. The Lord added daily such as were saved - From their sins: from the guilt and power of them.

III

1. The ninth hour - The Jews divided the time from sunrise to sunset into twelve hours; which were consequently of unequal length at different times of the year, as the days were longer or shorter. The third hour therefore was nine in the morning; the ninth, three in the afternoon; but not exactly. For the third hour was the middle space between sunrise and noon; which, if the sun rose at five, (the earliest hour of its rising in that climate,) was half an hour after eight: if at seven (the latest hour of its rising there) was half an hour after nine. The chief hours of prayer were the third and ninth; at which seasons the morning and evening sacrifices were offered, and incense (a kind of emblem representing prayer) burnt on the golden altar.

2. At the gate of the temple, called Beautiful - This gate was added by Herod the Great, between the court of the Gentiles and that of Israel. It was thirty cubits high, and fifteen broad, and made of Corinthian brass, more pompous in its workmanship and splendour than those that were covered with silver and gold.

6. Then said Peter, Silver and gold have I none - How unlike his supposed successor! Can the bishop of Rome either say or do the same?

12. Peter answered the people - Who were running together, and inquiring into the circumstances of the fact.

13. The God of our fathers - This was wisely introduced in the beginning of his discourse, that it might appear they taught no new religion, inconsistent with that of Moses, and were far from having the least design to divert their regards from the God of Israel. Hath glorified his Son - By this miracle, whom ye delivered up - When God had given him to you, and when ye ought to have received him as a most precious treasure, and to have preserved him with all your power.

14. Ye renounced the Holy One - Whom God had marked out as such; and the Just One - Even in the judgment of Pilate.

16. His name - Himself: his power and love. The faith which is by him - Of which he is the giver, as well as the object.

17. And now, brethren -- a word full of courtesy and compassion, I know - He speaks to their heart, that through ignorance ye did it - which lessened, though it could not take away, the guilt. As did also your rulers - The prejudice lying from the authority of the chief priests and elders, he here removes, but with great tenderness. He does not call them our, but your rulers. For as the Jewish dispensation ceased at the death of Christ, consequently so did the authority of its rulers.

18. But God - Who was not ignorant, permitted this which he had foretold, to bring good out of it.

19. Be converted - Be turned from sin and Satan unto God. See chap. xxvi, 20. But this term, so common in modern writings, very rarely occurs in Scripture: perhaps not once in the sense we now use it, for an entire change from vice to holiness. That the times of refreshing - Wherein God largely bestows his refreshing grace, may come - To you also. To others they will assuredly come, whether ye repent or no.

20. And he may send - The apostles generally speak of our Lord's second coming, as being just at hand. Who was before appointed - Before the foundation of the world.

21. Till the times of the restitution of all things - The apostle here comprises at once the whole course of the times of the New Testament, between our Lord's ascension and his coming in glory. The most eminent of these are the apostolic age, and that of the spotless Church, which will consist of all the Jews and Gentiles united, after all persecutions and apostacies are at an end.

22. The Lord shall raise you up a prophet like unto me - And that in many particulars. Moses instituted the Jewish Church: Christ instituted the Christian. With the prophesying of Moses was soon joined the effect, the deliverance of Israel from Egypt: with the prophesying of Christ that grand effect, the deliverance of his people from sin and death. Those who could not hear the voice of God, yet desired to hear that of Moses. Much more do those who are wearied with the law, desire to hear the voice of Christ. Moses spake to the people all, and only those things, which God had commanded him: so did Christ. But though he was like Moses, yet he was infinitely superior to him, in person, as well as in office. Deut. xviii, 15.

23. Every soul who will not hear that prophet, shall be destroyed from among the people - One cannot imagine a more masterly address than this, to warn the Jews of the dreadful consequence of their infidelity, in the very words of their favourite prophet, out of a pretended zeal for whom they rejected Christ.

24. These days - The days of the Messiah.

25. Ye are the sons of the prophets and of the covenant - That in, heirs of the prophecies. To you properly, as the first heirs, belong the prophecies and the covenant. Gen. xii, 3.

26. To bless you, by turning you from your iniquities - Which is the great Gospel blessing.

IV

1. And as they were speaking to the people, the priests - came upon them - So wisely did God order, that they should first bear a full testimony to the truth in the temple, and then in the great council; to which they could have had no access, had they not been brought before it as criminals.

2. The priests being grieved - That the name of Jesus was preached to the people; especially they were offended at the doctrine of his resurrection; for as they had put him to death, his rising again proved him to be the Just One, and so brought his blood upon their heads. The priests were grieved, lest their office and temple services should decline, and Christianity take root, through the preaching of the apostles, and their power of working miracles: the captain of the temple - Being concerned to prevent all sedition and disorder, the Sadducees - Being displeased at the overturning of all their doctrines, particularly with regard to the resurrection.

4. The number of the men - Beside women and children, were about five thousand - So many did our Lord now feed at once with the bread from heaven!

5. Rulers, and elders, and scribes - Who were eminent for power, for wisdom, and for learning.

6. Annas, who had been the high priest, and Caiaphas, who was so then.

7. By what name - By what authority, have ye done this? - They seem to speak ambiguously on purpose.

8. Then Peter, filled with the Holy Ghost - That moment. God moves his instruments, not when they please, but just when he sees it needful. Ye rulers - He gives them the honour due to their office.

10. Be it known to you all - Probably the herald of God proclaimed this with a loud voice. Whom God hath raised from the dead - They knew in their own consciences that it was so. And though they had hired the soldiers to tell a most senseless and incredible tale to the contrary, Matt. xxviii, 12, 15, yet it is observable, they did not, so far as we can learn, dare to plead it before Peter and John.

11. Psalm cxviii, 22.

12. There is no other name whereby we must be saved - The apostle uses a beautiful gradation, from the temporal deliverance which had been wrought for the poor cripple, by the power of Christ, to that of a much nobler and more important kind, which is wrought by Christ for impotent and sinful souls. He therein follows the admirable custom of his great Lord and Master, who continually took occasion from earthly to speak of spiritual things.

13. Illiterate and uneducated men - Even by such men (though not by such only) hath God in all ages caused his word to be preached before the world.

17. Yet that it spread no farther - For they look upon it as a mere gangrene. So do all the world upon genuine Christianity. Let us severely threaten them - Great men, ye do nothing. They have a greater than you to flee to.

18. They charged them not to speak - Privately; nor teach - Publicly.

19. Whether it be just to obey you rather than God, judge ye - Was it not by the same spirit, that Socrates, when they were condemning him to death, for teaching the people, said, "O ye Athenians, I embrace and love you; but I will obey God rather than you. And if you would spare my life on condition I should cease to teach my fellow citizens, I would die a thousand times rather than accept the proposal."

21. They all glorified God - So much wiser were the people than those who were over them.

24. The sense is, Lord, thou hast all power. And thy word is fulfilled. Men do rage against thee: but it is in vain.

25. Psalm ii, 1.

27. Whom thou hast anointed - To be king of Israel.

28. The sense is, but they could do no more than thou wast pleased to permit, according to thy determinate counsel, to save mankind by the sufferings of thy Son. And what was needful for this end, thou didst before determine to permit to be done.

30. Thou stretchest forth thy hand - Exertest thy power.

31. They were all filled - Afresh; and spake the word with boldness - So their petition was granted.

32. And the multitude of them that believed - Every individual person were of one heart and one soul - Their love, their hopes, their passions joined: and not so much as one - In so great a multitude: this was a necessary consequence of that union of heart; said that aught of the things which he had was his own - It is impossible any one should, while all were of one soul. So long as that truly Christian love continued, they could not but have all things common.

33. And great grace - A large measure of the inward power of the Holy Ghost, was upon them all - Directing all their thoughts, words, and actions.

34. For neither was there any one among them that wanted - We may observe, this is added as the proof that great grace was upon them all. And it was the immediate, necessary consequence of it: yea, and must be to the end of the world. In all ages and nations, the same cause, the same degree of grace, could not but in like circumstances produce the same effect. For whosoever were possessors of houses and lands sold them - Not that there was any particular command for this; but there was great grace and great love: of which this was the natural fruit.

35. And distribution was made - At first by the apostles themselves, afterward by them whom they appointed.

36. A son of consolation - Not only on account of his so largely assisting the poor with his fortune; but also of those peculiar gifts of the Spirit, whereby he was so well qualified both to comfort and to exhort.

37. Having an estate - Probably of considerable value. It is not unlikely that it was in Cyprus. Being a Levite, he had no portion, no distinct inheritance in Israel.

1. But a certain man named Ananias - It is certain, not a believer, for all that believed were of one heart and of one soul: probably not baptized; but intending now to offer himself for baptism.

2. And bringing a certain part - As if it had been the whole: perhaps saying it was so.

3. To lie to the Holy Ghost - Who is in us. And to keep back - Here was the first instance of it. This was the first attempt to bring propriety of goods into the Christian Church.

4. While it remained, did it not remain thine? - It is true, whosoever among the Christians (not one excepted) had houses or lands, sold them, and laid the price at the feet of the apostles. But it was in his own choice to be a Christian or not: and consequently either to sell his land, or keep it. And when it was sold, was it not in thy power? - For it does not appear that he professed himself a Christian when he sold it. Why hast thou conceived this thing in thy heart? - So profanely to dissemble on so solemn an occasion? Thou hast not lied to men only, but to God also. Hence the Godhead of the Holy Ghost evidently appears: since lying to him, ver. 3, is lying to God.

5. And Ananias fell down and expired - And this severity was not only just, considering that complication of vain glory, covetousness, fraud, and impiety, which this action contained: but it was also wise and gracious, as it would effectually deter any others from following his example. It was likewise a convincing proof of the upright conduct of the apostles, in managing the sums with which they were intrusted; and in general of their Divine mission. For none can imagine that Peter would have had the assurance to pronounce, and much less the power to execute such a sentence, if he had been guilty himself of a fraud of the same kind; or had been belying the Holy Ghost in the whole of his pretensions to be under his immediate direction.

7. About the space of three hours - How precious a space! The woman had a longer time for repentance.

8. If ye sold the land for so much - Naming the sum.

10. The Church - This is the first time it is mentioned: and here is a native specimen of a New Testament Church; which is a company of men, called by the Gospel, grafted into Christ by baptism, animated by love, united by all kind of fellowship, and disciplined by the death of Ananias and Sapphira.

12. And they were all - All the believers.

13. None of the rest - No formalists or hypocrites, durst join themselves - In an outward show only, like Ananias and Sapphira.

14. But so much the more were true believers added, because unbelievers kept at a distance.

17. The high priest - and the sect of the Sadducees - A goodly company for the priest! He, and these deniers of any angel or resurrection, were filled with zeal - Angry, bitter, persecuting zeal.

20. The words of this - That is, these words of life: words which show the way to life everlasting.

23. We found the prison shut - The angel probably had shut the doors again.

24. They doubted what this should be - They were even at their wit's end. The world, in persecuting the children of God, entangle themselves in numberless difficulties.

28. Did not we strictly command you, not to teach? - See the poor cunning of the enemies of the Gospel. They make laws and interdicts at their pleasure, which those who obey God cannot but break; and then take occasion thereby to censure and punish the innocent, as guilty. Ye would bring the blood of this man upon us - An artful and invidious word. The apostles did not desire to accuse any man. They simply declared the naked truth.

29. Then Peter - In the name of all the apostles, said - He does not now give them the titles of honour, which he did before, chap. iv, 8; but enters directly upon the subject, and justifies what he had done. This is, as it were, a continuation of that discourse, but with an increase of severity.

30. Hath raised up Jesus - Of the seed of David, according to the promises made to our fathers.

31. Him hath God exalted - From the grave to heaven; to give repentance - Whereby Jesus is received as a Prince; and forgiveness of sins - Whereby he is received as a saviour. Hence some infer, that repentance and faith are as mere gifts as remission of sins. Not so: for man co-operates in the former, but not in the latter. God alone forgives sins.

32. And also the Holy Ghost - A much greater witness.

34. But a certain Pharisee - And as such believing the resurrection of the dead; a doctor, or teacher of the law - That is, a scribe, and indeed one of the highest rank; had in honour by all the people - Except the Sadducees; rising up in the council - So God can raise defenders of his servants, whensoever and wheresoever he pleases.

36. Before these days - He prudently mentions the facts first, and then makes the inference.

38. Let them alone - In a cause which is manifestly good, we should immediately join. In a cause, on the other hand, which is manifestly evil, we should immediately oppose. But in a sudden, new, doubtful occurrence, this advice is eminently useful. If this counsel or this work - He seems to correct himself, as if it were some sudden work, rather than a counsel or design. And so it was. For the apostles

had no counsel, plan, or design of their own; but were mere instruments in the hand of God, working just as he led them from day to day.

41. Rejoicing - to suffer shame - This is a sure mark of the truth, joy in affliction, such is true, deep, pure.

VI

1. There arose a murmuring - Here was the first breach made on those who were before of one heart and of one soul. Partiality crept in unawares on some; and murmuring on others. Ah Lord! how short a time did pure, genuine, undefiled Christianity remain in the world! O the depth! How unsearchable are thy counsels! marvelous are thy ways, O King of saints! The Hellenists were Jews born out of Palestine. They were so called, because they used the Greek as their other tongue. In this partiality of the Hebrews, and murmuring of the Hellenists, were the needs of a general persecution sown. Did God ever, in any age or country, withdraw his restraining providence, and let loose the world upon the Christians, till there was a cause among themselves? Is not an open, general persecution, always both penal and medicinal? A punishment of those that will not accept of milder reproofs, as well as a medicine to heal their sickness? And at the same time a means both of purifying and strengthening those whose heart is still right with God.

2. It is not right that we should leave the word of God and serve tables - In the first Church, the primary business of apostles, evangelists, and bishops, was to preach the word of God; the secondary, to take a kind of paternal care (the Church being then like a family,) for the food, especially of the poor, the strangers, and the widows. Afterward, the deacons of both sexes were constituted for this latter business. And whatever time they had to spare from this, they employed in works of spiritual mercy. But their proper office was, to take care of the poor. And when some of them afterward preached the Gospel, they did this not by virtue of their deaconship, but of another commission, that of evangelists, which they probably received, not before, but after they were appointed deacons. And it is not unlikely that others were chosen deacons, or stewards, in their room, when any of these commenced evangelists.

3. Of good report - That there may be no room to suspect them of partiality or injustice. Full of the Holy Ghost and wisdom - For it is not a light matter to dispense even the temporal goods of the Church. To do even this well, a large measure both of the gifts and grace of God is requisite. Whom we will set over this business - It would have been happy for the Church, had its ordinary ministers in every age taken the same care to act in concert with the people committed to their charge, which the apostles themselves, extraordinary as their office was, did on this and other occasions.

4. We will constantly attend to prayer, and to the ministry of the word - This is doubtless the proper business of a Christian bishop: to speak to God in prayer; to men in preaching his word, as an ambassador for Christ.

5. And they chose - It seems seven Hellenists, as their names show. And Nicholas a proselyte - To whom the proselytes would the more readily apply.

7. And the word of God grew - The hindrances being removed.

9. There arose certain of the synagogue which is called - It was one and the same synagogue which consisted of these several nations. Saul of Cilicia was doubtless a member of it; whence it is not at all improbable, that Gamaliel presided over it. Libertines - So they were styled, whose fathers were once slaves, and afterward made free. This was the ease of many Jews who had been taken captive by the Romans.

14. We have heard him say - So they might. But yet the consequence they drew would not follow.

15. As the face of an angel - Covered with supernatural lustre. They reckoned his preaching of Jesus to be the Christ was destroying Moses and the law; and God bears witness to him, with the same glory as he did to Moses, when he gave the law by him.

VII

2. And he said - St. Stephen had been accused of blasphemy against Moses, and even against God; and of speaking against the temple and the law, threatening that Jesus would destroy the one, and change the other. In answer to this accusation, rehearsing as it were the articles of his historical creed, he speaks of God with high reverence, and a grateful sense of a long series of acts of goodness to the Israelites, and of Moses with great respect, on account of his important and honourable employments under God: of the temple with regard, as being built to the honour of God; yet not with such superstition as the Jews; putting them in mind, that no temple could comprehend God. And he was going on, no doubt, when he was interrupted by their clamour, to speak to the last point, the destruction of the temple, and the change of the law by Christ. Men, brethren, and fathers, hearken - The sum of his discourse is this: I acknowledge the glory of God revealed to the fathers, ver. 2; the calling of Moses, ver. 34, &c.; the dignity of the law, verses 8, 38, 44; the holiness of this place, verses 7, 45, 47. And

indeed the law is more ancient than the temple; the promise more ancient than the law. For God showed himself the God of Abraham, Isaac, Jacob, and their children freely, ver. 2, &c.; 9, &c.; 17,&c.; 32, 34, 35; and they showed faith and obedience to God, ver. 4, 20, &c., 23, particularly by their regard for the law, ver. 8, and the promised land, ver. 16. Meantime, God never confined his presence to this one place or to the observers of the law. For he hath been acceptably worshipped before the law was given, or the temple built, and out of this land, ver. 2, 9, 33, 44. And that our fathers and their posterity were not tied down to this land, their various sojournings, ver. 4, &c.; 14, 29, 44, and exile, ver. 43, show. But you and your fathers have always been evil, ver. 9; have withstood Moses, ver. 25, &c., 39, &c.; have despised the land, ver. 39, forsaken God, ver. 40, &c., superstitiously honoured the temple, ver. 48, resisted God and his Spirit, ver. 50, killed the prophets and the Messiah himself, ver. 51, and kept not the law for which ye contend, ver. 53. Therefore God is not bound to you; much less to you alone. And truly this solemn testimony of Stephen is most worthy of his character, as a man full of the Holy Ghost, and of faith and power: in which, though he does not advance so many regular propositions, contradictory to those of his adversaries, yet he closely and nervously answers them all. Nor can we doubt but he would, from these premises, have drawn inferences touching the destruction of the temple, the abrogation of the Mosaic law, the punishment of that rebellious people; and above all, touching Jesus of Nazareth, the true Messiah, had not his discourse been interrupted by the clamours of the multitude, stopping their ears, and rushing upon him. Men, brethren, and fathers - All who are here present, whether ye are my equals in years, or of more advanced age. The word which in this and in many other places is rendered men is a mere expletive. The God of glory - The glorious God, appeared to Abraham before he dwelt in Haran - Therefore Abraham knew God, long before he was in this land. Gen. xii, 1.

3. Which I will show thee - Abraham knew not where he went.

4. After his father was dead - While Terah lived, Abraham lived partly with him, partly in Canaan: but after he died, altogether in Canaan.

5. No, not to set his foot on - For the field mentioned, ver. 16, he did not receive by a Divine donation, but bought it; even thereby showing that he was a stranger in the land.

6. Gen. xv, 13.

7. They shall serve me - Not the Egyptians.

8. And so he begat Isaac - After the covenant was given, of which circumcision was the seal. Gen. xvii, 10.

9. But God was with him - Though he was not in this land. Gen. xxxvii, 28.

12. Sent our fathers first - Without Benjamin.

14. Seventy-five souls - So the seventy interpreters, (whom St. Stephen follows,) one son and a grandson of Manasseh, and three children of Ephraim, being added to the seventy persons mentioned Gen. xlvi, 27.

16. And were carried over to Shechem - It seems that St. Stephen, rapidly running over so many circumstances of history, has not leisure (nor was it needful where they were so well known) to recite them all distinctly. Therefore he here contracts into one, two different sepulchres, places, and purchases, so as in the former history, to name the buyer, omitting the seller, in the latter, to name the seller, omitting the buyer. Abraham bought a burying place of the children of Heth, Gen. xxiii. Gen. xxiii, 1-20 There Jacob was buried. Jacob bought a field of the children of Hamor. There Joseph was buried. You see here, how St. Stephen contracts these two purchases into one. This concise manner of speaking, strange as it seems to us, was common among the Hebrews; particularly, when in a case notoriously known, the speaker mentioned but part of the story, and left the rest, which would have interrupted the current of his discourse, to be supplied in the mind of the hearer. And laid in the sepulchre that Abraham bought - The first land which these strangers bought was for a sepulchre. They sought for a country in heaven. Perhaps the whole sentence might be rendered thus: So Jacob went down into Egypt and died, he and our fathers, and were carried over to Shechem, and laid by the sons (that is, decendants) of Hamor, the father of Shechem, in the sepulchre that Abraham bought for a sum of money.

17. Exod. i, 7.

18. Another king - Probably of another family.

19. Exposed - Cast out to perish by hunger or wild beasts.

20. In which time - A sad but a seasonable time. Exod. ii, 2.

21. Pharaoh's daughter took him up - By which means, being designed for a kingdom, he had all those advantages of education, which he could not have had, if he had not been exposed.

22. In all the wisdom of the Egyptians - Which was then celebrated in all the world, and for many ages after. And mighty in words - Deep, solid, weighty, though not of a ready utterance.

23. It came into his heart - Probably by an impulse from God.

24. Seeing one wronged - Probably by one of the task masters.

25. They understood it not - Such was their stupidity and sloth; which made him afterward unwilling to go to them.

26. He showed himself - Of his own accord, unexpectedly.

27. Who appointed thee - "Under the presence of the want of a call by man, the instruments of God are often rejected."

30. The angel - The Son of God; as appears from his styling himself Jehovah. In a flame of fire - Signifying the majesty of God then present. Exod. iii, 2.

33. Then said the Lord, Loose thy shoes - An ancient token of reverence; for the place is holy ground - The holiness of places depends on the peculiar presence of God there.

35. This Moses whom they refused - Namely, forty years before. Probably, not they, but their fathers did it, and God imputes it to them. So God frequently imputes the sins of the fathers to those of their children who are of the same spirit. Him did God send to be a deliverer - Which is much more than a judge; by the hand of - That is, by means of the angel - This angel who spoke to Moses on Mount Sinai expressly called himself Jehovah, a name which cannot, without the highest presumption, be assumed by any created angel, since he whose name alone is Jehovah, is the Most High over all the earth, Psalm lxxxiii, 18. Psalm lxxxii, 18. It was therefore the Son of God who delivered the law to Moses, under the character of Jehovah, and who is here spoken of as the angel of the covenant, in respect of his mediatorial office.

37. The Lord will raise you up a prophet - St. Stephen here shows that there is no opposition between Moses and Christ. Deut. xviii, 15

38. This is he - Moses. With the angel, and with our fathers - As a mediator between them. Who received the living oracles - Every period beginning with, And the Lord said unto Moses, is properly an oracle. But the oracles here intended are chiefly the ten commandments. These are termed living, because all the word of God, applied by his Spirit, is living and powerful, Heb. iv, 12, enlightening the eyes, rejoicing the heart, converting the soul, raising the dead. Exod. xix, 3.

40. Make us gods to go before us - Back into Egypt. Exod. xxxii, 1.

41. And they made a calf - In imitation of Apis, the Egyptian god: and rejoiced in the works of their hands - In the God they had made.

42. God turned - From them in anger; and gave them up - Frequently from the time of the golden calf, to the time of Amos, and afterward. The host of heaven - The stars are called an army or host, because of their number, order, and powerful influence. In the book of the prophets - Of the twelve prophets, which the Jews always wrote together in one book. Have ye offered - The passage of Amos referred to, chap. v, 25, &c., Amos v, 25 consists of two parts; of which the former confirms ver. 41, of the sin of the people; the latter the beginning of ver. 42, concerning their punishment. Have ye offered to me - They had offered many sacrifices; but God did not accept them as offered to him, because they sacrificed to idols also; and did not sacrifice to him with an upright heart. Amos v, 25.

43. Ye took up - Probably not long after the golden calf: but secretly; else Moses would have mentioned it. The shrine - A small, portable chapel, in which was the image of their god. Moloch was the planet Mars, which they worshipped under a human shape. Remphan, that is, Saturn, they represented by a star. And I will carry you beyond Babylon - That is, beyond Damascus (which is the word in Amos) and Babylon. This was fulfilled by the king of Assyria, 2 Kings xvii, 6.

44. Our fathers had the tabernacle of the testimony - The testimony was properly the two tables of stone, on which the ten commandments were written. Hence the ark which contained them is frequently called the ark of the testimony; and the whole tabernacle in this place. The tabernacle of the testimony - according to the model which he had seen - When he was caught up in the visions of God on the mount.

45. Which our fathers having received - From their ancestors; brought into the possession of the Gentiles - Into the land which the Gentiles possessed before. So that God's favour is not a necessary consequence of inhabiting this land. All along St. Stephen intimates two things:

1. That God always loved good men in every land:
2. That he never loved bad men even in this. Josh iii, 14.

46. Who petitioned to find a habitation for the God of Jacob - But he did not obtain his petition: for God remained without any temple till Solomon built him a house. Observe how wisely the word is chosen with respect to what follows.

48. Yet the Most High inhabiteth not temples made with hands - As Solomon declared at the very dedication of the temple, 1 Kings viii, 27. The Most High - Whom as such no building can contain. Isaiah lxvi, 1.

49. What is the place of my rest? - Have I need to rest?

51. Ye stiff necked - Not bowing the neck to God's yoke; and uncircumcised in heart - So they showed themselves, ver. 54; Act vii, 54 and ears - As they showed, ver. 57. Act vii, 57 So far were they from receiving the word of God into their hearts, that they would not hear it even with their ears. Ye - And your fathers, always - As often as ever ye are called, resist the Holy Ghost - Testifying by the prophets of Jesus, and the whole truth. This is the sum of what he had shown at large.

53. Who have received the law by the administration of angels - God, when he gave the law on Mount Sinai, was attended with thousands of his angels, Gal. iii, 19; Psalm lxviii, 17.

55. But he looking steadfastly up to heaven, saw the glory of God - Doubtless he saw such a glorious representation, God miraculously operating on his imagination, as on Ezekiel's, when he sat in his house at Babylon, and saw Jerusalem, and seemed to himself transported thither, chap. viii, 1-4. And probably other martyrs, when called to suffer the last extremity, have had extraordinary assistance of some similar kind.

56. I see the Son of man standing - As if it were just ready to receive him. Otherwise he is said to sit at the right hand of God.

57. They rushed upon him - Before any sentence passed.

58. The witnesses laid down their clothes at the feet of a young man, whose name was Saul - O Saul, couldst thou have believed, if one had told thee, that thou thyself shouldst be stoned in the same cause? and shouldst triumph in committing thy soul likewise to that Jesus whom thou art now blaspheming? His dying prayer reached thee, as well as many others. And the martyr Stephen, and Saul the persecutor, (afterward his brother both in faith and martyrdom,) are now joined in everlasting friendship, and dwell together in the happy company of those who have made their robes white in the blood of the Lamb.

59. And they stoned Stephen, invoking and saying, Lord Jesus, receive my spirit - This is the literal translation of the words, the name of God not being in the original. Nevertheless such a solemn prayer to Christ, in which a departing soul is thus committed into his hands, is such an act of worship, as no good man could have paid to a mere creature; Stephen here worshipping Christ in the very same manner in which Christ worshipped the Father on the cross.

VIII

1. At that time there was great persecution against the Church - Their adversaries having tasted blood, were the more eager. And they were all dispersed - Not all the Church: if so, who would have remained for the apostles to teach, or Saul to persecute? But all the teachers except the apostles, who, though in the most danger, stayed with the flock.

2. Devout men - Who feared God more than persecution. And yet were they not of little faith? Else they would not have made so great lamentation.

3. Saul made havoc of the Church - Like some furious beast of prey. So the Greek word properly signifies. Men and women - Regarding neither age nor sex.

4. Therefore they that were dispersed went everywhere - These very words are reassumed, after as it were a long parenthesis, chap. xi, 19, and the thread of the story continued.

5. Stephen - Being taken away, Philip, his next colleague, (not the apostle,) rises in his place.

9. A certain man - using magic - So there was such a thing as witchcraft once! In Asia at least, if not in Europe or America.

12. But when they believed - What Philip preached, then they saw and felt the real power of God, and submitted thereto.

13. And Simon believed - That is, was convinced of the truth.

14. And the apostles hearing that Samaria - The inhabitants of that country, had received the word of God - By faith, sent Peter and John - He that sends must be either superior, or at least equal, to him that is sent. It follows that the college of the apostles was equal if not superior to Peter.

15. The Holy Ghost - In his miraculous gifts? Or his sanctifying graces? Probably in both.

18. Simon offered them money - And hence the procuring any ministerial function, or ecclesiastical benefice by money, is termed Simony.

21. Thou hast neither part - By purchase, nor lot - Given gratis, in this matter - This gift of God. For thy heart is not right before God - Probably St. Peter discerned this long before he had declared it; although it does not appear that God gave to any of the apostles a universal power of discerning the hearts of all they conversed with; any more than a universal power of healing all the sick they came near. This we are sure St. Paul had not; though he was not inferior to the chief of the apostles. Otherwise he would not have suffered the illness of Epaphroditus to have brought him so near to death, Phil. ii, 25-27; nor have left so useful a fellow labourer as Trophimus sick at Miletus, 2 Tim. iv, 20.

22. Repent - if perhaps the thought of thy heart may be forgiven thee - Without all doubt if he had repented, he would have been forgiven. The doubt was, whether he would repent. Thou art in the gall of bitterness - In the highest degree of wickedness, which is bitterness, that is, misery to the soul; and in the bond of iniquity - Fast bound therewith.

26. The way which is desert - There were two ways from Jerusalem to Gaza, one desert, the other through a more populous country.

27. An eunuch - Chief officers were anciently called eunuchs, though not always literally such; because such used to be chief ministers in the eastern courts. Candace, queen of the Ethiopians - So all the queens of Ethiopia were called.

28. Sitting in his chariot, he read the Prophet Isaiah - God meeteth those that remember him in his

ways. It is good to read, hear, seek information even in a journey. Why should we not redeem all our time?

30. And Philip running to him, said, Understandest thou what thou readest? - He did not begin about the weather, news, or the like. In speaking for God, we may frequently come to the point at once, without circumlocution.

31. He desired Philip to come up and sit with him - Such was his modesty, and thirst after instruction.

32. The portion of Scripture - By reading that very chapter, the fifty-third of Isaiah, many Jews, yea, and atheists, have been converted. Some of them history records. God knoweth them all. Isaiah liii, 7

33. In his humiliation his judgment was taken away - That is, when he was a man, he had no justice shown him. To take away a person's judgment, is a proverbial phrase for oppressing him. And who shall declare, or count his generation - That is, who can number his seed, Isaiah liii, 10; which he hath purchased by laying down his life?

36. And as they went on the way they came to a certain water - Thus, even the circumstances of the journey were under the direction of God. The kingdom of God suits itself to external circumstances, without any violence, as air yields to all bodies, and yet pervades all. What hindereth me to be baptized? - Probably he had been circumcised: otherwise Cornelius would not have been the first fruits of the Gentiles.

38. And they both went down - Out of the chariot. It does not follow that he was baptized by immersion. The text neither affirms nor intimates any thing concerning it.

39. The Spirit of the Lord caught away Philip - Carried him away with a miraculous swiftness, without any action or labour of his own. This had befallen several of the prophets.

40. But Philip was found at Azotus - Probably none saw him, from his leaving the eunuch, till he was there.

IX

1. Acts xxii, 3, &c.; Acts xxvi, 9, &c.

2. Bound - By the connivance, if not authority, of the governor, under Aretas the king. See Acts ix, 14, 24.

3. And suddenly - When God suddenly and vehemently attacks a sinner, it is the highest act of mercy. So Saul, when his rage was come to the height, is taught not to breathe slaughter. And what was wanting in time to confirm him in his discipleship, is compensated by the inexpressible terror he sustained. By his also the suddenly constituted apostle was guarded against the grand snare into which novices are apt to fall.

4. He heard a voice - Severe, yet full of grace.

5. To kick against the goads - is a Syriac proverb, expressing an attempt that brings nothing but pain.

6. It shall be told thee - So God himself sends Saul to be taught by a man, as the angel does Cornelius, chap. x, 5. Admirable condescension! that the Lord deals with us by men, like ourselves.

7. The men - stood - Having risen before Saul; for they also fell to the ground, chap. xxvi, 14. It is probable they all journeyed on foot. Hearing the noise - But not an articulate voice. And seeing the light, but not Jesus himself, chap. xxvi, 13, &c.

9. And he was three days - An important season! So long he seems to have been in the pangs of the new birth. Without sight - By scales growing over his eyes, to intimate to him the blindness of the state he had been in, to impress him with a deeper sense of the almighty power of Christ, and to turn his thoughts inward, while he was less capable of conversing with outward objects. This was likewise a manifest token to others, of what had happened to him in his journey, and ought to have humbled and convinced those bigoted Jews, to whom he had been sent from the sanhedrim.

11. Behold he is praying - He was shown thus to Ananias.

12. A man called Ananias - His name also was revealed to Saul.

13. But he answered - How natural it is to reason against God.

14. All that call on thy name - That is, all Christians.

15. He is a chosen vessel to bear my name - That is, to testify of me. It is undeniable, that some men are unconditionally chosen or elected, to do some works for God

16. For I - Do thou as thou art commanded. I will take care of the rest; will show him - In fact, through the whole course of his ministry. How great things he must suffer - So far will he be now from persecuting others.

17. The Lord hath sent me - Ananias does not tell Saul all which Christ had said concerning him. It was not expedient that he should know yet to how great a dignity he was called.

24. They guarded the gates day and night - That is, the governor did, at their request, 2 Cor. xi, 32.

Wesley's Notes on the Bible - The New Testament

26. And coming to Jerusalem - Three years after, Gal. i, 18. These three years St. Paul passes over, chap. xxii, 17, likewise.

27. To the apostles - Peter and James, Gal. i, 18, 19. Gal. i, 18,

19 And declared - He who has been an enemy to the truth ought not to be trusted till he gives proof that he is changed.

31. Then the Church - The whole body of Christian believers, had peace - Their bitterest persecutor being converted. And being built up - In holy, loving faith, continually increasing, and walking in - That is, speaking and acting only from this principle, the fear of God and the comfort of the Holy Ghost - An excellent mixture of inward and outward peace, tempered with filial fear.

35. Lydda was a large town, one day's journey from Jerusalem. It stood in the plain or valley of Sharon, which extended from Caesarea to Joppa, and was noted for its fruitfulness.

36. Tabitha, which is by interpretation Dorcas - She was probably a Hellenist Jew, known among the Hebrews by the Syriac name Tabitha, while the Greeks called her in their own language, Dorcas. They are both words of the same import, and signify a roe or fawn.

38. The disciples sent to him - Probably none of those at Joppa had the gift of miracles. Nor is it certain that they expected a miracle from him.

39. While she was with the in - That is, before she died.

40. Peter having put them all out - That he might have the better opportunity of wrestling with God in prayer, said, Tabitha, arise. And she opened her eyes, and seeing Peter, sat up - Who can imagine the surprise of Dorcas, when called back to life? Or of her friends, when they saw her alive? For the sake of themselves, and of the poor, there was cause of rejoicing, and much more, for such a confirmation of the Gospel. Yet to herself it was matter of resignation, not joy, to be called back to these scenes of vanity: but doubtless, her remaining days were still more zealously spent in the service of her saviour and her God. Thus was a richer treasure laid up for her in heaven, and she afterward returned to a more exceeding weight of glory, than that from which so astonishing a providence had recalled her for a season.

X

1. And there was a certain man - The first fruits of the Gentiles, in Cesarea - Where Philip had been before, chap. viii, 40; so that the doctrine of salvation by faith in Jesus was not unknown there. Cesarea was the seat of the civil government, as Jerusalem was of the ecclesiastical. It is observable, that the Gospel made its way first through the metropolitan cities. So it first seized Jerusalem and afterward Cesarea: afterward Philippi, Athens, Corinth, Ephesus, Rome itself. A centurion, or captain, of that called the Italian band - That is, troop or company.

2. Who gave much alms to the people - That is, to the Jews, many of whom were at that time extremely poor.

3. He saw in a vision - Not in a trance, like Peter: plainly, so as to leave one not accustomed to things of this kind no room to suspect any imposition.

4. Thy prayers and thine alms are come up for a memorial before God - Dare any man say, These were only splendid sins? Or that they were an abomination before God? And yet it is certain, in the Christian sense Cornelius was then an unbeliever. He had not then faith in Christ. So certain it is, that every one who seeks faith in Christ, should seek it in prayer, and doing good to all men: though in strictness what is not exactly according to the Divine rule must stand in need of Divine favour and indulgence.

8. A devout soldier - How many such attendants have our modern officers? A devout soldier would now be looked upon as little better than a deserter from his colours.

10. And he became very hungry - At the usual meal time. The symbols in visions and trances, it is easy to observe, are generally suited to the state of the natural faculties.

11. Tied at the corners - Not all in one knot, but each fastened as it were up to heaven.

14. But Peter said, In nowise, Lord - When God commands a strange or seemingly improper thing, the first objection frequently finds pardon. But it ought not to be repeated. This doubt and delay of St. Peter had several good effects. Hereby the will of God in this important point was made more evident and incontestable. And Peter also, having been so slow of belief himself, could the more easily bear the doubting of his brethren, chap. xi, 2, &c.

15. What God hath purified - Hath made and declared clean. Nothing but what is clean can come down from heaven. St. Peter well remembered this saying in the council at Jerusalem, chap. xv, 9.

16. This was done thrice - To make the deeper impression.

17. While Peter doubted in himself, behold the men - Frequently the things which befall us within and from without at the same time, are a key to each other. The things which thus concur and agree together, ought to be diligently attended to.

19. Behold three men seek thee, arise therefore and go down, and go with them, doubting nothing

- How gradually was St. Peter prepared to receive this new admonition of the Spirit! Thus God is went to lead on his children by degrees, always giving them light for the present hour.

24. Cornelius was waiting for them - Not engaging himself in any secular business during that solemn time, but being altogether intent on this one thing.

26. I myself also am a man - And not God, who alone ought to be worshipped, Matt. iv, 10. Have all his pretended successors attended to this?

28. But God hath showed me - He speaks sparingly to them of his former doubt, and his late vision.

29. I ask for what intent ye have sent for me? - St. Peter knew this already. But he puts Cornelius on telling the story, both that the rest might be informed, and Cornelius himself more impressed by the narration: the repetition of which, even as we read it, gives a new dignity and spirit to Peter's succeeding discourse,

30. Four days ago I was fasting - The first of these days he had the vision; the second his messengers came to Joppa; on the third, St. Peter set out; and on the fourth, came to Cesarea.

31. Thy prayer is heard - Doubtless he had been praying for instruction, how to worship God in the most acceptable manner.

33. Now therefore we are all present before God - The language of every truly Christian congregation.

34. I perceive of a truth - More clearly than ever, from such a concurrence of circumstances. That God is not a respecter of persons - Is not partial in his love. The words mean, in a particular sense, that he does not confine his love to one nation; in a general, that he is loving to every man, and willeth all men should be saved.

35. But in every nation he that feareth God and worketh righteousness - He that, first, reverences God, as great, wise, good, the cause, end, and governor of all things; and secondly, from this awful regard to him, not only avoids all known evil, but endeavours, according to the best light he has, to do all things well; is accepted of him - Through Christ, though he knows him not. The assertion is express, and admits of no exception. He is in the favour of God, whether enjoying his written word and ordinances or not. Nevertheless the addition of these is an unspeakable blessing to those who were before in some measure accepted. Otherwise God would never have sent an angel from heaven to direct Cornelius to St. Peter.

36. This is the word which God sent - When he sent his Son into the world, preaching - Proclaiming by him-peace between God and man, whether Jew or Gentile, by the God-man. He is Lord of both; yea, Lord of and over all.

37. Ye know the word which was published - You know the facts in general, the meaning of which I shall now more particularly explain and confirm to you. The baptism which John preached - To which he invited them by his preaching, in token of their repentance. This began in Galilee, which is near Cesarea.

38. How God anointed Jesus - Particularly at his baptism, thereby inaugurating him to his office: with the Holy Ghost and with power - It is worthy our remark, that frequently when the Holy Ghost is mentioned there is added a word particularly adapted to the present circumstance. So the deacons were to be full of the Holy Ghost and wisdom, chap. vi, 3. Barnabas was full of the Holy Ghost and faith, chap. xi, 24. The disciples were filled with joy, and with the Holy Ghost, chap. xiii, 52. And here, where his mighty works are mentioned, Christ himself is said to be anointed with the Holy Ghost and with power. For God was with him-He speaks sparingly here of the majesty of Christ, as considering the state of his hearers.

41. Not now to all the people - As before his death; to us who did eat and drink with him - That is, conversed familiarly and continually with him, in the time of his ministry.

42. It is he who is ordained by God the Judge of the living and the dead - Of all men, whether they are alive at his coming, or had died before it. This was declaring to them, in the strongest terms, how entirely their happiness depended on a timely and humble subjection to him who was to be their final Judge.

43. To him give all the prophets witness - Speaking to heathens he does not quote any in particular; that every one who believeth in him - Whether he be Jew or Gentile; receiveth remission of sins - Though he had not before either feared God, or worked righteousness.

44. The Holy Ghost fell on all that were hearing the word - Thus were they consecrated to God, as the first fruits of the Gentiles. And thus did God give a clear and satisfactory evidence, that he had accepted them as well as the Jews.

45. The believers of the circumcision - The believing Jews.

47. Can any man forbid water, that these should not be baptized, who have received the Holy Ghost? - He does not say they have the baptism of the Spirit; therefore they do not need baptism with water. But just the contrary: if they have received the Spirit, then baptize them with water. How easily is this question decided, if we will take the word of God for our rule! Either men have received the Holy

Ghost or not. If they have not, Repent, saith God, and be baptized, and ye shall receive the gift of the Holy Ghost. If they have, if they are already baptized with the Holy Ghost, then who can forbid water?

48. In the name of the Lord - Which implies the Father who anointed him, and the Spirit with which he was anointed to his office. But as the Gentiles had before believed in God the Father, and could not but now believe in the Holy Ghost, under whose powerful influence they were at this very time, there was the less need of taking notice, that they were baptized into the belief and profession of the sacred Three: though doubtless the apostle administered the ordinances in that very form which Christ himself had prescribed.

XI

4. Peter laid all things before them - So he did not take it ill to be questioned, nor desire to be treated as infallible. And he answers the more mildly because it related to a point which he had not readily believed himself.

5. Being in a trance - Which suspends the use of the outward senses.

14. Saved - With the full Christian salvation, in this world and the world to come.

17. To us, when we believed - The sense is, because we believed, not because we were circumcised, was the Holy Ghost given to us. What was I - A mere instrument in God's hand. They had inquired only concerning his eating with the Gentiles. He satisfies them likewise concerning his baptizing them, and shows that he had done right in going to Cornelius, not only by the command of God, but also by the event, the descent of the Holy Ghost. And who are we that we should withstand God? Particularly by laying down rules of Christian communion which exclude any whom he has admitted into the Church of the first born, from worshipping God together. O that all Church governors would consider how bold an usurpation this is on the authority of the supreme Lord of the Church! O that the sin of thus withstanding God may not be laid to the charge of those, who perhaps with a good intention, but in an over fondness for their own forms, have done it, and are continually doing it.

18. They glorified God - Being thoroughly satisfied. Repentance unto life - True repentance is a change from spiritual death to spiritual life, and leads to life everlasting.

19. They who had been dispersed - St. Luke here resumes the thread of his narration, in the very words wherewith he broke it off, chap. viii. 6. As far as Phenicia to the north, Cyprus to the west, and Antioch to the east.

20. Some of them were men of Cyprus and Cyrene - Who were more accustomed to converse with the Gentiles. Who coming into Antioch - Then the capital of Syria, and, next to Rome and Alexandria, the most considerable city of the empire. Spake to the Greeks - As the Greeks were the most celebrated of the Gentile nations near Judea, the Jews called all the Gentiles by that name. Here we have the first account of the preaching the Gospel to the idolatrous Gentiles. All those to whom it had been preached before, did at least worship one God, the God of Israel.

21. And the hand of the Lord - That is, the power of his Spirit.

26. And the disciples were first called Christians at Antioch - Here it was that they first received this standing appellation. They were before termed Nazarenes and Galileans.

28. Agabus rising up - In the congregation. All the world - The word frequently signifies all the Roman empire. And so it is doubtless to be taken here.

29. Then - Understanding the distress they would otherwise be in on that account, the disciples determined to send relief to the brethren in Judea - Who herein received a manifest proof of the reality of their conversion.

30. Sending it to the elders - Who gave it to the deacons, to be distributed by them, as every one had need.

XII

1. About that time - So wisely did God mix rest and persecution in due time and measure succeeding each other. Herod - Agrippa; the latter was his Roman, the former his Syrian name. He was the grandson of Herod the Great, nephew to Herod Antipas, who beheaded John the Baptist; brother to Herodias, and father to that Agrippa before whom St. Paul afterward made his defense. Caligula made him king of the tetrarchy of his uncle Philip, to which he afterward added the territories of Antipas. Claudius made him also king of Judea, and added thereto the dominions of Lysanias.

2. James the brother of John - So one of the brothers went to God the first, the other the last of the apostles.

3. Then were the days of unleavened bread - At which the Jews came together from all parts.

4. Four quaternions - Sixteen men, who watched by turns day and night.

5. Continual prayer was made for him - Yet when their prayer was answered, they could scarce believe it, ver. 15. But why had they not prayed for St. James also? Because he was put to death as soon

as apprehended.

6. Peter was sleeping - Easy and void of fear; between two soldiers - Sufficiently secured to human appearance.

7. His chains - With which his right arm was bound to one of the soldiers, and his left arm to the other.

8. Gird thyself - Probably he had put off his girdle, sandals, and upper garment, before he lay down to sleep.

10. The first and second ward - At each of which doubtless was a guard of soldiers. The gate opened of its own accord - Without either Peter or the angel touching it. And they went on through one street - That Peter might know which way to go. And the angel departed from him - Being himself sufficient for what remained to be done.

11. Now I know of a truth - That this is not a vision, ver. 9.

12. And having considered - What was best to be done. Many were gathered together - At midnight.

13. The gate - At some distance from the house; to hearken - If any knocked.

14. And knowing Peter's voice - Bidding her open the door.

15. They said, Thou art mad - As we say, Sure you are not in your senses to talk so. It is his angel - It was a common opinion among the Jews, that every man had his particular guardian angel, who frequently assumed both his shape and voice. But this is a point on which the Scriptures are silent.

17. Beckoning to them - Many of whom being amazed, were talking together. And he said, Show these things to James - The brother or kinsman of our Lord, and author of the epistle which bears his name. He appears to have been a person of considerable weight and importance, probably the chief overseer of that province, and of the Church in Jerusalem in particular. He went into another place - Where he might be better concealed till the storm was over.

19. Herod commanded them to be put to death - And thus the wicked suffered in the room of the righteous. And going down from Judea - With shame, for not having brought forth Peter, according to his promise.

20. Having gained Blastus - To their side, they sued for, and obtained peace - Reconciliation with Herod. And so the Christians of those parts were, by the providence of God, delivered from scarcity. Their country was nourished - Was provided with, corn, by the king's country - Thus Hiram also, king of Tyre, desired of Solomon food or corn for his household, 1 Kings v, 9.

21. And on a set day - Which was solemnized yearly, in honour of Claudius Caesar; Herod, arrayed in royal apparel - In a garment so wrought with silver, that the rays of the rising sun striking upon, and being reflected from it, dazzled the eyes of the beholders. The people shouted, It is the voice of a God - Such profane flattery they frequently paid to princes. But the commonness of a wicked custom rather increases than lessens the guilt of it.

23. And immediately - God does not delay to vindicate his injured honour; an angel of the Lord smote him - Of this other historians say nothing: so wide a difference there is between Divine and human history! An angel of the Lord brought out Peter; an angel smote Herod. Men did not see the instruments in either case. These were only known to the people of God. Because he gave not glory to God - He willingly received it to himself, and by this sacrilege filled up the measure of his iniquities. So then vengeance tarried not. And he was eaten by worms, or vermin - How changed! And on the fifth day expired in exquisite torture. Such was the event! The persecutor perished, and the Gospel grew and multiplied.

25. Saul returned - To Antioch; taking John, surnamed Mark - The son of Mary, (at whose house the disciples met, to pray for Peter,) who was sister to Barnabas.

XIII

1. Manaen, who had been brought up with Herod - His foster brother, now freed from the temptations of a court.

2. Separate me Barnabas and Saul for the work to which I have called them - This was not ordaining them. St. Paul was ordained long before, and that not of men, neither by man: it was only inducting him to the province for which our Lord had appointed him from the beginning, and which was now revealed to the prophets and teachers. In consequence of this they fasted, prayed, and laid their hands on them, a rite which was used not in ordination only, but in blessing, and on many other occasions.

3. Then having fasted - Again. Thus they did also, chap. xiv, 23.

5. In the synagogues - Using all opportunities that offered.

6. Paphos was on the western, Salamis on the eastern part of the island.

7. The proconsul - The Roman governor of Cyprus, a prudent man - And therefore not overswayed by Elymas, but desirous to inquire farther.

Wesley's Notes on the Bible - The New Testament

9. Then Saul, who was also called Paul - It is not improbable, that coming now among the Romans, they would naturally adapt his name to their own language, and so called him Paul instead of Saul. Perhaps the family of the proconsul might be the first who addressed to or spoke of him by this name. And from this time, being the apostle of the Gentiles, he himself used the name which was more familiar to them.

10. O full of all guile - As a false prophet, and all mischief - As a magician. Thou son of the devil - A title well suited to a magician; and one who not only was himself unrighteous, but laboured to keep others from all goodness. Wilt thou not cease to pervert the right ways of the Lord? - Even now thou hast heard the truth of the Gospel.

11. And immediately a mist - Or dimness within, and darkness without, fell upon him.

12. Being astonished at the doctrine of the Lord - Confirmed by such a miracle.

13. John withdrawing from them returned - Tired with the fatigue, or shrinking from danger.

14. Antioch in Pisidia - Different from the Antioch mentioned ver. 1.

15. And after the reading of the law and the prophets, the chief of the synagogue sent to them - The law was read over once every year, a portion of it every Sabbath: to which was added a lesson taken out of the prophets. After this was over, any one might speak to the people, on any subject he thought convenient. Yet it was a circumstance of decency which Paul and Barnabas would hardly omit, to acquaint the rulers with their desire of doing it: probably by some message before the service began.

16. Ye that fear God - Whether proselytes or heathens.

17. The God - By such a commemoration of God's favours to their fathers, at once their minds were conciliated to the speaker, they were convinced of their duty to God, and invited to believe his promise, and the accomplishment of it. The six verses 17-22, contain the whole sum of the Old Testament. Of this people - Paul here chiefly addresses himself to those whom he styles, Ye that fear God: he speaks of Israel first; and ver. 26, speaks more directly to the Israelites themselves. Chose - And this exalted the people; not any merit or goodness of their own, Ezek. xx, 5. Our fathers - Abraham and his posterity. Isaiah i, 2.

18. Deut. i, 31.

19. Seven nations - Enumerated Deut. vii, 1; about four hundred and fifty years - That is, from the choice of the fathers to the dividing of the land; it was about four hundred and fifty years.

21. He gave them Saul forty years - Including the time wherein Samuel judged Israel.

22. Having removed him - Hence they might understand that the dispensations of God admit of various changes. I have found David, a man after my own heart - This expression is to be taken in a limited sense. David was such at that time, but not at all times. And he was so, in that respect, as he performed all God's will, in the particulars there mentioned: But he was not a man after God's own heart, in other respects, wherein he performed his own will. In the matter of Uriah, for instance, he was as far from being a man after God's own heart as Saul himself was. It is therefore a very gross, as well as dangerous mistake, to suppose this is the character of David in every part of his behaviour. We must beware of this, unless we would recommend adultery and murder as things after God's own heart. 1 Sam. xvi, 12, 13.

24. John having first preached - He mentions this, as a thing already known to them. And so doubtless it was. For it gave so loud an alarm to the whole Jewish nation, as could not but be heard of in foreign countries, at least as remote as Pisidia.

25. His course - His work was quickly finished, and might therefore well be termed a course or race. Luke iii, 16.

27. For they that dwell at Jerusalem, and their rulers - He here anticipates a strong objection, "Why did not they at Jerusalem, and especially their rulers, believe?" They know not him, because they understood not those very prophets whom they read or heard continually. Their very condemning him, innocent as he was, proves that they understood not the prophecies concerning him.

29. They fulfilled all things that were written of him - So far could they go, but no farther.

31. He was seen many days by them who came up with him from Galilee to Jerusalem - This last journey both presupposes all the rest, and was the most important of all.

33. Thou art my Son, this day have I begotten thee - It is true, he was the Son of God from eternity. The meaning therefore is, I have this day declared thee to be my Son. As St. Paul elsewhere, declared to be the Son of God with power, by the resurrection from the dead, Rom. i, 4. And it is with peculiar propriety and beauty that God is said to have begotten him, on the day when he raised him from the dead, as he seemed then to be born out of the earth anew. Psalm ii, 7.

34. No more to return to corruption - That is, to die no more. I will give you the sure mercies of David - The blessings promised to David in Christ. These are sure, certain, firm, solid, to every true believer in him. And hence the resurrection of Christ necessarily follows; for without this, those blessings could not be given. Isaiah lv, 3.

35. He saith - David in the name of the Messiah. Psalm xvi, 10.

36. David, having served the will of God in his generation, fell asleep - So his service extended

not itself beyond the bounds of the common age of man: but the service of the Messiah to all generations, as his kingdom to all ages. Served the will of God - Why art thou here thou who art yet in the world? Is it not that thou also mayest serve the will of God? Art thou serving it now? Doing all his will? And was added to his fathers - Not only in body. This expression refers to the soul also, and supposes the immortality of it.

39. Everyone that believeth is justified from all things - Has the actual forgiveness of all his sins, at the very time of his believing; from which ye could not be justified - Not only ye cannot now; but ye never could. For it afforded no expiation for presumptuous sins. By the law of Moses - The whole Mosaic institution! The division of the law into moral and ceremonial was not so common among the Jews, as it is among us. Nor does the apostle here consider it at all: but Moses and Christ are opposed to each other.

40. Beware - A weighty and seasonable admonition. No reproof is as yet added to it.

41. I work a work which ye will in nowise believe - This was originally spoken to those, who would not believe that God would ever deliver them from the power of the Chaldeans. But it is applicable to any who will not believe the promises, or the works of God. Hab. i, 5.

42. When the Jews were going out - Probably many of them, not bearing to hear him, went out before he had done. The Sabbath between - So the Jews call to this day the Sabbath between the first day of the month Tisri (on which the civil year begins) and the tenth of the same month, which is the solemn day of expiation.

43. Who speaking to them - More familiarly, persuaded them to continue - For trials were at hand, in the grace of God - That is, to adhere to the Gospel or Christian faith.

46. Then Paul and Barnabas speaking boldly, said - Those who hinder others must be publicly reproved. It was necessary - Though ye are not worthy: he shows that he had not preached to them, from any confidence of their believing, but seeing ye judge yourselves unworthy of eternal life - They indeed judged none but themselves worthy of it. Yet their rejecting of the Gospel was the same as saying, "We are unworthy of eternal life." Behold! - A thing now present! An astonishing revolution! We turn to the Gentiles - Not that they left off preaching to the Jews in other places. But they now determined to lose no more time at Antioch on their ungrateful countrymen, but to employ themselves wholly in doing what they could for the conversion of the Gentiles there.

47. For so hath the Lord commanded us - By sending us forth, and giving us an opportunity of fulfilling what he had foretold. I have set thee - The Father speaks to Christ. Isaiah xlix, 6.

48. As many as were ordained to eternal life - St. Luke does not say fore-ordained. He is not speaking of what was done from eternity, but of what was then done, through the preaching of the Gospel. He is describing that ordination, and that only, which was at the very time of hearing it. During this sermon those believed, says the apostle, to whom God then gave power to believe. It is as if he had said, "They believed, whose hearts the Lord opened;" as he expresses it in a clearly parallel place, speaking of the same kind of ordination, chap. xvi, 14, &c. It is observable, the original word is not once used in Scripture to express eternal predestination of any kind. The sum is, all those and those only, who were now ordained, now believed. Not that God rejected the rest: it was his will that they also should have been saved: but they thrust salvation from them. Nor were they who then believed constrained to believe. But grace was then first copiously offered them. And they did not thrust it away, so that a great multitude even of Gentiles were converted. In a word, the expression properly implies, a present operation of Divine grace working faith in the hearers.

XIV

1. They so spake - Persecution having increased their strength.

9. He had faith to be healed - He felt the power of God in his soul; and thence knew it was sufficient to heal his body also.

11. The gods are come down - Which the heathens supposed they frequently did; Jupiter especially. But how amazingly does the prince of darkness blind the minds of them that believe not! The Jews would not own Christ's Godhead, though they saw him work numberless miracles. On the other hand, the heathens seeing mere men work one miracle, were for deifying them immediately.

13. The priest of Jupiter - Whose temple and image were just without the gate of the city, brought garlands - To put on the victims, and bulls - The usual offerings to Jupiter.

14. They sprang in among the people, crying out - As in a fire, or other sudden and great danger.

15. To turn from these vanities - From worshipping any but the true God. He does not deign to call them gods; unto the living God - Not like these dead idols; who made the heaven and the earth, the sea - Each of which they supposed to have its own gods.

16. Who in times past - He prevents their objection, "But if these things are so, we should have heard them from our fathers." Suffered - An awful judgment, all nations - The multitude of them that err does not turn error into truth, to walk in their own ways - The idolatries which they had chosen.

17. He left not himself without witness - For the heathens had always from God himself a testimony both of his existence and of his providence; in that he did good - Even by punishments he testifies of himself; but more peculiarly by benefits; giving rain - By which air, earth, and sea, are, as it were, all joined together; from heaven - The seat of God; to which St. Paul probably pointed while he spoke, filling the body with food, the soul with gladness.

19. Who persuaded the multitude - Moved with equal ease either to adore or murder him.

20. But as the disciples stood round - Probably after sunset. The enraged multitude would scarce have suffered it in the day time: he rose and went into the city - That he should be able to do this, just after he had been left for dead, was a miracle little less than a resurrection from the dead. Especially considering the manner wherein the Jewish malefactors were stoned. The witnesses first threw as large a stone as they could lift, with all possible violence upon his head, which alone was sufficient to dash the skull in pieces. All the people then joined, as long as any motion or token of life remained.

23. When they had ordained them presbyters in every Church - Out of those who were themselves but newly converted. So soon can God enable even a babe in Christ to build up others in the common faith: they commended them to the Lord - An expression implying faith in Christ, as well as love to the brethren.

25. Perga and Attalia were cities of Pamphylia.

26. Recommended to the grace - Or favour, of God, for the work which they had fulfilled - This shows the nature and design of that laying on of hands, which was mentioned chap. xiii, 3.

XV

1. Coming down from Judea - Perhaps to supply what they thought Paul and Barnabas had omitted.

2. They (the brethren) determined that Paul and Barnabas, and certain others should go up to Jerusalem about this question - This is the journey to which St. Paul refers, Gal. ii, 1, 2, when he says he went up by Revelation: which is very consistent with this; for the Church in sending them might be directed by a Revelation made either immediately to St. Paul, or to some other person, relating to so important an affair. Important indeed it was, that these Jewish impositions should be solemnly opposed in time; because multitudes of converts were still zealous for the law, and ready to contend for the observance of it. Indeed many of the Christians of Antioch would have acquiesced in the determination of Paul alone. But as many others might have prejudices against him, for his having been so much concerned for the Gentiles, it was highly expedient to take the concurrent judgment of all the apostles on this occasion.

4. They were received - That is solemnly welcomed.

5. But certain Pharisees - For even believers are apt to retain their former turn of mind, and prejudices derived therefrom. The law of Moses - The whole law, both moral and ritual.

7. After much debate - It does not appear that this was among the apostles themselves. But if it had, if they themselves had debated at first, yet might their final decision be from an unerring direction. For how really soever they were inspired, we need not suppose their inspiration was always so instantaneous and express, as to supersede any deliberation in their own minds, or any consultation with each other. Peter rose up - This is the last time he is mentioned in the Acts.

8. God bare them witness - That he had accepted them, by giving them the Holy Ghost.

9. Purifying - This word is repeated from chap. x, 15; their hearts - The heart is the proper seat of purity; by faith - Without concerning themselves with the Mosaic law.

10. Now therefore - Seeing these things are so: why tempt ye God? - Why do ye provoke him to anger, by putting so heavy a yoke on their neck?

11. The Lord Jesus - He does not here say our Lord; because in this solemn place he means the Lord of all, we - Jews, shall be saved even as they - Gentiles, namely, through the grace of the Lord Jesus, not by our observance of the ceremonial law.

12. Miracles and wonders - By which also what St. Peter had said was confirmed.

14. Simon hath declared - James, the apostle of the Hebrews, calls Peter by his Hebrew name. To take out of them a people for his name - That is to believe in him, to be called by his name.

15. To this agree - St. Peter had urged the plain fact, which St. James confirms by Scripture prophecy. The words of the prophets - One of whom is immediately cited.

16. After this - After the Jewish dispensation expires. I will build again the fallen tabernacle of David - By raising from his seed the Christ, who shall build on the ruins of his fallen tabernacle a spiritual and eternal kingdom. Amos ix, 11.

17. The Gentiles on whom my name is called - That is, who are called by my name; who are my people.

18. Known unto God are all his works from eternity - Which the apostle infers from the prophecy itself, and the accomplishment of it. And this conversion of the Gentiles being known to him from

eternity, we ought not to think a new or strange thing. It is observable, he does not speak of God's works in the natural world, (which had been nothing to his present purpose,) but of his dealing with the children of men. Now he could not know these, without knowing the characters and actions of particular persons, on a correspondence with which the wisdom and goodness of his providential dispensations is founded. For instance, he could not know how he would deal with heathen idolaters (whom he was now calling into his Church) without knowing there would be heathen idolaters: and yet this was a thing purely contingent, a thing as dependent on the freedom of the human mind, as any we can imagine. This text, therefore, among a thousand more, is an unanswerable proof, that God foreknows future contingencies, though there are difficulties relating hereto which men cannot solve.

20. To abstain from fornication - Which even the philosophers among the heathens did not account any fault. It was particularly frequent in the worship of their idols, on which account they are here named together. And from things strangled - That is, from whatever had been killed, without pouring out the blood. When God first permitted man to eat flesh, he commanded Noah, and in him all his posterity, whenever they killed any creature for food, to abstain from the blood thereof. It was to be poured upon the ground as water: doubtless in honour of that blood which was in due time poured out for the sin of the world.

21. Perhaps the connection is, To the Jews we need write nothing on these heads; for they hear the law continually.

22. With the whole Church - Which therefore had a part therein; to send chosen men - Who might put it beyond all dispute, that this was the judgment of the apostles and all the brethren.

23. Writing thus, and sending it by their hand - The whole conduct of this affair plainly shows that the Church in those days had no conception of St. Peter's primacy, or of his being the chief judge in controversies. For the decree is drawn up, not according to his, but the Apostle James's proposal and direction: and that in the name, not of St. Peter, but of all the apostles and elders, and of the whole Church. Nay, St. Peter's name is not mentioned at all, either in the order for sending to Jerusalem on the question, ver. 2, or in the address of the messengers concerning it, ver. 4, or in the letter which was written in answer.

24. Forasmuch as, &c. - The simplicity, weightiness, and conciseness of this letter are highly observable.

26. Men that have hazarded their lives - This is spoken of Paul and Barnabas.

27. Who will tell you the same things - Which we have written.

28. These necessary things - All of these were necessary for that time. But the first of them was not necessary long; and the direction concerning it was therefore repealed by the same Spirit, as we read in the former Epistle to the Corinthians.

29. Blood - The eating which was never permitted the children of God from the beginning of the world. Nothing can be clearer than this. For,

1. From Adam to Noah no man ate flesh at all; consequently no man then ate blood.

2. When God allowed Noah and his posterity to eat flesh, he absolutely forbade them to eat blood; and accordingly this, with the other six precepts of Noah, was delivered down from Noah to Moses.

3. God renewed this prohibition by Moses, which was not repealed from the time of Moses till Christ came.

4. Neither after his coming did any presume to repeal this decree of the Holy Ghost, till it seemed good to the bishop of Rome so to do, about the middle of the eighth century.

5. From that time those Churches which acknowledged his authority held the eating of blood to be an indifferent thing. But,

6. In all those Churches which never did acknowledge the bishop of Rome's authority, it never was allowed to eat blood; nor is it allowed at this day. This is the plain fact; let men reason as plausibly as they please on one side or the other. From which keeping yourselves ye will do well - That is, ye will find a blessing. This gentle manner of concluding was worthy the apostolical wisdom and goodness. But how soon did succeeding councils of inferior authority change it into the style of anathemas! Forms which have proved an occasion of consecrating some of the most devilish passions under the most sacred names; and like some ill-adjusted weapons of war, are most likely to hurt the hand from which they are thrown.

35. Paul and Barnabas abode in Antioch - And it was during this time that Peter came down from Jerusalem, and that St. Paul withstood him to the face, for separating himself from the Gentiles, Gal. ii, 11, &c.

36. Let us go and visit the brethren in every city where we have preached - This was all that St. Paul designed at first; but it was not all that God designed by his journey, whose providence carried him much farther than he intended. And see how they do - How their souls prosper: how they grow in faith, hope love: what else ought to be the grand and constant inquiry in every ecclesiastical visitation? Reader, how dost thou do?

37. Barnabas counselled to take John - His kinsman.

38. But Paul thought it not right - To trust him again, who had deserted them before: who had shrunk from the labour and danger of converting those they were now going to confirm.

39. And there was a sharp contention - Literally, a paroxysm, or fit of a fever. But nothing in the text implies that the sharpness was on both sides. It is far more probable that it was not; that St. Paul, who had the right on his side, as he undoubtedly had,) maintained it with love. And Barnabas taking Mark with him, sailed away to Cyprus - Forsaking the work in which he was engaged, he went away to his own country.

40. But Paul departed - Held on his intended course: being recommended by the brethren to the grace of God - We do not find that Barnabas stayed for this. O how mighty is the grace of God! which in the midst of the world, in the midst of sin, among so many snares of Satan, and in spite of the incredible weakness and depravity of nature, yet overcomes all opposition, sanctifies, sustains, and preserves us to the end! It appears not only that Paul and Barnabas were afterward thoroughly reconciled, 1 Cor. ix, 6; Gal. ii, 9; but also that John was again admitted by St. Paul as a companion in his labours, Colossians iv, 10; Phil. i, 24; 2 Tim. iv, 11.

XVI

3. He took and circumcised him because of the Jews - The unbelieving Jews, to whom he designed he should preach. For they would not have conversed with him at all, so long as he was uncircumcised.

6. And having gone through Phrygia - And spoken there what was sufficient, as well as in the region of Galatia, being forbid by the Spirit (probably by an inward dictate) to speak as yet in the proconsular Asia, the time for it not being come.

7. Coming to Mysia, and passing it by, as being a part of Asia, they attempted to go into Bithynia; but the Spirit suffered them not - Forbidding them as before. Sometimes a strong impression, for which we are not able to give any account, is not altogether to be despised.

9. A vision appeared to Paul by night - It was not a dream, though it was by night. No other dream is mentioned in the New Testament than that of Joseph and of Pilate's wife. A man of Macedonia - Probably an angel clothed in the Macedonian habit, or using the language of the country, and representing the inhabitants of it. Help us - Against Satan, ignorance, and sin.

10. We sought to go into Macedonia - This is the first place in which St. Luke intimates his attendance on the apostle. And here he does it only in an oblique manner. Nor does he throughout the history once mention his own name, or any one thing which he did or said for the service of Christianity; though Paul speaks of him in the most honourable terms, Colossians iv, 14; 2 Tim. iv, 11; and probably as the brother whose praise in the Gospel went through all the Churches, 2 Cor. viii, 18. The same remark may be made on the rest of the sacred historians, who every one of them show the like amiable modesty.

11. We ran with a straight course - Which increased their confidence that God had called them.

12. The first city - Neapolis was the first city they came to in that part of Macedonia which was nearest to Asia: in that part which was farthest from it, Philippi. The river Strymon ran between them. Philippi was a Roman colony.

13. We went out of the gate - The Jews usually held their religious assemblies (either by choice or constraint) at a distance from the heathens: by a river side - Which was also convenient for purifying themselves. Where prayer was wont to be made - Though it does not appear there was any house built there. We spake - At first in a familiar manner. Paul did not immediately begin to preach.

14. A worshipper of God - Probably acquainted with the prophetic writings whose heart the Lord opened - The Greek word properly refers to the opening of the eyes: and the heart has its eyes, Eph. i, 18. These are closed by nature and to open them is the peculiar work of God.

15. She was baptized and her family - Who can believe that in so many families there was no infant? Or that the Jews, who were so long accustomed to circumcise their children, would not now devote them to God by baptism? She entreated us - The souls of the faithful cleave to those by whom they were gained to God. She constrained us - By her importunity. They did not immediately comply, lest any should imagine they sought their own profit by coming into Macedonia.

17. These men are - A great truth: but St. Paul did not need, nor would accept, of such testimony.

19. The magistrates - The supreme magistrates of the city. In the next verse they are called by a title which often signifies pretors. These officers exercised both the military and civil authority.

20. Being Jews - A nation peculiarly despised by the Romans.

21. And teach customs which it is not lawful for us to receive - The world has received all the rules and doctrines of all the philosophers that ever were. But this is a property of Gospel truth: it has something in it peculiarly intolerable to the world.

23. They laid many stripes upon them - Either they did not immediately say they were Romans, or in the tumult it was not regarded. Charging the jailer - Perhaps rather to quiet the people than because they thought them criminal.

24. Secured their feet in the stocks - These were probably those large pieces of wood, in use among the Romans, which not only loaded the legs of the prisoner, but also kept them extended in a very painful manner.

25. Paul and Silas sung a hymn to God - Notwithstanding weariness, hunger stripes, and blood. And the prisoners heard - A song to which they were not accustomed.

28. But Paul cried - As they were all then in the dark, it is not easy to say, how Paul knew of the jailer's purpose; unless it were by some immediate notice from God, which is by no means incredible. With a loud voice - Through earnestness, and because he was at some distance. Do thyself no harm - Although the Christian faith opens the prospect into another life, yet it absolutely forbids and effectually prevents a man's discharging himself from this.

30. Sirs - He did not style them so the day before. What must I do to be saved? - From the guilt I feel and the vengeance I fear? Undoubtedly God then set his sins in array before him, and convinced him in the clearest and strongest manner that the wrath of God abode upon him.

31. Thou shalt be saved and thy household - If ye believe. They did so, and were saved.

33. He washed their stripes - It should not be forgot, that the apostles had not the power of working miraculous cures when they pleased, either on themselves, or their dearest friends. Nor was it expedient they should, since it would have frustrated many wise designs of God, which were answered by their sufferings.

34. He set a table before them and rejoiced - Faith makes a man joyful, prudent, liberal.

35. The pretors sent - Being probably terrified by the earthquake; saying, Let those men go - How different from the charge given a few hours before! And how great an ease of mind to the jailer!

37. They have beaten us publicly, being Roman - St. Paul does not always plead this privilege. But in a country where they were entire strangers, such treatment might have brought upon them a suspicion of having been guilty of some uncommon crime, and so have hindered the course of the Gospel.

40. When they had seen the brethren, they comforted them and departed - Though many circumstances now invited their stay, yet they wisely complied with the request of the magistrates, that they might not seem to express any degree of obstinacy or revenge, or give any suspicion of a design to stir up the people.

XVII

1. And taking their journey through Amphipolis and Apollonia - St. Luke seems to have been left at Philippi; and to have continued in those parts, travelling from place to place among the Churches, till St. Paul returned thither. For here he leaves off speaking of himself as one of St. Paul's company; neither does he resume that style, till we find them together there, chap. xx, 5, 6. After this he constantly uses it to the end of the history. Amphipolis and Apollonia were cities of Macedonia.

2. And Paul, according to his custom - Of doing all things, as far as might be, in a regular manner, went in to them three Sabbath days - Not excluding the days between.

4. Of the principal women, not a few - Our free thinkers pique themselves upon observing, that women are more religious than men; and this, in compliment both to religion and good manners, they impute to the weakness of their understandings. And indeed as far as nature can go, in imitating religion by performing the outward acts of it, this picture of religion may make a fairer show in women than in men, both by reason of their more tender passions, and their modesty, which will make those actions appear to more advantage. But in the case of true religion, which always implies taking up the cross, especially in time of persecution, women lie naturally under a great disadvantage, as having less courage than men. So that their embracing the Gospel was a stronger evidence of the power of him whose strength is perfected in weakness, as a stronger assistance of the Holy Spirit was needful for them to overcome their natural fearfulness.

11. These were more ingenuous - Or generous. To be teachable in the things of God is true generosity of soul. The receiving the word with all readiness of mind, and the most accurate search into the truth, are well consistent.

12. Many of the - Of the Jews. And of the Grecian women - Who were followed by their husbands.

16. While Paul was waiting for the - Having no design, as it seems, to preach at Athens, but his zeal for God drew him into it unawares, without staying till his companions came.

18. Some of the Epicurean and Stoic philosopher - The Epicureans entirely denied a providence, and held the world to be the effect of mere chance; asserting sensual pleasure to be man's chief good, and that the soul and body died together. The Stoics held, that matter was eternal; that all things were governed by irresistible fate; that virtue was its own sufficient reward, and vice its own sufficient punishment. It is easy to see, how happily the apostle levels his discourse at some of the most important errors of each, while, without expressly attacking either, he gives a plain summary of his own religious principles. What would this babbler say? - Such is the language of natural reason, full of, and satisfied

with itself. Yet even here St. Paul had some fruit; though nowhere less than at Athens. And no wonder, since this city was a seminary of philosophers, who have ever been the pest of true religion. He seemeth to be a proclaimer - This he returns upon them at the 23rd verse; of strange gods - Such as are not known even at Athens. Because he preached to them Jesus and the resurrection - A God and a goddess. And as stupid as this mistake was, it is the less to be wondered at, since the Athenians might as well count the resurrection a deity, as shame, famine, and many others.

19. The Areopagus, or hill of Mars, (dedicated to Mars, the heathen God of war,) was the place where the Athenians held their supreme court of judicature. But it does not appear he was carried thither as a criminal. The original number of its Judges was twelve; but afterward it increased to three hundred. These were generally men of the greatest families in Athens, and were famed for justice and integrity.

21. And the strangers sojourning there - And catching the distemper of them. Some new thing - The Greek word signifies some newer thing. New things quickly grew cheap, and they wanted those that were newer still.

22. Then Paul standing in the midst of the Areopagus - An ample theatre; said - Giving them a lecture of natural divinity, with admirable wisdom, acuteness, fulness, and courtesy. They inquire after new things: Paul in his divinely philosophical discourse, begins with the first, and goes on to the last things, both which were new things to them. He points out the origin and the end of all things, concerning which they had so many disputes, and equally refutes both the Epicurean and Stoic. I perceive - With what clearness and freedom does he speak! Paul against Athens!

23. I found an altar - Some suppose this was set up by Socrates, to express in a covert way his devotion to the only true God, while he derided the plurality of the heathen gods, for which he was condemned to death: and others, that whoever erected this altar, did it in honour to the God of Israel, of whom there was no image, and whose name Jehovah was never made known to the idolatrous Gentiles. Him proclaim I unto you - Thus he fixes the wandering attention of these blind philosophers; proclaiming to them an unknown, and yet not a new God.

24. God who made the world - Thus is demonstrated even to reason, the one true, good God; absolutely different from the creatures, from every part of the visible creation.

25. Neither is he served as though he needed any thing - or person - The Greek word equally takes in both. To all - That live and breathe;-in him we live; and breathe - In him we move. By breathing life is continued. I breathe this moment: the next is not in my power: and all things - For in him we are. So exactly do the parts of this discourse answer each other.

26. He hath made of one blood the whole nation of men - By this expression the apostle showed them in the most unaffected manner, that though he was a Jew, be was not enslaved to any narrow views, but looked on all mankind as his brethren: having determined the times - That it is God who gave men the earth to inhabit, Paul proves from the order of times and places, showing the highest wisdom of the Disposer, superior to all human counsels. And the bounds of their habitation - By mountains, seas, rivers, and the like.

27. If haply - The way is open; God is ready to be found. But he will lay no force upon man; they might feel after him - This is in the midst between seeking and finding. Feeling being the lowest and grossest of all our senses, is fitly applied to the low knowledge of God; though he be not far from every one of us - We need not go far to seek or find him. He is very near us; in us. It is only perverse reason which thinks he is afar off.

28. In him - Not in ourselves, we live, and move, and have our being - This denotes his necessary, intimate, and most efficacious presence. No words can better express the continual and necessary dependence of all created beings, in their existence and all their operations, on the first and almighty cause, which the truest philosophy as well as divinity teaches. As certain also of your own poets have said - Aratus, whose words these are, was an Athenian, who lived almost three hundred years before this time. They are likewise to be found, with the alteration of one letter only, in the hymn of Cleanthes to Jupiter or the supreme being, one of the purest and finest pieces of natural religion in the whole world of Pagan antiquity.

29. We ought not to think - A tender expression especially in the first per son plural. As if he had said, Can God himself be a less noble being than we who are his offspring? Nor does he only here deny, that these are like God, but that they have any analogy to him at all, so as to be capable of representing him.

30. The times of ignorance - What! does he object ignorance to the knowing Athenians? Yes, and they acknowledge it by this very altar. God overlooked - As one paraphrases, "The beams of his eye did in a manner shoot over it." He did not appear to take notice of them, by sending express messages to them as he did to the Jews. But now - This day, this hour, saith Paul, puts an end to the Divine forbearance, and brings either greater mercy or punishment. Now he commandeth all men everywhere to repent - There is a dignity and grandeur in this expression, becoming an ambassador from the King of heaven. And this universal demand of repentance declared universal guilt in the strongest manner, and admirably confronted the pride of the haughtiest Stoic of them all. At the same time it bore down the

idle plea of fatality. For how could anyone repent of doing what he could not but have done?

31. He hath appointed a day in which he will judge the world - How fitly does he speak this, in their supreme court of justice? By the man - So he speaks, suiting himself to the capacity of his hearers. Whereof he hath given assurance to all men, in that he hath raised him from the dead - God raising Jesus demonstrated hereby, that he was to be the glorious Judge of all. We are by no means to imagine that this was all which the apostle intended to have said, but the indolence of some of his hearers and the petulancy of others cut him short.

32. Some mocked - Interrupting him thereby. They took offense at that which is the principal motive of faith, from the pride of reason. And having once stumbled at this, they rejected all the rest.

33. So Paul departed - Leaving his hearers divided in their judgment.

34. Among whom was even Dionysius the Areopagite - One of the Judges of that court: on whom some spurious writings have been fathered in later ages, by those who are fond of high sounding nonsense.

XVIII

1. Paul departing from Athens - He did not stay there long. The philosophers there were too easy, too indolent, and too wise in their own eyes to receive the Gospel.

2. Claudius, the Roman emperor, had commanded all the Jews to depart from Rome - All who were Jews by birth. Whether they were Jews or Christians by religion, the Roman were too stately to regard.

3. They were tent makers by trade - For it was a rule among the Jews (and why is it not among the Christians?) to bring up all their children to some trade, were they ever so rich or noble.

5. And when Silas and Timotheus were come from Macedonia - Silas seems to have stayed a considerable time at Berea: but Timotheus had come to the apostle while he was at Athens, and been sent by him to comfort and confirm the Church at Thessalonica, 1 Thess. iii, 1-5. But now at length both Silas and Timotheus came to the apostle at Corinth. Paul was pressed in spirit - The more probably from what Silas and Timotheus related. Every Christian ought diligently to observe any such pressure in his own spirit, and if it agree with Scripture, to follow it: if he does not he will feel great heaviness.

6. He shook his raiment - To signify he would from that time refrain from them: and to intimate, that God would soon shake them off as unworthy to be numbered among his people. I am pure - None can say this but he that has born a full testimony against sin. From henceforth I will go to the Gentiles - But not to them altogether. He did not break off all intercourse with the Jews even at Corinth. Only he preached no more in their synagogue.

7. He went into the house of one named Justus - A Gentile, and preached there, though probably he still lodged with Aquila.

8. And many hearing - The conversation of Crispus, and the preaching of Paul.

10. I am with thee: therefore fear not all the learning, politeness, grandeur, or power of the inhabitants of this city. Speak and hold not thy peace - For thy labour shall not be in vain. For I have much people in this city - So he prophetically calls them that afterward believed.

11. He continued there a year and six months - A long time! But how few souls are now gained in a longer time than this? Who is in the fault? Generally both teachers and hearers.

12. When Gallio was proconsul of Achaia - Of which Corinth was the chief city. This Gallio, the brother of the famous Seneca, is much commended both by him and by other writers, for the sweetness and generosity of his temper, and easiness of his behaviour. Yet one thing he lacked! But he knew it not and had no concern about it.

15. But if it be - He speaks with the utmost coolness and contempt, a question of names - The names of the heathen gods were fables and shadows. But the question concerning the name of Jesus is of more importance than all things else under heaven. Yet there is this singularity (among a thousand others) in the Christian religion, that human reason, curious as it is in all other things, abhors to inquire into it.

17. Then they all took Sosthenes - The successor of Crispus, and probably Paul's chief accuser, and beat him - It seems because he had occasioned them so much trouble to no purpose, before the judgment seat - One can hardly think in the sight of Gallio, though at no great distance from him. And it seems to have had a happy effect. For Sosthenes himself was afterward a Christian, 1 Cor. i, 1.

18. Paul continued many days - After the year and six months, to confirm the brethren. Aquila having shaved his head - As was the custom in a vow, chap. xxi, 24; Num. vi, 18. At Cenchrea - A seaport town, at a small distance from Corinth.

21. I must by all means keep the feast at Jerusalem - This was not from any apprehension that he was obliged in conscience to keep the Jewish feasts; but to take the opportunity of meeting a great number of his countrymen to whom he might preach Christ, or whom he might farther instruct, or free from the prejudices they had imbibed against him. But I will return to you - So he did, chap. xix, 1.

22. And landing at Cesarea, he went up - Immediately to Jerusalem; and saluted the Church - Eminently so called, being the mother Church of Christian believers: and having kept the feast there, he went down from thence to Antioch.

23. He went over the country of Galatia and Phrygia - It is supposed, spending about four years therein, including the time he stayed at Ephesus.

24. An eloquent man, mighty in the Scriptures - Of the Old Testament. Every talent may be of use in the kingdom of God, if joined with the knowledge of the Scriptures and fervour of spirit.

25. This man had been instructed - Though not perfectly, in the way of the Lord - In the doctrine of Christ. Knowing only the baptism of John - Only what John taught those whom he baptized, namely, to repent and believe in a Messiah shortly to appear.

26. He spake - Privately; and taught publicly. Probably he returned to live at Alexandria, soon after he had been baptized by John; and so had no opportunity of being fully acquainted with the doctrines of the Gospel, as delivered by Christ and his apostles. And explained to him the way of God more perfectly - He who knows Christ, is able to instruct even those that are mighty in the Scriptures.

27. Who greatly helped through grace - It is through grace only that any gift of any one is profitable to another. Them that had believed - Apollos did not plant, but water. This was the peculiar gift which he had received. And he was better able to convince the Jews, than to convert the heathens.

XIX

1. Having passed through - Galatia and Phrygia, which were termed the upper parts of Asia Minor. Certain disciples - Who had been formerly baptized by John the Baptist, and since imperfectly instructed in Christianity.

2. Have ye received the Holy Ghost? - The extraordinary gifts of the Spirit, as well as his sanctifying graces? We have not so much as heard - Whether there be any such gifts.

3. Into what were ye baptized - Into what dispensation? To the sealing of what doctrine? Into John's baptism - We were baptized by John and believe what he taught.

4. John baptized - That is, the whole baptism and preaching of John pointed at Christ. After this John is mentioned no more in the New Testament. Here he gives way to Christ altogether.

5. And hearing this, they were baptized - By some other. Paul only laid his hands upon them. They were baptized - They were baptized twice; but not with the same baptism. John did not administer that baptism which Christ afterward commanded, that is, in the name of the Father, Son, and Holy Ghost.

9. The way - The Christian way of worshipping God. He departed - Leaving them their synagogue to themselves. Discoursing daily - Not on the Sabbath only, in the school of one Tyrannus - Which we do not find was any otherwise consecrated, than by preaching the Gospel there.

10. All who desired it among the inhabitants of the proconsular Asia, now heard the word: St. Paul had been forbidden to preach it in Asia before, chap. xvi, 6. But now the time was come.

11. Special miracles - Wrought in a very uncommon manner.

12. Evil spirits - Who also occasioned many of those diseases, which yet might appear to be purely natural.

13. Exorcists - Several of the Jews about this time pretended to a power of casting out devils, particularly by certain arts or charms, supposed to be derived from Solomon. Undertook to name - Vain undertaking! Satan laughs at all those who attempt to expel him either out of the bodies or the souls of men but by Divine faith. All the light of reason is nothing to the craft or strength of that subtle spirit. His craft cannot be known but by the Spirit of God nor can his strength be conquered but by the power of faith.

17. And the name of the Lord Jesus was magnified - So that even the malice of the devil wrought for the furtherance of the Gospel.

18. Many came confessing - Of their own accord, and openly declaring their deeds - The efficacy of God's word, penetrating the inmost recesses of their soul, wrought that free and open confession to which perhaps even torments would not have compelled them.

19. Curious arts - Magical arts, to which that soft appellation was given by those who practiced them. Ephesus was peculiarly famous for these. And as these practices were of so much reputation there, it is no wonder the books which taught them should bear a great price. Bringing their books together - As it were by common consent, burnt them - Which was far better than selling them, even though the money had been given to the poor. Fifty thousand pieces of silver - If these pieces of silver be taken for Jewish shekels, the sum will amount to six thousand two hundred and fifty pounds.

20. So powerfully did the word of God grow - In extent, and prevail - In power and efficacy.

21. After these things were ended - Paul sought not to rest, but pressed on, as if he had yet done nothing. He is already possessed of Ephesus and Asia. He purposes for Macedonia and Achaia. He has his eye upon Jerusalem, then upon Rome; afterward on Spain, Rom. xv, 28. No Caesar, no Alexander the Great, no other hero, comes up to the magnanimity of this little Benjamite. Faith and love to God

and man had enlarged his heart, even as the sand of the sea.

24. Silver shrines - Silver models of that famous temple, which were bought not only by the citizens, but by strangers from all parts. The artificers - The other silversmiths.

25. The workmen - Employed by him and them.

26. Saying, that they are not gods which are made with hands - This manifestly shows, that the contrary opinion did then generally prevail, namely, that there was a real Divinity in their sacred images. Though some of the later heathens spoke of them just as the Romanists do now.

27. There is danger, not only that this our craft [trade] should come into disgrace, but also that the temple of the great goddess Diana should be despised - No wonder a discourse should make so deep an impression, which was edged both by interest and superstition. The great goddess was one of the standing titles of Diana. Her majesty destroyed - Miserable majesty, which was capable of being thus destroyed! Whom all Asia and the world - That is, the Roman empire, worshippeth - Although under a great variety of titles and characters. But the multitude of those that err does not turn error into truth.

29. They rushed with one accord - Demetrius and his company, into the theatre - Where criminals were wont to be thrown to the wild beasts, dragging with them Gaius and Aristarchus - When they could not find Paul. Probably they hoped to oblige them to fight with the wild beasts, as some think St. Paul had done before.

30. When Paul would have gone in to the people - Being above all fear, to plead the cause of his companions, and prove they are not gods which are made with hands.

31. The principal officers of Asia - The Asian priests, who presided over the public games, which they were then celebrating in honour of Diana.

32. The greater part did not know for what they were come together - Which is commonly the case in such an assembly.

33. And they thrust forward - Namely, the artificers and workmen, Alexander - Probably some well-known Christian whom they saw in the crowd: the Jews pushing him on - To expose him to the more danger. And Alexander waving with his hand - In token of desiring silence, would have made a defense - For himself and his brethren.

34. But when they knew that he was a Jew - And consequently an enemy to their worship of images; they prevented him, by crying, Great is Diana of the Ephesians.

35. The register - Probably the chief governor of the public games. The image which fell down from Jupiter - They believed that very image of Diana, which stood in her temple, fell down from Jupiter in heaven. Perhaps he designed to insinuate, as if falling down from Jupiter, it was not made with hands, and so was not that sort of idols which Paul had said were no gods.

37. Nor blasphemers of your goddess - They simply declared the one God, and the vanity of idols in general.

38. There are proconsuls - One in every province. There was one at Ephesus.

39. In a lawful assembly - In such a regular assembly as has authority to judge of religious and political affairs.

40. This concourse - He wisely calls it by an inoffensive name.

XX

1. After the tumult was ceased - So Demetrius gained nothing. Paul remained there till all was quiet.

2. He came into Greece - That part of it which lay between Macedonia and Achaia.

3. An ambush being laid for him - In his way to the ship.

4. To Asia - There some of them left him. But Trophimus went with him to Jerusalem, chap. xxi, 29. Aristarchus, even to Rome,. xxvii, 2.

6. We set sail - St. Luke was now with St. Paul again, as we learn from his manner of expressing himself.

7. To break bread - That is, to celebrate the Lord's Supper; continued his discourse - Through uncommon fervour of spirit.

8. There were many lamps in the room where they were assembled - To prevent any possible scandal.

9. In the window - Doubtless kept open, to prevent heat, both from the lamps and the number of people.

10. Paul fell or him - It is observable, our Lord never used this gesture. But Elijah and Elisha did as well as Paul. His life is in him - He is alive again.

11. So departed - Without taking any rest at all.

12. And they brought the young man alive - But alas! How many of those who have allowed themselves to sleep under sermons, or as it were to dream awake, have slept the sleep of eternal death, and fallen to rise no more!

13. Being himself to go on foot - That he might enjoy the company of his Christian brethren a little longer, although he had passed the night without sleep, and though Assos was of difficult and dangerous access by land.

14. Mitylene - Was a city and part of the isle of Lesbos, about seven miles distant from the Asiatic coast.

16. For Paul had determined to sail by Ephesus - Which lay on the other side of the bay. He hasted to be at Jerusalem on the day of pentecost - Because then was the greatest concourse of people.

17. Sending to Ephesus, he called the elders of the Church - These are called bishops in the 28th verse, (rendered overseers in our translation.) Perhaps elders and bishops were then the same; or no otherwise different than are the rector of a parish and his curates.

18. Ye know - Happy is he who can thus appeal to the conscience of his hearers.

19. Serving - See the picture of a faithful servant! The Lord - Whose the church is, with all humility, and with tears, and trials - These are the concomicants of it. The service itself is described more particularly in the following verse. This humility he recommends to the Ephesians themselves, Eph. iv, 2. His tears are mentioned again, verse 31, as also 2 Cor. ii, 4; Phil. iii, 18. These passages laid together supply us with the genuine character of St. Paul. Holy tears, from those who seldom weep on account of natural occurrences, are no mean specimen of the efficacy and proof of the truth of Christianity. Yet joy is well consistent therewith, ver. 24. The same person may be sorrowful, yet always rejoicing.

20. I have preached - Publicly; and taught - From house to house. Else he had not been pure from their blood. For even an apostle could not discharge his duty by public preaching only. How much less can an ordinary pastor!

21. Repentance toward God - The very first motion of the soul toward God is a kind of repentance.

22. Bound by the Spirit - Strongly impelled by him.

23. Save that - Only this I know in general; the Holy Ghost witnesseth - By other persons. Such was God's good pleasure to reveal these things to him, not immediately, but by the ministry of others.

24. Nor do I count my life precious - It adds great force to this and all the other passages of Scripture, in which the apostles express their contempt of the world, that they were not uttered by persons like Seneca and Antoninus, who talked elegantly of despising the world in the full affluence of all its enjoyments; but by men who daily underwent the greatest calamities, and exposed their lives in proof of their assertions.

25. Ye shall see my face no more - He wisely inserts this, that what follows might make the deeper impression.

27. For I have not shunned - Otherwise if any had perished, their blood would have been on his head.

28. Take heed therefore - I now devolve my care upon you; first to yourselves; then to the flock over which the Holy Ghost hath made you overseers - For no man, or number of men upon earth, can constitute an overseer, bishop, or any other Christian minister. To do this is the peculiar work of the Holy Ghost: to feed the Church of God - That is, the believing, loving, holy children of God; which he hath purchased - How precious is it then in his sight! with his own blood - For it is the blood of the only begotten Son of God, 1 John i, 7.

29. Grievous wolves - From without, namely, false apostles. They had, not yet broke in on the Church at Ephesus.

30. Yea, from among yourselves men will arise - Such were the Nicolaitans, of whom Christ complains, Rev. ii, 6; to draw away disciples - From the purity of the Gospel and the unity of the body.

31. I ceased not to warn every one night and day - This was watching indeed! Who copies after this example?

32. The word of his grace - It is the grand channel of it, to believers as well as unbelievers. Who is able to build you up - To confirm and increase your faith, love, holiness. God can thus build us up, without any instrument. But he does build us up by them. O beware of dreaming that you have less need of human teachers after you know Christ than before! And to give you an inheritance - Of eternal glory, among them that are sanctified - And so made meet for it. A large number of these Paul doubtless knew, and remembered before God.

33. I have coveted - Here the apostle begins the other branch of his farewell discourse, like old Samuel, 1 Sam. xii, 3, taking his leave of the children of Israel.

34. These hands - Callous, as you see, with labour. Who is he that envies such a bishop or archbishop as this?

35. I have showed you - Bishops, by my example, all things - And this among the rest; that thus labouring - So far as the labours of your office allow you time; ye ought to help the weak - Those who are disabled by sickness, or any bodily infirmity, from maintaining themselves by their own labour. And to remember - Effectually, so as to follow it; the word which he himself said - Without doubt his disciples remembered many of his words which are not recorded. It is happier to give - To imitate God,

and have him, as it were, indebted to us.

37. They all wept - Of old, men, yea, the best and bravest of men, were easily melted into tears; a thousand instances of which might be produced from profane as well as sacred writers. But now, notwithstanding the effeminacy which almost universally prevails, we leave those tears to women and children.

38. Sorrowing most for that word which he spake, that they should see his face no more - What sorrow will be in the great day, when God shall speak that word to all who are found on the left hand, that they shall see his face no more!

XXI

1. And when we were torn away from the in - Not without doing violence both to ourselves and them.

3. We landed at Tyre - That there should be Christians there was foretold, Psalm lxxxvii, 4. What we read in that Psalm of the Philistines and Ethiopians also may be compared with chap. viii, 40; xxvii, 4.

4. And finding disciples, we tarried there seven days - In order to spend a Sabbath with them. Who told Paul by the Spirit - That afflictions awaited him at Jerusalem. This was properly what they said by the Spirit. They themselves advised him not to go up. The disciples seemed to understand their prophetic impulse to be an intimation from the Spirit, that Paul, if he were so minded, might avoid the danger, by not going to Jerusalem.

7. Having finished our voyage - From Macedonia, chap. xx, 6, we came to Ptolemais - A celebrated city on the sea coast, anciently called Accos. It is now, like many other once noble cities, only a heap of ruins.

8. We came to Cesarea - So called from a stately temple which Herod the Great dedicated there to Augustus Caesar. It was the place where the Roman governor of Judea generally resided and kept his court. The evangelist, who was one of the seven deacons - An evangelist is a preacher of the Gospel to those who had never heard it, as Philip had done to the Samaritans, to the Ethiopian eunuch, and to all the towns from Azotus to Cesarea, chap. viii, 5, 26, 40. It is not unlikely he spent the following years preaching in Tyre and Sidon, and the other heathen cities in the neighbourhood of Galilee, his house being at Cesarea, a convenient situation for that purpose. We abode with him - We lodged at his house during our stay at Cesarea.

10. A certain prophet came - The nearer the event was, the more expressed were the predictions which prepared Paul for it.

11. Binding his own feet and hands - In the manner that malefactors were wont to be bound when apprehended. So shall the Jews bind the man whose girdle this is - St. Paul's bonds were first particularly foretold at Cesarea, to which he afterward came in bonds, chap. xxiii, 33.

12. Both we, (his fellow travelers,) and they of the place, besought him not to go up to Jerusalem - St. Paul knew that this prediction had the force of a command. They did not know this.

13. Breaking my heart - For the apostles themselves were not void of human affections. I am ready not only to be bound, but to die - And to him that is ready for it, the burden is light.

14. And when he would not be persuaded - This was not obstinacy, but true Christian resolution. We should never be persuaded, either to do evil, or to omit doing any good which is in our power; saying, the will of the Lord be done - Which they were satisfied Paul knew.

15. We took up our carriages - Our baggage; which probably went by sea before. What they took with them now in particular was the alms they were carrying to Jerusalem, chap. xxiv, 17.

16. The disciples brought us to one Mnason, a Cyprian, an old disciple - He was a native of Cyprus, but an inhabitant of Jerusalem, and probably one of the first converts there.

18. Paul went in with us - That it might appear we are all of one mind, to James - Commonly called the Lord's brother; the only apostle then presiding over the Churches in Judea.

20. They are all zealous for the law - For the whole Mosaic dispensation. How astonishing is this! Did none of the apostles, beside St. Paul, know that this dispensation was now abolished? And if they did both know and testify this, how came their hearers not to believe them?

21. They have been informed concerning thee, that thou teachest the Jews - not to circumcise their children, nor to walk after the customs - Of the Mosaic law. And so undoubtedly he did. And so he wrote to all the Churches in Galatia, among whom were many Jews. Yea, and James himself had long before assented to Peter, affirming before all the apostles and all the brethren, chap. xv, 10, That this very law was a yoke which (said he) neither our fathers nor we were able to bear - Amazing! that they did not know this! Or, that if they did, they did not openly testify it at all hazards, to every Jewish convert in Jerusalem!

22. What is it therefore - What is to be done? The multitude must needs come together - They will certainly gather together in a tumultuous manner, unless they be some way pacified.

23. *Therefore - To obviate their prejudice against thee: do this that we say to thee - Doubtless they meant this advice well: but could Paul follow it in godly sincerity? Was not the yielding so far to the judgment of others too great a deference to be paid to any mere men?

24. *And all will know - that thou thyself walkest orderly, keeping the law* - Ought he not, without any reverence to man, where the truth of God was so deeply concerned, to have answered plainly, I do not keep the Mosaic law; neither need any of you. Yea, Peter doth not keep the law. And God himself expressly commanded him not to keep it; ordering him to go in to men uncircumcised, and to eat with them, chap. xi, 3, which the law utterly forbids.

26. *Then Paul took the men* - Yielding his own judgment to their advice, which seemed to flow not out of spiritual but carnal wisdom; seeming to be what he really was not: making as if he believed the law still in force. *Declaring* - Giving notice to the priests in waiting, that he designed to accomplish the days of purification, till all the sacrifice should be offered, as the Mosaic law required, Num. vi, 13.

27. *And when the seven days were about to be accomplished* - When after giving notice to the priests, they were entering upon the accomplishment of those days. It was toward the beginning of them that Paul was seized. *The Jews that were from Asia* - Some of those Jews who came from Asia to the feast.

28. *Against the people* - The Jewish nation; *and the law* - Of Moses; *and this place* - The temple. *Yea, and hath even brought Greeks into the temple* - They might come into the outer court. But they imagined Paul had brought then into the inner temple, and had thereby polluted it.

30. *And immediately the gates were shut* - Both to prevent any further violation of the temple; and to prevent Paul's taking sanctuary at the horns of the altar.

31. *And as they went about to kill him* - It was a rule among the Jews, that any uncircumcised person who came into the inner temple, might be stoned without farther process. And they seemed to think Paul, who brought such in thither, deserved no better treatment. *Word came to the tribune* - A cohort or detachment of soldiers, belonging to the Roman legion, which lodged in the adjacent castle of Antonia, were stationed on feast days near the temple, to prevent disorders. It is evident, Lysias himself was not present, when the tumult began. Probably he was the oldest Roman tribune (or colonel) then at Jerusalem. And as such he was the commanding officer of the legion quartered at the castle.

33. *Then the tribune - Having made his way through the multitude, came near and took him* - And how many great ends of providence were answered by this imprisonment? This was not only a means of preserving his life, (after he had suffered severely for worldly prudence,) but gave him an opportunity of preaching the Gospel safely, in spite of all tumult, chap. xxii, 22, yea, and that in those places to which otherwise he could have had no access, verse 40. *And commanded him to be bound with two chains* - Taking it for granted he was some notorious offender. And thus the prophecy of Agabus was fulfilled, though by the hands of a Roman.

35. *When he came upon the stairs* - The castle of Antonia was situate on a rock fifty cubits high, at that corner of the outward temple, where the western and northern porticos joined, to each of which there were stairs descending from it.

37. *As Paul was about to be brought into the castle* - The wisdom of God taught to make use of that very time and place.

38. *Art not thou that Egyptian* - Who came into Judea when Felix had been some years governor there! Calling himself a prophet, he drew much people after him; and having brought them through the wilderness, led them to Mount Olivet, promising that the walls of the city should fall down before them. But Felix marching out of Jerusalem against him, his followers quickly dispersed, many of whom were taken or slain; but he himself made his escape.

40. *In the Hebrew tongue* - That dialect of it, which was then commonly spoken at Jerusalem.

XXII

1. *Hear ye now my defense* - Which they could not hear before for the tumult.

3. *I am verily* - This defense answers all that is objected, chap. xxi, 28. As there, so here also mention is made of the person of Paul, ver. 3, of the people and the law, ver. 3, 5, 12; of the temple, ver. 17; of teaching all men, ver. 15-17, 21; and of the truth of his doctrine, ver. 6. But he speaks closely and nervously, in few words, because the time was short. *But brought up at the feet of Gamaliel* - The scholars usually sat on low seats, or upon mats on the floor, at the feet of their masters, whose seats were raised to a considerable height. *Accurately instructed* - The learned education which Paul had received was once no doubt the matter of his boasting and confidence. Unsanctified learning made his bonds strong, and furnished him with numerous arguments against the Gospel. Yet when the grace of God had changed his heart, and turned his accomplishments into another channel, he was the fitter instrument to serve God's wise and merciful purposes, in the defense and propagation of Christianity.

4. *And persecuted this way* - With the same zeal that you do now. *Binding both men and women* - How much better was his condition, now he was bound himself.

5. *The high priest is my witness* - Is able to testify. *The brethren* -- Jews: so this title was not peculiar to the Christians.

6. *About noon* - All was done in the face of the sun. *A great light shone* - By whatever method God reveals himself to us, we shall have everlasting cause to recollect it with pleasure. Especially when he has gone in any remarkable manner out of his common way for this gracious purpose. If so, we should often dwell on the particular circumstances, and be ready, on every proper occasion, to recount those wonders of power and love, for the encouragement and instruction of others.

9. *They did not hear the voice* - Distinctly; but only a confused noise.

12. *A devout man according to the law* - A truly religious person, and though a believer in Christ, yet a strict observer of the law of Moses.

16. *Be baptized, and wash away thy sins* - Baptism administered to real penitents, is both a means and seal of pardon. Nor did God ordinarily in the primitive Church bestow this on any, unless through this means.

17. *When I was returned to Jerusalem* - From Damascus, *and was praying in the temple* - Whereby he shows that he still paid the temple its due honour, as the house of prayer. *I was in a trance* - Perhaps he might continue standing all the while, so that any who were near him would hardly discern it.

18. *And I saw him* - Jesus, *saying to me, Depart quickly out of Jerusalem* - Because of the snares laid for thee: and in order to preach where they will hear.

19. *And I said* - It is not easy for a servant of Christ, who is himself deeply impressed with Divine truths, to imagine to what a degree men are capable of hardening their hearts against thee. He is often ready to think with Paul, It is impossible for any to resist such evidence. But experience makes him wiser and shows that wilful unbelief is proof against all truth and reason.

20. *When the blood of thy martyr Stephen was shed, I also was standing by* - A real convert still retains the remembrance of his former sins. He confesses thorn and is humbled for them, all the days of his life.

22. *And they heard him to this word* - Till he began to speak of his mission to the Gentiles, and this too in such a manner as implied that the Jews were in danger of being cast off.

23. *They rent their garments* - In token of indignation and horror at this pretended blasphemy, *and cast dust into the air* - Through vehemence of rage, which they knew not how to vent.

25. *And as they* - The soldiers ordered by the tribune, *were binding him with thongs* - A freeman of Rome might be bound with a chain and beaten with a staff: but he might not be bound with thongs, neither scourged, or beaten with rods: *Paul said to the centurion* - The captain, who stood by to see the orders of the tribune executed.

26. *Consider what thou art about to do; for this man is a Roman* - Yea, there was a stronger reason to consider. For this man was a servant of God.

28. *But I was free born* - Not barely as being born at Tarsus; for this was not Roman colony. But probably either his father, or some of his ancestors, had been made free of Rome, for some military service. We learn hence, that we are under no obligation as Christians to give up our civil privileges (which we are to receive and prize as the gift of God) to every insolent invader. In a thousand circumstances, gratitude to God, and duty to men, will oblige us to insist upon them; and engage us to strive to transmit them improved, rather than impaired to posterity.

XXIII

1. *And Paul earnestly beholding the council* - Professing a clear conscience by his very countenance; and likewise waiting to see whether any of them was minded to ask him any question, *said, I have lived in all good conscience before God till this day* - He speaks chiefly of the time since he became a Christian. For none questioned him concerning what he had been before. And yet even in his unconverted state, although he was in an error, yet he had acted from conscience, before God - Whatever men may think or say of me.

3. *Then said Paul* - Being carried away by a sudden and prophetic impulse. *God is about to smite thee, thou whited wall* - Fair without; full of dirt and rubbish within. And he might well be so termed, not only as he committed this outrage, while gravely sitting on the tribunal of justice but also as, at the same time that he stood high in the esteem of the citizens, he cruelly defrauded the priests of their legal subsistence, so that some of them even perished for want. And God did remarkably smite him; for about five years after this, his house being reduced to ashes, in a tumult begun by his own son, he was besieged in the royal palace; where having hid himself in an old aqueduct, he was dragged out and miserably slain.

5. *I was not aware, brethren, that it was the high priest* - He seems to mean, I did not advert to it, in the prophetic transport of my mind: but he does not add, that his not adverting to it proceeded from the power of the Spirit coming upon him; as knowing they were not able to bear it. This answer admirably shows the situation of mind he was then in, partly with regard to the bystanders, whom he

thus softens, adding also the title of brethren, and justifying their reproof by the prohibition of Moses; partly with regard to himself, who, after that singular transport subsided, was again under the direction of the general command. Exod. xxii, 28.

6. I am a Pharisee, the son of a Pharisee: for the hope of the resurrection of the dead am I called in question - So he was in effect; although not formally, or explicitly.

8. The Pharisees confess both - Both the resurrection, and the existence of angels and separate spirits.

9. And the scribes of the Pharisees' side arising - Every sect contains both learned and unlearned. The former used to be the mouth of the party. If a spirit - St. Paul in his speech from the stairs had affirmed, that Jesus, whom they knew to have been dead, was alive, and that he had spoken to him from heaven, and again in a vision. So they add nothing, only they construe it in their own way, putting an angel or spirit for Jesus.

11. And the night following, the Lord Jesus - What Paul had before purposed in spirit, chap. xix, 21, God now in due time confirms. Another declaration to the same effect is made by an angel of God, chap. xxvii, 23. And from the 23rd chapter the sum of this book turns on the testimony of Paul to the Romans. How would the defenders of St. Peter's supremacy triumph, could they find out half as much ascribed to him! Be of good courage, Paul - As he laboured under singular distresses and persecutions, so he was favoured with extraordinary assurances of the Divine assistance. Thou must testify - Particular promises are usually given when all things appear desperate. At Rome also - Danger is nothing in the eyes of God: all hindrances farther his work. A promise of what is afar off, implies all that necessarily lies between. Paul shall testify at Rome: therefore he shall come to Rome; therefore he shall escape the Jews, the sea, the viper.

12. Some of the Jews bound themselves - Such execrable vows were not uncommon among the Jews. And if they were prevented from accomplishing what they had vowed, it was an easy matter to obtain absolution from their rabbis.

15. Now therefore ye - Which they never scrupled at all, as not doubting but they were doing God service.

17. And Paul - Though he had an express promise of it from Christ, was not to neglect any proper means of safety.

19. And the tribune taking him by the hand - In a mild, condescending way. Lysias seems to have conducted this whole affair with great integrity, humanity, and prudence.

24. Provide beasts - If a change should be necessary, to set Paul on - So we read of his riding once; but not by choice.

27. Having learned that he was a Roman - True; but not before he rescued him. Here he uses art.

31. The soldiers brought him by night to Antipatris - But not the same night they set out. For Antipatris was about thirty-eight of our miles northwest of Jerusalem. Herod the Great rebuilt it, and gave it this name in honour of his father Antipater: Cesarea was near seventy miles from Jerusalem, and about thirty from Antipatris.

35. In Herod's palace - This was a palace and a court built by Herod the Great. Probably some tower belonging to it might be used for a kind of state prison.

XXIV

1. Ananias - Who would spare no trouble on the occasion, with several of the elders, members of the sanhedrim.

2. Tertullus began - A speech how different from St. Paul's; which is true, modest, solid, and without paint. Felix was a man of the most infamous character, and a plague to all the provinces over which he presided.

4. But that I may not trouble thee any further - By trespassing either on thy patience or modesty. The eloquence of Tertullus was as bad as his cause: a lame introduction, a lame transition, and a lame conclusion. Did not God confound the orator's language?

10. Knowing - for several years thou hast been a judge over this nation - And so not unacquainted with our religious rites and customs, and consequently more capable of understanding and deciding a cause of this nature. There was no flattery in this. It was a plain fact. He governed Judea six or seven years. I answer for myself - As it may be observed, his answer exactly corresponds with the three articles of Tertullus's charge: sedition, heresy, and profanation of the temple. As to the first, he suggests, that he had not been long enough at Jerusalem to form a party and attempt an insurrection: (for it was about twelve days since he came up thither; five of which he had been at Cesarea, ver. 1; one or two were spent in his journey thither, and most of the rest he had been confined at Jerusalem.) And he challenges them, in fact, to produce any evidence of such practices, ver. 11-13. As to the second, he confesses himself to be a Christian; but maintains this to be a religion perfectly agreeable to the law and the prophets, and therefore deserving a fair reception, ver. 14, 16. And as for profaning the temple, he

observes that he behaved there in a most peaceful and regular manner, so that his innocence had been manifest even before the sanhedrim, where the authors of the tumult did not dare to appear against him.

14. After the way which they call heresy - This appellation St. Paul corrects. Not that it was then an odious word; but it was not honourable enough. A party or sect (so that word signifies) is formed by men. This way was prescribed by God. The apostle had now said what was sufficient for his defense; but having a fair occasion, he makes an ingenuous confession of his faith in this verse, his hope in the next, his love in the 17th. verse. So worship I the God of my fathers - This was a very proper plea before a Roman magistrate; as it proved that he was under the protection of the Roman laws, since the Jews were so: whereas had he introduced the worship of new gods he would have forfeited that protection. Believing all things which are written - Concerning the Messiah.

15. Both of the just and of the unjust - In a public court this was peculiarly proper to be observed.

16. For this cause - With a view to this, I also exercise myself - As well as they.

19. Who ought to have been present before thee - But the world never commit greater blunders, even against its own laws, than when it is persecuting the children of God.

21. Unless they think me blamable for this one word - Which nevertheless was the real truth. chap. xxiii, 6.

22. After I have been more accurately informed - Which he afterward was; and he doubtless (as well as Festus and Agrippa) transmitted a full account of these things to Rome.

23. He commanded the centurion to let him have liberty - To be only a prisoner at large. Hereby the Gospel was spread more and more; not to the satisfaction of the Jews. But they could not hinder it.

24. And after Paul had been kept some days in this gentle confinement at Cesarea, Felix, who had been absent for a short time, coming thither again, with Drusilla, his wife - The daughter of Herod Agrippa, one of the finest women of that age. Felix persuaded her to forsake her husband, Azizus, king of Emessa, and to be married to himself, though a heathen. She was afterward, with a son she had by Felix, consumed in an eruption of Mount Vesuvius. Concerning the faith in Christ - That is, the doctrine of Christ.

25. And as he reasoned of justice, temperance, and judgment to come - This was the only effectual way of preaching Christ to an unjust, lewd judge. Felix being terrified - How happily might this conviction have ended, had he been careful to pursue the views which were then opening upon his mind! But, like thousands, he deferred the consideration of these things to a more convenient season. A season which, alas! never came. For though he heard again, he was terrified no more. In the meantime we do not find Drusilla, though a Jewess, was thus alarmed. She had been used to hear of a future judgment: perhaps too she trusted to the being a daughter of Abraham, or to the expiation of the law, and so was proof against the convictions which seized on her husband, though a heathen. Let this teach us to guard against all such false dependencies as tend to elude those convictions that might otherwise be produced in us by the faithful preaching of the word of God. Let us stop our ears against those messengers of Satan, who appear as angels of light; who would teach us to reconcile the hope of salvation with a corrupt heart or an unholy life. Go thy way for this time - O how will every damned soul one day lament his having neglected such a time as this!

26. He hoped also - An evil hope: so when he heard his eye was not single. No marvel then that he profited nothing by all St. Paul's discourses: that money would be given - By the Christians for the liberty of so able a minister. And waiting for this, unhappy Felix fell short of the treasure of the Gospel.

27. But after two years - After St. Paul had been two years a prisoner, Felix desiring to gratify the Jews, left Paul bound - Thus men of the world, to gratify one another, stretch forth their hands to the things of God! Yet the wisdom of Felix did not profit him, did not satisfy the Jews at all. Their accusations followed him to Rome, and had utterly ruined him, but for the interest which his brother Pallas had with Nero.

XXV

2. Then the high priest and the chief of the Jews appeared against Paul - In so long a time their rage was not cooled. So much louder a call had Paul to the Gentiles.

4. But Festus answered - So Festus's care to preserve the imperial privileges was the means of preserving Paul's life. By what invisible springs does God govern the world! With what silence, and yet with what wisdom and energy!

5. Let those of you who are able - Who are best able to undertake the journey, and to manage the cause. If there be any wickedness in him - So he does not pass sentence before he hears the cause.

6. Not more than ten days - A short space for a new governor to stay at such a city as Jerusalem. He could not with any convenience have heard and decided the cause of Paul within that time.

7. Bringing many accusations - When many accusations are heaped together, frequently not one of them is true.

8. While he answered - To a general charge a general answer was sufficient.

Wesley's Notes on the Bible - The New Testament

9. Art thou willing to go up to Jerusalem - Festus could have ordered this without asking Paul. But God secretly overruled the whole, that he might have an occasion of appealing to Rome.

10. I am standing at Caesar's judgment seat - For all the courts of the Roman governors were held in the name of the emperor, and by commission from him. No man can give me up - He expresses it modestly: the meaning is, Thou canst not. I appeal to Caesar - Which any Roman citizen might do before sentence was passed.

12. The council - It was customary for a considerable number of persons of distinction to attend the Roman governors. These constituted a kind of council, with whom they frequently advised.

13. Agrippa - The son of Herod Agrippa, chap. xii, 1; and Bernice - His sister, with whom he lived in a scandalous familiarity. This was the person whom Titus Vespasian so passionately loved, that he would have made her empress, had not the clamours of the Roman prevented it.

15. Desiring judgment against him - As upon a previous conviction, which they falsely pretended.

16. It is not the custom of the Roman - How excellent a rule, to condemn no one unheard! A rule, which as it is common to all nations, (courts of inquisition only excepted,) so it ought to direct our proceedings in all affairs, not only in public, but private life.

18. Such things as I supposed - From their passion and vehemence.

19. But had certain questions - How coldly does he mention the things of the last importance! And about one Jesus - Thus does Festus speak of Him, to whom every knee shall bow! Whom Paul affirmed to be alive - And was this a doubtful question? But why, O Festus, didst thou doubt concerning it? Only because thou didst not search into the evidence of it. Otherwise that evidence might have opened to thee, till it had grown up into full conviction; and thy illustrious prisoner have led thee into the glorious liberty of the children of God.

23. With the tribunes and principal men of the city - The chief officers, both military and civil.

XXVI

And Paul stretching forth his hand - Chained as it was: a decent expression of his own earnestness, and proper to engage the attention of his hearers; answered for himself - Not only refuting the accusations of the Jews, but enlarging upon the faith of the Gospel.

2. King Agrippa - There is a peculiar force in thus addressing a person by name. Agrippa felt this.

3. Who art accurately acquainted - Which Festus was not; with the customs - In practical matters; and questions - In speculative. This word Festus had used in the absence of Paul, chap. xxv, 19, who, by the Divine leading, repeats and explains it. Agrippa had had peculiar advantages for an accurate knowledge of the Jewish customs and questions, from his education under his father Herod, and his long abode at Jerusalem. Nothing can be imagined more suitable or more graceful, than this whole discourse of Paul before Agrippa; in which the seriousness of the Christian, the boldness of the apostle, and the politeness of the gentleman and the scholar, appear in a most beautiful contrast, or rather a most happy union.

4. From my youth, which was from the beginning - That is, which was from the beginning of my youth.

5. If they would testify - But they would not, for they well knew what weight his former life must add to his present testimony.

6. And now - This and the two following verses are in a kind of ver. 6, 7, 8 parenthesis, and show that what the Pharisees rightly taught concerning the resurrection, Paul likewise asserted at this day. The ninth verse is connected with the fifth. For Pharisaism ver. 9, 5 impelled him to persecute. I stand in judgment for the hope of the promise - Of the resurrection. So it was in effect. For unless Christ had risen, there could have been no resurrection of the dead. And it was chiefly for testifying the resurrection of Christ, that the Jews still persecuted him.

7. Our twelve tribes - For a great part of the ten tribes also had at various times returned from the east to their own country, James i, 1; 1 Pet. i, 1. Worshipping continually night and day - That is, this is what they aim at in all their public and private worship.

8. Is it judged by you an incredible thing - It was by Festus, chap. xxv, 19, to whom Paul answers as if he had heard him discourse.

9. I thought - When I was a Pharisee: that I ought to do many things - Which he now enumerates.

10. I shut up many of the saints - Men not only innocent, but good, just, holy. I gave my vote against them - That is, I joined with those who condemned them. Perhaps the chief priests did also give him power to vote on these occasions.

11. I compelled them - That is, some of them; to blaspheme - This is the most dreadful of all! Repent, ye enemies of the Gospel. If Spira, who was compelled, suffered so terribly, what will become of those who compel, like Saul, but do not repent like him.

12. Acts ix, 2.

13. O King - Most seasonably, in the height of the narration, does he thus fix the king's attention.

Above the brightness of the sun - And no marvel. For what is the brightness of this created sun, to the Sun of righteousness, the brightness of the Father's glory?

14. In the Hebrew tongue - St. Paul was not now speaking in Hebrew: when he was, chap. xxiii, 7, he did not add, In the Hebrew tongue. Christ used this tongue both on earth and from heaven.

17. Delivering thee from the people - The Jews and the Gentiles, to whom, both Jews and Gentiles, I now send thee - Paul gives them to know, that the liberty he enjoys even in bonds, was promised to him, as well as his preaching to the Gentiles. I, denotes the authority of the sender. Now, the time whence his mission was dated. For his apostleship, as well as his conversion, commenced at this moment.

18. To open - He opens them, who sends Paul; and he does it by Paul who is sent; their eyes - Both of the Jews and Gentiles: that they may turn - Through the power of the Almighty, from the spiritual darkness wherein they were involved, to the light of Divine knowledge and holiness, and from the power of Satan, who now holds them in sin, guilt, and misery, to the love and happy service of God: that they may receive through faith - (He seems to place the same blessings in a fuller light,) pardon, holiness, and glory.

19. From that time - Having received power to obey, I was not disobedient - I did obey, I used that power, Gal. i, 16. So that even this grace whereby St. Paul was influenced was not irresistible.

20. I declared - From that hour to this, both to Jew and Gentile, that they should repent - This repentance, we may observe, is previous both to inward and outward holiness.

21. For these things - The apostle now applies all that he had said.

22. Having obtained help from God - When all other help failed, God sent the Roman from the castle, and so fulfilled the promise he had made, ver. 17.

24. Festus said, Paul, thou art beside thyself - To talk of men's rising from the dead! And of a Jew's enlightening not only his own nation, but tho polite and learned Greeks and Romans! Nay, Festus, it is thou that art beside thyself. That strikest quite wide of the mark. And no wonder: he saw that nature did not act in Paul; but the grace that acted in him he did not see. And therefore he took all this ardour which animated the apostle for a mere start of learned phrensy.

25. I am not mad, most excellent Festus - The style properly belonging to a Roman propretor. How inexpressibly beautiful is this reply! How strong! yet how decent and respectful! Mad men seldom call men by their names, and titles of honour. Thus also St. Paul refutes the charge. But utter the words of truth (confirmed in the next verse) and sobriety - The very reverse of madness. And both these remain, even when the men of God act with the utmost vehemence.

26. For the king knoweth of these things - St. Paul having refuted Festus, pursues his purpose, returning naturally, and as it were, step by step, from Festus to Agrippa. To whom I speak with freedom - This freedom was probably one circumstance which Festus accounted madness.

27. King Agrippa, believest thou the prophets? - He that believes these, believes Paul, yea, and Christ. The apostle now comes close to his heart. What did Agrippa feel when he heard this? I know that thou believest! - Here Paul lays so fast hold on the king that he can scarce make any resistance.

28. Then Agrippa said unto Paul, Almost thou persuadest me to be a Christian! - See here, Festus altogether a heathen, Paul alogether a Christian, Agrippa halting between both. Poor Agrippa! But almost persuaded! So near the mark, and yet fall short! Another step, and thou art within the vail. Reader, stop not with Agrippa; but go on with Paul.

29. I would to God - Agrippa had spoke of being a Christian, as a thing wholly in his own power. Paul gently corrects this mistake; intimating, it is the gift and the work of God; that all that hear me - It was modesty in St. Paul, not to apply directly to them all; yet he looks upon them and observes them; were such as I am - Christians indeed; full of righteousness, peace, and joy in the Holy Ghost. He speaks from a full sense of his own happiness, and an overflowing love to all.

30. And as he said this, the king rose up - An unspeakably precious moment to Agrippa. Whether he duly improved it or no, we shall see in that day.

31. This man doth nothing worthy of death, or of bonds - They speak of his whole life, not of one action only. And could ye learn nothing more than this from that discourse? A favourable judgment of such a preacher, is not all that God requires.

XXVII

1. As soon as it was determined to sail - As being a shorter and less expensive passage to Rome.

2. Adramyttium - was a sea port of Mysia. Aristarchus and Luke went with Paul by choice, not being ashamed of his bonds.

3. Julius treating Paul courteously - Perhaps he had heard him make his defense.

4. We sailed under Cyprus - Leaving it on the left hand.

7. Cnidus - was a cape and city of Caria.

8. The Fair Havens still retain the name. But the city of Lasea is now utterly lost, together with

many more of the hundred cities for which Crete was once so renowned.

9. The fast, or day of atonement, was kept on the tenth of Tisri, that is, the 25th of September. This was to them an ill time of sailing; not only because winter was approaching, but also because of the sudden storms, which are still common in the Mediterranean at that time of the year. Paul exhorted them - Not to leave Crete. Even in external things, faith exerts itself with the greatest presence of mind, and readiness of advice.

10. Saying to them - To the centurion and other officers.

11. The centurion regarded the master - And indeed it is a general rule, believe an artificer in his own art. Yet when there is the greatest need, a real Christian will often advise even better than him.

12. Which is a haven - Having a double opening, one to the southwest, the other to the northwest.

14. There arose against it - The south wind; a tempestuous wind, called in those parts Euroclydon. This was a kind of hurricane, not carrying them any one way, but tossing them backward and forward. These furious winds are now called levanters, and blow in all directions from the northeast to the southeast.

16. We were hardly able to get masters of the boat - To prevent its being staved.

18. They lightened the ship - Casting the heavy goods into the sea.

19. We cast out the tackling of the ship - Cutting away even those masts that were not absolutely necessary.

20. Neither sun nor stars appeared for many days - Which they could the less spare, before the compass was found out.

21. This loss - Which is before your eyes.

23. The God whose I am, and whom I serve - How short a compendium of religion! Yet how full! Comprehending both faith, hope, and love.

24. God hath given - Paul had prayed for them. And God gave him their lives; perhaps their souls also. And the centurion, subserving the providence of God, gave to Paul the lives of the prisoners. How wonderfully does his providence reign in the most contingent things! And rather will many bad men be preserved with a few good, (so it frequently happens,) than one good man perish with many bad. So it was in this ship: so it is in the world. Thee - At such a time as this, there was not the same danger, which might otherwise have been, of St. Paul's seeming to speak out of vanity, what he really spoke out of necessity. All the souls - Not only all the prisoners, as Julius afterward did, ver. 43; ask for souls, they shall be given thee: yea, more than thou hopest for, that sail with thee - So that Paul, in the sight of God, was the master and pilot of the ship.

27. The fourteenth night - Since they left Crete, ver. 18, 19. In the Adriatic sea - So the ancients called all that part of the Mediterranean, which lay south of Italy.

30. The sailors were attempting to flee out of the ship - Supposing the boat would go more safely over the shallows.

31. Unless these mariners abide in the ship - Without them ye know not how to manage her, ye cannot be saved - He does not say we. That they would not have regarded. The soldiers were not careful for the lives of the prisoners: nor was Paul careful for his own. We may learn hence, to use the most proper means for security and success, even while we depend on Divine Providence, and wait for the accomplishment of God's own promise. He never designed any promise should encourage rational creatures to act in an irrational manner; or to remain inactive, when he has given them natural capacities of doing something, at least, for their own benefit. To expect the accomplishment of any promise, without exerting these, is at best vain and dangerous presumption, if all pretense of relying upon it be not profane hypocrisy.

33. Ye continue fasting, having taken nothing - No regular meal, through a deep sense of their extreme danger. Let us not wonder then, if men who have a deep sense of their extreme danger of everlasting death, for a time forget even to eat their bread, or to attend to their worldly affairs. Much less let us censure that as madness, which may be the beginning of true wisdom.

34. This is for your preservation - That ye may be the better able to swim to shore.

36. Then they were all encouraged - By his example, as well as words.

38. Casting out the wheat - So firmly did they now depend on what St. Paul had said.

39. They did not know the land - Which they saw near them: having a level shore.

40. Loosing the rudder bands - Their ships had frequently two rudders, one on each side. were fastened while they let the ship drive; but were now loosened, when they had need of them to steer her into the creek.

41. A place where two seas met - Probably by reason of a sand bank running parallel with the shore.

42. The counsel - Cruel, unjust, ungrateful.

44. They all escaped safe to land - And some of them doubtless received the apostle as a teacher sent from God. These would find their deliverance from the fury of the sea, but an earnest of an infinitely greater deliverance, and are long ere this lodged with him in a more peaceful harbour than

Malta, or than the earth could afford.

XXVIII

1. Melita or Malta, is about twelve miles broad, twenty long, and sixty distant from Sicily to the south. It yields abundance of honey, (whence its name was taken,) with much cotton, and is very fruitful, though it has only three feet depth of earth above the solid rock. The Emperor Charles the Fifth gave it, in 1530, to the knights of Rhodes, driven out of Rhodes by the Turks. They are a thousand in number, of whom five hundred always reside on the island.

2. And the barbarians - So the Roman and Greeks termed all nations but their own. But surely the generosity shown by these uncultivated inhabitants of Malta, was far more valuable than all the varnish which the politest education could give, where it taught not humanity and compassion.

4. And when the barbarians saw - they said - Seeing also his chains, Doubtless this man is a murderer - Such rarely go unpunished even in this life; whom vengeance hath not suffered to live - They look upon him as a dead man already. It is with pleasure that we trace among these barbarians the force of conscience, and the belief of a particular providence: which some people of more learning have stupidly thought it philosophy to despise. But they erred in imagining, that calamities must always be interpreted as judgments. Let us guard against this, lest, like them, we condemn not only the innocent, but the excellent of the earth.

5. Having shaken off the venomous animal, he suffered no harm - The words of an eminent modern historian are, "No venomous kind of serpent now breeds in Malta, neither hurts if it be brought thither from another place. Children are seen there handling and playing even with scorpions; I have seen one eating them." If this be so, it seems to be fixed by the wisdom of God, as an eternal memorial of what he once wrought there.

6. They changed their minds, and said he was a God - Such is the stability of human reason! A little before he was a murderer; and presently he is a God: (just as the people of Lystra; one hour sacrificing, and the next stoning:) nay, but there is a medium. He is neither a murderer nor a God, but a man of God. But natural men never run into greater mistakes, than in judging of the children of God.

7. The chief man of the island - In wealth if not in power also. Three days - The first three days of our stay on the island.

11. Whose sign was - It was the custom of the ancients to have images on the head of their ships, from which they took their names. Castor and Pollux - Two heathen gods who were thought favourable to mariners.

15. The brethren -- that is, the Christians, came out thence to meet us - It is remarkable that there is no certain account by whom Christianity was planted at Rome. Probably some inhabitants of that city were at Jerusalem on the day of pentecost, chap. ii, 10; and being then converted themselves, carried the Gospel thither at their return. Appii-Forum was a town fifty-one miles from Rome; the Three Taverns about thirty. He took courage - He saw Christ was at Rome also, and now forgot all the troubles of his journey.

16. With the soldier - To whom he was chained, as the Roman custom was.

17. And after three days - Given to rest and prayer, Paul called the chief of the Jews together - He always sought the Jews first; but being now bound, he could not so conveniently go round to them. Though I have done nothing - Seeing him chained, they might have suspected he had. Therefore he first obviates this suspicion.

19. When the Jews opposed it - He speaks tenderly of them, not mentioning their repeated attempts to murder him. Not that I had any thing to accuse my nation of - Not that I had any design to accuse others, but merely to defend myself.

20. The hope of Israel - What Israel hopes for, namely, the Messiah and the resurrection.

21. We have neither received letters concerning thee - There must have been a peculiar providence in this, nor has any of the brethren -- the Jews, related - Professedly, in a set discourse, or spoke - Occasionally, in conversation, any evil of thee - How must the bridle then have been in their mouth!

22. This sect we know is everywhere spoken against - This is no proof at all of a bad cause, but a very probable mark of a good one.

23. To whom he expounded, testifying the kingdom of God, and persuading them concerning Jesus - These were his two grand topics,

1. That the kingdom of the Messiah was of a spiritual, not temporal nature:

2. That Jesus of Nazareth was the very person foretold, as the Lord of that kingdom. On this head he had as much need to persuade as to convince, their will making as strong a resistance as their understanding.

24. And some believed the things that were spoken - With the heart, as well as understanding.

25. Well spake the Holy Ghost to your fathers - Which is equally applicable to you.

26. Hearing ye shall hear - That is, ye shall most surely hear, and shall not understand - The words

manifestly denote a judicial blindness, consequent upon a wilful and obstinate resistance of the truth. First they would not, afterward they could not, believe. Isaiah vi, 9, &c.; Matt. xiii, 14; John xii, 40.

28. The salvation of God is sent to the Gentiles - Namely, from this time. Before this no apostle had been at Rome. St. Paul was the first.

30. And Paul continued two whole years - After which this book was written, long before St. Paul's death, and was undoubtedly published with his approbation by St. Luke, who continued with him to the last, 2 Tim. iv, 11. And received all that came to him - Whether they were Jews or Gentiles. These two years completed twenty-five years after our saviour's passion. Such progress had the Gospel made by that time, in the parts of the world which lay west of Jerusalem, by the ministry of St. Paul among the Gentiles. How far eastward the other apostles had carried it in the same time, history does not inform us.

31. No man forbidding him - Such was the victory of the word of God. While Paul was preaching at Rome, the Gospel shone with its highest lustre. Here therefore the Acts of the Apostles end; and end with great advantage. Otherwise St. Luke could easily have continued his narrative to the apostle's death.

John Wesley

NOTES ON ST PAUL'S EPISTLE TO THE ROMANS

MANY of the writings of the New Testament are written in the form of epistles. Such are not only those of St. Paul, James, Peter, Jude, but also both the treatises of St. Luke, and all the writings of St. John. Nay, we have seven epistles herein which the Lord Jesus himself sent by the hand of John to the seven churches; yea, the whole Rev. is no other than an epistle from Him. Concerning the epistles of St. Paul, we may observe, he writes in a very different manner to those churches which he had planted himself, and to those who had not seen his face in the flesh. In his letters to the former, a loving or sharp familiarity appears, as their behaviour was more or less suitable to the gospel. To the latter, he proposes the pure, unmixed gospel, in a more general and abstract manner. As to the time wherein he wrote his epistles, it is probable he wrote about the year of Christ, according to the common reckoning, 48 From Corinth, The Epistle to the Thessalonians. 49 From Phrygia, To the Galatians. 52 From Ephesus, The First to the Corinthians. From Troas, The First Epistle to Timothy. From Macedonia,The Second to the Corinthians, and that to Titus. From Corinth, To the Romans. 57 From Rome, To the Philippians, to Philemon, the Ephesians, and Colossians. 53 From Italy, To the Hebrews. 66 From Rome, The Second to Timothy. As to the general epistles, it seems, St. James wrote a little before his death, which was A. D. 63. St. Peter, who was martyred in the year 67, wrote his latter epistle a little before his death, and not long after his former. St. Jude wrote after him, when the mystery of iniquity was gaining ground swiftly. St. John is believed to have wrote all his epistles a little before his departure. The Revelation he wrote A. D. 96. That St. Paul wrote this epistle from Corinth we may learn from his commending to the Roman Phebe, a servant of the church of Cenchrea, chap. xvi, 1, a port of Corinth; and from his mentioning the salutations of Caius and Erastus, chap. xvi, 23, who were both Corinthians. Those to whom he wrote seem to have been chiefly foreigners, both Jews and gentiles, whom business drew from other provinces; as appears, both by his writing in Greek, and by his salutations of several former acquaintance. His chief design herein is to show,

1, That neither the gentiles by the law of nature, nor the Jews by the law of Moses, could obtain justification before God; and that therefore it was necessary for both to seek it from the free mercy of God by faith.

2, That God has an absolute right to show mercy on what terms he pleases, and to withhold it from those who will not accept it on his own terms. This Epistle consists of five parts: -

I. The introduction, C.i.1-15

II. The proposition briefly proved,
    1. Concerning faith and justification,
    2. Concerning salvation,
    3. Concerning the equality of believers, Jews or gentiles, 16-17 To these three parts, whereof The first is treated of, C.i.18-iv. The second, C.v-viii. The third, C.ix.-xi not only the treatise itself, but also the exhortation, answers in the same order.

III. The treatise,
    1. Concerning justification, which is, (1.) Not by works, for C.i.18 The gentiles, C.ii.1-10 The Jews, and 11-29 Both together are under sin, C.iii.1-20 (2.) But by faith, 21-31 as appears by the example of Abraham, and the testimony of David, C.iv.1-25
    2. Concerning salvation, C.v.-viii.
    3. Concerning the equal privileges of Jewish and gentile believers, C.ix.-xi.

IV. The exhortation, C.xii.1-2
    1. Concerning faith and its fruits, love and practical holiness, 3-21 C.xiii.1-10
    2. Concerning salvation, 11-14
    3. Of the conjunction of Jews and gentiles,. C.xiv.1-xv.13

V. The conclusion, 14-xvi.25 To express the design and contents of this epistle a little more at large: The apostle labours throughout to fix in those to whom he writes a deep sense of the excellency of the gospel, and to engage them to act suitably to it. For this purpose, after a general salutation, chap. i, 1-7, and profession of his affection for them, chap. i, 8-15, he declares he shall not be ashamed openly to maintain the gospel at Rome, seeing it is the powerful instrument of salvation, both to Jews and gentiles, by means of faith, chap. i, 16, 17. And, in order to demonstrate this, he shows,

1. That the world greatly needed such a dispensation, the gentiles being in a most abandoned state, chap. i, 18-32, and the Jews, though condemning others, being themselves no better, chap. ii, 1- 29; as, not withstanding some cavils, which he obviates, chap. iii, 1-8, their own scriptures testify, chap. iii, 9-19. So that all were under a necessity of seeking justification by this method, chap. iii, 20-31.

2. That Abraham and David themselves sought justification by faith, and not by works, chap. iv, 1-25.

3. That all who believe are brought into so happy a state, as turns the greatest afflictions into a matter of joy, chap. v, 1-11.

4. That the evils brought on mankind by Adam are abundantly recompensed to all that believe in Christ, chap. v, 12-21.

5. That, far from dissolving the obligations to practical holiness, the gospel increases them by peculiar obligations, chap. vi, 1-23. In order to convince them of these things the more deeply, and to remove their fondness for the Mosaic law, now they were married to Christ by faith in him, chap. vii, 1-6, he shows how unable the motives of the law were to produce that holiness which believers obtain by a living faith in the gospel, chap. vii, 7-25, viii, 1, 2, and then gives a more particular view of those things which rendered the gospel effectual to this great end, chap. viii, 3-39. That even the gentiles, if they believed, should have a share in these blessings, and that the Jews, if they believed not, should be excluded from them, being a point of great importance, the apostle bestows the ninth, tenth, and eleventh chapters in settling it. He begins the ninth chapter by expressing his tender love and high esteem for the Jewish nation, chap. ix, 1-5, and then shows,

1. That God's rejecting great part of the seed of Abraham, yea, and of Isaac too, was undeniable fact, chap. ix, 6-13.

2. That God had not chosen them to such peculiar privileges for any kind of goodness either in them or their fathers, chap. ix, 14- 24.

3. That his accepting the gentiles, and rejecting many of the Jews, had been foretold both by Hosea and Isaiah, chap. ix, 25-33.

4. That God had offered salvation to Jews and gentiles on the same terms, though the Jews had rejected it, chap. x, 1-21.

5. That though the rejection of Israel for their obstinacy was general, yet it was not total; there being still a remnant among them who did embrace the gospel, chap. xi, 1-10.

6. That the rejection of the rest was not final, but in the end all Israel should be saved, chap. xi, 11-31.

7. That, meantime, even their obstinacy and rejection served to display the unsearchable wisdom and love of God, chap. xi, 32- 36. The rest of the epistle contains practical instructions and exhortations. He particularly urges,

1. An entire consecration of themselves to God, and a care to glorify Him by a faithful improvement of their several talents, chap. vii, 1-11.

2. Devotion, patience, hospitality, mutual sympathy, humility, peace, and meekness, chap. vii, 12-21.

3. Obedience to magistrates, justice in all its branches, love the fulfilling of the law, and universal holiness, chap. viii, 1-14.

4. Mutual candour between those who differed in judgment, touching the observance of the Mosaic law, chap. xiv, 1-23, xv, 1- 17; in enforcing which he is led to mention the extent of his own labours, and his purpose of visiting the Romans; in the mean time recommending himself to their prayers, chap. xv, 18-33. And, after many salutations, chap. xvi, 1-16, and a caution against those who caused divisions, he concludes with a suitable blessing and doxology, chap. xvi, 17-27.

ROMANS

I

1. Paul, a servant of Jesus Christ -To this introduction the conclusion answers, chap. xv, 15, &c. Called to be an apostle - And made an apostle by that calling. While God calls, he makes what he calls. As the Judaizing teachers disputed his claim to the apostolical office, it is with great propriety that he asserts it in the very entrance of an epistle wherein their principles are entirely overthrown. And various other proper and important thoughts are suggested in this short introduction; particularly the prophecies

concerning the gospel, the descent of Jesus from David, the great doctrines of his Godhead and resurrection, the sending the gospel to the gentiles, the privileges of Christians, and the obedience and holiness to which they were obliged in virtue of their profession. Separated - By God, not only from the bulk of other men, from other Jews, from other disciples, but even from other Christian teachers, to be a peculiar instrument of God in spreading the gospel.

2. Which he promised before - Of old time, frequently, solemnly. And the promise and accomplishment confirm each other. Deut. xviii, 18; Isa. ix, 6, 7; Chapter liii; lxi; Jer. xxiii, 5.

3. Who was of the seed of David according to the flesh - That is, with regard to his human nature. Both the natures of our saviour are here mentioned; but the human is mentioned first, because the divine was not manifested in its full evidence till after his resurrection.

4. But powerfully declared to be the Son of God, according to the Spirit of Holiness - That is, according to his divine nature. By the resurrection from the dead - For this is both the fountain and the object of our faith; and the preaching of the apostles was the consequence of Christ's resurrection.

5. By whom we have received - I and the other apostles. Grace and apostleship - The favour to be an apostle, and qualifications for it. For obedience to the faith in all nations - That is, that all nations may embrace the faith of Christ. For his name - For his sake; out of regard to him.

6. Among whom - The nations brought to the obedience of faith. Are ye also - But St. Paul gives them no preeminence above others.

7. To all that are in Rome - Most of these were heathens by birth, ver. 13, though with Jews mixed among them. They were scattered up and down in that large city, and not yet reduced into the form of a church. Only some had begun to meet in the house of Aquila and Priscilla. Beloved of God - And from his free love, not from any merit of yours, called by his word and his Spirit to believe in him, and now through faith holy as he is holy. Grace - The peculiar favour of God. And peace - All manner of blessings, temporal, spiritual, and eternal. This is both a Christian salutation and an apostolic benediction. From God our Father, and the Lord Jesus Christ - This is the usual way wherein the apostles speak, "God the Father," "God our Father." Nor do they often, in speaking of him, use the word Lord, as it implies the proper name of God, Jehovah. In the Old Testament, indeed, the holy men generally said, "The Lord our God;" for they were then, as it were, servants; whereas now they are sons: and sons so well know their father, that they need not frequently mention his proper name. It is one and the same peace, and one and the same grace, which is from God and from Jesus Christ. Our trust and prayer fix on God, as he is the Father of Christ; and on Christ, as he presents us to the Father.

8. I thank - In the very entrance of this one epistle are the traces of all spiritual affections; but of thankfulness above all, with the expression of which almost all St. Paul's epistles begin. He here particularly thanks God, that what otherwise himself should have done, was done at Rome already. My God - This very word expresses faith, hope, love, and consequently all true religion. Through Jesus Christ - The gifts of God all pass through Christ to us; and all our petitions and thanksgivings pass through Christ to God. That your faith is spoken of - In this kind of congratulations St. Paul describes either the whole of Christianity, as Colossians i, 3, &c.; or some part of it, as 1 Cor. i, 5. Accordingly here he mentions the faith of the Romans, suitably to his design, ver. 12, 17. Through the whole world - This joyful news spreading everywhere, that there were Christians also in the imperial city. And the goodness and wisdom of God established faith in the chief cities; in Jerusalem and Rome particularly; that from thence it might be diffused to all nations.

9. God, whom I serve - As an apostle. In my spirit - Not only with my body, but with my inmost soul. In the gospel - By preaching it.

10. Always - In all my solemn addresses to God. If by any means now at length - This accumulation of particles declares the strength of his desire.

11. That I may impart to you - Face to face, by laying on of hands, prayer, preaching the gospel, private conversation. Some spiritual gift - With such gifts the Corinthians, who had enjoyed the presence of St. Paul, abounded, 1 Cor. i, 7; xii, 1; xiv, 1. So did the Galatians likewise, Gal. iii, 5; and, indeed, all those churches which had had the presence of any of the apostles had peculiar advantages in this kind, from the laying on of their hands, Acts xix, 6; viii, 17, &c., 2 Tim. i, 6. But as yet the Roman were greatly inferior to them in this respect; for which reason the apostle, in the twelfth chapter also, says little, if any thing, of their spiritual gifts. He therefore desires to impart some, that they might be established; for by these was the testimony of Christ confirmed among them. That St. Peter had no more been at Rome than St. Paul, at the time when this epistle was written, appears from the general tenor thereof, and from this place in particular: for, otherwise, what St. Paul wishes to impart to the Roman would have been imparted already by St. Peter.

12. That is, I long to be comforted by the mutual faith both of you and me - He not only associates the Roman with, but even prefers them before, himself. How different is this style of the apostle from that of the modern court of Rome!

13. Brethren - A frequent, holy, simple, sweet, and yet grand, appellation. The apostles but rarely address persons by their names; 'O ye Corinthians," "O Timotheus." St. Paul generally uses this

appellation, " Brethren;" sometimes in exhortation, " My beloved," or, " My beloved brethren;" St. James, "Brethren;" "My brethren," My beloved brethren;" St. Peter and Jude always, " Beloved;" St. John frequently, " Beloved;" once, " Brethren;" oftener than once, My little children." Though I have been hindered hitherto - Either by business, see chap. xv, 22; or persecution, 1 Thess. ii, 2; or the Spirit, Acts xvi, 7. That I might have some fruit - Of my ministerial labours. Even as I have already had from the many churches I have planted and watered among the other gentiles.

14. To the Greeks and the barbarians - He includes the Roman under the Greeks; so that this division comprises all nations. Both to the wise, and the unwise - For there were unwise even among the Greeks, and wise even among the barbarians. I am a debtor to all - I am bound by my divine mission to preach the gospel to them.

16. For I am not ashamed of the gospel - To the world, indeed, it is folly and weakness, 1 Cor. i, 18; therefore, in the judgment of the world, he ought to be ashamed of it; especially at Rome, the head and theatre of the world. But Paul is not ashamed, knowing it is the power of God unto salvation to every one that believeth - The great and gloriously powerful means of saving all who accept salvation in God's own way. As St. Paul comprises the sum of the gospel in this epistle, so he does the sum of the epistle in this and the following verse. Both to the Jew, and to the gentile - There is a noble frankness, as well as a comprehensive sense, in these words, by which he, on the one hand, shows the Jews their absolute need of the gospel; and, on the other, tells the politest and greatest nation in the world both that their salvation depended on receiving it, and that the first offers of it were in every place to be made to the despised Jews.

17. The righteousness of God - This expression sometimes means God's eternal, essential righteousness, which includes both justice and mercy, and is eminently shown in condemning sin, and yet justifying the sinner. Sometimes it means that righteousness by which a man, through the gift of God, is made and is righteous; and that, both by receiving Christ through faith, and by a conformity to the essential righteousness of God. St. Paul, when treating of justification, means hereby the righteousness of faith; therefore called the righteousness of God, because God found out and prepared, reveals and gives, approves and crowns it. In this verse the expression means, the whole benefit of God through Christ for the salvation of a sinner. Is revealed - Mention is made here, and ver. 18, of a twofold Revelation, - of wrath and of righteousness: the former, little known to nature, is revealed by the law; the latter, wholly unknown to nature, by the gospel. That goes before, and prepares the way; this follows. Each, the apostle says, is revealed at the present time, in opposition to the times of ignorance. From faith to faith - By a gradual series of still clearer and clearer promises. As it is written - St. Paul had just laid down three propositions:

1. Righteousness is by faith, ver. xvii,
2. Salvation is by righteousness, ver. xvi,
3. Both to the Jews and to the gentiles, ver. 16. Now all these are confirmed by that single sentence, The just shall live by faith - Which was primarily spoken of those who preserved their lives, when the Chaldeans besieged Jerusalem, by believing the declarations of God, and acting according to them. Here it means, He shall obtain the favour of God, and continue therein by believing. Hab. ii, 4

18. For - There is no other way of obtaining life and salvation. Having laid down his proposition, the apostle now enters upon the proof of it. His first argument is, The law condemns all men, as being under sin. None therefore is justified by the works of the law. This is treated of chap. iii, 20. And hence he infers, Therefore justification is by faith. The wrath of God is revealed - Not only by frequent and signal interpositions of divine providence, but likewise in the sacred oracles, and by us, his messengers. From heaven - This speaks the majesty of Him whose wrath is revealed, his all-seeing eye, and the extent of his wrath: whatever is under heaven is under the effects of his wrath, believers in Christ excepted. Against all ungodliness and unrighteousness - These two are treated of, ver. 23, &c. Of men - He is speaking here of the gentiles, and chiefly the wisest of them. Who detain the truth - For it struggles against their wickedness. In unrighteousness - The word here includes ungodliness also.

19. For what is to be known of God - Those great principles which are indispensably necessary to be known. Is manifest in them; for God hath showed it to them - By the light which enlightens every man that cometh into the world.

20. For those things of him which are invisible, are seen - By the eye of the mind. Being understood - They are seen by them, and them only, who use their understanding

21. Because, knowing God - For the wiser heathens did know that there was one supreme God; yet from low and base considerations they conformed to the idolatry of the vulgar. They did not glorify him as God, neither were thankful - They neither thanked him for his benefits, nor glorified him for his divine perfection. But became vain - Like the idols they worshipped. In their reasonings - Various, uncertain, foolish. What a terrible instance have we of this in the writings of Lucretius! What vain reasonings, and how dark a heart, amidst so pompous professions of wisdom!

23. And changed - With the utmost folly. Here are three degrees of ungodliness and of punishment: the first is described, ver. 21- 24; the second, ver. 25-27; the third, in ver. 28, and following

verses. The punishment in each case is expressed by God gave them up. If a man will not worship God as God, he is so left to himself that he throws away his very manhood. Reptiles - Or creeping things; as beetles, and various kinds of serpents.

24. Wherefore - One punishment of sin is from the very nature of it, as ver. 27; another, as here, is from vindictive justice. Uncleanness - Ungodliness and uncleanness are frequently joined, 1 Thess. iv, 5 as are the knowledge of God and purity. God gave them up - By withdrawing his restraining grace.

25. Who changed the truth - The true worship of God. Into a lie - False, abominable idolatries. And worshipped - Inwardly. And served - Outwardly.

26. Therefore God gave them up to vile affections - To which the heathen Roman were then abandoned to the last degree; and none more than the emperors themselves.

27. Receiving the just recompense of their error - Their idolatry being punished with that unnatural lust, which was as horrible a dishonour to the body, as their idolatry was to God.

28. God gave them up to an undiscerning mind - Treated of, ver. 32. To do things not expedient - Even the vilest abominations, treated of ver. 29-31.

29. Filled with all injustice - This stands in the first place; unmercifulness, in the last. Fornication - Includes here every species of uncleanness. Maliciousness - The Greek word properly implies a temper which delights in hurting another, even without any advantage to itself.

30. Whisperers - Such as secretly defame others. Backbiters - Such as speak against others behind their back. Haters of God - That is, rebels against him, deniers of his providence, or accusers of his justice in their adversities; yea, having an inward heart- enmity to his justice and holiness. Inventors of evil things - Of new pleasures, new ways of gain, new arts of hurting, particularly in war.

31. Covenant-breakers - It is well known, the Romans, as a nation, from the very beginning of their commonwealth, never made any scruple of vacating altogether the most solemn engagement, if they did not like it, though made by their supreme magistrate, in the name of the whole people. They only gave up the general who had made it, and then supposed themselves to be at full liberty. Without natural affection - The custom of exposing their own new - born children to perish by cold, hunger, or wild beasts, which so generally prevailed in the heathen world, particularly among the Greeks and Romans, was an amazing instance of this; as is also that of killing their aged and helpless parents, now common among the American heathens.

32. Not only do the same, but have pleasure in those that practice them - This is the highest degree of wickedness. A man may be hurried by his passions to do the thing he hates; but he that has pleasure in those that do evil, loves wickedness for wickedness' sake. And hereby he encourages them in sin, and heaps the guilt of others upon his own head.

II

1. Therefore - The apostle now makes a transition from the gentiles to the Jews, till, at ver. 6, he comprises both. Thou art inexcusable - Seeing knowledge without practice only increases guilt. O man - Having before spoken of the gentile in the third person, he addresses the Jew in the second person. But he calls him by a common appellation, as not acknowledging him to be a Jew. See verses 17, 28. Whosoever thou art that Judgest - Censurest, condemnest. For in that thou Judgest the other - The heathen. Thou condemnest thyself; for thou doest the same things - In effect; in many instances.

2. For we know - Without thy teaching That the judgment of God - Not thine, who exceptest thyself from its sentence. Is according to truth - Is just, making no exception, ver. 5, 6, 11; and reaches the heart as well as the life, ver. 16.

3. That thou shalt escape - Rather than the gentile.

4. Or despisest thou - Dost thou go farther still, - from hoping to escape his wrath, to the abuse of his love?. The riches - The abundance. Of his goodness, forbearance, and longsuffering - Seeing thou both hast sinned, dost sin, and wilt sin. All these are afterwards comprised in the single word goodness. Leadeth thee - That is, is designed of God to lead or encourage thee to it.

5. Treasurest up wrath - Although thou thinkest thou art treasuring up all good things. O what a treasure may a man lay up either way, in this short day of life! To thyself - Not to him whom thou Judgest. In the day of wrath, and Revelation, and righteous judgment of God - Just opposite to "the goodness and forbearance and longsuffering" of God. When God shall be revealed, then shall also be "revealed" the secrets of men's hearts, ver. 16. Forbearance and Revelation respect God, and are opposed to each other; longsuffering and righteous judgment respect the sinner; goodness and wrath are words of a more general import.

6. Prov. xxiv, 12

7. To them that seek for glory - For pure love does not exclude faith, hope, desire, 1 Cor. xv, 58.

8. But to them that are contentious - Like thee, O Jew, who thus fightest against God. The character of a false Jew is disobedience, stubbornness, impatience. Indignation and wrath, tribulation and anguish - Alluding to Psalm lxxviii, xlix, "He cast upon them," the Egyptians. "the fierceness of his

anger, wrath, and indignation, and trouble;" and finely intimating, that the Jews would in the day of vengeance be more severely punished than even the Egyptians were when God made their plagues so wonderful.

9. *Of the Jew first* - Here we have the first express mention of the Jews in this chapter. And it is introduced with great propriety. Their having been trained up in the true religion, and having had Christ and his apostles first sent to them, will place them in the foremost rank of the criminals that obey not the truth.

10. *But glory* - Just opposite to "wrath," from the divine approbation. *honour* - Opposite to "indignation," by the divine appointment; and peace now and forever, opposed to tribulation and anguish.

11. *For there is no respect of persons with God* - He will reward every one according to his works. But this is well consistent with his distributing advantages and opportunities of improvement, according to his own good pleasure.

12. *For as many as have sinned* - He speaks as of the time past, for all time will be past at the day of judgment. *Without the law* - Without having any written law. Shall also perish without the law - Without regard had to any outward law; being condemned by the law written in their hearts. The word also shows the agreement of the manner of sinning, with the manner of suffering. *Perish* - He could not so properly say, Shall be judged without the law.

13. *For not the hearers of the law are, even now, just before God, but the doers of the law shall be justified* - Finally acquitted and rewarded a most sure and important truth, which respects the gentiles also, though principally the Jews. St. Paul speaks of the former, ver. 14, &c.; of the latter, ver. 17, &c. Here is therefore no parenthesis; for the sixteenth verse also depends on the fifteenth, not on the twelfth. Rom. ii, 16, 15, 12.

14. *For when the gentiles* - That is, any of them. St. Paul, having refuted the perverse judgment of the Jews concerning the heathens, proceeds to show the just judgment of God against them. He now speaks directly of the heathens, in order to convince the heathens. Yet the concession he makes to these serves more strongly to convince the Jews. *Do by nature* - That is, without an outward rule; though this also, strictly speaking, is by preventing grace. *The things contained in the law* - The ten commandments being only the substance of the law of nature. These, not having the written law, are a law unto themselves - That is, what the law is to the Jews, they are, by the grace of God, to themselves; namely, a rule of life.

15. *Who show* - To themselves, to other men, and, in a sense, to God himself. *The work of the law* - The substance, though not the letter, of it. *Written on their hearts* - By the same hand which wrote the commandments on the tables of stone. *Their conscience* - There is none of all its faculties which the soul has less in its power than this. *Bearing witness* - In a trial there are the plaintiff, the defendant, and the witnesses. Conscience and sin itself are witnesses against the heathens. Their thoughts sometimes excuse, sometimes condemn, them. *Among themselves* - Alternately, like plaintiff and defendant. *Accusing or even defending them* - The very manner of speaking shows that they have far more room to accuse than to defend.

16. *In the day* - That is, who show this in the day. Everything will then be shown to be what it really is. In that day will appear the law written in their hearts as it often does in the present life. *When God shall judge the secrets of men* - On secret circumstances depends the real quality of actions, frequently unknown to the actors themselves, ver. 29. Men generally form their judgments, even of themselves merely from what is apparent. *According to my gospel* - According to the tenor of that gospel which is committed to my care. Hence it appears that the gospel also is a law.

17. *But if thou art called a Jew* - This highest point of Jewish glorying, after a farther description of it interposed, ver. 17-20, and refuted, ver. 21-24, is itself refuted, ver. 25, &c. The description consists of twice five articles; of which the former five, ver. 17, 18, show what he boasts of in himself; the other five, ver. 19, 20, what he glories in with respect to others. The first particular of the former five answers to the first of the latter; the second, to the second, and so on. *And restest in the law* - Dependest on it, though it can only condemn thee. *And gloriest in God* - As thy God; and that, too, to the exclusion of others.

19. *Blind, in darkness, ignorant, babes* - These were the titles which the Jews generally gave the gentiles.

20. *Having the form of knowledge and truth* - That is, the most accurate knowledge of the truth.

21. *Thou dost not teach thyself* - He does not teach himself who does not practice what he teaches. *Dost thou steal, commit adultery, commit sacrilege* - Sin grievously against thy neighbour, thyself, God. St. Paul had shown the gentiles, first their sins against God, then against themselves, then against their neighbours. He now inverts the order: for sins against God are the most glaring in an heathen, but not in a Jew. *Thou that abhorrest idols* - Which all the Jews did, from the time of the Babylonish captivity. *Thou committest sacrilege* - Doest what is worse, robbing Him "who is God over all" of the glory which is due to him. None of these charges were rashly advanced against the Jews of that age; for, as their own

historian relates, some even of the priests lived by rapine, and others in gross uncleanness. And as for sacrilegiously robbing God and his altar, it had been complained of ever since Malachi; so that the instances are given with great propriety and judgment.

24. Isaiah lii, 5

25. Circumcision indeed profiteth - He does not say, justifies. How far it profited is shown in the third and fourth chapters. Thy circumcision is become uncircumcision - is so already in effect. Thou wilt have no more benefit by it than if thou hadst never received it. The very same observation holds with regard to baptism.

26. If the uncircumcision - That is, a person uncircumcised. Keep the law - Walk agreeably to it. Shall not his uncircumcision be counted for circumcision - In the sight of God?

27. Yea, the uncircumcision that is by nature - Those who are, literally speaking, uncircumcised. Fulfilling the law - As to the substance of it. Shall judge thee - Shall condemn thee in that day. Who by the letter and circumcision - Who having the bare, literal, external circumcision, transgressest the law.

28. For he is not a Jew - In the most important sense, that is, one of God's beloved people. Who is one in outward show only; neither is that the true, acceptable circumcision, which is apparent in the flesh.

29. But he is a Jew - That is, one of God's people. Who is one inwardly - In the secret recesses of his soul. And the acceptable circumcision is that of the heart - Referring to Deut. xxx, 6; the putting away all inward impurity. This is seated in the spirit, the inmost soul, renewed by the Spirit of God. And not in the letter - Not in the external ceremony. Whose praise is not from men, but from God - The only searcher of the heart.

III

1. What then, may some say, is the advantage of the Jew, or of the circumcision - That is, those that are circumcised, above the gentiles?

2. Chiefly in that they were intrusted with the oracles of God - The scriptures, in which are so great and precious promises. Other prerogatives will follow, chap. ix, 4-5. St. Paul here singles out this by which, after removing the objection, he will convict them so much the more.

3. Shall their unbelief disannul the faithfulness of God - Will he not still make good his promises to them that do believe?

4. Psalm ii, 4.

5. But, it may be farther objected, if our unrighteousness be subservient to God's glory, is it not unjust in him to punish us for it? I speak as a man - As human weakness would be apt to speak.

6. God forbid - By no means. If it were unjust in God to punish that unrighteousness which is subservient to his own glory, how should God judge the world - Since all the unrighteousness in the world will then commend the righteousness of God.

7. But, may the objector reply, if the truth of God hath abounded - Has been more abundantly shown. Through my lie - If my lie, that is, practice contrary to truth, conduces to the glory of God, by making his truth shine with superior advantage. Why am I still judged as a sinner - Can this be said to be any sin at all? Ought I not to do what would otherwise be evil, that so much "good may come?" To this the apostle does not deign to give a direct answer, but cuts the objector short with a severe reproof.

8. Whose condemnation is just - The condemnation of all who either speak or act in this manner. So the apostle absolutely denies the lawfulness of " doing evil," any evil, "that good may come."

9. What then - Here he resumes what he said, verse 1. Rom. iii, 1. Under sin - Under the guilt and power of it: the Jews, by transgressing the written law; the gentiles, by transgressing the law of nature.

10. As it is written - That all men are under sin appears from the vices which have raged in all ages. St. Paul therefore rightly cites David and Isaiah, though they spoke primarily of their own age, and expressed what manner of men God sees, when he "looks down from heaven;" not what he makes them by his grace. There is none righteous - This is the general proposition. The particulars follow: their dispositions and designs, ver. 11, 12; their discourse, ver. 13, 14; their actions, ver. 16-18. Psalm xiv, 1, &c.

11. There is none that understandeth - The things of God.

12. They have all turned aside - From the good way. They are become unprofitable - Helpless impotent, unable to profit either themselves or others.

13. Their throat - Is noisome and dangerous as an open sepulchre. Observe the progress of evil discourse, proceeding out of the heart, through the throat, tongue, lips, till the whole mouth is filled therewith. The poison of asps - Infectious, deadly backbiting, tale-bearing, evil-speaking, is under (for honey is on) their lips. An asp is a venomous kind of serpent. Psalm v, 9; Psalm cxl, 3.

14. Cursing - Against God. Bitterness - Against their neighbour. Psalm x, 7.

15. Isaiah lix, 7, 8

17. Of peace - Which can only spring from righteousness.

18. The fear of God is not before their eyes - Much less is the love of God in their heart. Psalm xxxvi, 1.

19. Whatsoever the law - The Old Testament. Saith, it saith to them that are under the law - That is, to those who own its authority; to the Jews, and not the gentiles. St. Paul quoted no scripture against them, but pleaded with them only from the light of nature. Every mouth - Full of bitterness, ver. 14, and yet of boasting, ver. 27. May become guilty - May be fully convicted, and apparently liable to most just condemnation. These things were written of old, and were quoted by St. Paul, not to make men criminal, but to prove them so.

20. No flesh shall be justified - None shall be forgiven and accepted of God. By the works of the law - On this ground, that he hath kept the law. St. Paul means chiefly the moral part of it, ver. 9, 19 chap. ii, 21,

26; &c. which alone is not abolished, ver. 31. And it is not without reason, that he so often mentions the works of the law, whether ceremonial or moral; for it was on these only the Jews relied, being wholly ignorant of those that spring from faith. For by the law is only the knowledge of sin - But no deliverance either from the guilt or power of it.

21. But now the righteousness of God - That is, the manner of becoming righteous which God hath appointed. Without the law - Without that previous obedience which the law requires; without reference to the law, or dependence on it. Is manifested - In the gospel. Being attested by the Law itself, and by the Prophets - By all the promises in the Old Testament.

22. To all - The Jews. And upon all - The gentiles That believe: for there is no difference - Either as to the need of justification, or the manner of it.

23. For all have sinned - In Adam, and in their own persons; by a sinful nature, sinful tempers, and sinful actions. And are fallen short of the glory of God - The supreme end of man; short of his image on earth, and the enjoyment of him in heaven.

24. And are justified - Pardoned and accepted. Freely - Without any merit of their own. By his grace - Not their own righteousness or works. Through the redemption - The price Christ has paid. Freely by his grace - One of these expressions might have served to convey the apostle's meaning; but he doubles his assertion, in order to give us the fullest conviction of the truth, and to impress us with a sense of its peculiar importance. It is not possible to find words that should more absolutely exclude all consideration of our own works and obedience, or more emphatically ascribe the whole of our justification to free, unmerited goodness.

25. Whom God hath set forth - Before angels and men. A propitiation - To appease an offended God. But if, as some teach, God never was offended, there was no need of this propitiation. And, if so, Christ died in vain. To declare his righteousness - To demonstrate not only his clemency, but his justice; even that vindictive justice whose essential character and principal office is, to punish sin. By the remission of past sins - All the sins antecedent to their believing.

26. For a demonstration of his righteousness - Both of his justice and mercy. That he might be just - Showing his justice on his own Son. And yet the merciful justifier of every one that believeth in Jesus. That he might be just - Might evidence himself to be strictly and inviolably righteous in the administration of his government, even while he is the merciful justifier of the sinner that believeth in Jesus. The attribute of justice must be preserved inviolate; and inviolate it is preserved, if there was a real infliction of punishment on our saviour. On this plan all the attributes harmonize; every attribute is glorified, and not one superseded no, nor so much as clouded.

27. Where is the boasting then of the Jew against the gentile? It is excluded. By what law? of works? Nay - This would have left room for boasting. But by the law of faith - Since this requires all, without distinction, to apply as guilty and helpless sinners, to the free mercy of God in Christ. The law of faith is that divine constitution which makes faith, not works, the condition of acceptance.

28. We conclude then that a man is justified by faith - And even by this, not as it is a work, but as it receives Christ; and, consequently, has something essentially different from all our works whatsoever.

29. Surely of the gentiles also - As both nature and the scriptures show.

30. Seeing it is one God who - Shows mercy to both, and by the very same means.

31. We establish the law - Both the authority, purity, and the end of it; by defending that which the law attests; by pointing out Christ, the end of it; and by showing how it may be fulfilled in its purity.

IV

Having proved it by argument, he now proves by example, and such example as must have greater weight with the Jews than any other.

1. That justification is by faith:
2. That it is free for the gentiles.

1. That our father Abraham hath found - Acceptance with God. According to the flesh - That is, by works.

2. The meaning is, If Abraham had been justified by works, he would have had room to glory. But he had not room to glory. Therefore he was not justified by works.

3. Abraham believed God - That promise of God concerning the numerousness of his seed, Gen. xv, 5, 7; but especially the promise concerning Christ, Gen. xii, 3, through whom all nations should be blessed. And it was imputed to him for righteousness - God accepted him as if he had been altogether righteous. Gen. xv, 6.

4. Now to him that worketh - All that the law requires, the reward is no favour, but an absolute debt. These two examples are selected and applied with the utmost judgment and propriety. Abraham was the most illustrious pattern of piety among the Jewish patriarchs. David was the most eminent of their kings. If then neither of these was justified by his own obedience, if they both obtained acceptance with God, not as upright beings who might claim it, but as sinful creatures who must implore it, the consequence is glaring It is such as must strike every attentive understanding, and must affect every individual person.

5. But to him that worketh not - It being impossible he should without faith. But believeth, his faith is imputed to him for righteousness - Therefore God's affirming of Abraham, that faith was imputed to him for righteousness, plainly shows that he worked not; or, in other words, that he was not justified by works, but by faith only. Hence we see plainly how groundless that opinion is, that holiness or sanctification is previous to our justification. For the sinner, being first convinced of his sin and danger by the Spirit of God, stands trembling before the awful tribunal of divine justice; and has nothing to plead, but his own guilt, and the merits of a Mediator. Christ here interposes; justice is satisfied; the sin is remitted, and pardon is applied to the soul, by a divine faith wrought by the Holy Ghost, who then begins the great work of inward sanctification. Thus God justifies the ungodly, and yet remains just, and true to all his attributes! But let none hence presume to "continue in sin;" for to the impenitent, God "is a consuming fire." On him that justifieth the ungodly - If a man could possibly be made holy before he was justified, it would entirely set his justification aside; seeing he could not, in the very nature of the thing, be justified if he were not, at that very time, ungodly.

6. So David also - David is fitly introduced after Abraham, because be also received and delivered down the promise. Affirmeth - A man is justified by faith alone, and not by works. Without works-That is, without regard to any former good works supposed to have been done by him.

7. Happy are they whose sins are covered - With the veil of divine mercy. If there be indeed such a thing as happiness on earth, it is the portion of that man whose iniquities are forgiven, and who enjoys the manifestation of that pardon. Well may he endure all the afflictions of life with cheerfulness, and look upon death with comfort. O let us not contend against it, but earnestly pray that this happiness may be ours! Psalm xxxii, 1, 2.

9. This happiness - Mentioned by Abraham and David. On the circumcision - Those that are circumcised only. Faith was imputed to Abraham for righteousness - This is fully consistent with our being justified, that is, pardoned and accepted by God upon our believing, for the sake of what Christ hath done and suffered. For though this, and this alone, be the meritorious cause of our acceptance with God, yet faith may be said to be "imputed to us for righteousness," as it is the sole condition of our acceptance. We may observe here, forgiveness, not imputing sin, and imputing righteousness, are all one.

10. Not in circumcision - Not after he was circumcised; for he was justified before Ishmael was born, Gen. xv, 1-21; but he was not circumcised till Ishmael was thirteen years old, Gen. xvii, 25.

11. And - After he was justified. He received the sign of circumcision - Circumcision, which was a sign or token of his being in covenant with God. A seal - An assurance on God's part, that he accounted him righteous, upon his believing, before he was circumcised. Who believe in uncircumcision - That is, though they are not circumcised.

12. And the father of the circumcision - Of those who are circumcised, and believe as Abraham did. To those who believe not, Abraham is not a father, neither are they his seed.

13. The promise, that he should be the heir of the world - Is the same as that he should be "the father of all nations," namely, of those in all nations who receive the blessing. The whole world was promised to him and them conjointly. Christ is the heir of the world, and of all things; and so are all Abraham's seed, all that believe in him with the faith of Abraham

14. If they only who are of the law - Who have kept the whole law. Are heirs, faith is made void - No blessing being to be obtained by it; and so the promise is of no effect.

15. Because the law - Considered apart from that grace, which though it was in fact mingled with it, yet is no part of the legal dispensation, is so difficult, and we so weak and sinful, that, instead of bringing us a blessing, it only worketh wrath; it becomes to us an occasion of wrath, and exposes us to punishment as transgressors. Where there is no law in force, there can be no transgression of it.

16. Therefore it - The blessing. Is of faith, that it might be of grace - That it might appear to flow from the free love of God, and that the promise might be firm, sure, and effectual, to all the spiritual seed of Abraham; not only Jews, but gentiles also, if they follow his faith.

17. Before God - Though before men nothing of this appeared, those nations being then unborn. As quickening the dead - The dead are not dead to him and even the things that are not, are before God. And calling the things that are not - Summoning them to rise into being, and appear before him. The seed of Abraham did not then exist; yet God said, "So shall thy seed be." A man can say to his servant actually existing, Do this; and he doeth it: but God saith to the light, while it does not exist, Go forth; and it goeth. Gen. xvii, 5. 18-21. The Apostle shows the power and excellence of that faith to which he ascribes justification. Who against hope - Against all probability, believed and hoped in the promise. The same thing is apprehended both by faith and hope; by faith, as a thing which God has spoken; by hope, as a good thing which God has promised to us. So shall thy seed be - Both natural and spiritual, as the stars of heaven for multitude. Gen. xv, 5.

23. On his account only - To do personal honour to him.

24. But on ours also - To establish us in seeking justification by faith, and not by works; and to afford a full answer to those who say that, " to be justified by works means only, by Judaism; to be justified by faith means, by embracing Christianity, that is, the system of doctrines so called." Sure it is that Abraham could not in this sense be justified either by faith or by works; and equally sure that David (taking the words thus) was justified by works, and not by faith. Who raised up Jesus from the dead - As he did in a manner both Abraham and Sarah. If we believe on him who raised up Jesus - God the Father therefore is the proper object of justifying faith. It is observable, that St. Paul here, in speaking both of our faith and of the faith of Abraham, puts a part for the whole. And he mentions that part, with regard to Abraham, which would naturally affect the Jews most.

25. Who was delivered - To death. For our offenses - As an atonement for them. And raised for our justification - To empower us to receive that atonement by faith.

V

1. Being justified by faith - This is the sum of the preceding chapters. We have peace with God - Being enemies to God no longer, ver. 10; neither fearing his wrath, ver. 9. We have peace, hope, love, and power over sin, the sum of the fifth, sixth, seventh, and eighth chapters. These are the fruits of justifying faith: where these are not, that faith is not.

2. Into this grace - This state of favour.

3. We glory in tribulations also - Which we are so far from esteeming a mark of God's displeasure, that we receive them as tokens of his fatherly love, whereby we are prepared for a more exalted happiness. The Jews objected to the persecuted state of the Christians as inconsistent with the people of the Messiah. It is therefore with great propriety that the apostle so often mentions the blessings arising from this very thing.

4. And patience works more experience of the sincerity of our grace, and of God's power and faithfulness.

5. Hope shameth us not - That is, gives us the highest glorying. We glory in this our hope, because the love of God is shed abroad in our hearts - The divine conviction of God's love to us, and that love to God which is both the earnest and the beginning of heaven. By the Holy Ghost - The efficient cause of all these present blessings, and the earnest of those to come.

6. How can we now doubt of God's love? For when we were without strength - Either to think, will, or do anything good. In due time - Neither too soon nor too late; but in that very point of time which the wisdom of God knew to be more proper than any other. Christ died for the ungodly - Not only to set them a pattern, or to procure them power to follow it. It does not appear that this expression, of dying for any one, has any other signification than that of rescuing the life of another by laying down our own.

7. A just man - One who gives to all what is strictly their due The good man - One who is eminently holy; full of love, of compassion, kindness, mildness, of every heavenly and amiable temper. Perhaps-one-would-even-dare to die - Every word increases the strangeness of the thing, and declares even this to be something great and unusual.

8. But God recommendeth - A most elegant expression. Those are wont to be recommended to us, who were before either unknown to, or alienated from, us. While we were sinners - So far from being good, that we were not even just.

9. By his blood - By his bloodshedding. We shall be saved from wrath through him - That is, from all the effects of the wrath of God. But is there then wrath in God? Is not wrath a human passion? And how can this human passion be in God? We may answer this by another question: Is not love a human passion? And how can this human passion be in God? But to answer directly: wrath in man, and so love in man, is a human passion. But wrath in God is not a human passion; nor is love, as it is in God. Therefore the inspired writers ascribe both the one and the other to God only in an analogical sense.

10. If - As sure as; so the word frequently signifies; particularly in this and the eighth chapter. We shalt be saved - Sanctified and glorified. Through his life - "Whoever liveth to make intercession for

us."

11. And not only so, but we also glory - The whole sentence, from the third to the eleventh verse, may be taken together thus: We not only "rejoice in hope of the glory of God," but also in the midst of tribulations we glory in God himself through our Lord Jesus Christ, by whom we have now received the reconciliation.

12. Therefore - This refers to all the preceding discourse; from which the apostle infers what follows. He does not therefore properly make a digression, but returns to speak again of sin and of righteousness. As by one man - Adam; who is mentioned, and not Eve, as being the representative of mankind. Sin entered into the world - Actual sin, and its consequence, a sinful nature. And death - With all its attendants. It entered into the world when it entered into being; for till then it did not exist. By sin - Therefore it could not enter before sin. Even so - Namely, by one man. In that - So the word is used also, 2 Cor. v, 4. All sinned - In Adam. These words assign the reason why death came upon all men; infants themselves not excepted, in that all sinned.

13. For until the law sin was in the world - All, I say, had sinned, for sin was in the world long before the written law; but, I grant, sin is not so much imputed, nor so severely punished by God, where there is no express law to convince men of it. Yet that all had sinned, even then, appears in that all died.

14. Death reigned - And how vast is his kingdom! Scarce can we find any king who has as many subjects, as are the kings whom he hath conquered. Even over them that had not sinned after the likeness of Adam's transgression - Even over infants who had never sinned, as Adam did, in their own persons; and over others who had not, like him, sinned against an express law. Who is the figure of him that was to come - Each of them being a public person, and a federal head of mankind. The one, the fountain of sin and death to mankind by his offense; the other, of righteousness and life by his free gift. Thus far the apostle shows the agreement between the first and second Adam: afterward he shows the differences between them. The agreement may be summed up thus: As by one man sin entered into the world, and death by sin; so by one man righteousness entered into the world, and life by righteousness. As death passed upon all men, in that all had sinned; so life passed upon all men, (who are in the second Adam by faith,) in that all are justified. And as death through the sin of the first Adam reigned even over them who had not sinned after the likeness of Adam's transgression; so through the righteousness of Christ, even those who have not obeyed, after the likeness of his obedience, shall reign in life. We may add, As the sin of Adam, without the sins which we afterwards committed, brought us death; so the righteousness of Christ, without the good works which we afterwards perform, brings us life: although still every good, as well as evil, work, will receive its due reward.

15. Yet not - St. Paul now describes the difference between Adam and Christ; and that much more directly and expressly than the agreement between them. Now the fall and the free gift differ,

1. In amplitude, ver. 15.

2. He from whom sin came, and He from whom the free gift came, termed also "the gift of righteousness," differ in power, ver. 16.

3. The reason of both is subjoined, ver. 17.

4. This premised, the offense and the free gift are compared, with regard to their effect, ver. 18, and with regard to their cause, ver. 19.

16. The sentence was by one offense to Adam's condemnation - Occasioning the sentence of death to pass upon him, which, by consequence, overwhelmed his posterity. But the free gift is of many offenses unto justification - Unto the purchasing it for all men, notwithstanding many offenses.

17. There is a difference between grace and the gift. Grace is opposed to the offense; the gift, to death, being the gift of life.

18. Justification of life - Is that sentence of God, by which a sinner under sentence of death is adjudged to life.

19. As by the disobedience of one man many (that is, all men) were constituted sinners - Being then in the loins of their first parent, the common head and representative of them all. So by the obedience of one - By his obedience unto death; by his dying for us. Many - All that believe. Shall be constituted righteous - Justified, pardoned.

20. The law came in between - The offense and the free gift. That the offense might abound - That is, the consequence (not the design) of the law's coming in was, not the taking away of sin, but the increase of it. Yet where sin abounded, grace did much more abound - Not only in the remission of that sin which Adam brought on us, but of all our own; not only in remission of sins, but infusion of holiness; not only in deliverance from death, but admission to everlasting life, a far more noble and excellent life than that which we lost by Adam's fall.

21. That as sin had reigned - so grace also might reign - Which could not reign before the fall; before man had sinned. Through righteousness to eternal life by Jesus Christ our Lord - Here is pointed out the source of all our blessings, the rich and free grace of God. The meritorious cause; not any works of righteousness of man, but the alone merits of our Lord Jesus Christ. The effect or end of all; not only pardon, but life; divine life, leading to glory.

VI

1. The apostle here sets himself more fully to vindicate his doctrine from the consequence above suggested, chap. iii, 7, 8. He had then only in strong terms denied and renounced it: here he removes the very foundation thereof.

2. Dead to sin - Freed both from the guilt and from the power of it.

3. As many as have been baptized into Jesus Christ have been baptized into his death - In baptism we, through faith, are ingrafted into Christ; and we draw new spiritual life from this new root, through his Spirit, who fashions us like unto him, and particularly with regard to his death and resurrection.

4. We are buried with him - Alluding to the ancient manner of baptizing by immersion. That as Christ was raised from the dead by the glory - Glorious power. Of the Father, so we also, by the same power, should rise again; and as he lives a new life in heaven, so we should walk in newness of life. This, says the apostle, our very baptism represents to us.

5. For - Surely these two must go together; so that if we are indeed made conformable to his death, we shall also know the power of his resurrection.

6. Our old man - Coeval with our being, and as old as the fall; our evil nature; a strong and beautiful expression for that entire depravity and corruption which by nature spreads itself over the whole man, leaving no part uninfected. This in a believer is crucified with Christ, mortified, gradually killed, by virtue of our union with him. That the body of sin - All evil tempers, words, and actions, which are the "members" of the "old man," Colossians iii, 5, might be destroyed.

7. For he that is dead - With Christ. Is freed from the guilt of past, and from the power of present, sin, as dead men from the commands of their former masters.

8. Dead with Christ - Conformed to his death, by dying to sin.

10. He died to sin - To atone for and abolish it. He liveth unto God - A glorious eternal life, such as we shall live also.

12. Let not sin reign even in your mortal body - It must be subject to death, but it need not be subject to sin.

13. Neither present your members to sin - To corrupt nature, a mere tyrant. But to God - Your lawful King.

14. Sin shall not have dominion over you - It has neither right nor power. For ye are not under the law - A dispensation of terror and bondage, which only shows sin, without enabling you to conquer it. But under grace - Under the merciful dispensation of the gospel, which brings complete victory over it to every one who is under the powerful influences of the Spirit of Christ.

17. The form of doctrine into which ye have been delivered - Literally it is, The mould into which ye have been delivered; which, as it contains a beautiful allusion, conveys also a very instructive admonition; intimating that our minds, all pliant and ductile, should be conformed to the gospel precepts, as liquid metal, take the figure of the mould into which they are cast.

18. Being then set free from sin - We may see the apostles method thus far at one view: - Chap. Ver.

1. Bondage to sin chap. iii, 9
2. The knowledge of sin by the law; a sense of God's wrath; inward death chap. iii, 20
3. The Revelation of the righteousness of God in Christ through the gospel chap. iii, 21
4. The center of all, faith, embracing that righteousness chap. iii, 22
5. Justification, whereby God forgives all past sin, and freely accepts the sinner chap. iii, 24
6. The gift of the Holy Ghost; a sense of chap. v, 5, God's love new inward life ver. 4
7. The free service of righteousness ver. 12

19. I speak after the manner of men - Thus it is necessary that the scripture should let itself down to the language of men. Because of the weakness of your flesh - Slowness of understanding flows from the weakness of the flesh, that is, of human nature. As ye have presented your members servants to uncleanness and iniquity unto iniquity, so now present your members servants of righteousness unto holiness - Iniquity (whereof uncleanness is an eminent part) is here opposed to righteousness; and unto iniquity is the opposite of unto holiness. Righteousness here is a conformity to the divine will; holiness, to the whole divine nature. Observe, they who are servants of righteousness go on to holiness; but they who are servants to iniquity get no farther. Righteousness is service, because we live according to the will of another; but liberty, because of our inclination to it, and delight in it.

20. When ye were the servants of sin, ye were free from righteousness - In all reason, therefore, ye ought now to be free from unrighteousness; to be as uniform and zealous in serving God as ye were in serving the devil.

21. Those things - He speaks of them as afar off.

23. Death - Temporal, spiritual, and eternal. Is the due wages of sin; but eternal life is the gift of God - The difference is remarkable. Evil works merit the reward they receive: good works do not. The former demand wages: the latter accept a free gift.

VII

1. The apostle continues the comparison between the former and the present state of a believer, and at the same time endeavours to wean the Jewish believers from their fondness for the Mosaic law. I speak to them that know the law - To the Jews chiefly here. As long - So long, and no longer. As it liveth - The law is here spoken of, by a common figure, as a person, to which, as to an husband, life and death are ascribed. But he speaks indifferently of the law being dead to us, or we to it, the sense being the same.

2. She is freed from the law of her husband - From that law which gave him a peculiar property in her.

4. Thus ye also - Are now as free from the Mosaic law as an husband is, when his wife is dead. By the body of Christ - Offered up; that is, by the merits of his death, that law expiring with him.

5. When ye were in the flesh - Carnally minded, in a state of nature; before we believed in Christ. Our sins which were by the law - Accidentally occasioned, or irritated thereby. Wrought in our members - Spread themselves all over the whole man.

6. Being dead to that whereby we were held - To our old husband, the law. That we might serve in newness of spirit - In a new, spiritual manner. And not in the oldness of the letter - Not in a bare literal, external way, as we did before.

7. What shall we say then - This is a kind of a digression, to the beginning of the next chapter, wherein the apostle, in order to show in the most lively manner the weakness and inefficacy of the law, changes the person and speaks as of himself, concerning the misery of one under the law. This St. Paul frequently does, when he is not speaking of his own person, but only assuming another character, chap. iii, 5, 1 Cor. x, 30, 1 Cor. iv, 6. The character here assumed is that of a man, first ignorant of the law, then under it and sincerely, but ineffectually, striving to serve God. To have spoken this of himself, or any true believer, would have been foreign to the whole scope of his discourse; nay, utterly contrary thereto, as well as to what is expressly asserted, chap. viii, 2. Is the law sin - Sinful in itself, or a promoter of sin. I had not known lust - That is, evil desire. I had not known it to be a sin; nay, perhaps I should not have known that any such desire was in me: it did not appear, till it was stirred up by the prohibition.

8. But sin - My inbred corruption. Taking occasion by the commandment - Forbidding, but not subduing it, was only fretted, and wrought in me so much the more all manner of evil desire. For while I was without the knowledge of the law, sin was dead - Neither so apparent, nor so active; nor was I under the least apprehensions of any danger from it.

9. And I was once alive without the law - Without the close application of it. I had much life, wisdom, virtue, strength: so I thought. But when the commandment - That is, the law, a part put for the whole; but this expression particularly intimates its compulsive force, which restrains, enjoins, urges, forbids, threatens. Came - In its spiritual meaning, to my heart, with the power of God. Sin revived, and I died - My inbred sin took fire, and all my virtue and strength died away; and I then saw myself to be dead in sin, and liable to death eternal.

10. The commandment which was intended for life - Doubtless it was originally intended by God as a grand means of preserving and increasing spiritual life, and leading to life everlasting.

11. Deceived me - While I expected life by the law, sin came upon me unawares and slew all my hopes.

12. The commandment - That is, every branch of the law. Is holy, and just, and good - It springs from, and partakes of, the holy nature of God; it is every way just and right in itself; it is designed wholly for the good of man.

13. Was then that which is good made the cause of evil to me; yea, of death, which is the greatest of evil? Not so. But it was sin, which was made death to me, inasmuch as it wrought death in me even by that which is good - By the good law. So that sin by the commandment became exceeding sinful - The consequence of which was, that inbred sin, thus driving furiously in spite of the commandment, became exceeding sinful; the guilt thereof being greatly aggravated.

14. I am carnal - St. Paul, having compared together the past and present state of believers, that "in the flesh," ver. 5, and that "in the spirit," ver. 6, in answering two objections, (Is then the law sin? ver. 7, and, Is the law death? ver. 13,) interweaves the whole process of a man reasoning, groaning, striving, and escaping from the legal to the evangelical state. This he does from ver. 7, to the end of this chapter. Sold under sin - Totally enslaved; slaves bought with money were absolutely at their master's disposal.

16. It is good - This single word implies all the three that were used before, ver. 12, "holy, just, and good."

17. It is no more I that can properly be said to do it, but rather sin that dwelleth in me - That makes, as it were, another person, and tyrannizes over me.

18. In my flesh - The flesh here signifies the whole man as he is by nature.

21. I find then a law - An inward constraining power, flowing from the dictate of corrupt nature.

22. *For I delight in the law of God* - This is more than "I consent to," ver. 16. The day of liberty draws near. *The inward man* - Called the mind, ver. 23, 25.

23. *But I see another law in my members* - Another inward constraining power of evil inclinations and bodily appetites. *Warring against the law of my mind* - The dictate of my mind, which delights in the law of God. *And captivating me* - In spite of all my resistance

24. *Wretched man that I am* - The struggle is now come to the height; and the man, finding there is no help in himself, begins almost unawares to pray, Who shall deliver me? He then seeks and looks for deliverance, till God in Christ appears to answer his question. The word which we translate deliver, implies force. And indeed without this there can be no deliverance. *The body of this death* - That is, this body of death; this mass of sin, leading to death eternal, and cleaving as close to me as my body to my soul. We may observe, the deliverance is not wrought yet.

25. *I thank God through Jesus Christ our Lord* - That is, God will deliver me through Christ. But the apostle, as his frequent manner is, beautifully interweaves his assertion with thanksgiving; the hymn of praise answering in a manner to the voice of sorrow, "Wretched man that I am!" So then - He here sums up the whole, and concludes what he began, ver. 7. *I myself* - Or rather that I, the person whom I am personating, till this deliverance is wrought. *Serve the law of God with my mind* - My reason and conscience declare for God. *But with my flesh the law of sin* - But my corrupt passions and appetites still rebel. The man is now utterly weary of his bondage, and upon the brink of liberty.

VIII

1. *There is therefore now no condemnation* - Either for things present or past. Now he comes to deliverance and liberty. The apostle here resumes the thread of his discourse, which was interrupted, chap. vii, 7.

2. *The law of the Spirit* - That is, the gospel. *Hath freed me from the law of sin and death* - That is, the Mosaic dispensation.

3. *For what the law* - Of Moses. *Could not do, in that it was weak through the flesh* - Incapable of conquering our evil nature. If it could, God needed not to have sent his own Son *in the likeness of sinful flesh* - We with our sinful flesh were devoted to death. But God sending his own Son, in the likeness of that flesh, though pure from sin, condemned that sin which was in our flesh; gave sentence, that sin should be destroyed, and the believer wholly delivered from it.

4. *That the righteousness of the law* - The holiness it required, described, ver. 11. *Might be fulfilled in us, who walk not after the flesh, but after the Spirit* - Who are guided in all our thoughts, words, and actions, not by corrupt nature, but by the Spirit of God. From this place St. Paul describes primarily the state of believers, and that of unbelievers only to illustrate this.

5. *They that are after the flesh* - Who remain under the guidance of corrupt nature. *Mind the things of the flesh* - Have their thoughts and affections fixed on such things as gratify corrupt nature; namely, on things visible and temporal; on things of the earth, on pleasure, (of sense or imagination,) praise, or riches. *But they who are after the Spirit* - Who are under his guidance. *Mind the things of the Spirit* - Think of, relish, love things invisible, eternal; the things which the Spirit hath revealed, which he works in us, moves us to, and promises to give us.

6. *For to be carnally minded* - That is, to mind the things of the flesh. *Is death* - The sure mark of spiritual death, and the way to death everlasting. *But to be spiritually minded* - That is, to mind the things of the Spirit. *Is life* - A sure mark of spiritual life, and the way to life everlasting. And attended *with peace* - The peace of God, which is the foretaste of life everlasting; and peace with God, opposite to the enmity mentioned in the next verse.

7. *Enmity against God* - His existence, power, and providence.

8. *They who are in the flesh* - Under the government of it.

9. *In the Spirit* - Under his government. *If any man have not the Spirit of Christ* - Dwelling and governing in him. *He is none of his* - He is not a member of Christ; not a Christian; not in a state of salvation. A plain, express declaration, which admits of no exception. He that hath ears to hear, let him hear!

10. *Now if Christ be in you* - Where the Spirit of Christ is, there is Christ. *The body indeed is dead* - Devoted to death. *Because of sin* - Heretofore committed. *But the Spirit is life* - Already truly alive. *Because of righteousness* - Now attained. From ver. 13, St. Paul, having finished what he had begun, chap. vi, 1, describes purely the state of believers.

12. *We are not debtors to the flesh* - We ought not to follow it.

13. *The deeds of the flesh* - Not only evil actions, but evil desires, tempers, thoughts. *If ye mortify* - Kill, destroy these. *Ye shall live* - The life of faith more abundantly here, and hereafter the life of glory.

14. *For as many as are led by the Spirit of God* - In all the ways of righteousness. *They are the sons of God* - Here St. Paul enters upon the description of those blessings which he comprises, ver. 30,

in the word glorified; though, indeed, he does not describe mere glory, but that which is still mingled with the cross. The sum is, through sufferings to glory.

15. For ye - Who are real Christians. Have not received the spirit of bondage - The Holy Ghost was not properly a spirit of bondage, even in the time of the Old Testament. Yet there was something of bondage remaining even in those who then had received the Spirit. Again - As the Jews did before. We - All and every believer. Cry - The word denotes a vehement speaking, with desire, confidence, constancy. Abba, Father - The latter word explains the former. By using both the Syriac and the Greek word, St. Paul seems to point out the joint cry both of the Jewish and gentile believers. The spirit of bondage here seems directly to mean, those operations of the Holy Spirit by which the soul, on its first conviction, feels itself in bondage to sin, to the world, to Satan, and obnoxious to the wrath of God. This, therefore, and the Spirit of adoption, are one and the same Spirit, only manifesting itself in various operations, according to the various circumstances of the persons.

16. The same Spirit beareth witness with our spirit - With the spirit of every true believer, by a testimony distinct from that of his own spirit, or the testimony of a good conscience. Happy they who enjoy this clear and constant.

17. Joint heirs - That we may know it is a great inheritance which God will give us for he hath given a great one to his Son. If we suffer with him - Willingly and cheerfully, for righteousness' sake. This is a new proposition, referring to what follows.

18. For I reckon - This verse gives the reason why he but now mentioned sufferings and glory. When that glory "shall be revealed in us," then the sons of God will be revealed also.

19. For the earnest expectation - The word denotes a lively hope of something drawing near, and a vehement longing after it. Of the creation - Of all visible creatures, believers excepted, who are spoken of apart; each kind, according as it is capable. All these have been sufferers through sin; and to all these (the finally impenitent excepted) shall refreshment redound from the glory of the children of God. Upright heathens are by no means to be excluded from this earnest expectation: nay, perhaps something of it may at some times be found even in the vainest of men; who (although in the hurry of life they mistake vanity for liberty, and partly stifle, partly dissemble, their groans, yet) in their sober, quiet, sleepless, afflicted hours, pour forth many sighs in the ear of God.

20. The creation was made subject to vanity - Abuse, misery, and corruption. By him who subjected it - Namely, God, Gen. iii, 17, v, 29. Adam only made it liable to the sentence which God pronounced; yet not without hope.

21. The creation itself shall be delivered - Destruction is not deliverance: therefore whatsoever is destroyed, or ceases to be, is not delivered at all. Will, then, any part of the creation be destroyed? Into the glorious liberty - The excellent state wherein they were created.

22. For the whole creation groaneth together - With joint groans, as it were with one voice. And travaileth - Literally, is in the pains of childbirth, to be delivered of the burden of the curse. Until now - To this very hour; and so on till the time of deliverance.

23. And even we, who have the first-fruits of the Spirit - That is, the Spirit, who is the first-fruits of our inheritance. The adoption - Persons who had been privately adopted among the Roman were often brought forth into the forum, and there publicly owned as their sons by those who adopted them. So at the general resurrection, when the body itself is redeemed from death, the sons of God shall be publicly owned by him in the great assembly of men and angels. The redemption of our body - From corruption to glory and immortality.

24. For we are saved by hope - Our salvation is now only in hope. We do not yet possess this full salvation.

26. Likewise the Spirit - Nay, not only the universe, not only the children of God, but the Spirit of God also himself, as it were, groaneth, while he helpeth our infirmities, or weaknesses. Our understandings are weak, particularly in the things of God our desires are weak; our prayers are weak. We know not - Many times. What we should pray for - Much less are we able to pray for it as we ought: but the Spirit maketh intercession for us - In our hearts, even as Christ does in heaven. With groanings - The matter of which is from ourselves, but the Spirit forms them; and they are frequently inexpressible, even by the faithful themselves.

27. But he who searcheth the hearts - Wherein the Spirit dwells and intercedes. Knoweth - Though man cannot utter it. What is the mind of the Spirit, for he maketh intercession for the saints - Who are near to God. According to God - According to his will, as is worthy of God. and acceptable to him.

28. And we know - This in general; though we do not always know particularly what to pray for. That all things - Ease or pain, poverty or riches, and the ten thousand changes of life. Work together for good - Strongly and sweetly for spiritual and eternal good. To them that are called according to his purpose - His gracious design of saving a lost world by the death of his Son. This is a new proposition. St. Paul, being about to recapitulate the whole blessing contained in justification, (termed "glorification," ver. 30,) first goes back to the purpose or decree of God, which is frequently mentioned in holy writ. To explain this (nearly in the words of an eminent writer) a little more at large:-When a

Wesley's Notes on the Bible - The New Testament

man has a work of time and importance before him, he pauses, consults, and contrives; and when he has laid a plan, resolves or decrees to proceed accordingly. Having observed this in ourselves, we are ready to apply it to God also; and he, in condescension to us has applied it to himself. The works of providence and redemption are vast and stupendous, and therefore we are apt to conceive of God as deliberating and consulting on them, and then decreeing to act according to "the counsel of his own will;" as if, long before the world was made, he had been concerting measures both as to the making and governing of it, and had then writ down his decrees, which altered not, any more than the laws of the Medes and Persians. Whereas, to take this consulting and decreeing in a literal sense, would be the same absurdity as to ascribe a real human body and human passions to the ever-blessed God. This is only a popular representation of his infallible knowledge and unchangeable wisdom; that is, he does all things as wisely as a man can possibly do, after the deepest consultation, and as steadily pursues the most proper method as one can do who has laid a scheme beforehand. But then, though the effects be such as would argue consultation and consequent decrees in man, yet what need of a moment's consultation in Him who sees all things at one view? Nor had God any more occasion to pause and deliberate, and lay down rules for his own conduct from all eternity, than he has now. What was there any fear of his mistaking afterwards, if he had not beforehand prepared decrees, to direct him what he was to do? Will any man say, he was wiser before the creation than since? or had he then more leisure, that he should take that opportunity to settle his affairs, and make rules (or himself, from which he was never to vary? He has doubtless the same wisdom and all other perfections at this day which he had from eternity; and is now as capable of making decrees, or rather has no more occasion for them now than formerly: his understanding being always equally clear and bright, his wisdom equally infallible.

29. Whom he foreknew, he also predestinated conformable to the image of his Son - Here the apostle declares who those are whom he foreknew and predestinated to glory; namely, those who are conformable to the image of his Son. This is the mark of those who are foreknown and will be glorified, 2 Tim. ii, 19. Phil. iii, 10, 21.

30. Them he - In due time. Called - By his gospel and his Spirit. And whom he called - When obedient to the heavenly calling, Acts xxvi, 19. He also justified - Forgave and accepted. And whom he justified - Provided they "continued in his goodness," chap. xi, 22, he in the end glorified - St. Paul does not affirm, either here or in any other part of his writings, that precisely the same number of men are called, justified, and glorified. He does not deny that a believer may fall away and be cut off between his special calling and his glorification, chap. xi, 22. Neither does he deny that many are called who never are justified. He only affirms that this is the method whereby God leads us step by step toward heaven. He glorified - He speaks as one looking back from the goal, upon the race of faith. Indeed grace, as it is glory begun, is both an earnest and a foretaste of eternal glory.

31. What shall we say then to these things - Related in the third, fifth, and eighth chapters? As if he had said, We cannot go, think, or wish anything farther. If God be for us - Here follow four periods, one general and three particular. Each begins with glorying in the grace of God, which is followed by a question suitable to it, challenging all opponents to all which, "I am persuaded," &c., is a general answer. The general period is, If God be for us, who can be against us? The first particular period, relating to the past time, is, He that spared not his own Son, how shall he not freely give us all things? The second, relating to the present, is, It is God that justifieth. Who is he that condemneth? The third, relating to the future, is, It is Christ that died - Who shall separate us from the love of Christ?

32. He that - This period contains four sentences: He spared not his own Son; therefore he will freely give us all things. He delivered him up for us all; therefore, none can lay anything to our charge. Freely - For all that follows justification is a free gift also. All things - Needful or profitable for us.

33. God's elect - The above-cited author observes, that long before the coming of Christ the heathen world revolted from the true God, and were therefore reprobated, or rejected. But the nation of the Jews were chosen to be the people of God, and were therefore styled, "the children" or "sons of God," Deut. xiv, 1; "holy people," Deut. vii, 6; xiv, 2; "a chosen seed," Deut. iv, 37; "the elect," Isaiah xli, 8, 9; xliii, 10; "the called of God," Isaiah xlviii, 12. And these titles were given to all the nation of Israel, including both good and bad. Now the gospel having the most strict connection with the Books of the Old Testament, where these phrases frequently occur; and our Lord and his apostles being native Jews, and beginning to preach in the land of Israel, the language in which they preached would of course abound with the phrases of the Jewish nation. And hence it is easy to see why such of them as would not receive him were styled reprobated. For they no longer continued to be the people of God; whereas this and those other honourable titles were continued to all such Jews as embraced Christianity. And the same appellations which once belonged to the Jewish nation were now given to the gentile Christians also together with which they were invested with all the privileges of "the chosen people of God;" and nothing could cut them off from these but their own wilful apostasy. It does not appear that even good men were ever termed God's elect till above two thousand years from the creation. God's electing or choosing the nation of Israel, and separating them from the other nations, who were sunk in idolatry and all wickedness, gave the first occasion to this sort of language. And as the separating the

Christians from the Jews was a like event, no wonder it was expressed in like words and phrases only with this difference, the term elect was of old applied to all the members of the visible church; whereas in the New Testament it is applied only to the members of the invisible.

34. Yea rather, that is risen - Our faith should not stop at his death, but be exercised farther on his resurrection, kingdom, second coming. Who maketh intercession for us - Presenting there his obedience, his sufferings, his prayers, and our prayers sanctified through him.

35. Who shall separate us from the love of Christ - Toward us? Shall affliction or distress - He proceeds in order, from less troubles to greater: can any of these separate us from his protection in it; and, if he sees good, deliverance from it?

36. All the day - That is, every day, continually. We are accounted - By our enemies; by ourselves. Psalm xliv, 22.

37. We more than conquer - We are not only no losers, but abundant gainers, by all these trials. This period seems to describe the full assurance of hope.

38. I am persuaded - This is inferred from the thirty-fourth verse, in an admirable order: - Neither death" shall hurt us; For "Christ is dead:" "Nor life;" 'is risen" Nor angels, nor principalities, nor powers; nor things pre- sent, nor things to come;" "is at the right hand of God:" "Nor height, nor depth, nor any other creature;" "maketh intercession for us." Neither death - Terrible as it is to natural men; a violent death in particular, ver. 36. Nor life - With all the affliction and distress it can bring, ver. 35; or a long, easy life; or all living men. Nor angels - Whether good (if it were possible they should attempt it) or bad, with all their wisdom and strength. Nor principalities, nor powers - Not even those of the highest rank, or the most eminent power. Nor things present - Which may befall us during our pilgrimage; or the whole world, till it passeth away. Nor things to come - Which may occur either when our time on earth is past, or when time itself is at an end, as the final judgment, the general conflagration, the everlasting fire. Nor height, nor depth - The former sentence respected the differences of times; this, the differences of places. How many great and various things are contained in these words, we do not, need not, cannot know yet. The height - In St. Paul's sublime style, is put for heaven. The depth - For the great abyss: that is, neither the heights, I will not say of walls, mountains, seas, but, of heaven itself, can move us; nor the abyss itself, the very thought of which might astonish the boldest creature. Nor any creature - Nothing beneath the Almighty; visible enemies he does not even deign to name. Shall be able - Either by force, ver. 35; or by any legal claim, ver. 33, &c. To separate us from the love of God in Christ - Which will surely save, protect, deliver us who believe in, and through, and from, them all.

IX

In this chapter St. Paul, after strongly declaring his love and esteem for them, sets himself to answer the grand objection of his countrymen; namely, that the rejection of the Jews and reception of the gentiles was contrary to the word of God. That he had not here the least thought of personal election or reprobation is manifest,

1. Because it lay quite wide of his design, which was this, to show that God's rejecting the Jews and receiving the gentiles was consistent with his word

2. Because such a doctrine would not only have had no tendency to convince, but would have evidently tended to harden, the Jews;

3. Because when he sums up his argument in the close of the chapter, he has not one word, or the least intimation, about it.

1. In Christ - This seems to imply an appeal to him. In the Holy Ghost - Through his grace.

2. I have great sorrow - A high degree of spiritual sorrow and of spiritual Joy may consist together, chap. viii, 39. By declaring his sorrow for the unbelieving Jews, who excluded themselves from all the blessings he had enumerated, he shows that what he was now about to speak, he did not speak from any prejudice to them.

3. I could wish - Human words cannot fully describe the motions of souls that are full of God. As if he had said, I could wish to suffer in their stead; yea, to be an anathema from Christ in their place. In how high a sense he wished this, who can tell, unless himself had been asked and had resolved the question? Certainly he did not then consider himself at all, but only others and the glory of God. The thing could not be; yet the wish was pious and solid; though with a tacit condition, if it were right and possible.

4. Whose is the adoption, &c. - He enumerates six prerogatives, of which the first pair respect God the Father, the second Christ, the third the Holy Ghost. The adoption and the glory - That is, Israel is the first-born child of God, and the God of glory is their God, Deut. iv, 7; Psalm cvi, 20. These are relative to each other. At once God is the Father of Israel, and Israel are the people of God. He speaks not here of the ark, or any corporeal thing. God himself is "the glory of his people Israel." And the covenants, and the giving of the law - The covenant was given long before the law. It is termed covenants, in the plural, because it was so often and so variously repeated, and because there were two dispositions of it,

Gal. iv, 24, frequently called two covenants; the one promising, the other exhibiting the promise. And the worship, and the promises - The true way of worshipping God; and all the promises made to the fathers.

5. To the preceding, St. Paul now adds two more prerogatives. Theirs are the fathers - The patriarchs and holy men of old, yea, the Messiah himself. Who is over all, God blessed forever - The original words imply the self-existent, independent Being, who was, is, and is to come. Over all - The supreme; as being God, and consequently blessed forever. No words can more dearly express his divine, supreme majesty, and his gracious sovereignty both over Jews and, gentiles.

6. Not as if - The Jews imagined that the word of God must fail if all their nation were not saved. This St. Paul now refutes, and proves that the word itself had foretold their falling away. The word of God - The promises of God to Israel. Had fallen to the ground - This could not be. Even now, says the apostle, some enjoy the promises; and hereafter "all Israel shall be saved." This is the sum of the ninth, tenth, and eleventh chapters. For - Here he enters upon the proof of it. All are not Israel, who are of Israel - The Jews vehemently maintained the contrary; namely, that all who were born Israelites, and they only, were the people of God. The former part of this assertion is refuted here, the latter, ver. 24, &c. The sum is, God accepts all believers, and them only; and this is no way contrary to his word. Nay, he hath declared in his word, both by types and by express testimonies, that believers are accepted as the "children of the promise," while unbelievers are rejected, though they are "children after the flesh." All are not Israel - Not in the favour of God. Who are lineally descended of Israel.

7. Neither because they are lineally the seed of Abraham, will it follow that they are all children of God - This did not hold even in Abraham's own family; and much less in his remote descendants. But God then said, In Isaac shall thy seed be called - That is, Isaac, not Ishmael, shall be called thy seed; that seed to which the promise is made.

8. That is, Not the children, &c. - As if he had said, This is a clear type of things to come; showing us, that in all succeeding generations, not the children of the flesh, the lineal descendants of Abraham, but the children of the promise, they to whom the promise is made, that is, believers, are the children of God. Gen. xxi, 12

9. For this is the word of the promise - By the power of which Isaac was conceived, and not by the power of nature. Not, Whosoever is born of thee shall be blessed, but, At this time - Which I now appoint. I will come, and Sarah shall have a son - And he shall inherit the blessing. Gen. xviii, 10.

10. And that God's blessing does not belong to all the descendants of Abraham, appears not only by this instance, but by that of Esau and Jacob, who was chosen to inherit the blessing, before either of them had done good or evil. The apostle mentions this to show, that neither were their ancestors accepted through any merit of their own. That the purpose of God according to election might stand - Whose purpose was, to elect or choose the promised seed. Not of works - Not for any preceding merit in him he chose. But of him that called - Of his own good pleasure who called to that privilege whom he saw good.

12. The elder - Esau. Shall serve the younger - Not in person, for he never did; but in his posterity. Accordingly the Edomites were often brought into subjection by the Israelites. Gen. xxv, 23.

13. As it is written - With which word in Genesis, spoken so long before, that of Malachi agrees. I have loved Jacob - With a peculiar love; that is, the Israelites, the posterity of Jacob. And I have, comparatively, hated Esau - That is, the Edomites, the posterity of Esau. But observe,

1. This does not relate to the person of Jacob or Esau
2. Nor does it relate to the eternal state either of them or their posterity. Thus far the apostle has been proving his proposition, namely, that the exclusion of a great part of the seed of Abraham, yea, and of Isaac, from the special promises of God, was so far from being impossible, that, according to the scriptures themselves, it had actually happened. He now introduces and refutes an objection. Mal. i, 2, 3.

14. Is there injustice with God - Is it unjust in God to give Jacob the blessing rather than Esau? or to accept believers, and them only. God forbid - In no wise. This is well consistent with justice; for he has a right to fix the terms on which he will show mercy, according to his declaration to Moses, petitioning for all the people, after they had committed idolatry with the golden calf. I will have mercy on whom I will have mercy - According to the terms I myself have fixed. And I will have compassion on whom I will have compassion - Namely, on those only who submit to my terms, who accept of it in the way that I have appointed.

15. Exod. xxxiii, 19.

16. It - The blessing. Therefore is not of him that willeth, nor of him that runneth - It is not the effect either of the will or the works of man, but of the grace and power of God. The will of man is here opposed to the grace of God, and man's running, to the divine operation. And this general declaration respects not only Isaac and Jacob, and the Israelites in the time of Moses, but likewise all the spiritual children of Abraham, even to the end of the world.

17. Moreover - God has an indisputable right to reject those who will not accept the blessings on his own terms. And this he exercised in the case of Pharaoh; to whom, after many instances of

stubbornness and rebellion, he said, as it is recorded in scripture, For this very thing have I raised thee up - That is, Unless thou repent, this will surely be the consequence of my raising thee up, making thee a great and glorious king, that my power will be shown upon thee, (as indeed it was, by overwhelming him and his army in the sea,) and my name declared through all the earth - As it is at this day. Perhaps this may have a still further meaning. It seems that God was resolved to show his power over the river, the insects, other animals, (with the natural causes of their health, diseases, life, and death,) over the meteors, the air, the sun, (all of which were worshipped by the Egyptians, from whom other nations learned their idolatry,) and at once over all their gods, by that terrible stroke of slaying all their priests, and their choicest victims, the firstborn of man and beast; and all this with a design, not only to deliver his people Israel, (for which a single act of omnipotence would have sufficed,) but to convince the Egyptians, that the objects of their worship were but the creatures of Jehovah, and entirely in his power, and to draw them and the neighbouring nations, who should hear of all these wonders, from their idolatry, to worship the one God. For the execution of this design, (in order to the display of the divine power over the various objects of their worship, in variety of wonderful acts, which were at the same time just punishments for their cruel oppression of the Israelites,) God was pleased to raise to the throne of an absolute monarchy, a man, not whom he had made wicked on purpose, but whom he found so, the proudest, the most daring and obstinate of all the Egyptian princes; and who, being incorrigible, well deserved to be set up in that situation, where the divine judgments fell the heaviest. Exod. ix, 16.

18. So then - That is, accordingly he does show mercy on his own terms, namely, on them that believe. And whom he willeth - Namely, them that believe not. He hardeneth - Leaves to the hardness of their hearts.

19. Why doth he still find fault - The particle still is strongly expressive of the objector's sour, morose murmuring. For who hath resisted his will - The word his likewise expresses his surliness and aversion to God, whom he does not even deign to name.

20. Nay, but who art thou, O man - Little, impotent, ignorant man. That repliest against God - That accusest God of injustice, for himself fixing the terms on which he will show mercy? Shall the thing formed say to him that formed it, Why hast thou made me thus - Why hast thou made me capable of honour and immortality, only by believing?

21. Hath not the potter power over the clay - And much more hath not God power over his creatures, to appoint one vessel, namely, the believer, to honour, and another, the unbeliever, to dishonour? If we survey the right which God has over us, in a more general way, with regard to his intelligent creatures, God may be considered in two different views, as Creator, Proprietor, and Lord of all; or, as their moral Governor, and Judge. God, as sovereign Lord and Proprietor of all, dispenses his gifts or favours to his creatures with perfect wisdom, but by no rules or methods of proceeding that we are acquainted with. The time when we shall exist, the country where we shall live, our parents, our constitution of body and turn of mind; these, and numberless other circumstances, are doubtless ordered with perfect wisdom, but by rules that lie quite out of our sight. But God's methods of dealing with us, as our Governor and Judge, are clearly revealed and perfectly known; namely, that he will finally reward every man according to his works: "He that believeth shalt be saved, and he that believeth not shall be damned." Therefore, though "He hath mercy on whom he willeth, and whom he willeth he hardeneth," that is, suffers to be hardened in consequence of their obstinate wickedness; yet his is not the will of an arbitrary, capricious, or tyrannical being. He wills nothing but what is infinitely wise and good; and therefore his will is a most proper rule of judgment. He will show mercy, as he hath assured us, to none but true believers, nor harden any but such as obstinately refuse his mercy. Jer. xviii, 6, 7

22. What if God, being willing - Referring to ver. 18, 19. That is, although it was now his will, because of their obstinate unbelief, To show his wrath - Which necessarily presupposes sin. And to make his power known - This is repeated from the seventeenth verse. Yet endured - As he did Pharaoh. With much longsuffering - Which should have led them to repentance. The vessels of wrath - Those who had moved his wrath by still rejecting his mercy. Fitted for destruction - By their own wilful and final impenitence. Is there any injustice in this?

23. That he might make known - What if by showing such longsuffering even to "the vessels of wrath," he did the more abundantly show the greatness of his glorious goodness, wisdom, and power, on the vessels of mercy; on those whom he had himself, by his grace, prepared for glory. Is this any injustice?

24. Even us - Here the apostle comes to the other proposition, of grace free for all, whether Jew or gentile. Of the Jews - This he treats of, ver. 25. Of the gentiles - Treated of in the same verse.

25. Beloved - As a spouse. Who once was not beloved - Consequently, not unconditionally elected. This relates directly to the final restoration of the Jews. Hosea ii, 23

26. There shall they be called the sons of God - So that they need not leave their own country and come to Judea. Hosea i, 10

27. But Isaiah testifies, that (as many gentiles will be accepted, so) many Jews will be rejected; that out of all the thousands of Israel, a remnant only shall be saved. This was spoken originally of the

few that were saved from the ravage of Sennacherib's army. Isaiah x, 22, 23

28. For he is finishing or cutting short his account - In rigorous justice, will leave but a small remnant. There will be so general a destruction, that but a small number will escape.

29. As Isaiah had said before - Namely, Isaiah i, 9, concerning those who were besieged in Jerusalem by Rezin and Pekah. Unless the Lord had left us a seed - Which denotes,

1. The present paucity:

2. The future abundance. We had been as Sodom - So that it is no unexampled thing for the main body of the Jewish nation to revolt from God, and perish in their sin.

30. What shall we say then - What is to be concluded from all that has been said but this, That the gentiles, who followed not after righteousness - Who a while ago had no knowledge of, no care or thought about, it. Have attained to righteousness - Or justification. Even the righteousness which is by faith. This is the first conclusion we may draw from the preceding observations. The second is, that Israel - The Jews Although following after the law of righteousness - That law which, duly used, would have led them to faith, and thereby to righteousness. Have not attained to the law of righteousness - To that righteousness or justification which is one great end of the law

32. And wherefore have they not? Is it because God eternally decreed they should not? There is nothing like this to be met with but agreeable to his argument the apostle gives us this good reason for it, Because they sought it not by faith - Whereby alone it could be attained. But as it were - In effect, if not professsedly, by works. For they stumbled at that stumblingstone - Christ crucified.

33. As it is written - Foretold by their own prophet. Behold, I lay in Zion - I exhibit in my church, what, though it is in truth the only sure foundation of happiness, yet will be in fact a stumblingstone and rock of offense - An occasion of ruin to many, through their obstinate unbelief. Isaiah viii, 14; Isaiah xxviii, 16

X

1. My prayer to God is, that they may be saved - He would not have prayed for this, had they been absolutely reprobated.

2. They have a zeal, but not according to knowledge - They had zeal without knowledge; we have knowledge without zeal.

3. For they being ignorant of the righteousness of God - Of the method God has established for the justification of a sinner. And seeking to establish their own righteousness - Their own method of acceptance with God. Have not submitted to the righteousness of God - The way of justification which he hath fixed.

4. For Christ is the end of the law - The scope and aim of it. It is the very design of the law, to bring men to believe in Christ for justification and salvation. And he alone gives that pardon and life which the law shows the want of, but cannot give. To every one - Whether Jew or gentile, treated of, ver. 11, &c. That believeth - Treated of, ver. 5.

5. For Moses describeth the only righteousness which is attainable by the law, when he saith, The man who doeth these things shall live by them - that is, he that perfectly keeps all these precepts in every point, he alone may claim life and salvation by them. But this way of justification is impossible to any who have ever transgressed any one law in any point. Lev. xviii, 5

6. But the righteousness which is by faith - The method of becoming righteous by believing. Speaketh a very different language, and may be considered as expressing itself thus: (to accommodate to our present subject the words which Moses spake, touching the plainness of his law:) Say not in thy heart, Who shall ascend into heaven, as if it were to bring Christ down: or, Who shall descend into the grave, as if it were to bring him again from the dead - Do not imagine that these things are to be done now, in order to procure thy pardon and salvation. Deut. xxx, 14.

8. But what saith he - Moses. Even these words, so remarkably applicable to the subject before us. All is done ready to thy hand. The word is nigh thee - Within thy reach; easy to be understood, remembered, practiced. This is eminently true of the word of faith - The gospel. Which we preach - The sum of which is, If thy heart believe in Christ, and thy life confess him, thou shalt be saved.

9. If thou confess with thy mouth - Even in time of persecution, when such a confession may send thee to the lions.

10. For with the heart - Not the understanding only. Man believeth to righteousness - So as to obtain justification. And with the mouth confession is made - So as to obtain final salvation. Confession here implies the whole of outward, as believing does the root of all inward, religion.

11. Isaiah xxviii, 16.

12. The same Lord of all is rich - So that his blessings are never to be exhausted, nor is he ever constrained to hold his hand. The great truth proposed in ver. 11 is so repeated here, and in ver. 13, and farther confirmed, ver. 14, 15, as not only to imply, that "whosoever calleth upon him shall be saved;" but also that the will of God is, that all should savingly call upon him.

13. Joel ii, 32.

15. But how shall they preach, unless they be sent - Thus by a chain of reasoning, from God's will that the gentiles also should "call upon him," St. Paul infers that the apostles were sent by God to preach to the gentiles also. The feet - Their very footsteps; their coming. Isaiah lii, 7.

16. Isaiah liii, 1.

17. Faith, indeed, ordinarily cometh by hearing; even by hearing the word of God.

18. But their unbelief was not owing to the want of hearing For they have heard. Yes verily - So many nations have already heard the preachers of the gospel, that I may in some sense say of them as David did of the lights of heaven. Psalm xxix, 4

19. But hath not Israel known - They might have known, even from Moses and Isaiah, that many of the gentiles would be received, and many of the Jews rejected. I will provoke you to jealousy by them that are not a nation - As they followed gods that were not gods, so he accepted in their stead a nation that was not a nation; that is, a nation that was not in covenant with God. A foolish nation - Such are all which know not God. Deut. xxxii, 21

20. But Isaiah is very bold - And speaks plainly what Moses but intimated. Isaiah lxv, 1, 2.

21. An unbelieving and gainsaying people - Just opposite to those who believed with their hearts, and made confession with their mouths.

XI

1. Hath God rejected his whole people - All Israel? In no wise. Now there is "a remnant" who believe, ver. 5; and hereafter "all Israel will be saved," ver. 26.

2. God hath not rejected that part of his people whom he foreknew - Speaking after the manner of men. For, in fact, knowing and foreknowing are the same thing with God, who knows or sees all things at once, from everlasting to everlasting. Know ye not - That in a parallel case, amidst a general apostasy, when Elijah thought the whole nation was fallen into idolatry, God "knew" there was "a remnant" of true worshippers.

3. 1 Kings xix, 10.

4. To Baal - Nor to the golden calves.

5. According to the election of grace - According to that gracious purpose of God, "He that believeth shall be saved."

6. And if by grace, then it is no more of works - Whether ceremonial or moral. Else grace is no longer grace - The very nature of grace is lost. And if it be of works, then it is no more grace: else work is no longer work - But the very nature of it is destroyed. There is something so absolutely inconsistent between the being justified by grace, and the being justified by works, that, if you suppose either, you of necessity exclude the other. For what is given to works is the payment of a debt; whereas grace implies an unmerited favour. So that the same benefit cannot, in the very nature of things, be derived from both.

7. What then - What is the conclusion from the whole? It is this: that Israel in general hath not obtained justification; but those of them only who believe. And the rest were blinded - By their own wilful prejudice.

8. God hath at length withdrawn his Spirit, and so given them up to a spirit of slumber; which is fulfilled unto this day. Isaiah xxix, 10

9. And David saith - In that prophetic imprecation, which is applicable to them, as well as to Judas. A recompence - Of their preceding wickedness. So sin is punished by sin; and thus the gospel, which should have fed and strengthened their souls, is become a means of destroying them. Psalm lxix, 22, 23

11. Have they stumbled so as to fall - Totally and finally? No But by their fall - Or slip: it is a very soft word in the original. Salvation is come to the gentiles - See an instance of this, Acts xiii, 46. To provoke them - The Jews themselves, to jealousy.

12. The first part of this verse is treated of, ver. 13, &c.; the latter, How much more their fulness, (that is, their full conversion,) ver. 23, &c. So many prophecies refer to this grand event, that it is surprising any Christian can doubt of it. And these are greatly confirmed by the wonderful preservation of the Jews as a distinct people to this day. When it is accomplished, it will be so strong a demonstration, both of the Old and New Testament Revelation, as will doubtless convince many thousand Deists, in countries nominally Christian; of whom there will, of course, be increasing multitudes among merely nominal Christians. And this will be a means of swiftly propagating the gospel among Mahometans and Pagans; who would probably have received it long ago, had they conversed only with real Christians.

13. I magnify my office - Far from being ashamed of ministering to the gentiles, I glory therein; the rather, as it may be a means of provoking my brethren to jealousy.

14. My flesh - My kinsmen.

15. Life from the dead - Overflowing life to the world, which was dead.

16. **And this will surely come to pass. For if the first fruits be holy, so is the lump** - The consecration of them was esteemed the consecration of all and so the conversion of a few Jews is an earnest of the conversion of all the rest. **And if the root be holy** - The patriarchs from whom they spring, surely God will at length make their descendants also holy.

17. **Thou** - O gentile. **Being a wild olive tree** - Had the graft been nobler than the stock, yet its dependance on it for life and nourishment would leave it no room to boast against it. How much less, when, contrary to what is practiced among men, the wild olive tree is engrafted on the good!

18. **Boast not against the branches** - Do not they do this who despise the Jews? or deny their future conversion?

20. **They were broken off for unbelief, and thou standest by faith** - Both conditionally, not absolutely: if absolutely, there might have been room to boast. **By faith** - The free gift of God, which therefore ought to humble thee.

21. **Be not highminded, but fear** - We may observe, this fear is not opposed to trust, but to pride and security.

22. **Else shalt thou** - Also, who now "standest by faith," be both totally and finally cut off.

24. **Contrary to nature** - For according to nature, we graft the fruitful branch into the wild stock; but here the wild branch is grafted into the fruitful stock.

25. St. Paul calls any truth known but to a few, a mystery. Such had been the calling of the gentiles: such was now the conversion of the Jews. **Lest ye should be wise in your own conceits** - Puffed up with your present advantages; dreaming that ye are the only church; or that the church of Rome cannot fail. Hardness in part is happened to Israel, till - Israel therefore is neither totally nor finally rejected. **The fulness of the gentiles be come in** - Till there be a vast harvest amongst the heathens.

26. **And so all Israel shall be saved** - Being convinced by the coming of the gentiles. But there will be a still larger harvest among the gentiles, when all Israel is come in. **The deliverer shall come** - Yea, the deliverer is come; but not the full fruit of his coming. Isaiah lix, 20

28. **They are now enemies** - To the gospel, to God, and to themselves, which God permits. **For your sake: but as for the election** - That part of them who believe, they are beloved.

29. **For the gifts and the calling of God are without repentance** - God does not repent of his gifts to the Jews, or his calling of the gentiles.

32. **For God hath shut up all together in disobedience** - Suffering each in their turn to revolt from him. First, God suffered the gentiles in the early age to revolt, and took the family of Abraham as a peculiar seed to himself. Afterwards he permitted them to fall through unbelief, and took in the believing gentiles. And he did even this to provoke the Jews to jealousy, and so bring them also in the end to faith. This was truly a mystery in the divine conduct, which the apostle adores with such holy astonishment.

33. **O the depth of the riches, and wisdom, and knowledge of God** - In the ninth chapter, St. Paul had sailed but in a narrow sea: now he is in the ocean. The depth of the riches is described, ver. 35; the depth of wisdom, ver. 34; the depth of knowledge, in the latter part of this verse. Wisdom directs all things to the best end; knowledge sees that end. **How unsearchable are his judgments** - With regard to unbelievers. **His ways** - With regard to believers. His ways are more upon a level; His judgments "a great deep." But even his ways we cannot trace.

34. **Who hath known the mind of the Lord** - Before or any farther than he has revealed it. Isaiah xl, 13.

35. **Given to him** - Either wisdom or power?

36. **Of him** - As the Creator. **Through him** - As the Preserver. **To him** - As the ultimate end, are all things. To him be the glory of his riches, wisdom, knowledge. **Amen** - A concluding word, in which the affection of the apostle, when it is come to the height, shuts up all.

XII

1. **I exhort you** - St. Paul uses to suit his exhortations to the doctrines he has been delivering. So here the general use from the whole is contained in the first and second verses. The particular uses follow, from the third verse to the end of the Epistle. **By the tender mercies of God** - The whole sentiment is derived from Romans. The expression itself is particularly opposed to "the wrath of God," chap. i, 18. It has a reference here to the entire gospel, to the whole economy of grace or mercy, delivering us from "the wrath of God," and exciting us to all duty. **To present** - So chap. vi, 13; xvi, 19; now actually to exhibit before God. **Your bodies** - That is, yourselves; a part is put for the whole; the rather, as in the ancient sacrifices of beasts, the body was the whole. These also are particularly named in opposition to that vile abuse of their bodies mentioned, chap. i, 24. Several expressions follow, which have likewise a direct reference to other expressions in the same chapter. **A sacrifice** - Dead to sin and living - By that life which is mentioned, chap. i, 17; vi, 4, &c. **Holy** - Such as the holy law requires, chap. vii, 12. **Acceptable** - chap. viii, 8. **Which is your reasonable service** - The worship of the heathens

was utterly unreasonable, chap. i, 18, &c.; so was the glorying of the Jews, chap. ii, 3, &c. But a Christian acts in all things by the highest reason, from the mercy of God inferring his own duty.

2. And be not conformed - Neither in judgment, spirit, nor behaviour. To this world - Which, neglecting the will of God, entirely follows its own. That ye may prove - Know by sure trial; which is easily done by him who has thus presented himself to God. What is that good, and acceptable, and perfect will of God - The will of God is here to be understood of all the preceptive part of Christianity, which is in itself so excellently good, so acceptable to God, and so perfective of our natures.

3. And I say - He now proceeds to show what that will of God is. Through the grace which is given to me - He modestly adds this, lest he should seem to forget his own direction. To every one that is among you - Believers at Rome. Happy, had they always remembered this! The measure of faith - Treated of in the first and following chapters, from which all other gifts and graces flow.

5. So we - All believers. Are one body - Closely connected together in Christ, and consequently ought to be helpful to each other.

6. Having then gifts differing according to the grace which is given us - Gifts are various: grace is one. Whether it be prophecy - This, considered as an extraordinary gift, is that whereby heavenly mysteries are declared to men, or things to come foretold. But it seems here to mean the ordinary gift of expounding scripture. Let us prophesy according to the analogy of faith - St. Peter expresses it, "as the oracles of God;" according to the general tenor of them; according to that grand scheme of doctrine which is delivered therein, touching original sin, justification by faith, and present, inward salvation. There is a wonderful analogy between all these; and a close and intimate connection between the chief heads of that faith "which was once delivered to the saints." Every article therefore concerning which there is any question should be determined by this rule; every doubtful scripture interpreted according to the grand truths which run through the whole.

7. Ministering - As deacons. He that teacheth - Catechumens; for whom particular instructors were appointed. He that exhorteth - Whose peculiar business it was to urge Christians to duty, and to comfort them in trials.

8. He that presideth - That hath the care of a flock. He that showeth mercy - In any instance. With cheerfulness - Rejoicing that he hath such an opportunity.

9. Having spoken of faith and its fruit, ver. 3, &c., he comes now to love. The ninth, tenth, and eleventh verses refer to chapter the seventh; the twelfth verse to chapter the eighth; the thirteenth verse, of communicating to the saints, whether Jews or gentiles, to chapter the ninth, &c. Part of the sixteenth verse is repeated from chap. xi, 25. Abhor that which is evil; cleave to that which is good - Both inwardly and outwardly, whatever ill-will or danger may follow.

10. In honour preferring one another - Which you will do, if you habitually consider what is good in others, and what is evil in yourselves.

11. Whatsoever ye do, do it with your might. In every business diligently and fervently serving the Lord - Doing all to God, not to man.

12. Rejoicing in hope - Of perfect holiness and everlasting happiness. Hitherto of faith and love; now of hope also, see the fifth and eighth chapters; afterwards of duties toward others; saints, ver. 13 persecutors, ver. 14 friends, strangers, enemies, ver. 15, &c.

13. Communicate to the necessities of the saints - Relieve all Christians that are in want. It is remarkable, that the apostle, treating expressly of the duties flowing from the communion of saints, yet never says one word about the dead. Pursue hospitality - Not only embracing those that offer, but seeking opportunities to exercise it.

14. Curse not - No, not in your heart.

15. Rejoice - The direct opposite to weeping is laughter; but this does not so well suit a Christian.

16. Mind not high things - Desire not riches, honour, or the company of the great.

17. Provide - Think beforehand; contrive to give as little offense as may be to any.

19. Dearly beloved - So he softens the rugged spirit. Revenge not yourselves, but leave that to God. Perhaps it might more properly be rendered, leave room for wrath; that is, the wrath of God, to whom vengeance properly belongs. Deut. xxxii, 35

20. Feed him - With your own hand: if it be needful, even put bread into his mouth. Heap coals of fire upon his head - That part which is most sensible. "So artists melt the sullen ore of lead, By heaping coals of fire upon its head; In the kind warmth the metal learns to glow, And pure from dross the silver runs below." Prov. xxv, 21, &c.

21. And if you see no present fruit, yet persevere. Be not overcome with evil - As all are who avenge themselves. But overcome evil with good. Conquer your enemies by kindness and patience.

XIII

1. St. Paul, writing to the Romans, whose city was the seat of the empire, speaks largely of obedience to magistrates: and this was also, in effect, a public apology for the Christian religion. Let every soul be subject to the supreme powers - An admonition peculiarly needful for the Jews. Power, in the singular number, is the supreme authority; powers are they who are invested with it. That is more readily acknowledged to be from God than these. The apostle affirms it of both. They are all from God, who constituted all in general, and permits each in particular by his providence. The powers that be are appointed by God - It might be rendered, are subordinate to, or, orderly disposed under, God; implying, that they are God's deputies or vicegerents and consequently, their authority being, in effect, his, demands our conscientious obedience.

2. Whosoever resisteth the power - In any other manner than the laws of the community direct. Shall receive condemnation - Not only from the magistrate, but from God also.

3. For rulers are - In the general, notwithstanding some particular exceptions. A terror to evil works - Only. Wouldest thou then not be afraid - There is one fear which precedes evil actions, and deters from them: this should always remain. There is another fear which follows evil actions: they who do well are free from this.

4. The sword - The instrument of capital punishment, which God authorizes him to inflict.

5. Not only for fear of wrath - That is, punishment from man. But for conscience' sake - Out of obedience to God.

6. For this cause - Because they are the ministers (officers) of God for the public good. This very thing - The public good.

7. To all - Magistrates. Tribute - Taxes on your persons or estates. Custom - For goods exported or imported. Fear - Obedience. honour - Reverence. All these are due to the supreme power.

8. From our duty to magistrates he passes on to general duties. To love one another - An eternal debt, which can never be sufficiently discharged; but yet if this be rightly performed, it discharges all the rest. For he that loveth another - As he ought. Hath fulfilled the whole law - Toward his neighbour.

9. If there be any other - More particular. Commandment - Toward our neighbour; as there are many in the law. It is summed up in this - So that if you was not thinking of it, yet if your heart was full of love, you would fulfil it.

10. Therefore love is the fulfilling of the law - For the same love which restrains from all evil, incites us to all good.

11. And do this - Fulfil the law of love in all the instances above mentioned. Knowing the season - Full of grace, but hasting away. That it is high time to awake out of sleep - How beautifully is the metaphor carried on! This life, a night; the resurrection, the day; the gospel shining on the heart, the dawn of this day; we are to awake out of sleep; to rise up and throw away our night-clothes, fit only for darkness, and put on new; and, being soldiers, we are to arm, and prepare for fight, who are encompassed with so many enemies. The day dawns when we receive faith, and then sleep gives place. Then it is time to rise, to arm, to walk, to work, lest sleep steal upon us again. Final salvation, glory, is nearer to us now, than when we first believed - It is continually advancing, flying forward upon the swiftest wings of time. And that which remains between the present hour and eternity is comparatively but a moment.

13. Banqueting - Luxurious, elegant feasts.

14. But put ye on the Lord Jesus Christ - Herein is contained the whole of our salvation. It is a strong and beautiful expression for the most intimate union with him, and being clothed with all the graces which were in him. The apostle does not say, Put on purity and sobriety, peacefulness and benevolence; but he says all this and a thousand times more at once, in saying, Put on Christ. And make not provision - To raise foolish desires, or, when they are raised already, to satisfy them.

XIV

1. Him that is weak - Through needless scruples. Receive - With all love and courtesy into Christian fellowship. But not to doubtful disputations - About questionable points.

2. All things - All sorts of food, though forbidden by the law.

3. Despise him that eateth not - As over-scrupulous or superstitious. Judge him that eateth - As profane, or taking undue liberties. For God hath received him - Into the number of his children, notwithstanding this.

5. One day above another - As new moons, and other Jewish festivals. Let every man be fully persuaded - That a thing is lawful, before he does it.

6. Regardeth it to the Lord - That is, out of a principle of conscience toward God. To the Lord he doth not regard it - He also acts from a principle of conscience. He that eateth not - Flesh. Giveth God thanks - For his herbs.

7. None of us - Christians, in the things we do. Liveth to himself - Is at his own disposal; doeth his own will.

10. Or why dost thou despise thy brother - Hitherto the apostle as addressed the weak brother: now he speaks to the stronger.

11. As I live - An oath proper to him, because he only possesseth life infinite and independent. It is Christ who is here termed both Lord and God; as it is he to whom we live, and to whom we die. Every tongue shall confess to God - Shall own him as their rightful Lord; which shall then only be accomplished in its full extent. The Lord grant we may find mercy in that day; and may it also be imparted to those who have differed from us! yea, to those who have censured and condemned us for things which we have done from a desire to please him, or refused to do from a fear of offending him. Isaiah xlv, 23

13. But judge this rather - Concerning ourselves. Not to lay a stumblingblock - By moving him to do as thou doest, though against his conscience. Or a scandal - Moving him to hate or judge thee.

14. I am assured by the Lord Jesus - Perhaps by a particular Revelation. That there is nothing - Neither flesh nor herbs. Unclean of itself - Unlawful under the gospel.

15. If thy brother is grieved - That is, wounded, led into sin. Destroy not him for whom Christ died - So we see, he for whom Christ died may be destroyed. With thy meat - Do not value thy meat more than Christ valued his life.

16. Let not then your good and lawful liberty be evil spoken of - By being offensive to others.

17. For the kingdom of God - That is, true religion, does not consist in external observances. But in righteousness - The image of God stamped on the heart; the love of God and man, accompanied with the peace that passeth all understanding, and joy in the Holy Ghost.

18. In these - Righteousness, peace, and joy. Men - Wise and good men.

19. Peace and edification are closely joined. Practical divinity tends equally to peace and to edification. Controversial divinity less directly tends to edification, although sometimes, as they of old, we cannot build without it, Neh. iv, 17.

20. The work of God - Which he builds in the soul by faith, and in the church by concord. It is evil to that man who eateth with offense - So as to offend another thereby.

21. Thy brother stumbleth - By imitating thee against his conscience, contrary to righteousness. Or is offended - At what thou doest to the loss of his peace. Or made weak - Hesitating between imitation and abhorrence, to the loss of that joy in the Lord which was his strength.

22. Hast thou faith - That all things are pure? Have it to thyself before God - In circumstances like these, keep it to thyself, and do not offend others by it. Happy is he that condemneth not himself - By an improper use of even innocent things! and happy he who is free from a doubting conscience! He that has this may allow the thing, yet condemn himself for it.

23. Because it is not of faith - He does not believe it lawful and, in all these cases, whatsoever is not of faith is sin - Whatever a man does without a full persuasion of its lawfulness, it is sin to him.

XV

1. We who are strong - Of a clearer judgment, and free from these scruples. And not to please ourselves - Without any regard to others.

2. For his good - This is a general word: edification is one species of good.

3. But bore not only the infirmities, but reproaches, of his brethren; and so fulfilled that scripture. Psalm lxix, 9

4. Aforetime - In the Old Testament. That we through patience and consolation of the scriptures may have hope - That through the consolation which God gives us by these, we may have patience and a joyful hope.

5. According to the power of Christ Jesus.

6. That ye - Both Jews and gentiles, believing with one mind, and confessing with one mouth.

7. Receive ye one another - Weak and strong, with mutual love.

8. Now I say - The apostle here shows how Christ received us. Christ Jesus-Jesus is the name, Christ the surname. The latter was first known to the Jews; the former, to the gentiles. Therefore he is styled Jesus Christ, when the words stand in the common, natural order. When the order is inverted, as here, the office of Christ is more solemnly considered. Was a servant - Of his Father. Of the circumcision - For the salvation of the circumcised, the Jews. For the truth of God - To manifest the truth and fidelity of God.

9. As it is written - In the eighteenth Psalm, here the gentiles and Jews are spoken of as joining in the worship of the God of Israel. Psalm xviii, 49

10. Deut. xxxii, 43.

11. Psalm cxvii, 1.

12. There shall be the root of Jesse - That kings and the Messiah should spring from his house,

was promised to Jesse before it was to David. In him shall the gentiles hope - Who before had been "without hope," Eph. ii, 12. Isaiah xi, 10

13. Now the God of hope - A glorious title of God, but till now unknown to the heathens; for their goddess Hope, like their other idols, was nothing; whose temple at Rome was burned by lightning. It was, indeed, built again not long after, but was again burned to the ground.

14. There are several conclusions of this Epistle. The first begins at this verse; the second, chap. xvi, 1; the third, chap. xvi, 17; the fourth, chap. xvi, 21; and the fifth, chap. xvi, 25; Ye are full of goodness - By being created anew. And filled with all knowledge - By long experience of the things of God. To admonish - To instruct and confirm.

15. Because of the grace - That is, because I am an apostle of the gentiles.

16. The offering up of the gentiles - As living sacrifices.

17. I have whereof to glory through Jesus Christ - All my glorying is in and through him.

18. By word - By the power of the Spirit. By deed - Namely, through "mighty signs and wonders."

20. Not where Christ had been named - These places he generally declined, though not altogether, having an holy ambition (so the Greek word means) to make the first proclamation of the gospel in places where it was quite unheard of, in spite of all the difficulty and dangers that attended it. Lest I should only build upon another man's foundation - The providence of God seemed in a special manner, generally, to prevent this, though not entirely, lest the enemies of the apostle, who sought every occasion to set light by him, should have had room to say that he was behind other apostles, not being sufficient for planting of churches himself, but only for preaching where others had been already; or that he declined the more difficult part of the ministry

21. Isaiah lii, 15.

22. Therefore I have been long hindered from coming to you - Among whom Christ had been named.

23. Having no longer place in these parts - Where Christ has now been preached in every city.

24. Into Spain - Where the gospel had not yet been preached. If first I may be somewhat satisfied with your company - How remarkable is the modesty with which he speaks! They might rather desire to be satisfied with his. Somewhat satisfied - Intimating the shortness of his stay; or, perhaps, that Christ alone can throughly satisfy the soul.

26. The poor of the saints that are in Jerusalem - It can by no means be inferred from this expression, that the community of goods among the Christians was then ceased. All that can be gathered from it is, that in this time of extreme dearth, Acts xi, 28, 29, some of the church in Jerusalem were in want; the rest being barely able to subsist themselves, but not to supply the necessities of their brethren.

27. It hath pleased them; and they are their debtors - That is, they are bound to it, in justice as well as mercy. Spiritual things - By the preaching of the gospel. Carnal things - Things needful for the body.

28. When I have sealed to them this fruit - When I have safely delivered to them, as under seal, this fruit of their brethren's love. I will go by you into Spain - Such was his design; but it does not appear that Paul went into Spain. There are often holy purposes in the minds of good men, which are overruled by the providence of God so as never to take effect. And yet they are precious in the sight of God.

30. I beseech you by the love of the Spirit - That is, by the love which is the genuine fruit of the Spirit. To strive together with me in your prayers - He must pray himself, who would have others strive together with him in prayer. Of all the apostles, St. Paul alone is recorded to desire the prayers of the faithful for himself. And this he generally does in the conclusions of his Epistles; yet not without making a difference. For he speaks in one manner to them whom he treats as his children, with the gravity or even severity of a father, such as Timothy, Titus, the Corinthians, and Galatians; in another, to them whom he treats rather like equals, such as the Romans, Ephesians, Thessalonians, Colossians, Hebrews.

31. That I may be delivered - He is thus urgent from a sense of the importance of his life to the church. Otherwise he would have rejoiced "to depart, and to be with Christ." And that my service may be acceptable - In spite of all their prejudices; to the end the Jewish and gentile believers may be knit together in tender love.

32. That I may come to you - This refers to the former, With joy - To the latter, part of the preceding verse.

XVI

1. I commend unto you Phebe - The bearer of this letter. A servant - The Greek word is a deaconness. Of the church in Cenchrea - In the apostolic age, some grave and pious women were appointed deaconnesses in every church. It was their office, not to teach publicly, but to visit the sick, the women in particular, and to minister to them both in their temporal and spiritual necessities.

2. In the Lord - That is, for the Lord's sake, and in a Christian manner. St. Paul seems fond of this

expression.

4. *Who have for my life, as it were, laid down their own necks* - That is, exposed themselves to the utmost danger. *But likewise all the churches of the gentiles* - Even that at Rome, for preserving so valuable a life.

5. *Salute the church that is in their house* - Aquila had been driven from Rome in the reign of Claudius, but was now returned, and performed the same part there which Caius did at Corinth, ver. 23. Where any Christian had a large house, there they all assembled together though as yet the Christians at Rome had neither bishops nor deacons. So far were they from any shadow of papal power. Nay, there does not appear to have been then in the whole city any more than one of these domestic churches. Otherwise there can be no doubt but St. Paul would have saluted them also. *Epenetus* - Although the apostle had never been at Rome, yet had he many acquaintance there. But here is no mention of Linus or Cemens; whence it appears, they did not come to Rome till after this. *The firstfruits of Asia* - The first convert in the proconsular Asia.

7. *Who are of note among the apostles* - They seem to have been some of the most early converts. *Fellowprisoners* - For the gospel's sake.

9. *Our fellowlabourer* - Mine and Timothy's, verse 21.

11. *Those of the family of Aristobulus and Narcissus, who are in the Lord* - It seems only part of their families were converted. Probably, some of them were not known to St. Paul by face, but only by character. Faith does not create moroseness, but courtesy, which even the gravity of an apostle did not hinder.

12. *Salute Tryphena and Tryphosa* - Probably they were two sisters.

13. *Salute Rufus* - Perhaps the same that is mentioned, Mark xv, 21. *And his mother and mine* - This expression may only denote the tender care which Rufus's mother had taken of him.

14. *Salute Asyncritus, Phlegon, &c.* - He seems to join those together, who were joined by kindred, nearness of habitation, or any other circumstance. It could not but encourage the poor especially, to be saluted by name, who perhaps did not know that the apostle bad ever heard of them. It is observable, that whilst the apostle forgets none who are worthy, yet he adjusts the nature of his salutation to the degrees of worth in those whom he salutes.

15. *Salute all the saints* - Had St. Peter been then at Rome, St. Paul would doubtless have saluted him by name; since no one in this numerous catalogue was of an eminence comparable to his. But if he was not then at Rome, the whole Roman tradition, with regard to the succession of their bishops, fails in the most fundamental article.

16. *Salute one another with an holy kiss* - Termed by St. Peter, "the kiss of love," 1 Pet. v, 14. So the ancient Christians concluded all their solemn offices; the men saluting the men, and the women the women. And this apostolical custom seems to have continued for some ages in all Christian churches.

17. *Mark them who cause divisions* - Such there were, therefore, at Rome also. *Avoid them* - Avoid all unnecessary intercourse with them.

18. *By good words* - Concerning themselves, making great promises. *And fair speeches* - Concerning you, praising and flattering you. *The harmless* - Who, doing no ill themselves, are not upon their guard against them that do.

19. *But I would have you* - Not only obedient, but discreet also. *Wise with regard to that which is good* - As knowing in this as possible. *And simple with regard to that which is evil* - As ignorant of this as possible.

20. *And the God of peace* - The Author and Lover of it, giving a blessing to your discretion. *Shall bruise Satan under your feet* - Shall defeat all the artifices of that sower of tares, and unite you more and more together in love.

21. *Timotheus my fellowlabourer* - Here he is named even before St. Paul's kinsmen. But as he had never been at Rome, he is not named in the beginning of the epistle.

22. *I Tertius, who wrote this epistle, salute you* - Tertius, who wrote what the apostle dictated, inserted this, either by St. Paul's exhortation or ready permission. *Caius* - The Corinthian, 1 Cor. i, 14. *My host, and of the whole church* - Who probably met for some time in his house.

23. *The chamberlain of the city* - Of Corinth.

25. *Now to him who is able* - The last words of this epistle exactly answer the first, chapter i, 1-v, chap. i, 1-v, in particular, concerning the power of God, the gospel, Jesus Christ, the scriptures, the obedience of faith, all nations. *To establish you* - Both Jews and gentiles. *According to my gospel, and the preaching of Jesus Christ* - That is, according to the tenor of the gospel of Jesus Christ, which I preach. *According to the Revelation of the mystery* - Of the calling of the gentiles, which, as plainly as it was foretold in the Prophets, was still hid from many even of the believing Jews.

26. *According to the commandment* - The foundation of the apostolical office. *Of the eternal God* - A more proper epithet could not be. A new dispensation infers no change in God. Known unto him are all his works, and every variation of them, from eternity. *Made known to all nations* - Not barely that they might know, but enjoy it also, through obeying the faith.

27. To the only wise God - Whose manifold wisdom is known in the church through the gospel, Eph. iii, 10. "To him who is able," and, to the wise God," are joined, as 1 Cor. i, 24, where Christ is styled "the wisdom of God," and "the power of God." To him be glory through Christ Jesus forever - And let every believer say, Amen!

John Wesley

NOTES ON ST. PAUL'S FIRST EPISTLE TO THE CORINTHIANS

CORINTH was a city of Achaia, situate on the isthmus which joins Peloponnesus, now called the Morea, to the rest of Greece. Being so advantageously situated for trade, the inhabitants of it abounded in riches, which, by too natural a consequence, led them into luxury, lewdness, and all manner of vice. Yet even here St. Paul planted a numerous church, chiefly of heathen converts; to whom, about three years after he had left Corinth, he wrote this epistle from Ephesus; as well to correct various disorders of which they were guilty, as to answer some questions which they had proposed to him. The Epistle consists of: The inscription Chap. i. 1-3

I. The treatise itself, in which is,
1. An exhortation to concord, beating down all glorying in the flesh, 4- iv.21
2. A reproof,
1. For not excommunicating the incestuous person, v. 1-13
2. For going to law before heathen Judges, vi. 1-11
3. A dissuasive from fornication, 12-20
4. An answer to the questions they had proposed concerning marriage, vii. 1, 10, 25, 36, 39
5. Concerning things sacrificed to idols, viii. 1- ix. 1
6. Concerning the veiling of women, 2-16
7. Concerning the Lord's supper, 17-34
8. Concerning spiritual gifts, xii. xiii. xiv
9. Concerning the resurrection, xv. 1-58
10. Concerning the collection for the poor, the coming of himself, of Timothy, of Apollos, the sum of all, xvi, 1, 5, 10, 12, 13, 14
II. The conclusion, 15, 17, 19-24

1st CORINTHIANS

I

1. *Paul, called to be an apostle* - There is great propriety in every clause of the salutation, particularly in this, as there were some in the church of Corinth who called the authority of his mission in question. *Through the will of God* - Called "the commandment of God," 1 Tim. i, 1 This was to the churches the ground of his authority; to Paul himself, of an humble and ready mind. By the mention of God, the authority of man is excluded, Gal. i, 1; by the mention of the will of God, the merit of Paul, chap. xv, 8, &c. *And Sosthenes* - A Corinthian, St. Paul's companion in travel. It was both humility and prudence in the apostle, thus to join his name with his own, in an epistle wherein he was to reprove so many irregularities. *Sosthenes the brother* - Probably this word is emphatical; as if he had said, Who, from a Jewish opposer of the gospel, became a faithful brother.

2. *To the church of God which is in Corinth* - St. Paul, writing in a familiar manner to the Corinthians, as also to the Thessalonians and Galatians, uses this plain appellation. To the other churches he uses a more solemn address. *Sanctified through Jesus Christ* - And so undoubtedly they were in general, notwithstanding some exceptions. *Called* - Of Jesus Christ, Rom. i, 6 *And* - As the fruit of that calling made holy. *With all that in every place* - Nothing could better suit that catholic love which St. Paul labours to promote in this epistle, than such a declaration of his good wishes for every true Christian upon earth. *Call upon the name of our Lord Jesus Christ* - This plainly implies that all Christians pray to Christ, as well as to the Father through him.

4. *Always* - Whenever I mention you to God in prayer.

5. *In all utterance and knowledge* - Of divine things. These gifts the Corinthians particularly admired. Therefore this congratulation naturally tended to soften their spirits, and I make way for the reproofs which follow.

6. *The testimony of Christ* - The gospel. *Was confirmed among you* - By these gifts attending it. They knew they had received these by the hand of Paul: and this consideration was highly proper, to revive in them their former reverence and affection for their spiritual father.

7. *Waiting* - With earnest desire. *For the glorious Revelation of our Lord Jesus Christ* - A sure mark of a true or false Christian, to long for, or dread, this Revelation.

8. *Who will also* - if you faithfully apply to him. Confirm you to the end. *In the day of Christ* - Now it is our day, wherein we are to work out our salvation; then it will be eminently the day of Christ, and of his glory in the saints.

9. *God is faithful* - To all his promises; and therefore "to him that hath shall be given." *By whom ye are called* - A pledge of his willingness to save you unto the uttermost.

10. *Now I exhort you* - Ye have faith and hope; secure love also. *By the endearing name of our Lord Jesus Christ* - Infinitely preferable to all the human names in which ye glory. *That ye all speak the same thing* - They now spoke different things, ver. 12 *And that there be no schisms among you* - No alienation of affection from each other. Is this word ever taken in any other sense in scripture? *But that ye be joined in the same mind* - Affections, desires. *And judgment* - Touching all the grand truths of the gospel.

11. *It hath been declared to me by them of the family of Chloe* - Whom some suppose to have been the wife of Stephanas, and the mother of Fortunatus and Achaicus. By these three the Corinthians had sent their letter to St. Paul, chap. xvi, 17. *That there are contentions* - A word equivalent with schisms in the preceding verse.

12. *Now this I say* - That is, what I mean is this: there are various parties among you, who set themselves, one against an other, in behalf of the several teachers they admire. *And I of Christ* - They spoke well, if they had not on this pretense despised their teachers, chap. iv, 8 Perhaps they valued themselves on having heard Christ preach in his own person.

13. *Is Christ divided* - Are not all the members still under one head? Was not he alone crucified for you all; and were ye not all baptized in his name? The glory of Christ then is not to be divided between him and his servants; neither is the unity of the body to be torn asunder, seeing Christ is one still.

14. *I thank God* - (A pious phrase for the common one, "I rejoice,") that, in the course of his providence, I baptized none of you, but Crispus, once the ruler of the synagogue, and Caius.

15. *Lest any should say that I had baptized in my own name* - In order to attach them to myself.

16. *I know not* - That is, it does not at present occur to my memory, that I baptized any other.

17. *For God did not send me to baptize* - That was not my chief errand: those of inferior rank and abilities could do it: though all the apostles were sent to baptize also, Matt. xxviii, 19 *But to preach the gospel* - So the apostle slides into his general proposition: but *not with wisdom of speech* - With the artificial ornaments of discourse, invented by human wisdom. *Lest the cross of Christ should be made of none effect* - The whole effect of St. Paul's preaching was owing to the power of God accompanying the plain declaration of that great truth, "Christ bore our sins upon the cross." But this effect might have been imputed to another cause, had he come with that wisdom of speech which they admired.

18. *To them that perish* - By obstinately rejecting the only name whereby they can be saved. *But to us who are saved* - Now saved from our sins, and in the way to everlasting salvation, it is the great instrument of the power of God.

19. *For it is written* - And the words are remarkably applicable to this great event. Isaiah xxix, 14

20. *Where is the wise?* &c. - The deliverance of Judea from Sennacherib is what Isaiah refers to in these words; in a bold and beautiful allusion to which, the apostle in the clause that follows triumphs over all the opposition of human wisdom to the victorious gospel of Christ. What could the wise men of the gentiles do against this? or the Jewish scribes? or *the disputers of this world?* - Those among both, who, proud of their acuteness, were fond of controversy, and thought they could confute all opponents. *Hath not God made foolish the wisdom of this world* - That is, shown it to be very foolishness. Isaiah xxxiii, 18

21. *For since in the wisdom of God* - According to his wise disposals, leaving them to make the trial. *The world* - Whether Jewish or gentile, by all its boasted *wisdom knew not God* - Though the whole creation declared its Creator, and though he declared himself by all the prophets; it pleased God, by a way which those who perish count mere foolishness, to save them that believe.

22. For whereas the Jews demand of the apostles, as they did of their Lord, more signs still, after all they have seen already; and *the Greeks*, or gentiles, *seek wisdom* - The depths of philosophy, and the charms of eloquence.

23. *We go on to preach*, in a plain and historical, not rhetorical or philosophical, manner, *Christ crucified, to the Jews a stumblingblock* - Just opposite to the "signs" they demand. *And to the Greeks foolishness* - A silly tale, just opposite to the wisdom they seek.

24. *But to them that are called* - And obey the heavenly calling. *Christ* - With his cross, his death, his life, his kingdom. And they experience, first, that he is the power, then, that he is the wisdom, of God.

25. *Because the foolishness of God* - The gospel scheme, which the world judge to be mere foolishness, is wiser than the wisdom of men; and, weak as they account it, stronger than all the strength of men.

26. *Behold your calling* - What manner of men they are whom God calls. *That not many wise men after the flesh* - In the account of the world. *Not many mighty* - Men of power and authority.

28. *Things that are not* - The Jews frequently called the gentiles, "Them that are not," 2 Esdras vi. 56, 57. In so supreme contempt did they hold them. *The things that are* - In high esteem.

29. *That no flesh* - A fit appellation. Flesh is fair, but withering as grass. *May glory before God* - In God we ought to glory.

30. *Of him* - Out of his free grace and mercy. Are ye Engrafted into Christ Jesus, who is made unto us that believe wisdom, who were before utterly foolish and ignorant. *Righteousness* - The sole ground of our justification, who were before under the wrath and curse of God. *Sanctification* - A principle of universal holiness, whereas before we were altogether dead in sin. *And redemption* - That is, complete deliverance from all evil, and eternal bliss both of soul and body.

31. *Let him glory in the Lord* - Not in himself, not in the flesh, not in the world. Jer. ix, 23, 24

II

1. *And I accordingly came to you, not with loftiness of speech or of wisdom* - I did not affect either deep wisdom or eloquence. *Declaring the testimony of God* - What God gave me to testify concerning his Son.

2. *I determined not to know anything* - To wave all my other knowledge, and not to preach anything, *save Jesus Christ, and him crucified* - That is, what he did, suffered, taught. A part is put for the whole.

3. *And I was with you* - At my first entrance. *In weakness* - Of body, 2 Cor. xii, 7 *And in fear* - Lest I should offend any. *And in much trembling* - The emotion of my mind affecting my very body.

4. *And my speech in private, as well as my public preaching, was not with the persuasive words of human wisdom,* such as the wise men of the world use; *but with the demonstration of the Spirit and of power* - With that powerful kind of demonstration, which flows from the Holy Spirit; which works on the conscience with the most convincing light, and the most persuasive evidence.

5. *That your faith might not be built on the wisdom or power of man, but on the wisdom and power of God.*

6. *Yet we speak wisdom* - Yea, the truest and most excellent wisdom. *Among the perfect* - Adult, experienced Christians. By wisdom here he seems to mean, not the whole Christian doctrine, but the most sublime and abstruse parts of it. *But not the wisdom admired and taught by the men of this world, nor of the rulers of this world,* Jewish or heathen, *that come to nought* - Both they and their wisdom, and the world itself.

7. *But we speak the mysterious wisdom of God, which was hidden* for many ages from all the world, and is still hidden even from "babes in Christ;" much more from all unbelievers. *Which God ordained before the world* - So far is this from coming to nought, like worldly wisdom. *For our glory* - Arising from the glory of our Lord, and then to be revealed when all worldly glory vanishes.

8. *Had they known it* - That wisdom. *They would not have crucified* - Punished as a slave. *The Lord of glory* - The giving Christ this august title, peculiar to the great Jehovah, plainly shows him to be the supreme God. In like manner the Father is styled, "the Father of glory," Eph. i, 17; and the Holy Ghost, "the Spirit of glory," 1 Pet. iv, 14. The application of this title to all the three, shows that the Father, Son, and Holy Ghost are "the God of glory;" as the only true God is called, Psalm xxix, 3, and Acts vii, 2.

9. But this ignorance of theirs fulfils what is written concerning the blessings of the Messiah's kingdom. *No natural man hath either seen, heard, or known, the things which God hath prepared,* saith the prophet, *for them that love him.* Isaiah lxiv, 4

10. *But God hath revealed* - Yea, and "freely given," ver. 12. *Them to us* - Even inconceivable peace, and joy unspeakable. *By his Spirit* - Who intimately and fully knows them. *For the Spirit searcheth even the deep things of God* - Be they ever so hidden and mysterious; the depths both of his nature and his kingdom.

11. *For what man knoweth the things of a man* - All the inmost recesses of his mind; although men are all of one nature, and so may the more easily know one another. *So the things of God knoweth no one but the Spirit* - Who, consequently, is God.

12. *Now we have received, not the spirit of the world* - This spirit is not properly received; for the men of the world always had it. *But Christians receive the Spirit of God,* which before they had not.

13. *Which also we speak* - As well as know. *In words taught by the Holy Spirit* - Such are all the words of scripture. How high a regard ought we, then, to retain for them! *Explaining spiritual things by spiritual words;* or, adapting spiritual words to spiritual things - Being taught of the Spirit to express the

things of the Spirit.

14. But the natural man - That is, every man who hath not the Spirit; who has no other way of obtaining knowledge, but by his senses and natural understanding. Receiveth not - Does not understand or conceive. The things of the Spirit - The things revealed by the Spirit of God, whether relating to his nature or his kingdom. For they are foolishness to him - He is so far from understanding, that he utterly despises, them Neither can he know them - As he has not the will, so neither has he the power. Because they are spiritually discerned - They can only be discerned by the aid of that Spirit, and by those spiritual senses, which he has not.

15. But the spiritual man - He that hath the Spirit. Discerneth all the things of God whereof we have been speaking. Yet he himself is discerned by no man - No natural men. They neither understand what he is, nor what he says.

16. Who - What natural man. We - Spiritual men; apostles in particular. Have - Know, understand. The mind of Christ - Concerning the whole plan of gospel salvation. Isaiah xl, 13

III

1. And I, brethren -- he spoke before, ver. 1, of his entrance, now of his progress, among them. Could not speak to you as unto spiritual - Adult, experienced Christians. But as unto men who were still in great measure carnal, as unto babes in Christ - Still weak in grace, though eminent in gifts, chap. i, 5.

2. I fed you, as babes, with milk - The first and plainest truths of the gospel. So should every preacher suit his doctrine to his hearers.

3. For while there is among you emulation in your hearts, strife in your words, and actual divisions, are ye not carnal, and walk according to men - As mere men; not as Christians, according to God.

4. I am of Apollos - St. Paul named himself and Apollos, to show that he would condemn any division among them, even though it were in favour of himself, or the dearest friend he had in the world. Are ye not carnal - For the Spirit of God allows no party zeal.

5. Ministers - Or servants. By whom ye believed, as the Lord, the Master of those servants, gave to every man.

7. God that giveth the increase - Is all in all: without him neither planting nor watering avails.

8. But he that planteth and he that watereth are one - Which is another argument against division. Though their labours are different. they are all employed in one general work, - the saving souls. Hence he takes occasion to speak of the reward of them that labour faithfully, and the awful account to be given by all. Every man shall receive his own peculiar reward according to his own peculiar labour - Not according to his success; but he who labours much, though with small success, shall have a great reward. Has not all this reasoning the same force still? The ministers are still surely instruments in God's hand, and depend as entirely as ever on his blessing, to give the increase to their labours. Without this, they are nothing: with it, their part is so small, that they hardly deserve to be mentioned. May their hearts and hands be more united; and, retaining a due sense of the honour God doeth them in employing them, may they faithfully labour, not as for themselves, but for the great Proprietor of all, till the day come when he will reward them in full proportion to their fidelity and diligence!

9. For we are all fellowlabourers - God's labourers, and fellowlabourers with each other. Ye are God's husbandry - This is the sum of what went before: it is a comprehensive word, taking in both a field, a garden, and a vineyard. Ye are God's building - This is the sum of what follows.

10. According to the grace of God given to me - This he premises, lest he should seem to ascribe it to himself. Let every one take heed how he buildeth thereon - That all his doctrines may be consistent with the foundation.

11. For other foundation - On which the whole church: and all its doctrines, duties, and blessings may be built. Can no man lay than what is laid - In the counsels of divine wisdom, in the promises and prophecies of the Old Testament, in the preaching of the apostles, St. Paul in particular. Which is Jesus Christ - Who, in his person and offices, is the firm, immovable Rock of Ages, every way sufficient to bear all the weight that God himself, or the sinner, when he believes, can lay upon him.

12. If any one build gold, silver, costly stones - Three sorts of materials which will bear the fire; true and solid doctrines. Wood, hay, stubble - Three which will not bear the fire. Such are all doctrines, ceremonies, and forms of human invention; all but the substantial, vital truths of Christianity.

13. The time is coming when every one's work shall be made manifest: for the day of the Lord, that great and final day, shall declare it - To all the world. For it is revealed - What faith beholds as so certain and so near is spoken of as already present. By fire; yea, the fire shall try every one's work, of what sort it is - The strict process of that day will try every man's doctrines, whether they come up to the scripture standard or not. Here is a plain allusion to the flaming light and consuming heat of the general conflagration. But the expression, when applied to the trying of doctrines, and consuming those that are wrong, is evidently figurative; because no material fire can have such an effect on what is of a moral

nature. And therefore it is added, he who builds wood, hay, or stubble, shall be saved as through the fire - Or, as narrowly as a man escapes through the fire, when his house is all in flames about him. This text, then, is so far from establishing the Romanish purgatory, that it utterly overthrows it. For the fire here mentioned does not exist till the day of judgment: therefore, if this be the fire of purgatory, it follows that purgatory does not exist before the day of judgment.

14. He shall receive a reward - A peculiar degree of glory. Some degree even the other will receive, seeing he held the foundation; though through ignorance he built thereon what would not abide the fire.

15. He shall suffer loss - The loss of that peculiar degree of glory.

16. Ye - All Christians. Are the temple of God - The most noble kind of building, ver. 9.

17. If any man destroy the temple of God - Destroy a real Christian, by schisms, or doctrines fundamentally wrong. Him shall God destroy - He shall not be saved at all; not even as through the fire."

18. Let him become a fool in this world - Such as the world accounts so. That he may become wise - In God's account.

19. For all the boasted wisdom of the world is mere foolishness in the sight of God. He taketh the wise in their own craftiness - Not only while they think they are acting wisely, but by their very wisdom, which itself is their snare, and the occasion of their destruction. Job v, 13.

20. That they are but vain - Empty, foolish; they and all their thoughts. Psalm xciv, 11.

21. Therefore - Upon the whole. Let none glory in men - So as to divide into parties on their account. For all things are yours - and we in particular. We are not your lords, but rather your servants.

22. Whether Paul or Apollos, or Cephas - We are all equally yours, to serve you for Christ's sake. Or the world - This leap from Peter to the world greatly enlarges the thought, and argues a kind of impatience of enumerating the rest. Peter and every one in the whole world, however excellent in gifts, or grace, or office, are also your servants for Christ's sake. Or life, or death - These, with all their various circumstances, are disposed as will be most for your advantage. Or things present - On earth. Or things to come - In heaven. Contend, therefore, no more about these little things; but be ye united in love, as ye are in blessings.

23. And ye are Christ's - His property, his subjects. his members. And Christ is God's - As Mediator, he refers all his services to his Father's glory.

IV

1. Let a man account us, as servants of Christ - The original word properly signifies such servants as laboured at the oar in rowing vessels; and, accordingly, intimates the pains which every faithful minister takes in his Lord's work. O God, where are these ministers to be found? Lord, thou knowest. And stewards of the mysteries of God - Dispenseth of the mysterious truths of the gospel.

3. Yea, I judge not myself - My final state is not to be determined by my own judgment.

4. I am not conscious to myself of anything evil; yet am I not hereby justified - I depend not on this, as a sufficient justification of myself in God's account. But he that judgeth me is the Lord - By his sentence I am to stand or fall.

5. Therefore judge nothing before the time - Appointed for judging all men. Until the Lord come, who, in order to pass a righteous judgment, which otherwise would be impossible, will both bring to light the things which are now covered with impenetrable darkness, and manifest the most secret springs of action, the principles and intentions of every heart. And then shall every one - Every faithful steward, have praise of God.

6. These things - Mentioned, chap. i, 10, &c. I have by a very obvious figure transferred to myself and Apollos - And Cephas, instead of naming those particular preachers at Corinth, to whom ye are so fondly attached. That ye may learn by us - From what has been said concerning us, who, however eminent we are, are mere instruments in God's hand. Not to think of any man above what is here written - Or above what scripture warrants. chap. iii, 7

7. Who maketh thee to differ - Either in gifts or graces. As if thou hadst not received it - As if thou hadst it originally from thyself.

8. Now ye are full - The Corinthians abounded with spiritual gifts; and so did the apostles: but the apostles, by continual want and sufferings, were kept from self- complacency. The Corinthians suffering nothing, and having plenty of all things, were pleased with and applauded themselves; and they were like children who, being raised in the world, disregard their poor parents. Now ye are full, says the apostle, in a beautiful gradation, ye are rich, ye have reigned as kings - A proverbial expression, denoting the most splendid and plentiful circumstances. Without any thought of us. And I would ye did reign - In the best sense: I would ye had attained the height of holiness. That we might reign with you - Having no more sorrow on your account, but sharing in your happiness.

9. God hath set forth us last, as appointed to death - Alluding to the Roman custom of bringing

forth those persons last on the stage, either to fight with each other, or with wild beasts, who were devoted to death; so that, if they escaped one day, they were brought out again and again, till they were killed.

10. We are fools, in the account of the world, for Christ's sake, but ye are wise in Christ - Though ye are Christians, ye think yourselves wise; and ye have found means to make the world think you so too. We are weak - In presence, in infirmities, in sufferings. But ye are strong - In just opposite circumstances.

11. And are naked - Who can imagine a more glorious triumph of the truth, than that which is gained in these circumstances when St. Paul, with an impediment in his speech, and a person rather contemptible than graceful, appeared in a mean, perhaps tattered, dress before persons of the highest distinction, and yet commanded such attention. and made such deep impressions upon them!

12. We bless-suffer it-intreat - We do not return revilings, persecution, defamation; nothing but blessing.

13. We are made as the filth of the world, and offscouring of all things - Such were those poor wretches among the heathens, who were taken from the dregs of the people, to be offered as expiatory sacrifices to the infernal gods. They were loaded with curses, affronts, and injuries, all the way they went to the altars; and when the ashes of those unhappy men were thrown into the sea, these very names were given them in the ceremony.

14. I do not write these things to shame you, but as my beloved children I warn you - It is with admirable prudence and sweetness the apostle adds this, to prevent any unkind construction of his words.

15. I have begotten you - This excludes not only Apollos, his successor, but also Silas and Timothy, his companions; and the relation between a spiritual father and his children brings with it an inexpressible nearness and affection.

16. Be ye followers of me - In that spirit and behaviour which I have so largely declared.

17. My beloved son - Elsewhere he styles him "brother," 2 Cor. i, 1; but here paternal affection takes place. As I teach - No less by example than precept.

18. Now some are puffed up - St. Paul saw, by a divine light, the thoughts which would arise in their hearts. As if I would not come - Because I send Timothy.

19. I will know - He here shows his fatherly authority Not the big, empty speech of these vain boasters, but how much of the power of God attends them.

20. For the kingdom of God - Real religion, does not consist in words, but in the power of God ruling the heart.

21. With a rod - That is, with severity.

V

1. Fornication - The original word implies criminal conversation of any kind whatever. His father's wife - While his father was alive.

2. Are ye puffed up? Should ye not rather have mourned - Have solemnly humbled yourselves, and at that time of solemn mourning have expelled that notorious sinner from your communion?

3. I verily, as present in spirit - Having a full (it seems, a miraculous) view of the whole fact. Have already, as if I were actually present, judged him who hath so scandalously done this.

4. And my spirit - Present with you. With the power of the Lord Jesus Christ - To confirm my sentence.

5. To deliver such an one - This was the highest degree of punishment in the Christian church; and we may observe, the passing this sentence was the act of the apostle, not of the Corinthians. To Satan - Who was usually permitted, in such cases, to inflict pain or sickness on the offender. For the destruction - Though slowly and gradually. Of the flesh - Unless prevented by speedy repentance.

6. Your glorying - Either in your gifts or prosperity, at such a time as this, is not good. Know ye not that a little leaven - One sin, or one sinner. Leaveneth the whole lump - Diffuses guilt and infection through the whole congregation.

7. Purge out therefore the old leaven - Both of sinners and of sin. That ye may be a new lump, as ye are unleavened - That is, that being unleavened ye may be a new lump, holy unto the Lord. For our passover is slain for us - The Jewish passover, about the time of which this epistle was wrote, ver. 11, was only a type of this. What exquisite skill both here and everywhere conducts the zeal of the inspired writer! How surprising a transition is here, and yet how perfectly natural! The apostle, speaking of the incestuous criminal, slides into his darling topic, - crucified saviour. Who would have expected it on such an occasion. Yet, when it is thus brought in, who does not see and admire both the propriety of the subject, and the delicacy of its introduction?

8. Therefore let us keep the feast - Let us feed on him by faith. Here is a plain allusion to the Lord's supper, which was instituted in the room of the passover. Not with the old leaven - Of

heathenism or Judaism. Malignity is stubbornness in evil. Sincerity and truth seem to be put here for the whole of true, inward religion.

9. I wrote to you in a former epistle - And, doubtless, both St. Paul and the other apostles wrote many things which are not extant now. Not to converse - Familiarly; not to contract any intimacy or acquaintance with them, more than is absolutely necessary.

10. But I did not mean that you should altogether refrain from conversing with heathens, though they are guilty in some of these respects. Covetous, rapacious, idolaters - Sinners against themselves, their neighbour, God. For then ye must go out of the world - Then all civil commerce must cease. So that going out of the world, which some account a perfection, St. Paul accounts an utter absurdity.

11. Who is named a brother - That is, a Christian; especially if a member of the same congregation. Rapacious - Guilty of oppression, extortion, or any open injustice. No, not to eat with him - Which is the lowest degree of familiarity.

12. I speak of Christians only. For what have I to do to judge heathens? But ye, as well as I, judge those of your own community.

13. Them that are without God will judge - The passing sentence on these he hath reserved to himself. And ye will take away that wicked person - This properly belongs to you.

VI

1. The unjust - The heathens. A Christian could expect no justice from these. The saints - Who might easily decide these smaller differences in a private and friendly manner.

2. Know ye not - This expression occurs six times in this single chapter, and that with a peculiar force; for the Corinthians knew and gloried in it, but they did not practice. That the saints - After having been judged themselves. Shall judge the world - Shall be assessors with Christ in the judgment wherein he shall condemn all the wicked, as well angels as men, Matt. xix, 28 Rev. xx, 4.

4. Them who are of no esteem in the church - That is, heathens, who, as such, could be in no esteem with the Christians.

5. Is there not one among you, who are such admirers of wisdom, that is wise enough to decide such causes?

7. Indeed there is a fault, that ye quarrel with each other at all, whether ye go to law or no. Why do ye not rather suffer wrong - All men cannot or will not receive this saying. Many aim only at this, "I will neither do wrong, nor suffer it." These are honest heathens, but no Christians.

8. Nay, ye do wrong - Openly. And defraud - Privately. O how powerfully did the mystery of iniquity already work!

9. Idolatry is here placed between fornication and adultery, because they generally accompanied it. Nor the effeminate - Who live in an easy, indolent way; taking up no cross, enduring no hardship. But how is this? These good-natured, harmless people are ranked with idolaters and sodomites! We may learn hence, that we are never secure from the greatest sins, till we guard against those which are thought the least; nor, indeed, till we think no sin is little, since every one is a step toward hell.

11. And such were some of you: but ye are washed - From those gross abominations; nay, and ye are inwardly sanctified; not before, but in consequence of, your being justified in the name - That is, by the merits, of the Lord Jesus, through which your sins are forgiven. And by the Spirit of our God - By whom ye are thus washed and sanctified.

12. All things - Which are lawful for you. Are lawful for me, but all things are not always expedient - Particularly when anything would offend my weak brother; or when it would enslave my own soul. For though all things are lawful for me, yet I will not be brought under the power of any - So as to be uneasy when I abstain from it; for, if so, then I am under the power of it.

13. As if he had said, I speak this chiefly with regard to meats; (and would to God all Christians would consider it!) particularly with regard to those offered to idols, and those forbidden in the Mosaic law. These, I grant, are all indifferent, and have their use, though it is only for a time: then meats, and the organs which receive them, will together moulder into dust. But the case is quite otherwise with fornication. This is not indifferent, but at all times evil. For the body is for the Lord - Designed only for his service. And the Lord, in an important sense, for the body - Being the saviour of this, as well as of the soul; in proof of which God hath already raised him from the dead.

16. Gen. ii, 24.

17. But he that is joined to the Lord - By faith. Is one spirit with him - And shall he make himself one flesh with an harlot?

18. Flee fornication - All unlawful commerce with women, with speed, with abhorrence, with all your might. Every sin that a man commits against his neighbour terminates upon an object out of himself, and does not so immediately pollute his body, though it does his soul. But he that committeth fornication, sinneth against his own body - Pollutes, dishonours, and degrades it to a level with brute beasts.

Wesley's Notes on the Bible - The New Testament

19. And even your body is not, strictly speaking, your own even this is the temple of the Holy Ghost - Dedicated to him, and inhabited by him. What the apostle calls elsewhere "the temple of God," chap. iii, 16, 17, and "the temple of the living God," 2 Cor. vi, 16, he here styles the temple of the Holy Ghost; plainly showing that the Holy Ghost is the living God.

20. Glorify God with your body, and your spirit - Yield your bodies and all their members, as well as your souls and all their faculties, as instruments of righteousness to God. Devote and employ all ye have, and all ye are, entirely, unreservedly, and forever, to his glory.

VII

1. It is good for a man - Who is master of himself. Not to touch a women - That is, not to marry. So great and many are the advantages of a single life.

2. Yet, when it is needful, in order to avoid fornication, let every man have his own wife. His own - For Christianity allows no polygamy.

3. Let not married persons fancy that there is any perfection in living with each other, as if they were unmarried. The debt - This ancient reading seems far more natural than the common one.

4. The wife-the husband - Let no one forget this, on pretense of greater purity.

5. Unless it be by consent for a time - That on those special and solemn occasions ye may entirely give yourselves up to the exercises of devotion. Lest - If ye should long remain separate. Satan tempt you - To unclean thoughts, if not actions too.

6. But I say this - Concerning your separating for a time and coming together again. Perhaps he refers also to ver. 2.

7. For I would that all men were herein even as I - I would that all believers who are now unmarried would remain "eunuchs for the kingdom of heaven's sake" St. Paul, having tasted the sweetness of this liberty, wished others to enjoy it, as well as himself. But every one hath his proper gift from God - According to our Lord's declaration, "All men cannot receive this saying, save they," the happy few, to whom it is given," Matt. xix, 11.

8. It is good for them if they remain even as I - That St. Paul was then single is certain and from Acts vii, 58, compared with the following parts of the history, it seems probable that he always was so. It does not appear that this declaration, any more than ver. 1, hath any reference at all to a state of persecution.

10. Not I - Only. But the Lord - Christ; by his express command, Matt. v, 32.

11. But if she depart - Contrary to this express prohibition. And let not the husband put away his wife - Except for the cause of adultery.

12. To the rest - Who are married to unbelievers. Speak I - By Revelation from God, though our Lord hath not left any commandment concerning it. Let him not put her away - The Jews, indeed, were obliged of old to put away their idolatrous wives, Ezra x, 3; but their case was quite different. They were absolutely forbid to marry idolatrous women; but the persons here spoken of were married while they were both in a state of heathenism.

14. For the unbelieving husband hath, in many instances, been sanctified by the wife - Else your children would have been brought up heathens; whereas now they are Christians. As if he had said, Ye see the proof of it before your eyes.

15. A brother or a sister - A Christian man or woman. Is not enslaved - is at full liberty. In such cases: but God hath called us to peace - To live peaceably with them, if it be possible.

17. But as God hath distributed - The various stations of life, and various relations, to every one, let him take care to discharge his duty therein. The gospel disannuls none of these. And thus I ordain in all the churches - As a point of the highest concern.

19. Circumcision is nothing, and uncircumcision is nothing - Will neither promote nor obstruct our salvation. The one point is, keeping the commandments of God; "faith working by love."

20. In the calling - The outward state. Wherein he is - When God calls him. Let him not seek to change this, without a clear direction from Providence.

21. Care not for it - Do not anxiously seek liberty. But if thou canst be free, use it rather - Embrace the opportunity.

22. Is the Lord's freeman - Is free in this respect. The Greek word implies one that was a slave, but now is free. Is the bondman of Christ - Not free in this respect; not at liberty to do his own will.

23. Ye are bought with a price - Ye belong to God; therefore, where it can be avoided, do not become the bondslaves of men - Which may expose you to many temptations.

24. Therein abide with God - Doing all things as unto God, and as in his immediate presence. They who thus abide with God preserve an holy indifference with regard to outward things.

25. Now concerning virgins - Of either sex. I have no commandment from the Lord - By a particular Revelation. Nor was it necessary he should; for the apostles wrote nothing which was not divinely inspired: but with this difference, - sometimes they had a particular Revelation, and a special

commandment; at other times they wrote from the divine light which abode with them, the standing treasure of the Spirit of God. And this, also, was not their private opinion, but a divine rule of faith and practice. As one whom God hath made faithful in my apostolic office; who therefore faithfully deliver what I receive from him.

26, 27. *This is good for the present distress* - While any church is under persecution. *For a man to continue as he is* - Whether married or unmarried. St. Paul does not here urge the present distress as a reason for celibacy, any more than for marriage; but for a man's not seeking to alter his state, whatever it be, but making the best of it.

28. *Such will have trouble in the flesh* - Many outward troubles. *But I spare you* - I speak as little and as tenderly as possible.

29. *But this I say, brethren* -- with great confidence. *The time of our abode here is short.* It plainly follows, that even they who have wives be as serious, zealous, active, dead to the world, as devoted to God, as holy in all manner of conversation, as if they had none - By so easy a transition does the apostle slide from every thing else to the one thing needful; and, forgetting whatever is temporal, is swallowed up in eternity.

30. *And they that weep, as if they wept not* - "Though sorrowful, yet always rejoicing." *They that rejoice, as if they rejoiced not* - Tempering their joy with godly fear. *They that buy, as if they possessed not* - Knowing themselves to be only stewards, not proprietors.

31. *And they that use this world, as not abusing it* - Not seeking happiness in it, but in God: using every thing therein only in such a manner and degree as most tends to the knowledge and love of God. *For the whole scheme and fashion of this world* - This marrying, weeping, rejoicing, and all the rest, not only will pass, but now passeth away, is this moment flying off like a shadow.

32. *Now I would have you* - For this flying moment. *Without carefulness* - Without any incumbrance of your thoughts. *The unmarried man* - If he understand and use the advantage he enjoys- Careth only for the things of the Lord, how he may please the Lord.

33. *But the married careth for the things of the world* - And it in his duty so to do, so far as becomes a Christian. *How he may please his wife* - And provide all things needful for her and his family.

34. *There is a difference also between a wife and a virgin* - Whether the church be under persecution or not. *The unmarried woman* - If she know and use her privilege. Careth only for the things of the Lord - All her time, care, and thoughts center in this, how she may be holy both in body and spirit. This is the standing advantage of a single life, in all ages and nations. But who makes a suitable use of it?

35. *Not that I may cast a snare upon you* - Who are not able to receive this saying. *But for your profit* - Who are able. *That ye may resolutely and perseveringly wait upon the Lord* - The word translated *wait* signifies sitting close by a person, in a good posture to hear. So Mary sat at the feet of Jesus, Luke x, 39. *Without distraction* - Without having the mind drawn any way from its center; from its close attention to God; by any person, or thing, or care, or incumbrance whatsoever.

36. *But if any parent think he should otherwise act indecently* - Unbecoming his character. Toward his virgin daughter, if she be above age, (or of full age,) and need so require, ver. 9, *let them marry* - Her suitor and she.

37. *Having no necessity* - Where there is no such need. *But having power over his own will* - Which would incline him to desire the increase of his family, and the strengthening it by new relations.

38. *Doeth better* - If there be no necessity.

39. *Only in the Lord* - That is, only if Christians marry Christians: a standing direction, and one of the utmost importance.

40. *I also* - As well as any of you. *Have the Spirit of God* - Teaching me all things This does not imply any doubt; but the strongest certainty of it, together with a reproof of them for calling it in question. Whoever, therefore, would conclude from hence, that St. Paul was not certain he had the Spirit of Christ, neither understands the true import of the words, nor considers how expressly he lays claim to the Spirit, both in this epistle, chap. ii, 16, xiv, 37, and the other. 2 Cor. xiii, 3. Indeed, it may be doubted whether the word here and elsewhere translated *think*, does not always imply the fullest and strongest assurance. See chap. x, 12.

VIII

1. *Now concerning the next question you proposed. All of us have knowledge* - A gentle reproof of their self-conceit. *Knowledge without love always puffeth up. Love alone edifies* - Builds us up in holiness.

2. *If any man think he knoweth any thing* - Aright, unless so far he is taught by God. *He knoweth nothing yet as he ought to know* - Seeing there is no true knowledge without divine love.

3. *He is known* - That is, approved, by him. Psalm i, 6.

4. We know that an idol is nothing - A mere nominal god, having no divinity, virtue, or power.

5. For though there be that are called gods - By the heathens both celestial, (as they style them,) terrestrial, and infernal deities.

6. Yet to us - Christians. There is but one God - This is exclusive, not of the One Lord, as if he were an inferior deity; but only of the idols to which the One God is opposed. From whom are all things - By creation, providence, and grace. And we for him - The end of all we are, have, and do. And one Lord - Equally the object of divine worship. By whom are all things - Created, sustained, and governed. And we by him - Have access to the Father, and all spiritual blessings.

7. Some eat, with consciousness of the idol - That is, fancying it is something, and that it makes the meat unlawful to be eaten. And their conscience, being weak - Not rightly informed. Is defiled - contracts guilt by doing it.

8. But meat commendeth us not to God - Neither by eating, nor by refraining from it. Eating and not eating are in themselves things merely indifferent.

10. For if any one see thee who hast knowledge - Whom he believes to have more knowledge than himself, and who really hast this knowledge, that an idol is nothing-sitting down to an entertainment in an idol temple. The heathens frequently made entertainments in their temples, on what hath been sacrificed to their idols. Will not the conscience of him that is weak - Scrupulous. Be encouraged - By thy example. To eat - Though with a doubting conscience.

11. And through thy knowledge shall the weak brother perish, for whom Christ died? - And for whom thou wilt not lose a meal's meat, so far from dying for him! We see, Christ died even for them that perish.

12. Ye sin against Christ - Whose members they are.

13. If meat - Of any kind. Who will follow this example? What preacher or private Christian will abstain from any thing lawful in itself, when it offends a weak brother?

IX

1. Am I not free? am I not an apostle? - That is, Have not I the liberty of a common Christian? yea, that of an apostle? He vindicates his apostleship, chap. ix, 1-iii, his apostolical liberty, chap. ix, 4-19. Have I not seen Jesus Christ? - Without this he could not have been one of those first grand witnesses. Are not ye my work in the Lord - A full evidence that God hath sent me? And yet some, it seems, objected to his being an apostle, because he had not asserted his privilege in demanding and receiving such maintenance from the churches as was due to that office.

2. Ye are the seal of my apostleship - Who have received not only faith by my mouth, but all the gifts of the Spirit by my hands.

3. My answer to them who examine me - Concerning my apostleship. Is this - Which I have now given.

4. Have we not power - I and my fellowlabourers. To eat and to drink - At the expense of those among whom we labour.

5. Have we not power to lead about with us a sister, a wife - And to demand sustenance for her also? As well as the other apostles - Who therefore, it is plain, did this. And Peter - Hence we learn,

1. That St. Peter continued to live with his wife after he became an apostle:

2. That he had no rights as an apostle which were not common to St. Paul.

6. To forbear working - With our hands.

8. Do I speak as a man - Barely on the authority of human reason? Does not God also say, in effect, the same thing? The ox that treadeth out the corn - This was the custom in Judea, and many eastern nations. In several of them it is retained still. And at this day, horses tread out the corn in some parts of Germany.

9. Doth God - In this direction. Take care for oxen - Only? Hath he not a farther meaning? And so undoubtedly he hath in all the other Mosaic laws of this kind.

10. He who ploweth ought to plow in hope - Of reaping. This seems to be a proverbial expression. And he that thresheth in hope - Ought not to be disappointed, ought to eat the fruit of his labours. And ought they who labour in God's husbandry. Deut. xxv, 4

11. Is it a great matter if we shall reap as much of your carnal things - As is needful for our sustenance? Do you give us things of greater value than those you receive from us?

12. If others - Whether true or false apostles. Partake of this power - Have a right to be maintained. Do not we rather - On account of our having laboured so much more? Lest we should give any hindrance to the gospel - By giving an occasion of cavil or reproach.

14. Matt. x, 10

15. It were better for me to die than - To give occasion to them that seek occasion against me, 2 Cor. xi, 12.

17. Willingly - He seems to mean, without receiving anything. St. Paul here speaks in a manner

peculiar to himself. Another might have preached willingly, and yet have received a maintenance from the Corinthians. But if he had received anything from them, he would have termed it preaching unwillingly. And so, in the next verse, another might have used that power without abusing it. But his own using it at all, he would have termed abusing it. A dispensation is intrusted to me - Therefore I dare not refrain.

18. What then is my reward - That circumstance in my conduct for which I expect a peculiar reward from my great Master? That I abuse not - Make not an unseasonable use of my power which I have in preaching the gospel.

19. I made myself the servant of all - I acted with as self-denying a regard to their interest, and as much caution not to offend them, as if I had been literally their servant or slave. Where is the preacher of the gospel who treads in the same steps?

20. To the Jews I became as a Jew - Conforming myself in all things to their manner of thinking and living, so far as; I could with innocence. To them that are under the law - Who apprehend themselves to be still bound by the Mosaic law. As under the law - Observing it myself, while I am among them. Not that he declared this to be necessary, or refused to converse with those who did not observe it. This was the very thing which he condemned in St. Peter, Gal. ii, 14.

21. To them that are without the law - The heathens. As without the law - Neglecting its ceremonies. Being not without the law to God - But as much as ever under its moral precepts. Under the law to Christ - And in this sense all Christians will be under the law for ever.

22. I became as weak - As if I had been scrupulous too. I became all things to all men - Accommodating myself to all, so far as I could consistent with truth and sincerity.

24. Know ye not that - In those famous games which are kept at the isthmus, near your city. They who run in the foot race all run, though but one receiveth the prize - How much greater encouragement have you to run; since ye may all receive the prize of your high calling!

25. And every one that there contendeth is temperate in all things - To an almost incredible degree; using the most rigorous self denial in food, sleep, and every other sensual indulgence. A corruptible crown - A garland of leaves, which must soon wither. The moderns only have discovered that it is "legal" to do all this and more for an eternal crown than they did for a corruptible!

26. I so run, not as uncertainly - I look straight to the goal; I run straight toward it. I cast away every weight, regard not any that stand by. I fight not as one that beateth the air - This is a proverbial expression for a man's missing his blow, and spending his strength, not on his enemy, but on empty air.

27. But I keep under my body - By all kinds of self denial. And bring it into subjection - To my spirit and to God. The words are strongly figurative, and signify the mortification of the body of sin, "by an allusion to the natural bodies of those who were bruised or subdued in combat. Lest by any means after having preached - The Greek word means, after having discharged the office of an herald, (still carrying on the allusion,) whose office it was to proclaim the conditions, and to display the prizes. I myself should become a reprobate - Disapproved by the Judge, and so falling short of the prize. This single text may give us a just notion of the scriptural doctrine of election and reprobation; and clearly shows us, that particular persons are not in holy writ represented as elected absolutely and unconditionally to eternal life, or predestinated absolutely and unconditionally to eternal death; but that believers in general are elected to enjoy the Christian privileges on earth; which if they abuse, those very elect persons will become reprobate. St. Paul was certainly an elect person, if ever there was one; and yet he declares it was possible he himself might become a reprobate. Nay, he actually would have become such, if he had not thus kept his body under, even though he had been so long an elect person, a Christian, and an apostle.

X

1. Now - That ye may not become reprobates, consider how highly favoured your fathers were, who were God's elect and peculiar people, and nevertheless were rejected by him. They were all under the cloud - That eminent token of God's gracious presence, which screened them from the heat of the sun by day, and gave them light by night. And all passed through the sea - God opening a way through the midst of the waters. Exod. xiii, 21 Exod. xiv, 22

2. And were all, as it were, baptized unto Moses - initiated into the religion which he taught them. In the cloud and in the sea - Perhaps sprinkled here and there with drops of water from the sea or the cloud, by which baptism might be the more evidently signified.

3. And all ate the same manna, termed spiritual meat, as it was typical,

1. Of Christ and his spiritual benefits:
2. Of the sacred bread which we eat at his table. Exod. xvi, 15.

4. And all drank the same spiritual drink - Typical of Christ, and of that cup which we drink. For they drank out of the spiritual or mysterious rock, the wonderful streams of which followed them in their several journeyings, for many years, through the wilderness. And that rock was a manifest type of

Wesley's Notes on the Bible - The New Testament

Christ - The Rock of Eternity, from whom his people derive those streams of blessings which follow them through all this wilderness. Exod. xvii, 6.

5. Yet - Although they had so many tokens of the divine presence. They were overthrown - With the most terrible marks of his displeasure.

6. Now these things were our examples - Showing what we are to expect if, enjoying the like benefits, we commit the like sins. The benefits are set down in the same order as by Moses in Exodus; the sins and punishments in a different order; evil desire first, as being the foundation of all; next, idolatry, ver. 7, 14; then fornication, which usually accompanied it, ver. 8; the tempting and murmuring against God, in the following verses. As they desired - Flesh, in contempt of manna. Num. xi, 4

7. Neither be ye idolaters - And so, "neither murmur ye," ver. 10. The other cautions are given in the first person; but these in the second. And with what exquisite propriety does he vary the person! It would have been improper to say, Neither let us be idolaters; for he was himself in no danger of idolatry; nor probably of murmuring against Christ, or the divine providence. To play - That is, to dance, in honour of their idol. Exod. xxxii, 6.

8. And fell in one day three and twenty thousand - Beside the princes who were afterwards hanged, and those whom the Judges slew so that there died in all four and twenty thousand. Num. xxv, 1, 9.

9. Neither let us tempt Christ - By our unbelief. St. Paul enumerates five benefits, ver. 1-4; of which the fourth and fifth were closely connected together; and five sins, the fourth and fifth of which were likewise closely connected. In speaking of the fifth benefit, he expressly mentions Christ; and in speaking of the fourth sin, he shows it was committed against Christ. As some of them tempted him - This sin of the people was peculiarly against Christ; for when they had so long drank of that rock, yet they murmured for want of water. Num. xxi, 4, &c.

10. The destroyer - The destroying angel. Num. xiv, 1, 36

11. On whom the ends of the ages are come - The expression has great force. All things meet together, and come to a crisis, under the last, the gospel, dispensation; both benefits and dangers, punishments and rewards. It remains, that Christ come as an avenger and judge. And even these ends include various periods, succeeding each other.

12. The common translation runs, Let him that thinketh he standeth; but the word translated thinketh, most certainly strengthens, rather than weakens, the sense.

13. Common to man - Or, as the Greek word imports, proportioned to human strength. God is faithful - In giving the help which he hath promised. And he will with the temptation - Provide for your deliverance.

14. Flee from idolatry - And from all approaches to it.

16. The cup which we bless - By setting it apart to a sacred use, and solemnly invoking the blessing of God upon it. Is it not the communion of the blood of Christ - The means of our partaking of those invaluable benefits, which are the purchase of the blood of Christ. The communion of the body of Christ - The means of our partaking of those benefits which were purchased by the body of Christ - offered for us.

17. For it is this communion which makes us all one. We being many are yet, as it were, but different parts of one and the same broken bread, which we receive to unite us in one body.

18. Consider Israel after the flesh - Christians are the spiritual "Israel of God." Are not they who eat of the sacrifices partakers of the altar - Is not this an act of communion with that God to whom they are offered? And is not the case the same with those who eat of the sacrifices which have been offered to idols?

19. What say I then - Do I in saying this allow that an idol is anything divine? I aver, on the contrary, that what the heathens sacrifice, they sacrifice to devils. Such in reality are the gods of the heathens; and with such only can you hold communion in those sacrifices.

21. Ye cannot drink the cup of the Lord, and the cup of devils - You cannot have communion with both.

22. Do we provoke the Lord to jealousy - By thus caressing his rivals? Are we stronger than he - Are we able to resist, or to bear his wrath?

23. Supposing this were lawful in itself, yet it is not expedient, it is not edifying to my neighbour.

24. His own only, but another's welfare also.

25. The apostle now applies this principle to the point in question. Asking no questions - Whether it has been sacrificed or not.

26. For God, who is the Creator, Proprietor, and Disposer of the earth and all that is therein, hath given the produce of it to the children of men, to be used without scruple. Psalm xxiv, 1

28. For his sake that showed thee, and for conscience' sake - That is, for the sake of his weak conscience, lest it should be wounded.

29. Conscience I say, not thy own - I speak of his conscience, not thine. For why is my liberty judged by another's conscience - Another's conscience is not the standard of mine, nor is another's

persuasion the measure of my liberty.

30. If I by grace am a partaker - If I thankfully use the common blessings of God.

31. Therefore - To close the present point with a general rule, applicable not only in this, but in all cases, Whatsoever ye do - In all things whatsoever, whether of a religious or civil nature, in all the common, as well as sacred, actions of life, keep the glory of God in view, and steadily pursue in all this one end of your being, the planting or advancing the vital knowledge and love of God, first in your own soul, then in all mankind.

32. Give no offense - If, and as far as, it is possible.

33. Even as I, as much as lieth in me, please all men.

XI

2. I praise you - The greater part of you.

3. I would have you know - He does not seem to have given them any order before concerning this. The head of every man - Particularly every believer. Is Christ, and the head of Christ is God - Christ, as he is Mediator, acts in all things subordinately to his Father. But we can no more infer that they are not of the same divine nature, because God is said to be the head of Christ, than that man and woman are not of the same human nature, because the man is said to be the head of the woman.

4. Every man praying or prophesying - Speaking by the immediate power of God. With his head - And face. Covered - Either with a veil or with long hair. Dishonoureth his head - St. Paul seems to mean, As in these eastern nations veiling the head is a badge of subjection, so a man who prays or prophesies with a veil on his head, reflects a dishonour on Christ, whose representative he is.

5. But every woman - Who, under an immediate impulse of the Spirit, (for then only was a woman suffered to speak in the church,) prays or prophesies without a veil on her face, as it were disclaims subjection, and reflects dishonour on man, her head. For it is the same, in effect, as if she cut her hair short, and wore it in the distinguishing form of the men. In those ages, men wore their hair exceeding short, as appears from the ancient statues and pictures.

6. Therefore if a woman is not covered - If she will throw off the badge of subjection, let her appear with her hair cut like a man's. But if it be shameful far a woman to appear thus in public, especially in a religious assembly, let her, for the same reason, keep on her veil.

7. A man indeed ought not to veil his head, because he is the image of God - In the dominion he bears over the creation, representing the supreme dominion of God, which is his glory. But the woman is only matter of glory to the man, who has a becoming dominion over her. Therefore she ought not to appear, but with her head veiled, as a tacit acknowledgment of it.

8. The man is not - In the first production of nature.

10. For this cause also a woman ought to be veiled in the public assemblies, because of the angels - Who attend there, and before whom they should be careful not to do anything indecent or irregular.

11. Nevertheless in the Lord Jesus, there is neither male nor female - Neither is excluded; neither is preferred before the other in his kingdom.

12. And as the woman was at first taken out of the man, so also the man is now, in the ordinary course of nature, by the woman; but all things are of God - The man, the woman, and their dependence on each other.

13. Judge of yourselves - For what need of more arguments if so plain a case? Is it decent for a woman to pray to God - The Most High, with that bold and undaunted air which she must have, when, contrary to universal custom, she appears in public with her head uncovered?

14. For a man to have long hair, carefully adjusted, is such a mark of effeminacy as is a disgrace to him.

15. Given her - Originally, before the arts of dress were in being.

16. We have no such custom here, nor any of the other churches of God - The several churches that were in the apostles' time had different customs in things that were not essential; and that under one and the same apostle, as circumstances, in different places, made it convenient. And in all things merely indifferent the custom of each place was of sufficient weight to determine prudent and peaceable men. Yet even this cannot overrule a scrupulous conscience, which really doubts whether the thing be indifferent or no. But those who are referred to here by the apostle were contentious, not conscientious, persons.

18. In the church - In the public assembly. I hear there are schisms among you; and I partly believe it - That is, I believe it of some of you. It is plain that by schisms is not meant any separation from the church, but uncharitable divisions in it; for the Corinthians continued to be one church; and, notwithstanding all their strife and contention, there was no separation of any one party from the rest, with regard to external communion. And it is in the same sense that the word is used, chap. i, 10; chap. xii, 25; which are the only places in the New Testament, beside this, where church schisms are mentioned. Therefore, the indulging any temper contrary to this tender care of each other is the true

scriptural schism. This is, therefore, a quite different thing from that orderly separation from corrupt churches which later ages have stigmatized as schisms; and have made a pretense for the vilest cruelties, oppressions, and murders, that have troubled the Christian world. Both heresies and schisms are here mentioned in very near the same sense; unless by schisms be meant, rather, those inward animosities which occasion heresies; that is, outward divisions or parties: so that whilst one said, "I am of Paul," another, "I am of Apollos," this implied both schism and heresy. So wonderfully have later ages distorted the words heresy and schism from their scriptural meaning. Heresy is not, in all the Bible, taken for "an error in fundamentals," or in anything else; nor schism, for any separation made from the outward communion of others. Therefore, both heresy and schism, in the modern sense of the words, are sins that the scripture knows nothing of; but were invented merely to deprive mankind of the benefit of private judgment, and liberty of conscience.

19. There must be heresies - Divisions. Among you - In the ordinary course of things; and God permits them, that it may appear who among you are, and who are not, upright of heart.

20. Therefore - That is, in consequence of those schisms. It is not eating the Lord's supper - That solemn memorial of his death; but quite another thing.

21. For in eating what ye call the Lord's supper, instead of all partaking of one bread, each person brings his own supper, and eats it without staying for the rest. And hereby the poor, who cannot provide for themselves, have nothing; while the rich eat and drink to the full just as the heathens use to do at the feasts on their sacrifices.

22. Have ye not houses to eat and drink your common meals in? or do ye despise the church of God - Of which the poor are both the larger and the better part. Do ye act thus in designed contempt of them?

23. I received - By an immediate Revelation.

24. This is my body, which is broken for you - That is, this broken bread is the sign of my body, which is even now to be pierced and wounded for your iniquities. Take then, and eat of, this bread, in an humble, thankful, obediential remembrance of my dying love; of the extremity of my sufferings on your behalf, of the blessings I have thereby procured for you, and of the obligations to love and duty which I have by all this laid upon you.

25. After supper - Therefore ye ought not to confound this with a common meal. Do this in remembrance of me - The ancient sacrifices were in remembrance of sin: this sacrifice, once offered, is still represented in remembrance of the remission of sins.

26. Ye show forth the Lord's death - Ye proclaim, as it were, and openly avow it to God, and to all the world. Till he come - In glory.

27. Whosoever shall eat this bread unworthily - That is, in an unworthy, irreverent manner; without regarding either Him that appointed it, or the design of its appointment. Shall be guilty of profaning that which represents the body and blood of the Lord.

28. But let a man examine himself - Whether he know the nature and the design of the institution, and whether it be his own desire and purpose throughly to comply therewith.

29. For he that eateth and drinketh so unworthily as those Corinthians did, eateth and drinketh judgment to himself - Temporal judgments of various kinds, ver. 30. Not distinguishing the sacred tokens of the Lord's body - From his common food.

30. For this cause - Which they had not observed. Many sleep - In death.

31. If we would judge ourselves - As to our knowledge, and the design with which we approach the Lord's table. We should not be thus judged - That is, punished by God.

32. When we are thus judged, it is with this merciful design, that we may not be finally condemned with the world.

33. The rest - The other circumstances relating to the Lord's supper.

XII

1. Now concerning spiritual gifts - The abundance of these in the churches of Greece strongly refuted the idle learning of the Greek philosophers. But the Corinthians did not use them wisely, which occasioned St. Paul's writing concerning them. He describes,
   1. The unity of the body, ver. 1-xxvii,
   2. The variety of members and offices, ver. 27-30,
   3. The way of exercising gifts rightly, namely, by love, ver. 31, chap. xiii, 1. throughout: and adds,
   4. A comparison of several gifts with each other, in the chap. xiv, 1. fourteenth chapter.

2. Ye were heathens - Therefore, whatever gifts ye have received, it is from the free grace of God. Carried away - By a blind credulity. After dumb idols - The blind to the dumb; idols of wood and stone, unable to speak themselves, and much more to open your mouths, as God has done. As ye were led - By the subtlety of your priests.

3. Therefore - Since the heathen idols cannot speak themselves, much less give spiritual gifts to

others, these must necessarily be among Christians only. As no one speaking by the Spirit of God calleth Jesus accursed - That is, as none who does this, (which all the Jews and heathens did,) speaketh by the Spirit of God - Is actuated by that Spirit, so as to speak with tongues, heal diseases, or cast out devils. So no one can say, Jesus is the Lord - None can receive him as such; for, in the scripture language, to say, or to believe, implies an experimental assurance. But by the Holy Ghost - The sum is, None have the Holy Spirit but Christians: all Christians have this Spirit.

4. There are diversities of gifts, but the same Spirit - Divers streams, but all from one fountain. This verse speaks of the Holy Ghost, the next of Christ, the sixth of God the Father. The apostle treats of the Spirit, ver. 7, &c.; of Christ, ver. 12, &c.; of God, ver. 28, &c.

5. Administrations - Offices. But the same Lord appoints them all.

6. Operations - Effects produced. This word is of a larger extent than either of the former. But it is the same God who worketh all these effects in all the persons concerned.

7. The manifestation - The gift whereby the Spirit manifests itself. Is given to each - For the profit of the whole body.

8. The word of wisdom - A power of understanding and explaining the manifold wisdom of God in the grand scheme of gospel salvation. The word of knowledge - Perhaps an extraordinary ability to understand and explain the Old Testament types and prophecies.

9. Faith may here mean an extraordinary trust in God under the most difficult or dangerous circumstances. The gift of healing need not be wholly confined to the healing diseases with a word or a touch. It may exert itself also, though in a lower degree, where natural remedies are applied; and it may often be this, not superior skill, which makes some physicians more successful than others. And thus it may be with regard to other gifts likewise. As, after the golden shields were lost, the king of Judah put brazen in their place, so, after the pure gifts were lost, the power of God exerts itself in a more covert manner, under human studies and helps; and that the more plentifully, according as there is the more room given for it.

10. The working of other miracles. Prophecy - Foretelling things to come. The discerning - Whether men be of an upright spirit or no; whether they have natural or supernatural gifts for offices in the church; and whether they who profess to speak by inspiration speak from a divine, a natural, or a diabolical spirit.

11. As he willeth - The Greek word does not so much imply arbitrary pleasure, as a determination founded on wise counsel.

12. So is Christ - That is, the body of Christ, the church.

13. For by that one Spirit, which we received in baptism, we are all united in one body. Whether Jews or gentiles - Who are at the greatest distance from each other by nature. Whether slaves or freemen - Who are at the greatest distance by law and custom. We have all drank of one Spirit - In that cup, received by faith, we all imbibed one Spirit, who first inspired, and still preserves, the life of God in our souls.

15. The foot is elegantly introduced as speaking of the hand; the ear, of the eye; each, of a part that has some resemblance to it. So among men each is apt to compare himself with those whose gifts some way resemble his own, rather than with those who are at a distance, either above or beneath him. Is it therefore not of the body - Is the inference good? Perhaps the foot may represent private Christians; the hand, officers in the church; the eye, teachers; the ear, hearers.

16. The ear - A less noble part. The eye - The most noble.

18. As it hath pleased him - With the most exquisite wisdom and goodness.

20. But one body - And it is a necessary consequence of this unity, that the several members need one another.

21. Nor the head - The highest part of all. To the foot - The very lowest.

22. The members which appear to be weaker - Being of a more delicate and tender structure; perhaps the brains and bowels, or the veins, arteries, and other minute channels in the body.

23. We surround with more abundant honour - By so carefully covering them. More abundant comeliness - By the help of dress.

24. Giving more abundant honour to that which lacked - As being cared for and served by the noblest parts.

27. Now ye - Corinthians. Are the body and members of Christ - part of them, I mean, not the whole body.

28. First apostles - Who plant the gospel in the heathen nations. Secondly prophets - Who either foretel things to come, or speak by extra-ordinary inspiration, for the edification of the church. Thirdly teachers - Who precede even those that work miracles. Under prophets and teachers are comprised evangelists and pastors, Eph. iv, 11. Helps, governments - It does not appear that these mean distinct offices: rather, any persons might be called helps, from a peculiar dexterity in helping the distressed; and governments, from a peculiar talent for governing or presiding in assemblies.

31. Ye covet earnestly the best gifts - And they are worth your pursuit, though but few of you can

attain them. But there is a far more excellent gift than all these; and one which all may, yea, must attain or perish.

XIII

The necessity of love is shown, ver. 1-3. The nature and properties, ver. 4-7. The duration of it, ver. 8-13 Verse

1. Though I speak with all the tongues - Which are upon earth, and with the eloquence of an angel. And have not love - The love of God, and of all mankind for his sake, I am no better before God than the sounding instruments of brass, used in the worship of some of the heathen gods. Or a tinkling cymbal - This was made of two pieces of hollow brass, which, being struck together, made a tinkling, but very little variety of sound.

2. And though I have the gift of prophecy - Of foretelling future events. And understand all the mysteries - Both of God's word and providence. And all knowledge - Of things divine and human, that ever any mortal attained to. And though I have the highest degree of miracle working faith, and have not this love, I am nothing.

3. And though I - Deliberately, piece by piece. Give all my goods to feed the poor, yea, though I deliver up my body to be burned - Rather than I would renounce my religion. And have not the love - Hereafter described. It profiteth me nothing - Without this, whatever I speak, whatever I have, whatever I know, whatever I do, whatever I suffer, is nothing.

4. The love of God, and of our neighbour for God's sake, is patient toward, all men. It, suffers all the weakness, ignorance, errors, and infirmities of the children of God; all the malice and wickedness of the children of the world: and all this, not only for a time, but to the end. And in every step toward overcoming evil with good, it is kind, soft, mild, benign. It inspires the sufferer at once with the most amiable sweetness, and the most fervent and tender affection. Love acteth not rashly - Does not hastily condemn any one; never passes a severe sentence on a slight or sudden view of things. Nor does it ever act or behave in a violent, headstrong, or precipitate manner. Is not puffed up - Yea, humbles the soul to the dust.

5. It doth not behave indecently - Is not rude, or willingly offensive, to any. It renders to all their due - Suitable to time, person, and all other circumstances. Seeketh not her own - Ease, pleasure, honour, or temporal advantage. Nay, sometimes the lover of mankind seeketh not, in some sense, even his own spiritual advantage; does not think of himself, so long as a zeal for the glory of God and the souls of men swallows him up. But, though he is all on fire for these ends, yet he is not provoked to sharpness or unkindness toward any one. Outward provocations indeed will frequently occur; but he triumphs over all. Love thinketh no evil - Indeed it cannot but see and hear evil things, and know that they are so; but it does not willingly think evil of any; neither infer evil where it does not appear. It tears up, root and branch, all imagining of what we have not proof. It casts out all jealousies, all evil surmises, all readiness to believe evil.

6. Rejoiceth not in iniquity - Yea, weeps at either the sin or folly of even an enemy; takes no pleasure in hearing or in repeating it, but desires it may be forgotten forever. But rejoiceth in the truth - Bringing forth its proper fruit, holiness of heart and life. Good in general is its glory and joy, wherever diffused in all the world.

7. Love covereth all things - Whatever evil the lover of mankind sees, hears, or knows of any one, he mentions it to none; it never goes out of his lips, unless where absolute duty constrains to speak. Believeth all things - Puts the most favourable construction on everything, and is ever ready to believe whatever may tend to the advantage of any one character. And when it can no longer believe well, it hopes whatever may excuse or extenuate the fault which cannot be denied. Where it cannot even excuse, it hopes God will at length give repentance unto life. Meantime it endureth all things - Whatever the injustice, the malice, the cruelty of men can inflict. He can not only do, but likewise suffer, all things, through Christ who strengtheneth him.

8. Love never faileth - It accompanies to, and adorns us in, eternity; it prepares us for, and constitutes, heaven. But whether there be prophecies, they shall fail - When all things are fulfilled, and God is all in all. Whether there be tongues, they shall cease - One language shall prevail among all the inhabitants of heaven, and the low and imperfect languages of earth be forgotten. The knowledge likewise which we now so eagerly pursue, shall then vanish away - As starlight is lost in that of the midday sun, so our present knowledge in the light of eternity.

9. For we know in part, and we prophesy in part - The wisest of men have here but short, narrow, imperfect conceptions, even of the things round about them, and much more of the deep things of God. And even the prophecies which men deliver from God are far from taking in the whole of future events, or of that wisdom and knowledge of God which is treasured up in the scripture Revelation.

10. But when that which is perfect is come - At death and in the last day. That which is in part shall vanish away - Both that poor, low, imperfect, glimmering light, which is all the knowledge we

now can attain to; and these slow and unsatisfactory methods of attaining, as well as of imparting it to others.

11. In our present state we are mere infants in point of knowledge, compared to what we shall be hereafter. I put away childish things - Of my own accord, willingly, without trouble.

12. Now we see - Even the things that surround us. But by means of a glass - Or mirror, which reflects only their imperfect forms, in a dim, faint, obscure manner; so that our thoughts about them are puzzling and intricate, and everything is a kind of riddle us. But then - We shall see, not a faint reflection, but the objects themselves. Face to face - Distinctly. Now I know in part - Even when God himself reveals things to me, great part of them is still kept under the veil. But then I shall know even as also I am known - In a clear, full, comprehensive manner; in some measure like God, who penetrates the center of every object, and sees at one glance through my soul and all things.

13. Faith, hope, love - Are the sum of perfection on earth; love alone is the sum of perfection in heaven.

XIV

1. Follow after love - With zeal, vigour, courage, patience; else you can neither attain nor keep it. And - In their place, as subservient to this. Desire spiritual gifts; but especially that ye may prophesy - The word here does not mean foretelling things to come; but rather opening and applying the scripture.

2. He that speaketh in an unknown tongue speaks, in effect, not to men, but to God - Who alone understands him.

4. Edifieth himself - Only, on the most favourable supposition. The church - The whole congregation.

5. Greater - That is, more useful. By this alone are we to estimate all our gifts and talents.

6. Revelation - Of some gospel mystery. Knowledge - Explaining the ancient types and prophecies. Prophecy - Foretelling some future event. Doctrine - To regulate your tempers and lives. Perhaps this may be the sense of these obscure words.

7. How shall it be known what is piped or harped - What music can be made, or what end answered?

8. Who will prepare himself for the battle - Unless he understand what the trumpet sounds? suppose a retreat or a march.

9. Unless ye utter by the tongue - Which is miraculously given you. Words easy to be understood - By your hearers. Ye will speak to the air - A proverbial expression. Will utterly lose your labour.

11. I shall be a barbarian to him - Shall seem to talk unintelligible gibberish.

13. That he may be able to interpret - Which was a distinct gift.

14. If I pray in an unknown tongue - The apostle, as he did at ver. 6, transfers it to himself. My spirit prayeth - By the power of the Spirit I understand the words myself. But my understanding is unfruitful - The knowledge I have is no benefit to others.

15. I will pray with the spirit, but I will pray with the understanding also - I will use my own understanding, as well as the power of the Spirit. I will not act so absurdly, as to utter in a congregation what can edify none but myself.

16. Otherwise how shall he that filleth the place of a private person - That is, any private hearer. Say Amen - Assenting and confirming your words, as it was even then usual for the whole congregation to do.

19. With my understanding - In a rational manner; so as not only to understand myself, but to be understood by others.

20. Be not children in understanding - This is an admirable stroke of true oratory! to bring down the height of their spirits, by representing that wherein they prided themselves most, as mere folly and childishness. In wickedness be ye infants - Have all the innocence of that tender age. But in understanding be ye grown men - Knowing religion was not designed to destroy any of our natural faculties, but to exalt and improve them, our reason in particular.

21. It is written in the Law - The word here, as frequently, means the Old Testament. In foreign tongues will I speak to this people - And so he did. He spake terribly to them by the Babylonians, when they had set at nought what he had spoken by the prophets, who used their own language. These words received a farther accomplishment on the day of pentecost. Isaiah xxviii, 11.

22. Tongues are intended for a sign to unbelievers - To engage their attention, and convince them the message is of God. Whereas prophecy is not so much for unbelievers, as for the confirmation of them that already believe.

23. Yet - Sometimes prophecy is of more use, even to unbelievers, than speaking with tongues. For instance: If the whole church be met together - On some extraordinary occasion. It is probable, in so large a city, they ordinarily met in several places. And there come in ignorant persons - Men of learning might have understood the tongues in which they spoke. It is observable, St. Paul says here, ignorant

persons or unbelievers; but in the next verse, an unbeliever or an ignorant person. Several bad men met together hinder each other by evil discourse. Single persons are more easily gained.

24. He is convicted by all - who speak in their turns, and speak to the heart of the hearers. He is judged by all - Everyone says something to which his conscience bears witness.

25. The secrets of his heart are made manifest - Laid open, clearly described; in a manner which to him is most astonishing and utterly unaccountable. How many instances of it are seen at this day! So does God still point his word.

26. What a thing is it, brethren -- this was another disorder among them. Everyone hath a psalm - That is, at the same time one begins to sing a psalm; another to deliver a doctrine; another to speak in an unknown tongue; another to declare what has been revealed to him; another to interpret what the former is speaking; every one probably gathering a little company about him, just as they did in the schools of the philosophers. Let all be done to edification - So as to profit the hearers.

27. By two or three at most - Let not above two or three speak at one meeting. And that by course - That is, one after another. And let one interpret - Either himself, ver. 13; or, if he have not the gift, some other, into the vulgar tongue. It seems, the gift of tongues was an instantaneous knowledge of a tongue till then unknown, which he that received it could afterwards speak when he thought fit, without any new miracle.

28. Let him speak - That tongue, if he find it profitable to himself in his private devotions.

29. Let two or three of the prophets - Not more, at one meeting. Speak - One after another, expounding the scripture.

31. All - Who have that gift. That all may learn - Both by speaking and by hearing.

32. For the spirits of the prophets are subject to the prophets - But what enthusiast considers this? The impulses of the Holy Spirit, even in men really inspired, so suit themselves to their rational faculties, as not to divest them of the government of themselves, like the heathen priests under their diabolical possession. Evil spirits threw their prophets into such ungovernable ecstasies, as forced them to speak and act like madmen. But the Spirit of God left his prophets the clear use of their judgment, when, and how long, it was fit for them to speak, and never hurried them into any improprieties either as to the matter, manner, or time of their speaking.

34. Let your women be silent in the churches - Unless they are under an extraordinary impulse of the Spirit. For, in other cases, it is not permitted them to speak - By way of teaching in public assemblies. But to be in subjection - To the man whose proper office it is to lead and to instruct the congregation. Gen. iii, 16.

35. And even if they desire to learn anything - Still they are not to speak in public, but to ask their own husbands at home - That is the place, and those the persons to inquire of.

36. Are ye of Corinth either the first or the only Christians? If not, conform herein to the custom of all the churches.

37. Or spiritual - Endowed with any extraordinary gift of the Spirit. Let him - Prove it, by acknowledging that I now write by the Spirit.

38. Let him be ignorant - Be it at his own peril.

39. Therefore - To sum up the whole.

40. Decently - By every individual. In order - By the whole church.

XV

2. Ye are saved, if ye hold fast - Your salvation is begun, and will be perfected, if ye continue in the faith. Unless ye have believed in vain - Unless indeed your faith was only a delusion.

3. I received - From Christ himself. It was not a fiction of my own. Isaiah liii, 8, 9.

4. According to the scriptures - He proves it first from scripture, then from the testimony of a cloud of witnesses. Psalm xvi, 10.

5. By the twelve - This was their standing appellation; but their full number was not then present.

6. Above five hundred - Probably in Galilee. A glorious and incontestable proof! The greater part remain - Alive.

7. Then by all the apostles - The twelve were mentioned ver. 5. This title here, therefore, seems to include the seventy; if not all those, likewise, whom God afterwards sent to plant the gospel in heathen nations.

8. An untimely birth - It was impossible to abase himself more than he does by this single appellation. As an abortion is not worthy the name of a man, so he affirms himself to be not worthy the name of an apostle.

9. I persecuted the church - True believers are humbled all their lives, even for the sins they committed before they believed.

10. I laboured more than they all - That is, more than any of them, from a deep sense of the peculiar love God had shown me. Yet, to speak more properly, it is not I, but the grace of God that is

with me - This it is which at first qualified me for the work, and still excites me to zeal and diligence in it.

11. Whether I or they, so we preach - All of us speak the same thing.

12. How say some - Who probably had been heathen philosophers.

13. If there be no resurrection - If it be a thing flatly impossible.

14. Then is our preaching - From a commission supposed to be given after the resurrection. Vain - Without any real foundation.

15. If the dead rise not - If the very notion of a resurrection be, as they say, absurd and impossible.

17. Ye are still in your sins - That is, under the guilt of them. So that there needed something more than reformation, (which was plainly wrought,) in order to their being delivered from the guilt of sin even that atonement, the sufficiency of which God attested by raising our great Surety from the grave.

18. They who sleep in Christ - Who have died for him, or believing in him. Are perished - Have lost their life and being together.

19. If in this life only we have hope - If we look for nothing beyond the grave. But if we have a divine evidence of things not seen, if we have "a hope full of immortality," if we now taste of "the powers of the world to come," and see "the crown that fadeth not away," then, notwithstanding all our present trials, we are more happy than all men.

20. But now - St. Paul declares that Christians "have hope," not "in this life only." His proof of the resurrection lies in a narrow compass, ver. 12-19. Almost all the rest of the chapter is taken up in illustrating, vindicating, and applying it. The proof is short, but solid and convincing, that which arose from Christ's resurrection. Now this not only proved a resurrection possible, but, as it proved him to be a divine teacher, proved the certainty of a general resurrection, which he so expressly taught. The first fruit of them that slept - The earnest, pledge, and insurance of their resurrection who slept in him: even of all the righteous. It is of the resurrection of these, and these only, that the apostle speaks throughout the chapter.

22. As through Adam all, even the righteous, die, so through Christ all these shall be made alive - He does not say, "shall revive," (as naturally as they die,) but shall be made alive, by a power not their own.

23. Afterward - The whole harvest. At the same time the wicked shall rise also. But they are not here taken into the account.

24. Then - After the resurrection and the general judgment. Cometh the end - Of the world; the grand period of all those wonderful scenes that have appeared for so many succeeding generations. When he shall have delivered up the kingdom to the Father, and he (the Father) shall have abolished all adverse rule, authority, and power - Not that the Father will then begin to reign without the Son, nor will the Son then cease to reign. For the divine reign both of the Father and Son is from everlasting to everlasting. But this is spoken of the Son's mediatorial kingdom, which will then be delivered up, and of the immediate kingdom or reign of the Father, which will then commence. Till then the Son transacts the business which the Father hath given him, for those who are his, and by them as well as by the angels, with the Father, and against their enemies. So far as the Father gave the kingdom to the Son, the Son shall deliver it up to the Father, John xiii, 3. Nor does the Father cease to reign, when he gives it to the Son; neither the Son, when he delivers it to the Father: but the glory which he had before the world began, John xvii, 5; Heb. i, 8, will remain even after this is delivered up. Nor will he cease to be a king even in his human nature, Luke i, 33. If the citizens of the new Jerusalem" shall reign for ever," Rev. xxii, 5, how much more shall he?

25. He must reign - Because so it is written. Till he - the Father hath put all his enemies under his feet. Psalm cx, 1.

26. The last enemy that is destroyed is death - Namely, after Satan, Heb. ii, 14, and sin, ver. 56, are destroyed. In the same order they prevailed. Satan brought in sin, and sin brought forth death. And Christ, when he of old engaged with these enemies, first conquered Satan, then sin, in his death; and, lastly, death, in his resurrection. In the same order he delivers all the faithful from them, yea, and destroys these enemies themselves. Death he so destroys that it shall be no more; sin and Satan, so that they shall no more hurt his people.

27. Under him - Under the Son. Psalm viii, 6, 7

28. The Son also shall be subject - Shall deliver up the mediatorial kingdom. That the three-one God may be all in all - All things, (consequently all persons,) without any interruption, without the intervention of any creature, without the opposition of any enemy, shall be subordinate to God. All shall say, "My God, and my all." This is the end. Even an inspired apostle can see nothing beyond this.

29. Who are baptized for the dead - Perhaps baptized in hope of blessings to be received after they are numbered with the dead. Or, "baptized in the room of the dead" - Of them that are just fallen in the cause of Christ: like soldiers who advance in the room of their companions that fell just before their face.

30. Why are we - The apostles. Also in danger every hour - It is plain we can expect no amends in

this life.

31. I protest by your rejoicing, which I have - Which love makes my own. I die daily - I am daily in the very jaws of death. Beside that I live, as it were, in a daily martyrdom.

32. If to speak after the manner of men - That is, to use a proverbial phrase, expressive of the most imminent danger I have fought with wild beasts at Ephesus - With the savage fury of a lawless multitude, Acts xix, 29, &c. This seems to have been but just before. Let us eat, &c. - We might, on that supposition, as well say, with the Epicureans, Let us make the best of this short life, seeing we have no other portion.

33. Be not deceived - By such pernicious counsels as this. Evil communications corrupt good manners - He opposes to the Epicurean saying, a well - known verse of the poet Menander. Evil communications - Discourse contrary to faith, hope, or love, naturally tends to destroy all holiness.

34. Awake - An exclamation full of apostolical majesty. Shake off your lethargy! To righteousness - Which flows from the true knowledge of God, and implies that your whole soul be broad awake. And sin not - That is, and ye will not sin. Sin supposes drowsiness of soul. There is need to press this. For some among you have not the knowledge of God - With all their boasted knowledge, they are totally ignorant of what it most concerns them to know. I speak this to your shame - For nothing is more shameful, than sleepy ignorance of God, and of the word and works of God; in these especially, considering the advantages they had enjoyed.

35. But some one possibly will say, How are the dead raised up, after their whole frame is dissolved? And with what kind of bodies do they come again, after these are mouldered into dust?

36. To the inquiry concerning the manner of rising, and the quality of the bodies that rise, the Apostle answers first by a similitude, ver. 36-42, and then plainly and directly, ver. 42, 43. That which thou sowest, is not quickened into new life and verdure, except it die - Undergo a dissolution of its parts, a change analogous to death. Thus St. Paul inverts the objection; as if he had said, Death is so far from hindering life, that it necessarily goes before it.

37. Thou sowest not the body that shall be - Produced from the seed committed to the ground, but a bare, naked grain, widely different from that which will afterward rise out of the earth.

38. But God - Not thou, O man, not the grain itself, giveth it a body as it hath pleased him, from the time he distinguished the various Species of beings; and to each of the seeds, not only of the fruits, but animals also, (to which the Apostle rises in the following verse,) its own body; not only peculiar to that species, but proper to that individual, and arising out of the substance of that very grain.

39. All flesh - As if he had said, Even earthy bodies differ from earthy, and heavenly bodies from heavenly. What wonder then, if heavenly bodies differ from earthy? or the bodies which rise from those that lay in the grave?

40. There are also heavenly bodies - As the sun, moon, and stars; and there are earthy - as vegetables and animals. But the brightest lustre which the latter can have is widely different from that of the former.

41. Yea, and the heavenly bodies themselves differ from each other.

42. So also is the resurrection of the dead - So great is the difference between the body which fell, and that which rises. It is sown - A beautiful word; committed, as seed, to the ground. In corruption - Just ready to putrefy, and, by various degrees of corruption and decay, to return to the dust from whence it came. It is raised in incorruption - Utterly incapable of either dissolution or decay.

43. It is sown in dishonour - Shocking to those who loved it best, human nature in disgrace! It is raised in glory - Clothed with robes of light, fit for those whom the King of heaven delights to honour. It is sown in weakness - Deprived even of that feeble strength which it once enjoyed. It is raised in power - Endued with vigour, strength, and activity, such as we cannot now conceive.

44. It is sown in this world a merely animal body - Maintained by food, sleep, and air, like the bodies of brutes: but it is raised of a more refined contexture, needing none of these animal refreshments, and endued with qualities of a spiritual nature, like the angels of God.

45. The first Adam was made a living soul - God gave him such life as other animals enjoy: but the last Adam, Christ, is a quickening spirit - As he hath life in himself, so he quickeneth whom he will; giving a more refined life to their very bodies at the resurrection. Gen. ii, 7

47. The first man was from the earth, earthy; the second man is the Lord from heaven-The first man, being from the earth, is subject to corruption and dissolution, like the earth from which he came. The second man - St. Paul could not so well say, "Is from heaven, heavenly:" because, though man owes it to the earth that he is earthy, yet the Lord does not owe his glory to heaven. He himself made the heavens, and by descending from thence showed himself to us as the Lord. Christ was not the second man in order of time; but in this respect, that as Adam was a public person, who acted in the stead of all mankind, so was Christ. As Adam was the first general representative of men, Christ was the second and the last. And what they severally did, terminated not in themselves, but affected all whom they represented.

48. They that are earthy - Who continue without any higher principle. They that are heavenly -

Who receive a divine principle from heaven.

49. The image of the heavenly - Holiness and glory.

50. But first we must be entirely changed; for such flesh and blood as we are clothed with now, cannot enter into that kingdom which is wholly spiritual: neither doth this corruptible body inherit that incorruptible kingdom.

51. A mystery - A truth hitherto unknown; and not yet fully known to any of the sons of men. We - Christians. The Apostle considers them all as one, in their succeeding generations. Shall not all die - Suffer a separation of soul and body. But we shall all - Who do not die, be changed - So that this animal body shall become spiritual.

52. In a moment - Amazing work of omnipotence! And cannot the same power now change us into saints in a moment? The trumpet shall sound - To awaken all that sleep in the dust of the earth.

54. Death is swallowed up in victory - That is, totally conquered, abolished forever.

55. O death, where is thy sting? - Which once was full of hellish poison. O hades, the receptacle of separate souls, where is thy victory - Thou art now robbed of all thy spoils; all thy captives are set at liberty. Hades literally means the invisible world, and relates to the soul; death, to the body. The Greek words are found in the Septuagint translation of Hosea xiii, 14. Isaiah xxv, 8

56. The sting of death is sin - Without which it could have no power. But this sting none can resist by his own strength. And the strength of sin is the law - As is largely declared, Rom. vii, 7, &c.

57. But thanks be to God, who hath given us the victory - Over sin, death, and hades.

58. Be ye steadfast - In yourselves. Unmovable - By others; continually increasing in the work of faith and labour of love. Knowing your labour is not in vain in the Lord - Whatever ye do for his sake shall have its full reward in that day. Let us also endeavour, by cultivating holiness in all its branches, to maintain this hope in its full energy; longing for that glorious day, when, in the utmost extent of the expression, death shall be swallowed up forever, and millions of voices, after the long silence of the grave, shall burst out at once into that triumphant song, O death, where is thy sting? O hades, where is thy victory?

XVI

1. The saints - A more solemn and a more affecting word, than if he had said, the poor.

2. Let every one - Not the rich only: let him also that hath little, gladly give of that little. According as he hath been prospered - Increasing his alms as God increases his substance. According to this lowest rule of Christian prudence, if a man when he has or gains one pound give a tenth to God, when he has or gains an hundred he will give the tenth of this also. And yet I show unto you a more excellent way. He that hath ears to hear, let him hear. Stint yourself to no proportion at all. But lend to God all you can.

4. They shall go with me - To remove any possible suspicion.

5. I pass through Macedonia - I purpose going that way.

7. I will not see you now - Not till I have been in Macedonia.

8. I will stay at Ephesus - Where he was at this time.

9. A great door - As to the number of hearers. And effectual - As to the effects wrought upon them. And there are many adversaries - As there must always be where Satan's kingdom shakes. This was another reason for his staying there.

10. Without fear - Of any one's despising him for his youth. For he worketh the work of the Lord - The true ground of reverence to pastors. Those who do so, none ought to despise.

11. I look for him with the brethren -- that accompany him.

12. I besought him much - To come to you. With the brethren - Who were then going to Corinth. Yet he was by no means willing to come now - Perhaps lest his coming should increase the divisions among them.

13. To conclude. Watch ye - Against all your seen and unseen enemies. Stand fast in the faith - Seeing and trusting him that is invisible. Acquit yourselves like men - With courage and patience. Be strong - To do and suffer all his will.

15. The first fruits of Achaia - The first converts in that province.

16. That ye also - In your turn. Submit to such - So repaying their free service. And to every one that worketh with us and laboureth - That labours in the gospel either with or without a fellow- labourer.

17. I rejoice at the coming of Stephanas, and Fortunatus, and Achaiacus - Who were now returned to Corinth but the joy which their arrival had occasioned remained still in his heart. They have supplied what was wanting on your part - They have performed the offices of love, which you could not, by reason of your absence.

18. For they have refreshed my spirit and yours - Inasmuch as you share in my comfort. Such therefore acknowledge - With suitable love and respect.

19. Aquila and Priscilla had formerly made some abode at Corinth, and there St. Paul's

acquaintance with them began, Acts xviii, 1, 2.

21. *With my own hand* - What precedes having been written by an amanuensis.

22. *If any man love not the Lord Jesus Christ* - If any be an enemy to his person, offices, doctrines, or commands. *Let him be Anathema. Maran-atha*-Anathema signifies a thing devoted to destruction. It seems to have been customary with the Jews of that age, when they had pronounced any man an Anathema, to add the Syriac expression, Maran-atha, that is, "The Lord cometh;" namely, to execute vengeance upon him. This weighty sentence the apostle chose to write with his own hand; and to insert it between his salutation and solemn benediction, that it might be the more attentively regarded.

NOTES ON ST. PAUL'S SECOND EPISTLE TO THE CORINTHIANS

IN this epistle, written from Macedonia, within a year after the former, St. Paul beautifully displays his tender affection toward the Corinthians, who were greatly moved by the seasonable severity of the former, and repeats several of the admonitions he had there given them. In that he had written concerning the affairs of the Corinthians: in this he writes chiefly concerning his own; but in such a manner as to direct all he mentions of himself to their spiritual profit. The thread and connection of the whole epistle is historical: other things are interwoven only by way of digression. It contains,

I. The inscription, C. i. 1, 2

II. The treatise itself.
    1. In Asia I was greatly pressed; but God comforted me; as I acted uprightly; even in this, that I have not yet come to you; who ought to obey me, Cii. 11
    2. From Troas I hastened to Macedonia, spreading the gospel everywhere, the glorious charge of which I execute, according to its importance, Cvii. 1
    3. In Macedonia I received a joyful message concerning you, 2-16
    4. In this journey I had a proof of the liberality of the Macedonians, whose example ye ought to follow, C.viii.1-C.ix.15
    5. I am now on my way to you, armed with the power of Christ. Therefore obey, C.x 1-C.xiii.10 The conclusion 11-13

2nd CORINTHIANS

I

1. Timotheus our brother - St. Paul writing to Timotheus styled him his son; writing of him, his brother.

3. Blessed be the God and Father of our Lord Jesus Christ - A solemn and beautiful introduction, highly suitable to the apostolical spirit. The Father of mercies, and God of all comfort - Mercies are the fountain of comfort; comfort is the outward expression of mercy. God shows mercy in the affliction itself. He gives comfort both in and after the affliction. Therefore is he termed, the God of all comfort. Blessed be this God!

4. Who comforteth us in all our affliction, that we may be able to comfort them who are in any affliction - He that has experienced one kind of affliction is able to comfort others in that affliction. He that has experienced all kinds of affliction is able to comfort them in all.

5. For as the sufferings of Christ abound in us - The sufferings endured on his account. So our comfort also aboundeth through Christ - The sufferings were many, the comfort one; and yet not only equal to, but overbalancing, them all.

6. And whether we are afflicted, it is for your comfort and salvation - For your present comfort, your present and future salvation. Or whether we are comforted, it is for your comfort - That we may be the better able to comfort you. Which is effectual in the patient enduring the same sufferings which we also suffer - Through the efficacy of which you patiently endure the same kind of sufferings with us.

7. And our hope concerning you - Grounded on your patience in suffering for Christ's sake, is steadfast.

8. We would not have you ignorant, brethren, of the trouble which befell us in Asia - Probably the same which is described in the nineteenth chapter of the Acts. The Corinthians knew before that he had been in trouble: he now declares the greatness and the fruit of it. We were exceedingly pressed, above our strength - Above the ordinary strength even of an apostle.

9. Yea, we had the sentence of death in ourselves - We ourselves expected nothing but death.

10. We trust that he will still deliver - That we may at length be able to come to you.

Wesley's Notes on the Bible - The New Testament

11. **You likewise** - As well as other churches. **Helping with us by prayer, that for the gift** - Namely, my deliverance. **Bestowed upon us by means of many persons** - Praying for it, thanks may be given by many.

12. **For I am the more emboldened to look for this, because I am conscious of my integrity; seeing this is our rejoicing** - Even in the deepest adversity. **The testimony of our conscience** - Whatever others think of us. **That in simplicity** - Having one end in view, aiming singly at the glory of God. **And godly sincerity** - Without any tincture of guile, dissimulation, or disguise. **Not with carnal wisdom, but by the grace of God** - Not by natural, but divine, wisdom. **We have had our conversation in the world** - In the whole world; in every circumstance.

14. **Ye have acknowledged us in part** - Though not so fully as ye will do. **That we are your rejoicing** - That ye rejoice in having known us. **As ye also are ours** - As we also rejoice in the success of our labours among you; and we trust shall rejoice therein in the day of the Lord Jesus.

15. **In this confidence** - That is, being confident of this.

17. **Did I use levity** - Did I lightly change my purpose? **Do I purpose according to the flesh** - Are my purposes grounded on carnal or worldly considerations? **So that there should be with me yea and nay** - Sometimes one, sometimes the other; that is, variableness and inconstancy.

18. **Our word to you** - The whole tenor of our doctrine. **Hath not been yea and nay** - Wavering and uncertain.

19. **For Jesus Christ, who was preached by us** - That is, our preaching concerning him. **Was not yea and nay** - Was not variable and inconsistent with itself. **But was yea in him** - Always one and the same, centering in him.

20. **For all the promises of God are yea and amen in him** - Are surely established in and through him. They are yea with respect to God promising; amen, with respect to men believing; yea, with respect to the apostles; amen, with respect to their hearers.

21. **I say, to the glory of God** - For it is God alone that is able to fulfil these promises. **That establisheth us** - Apostles and teachers. **With you** - All true believers. In the faith of Christ; **and hath anointed us** - With the oil of gladness, with joy in the Holy Ghost, thereby giving us strength both to do and suffer his will.

22. **Who also hath sealed us** - Stamping his image on our hearts, thus marking and sealing us as his own property. **And given us the earnest of his Spirit** - There is a difference between an earnest and a pledge. A pledge is to be restored when the debt is paid; but an earnest is not taken away, but completed. Such an earnest is the Spirit. The first fruits of it we have Rom. viii, 23; and we wait for all the fulness.

23. **I call God for a record upon my soul** - Was not St. Paul now speaking by the Spirit? And can a more solemn oath be conceived? Who then can imagine that Christ ever designed to forbid all swearing? **That to spare you I came not yet to Corinth** - Lest I should be obliged to use severity. He says elegantly to Corinth, not to you, when be is intimating his power to punish.

24. **Not that we have dominion over your faith** - This is the prerogative of God alone. **But are helpers of your joy** - And faith from which it springs. **For by faith ye have stood** - To this day. We see the light in which ministers should always consider themselves, and in which they are to be considered by others. Not as having dominion over the faith of their people, and having a right to dictate by their own authority what they shall believe, or what they shall do; but as helpers of their joy, by helping them forward in faith and holiness. In this view, how amiable does their office appear! and how friendly to the happiness of mankind! How far, then, are they from true benevolence, who would expose it to ridicule and contempt!

II

1. **In grief** - Either on account of the particular offender, or of the church in general.

2. **For if I grieve you, who is he that cheereth me, but he that is grieved by me** - That is, I cannot be comforted myself till his grief is removed.

3. **And I wrote thus to you** - I wrote to you before in this determination, not to come to you in grief.

4. **From much anguish I wrote to you, not so much that ye might be grieved, as that ye might know by my faithful admonition my abundant love toward you.**

5. **He hath grieved me but in part** - Who still rejoice over the greater part of you. Otherwise I might burden you all.

6. **Sufficient for such an one** - With what a remarkable tenderness does St. Paul treat this offender! He never once mentions his name. Nor does he here so much as mention his crime. **By many** - Not only by the rulers of the church: the whole congregation acquiesced in the sentence.

10. **To whom ye forgive** - He makes no question of their complying with his direction. **Anything** - So mildly does he speak even of that heinous sin, after it was repented of. **In the person of Christ** - By

the authority wherewith he has invested me.

11. Lest Satan - To whom he had been delivered, and who sought to destroy not only his flesh, but his soul also. Get an advantage over us - For the loss of one soul is a common loss.

12. Now when I came to Troas - It seems, in that passage from Asia to Macedonia, of which a short account is given, Acts xx, 1, 2. Even though a door was opened to me - That is, there was free liberty to speak, and many were willing to hear: yet,

13. I had no rest in my spirit - From an earnest desire to know how my letter had been received. Because I did not find Titus - In his return from you. So I went forth into Macedonia - Where being much nearer, I might more easily be informed concerning you. The apostle resumes the thread of his discourse, chap. vii, 2, interposing an admirable digression concerning what he had done and suffered elsewhere, the profit of which he by this means derives to the Corinthians also; and as a prelude to his apology against the false apostles.

14. To triumph, implies not only victory, but an open manifestation of it. And as in triumphal processions, especially in the east, incense and perfumes were burned near the conqueror, the apostle beautifully alludes to this circumstance in the following verse: as likewise to the different effects which strong perfumes have upon different persons; some of whom they revive, while they throw others into the most violent disorders.

15. For we - The preachers of the gospel. Are to God a sweet odour of Christ - God is well-pleased with this perfume diffused by us, both in them that believe and are saved, treated of, chap. iii, 1; chap. iv, 2; and in them that obstinately disbelieve and, consequently, perish, treated of, chap. iv, 3-6.

16. And who is sufficient for these things - No man living, but by the power of God's Spirit.

17. For we are not as many, who adulterate the word of God - Like those vintners (so the Greek word implies) who mix their wines with baser liquors. But as of sincerity - Without any mixture. But as from God - This rises higher still; transmitting his pure word, not our own. In the sight of God - Whom we regard as always present, and noting every word of our tongue. Speak we - The tongue is ours, but the power is God's. In Christ - Words which he gives, approves, and blesses.

III

1. Do we begin again to recommend ourselves - Is it needful? Have I nothing but my own word to recommend me? St. Paul chiefly here intends himself; though not excluding Timotheus, Titus, and Silvanus. Unless we need - As if he had said, Do I indeed want such recommendation?

2. Ye are our recommendatory letter - More convincing than bare words could be. Written on our hearts - Deeply engraven there, and plainly legible to all around us.

3. Manifestly declared to be the letter of Christ - Which he has formed and published to the world. Ministered by us - Whom he has used herein as his instruments, therefore ye are our letter also. Written not in tables of stone - Like the ten commandments. But in the tender, living tables of their hearts - God having taken away the hearts of stone and given them hearts of flesh.

4. Such trust have we in God - That is, we trust in God that this is so.

5. Not that we are sufficient of ourselves - So much as to think one good thought; much less, to convert sinners.

6. Who also hath made us able ministers of the new covenant - Of the new, evangelical dispensation. Not of the law, fitly called the letter, from God's literally writing it on the two tables. But of the Spirit - Of the gospel dispensation, which is written on the tables of our hearts by the Spirit. For the letter - The law, the Mosaic dispensation. Killeth - Seals in death those who still cleave to it. But the Spirit - The gospel, conveying the Spirit to those who receive it. Giveth life - Both spiritual and eternal: yea, if we adhere to the literal sense even of the moral law, if we regard only the precept and the sanction as they stand in themselves, not as they lead us to Christ, they are doubtless a killing ordinance, and bind us down under the sentence of death.

7. And if the ministration of death - That is, the Mosaic dispensation, which proves such to those who prefer it to the gospel, the most considerable part of which was engraven on those two stones, was attended with so great glory.

8. The ministration of the Spirit - That is, the Christian dispensation.

9. The ministration of condemnation - Such the Mosaic dispensation proved to all the Jews who rejected the gospel whereas through the gospel (hence called the ministration of righteousness) God both imputed and imparted righteousness to all believers. But how can the moral law (which alone was engraven on stone) be the ministration of condemnation, if it requires no more than a sincere obedience, such as is proportioned to our infirm state? If this is sufficient to justify us, then the law ceases to be a ministration of condemnation. It becomes (flatly contrary to the apostle's doctrine) the ministration of righteousness.

10. It hath no glory in this respect, because of the glory that excelleth - That is, none in comparison of this more excellent glory. The greater light swallows up the less.

11. *That which remaineth* - That dispensation which remains to the end of the world; that spirit and life which remain forever.

12. *Having therefore this hope* - Being fully persuaded of this.

13. *And we do not act as Moses did, who put a veil over his face* - Which is to be understood with regard to his writings also. *So that the children of Israel could not look steadfastly to the end of that dispensation which is now abolished* - The end of this was Christ. The whole Mosaic dispensation tended to, and terminated in, him; but the Israelites had only a dim, wavering sight of him, of whom Moses spake in an obscure, covert manner.

14. *The same veil remaineth on their understanding unremoved* - Not so much as folded back, (so the word implies,) so as to admit a little, glimmering light. *On the public reading of the Old Testament* - The veil is not now on the face of Moses or of his writings, but on the reading of them, and on the heart of them that believe not. *Which is taken away in Christ* - That is, from the heart of them that truly believe on him.

16. *When it* - Their heart. *Shall turn to the Lord* - To Christ, by living faith. *The veil is taken away* - That very moment; and they see, with the utmost clearness, how all the types and prophecies of the law are fully accomplished in him.

17. *Now the Lord* - Christ is that Spirit of the law whereof I speak, to which the letter was intended to lead. *And where the Spirit of the Lord, Christ, is, there is liberty* - Not the veil, the emblem of slavery. There is liberty from servile fear, liberty from the guilt and from the power of sin, liberty to behold with open face the glory of the Lord.

18. *And, accordingly, all we that believe in him, beholding as in a glass* - In the mirror of the gospel. *The glory of the Lord* - His glorious love. *Are transformed into the same image* - Into the same love. *From one degree of this glory to another*, in a manner worthy of his almighty Spirit. What a beautiful contrast is here! Moses saw the glory of the Lord, and it rendered his face so bright, that he covered it with a veil; Israel not being able to bear the reflected light. We behold his glory in the glass of his word, and our faces shine too; yet we veil them not, but diffuse the lustre which is continually increasing, as we fix the eye of our mind more and more steadfastly on his glory displayed in the gospel.

IV

1. *Therefore having this ministry* - Spoken of, chap. iii, 6. *As we have received mercy* - Have been mercifully supported in all our trials. *We faint not* - We desist not in any degree from our glorious enterprise.

2. *But have renounced* - Set at open defiance. *The hidden things of shame* - All things which men need to hide, or to be ashamed of. *Not walking in craftiness* - Using no disguise, subtlety, guile. *Nor privily corrupting the pure word of God* - By any additions or alterations, or by attempting to accommodate it to the taste of the hearers.

3. *But if our gospel also* - As well as the law of Moses.

4. *The God of this world* - What a sublime and horrible description of Satan! He is indeed the God of all that believe not, and works in them with inconceivable energy. *Hath blinded* - Not only veiled, the eye of their understanding. *Illumination* - Is properly the reflection or propagation of light, from those who are already enlightened, to others. *Who is the image of God* - Hence also we may understand how great is the glory of Christ. He that sees the Son, sees the Father in the face of Christ. The Son exactly exhibits the Father to us.

5. *For* - The fault is not in us, neither in the doctrine they hear from us. *We preach not ourselves* - As able either to enlighten, or pardon, or sanctify you. *But Jesus Christ* - As your only wisdom, righteousness, sanctification. *And ourselves your servants* - Ready to do the meanest offices. *For Jesus' sake* - Not for honour, interest, or pleasure.

6. *For God hath shined in our hearts* - The hearts of all those whom the God of this world no longer blinds. God who is himself our light; not only the author of light, but also the fountain of it. *To enlighten us with the knowledge of the glory of God* - Of his glorious love, and of his glorious image. *In the face of Jesus Christ* - Which reflects his glory in another manner than the face of Moses did.

7. *But we* - Not only the apostles, but all true believers. *Have this treasure* - Of divine light, love, glory. *In earthen vessels* - In frail, feeble, perishing bodies. He proceeds to show, that afflictions, yea, death itself, are so far from hindering the ministration of the Spirit, that they even further it, sharpen the ministers, and increase the fruit. *That the excellence of the power*, which works these in us, *may undeniably appear to be of God*.

8. *We are troubled, &c.* - The four articles in this verse respect inward, the four in the next outward, afflictions. In each clause the former part shows the "earthen vessels;" the latter, "the excellence of the power." *Not crushed* - Not swallowed up in care and anxiety. *Perplexed* - What course to take, but never despairing of his power and love to carry us through.

10. Always - Wherever we go. Bearing about in the body the dying of the Lord Jesus - Continually expecting to lay down our lives like him. That the life also of Jesus might be manifested in our body - That we may also rise and be glorified like him.

11. For we who yet live - Who are not yet killed for the testimony of Jesus. Are always delivered unto death - Are perpetually in the very jaws of destruction; which we willingly submit to, that we may "obtain a better resurrection."

12. So then death worketh in us, but life in you - You live in peace; we die daily. Yet - Living or dying, so long as we believe, we cannot but speak.

13. Having the same spirit of faith - Which animated the saints of old; David, in particular, when he said, I believed, and therefore have I spoken - That is, I trusted in God, and therefore he hath put this song of praise in my mouth. We also speak - We preach the gospel, even in the midst of affliction and death, because we believe that God will raise us up from the dead, and will present us, ministers, with you, all his members, "faultless before his presence with exceeding joy." Psalm cxvi, 10.

15. For all things - Whether adverse or prosperous. Are for your sakes - For the profit of all that believe, as well as all that preach. That the overflowing grace - Which continues you alive both in soul and body. Might abound yet more through the thanksgiving of many - For thanksgiving invites more: abundant grace.

16. Therefore - Because of this grace, we faint not. The outward man - The body. The inward man - The soul.

17. Our light affliction - The beauty and sublimity of St. Paul's expressions here, as descriptive of heavenly glory, opposed to temporal afflictions, surpass all imagination, and cannot be preserved in any translation or paraphrase, which after all must sink infinitely below the astonishing original.

18. The things that are seen - Men, money, things of earth. The things that are not seen - God, grace, heaven.

V

1. Our earthly house - Which is only a tabernacle, or tent, not designed for a lasting habitation.

2. Desiring to be clothed upon - This body, which is now covered with flesh and blood, with the glorious house which is from heaven. Instead of flesh and blood, which cannot enter heaven, the rising body will be clothed or covered with what is analogous thereto, but incorruptible and immortal. Macarius speaks largely of this.

3. If being clothed - That is, with the image of God, while we are in the body. We shall not be found naked - Of the wedding garment.

4. We groan being burdened - The apostle speaks with exact propriety. A burden naturally expresses groans. And we are here burdened with numberless afflictions, infirmities, temptations. Not that we would be unclothed - Not that we desire to remain without a body. Faith does not understand that philosophical contempt of what the wise Creator has given. But clothed upon - With the glorious, immortal, incorruptible, spiritual body. That what is mortal - This present mortal body. May be swallowed up of life - Covered with that which lives forever.

5. Now he that hath wrought us to this very thing - This longing for immortality. Is God - For none but God, none less than the Almighty, could have wrought this in us.

6. Therefore we behave undauntedly - But most of all when we have death in view; knowing that our greatest happiness lies beyond the grave.

7. For we cannot clearly see him in this life, wherein we walk by faith only: an evidence, indeed, that necessarily implies a kind of "seeing him who is invisible;" yet as far beneath what we shall have in eternity, as it is above that of bare, unassisted reason.

8. Present with the Lord - This demonstrates that the happiness of the saints is not deferred till the resurrection.

9. Therefore we are ambitious - The only ambition which has place in a Christian. Whether present - In the body. Or absent - From it.

10. For we all - Apostles as well as other men, whether now present in the body, or absent from it. Must appear - Openly, without covering, where all hidden things will be revealed; probably the sins, even of the faithful, which were forgiven long before. For many of their good works, as their repentance, their revenge against sin, cannot other wise appear. But this will be done at their own desire, without grief, and without shame. According to what he hath done in the body, whether good or evil - In the body he did either good or evil; in the body he is recompensed accordingly.

11. Knowing therefore the terror of the Lord, we the more earnestly persuade men to seek his favour; and as God knoweth this, so, I trust, ye know it in your own consciences.

12. We do not say this, as if we thought there was any need of again recommending ourselves to you, but to give you an occasion of rejoicing and praising God, and to furnish you with an answer to those false apostles who glory in appearance, but not in heart, being condemned by their own

conscience.

13. For if we are transported beyond ourselves - Or at least, appear so to others, treated of, 2 Cor. v, 15-21, speaking or writing with uncommon vehemence. It is to God - He understands (if men do not) the emotion which himself inspires. If we be sober - Treated of, chap. vi, 1-10. If I proceed in a more calm, sedate manner. It is for your sakes - Even good men bear this, rather than the other method, in their teachers. But these must obey God, whoever is offended by it.

14. For the love of Christ - To us, and our love to him. Constraineth us - Both to the one and the other; beareth us on with such a strong, steady, prevailing influence, as winds and tides exert when they waft the vessel to its destined harbour. While we thus judge, that if Christ died for all, then are all, even the best of men, naturally dead - In a state of spiritual death, and liable to death eternal. For had any man been otherwise, Christ had not needed to have died for him.

15. And that he died for all - That all might be saved. That they who live - That all who live upon the earth. Should not henceforth - From the moment they know him. Live unto themselves - Seek their own honour, profit, pleasure. But unto him - In all righteousness and true holiness.

16. So that we from this time - That we knew the love of Christ. Know no one - Neither ourselves, nor you, neither the rest of the apostles, Gal. ii, 6, nor any other person. After the flesh - According to his former state, country, descent, nobility, riches, power, wisdom. We fear not the great. We regard not the rich or wise. We account not the least less than ourselves. We consider all, only in order to save all. Who is he that thus knows no one after the flesh? In what land do these Christians live? Yea, if we have known even Christ after the flesh - So as to love him barely with a natural love, so as to glory in having conversed with him on earth, so as to expect only temporal benefits from him.

17. Therefore if any one be in Christ - A true believer in him. There is a new creation - Only the power that makes a world can make a Christian. And when he is so created, the old things are passed away - Of their own accord, even as snow in spring. Behold - The present, visible, undeniable change! All things are become new - He has new life, new senses, new faculties, new affections, new appetites, new ideas and conceptions. His whole tenor of action and conversation is new, and he lives, as it were, in a new world. God, men, the whole creation, heaven, earth, and all therein, appear in a new light, and stand related to him in a new manner, since he was created anew in Christ Jesus.

18. And all these new things are from God, considered under this very notion, as reconciling us - The world, 2 Cor. v, 19, to himself.

19. Namely - The sum of which is, God - The whole Godhead, but more eminently God the Father. Was in Christ, reconciling the world - Which was before at enmity with God. To himself - So taking away that enmity, which could no otherwise be removed than by the blood of the Son of God.

20. Therefore we are ambassadors for Christ-we beseech you in Christ's stead - Herein the apostle might appear to some "transported beyond himself." In general he uses a more calm, sedate kind of exhortation, as in the beginning of the next chapter. What unparalleled condescension and divinely tender mercies are displayed in this verse! Did the judge ever beseech a condemned criminal to accept of pardon? Does the creditor ever beseech a ruined debtor to receive an acquittance in full? Yet our almighty Lord, and our eternal Judge, not only vouchsafes to offer these blessings, but invites us, entreats us, and, with the most tender importunity, solicits us, not to reject them.

21. He made him a sin offering, who knew no sin - A commendation peculiar to Christ. For us - Who knew no righteousness, who were inwardly and outwardly nothing but sin; who must have been consumed by the divine justice, had not this atonement been made for our sins. That we might be made the righteousness of God through him - Might through him be invested with that righteousness, first imputed to us, then implanted in us, which is in every sense the righteousness of God.

VI

1. We then not only beseech, but as fellow-labourers with you, who are working out your own salvation, do also exhort you, not to receive the grace of God - Which we have been now describing. In vain - We receive it by faith; and not in vain, if we add to this, persevering holiness.

2. For he saith - The sense is, As of old there was a particular time wherein God was pleased to pour out his peculiar blessing, so there is now. And this is the particular time: this is a time of peculiar blessing. Isaiah xlix, 8.

3. Giving, as far as in us lies, no offense, that the ministry be not blamed on our account.

4. But approving ourselves as the ministers of God - Such as his ministers ought to be. In much patience - Shown,

   1. In afflictions, necessities, distresses - All which are general terms.
   2. In stripes, imprisonments, tumults - Which are particular sorts of affliction, necessity, distress
   3. In labours, watchings, fastings - Voluntarily endured. All these are expressed in the plural number, to denote a variety of them. In afflictions, several ways to escape may appear, though none without difficulty in necessities, one only, and that a difficult one; in distresses, none at all appears.

5. In tumults - The Greek word implies such attacks as a man cannot stand against, but which bear him hither and thither by violence.

6. By prudence - Spiritual divine; not what the world terms so. Worldly prudence is the practical use of worldly wisdom: divine prudence is the due exercise of grace, making spiritual understanding go as far as possible. By love unfeigned - The chief fruit of the Spirit.

7. By the convincing and converting power of God - Accompanying his word; and also attesting it by divers miracles. By the armour of righteousness on the right hand and the left - That is, on all sides; the panoply or whole armour of God.

8. By honour and dishonour - When we are present. By evil report and good report - When we are absent. Who could bear honour and good report, were it not balanced by dishonour? As deceivers - Artful, designing men. So the world represents all true ministers of Christ. Yet true - Upright, sincere, in the sight of God.

9. As unknown - For the world knoweth us not, as it knew him not. Yet well known - To God, and to those who are the seals of our ministry. As dying, yet behold - Suddenly, unexpectedly, God interposes, and we live.

10. As sorrowing - For our own manifold imperfections, and for the sins and sufferings of our brethren. Yet always rejoicing - In present peace, love, power, and a sure hope of future glory. As having nothing, yet possessing all things - For all things are ours, if we are Christ's. What a magnificence of thought is this!

11. From the praise of the Christian ministry, which he began chap. ii, 14, he now draws his affectionate exhortation. O ye Corinthians - He seldom uses this appellation. But it has here a peculiar force. Our mouth is opened toward you - With uncommon freedom, because our heart is enlarged - In tenderness.

12. Ye are not straitened in us - Our heart is wide enough to receive you all. But ye are straitened in your own bowels - Your hearts are shut up, and so not capable of the blessings ye might enjoy.

13. Now for a recompence of the same - Of my parental tenderness. I speak as to my children - I ask nothing hard or grievous. Be ye also enlarged - Open your hearts, first to God, and then to us, so chap. viii, 5, that God may "dwell in you," 2 Cor. vi, 16; vii, 1; and that ye may "receive us," chap. vii, 2.

14. Be not unequally yoked with unbelievers - Christians with Jews or heathens. The apostle particularly speaks of marriage. But the reasons he urges equally hold against any needless intimacy with them. Of the five questions that follow, the three former contain the argument; the two latter, the conclusion.

15. What concord hath Christ - Whom ye serve. With Belial - To whom they belong.

16. What agreement hath the temple of God with idols - If God would not endure idols in any part of the land wherein he dwelt, how much less, under his own roof! He does not say, with the temple of idols, for idols do not dwell in their worshippers. As God hath said - To his ancient church, and in them to all the Israel of God. I will dwell in them, and walk in them - The former signifying his perpetual presence; the latter, his operation. And I will be to them a God, and they shall be to me a people - The sum of the whole gospel covenant. Lev. xxvi, 11, &c.

17. Touch not the unclean person - Keep at the utmost distance from him. And I will receive you - Into my house and family. Isaiah lii, 11; Zephaniah iii, 19, 20.

18. And ye shall be to me for sons and for daughters, saith the Lord Almighty - The promise made to Solomon, 1 Chr. xxviii, 6, is here applied to all believers; as the promise made particularly to Josh. is applied to them, Heb. xiii, 5. Who can express the worth, who can conceive the dignity, of this divine adoption? Yet it belongs to all who believe the gospel, who have faith in Christ. They have access to the Almighty; such free and welcome access, as a beloved child to an indulgent father. To him they may fly for aid in every difficulty, and from him obtain a supply in all their wants. Isaiah xliii, 6.

VII

1. Let us cleanse ourselves - This is the latter part of the exhortation, which was proposed, chap. vi, 1, and resumed, chap. vi, 14. From all pollution of the flesh - All outward sin. And of the spirit - All inward. Yet let us not rest in negative religion, but perfect holiness - Carrying it to the height in all its branches, and enduring to the end in the loving fear of God, the sure foundation of all holiness.

2. Receive us - The sum of what is said in this, as well as in the tenth and following chapters. We have hurt no man - In his person. We have corrupted no man - In his principles. We have defrauded no man - Of his property. In this he intimates likewise the good he had done them, but with the utmost modesty, as it were not looking upon it.

3. I speak not to condemn you - Not as if I accused you of laying this to my charge. I am so far from thinking so unkindly of you, that ye are in our hearts, to live and die with you - That is, I could rejoice to spend all my days with you.

4. I am filled with comfort - Of this he treats, 2 Cor. vii, 6, &c.; of his joy, 2 Cor. vii, 7, &c.; of both, 2 Cor. vii, 13.

5. Our flesh - That is, we ourselves. Had no rest from without - From the heathens. Were fightings - Furious and cruel oppositions. From within - From our brethren. Were fears - Lest they should be seduced.

7. Your earnest desire - To rectify what had been amiss. Your grief - For what had offended God, and troubled me.

8. I did repent - That is, I felt a tender sorrow for having grieved you, till I saw the happy effect of it.

10. The sorrow of the world - Sorrow that arises from worldly considerations. Worketh death - Naturally tends to work or occasion death, temporal, spiritual, and eternal.

11. How great diligence it wrought in you - Shown in all the following particulars. Yea, clearing of yourselves - Some had been more, some less, faulty; whence arose these various affections. Hence their apologizing and indignation, with respect to themselves; their fear and desire, with respect to the apostle; their zeal and revenge, with respect to the offender, yea, and themselves also. Clearing of yourselves - From either sharing in, or approving of, his sin. Indignation - That ye had not immediately corrected the offender. Fear - Of God's displeasure, or lest I should come with a rod. Vehement desire - To see me again. Zeal - For the glory of God, and the soul of that sinner. Yea, revenge - Ye took a kind of holy revenge upon yourselves, being scarce able to forgive yourselves. In all things ye - As a church. Have approved yourselves to be pure - That is, free from blame, since ye received my letter.

12. It was not only, or chiefly, for the sake of the incestuous person, or of his father; but to show my care over you.

VIII

1. We declare to you the grace of God - Which evidently appeared by this happy effect.

2. In a great trial of affliction - Being continually persecuted, harassed, and plundered.

4. Praying us with much entreaty - Probably St. Paul had lovingly admonished them not to do beyond their power.

5. And not as we hoped - That is, beyond all we could hope. They gave themselves to us, by the will of God - In obedience to his will, to be wholly directed by us.

6. As he had begun - When he was with you before.

9. For ye know - And this knowledge is the true source of love. The grace - The most sincere, most free, and most abundant love. He became poor - In becoming man, in all his life; in his death. Rich - In the favour and image of God.

12. A man - Every believer. Is accepted - With God. According to what he hath - And the same rule holds universally. Whoever acknowledges himself to be a vile, guilty sinner, and, in consequence of this acknowledgment, flies for refuge to the wounds of a crucified saviour, and relies on his merits alone for salvation, may in every circumstance of life apply this indulgent declaration to himself.

14. That their abundance - If need should so require. May be - At another time. A supply to your want: that there may be an equality - No want on one side, no superfluity on the other. It may likewise have a further meaning:-that as the temporal bounty of the Corinthians did now supply the temporal wants of their poor brethren in Judea, so the prayers of these might be a means of bringing down many spiritual blessings on their benefactors: so that all the spiritual wants of the one might be amply supplied; all the temporal of the other.

15. As it is written, He that had gathered the most had nothing over; and he that had gathered the least did not lack - That is, in which that scripture is in another sense fulfilled. Exod. xvi, 18

17. Being more forward - Than to need it, though he received it well.

18. We - I and Timothy. The brother - The ancients generally supposed this was St. Luke. Whose praise - For faithfully dispensing the gospel, is through all the churches.

19. He was appointed by the churches - Of Macedonia. With this gift - Which they were carrying from Macedonia to Jerusalem. For the declaration of our ready mind - That of Paul and his fellow-traveler, ready to be the servants of all.

22. With them - With Titus and Luke. Our brother - Perhaps Apollos.

23. My partner - In my cares and labours. The glory of Christ - Signal instruments of advancing his glory.

24. Before the churches - Present by their messengers.

IX

1. To write to you - Largely.
2. I boast to them of Macedonia - With whom he then was.
3. I have sent the above mentioned brethren before me.
5. Spoken of before - By me, to the Macedonians. Not as a matter of covetousness - As wrung by importunity from covetous persons.
6. He that soweth sparingly shall reap sparingly; he that soweth bountifully shall reap bountifully - A general rule. God will proportion the reward to the work, and the temper whence it proceeds.
7. Of necessity - Because he cannot tell how to refuse.
8. How remarkable are these words! Each is loaded with matter and increases all the way it goes. All grace - Every kind of blessing. That ye may abound to every good work - God gives us everything, that we may do good therewith, and so receive more blessings. All things in this life, even rewards, are, to the faithful, seeds in order to a future harvest. Prov. xxii, 9
9. He hath scattered abroad - (A generous word.) With a full hand, without any anxious thought which way each grain falls. His righteousness - His beneficence, with the blessed effects of it. Remaineth forever - Unexhausted, God still renewing his store. Psalm cxii, 9
10. And he who supplieth seed - Opportunity and ability to help others. And bread - All things needful for your own souls and bodies. Will continually supply you with that seed, yea, multiply it to you more and more. And increase the fruits of your righteousness - The happy effects of your love to God and man. Isaiah lv, 10
11. Which worketh by us thanksgiving to God - Both from us who distribute, and them who receive, your bounty.
13. Your avowed subjection - Openly testified by your actions. To all men - Who stand in need of it.
15. His unspeakable gift - His outward and inward blessings, the number and excellence of which cannot be uttered.

X

1. Now I Paul myself - - A strongly emphatical expression. Who when present am base among you - So, probably, some of the false teachers affirmed. Copying after the meekness and gentleness of Christ, entreat - Though I might command you.
2. Do not constrain me when present to be bold - To exert my apostolical authority. Who think of us as walking after the flesh - As acting in a cowardly or crafty manner.
3. Though we walk in the flesh - In mortal bodies, and, consequently, are not free from human weakness. Yet we do not war - Against the world and the devil. After the flesh - By any carnal or worldly methods. Though the apostle here, and in several other parts of this epistle, speaks in the plural number, for the sake of modesty and decency, yet he principally means himself. On him were these reflections thrown, and it is his own authority which he is vindicating.
4. For the weapons of our warfare - Those we use in this war. Are not carnal - But spiritual, and therefore mighty to the throwing down of strong holds - Of all the difficulties which men or devils can raise in our way. Though faith and prayer belong also to the Christian armour, Eph. vi, 15, &c., yet the word of God seems to be here chiefly intended.
5. Destroying all vain reasonings, and every high thing which exalteth itself - As a wall or rampart. Against the knowledge of God, and bringing every thought - Or, rather, faculty of the mind. Into captivity to the obedience of Christ - Those evil reasonings are destroyed. The mind itself, being overcome and taken captive, lays down all authority of its own, and entirely gives itself up to perform, for the time to come, to Christ its conqueror the obedience of faith.
6. Being in readiness to avenge all disobedience - Not only by spiritual censure, but miraculous punishments. When your obedience is fulfilled - When the sound part of you has given proof of your obedience, so that I am in no danger of punishing the innocent with the guilty.
7. Do ye look at the outward appearance of things - Does any of you judge of a minister of Christ by his person, or any outward circumstance? Let him again think this of himself - Let him learn it from his own reflection, before I convince him by a severer method.
8. I should not be ashamed - As having said more than I could make good.
9. I say this, that I may not seem to terrify you by letters - Threatening more than I can perform.
10. His bodily presence is weak - His stature, says St. Chrysostom, was low, his body crooked, and his head bald.
12. For we presume not - A strong irony. To equal ourselves - As partners of the same office. Or to compare ourselves - As partakers of the same labour. They among themselves limiting themselves - Choosing and limiting their provinces according to their own fancy.

13. But we will not, like them, boastingly extend ourselves beyond our measure, but according to the measure of the province which God hath allotted us - To me, in particular, as the apostle of the gentiles. A measure which reaches even unto you - God allotted to each apostle his province, and the measure or bounds thereof.

14. We are come even to you - By a gradual, regular process, having taken the intermediate places in our way, in preaching the gospel of Christ.

15. Having hope, now your faith is increased - So that you can the better spare us. To be enlarged by you abundantly - That is, enabled by you to go still further.

16. In the regions beyond you - To the west and south, where the gospel had not yet been preached.

XI

1. I wish ye would bear - So does he pave the way for what might otherwise have given offense. With my folly - Of commending myself; which to many may appear folly; and really would be so, were it not on this occasion absolutely necessary.

2. For - The cause of his seeming folly is expressed in this and the following verse; the cause why they should bear with him, 2 Cor. xi, 4.

3. But I fear - Love is full of these fears. Lest as the serpent - A most apposite comparison. Deceived Eve - Simple, ignorant of evil. By his subtilty - Which is in the highest degree dangerous to such a disposition. So your minds - We might therefore be tempted, even if there were no sin in us. Might be corrupted - Losing their virginal purity. From the simplicity that is in Christ - That simplicity which is lovingly intent on him alone, seeking no other person or thing.

4. If indeed - Any could show you another saviour, a more powerful Spirit, a better gospel. Ye might well bear with him - But this is impossible.

6. If I am unskilful in speech - If I speak in a plain, unadorned way, like an unlearned person. So the Greek word properly signifies.

7. Have I committed an offense - Will any turn this into an objection? In humbling myself - To work at my trade. That ye might be exalted - To be children of God.

8. I spoiled other churches - I, as it were, took the spoils of them: it is a military term. Taking wages (or pay, another military word) of them - When I came to you at first. And when I was present with you, and wanted - My work not quite supplying my necessities. I was chargeable to no man - Of Corinth.

9. For - I choose to receive help from the poor Macedonians, rather than the rich Corinthians! Were the poor in all ages more generous than the rich?

10. This my boasting shall not be stopped - For I will receive nothing from you.

11. Do I refuse to receive anything of you, because I love you not? God knoweth that is not the case.

12. Who desire any occasion - To censure me. That wherein they boast, they may be found even as we - They boasted of being "burdensome to no man." But it was a vain boast in them, though not in the apostle.

14. Satan himself is transformed - Uses to transform himself; to put on the fairest appearances.

15. Therefore it is no great, no strange, thing; whose end, notwithstanding all their disguises, shall be according to their works.

16. I say again - He premises a new apology to this new commendation of himself. Let no man think me a fool - Let none think I do this without the utmost necessity. But if any do think me foolish herein, yet bear with my folly.

17. I speak not after the Lord - Not by an express command from him; though still under the direction of his Spirit. But as it were foolishly - In such a manner as many may think foolish.

18. After the flesh - That is, in external things.

19. Being wise - A beautiful irony.

20. For ye suffer - Not only the folly, but the gross abuses, of those false apostles. If a man enslave you - Lord it over you in the most arbitrary manner. If he devour you - By his exorbitant demands; not - withstanding his boast of not being burdensome. If he take from you - By open violence. If he exalt himself - By the most unbounded self-commendation. If he smite you on the face - (A very possible case,) under pretense of divine zeal.

21. I speak with regard to reproach, as though we had been weak - I say, "Bear with me," even on supposition that the weakness be real which they reproach me with.

22. Are they Hebrews, Israelites, the seed of Abraham - These were the heads on which they boasted.

23. I am more so than they. In deaths often - Surrounding me in the most dreadful forms.

24. Five times I received from the Jews forty stripes save one - Which was the utmost that the law

allowed. With the Roman he sometimes pleaded his privilege as a Roman; but from the Jews he suffered all things.

25. Thrice I have been shipwrecked - Before his voyage to Rome. In the deep - Probably floating on some part of the vessel.

27. In cold and nakedness - Having no place where to lay my head; no convenient raiment to cover me; yet appearing before noble-men, governors, kings; and not being ashamed.

28. Beside the things which are from without - Which I suffer on the account of others; namely, the care of all the churches - A more modest expression than if he had said, the care of the whole church. All - Even those I have not seen in the flesh. St. Peter himself could not have said this in so strong a sense.

29. Who - So he had not only the care of the churches, but of every person therein. Is weak, and I am not weak - By sympathy, as well as by condescension. Who is offended - Hindered in, or turned out of, the good way. And I burn not - Being pained as though I had fire in my bosom.

30. I will glory of the things that concern my infirmities - Of what shows my weakness, rather than my strength.

32. The governor under Aretas - King of Arabia and Syria of which Damascus was a chief city, willing to oblige the Jews, kept the city - Setting guards at all the gates day and night.

33. Through a window - Of an house which stood on the city wall.

XII

1. It is not expedient - Unless on so pressing occasion. Visions are seen; Revelations, heard.

2. I knew a man in Christ - That is, a Christian. It is plain from 2 Cor. xii, 6, 7, that he means himself, though in modesty he speaks as of a third person. Whether in the body or out of the body I know not - It is equally possible with God to present distant things to the imagination in the body, as if the soul were absent from it, and present with them; or to transport both soul and body for what time he pleases to heaven; or to transport the soul only thither for a season, and in the mean time to preserve the body fit for its re-entrance. But since the apostle himself did not know whether his soul was in the body, or whether one or both were actually in heaven, it would be vain curiosity for us to attempt determining it. The third heaven - Where God is; far above the aerial and the starry heaven. Some suppose it was here the apostle was let into the mystery of the future state of the church; and received his orders to turn from the Jews and go to the gentiles.

3. Yea, I knew such a man - That at another time.

4. He was caught up into paradise - The seat of happy spirits in their separate state, between death and the resurrection. Things which it is not possible for man to utter - Human language being incapable of expressing them. Here he anticipated the joyous rest of the righteous that die in the Lord. But this rapture did not precede, but follow after, his being caught up to the third heaven: a strong intimation that he must first discharge his mission, and then enter into glory. And beyond all doubt, such a foretaste of it served to strengthen him in all his after trials, when he could call to mind the very joy that was prepared for him.

5. Of such an one I will - I might, glory; but I will not glory of myself - As considered in myself.

6. For if I should resolve to glory - Referring to, I might glory of such a glorious Revelation. I should not be a fool - That is, it could not justly be accounted folly to relate the naked truth. But I forbear - I speak sparingly of these things, for fear any one should think too highly of me - O where is this fear now to be found? Who is afraid of this?

7. There was given me - By the wise and gracious providence of God. A thorn in the flesh - A visitation more painful than any thorn sticking in the flesh. A messenger or angel of Satan to buffet me - Perhaps both visibly and invisibly; and the word in the original expresses the present, as well as the past, time. All kinds of affliction had befallen the apostle. Yet none of those did he deprecate. But here he speaks of one, as above all the rest, one that macerated him with weakness, and by the pain and ignominy of it prevented his being lifted up mere, or, at least, not less, than the most vehement head ache could have done; which many of the ancients say he laboured under. St. Paul seems to have had a fresh fear of these buffetings every moment, when he so frequently represses himself in his boasting, though it was extorted from him by the utmost necessity.

8. Concerning this - He had now forgot his being lifted up. I besought the Lord thrice - As our Lord besought his Father.

9. But he said to me - In answer to my third request. My grace is sufficient for thee - How tender a repulse! We see there may be grace where there is the quickest sense of pain. My strength is more illustriously displayed by the weakness of the instrument. Therefore I will glory in my weaknesses rather than my Revelations, that the strength of Christ may rest upon me - The Greek word properly means, may cover me all over like a tent. We ought most willingly to accept whatever tends to this end, however contrary to flesh and blood.

10. **Weaknesses** - Whether proceeding from Satan or men. **For when I am weak** - Deeply conscious of my weakness, then does the strength of Christ rest upon me.

11. **Though I am nothing** - Of myself.

14. **The third time** - Having been disappointed twice. **I seek not yours** - Your goods. **But you** - Your souls.

15. **I will gladly spend** - All I have. **And be spent** - Myself.

16. But some may object, though I did not burden you, though I did not take anything of you myself, yet being crafty I caught you with guile - I did secretly by my messengers what I would not do openly, or in person.

17. I answer this lying accusation by appealing to plain fact. **Did I make a gain of you by Titus** - Or any other of my messengers? You know the contrary. It should be carefully observed, that St. Paul does not allow, but absolutely denies, that he had caught them with guile; so that the common plea for guile, which has been often drawn from this text, is utterly without foundation.

18. **I desired Titus** - To go to you.

19. **Think ye that we again excuse ourselves** - That I speak this for my own sake? No. I speak all this for your sakes.

21. **Who had sinned before** - My last coming to Corinth. **Uncleanness** - Of married persons. **Lasciviousness** - Against nature.

XIII

1. **I am coming this third time** - He had been coming twice before, though he did not actually come.

2. **All the rest** - Who have since then sinned in any of these kinds. **I will not spare** - I will severely punish them.

4. **He was crucified through weakness** - Through the impotence of human nature. **We also are weak with him** - We appear weak and despicable by partaking of the same sufferings for his sake. **But we shall live with him** - Being raised from the dead. **By the power of God in you** - By that divine energy which is now in every believer, 2 Cor. xiii, 5.

5. **Prove yourselves** - Whether ye are such as can, or such as cannot, bear the test - This is the proper meaning of the word which we translate, reprobates. **Know ye not yourselves, that Jesus Christ is in you** - All Christian believers know this, by the witness and by the fruit of his Spirit. Some translate the words, Jesus Christ is among you; that is, in the church of Corinth; and understand them of the miraculous gifts and the power of Christ which attended the censures of the apostle.

6. **And I trust ye shall know** - By proving yourselves, not by putting my authority to the proof.

7. **I pray God that ye may do no evil** - To give me occasion of showing my apostolical power. **I do not desire to appear approved** - By miraculously punishing you. But that ye may do that which is good, **though we should be as reprobates** - Having no occasion to give that proof of our apostleship.

8. **For we can do nothing against the truth** - Neither against that which is just and right, nor against those who walk according to the truth of the gospel.

9. **For we rejoice when we are weak** - When we appear so, having no occasion to show our apostolic power. **And this we wish, even your perfection** - In the faith that worketh by love.

11. **Be perfect** - Aspire to the highest degree of holiness. **Be of good comfort** - Filled with divine consolation. **Be of one mind** - Desire, labour, pray for it, to the utmost degree that is possible.

13. **The grace** - Or favour. **Of our Lord Jesus Christ** - By which alone we can come to the Father. **And the love of God** - Manifested to you, and abiding in you. **And the communion** - Or fellowship. **Of the Holy Ghost** - In all his gifts and graces. It is with great reason that this comprehensive and instructive blessing is pronounced at the close of our solemn assemblies; and it is a very indecent thing to see so many quitting them, or getting into postures of remove, before this short sentence can be ended. How often have we heard this awful benediction pronounced! Let us study it more and more, that we may value it proportionably; that we may either deliver or receive it with a becoming reverence, with eyes and hearts lifted up to God, "who giveth the blessing out of Zion, and life forevermore."

John Wesley

NOTES ON ST. PAUL'S EPISTLE TO THE GALATIANS

THIS epistle is not written, as most of St. Paul's are, to the Christians of a particular city, but to those of a whole country in Asia Minor, the metropolis of which was Ancyra. These readily embraced the gospel; but, after St. Paul had left them, certain men came among them, who (like those mentioned, Acts xv, 1.) taught that it was necessary to be circumcised, and to keep the Mosaic law. They affirmed, that all the other apostles taught thus; that St. Paul was inferior to them; and that even he sometimes practiced and recommended the law, though at other times he opposed it. The first part, therefore, of this epistle is spent in vindicating himself and his doctrine; proving,

1. That he had it immediately from Christ himself; and that he was not inferior to the other apostles.
2. That it was the very same which the other apostles preached. And,
3. That his practice was consistent with his doctrine. The second contains proofs, drawn from the Old Testament, that the law and all its ceremonies were abolished by Christ. The third contains practical inferences, closed with his usual benediction. To be a little more distinct - This epistle contains,

I. The inscription, C.i. 1-5

II. The calling the Galatians back to the true gospel; wherein he
    1. Reproves them for leaving it, 6-10
    2. Asserts the authority of the gospel he had preached, who,
    1. Of a persecutor was made an apostle, by an immediate call from heaven, 11-17
    2. Was no way inferior to Peter himself, 18-C.ii. 21
    3. Defends justification by faith, and again reproves the Galatians, C.iii. 1-iv. 11
    4. Explains the same thing by an allegory taken out of the law itself, 12-31
    5. Exhorts them to maintain their liberty, C.v.1-12 warns them not to abuse it, and admonishes them to walk not after the flesh, but after the Spirit,. 13-C.vi. 10

III. The conclusion, 11-18

GALATIANS

I

1. Paul, an apostle - Here it was necessary for St. Paul to assert his authority; otherwise he is very modest in the use of this title. He seldom mentions it when he mentions others in the salutations with himself, as in the Epistles to the Philippians and Thessalonians; or when he writes about secular affairs, as in that to Philemon; nor yet in writing to the Hebrews because he was not properly their apostle. Not of men - Not commissioned from them, but from God the Father. Neither by man - Neither by any man as an instrument, but by Jesus Christ. Who raised him from the dead - Of which it was the peculiar business of an apostle to bear witness.

2. And all the brethren -- who agree with me in what I now write.

4. That he might deliver us from the present evil world - From the guilt, wickedness, and misery wherein it is involved, and from its vain and foolish customs and pleasures. According to the will of God - Without any merit of ours. St. Paul begins most of his epistles with thanksgiving; but, writing to the Galatians, he alters his style, and first sets down his main proposition, That by the merits of Christ alone, giving himself for our sins, we are justified: neither does he term them, as he does others, either saints," elect," or churches of God."

5. To whom be glory - For this his gracious will.

6. I marvel that ye are removed so soon - After my leaving you. From him who called you by the

219

grace of Christ - His gracious gospel, and his gracious power.

7. Which, indeed, is not properly another gospel. For what ye have now received is no gospel at all; it is not glad, but heavy, tidings, as setting your acceptance with God upon terms impossible to be performed. But there are some that trouble you - The same word occurs, Acts xv, 24. And would - If they were able. Subvert or overthrow the gospel of Christ - The better to effect which, they suggest, that the other apostles, yea, and I myself, insist upon the observance of the law.

8. But if we - I and all the apostles. Or an angel from heaven - If it were possible. Preach another gospel, let him be accursed - Cut off from Christ and God.

9. As - He speaks upon mature deliberation; after pausing, it seems, between the two verses. We - I and the brethren who are with me. Have said before - Many times, in effect, if not in terms. So I say - All those brethren knew the truth of the gospel. St. Paul knew the Galatians had received the true gospel.

10. For - He adds the reason why he speaks so confidently. Do I now satisfy men - Is this what I aim at in preaching or writing? If I still - Since I was an apostle. Pleased men - Studied to please them; if this were my motive of action; nay, if I did in fact please the men who know not God. I should not be the servant of Christ - Hear this, all ye who vainly hope to keep in favour both with God and with the world!

11. But I certify you, brethren -- he does not till now give them even this appellation. That the gospel which was preached by me among you is not according to man - Not from man, not by man, not suited to the taste of man.

12. For neither did I receive it - At once. Nor was I taught it - Slowly and gradually, by any man. But by the Revelation of Jesus Christ - Our Lord revealed to him at first, his resurrection, ascension, and the calling of the gentiles, and his own apostleship; and told him then, there were other things for which he would appear to him.

13. I Persecuted the church of God - That is, the believers in Christ.

14. Being zealous of the unwritten traditions - Over and above those written in the law.

15. But when it pleased God - He ascribes nothing to his own merits, endeavours, or sincerity. Who separated me from my mother's womb - Set me apart for an apostle, as he did Jeremiah for a prophet. Jer. i, 5. Such an unconditional predestination as this may consist, both with God's justice and mercy. And called me by his grace - By his free and almighty love, to be both a Christian and an apostle.

16. To reveal his Son in me - By the powerful operation of his Spirit, chap. iv, 6; as well as to me, by the heavenly vision. That I might preach him to others - Which I should have been ill qualified to do, had I not first known him myself. I did not confer with flesh and blood - Being fully satisfied of the divine will, and determined to obey, I took no counsel with any man, neither with my own reason or inclinations, which might have raised numberless objections.

17. Neither did I go up to Jerusalem - The residence of the apostles. But I immediately went again into Arabia, and returned again to Damascus - He presupposes the journey to Damascus, in which he was converted, as being known to them all.

18. Then after three years - Wherein I had given full proof of my apostleship. I went to visit Peter - To converse with him.

19. But other of the apostles I saw none, save James the brother (that is, the kinsman) of the Lord - Therefore when Barnabas is said to have "brought him into the apostles," Acts ix, 27, only St. Peter and St James are meant.

24. In me - That is, on my account.

II

1. Then fourteen years after - My first journey thither. I went up again to Jerusalem - This seems to be the journey mentioned Acts xv, 2; several passages here referring to that great council, wherein all the apostles showed that they were of the same judgment with him.

2. I went up - Not by any command from them, but by an express Revelation from God. And laid before them - The chief of the church in Jerusalem. The gospel which I preach among the gentiles - Acts xv, 4, touching justification by faith alone; not that they might confirm me therein, but that I might remove prejudice from them. Yet not publicly at first, but severally to those of eminence - Speaking to them one by one. Lest I should run, or should have run, in vain - Lest I should lose the fruit either of my present or past labours. For they might have greatly hindered this, had they not been fully satisfied both of his mission and doctrine. The word run beautifully expresses the swift progress of the gospel.

3. But neither was Titus who was with me - When I conversed with them. Compelled to be circumcised - A clear proof that none of the apostles insisted on the circumcising gentile believers. The sense is, And it is true, some of those false brethren would fain have compelled Titus to be circumcised; but I utterly refused it.

4. Because of false brethren -- who seem to have urged it. Introduced unawares - Into some of those private conferences at Jerusalem. Who had slipped in to spy out our liberty - From the ceremonial law. That they might, if possible, bring us into that bondage again.

5. To whom we did not yield by submission - Although in love he would have yielded to any. With such wonderful prudence did the apostle use his Christian liberty! circumcising Timothy, Acts xvi, 3, because of weak brethren, but not Titus, because of false brethren. That the truth of the gospel - That is, the true genuine gospel. Might continue with you - With you gentiles. So we defend, for your sakes, the privilege which you would give up.

6. And they who undoubtedly were something - Above all others. What they were - How eminent soever. It is no difference to me - So that I should alter either my doctrine or my practice. God accepteth no man's person - For any eminence in gifts or outward prerogatives. In that conference added nothing to me - Neither as to doctrine nor mission.

7. But when they saw - By the effects which I laid before them, ver. 8; Acts xv, 12. That I was intrusted with the gospel of the uncircumcision - That is, with the charge of preaching it to the uncircumcised heathens.

8. For he that wrought effectually in Peter for the apostleship of the circumcision - To qualify him for, and support him in, the discharge of that office to the Jews. Wrought likewise effectually in and by me - For and in the discharge of my office toward the gentiles.

9. And when James - Probably named first because he was bishop of the church in Jerusalem. And Cephas - Speaking of him at Jerusalem he calls him by his Hebrew name. And John - Hence it appears that he also was at the council, though he is not particularly named in the Acts. Who undoubtedly were pillars - The principal supporters and defenders of the gospel. Knew - After they had heard the account I gave them. The grace - Of apostleship. Which was given me, they - In the name of all. Gave to me and Barnabas - My fellow-labourer. The right hands of fellowship - They gave us their hands in token of receiving us as their fellow- labourers, mutually agreeing that we - I and those in union with me. Should go to the gentiles - Chiefly. And they - With those that were in union with them, chiefly to the circumcision - The Jews.

10. Of the poor - The poor Christians in Judea, who had lost all they had for Christ's sake.

11. But - The argument here comes to the height. Paul reproves Peter himself. So far was he from receiving his doctrine from man, or from being inferior to the chief of the apostles. When Peter - Afterwards, Came to Antioch - Then the chief of all the Gentile churches. I withstood him to the face, because he was to be blamed - For fear of man, ver. 12; for dissimulation, ver. 13; and for not walking uprightly. ver. 14.

13. And the other believing Jews - Who were at Antioch. Dissembled with him, so that even Barnabas was carried away with their dissimulation - Was born away, as with a torrent, into the same ill practice.

14. I said to Cephas before them all - See Paul single against Peter and all the Jews! If thou being a Jew, yet livest, in thy ordinary conversation, after the manner of the gentiles - Not observing the ceremonial law, which thou knowest to be now abolished. Why compellest thou the gentiles - By withdrawing thyself and all the ministers from them; either to judaize, to keep the ceremonial law, or to be excluded from church communion?

15. We - St. Paul, to spare St. Peter, drops the first person singular, and speaks in the plural number. ver. 18, he speaks in the first person singular again by a figure; and without a figure, ver. 19, &c. Who are Jews by nature - By birth, not proselytes only. And not sinners of the gentiles - That is, not sinful Gentiles; not such gross, enormous, abandoned sinners, as the heathens generally were.

16. Knowing that a man is not justified by the works of the law - Not even of the moral, much less the ceremonial, law. But by the faith of Jesus Christ - That is, by faith in him. The name Jesus was first known by the gentiles; the name Christ by the Jews. And they are not always placed promiscuously; but generally in a more solemn way of speaking, the Apostle says, Christ Jesus; in a more familiar, Jesus Christ. Even we - And how much more must the Gentiles, who have still less pretense to depend on their own works! Have believed - Knowing there is no other way. Because - Considering the demands of the law, and the fate of human nature, it is evident, that by the works of the law - By such an obedience as it requires. Shall no flesh living - No human creature, Jew or Gentile, be justified. Hitherto St. Paul had been considering that single question, "Are Christians obliged to observe the ceremonial law? But he here insensibly goes farther, and, by citing this scripture, shows that what he spoke directly of the ceremonial, included also the moral, law. For David undoubtedly did so, when he said, Psalm cxliii, 2, the place here referred to, "In thy sight shall no man living be justified;" which the Apostle likewise explains, Rom. iii, 19, 20, in such a manner as can agree to none but the moral law.

17. But if while we seek to be justified by Christ, we ourselves are still found sinners - If we continue in sin, will it therefore follow, that Christ is the minister or countenancer of sin?

18. By no means. For if I build again - By my sinful practice. The things which I destroyed - By my preaching, I only make myself - Or show myself, not Christ, to be a transgressor; the whole blame

lies on me, not him or his gospel. As if he had said, The objection were just, if the gospel promised justification to men continuing in sin. But it does not. Therefore if any who profess the gospel do not live according to it, they are sinners, it is certain, but not justified, and so the gospel is clear.

19. For I through the law - Applied by the Spirit to my heart, and deeply convincing me of my utter sinfulness and helplessness. Am dead to the law - To all hope of justification from it. That I may live to God - Not continue in sin. For this very end am I, in this sense, freed from the law, that I may be freed from sin.

20. The Apostle goes on to describe how he is freed from sin; how far he is from continuing therein. I am crucified with Christ - Made conformable to his death; "the body of sin is destroyed." Rom. vi, 6. And I - As to my corrupt nature. Live no longer - Being dead to sin. But Christ liveth in me - Is a fountain of life in my inmost soul, from which all my tempers, words, and actions flow. And the life that I now live in the flesh - Even in this mortal body, I live by faith in the Son of God - I derive every moment from that supernatural principle; from a divine evidence and conviction, that "he loved me, and delivered up himself for me."

21. Meantime I do not make void - In seeking to be justified by my own works. The grace of God - The free love of God in Christ Jesus. But they do, who seek justification by the law. For if righteousness is by the law - If men might be justified by their obedience to the law, moral or ceremonial. Then Christ died in vain - Without any necessity for it, since men might have been saved without his death; might by their own obedience have been both discharged from condemnation, and entitled to eternal life.

III

1. O thoughtless Galatians - He breaks in upon them with a beautiful abruptness. Who hath bewitched you - Thus to contradict both your own reason and experience. Before whose eyes Jesus Christ hath been as evidently set forth - By our preaching, as if he had been crucified among you.

2. This only would I learn of you - That is, this one argument might convince you. Did ye receive the witness and the fruit of the Spirit by performing the works of the law, or by hearing of and receiving faith?

3. Are ye so thoughtless - As not to consider what you have yourselves experienced? Having begun in the Spirit - Having set out under the light and power of the Spirit by faith, do ye now, when ye ought to be more spiritual, and more acquainted with the power of faith, expect to be made perfect by the flesh? Do you think to complete either your justification or sanctification, by giving up that faith, and depending on the law, which is a gross and carnal thing when opposed to the gospel?

4. Have ye suffered - Both from the zealous Jews and from the heathens. So many things - For adhering to the gospel. In vain - So as to lose all the blessings which ye might have obtained, by enduring to the end. If it be yet in vain - As if he had said, I hope better things, even that ye will endure to the end.

5. And, at the present time, Doth he that ministereth the gift of the Spirit to you, and worketh miracles among you, do it by the works of the law - That is, in confirmation of his preaching justification by works, or of his preaching justification by faith?

6. Doubtless in confirmation of that grand doctrine, that we are justified by faith, even as Abraham was. The Apostle, both in this and in the epistle to the Romans, makes great use of the instance of Abraham: the rather, because from Abraham the Jews drew their great argument, as they do this day, both for their own continuance in Judaism, and for denying the gentiles to be the church of God. Gen. xv, 6

7. Know then that they who are partakers of his faith, these, and these only, are the sons of Abraham, and therefore heirs of the promises made to him.

8. And the scripture - That is, the Holy Spirit, who gave the scripture. Foreseeing that God would justify the gentiles also by faith, declared before - So great is the excellency and fulness of the scripture, that all the things which can ever be controverted are therein both foreseen and determined. In or through thee - As the father of the Messiah, shall all the nations be blessed. Gen. xii, 3

9. So then all they, and they only, who are of faith - Who truly believe. Are blessed with faithful Abraham - Receive the blessing as he did, namely, by faith.

10. They only receive it. For as many as are of the works of the law - As God deals with on that footing, only on the terms the law proposes, are under a curse; for it is written, Cursed is every one who continueth not in all the things which are written in the law. Who continueth not in all the things - So it requires what no man can perform, namely, perfect, uninterrupted, and perpetual obedience. Deut. xxvii, 26

11. But that none is justified by his obedience to the law in the sight of God - Whatever may be done in the sight of man, is farther evident from the words of Habakkuk, The just shall live by faith - That is, the man who is accounted just or righteous before God, shall continue in a state of acceptance,

life, and salvation, by faith. This is the way God hath chosen. Hab. ii, 4.

12. And the law is not of faith - But quite opposite to it: it does not say, Believe; but, Do. Lev. xviii, 5

13. Christ - Christ alone. The abruptness of the sentence shows an holy indignation at those who reject so great a blessing. Hath redeemed us - Whether Jews or gentiles, at an high price. From the curse of the law - The curse of God, which the law denounces against all transgressors of it. Being made a curse for us - Taking the curse upon himself, that we might be delivered from it, willingly submitting to that death which the law pronounces peculiarly accursed. Deut. xxi, 23.

14. That the blessing of Abraham - The blessing promised to him. Might come on the gentiles - Also. That we - Who believe, whether Jews or gentiles. Might receive the promise of the Spirit - Which includes all the other promises. Through faith - Not by works; for faith looks wholly to the promise.

15. I speak after the manner of men - I illustrate this by a familiar instance, taken from the practice of men. Though it be but a man's covenant, yet, if it be once legally confirmed, none - No, not the covenanter himself, unless something unforeseen occur, which cannot be the case with God. Disannulleth, or addeth thereto - Any new conditions.

16. Now the promises were made to Abraham and his seed - Several promises were made to Abraham; but the chief of all, and which was several times repeated, was that of the blessing through Christ. He - That is, God. Saith not, And to seeds, as of many - As if the promise were made to several kinds of seed. But as of one - That is, one kind of seed, one posterity, one kind of sons. And to all these the blessing belonged by promise. Which is Christ - including all that believe in him. Gen. xxii, 18.

17. And this I say - What I mean is this. The covenant which was before confirmed of God - By the promise itself, by the repetition of it, and by a solemn oath, concerning the blessing all nations. Through Christ, the law which was four hundred and thirty years after - Counting from the time when the promise was first made to Abraham, Gen. xii, 2, 3. Doth not disannul, so as to make the promise of no effect - With regard to all nations, if only the Jewish were to receive it; yea, with regard to them also, if it was by works, so as to supersede it, and introduce another way of obtaining the blessing.

18. And again - This is a new argument. The former was drawn from the time, this from the nature, of the transaction. If the eternal inheritance be obtained by keeping the law, it is no more by virtue of the free promise - These being just opposite to each other. But it is by promise. Therefore it is not by the law.

19. It - The ceremonial law. Was added - To the promise. Because of transgressions - Probably, the yoke of the ceremonial law was inflicted as a punishment for the national sin of idolatry, Exod. xxxii, 1, at least the more grievous parts of it; and the whole of it was a prophetic type of Christ. The moral law was added to the promise to discover and restrain transgressions, to convince men of their guilt, and need of the promise, and give some check to sin. And this law passeth not away; but the ceremonial law was only introduced till Christ, the seed to or through whom the promise was made, should come. And it was ordained by angels in the hand of a mediator - It was not given to Israel, like the promise to Abraham, immediately from God himself; but was conveyed by the ministry of angels to Moses, and delivered into his hand as a mediator between God and them, to remind them of the great Mediator.

20. Now the mediator is not a mediator of one - There must be two parties, or there can be no mediator between them; but God who made the free promise to Abraham is only one of the parties. The other, Abraham, was not present at the time of Moses. Therefore in the promise Moses had nothing to do. The law, wherein he was concerned, was a transaction of quite another nature.

21. Will it follow from hence that the law is against, opposite to, the promises of God? By no means. They are well consistent. But yet the law cannot give life, as the promise doth. If there had been a law which could have given life - Which could have entitled a sinner to life, God would have spared his own Son, and righteousness, or justification. with all the blessings consequent upon it, would have been by that law.

22. But, on the contrary, the scripture wherein that law is written hath concluded all under sin - Hath shut them up together, (so the word properly signifies,) as in a prison, under sentence of death, to the end that all being cut off from expecting justification by the law, the promise might be freely given to them that believe.

23. But before faith - That is, the gospel dispensation. Came, we were kept - As in close custody. Under the law - The Mosaic dispensation. Shut up unto the faith which was to be revealed - Reserved and prepared for the gospel dispensation.

24. Wherefore the law was our schoolmaster unto Christ - It was designed to train us up for Christ. And this it did both by its commands, which showed the need we had of his atonement; and its ceremonies, which all pointed us to him.

25. But faith - That is, the gospel dispensation. Being come, we are no longer under that schoolmaster - The Mosaic dispensation.

26. For ye - Christians. Are all adult sons of God - And so need a schoolmaster no longer.

27. For as many of you as have testified your faith by being baptized in the name of Christ, have put on Christ - Have received him as your righteousness, and are therefore sons of God through him.

28. There is neither Jew nor Greek - That is, there is no difference between them; they are equally accepted through faith. There is neither male nor female - Circumcision being laid aside, which was peculiar to males, and was designed to put a difference, during that dispensation, between Jews and gentiles.

29. If ye are Christ's - That is, believers in him.

IV

1. Now - To illustrate by a plain similitude the preeminence of the Christian, over the legal, dispensation. The heir, as long as he is a child - As he is under age. Differeth nothing from a servant - Not being at liberty either to use or enjoy his estate. Though he be Lord - Proprietor of it all.

2. But is under tutors - As to his person. And stewards - As to his substance.

3. So we - The church of God. When we were children - In our minority, under the legal dispensation. Were in bondage - In a kind of servile state. Under the elements of the world - Under the typical observances of the law, which were like the first elements of grammar, the A B C of children; and were of so gross a nature, as hardly to carry our thoughts beyond this world.

4. But when the fulness of the time - Appointed by the Father, ver. 2. Was come, God sent forth - From his own bosom. His Son, miraculously made of the substance of a woman - A virgin, without the concurrence of a man. Made under the law - Both under the precept, and under the curse, of it.

5. To redeem those under the law - From the curse of it, and from that low, servile state. That we - Jews who believe. Might receive the adoption - All the privileges of adult sons.

6. And because ye - Gentiles who believe, are also thus made his adult sons, God hath sent forth the Spirit of his Son into your hearts likewise, crying, Abba, Father - Enabling you to call upon God both with the confidence, and the tempers, of dutiful children. The Hebrew and Greek word are joined together, to express the joint cry of the Jews and gentiles.

7. Wherefore thou - Who believest in Christ. Art no more a servant - Like those who are under the law. But a son - Of mature age. And if a son, then an heir of all the promises, and of the all- sufficient God himself.

8. Indeed then when ye knew not God, ye served them that by nature - That is, in reality. Are no gods - And so were under a far worse bondage than even that of the Jews. For they did serve the true God, though in a low, slavish manner.

9. But now being known of God - As his beloved children. How turn ye back to the weak and poor elements - Weak, utterly unable to purge your conscience from guilt, or to give that filial confidence in God. Poor - incapable of enriching the soul with such holiness and happiness as ye are heirs to. Ye desire to be again in bondage - Though of another kind; now to these elements, as before to those idols.

10. Ye observe days - Jewish sabbaths. And months - New moons. And times - As that of the passover, pentecost, and the feast of tabernacles. And years - Annual solemnities. it does not mean sabbatic years. These were not to be observed out of the land of Canaan.

11. The apostle here, dropping the argument, applies to the affections, ver. 11-20, and humbles himself to the Galatians, with an inexpressible tenderness.

12. Brethren, I beseech you, be as I am - Meet me in mutual love. For I am as ye were - I still love you as affectionately as ye once loved me. Why should I not? Ye have not injured me at all - I have received no personal injury from you.

13. I preached to you, notwithstanding infirmity of the flesh - That is, notwithstanding bodily weakness, and under great disadvantage from the despicableness of my outward appearance.

14. And ye did not slight my temptation - That is, ye did not slight or disdain me for my temptation, my "thorn in the flesh."

15. What was then the blessedness ye spake of - On which ye so congratulated one another.

17. They - The judaizing teachers who are come among you. Zealously affect you - Express an extraordinary regard for you. But not well - Their zeal is not according to knowledge; neither have they a single eye to your spiritual advantage. Yea, they would exclude you - From me and from the blessings of the gospel. That ye might affect - Love and esteem them.

18. In a good thing - In what is really worthy our zeal. True zeal is only fervent love.

19. My little children - He speaks as a parent, both with authority, and the most tender sympathy, toward weak and sickly children. Of whom I travail in birth again - As I did before, ver. 13, in vehement pain, sorrow, desire, prayer. Till Christ be formed in you - Till there be in you all the mind that was in him.

20. I could wish to be present with you now - Particularly in this exigence. And to change - Variously to attemper. My voice - He writes with much softness; but he would speak with more. The voice may more easily be varied according to the occasion than a letter can. For I stand in doubt of you -

So that I am at a loss how to speak at this distance.

21. Do ye not hear the law - Regard what it says.

22. Gen. xxi, 2, 9.

23. Was born after the flesh - In a natural way. By promise - Through that supernatural strength which was given Abraham in consequence of the promise.

24. Which things are an allegory - An allegory is a figurative speech, wherein one thing is expressed, and another intended. For those two sons are types of the two covenants. One covenant is that given from Mount Sinai, which beareth children to bondage - That is, all who are under this, the Jewish covenant, are in bondage. Which covenant is typified by Agar.

25. For this is Mount Sinai in Arabia - That is, the type of Mount Sinai. And answereth to - Resembles Jerusalem that now is, and is in bondage - Like Agar, both to the law and to the Romans.

26. But the other covenant is derived from Jerusalem that is above, which is free - Like Sarah from all inward and outward bondage, and is the mother of us all - That is, all who believe in Christ, are free citizens of the New Jerusalem.

27. For it is written - Those words in the primary sense promise a flourishing state to Judea, after its desolation by the Chaldeans. Rejoice. thou barren, that bearest not - Ye heathen nations, who, like a barren woman, were destitute, for many ages, of a seed to serve the Lord. Break forth and cry aloud for joy, thou that, in former time, travailedst not: for the desolate hath many more children than she that hath an husband - For ye that were so long utterly desolate shall at length bear more children than the Jewish church, which was of old espoused to God. Isaiah liv, 1.

28. Now we - Who believe, whether Jews or Gentiles. Are children of the promise - Not born in a natural way, but by the supernatural power of God. And as such we are heirs of the promise made to believing Abraham.

29. But as then, he that was born after the flesh persecuted him that was born after the Spirit, so it is now also - And so it will be in all ages and nations to the end of the world.

30. But what saith the scripture - Showing the consequence of this. Cast out the bondwoman and her son - Who mocked Isaac. In like manner will God cast out all who seek to be justified by the law; especially if they persecute them who are his children by faith. Gen. xxi, 10.

31. So then - To sum up all. We - Who believe. Are not children of the bondwoman - Have nothing to do with the servile Mosaic dispensation. But of the free - Being free from the curse and the bond of that law, and from the power of sin and Satan.

V

1. Stand fast therefore in the liberty - From the ceremonial law. Wherewith Christ hath made us - And all believers, free; and be not entangled again with the yoke of legal bondage.

2. If ye be circumcised - And seek to be justified thereby. Christ - The Christian institution. Will profit you nothing - For you hereby disclaim Christ, and all the blessings which are through faith in him.

3. I testify to every man - Every gentile. That is circumcised - He thereby makes himself a debtor - Obliges.

4. Therefore Christ is become of no effect to you - Who seek to be justified by the law. Ye are fallen from grace - Ye renounce the new covenant. Ye disclaim the benefit of this gracious dispensation.

5. For we - Who believe in Christ, Who are under the gospel dispensation. Through the Spirit - Without any of those carnal ordinances. Wait for - in sure confidence of attaining. The hope of righteousness - The righteousness we hope for, and full reward of it. This righteousness we receive of God through faith; and by faith we shall obtain the reward.

6. For in Christ Jesus - According to the institution which he hath established, according to the tenor of the Christian covenant. Neither circumcision - With the most punctual observance of the law. Nor uncircumcision - With the most exact heathen morality. Availeth anything - Toward present justification or eternal salvation. But faith - Alone; even that faith which worketh by love - All inward and outward holiness.

7. Ye did run well - In the race of faith. Who hath hindered you in your course, that ye should not still obey the truth?

8. This your present persuasion cometh not from God, who called you - to his kingdom and glory.

9. A little leaven leaveneth the whole lump - One troubler, ver. 10, troubles all.

10. Yet I have confidence that - After ye have read this. Ye will be no otherwise minded - Than I am, and ye were. But he that troubleth you - It seems to have been one person chiefly who endeavoured to seduce them. Shall bear his judgment - A heavy burden, already hanging over his head.

11. But if I still preach circumcision - As that troubler seems to have affirmed, probably taking occasion from his having circumcised Timothy. Why do I still suffer persecution? then is the offense of the cross ceased - The grand reason why the Jews were so offended at his preaching Christ crucified, and so bitterly persecuted him for it, was, that it implied the abolition of the law. Yet St. Paul did not

condemn the conforming, out of condescension to the weakness of any one, even to the ceremonial law; but he did absolutely condemn those who taught it as necessary to justification.

12. I would they were even cut off - From your communion; cast out of your church, that thus trouble you.

13. Ye have been called to liberty - From sin and misery, as well as from the ceremonial law. Only use not liberty for an occasion to the flesh - Take not occasion from hence to gratify corrupt nature. But by love serve one another - And hereby show that Christ has made you free.

14. For all the law is fulfilled in this, Thou shalt love thy neighbour as thyself - inasmuch as none can do this without loving God, 1 John iv, 12; and the love of God and man includes all perfection. Lev. xix, 18.

15. But if - On the contrary, in consequence of the divisions which those troublers have occasioned among you, ye bite one another by evil speaking. And devour one another - By railing and clamour. Take heed ye be not consumed one of another - By bitterness, strife, and contention, our health and strength, both of body and soul, are consumed, as well as our substance and reputation.

16. I say then - He now explains what he proposed, ver. 13. Walk by the Spirit - Follow his guidance in all things. And fulfil not - In anything. The desire of the flesh - Of corrupt nature.

17. For the flesh desireth against the Spirit - Nature desires what is quite contrary to the Spirit of God. But the Spirit against the flesh- - But the Holy Spirit on his part opposes your evil nature. These are contrary to each other - The flesh and the Spirit; there can be no agreement between them. That ye may not do the things which ye would- - That, being thus strengthened by the Spirit, ye may not fulfil the desire of the flesh, as otherwise ye would do.

18. But if ye are led by the Spirit - Of liberty and love, into all holiness. Ye are not under the law - Not under the curse or bondage of it; not under the guilt or the power of sin.

19. Now the works of the flesh - By which that inward principle is discovered. Are manifest - Plain and undeniable. Works are mentioned in the plural because they are distinct from, and often inconsistent with, each other. But "the fruit of the Spirit" is mentioned in the singular, ver. 22, as being all consistent and connected together. Which are these - He enumerates those "works of the flesh" to which the Galatians were most inclined; and those parts of "the fruit of the Spirit" of which they stood in the greatest need. Lasciviousness - The Greek word means anything inward or outward that is contrary to chastity, and yet short of actual uncleanness.

20. Idolatry, witchcraft - That this means witchcraft, strictly speaking, (not poisoning,) appears from its being joined with the worship of devil-gods, and not with murder. This is frequently and solemnly forbidden in the Old Testament. To deny therefore that there is, or ever was, any such thing, is, by plain consequence, to deny the authority both of the Old and New Testament. Divisions - In domestic or civil matters. Heresies are divisions in religious communities.

21. Revellings - Luxurious entertainments. Some of the works here mentioned are wrought principally, if not entirely, in the mind; and yet they are called "works of the flesh." Hence it is clear, the apostle does not by "the flesh" mean the body, or sensual appetites and inclinations only, but the corruption of human nature, as it spreads through all the powers of the soul, as well as all the members of the body. Of which I tell you before - Before the event, I forewarn you.

22. Love - The root of all the rest. Gentleness - Toward all men; ignorant and wicked men in particular. Goodness - The Greek word means all that is benign, soft, winning, tender, either in temper or behaviour.

23. Meekness - Holding all the affections and passions in even balance.

24. And they that are Christ's - True believers in him. Have thus crucified the flesh - Nailed it, as it were, to a cross whence it has no power to break loose, but is continually weaker and weaker. With its affections and desires - All its evil passions, appetites, and inclinations.

25. If we live by the Spirit - If we are indeed raised from the dead, and are alive to God, by the operation of his Spirit. Let us walk by the Spirit - Let us follow his guidance, in all our tempers, thoughts, words, and actions.

26. Be not desirous of vain glory - Of the praise or esteem of men. They who do not carefully and closely follow the Spirit, easily slide into this: the natural effects of which are, provoking to envy them that are beneath us, and envying them that are above us.

VI

1. Brethren, if a man be overtaken in any fault - By surprise, ignorance, or stress of temptation. Ye who are spiritual - Who continue to live and walk by the Spirit. Restore such an one - By reproof, instruction, or exhortation. Everyone who can, ought to help herein; only in the spirit of meekness - This is essential to a spiritual man; and in this lies the whole force of the cure. Considering thyself - The plural is beautifully changed into the singular. Let each take heed to himself. Lest thou also be tempted - Temptation easily and swiftly passes from one to another; especially if a man endeavours to cure

John Wesley

another without preserving his own meekness.

2. Bear ye one another's burdens - Sympathize with, and assist, each other, in all your weaknesses, grievances, trials. And so fulfil the law of Christ - The law of Christ (an uncommon expression) is the law of love: this our Lord peculiarly recommends; this he makes the distinguishing mark of his disciples.

3. If any one think himself to be something - Above his brethren, or by any strength of his own. When he is nothing, he deceiveth himself - He alone will bear their burdens, who knows himself to be nothing.

4. But let every man try his own work - Narrowly examine all he is, and all he doeth. And then he shall have rejoicing in himself - He will find in himself matter of rejoicing, if his works are right before God. And not in another - Not in glorying over others.

5. For every one shall bear his own burden - In that day shall give an account of himself to God.

6. Let him that is taught impart to him that teacheth all such temporal good things as he stands in need of.

7. God is not mocked - Although they attempt to mock him, who think to reap otherwise than they sow.

8. For he that now soweth to the flesh - That follows the desires of corrupt nature. Shall hereafter of the flesh - Out of this very seed. Reap corruption - Death everlasting. But he that soweth to the Spirit - That follows his guidance in all his tempers and conversation. Shall of the Spirit - By the free grace and power of God, reap life everlasting.

9. But let us not be weary in well doing - Let us persevere in sowing to the Spirit. For in due season - When the harvest is come, we shall reap, if we faint not.

10. Therefore as we have opportunity - At whatever time or place, and in whatever manner we can. The opportunity in general is our lifetime; but there are also many particular opportunities. Satan is quickened in doing hurt, by the shortness of the time, Rev. xii, 12. By the same consideration let us be quickened in doing good. Let us do good - In every possible kind, and in every possible degree. Unto all men - neighbours or strangers, good or evil, friends or enemies. But especially to them who are of the household of faith. For all believers are but one family.

11. Ye see how large a letter - St. Paul had not yet wrote a larger to any church. I have written with my own hand - He generally wrote by an amanuensis.

12. As many as desire to make a fair appearance in the flesh - To preserve a fair character. These constrain you - Both by their example and importunity. To be circumcised - Not so much from a principle of conscience, as lest they should suffer persecution - From the unbelieving Jews. For the cross of Christ - For maintaining that faith in a crucified saviour is alone sufficient for justification.

13. For neither they themselves keep the whole law - So far are they from a real zeal for it. But yet they desire to have you circumcised, that they may glory in your flesh - That they may boast of you as their proselytes, and make a merit of this with the other Jews.

14. But God forbid that I should glory - Should boast of anything I have, am, or do; or rely on anything for my acceptance with God, but what Christ hath done and suffered for me. By means of which the world is crucified to me - All the things and persons in it are to me as nothing. And I unto the world - I am dead to all worldly pursuits, cares, desires, and enjoyments.

15. For neither circumcision is anything, nor uncircumcision - Neither of these is of any account. But a new creation - Whereby all things in us become new.

16. And as many as walk according to this rule -

1. Glorying only in the cross of Christ.

2. Being crucified to the world. And,

3. Created anew. Peace and mercy be upon them, and upon the Israel, that is, the Church, of God - Which consists of all those, and those only, of every nation and kindred, who walk by this rule.

17. From henceforth let none trouble me - By quarrels and disputes. For I bear - And afflictions should not be added to the afflicted. In my body the marks of the Lord Jesus - The scars, marks, and brands of my sufferings for Him.

NOTES ON ST. PAUL'S EPISTLE TO THE EPHESIANS

EPHESUS was the chief city of that part of Asia, which was a Roman province. Here St. Paul preached for three years, Acts xx, 31; and from hence the gospel was spread throughout the whole province, Acts xix, 10. At his taking leave of the church there, he forewarned them both of great persecutions from without, and of divers heresies and schisms which would arise among themselves. And accordingly he writes this epistle, nearly resembling that to the Colossians, written about the same time, to establish them in the doctrine he had delivered, to arm them against false teachers, and to build them up in love and holiness, both of heart and conversation. He begins this, as most of his epistles, with thanksgiving to God for their embracing and adhering to the gospel. He shows the inestimable blessings and advantages they received thereby, as far above all the Jewish privileges, as all the wisdom and philosophy of the heathens. He proves that our Lord is the Head of the whole church; of angels and spirits, the church triumphant, and of Jews and gentiles, now equally members of the church militant. In the three last chapters he exhorts them to various duties, civil and religious, personal and relative, suitable to their Christian character, privileges, assistances, and obligations. In this epistle we may observe,

I. The inscription, Chap. i. 1, 2

II. The doctrine pathetically explained, which contains,
    1. Praise to God for the whole gospel blessing, 3-14 With thanksgiving and prayer for the saints, 15- ii. 10
    2. A more particular admonition concerning their once miserable, but now happy, condition, 11-12 A prayer for their establishment, iii. 1-19 A doxology, 20, 21

III. The exhortation,
    1. General: to walk worthy of their calling, agreeably to,
        1.The unity of the Spirit, and the diversity of his gifts, C.iv.1-16
        2.The difference between their former and their present state, 17- 24
    2. Particular To avoid,
    1. Lying, 25
    2. Anger, 26, 27
    3. Theft, 28
    4. Corrupt communication, 29, 30
    5. Bitterness, 31- 5. 2
    6. Uncleanness, 3-14
    7. Drunkenness, 15-21 With a commendation of the opposite virtues To do their duty, as,
    1. Wives and husbands, 22-33
    2. Children and parents, vi. 1-4
    3. Servants and masters, 5-9
    3. Final: to war the spiritual warfare, 10-20

IV. The conclusion, 21-24

John Wesley

EPHESIANS

I

1. By the will of God - Not by any merit of my own. To the saints who are at Ephesus - And in all the adjacent places. For this epistle is not directed to the Ephesians only, but likewise to all the other churches of Asia.

3. Blessed be the God and Father of our Lord Jesus Christ, who hath blessed us - God's blessing us is his bestowing all spiritual and heavenly blessings upon us. Our blessing God is the paying him our solemn and grateful acknowledgments, both on account of his own essential blessedness, and of the blessings which he bestows upon us. He is the God of our Lord Jesus Christ, as man and Mediator: he is his Father, primarily, with respect to his divine nature, as his only begotten Son; and, secondarily, with respect to his human nature, as that is personally united to the divine. With all spiritual blessings in heavenly things - With all manner of spiritual blessings, which are heavenly in their nature, original, and tendency, and shall be completed in heaven: far different from the external privileges of the Jews, and the earthly blessings they expected from the Messiah.

4. As he hath chosen us - Both Jews and gentiles, whom he foreknew as believing in Christ, 1 Pet. i, 2.

5. Having predestinated us to the adoption of sons - Having foreordained that all who afterwards believed should enjoy the dignity of being sons of God, and joint-heirs with Christ. According to the good pleasure of his will - According to his free, fixed, unalterable purpose to confer this blessing on all those who should believe in Christ, and those only.

6. To the praise of the glory of his grace - His glorious, free love without any desert on our part.

7. By whom we - Who believe. Have - From the moment we believe. Redemption - From the guilt and power of sin. Through his blood - Through what he hath done and suffered for us. According to the riches of his grace - According to the abundant overflowings of his free mercy and favour.

8. In all wisdom - Manifested by God in the whole scheme of our salvation. And prudence - Which be hath wrought in us, that we may know and do all his acceptable and perfect will.

9. Having made known to us - By his word and by his Spirit. The mystery of his will - The gracious scheme of salvation by faith, which depends on his own sovereign will alone. This was but darkly discovered under the law; is now totally hid from unbelievers; and has heights and depths which surpass all the knowledge even of true believers.

10. That in the dispensation of the fulness of the times - In this last administration of God's fullest grace, which took place when the time appointed was fully come. He might gather together into one in Christ - Might recapitulate, re-unite, and place in order again under Christ, their common Head. All things which are in heaven, and on earth - All angels and men, whether living or dead, in the Lord.

11. Through whom we - Jews. Also have obtained an inheritance - The glorious inheritance of the heavenly Canaan, to which, when believers, we were predestinated according to the purpose of him that worketh all things after the counsel of his own will - The unalterable decree, "He that believeth shall be delivered;" which will is not an arbitrary will, but flowing from the rectitude of his nature, else, what security would there be that it would be his will to keep his word even with the elect?

12. That we - Jews. Who first believed - Before the gentiles. So did some of them in every place. Here is another branch of the true gospel predestination: he that believes is not only elected to salvation, (if he endures to the end,) but is fore-appointed of God to walk in holiness, to the praise of his glory.

13. In whom ye - Gentiles. Likewise believed, after ye had heard the gospel - Which God made the means of your salvation; in whom after ye had believed - Probably some time after their first believing. Ye were sealed by that Holy Spirit of promise - Holy both in his nature and in his operations, and promised to all the children of God. The sealing seems to imply,

   1. A full impression of the image of God on their souls.
   2. A full assurance of receiving all the promises, whether relating to time or eternity.

14. Who, thus sealing us, is an earnest - Both a pledge and a foretaste of our inheritance. Till the redemption of the purchased possession - Till the church, which he has purchased with his own blood, shall be fully delivered from all sin and sorrow, and advanced to everlasting glory. To the praise of his glory - Of his glorious wisdom, power, and mercy.

15. Since I heard of your faith and love - That is, of their perseverance and increase therein.

16. I cease not - In all my solemn addresses to God. To give thanks for you, making mention of you in my prayers - So he did of all the churches, Col. i, 9.

17. That the Father of that infinite glory which shines in the face of Christ, from whom also we receive the glorious inheritance, ver. 18, may give you the Spirit of wisdom and Revelation - The same who is the Spirit of promise is also, in the progress of the faithful, the Spirit of wisdom and Revelation; making them wise unto salvation, and revealing to them the deep things of God. He is here speaking of that wisdom and Revelation which are common to all real Christians.

18. The eyes of your understanding - It is with these alone that we discern the things of God. Being first opened, and then enlightened - By his Spirit. That ye may know what is the hope of his calling - That ye may experimentally and delightfully know what are the blessings which God has called you to hope for by his word and his Spirit. And what is the riches of the glory of his inheritance in the saints - What an immense treasure of blessedness he hath provided as an inheritance for holy souls.

19. And what the exceeding greatness of his power toward us who believe - Both in quickening our dead souls, and preserving them in spiritual life. According to the power which he exerted in Christ, raising him from the dead - By the very same almighty power whereby he raised Christ; for no less would suffice.

20. And he hath seated him at his own right hand - That is, he hath exalted him in his human nature, as a recompence for his sufferings, to a quiet, everlasting possession of all possible blessedness, majesty, and glory.

21. Far above all principality, and power, and might, and dominion - That is, God hath invested him with uncontrollable authority over all demons in hell, all angels in heaven, and all the princes and potentates on earth. And every name that is named - We know the king is above all, though we cannot name all the officers of his court. So we know that Christ is above all, though we are not able to name all his subjects. Not only in this world, but also in that which is to come - The world to come is so styled, not because it does not yet exist, but because it is not yet visible. Principalities and powers are named now; but those also who are not even named in this world, but shall be revealed in the world to come, are all subject to Christ.

22. And he hath given him to be head over all things to the church - An head both of guidance and government, and likewise of life and influence, to the whole and every member of it. All these stand in the nearest union with him, and have as continual and effectual a communication of activity, growth, and strength from him, as the natural body from its head.

23. The fulness of him that filleth all in all - It is hard to say in what sense this can be spoken of the church; but the sense is easy and natural, if we refer it to Christ, who is the fulness of the Father.

II

1. And he hath quickened you - In the nineteenth and twentieth verses of the preceding chapter, St. Paul spoke of God's working in them by the same almighty power whereby he raised Christ from the dead. On the mention of this he, in the fulness of his heart, runs into a flow of thought concerning the glory of Christ's exaltation in the three following verses. He here resumes the thread of his discourse. Who were dead - Not only diseased, but dead; absolutely void of all spiritual life; and as incapable of quickening yourselves, as persons literally dead. In trespasses and sins-Sins seem to be spoken chiefly of the gentiles, who knew not God; trespasses, of the Jews, who had his law, and yet regarded it not, ver. 5. The latter herein obeyed the flesh; the former, the prince of the power of the air.

2. According to the course of this world - The word translated course properly means a long series of times, wherein one corrupt age follows another. According to the prince of the power of the air - The effect of which power all may perceive, though all do not understand the cause of it: a power unspeakably penetrating and widely diffused; but yet, as to its baneful influences, beneath the orb of believers. The evil spirits are united under one head, the seat of whose dominion is in the air. Here he sometimes raises storms, sometimes makes visionary representations, and is continually roving to and fro. The spirit that now worketh - With mighty power; and so he did, and doth in all ages. In the sons of disobedience - In all who do not believe and obey the gospel.

3. Among whom we - Jews. Also, formerly had our conversation: doing the will of the flesh - In gross, brutal sins. And of the mind - By spiritual, diabolical wickedness. In the former clause, flesh denotes the whole evil nature; in the latter, the body opposed to the soul. And were by nature - That is, in our natural state. Children of wrath - Having the wrath of God abiding on us, even as the gentiles. This expression, by nature, occurs also, Gal. iv, 8; Rom. ii, 14; and thrice in the eleventh chapter. But in none of these places does it signify, by custom, or practice, or customary practice, as a late writer affirms. Nor can it mean so here For this would make the apostle guilty of gross tautology, their customary sinning having been expressed already, in the former part of the verse. But all these passages agree in expressing what belongs to the nature of the persons spoken of.

4. Mercy removes misery: love confers salvation.

5. He hath quickened us together with Christ - In conformity to him, and by virtue of our union with him. By grace ye are saved - Grace is both the beginning and end. The apostle speaks indifferently either in the first or second person; the Jews and gentiles being in the same circumstance, both by nature and by grace. This text lays the axe to the very root of spiritual pride, and all glorying in ourselves. Therefore St. Paul, foreseeing the backwardness of mankind to receive it, yet knowing the absolute necessity of its being received, again asserts the very same truth, ver. 8, in the very same words.

6. And hath raised us up together - Both Jews and gentiles already in spirit; and ere long our

bodies too will be raised. And made us all sit together in heavenly places - This is spoken by way of anticipation. Believers are not yet possessed of their seats in heaven; but each of them has a place prepared for him.

7. The ages to come - That is, all succeeding ages.

8. By grace ye are saved through faith - Grace, without any respect to human worthiness, confers the glorious gift. Faith, with an empty hand, and without any pretense to personal desert, receives the heavenly blessing. And this is not of yourselves - This refers to the whole preceding clause, That ye are saved through faith, is the gift of God.

9. Not by works - Neither this faith nor this salvation is owing to any works you ever did, will, or can do.

10. For we are his workmanship - Which proves both that salvation is by faith, and that faith is the gift of God. Created unto good works - That afterwards we might give ourselves to them. Which God had before preprepared - The occasions of them: so we must still ascribe the whole to God. That we might walk in them - Though not be justified by them.

11. Wherefore remember - Such a remembrance strengthens faith, and increases gratitude. That ye being formerly gentiles in the flesh - Neither circumcised in body nor in spirit. Who were accordingly called the uncircumcision - By way of reproach. By that which is called the circumcision - By those who call themselves the circumcised, and think this a proof that they are the people of God; and who indeed have that outward circumcision which is performed by hands in the flesh.

12. Were at that time without Christ - Having no faith in, or knowledge of, him. Being aliens from the commonwealth of Israel - Both as to their temporal privileges and spiritual blessings. And strangers to the covenants of promise - The great promise in both the Jewish and Christian covenant was the Messiah. Having no hope - Because they had no promise whereon to ground their hope. And being without God - Wholly ignorant of the true God, and so in effect atheists. Such in truth are, more or less, all men, in all ages, till they know God by the teaching of his own Spirit. In the world - The wide, vain world, wherein ye wandered up and down, unholy and unhappy.

13. Far off - From God and his people. Nigh - Intimately united to both.

14. For he is our peace - Not only as he purchased it, but as he is the very bond and center of union. He who hath made both - Jews and gentiles, one church. The apostle describes,

1. The conjunction of the gentiles with Israel, ver. 14, 15. And,

2. The conjunction of both with God, ver. 15-18. Each description is subdivided into two parts. And the former part of the one, concerning abolishing the enmity, answers the former part of the other; the latter part of the one, concerning the evangelical decrees, the latter part of the other. And hath broken down the middle wall of partition - Alluding to that wall of old, which separated the court of Israel from the court of the gentiles. Such a wall was the ceremonial law, which Christ had now taken away.

15. Having abolished by his suffering in the flesh the cause of enmity between the Jews and gentiles, even the law of ceremonial commandments, through his decrees - Which offer mercy to all; see Colossians ii, 14. That he might form the two - Jew and gentile. Into one new man - one mystical body.

16. In one body - One church. Having slain - By his own death on the cross. The enmity - Which had been between sinners and God.

17. And he came - After his resurrection. And preached peace - By his ministers and his Spirit. To you - Gentiles. That were afar off - At the utmost distance from God. And to them that were nigh - To the Jews, who were comparatively nigh, being his visible church.

18. For through him, we both - Jews and gentiles. Have access - Liberty of approaching, by the guidance and aid of one Spirit to God as our Father. Christ, the Spirit, and the Father, the three-one God, stand frequently in the same order.

19. Therefore ye are no longer strangers, but citizens of the heavenly Jerusalem; no longer foreigners, but received into the very family of God.

20. And are built upon the foundation of the apostles and prophets - As the foundation sustains the building, so the word of God, declared by the apostles and prophets, sustains the faith of all believers. God laid the foundation by them; but Christ himself is the chief corner-stone of the foundation. Elsewhere he is termed the foundation itself, 1 Cor. iii, 11.

21. On whom all the building fitly framed together - The whole fabric of the universal church rises up like a great pile of living materials. Into an holy temple in the Lord - Dedicated to Christ, and inhabited by him, in which he displays his presence, and is worshipped and glorified. What is the temple of Diana of the Ephesians, whom ye formerly worshipped, to this?

III

1. **For this cause** - That ye may be so "built together," **I am a prisoner for you gentiles** - For your advantage, and for asserting your right to these blessings. This it was which so enraged the Jews against him.

2. **The dispensation of the grace of God given me in your behalf** - That is, the commission to dispense the gracious gospel; to you gentiles in particular. This they had heard from his own mouth.

3. **The mystery** - Of salvation by Christ alone, and that both to Jews and gentiles. **As I wrote before** - Namely, chap. i, 9, 10; the very words of which passage he here repeats.

5. **Which in other** - In former, ages was not so clearly or fully made known to the sons of men - To any man, no, not to Ezekiel, so often styled, "son of man;" nor to any of the ancient prophets. Those here spoken of are New Testament prophets.

6. **That the gentiles are joint-heirs** - Of God. **And of the same body** - Under Christ the head. **And joint-partakers of his promise** - The communion of the Holy Ghost.

7. **According to the gift of the grace of God** - That is, the apostle-ship which he hath graciously given me, and which he hath qualified me for. **By the effectual working of his power** - In me and by me.

8. **Unto me, who am less than the least of all saints, is this grace given** - Here are the noblest strains of eloquence to paint the exceeding low opinion the apostle had of himself, and the fulness of unfathomable blessings which are treasured up in Christ.

9. **What is the fellowship of the mystery** - What those mysterious blessings are whereof all believers jointly partake. **Which was, in a great measure, hidden from eternity by God, who, to make way for the free exercise of his love, created all things** - This is the foundation of all his dispensations.

10. **That the manifold wisdom of God might be made known by the church** - By what is done in the church, which is the theatre of the divine wisdom.

12. **By whom we have free access** - Such as those petitioners have, who are introduced to the royal presence by some distinguished favourite. **And boldness** - Unrestrained liberty of speech, such as children use in addressing an indulgent father, when, without fear of offending, they disclose all their wants, and make known all their requests.

13. **The not fainting is your glory.**

15. **Of whom** - The Father. The whole family of angels in heaven, saints in paradise, and believers on earth is named. Being the "children of God," (a more honourable title than "children of Abraham,") and depending on him as the Father of the family.

16. **The riches of his glory** - The immense fulness of his glorious wisdom, power, and mercy. **The inner man** - The soul.

17. **Dwell** - That is, constantly and sensibly abide.

18. **That being rooted and grounded** - That is, deeply fixed and firmly established, in love. **Ye may comprehend** - So far as an human mind is capable. **What is the breadth of the love of Christ** - Embracing all mankind. **And length** - From everlasting to everlasting. **And depth** - Not to be fathomed by any creature. **And height** - Not to be reached by any enemy.

19. **And to know** - But the apostle corrects himself, and immediately observes, it cannot be fully known. This only we know, that the love of Christ surpasses all knowledge. **That ye may be filled** - Which is the sum of all. **With all the fulness of God** - With all his light, love, wisdom, holiness, power, and glory. A perfection far beyond a bare freedom from sin.

20. **Now to him** - This doxology is admirably adapted to strengthen our faith, that we may not stagger at the great things the apostle has been praying for, as if they were too much for God to give, or for us to expect from him. **That is able** - Here is a most beautiful gradation. When he has given us exceeding, yea, abundant blessings, still we may ask for more. And he is able to do it. But we may think of more than we have asked. He is able to do this also. Yea, and above all this. **Above all we ask** - Above all we can think. Nay, exceedingly, abundantly above all that we can either ask or think.

21. **In the church** - On earth and in heaven.

IV

1. **I therefore, the prisoner of the Lord** - Imprisoned for his sake and for your sakes; for the sake of the gospel which he had preached amongst them. This was therefore a powerful motive to them to comfort him under it by their obedience.

3. **endeavouring to keep the unity of the Spirit** - That mutual union and harmony, which is a fruit of the Spirit. **The bond of peace is love.**

4. **There is one body** - The universal church, all believers throughout the world. **One Spirit, one Lord, one God and Father** - The ever-blessed Trinity. **One hope** - Of heaven.

5. **One outward baptism.**

6. **One God and Father of all** - That believe. **Who is above all** - Presiding over all his children,

operating through them all by Christ, and dwelling in all by his Spirit.

7. According to the measure of the gift of Christ - According as Christ is pleased to give to each.

8. Wherefore he saith - That is, in reference to which God saith by David, Having ascended on high, he led captivity captive - He triumphed over all his enemies, Satan, sin, and death, which had before enslaved all the world: alluding to the custom of ancient conquerors, who led those they had conquered in chains after them. And, as they also used to give donatives to the people, at their return from victory, so he gave gifts to men - Both the ordinary and extraordinary gifts of the Spirit. Psalm lxviii, 18.

9. Now this expression, He ascended, what is it, but that he descended - That is, does it not imply, that he descended first? Certainly it does, on the supposition of his being God. Otherwise it would not: since all the saints will ascend to heaven, though none of them descended thence. Into the lower parts of the earth - So the womb is called, Psalm cxxxix, 5; the grave, Psalm lxiii, 9.

10. He that descended - That thus amazingly humbled himself. Is the same that ascended - That was so highly exalted. That he might fill all things - The whole church, with his Spirit, presence, and operations.

11. And, among other his free gifts, he gave some apostles - His chief ministers and special witnesses, as having seen him after his resurrection, and received their commission immediately from him. And same prophets, and some evangelists - A prophet testifies of things to come; an evangelist of things past: and that chiefly by preaching the gospel before or after any of the apostles. All these were extraordinary officers. The ordinary were. Some pastors - Watching over their several flocks. And some teachers - Whether of the same or a lower order, to assist them, as occasion might require.

12. In this verse is noted the office of ministers; in the next, the aim of the saints; in the 14th, 15th, 16th, the way of growing in grace. And each of these has three parts, standing in the same order. For the perfecting the saints - The completing them both in number and their various gifts and graces. To the work of the ministry - The serving God and his church in their various ministrations. To the edifying of the body of Christ - The building up this his mystical body in faith, love, holiness.

13. Till we all - And every one of us. Come to the unity of the faith, and knowledge of the Son of God - To both an exact agreement in the Christian doctrine, and an experimental knowledge of Christ as the Son of God. To a perfect man - To a state of spiritual manhood both in understanding and strength. To the measure of the stature of the fulness of Christ - To that maturity of age and spiritual stature wherein we shall be filled with Christ, so that he will be all in all.

14. Fluctuating to and fro - From within, even when there is no wind. And carried about with every wind - From without; when we are assaulted by others, who are unstable as the wind. By the sleight of men - By their "cogging the dice;" so the original word implies.

15. Into him - Into his image and Spirit, and into a full union with him.

16. From whom the whole mystical body fitly joined together - All the parts being fitted for and adapted to each other, and most exactly harmonizing with the whole. And compacted - Knit and cemented together with the utmost firmness. Maketh increase by that which every joint supplieth - Or by the mutual help of every joint. According to the effectual working in the measure of every member - According as every member in its measure effectually works for the support and growth of the whole. A beautiful allusion to the human body, composed of different joints and members, knit together by various ligaments, and furnished with vessels of communication from the head to every part.

17. This therefore I say - He returns thither where he begun, ver. 1. And testify in the Lord - In the name and by the authority of the Lord Jesus. In the vanity of their mind - Having lost the knowledge of the true God, Rom. i, 21. This is the root of all evil walking.

18. Having their understanding darkened, through the ignorance that is in them - So that they are totally void of the light of God, neither have they any knowledge of his will. Being alienated from the life of God - Utter strangers to the divine, the spiritual life. Through the hardness of their hearts - Callous and senseless. And where there is no sense, there can be no life.

19. Who being past feeling - The original word is peculiarly significant. It properly means, past feeling pain. Pain urges the sick to seek a remedy, which, where there is no pain, is little thought of. Have given themselves up - Freely, of their own accord. Lasciviousness is but one branch of uncleanness, which implies impurity of every kind.

20. But ye have not so learned Christ - That is, ye cannot act thus, now ye know him, since you know the Christian dispensation allows of no sin.

21. Seeing ye have heard him - Teaching you inwardly by his Spirit. As the truth is in Jesus - According to his own gospel.

22. The old man - That is, the whole body of sin. All sinful desires are deceitful; promising the happiness which they cannot give.

23. The spirit of your mind - The very ground of your heart.

24. The new man - Universal holiness. After - In the very image of God.

25. Wherefore - Seeing ye are thus created anew, walk accordingly, in every particular. For we are

members one of another - To which intimate union all deceit is quite repugnant.

26. Be ye angry, and sin not - That is, if ye are angry, take heed ye sin not. Anger at sin is not evil; but we should feel only pity to the sinner. If we are angry at the person, as well as the fault, we sin. And how hardly do we avoid it. Let not the sun go down upon your wrath - Reprove your brother, and be reconciled immediately. Lose not one day. A clear, express command. Reader, do you keep it?

27. Neither give place to the devil - By any delay.

28. But rather let him labour - Lest idleness lead him to steal again. And whoever has sinned in any kind ought the more zealously to practice the opposite virtue. That he may have to give - And so be no longer a burden and nuisance, but a blessing, to his neighbours.

29. But that which is good - Profitable to the speaker and hearers. To the use of edifying - To forward them in repentance, faith, or holiness. That it may minister grace - Be a means of conveying more grace into their hearts. Hence we learn, what discourse is corrupt, as it were stinking in the nostrils of God; namely, all that is not profitable, not edifying, not apt to minister grace to the hearers.

30. Grieve not the Holy Spirit - By any disobedience. Particularly by corrupt discourse; or by any of the following sins. Do not force him to withdraw from you, as a friend does whom you grieve by unkind behaviour. The day of redemption - That is, the day of judgment, in which our redemption will be completed.

31. Let all bitterness - The height of settled anger, opposite to kindness, ver. 32. And wrath - Lasting displeasure toward the ignorant, and them that are out of the way, opposite to tenderheartedness. And anger - The very first risings of disgust at those that injure you, opposite to forgiving one another. And clamour - Or bawling. "I am not angry," says one; "but it is my way to speak so." Then unlearn that way: it is the way to hell. And evil speaking - Be it in ever so mild and soft a tone, or with ever such professions of kindness. Here is a beautiful retrogradation, beginning with the highest, and descending to the lowest, degree of the want of love.

32. As God, showing himself kind and tenderhearted in the highest degree, hath forgiven you.

V

1. Be ye therefore followers - Imitators. Of God - In forgiving and loving. O how much more honourable and more happy, to be an imitator of God, than of Homer, Virgil, or Alexander the Great!

3. But let not any impure love be even named or heard of among you - Keep at the utmost distance from it, as becometh saints.

4. Nor foolish talking - Tittle tattle, talking of nothing, the weather, fashions, meat and drink. Or jesting - The word properly means, wittiness, facetiousness, esteemed by the heathens an half- virtue. But how frequently even this quenches the Spirit, those who are tender of conscience know. Which are not convenient - For a Christian; as neither increasing his faith nor holiness.

6. Because of these things - As innocent as the heathens esteem them, and as those dealers in vain words would persuade you to think them.

8. Ye were once darkness - Total blindness and ignorance. Walk as children of light - Suitably to your present knowledge.

9. The fruit of the light - Opposite to " the unfruitful works of darkness," chap. iv, 11. Is in - That is, consists in. Goodness and righteousness and truth - Opposite to the sins spoken of, chap. iv, 25,&c.

11. Reprove them - To avoid them is not enough.

12. In secret - As flying the light.

13. But all things which are reproved, are thereby dragged out into the light, and made manifest - Shown in their proper colours, by the light. For whatsoever doth make manifest is light - That is, for nothing but light, yea, light from heaven, can make anything manifest.

14. Wherefore he - God. Saith - In the general tenor of his word, to all who are still in darkness. Awake thou that steepest - In ignorance of God and thyself; in stupid insensibility. And arise from the dead - From the death of sin. And Christ shall give thee light - Knowledge, holiness, happiness.

15. Circumspectly - Exactly, with the utmost accuracy, getting to the highest pitch of every point of holiness. Not as fools - Who think not where they are going, or do not make the best of their way.

16. With all possible care redeeming the time - Saving all you can for the best purposes; buying every possible moment out of the hands of sin and Satan; out of the hands of sloth, ease, pleasure, worldly business; the more diligently, because the present are evil days, days of the grossest ignorance, immorality, and profaneness.

17. What the will of the Lord is - In every time, place, and circumstance.

18. Wherein is excess - That is, which leads to debauchery of every kind. But be ye filled with the Spirit - In all his graces, who gives a more noble pleasure than wine can do.

19. Speaking to each other - By the Spirit. In the Psalms - Of David. And hymns - Of praise. And spiritual songs - On any divine subject. By there being no inspired songs, peculiarly adapted to the Christian dispensation, as there were to the Jewish, it is evident that the promise of the Holy Ghost to

believers, in the last days, was by his larger effusion to supply the lack of it. Singing with your hearts - As well as your voice. To the Lord - Jesus, who searcheth the heart.

20. Giving thanks - At all times and places. And for all things - Prosperous or adverse, since all work together for good. In the name of, or through, our Lord Jesus Christ - By whom we receive all good things.

22. In the following directions concerning relative duties, the inferiors are all along placed before the superiors, because the general proposition is concerning submission; and inferiors ought to do their duty, whatever their superiors do. Wives, submit yourselves to your own husbands - Unless where God forbids. Otherwise, in all indifferent things, the will of the husband is a law to the wife. As unto the Lord - The obedience a wife pays to her husband is at the same time paid to Christ himself; he being head of the wife, as Christ is head of the church.

23. The head - The governor, guide, and guardian of the wife. And he is the saviour of the body - The church, from all sin and misery.

24. In everything - Which is not contrary to any command of God.

25. Even as Christ loved the church - Here is the true model of conjugal affection. With this kind of affection, with this degree of it, and to this end, should husbands love their wives.

26. That he might sanctify it through the word - The ordinary channel of all blessings. Having cleansed it - From the guilt and power of sin. By the washing of water - In baptism; if, with "the outward and visible sign," we receive the "inward and spiritual grace."

27. That he might present it - Even in this world. To himself - As his spouse. A glorious church - All glorious within. Not having spot - Of impurity from any sin. Or wrinkle - Of deformity from any decay.

28. As their own bodies - That is, as themselves. He that loveth his wife loveth himself - Which is not a sin, but an indisputable duty.

29. His own flesh - That is, himself. Nourisheth and cherisheth - That is, feeds and clothes it.

30. For we - The reason why Christ nourishes and cherishes the church is, that close connection between them which is here expressed in the words of Moses, originally spoken concerning Eve. Are members - Are as intimately united to Christ, in a spiritual sense, as if we were literally "flesh of his flesh, and bone of his bone."

31. For this cause - Because of this intimate union. Gen. ii, 24.

VI

1. Children, obey your parents - In all things lawful. The will of the parent is a law to the child. In the Lord - For his sake. For this is right - Manifestly just and reasonable.

2. honour - That is, love, reverence, obey, assist, in all things. The mother is particularly mentioned, as being more liable to be slighted than the father. Which is the first commandment with a promise - For the promise implied in the second commandment does not belong to the keeping that command in particular, but the whole law. Exod. xx, 12

3. That thou mayest live long upon the earth - This is usually fulfilled to eminently dutiful children; and he who lives long and well has a long seed-time for the eternal harvest. But this promise, in the Christian dispensation, is to be understood chiefly in a more exalted and Spiritual sense.

4. And, ye fathers - Mothers are included; but fathers are named, as being more apt to be stern and severe. Provoke not your children to wrath - Do not needlessly fret or exasperate them. But bring them up - With all tenderness and mildness. In the instruction and discipline of the Lord - Both in Christian knowledge and practice.

5. Your masters according to the flesh - According to the present state of things: afterward the servant is free from his master. With fear and trembling - A proverbial expression, implying the utmost care and diligence. In singleness of heart - With a single eye to the providence and will of God.

6. Not with eye-service - Serving them better when under their eye than at other times. But doing the will of God from the heart - Doing whatever you do, as the will of God, and with your might.

7. Unto the Lord, and not to men - That is, rather than to men; and by making every action of common life a sacrifice to God; having an eye to him in all things, even as if there were no other master.

8. He shall receive the same - That is, a full and adequate recompence for it.

9. Do the same things to them - That is, act toward them from the same principle. Forbearing threatening - Behaving with gentleness and humanity, not in a harsh or domineering way.

10. Brethren - This is the only place in this epistle where he uses this compellation. Soldiers frequently use it to each other in the field. Be strong - Nothing less will suffice for such a fight: to be weak, and remain so, is the way to perish. In the power of his might - A very uncommon expression, plainly denoting what great assistance we need as if his might would not do, it must be the powerful exertion of his might.

11. Put on the whole armour of God - The Greek word means a complete suit of armour. Believers

are said to put on the girdle, breastplate, shoes; to take the shield of faith, and sword of the Spirit. The whole armour - As if the armour would scarce do, it must be the whole armour. This is repeated, ver. 13, because of the strength and subtilty of our adversaries, and because of an "evil day" of sore trial being at hand.

12. For our wrestling is not only, not chiefly, against flesh and blood - Weak men, or fleshly appetites. But against principalities, against powers - The mighty princes of all the infernal legions. And great is their power, and that likewise of those legions whom they command. Against the rulers of the world - Perhaps these principalities and powers remain mostly in the citadel of their kingdom of darkness. But there are other evil spirits who range abroad, to whom the provinces of the world are committed. Of the darkness - This is chiefly spiritual darkness. Of this age - Which prevails during the present state of things. Against wicked spirits - Who continually oppose faith, love, holiness, either by force or fraud; and labour to infuse unbelief, pride, idolatry malice, envy, anger, hatred. In heavenly places - Which were once their abode, and which they still aspire to, as far as they are permitted.

13. In the evil day - The war is perpetual; but the fight is one day less, another more, violent. The evil day is either at the approach of death, or in life; may be longer or shorter and admits of numberless varieties. And having done all, to stand - That ye may still keep on your armour, still stand upon your guard, still watch and pray; and thus ye will be enabled to endure unto the end, and stand with joy before the face of the Son of Man.

14. Having your loins girt about - That ye may be ready for every motion. With truth - Not only with the truths of the gospel, but with "truth in the inward parts;" for without this all our knowledge of divine truth will prove but a poor girdle "in the evil day." So our Lord is described, Isaiah xi, 5. And as a girded man is always ready to go on, so this seems to intimate an obedient heart, a ready will. Our Lord adds to the loins girded, the lights burning, Luke xii, 35; showing that watching and ready obedience are the inseparable companions of faith and love. And having on the breastplate of righteousness - The righteousness of a spotless purity, in which Christ will present us faultless before God, through the merit of his own blood. With this breastplate our Lord is described, Isaiah lix, 17. In the breast is the seat of conscience, which is guarded by righteousness. No armour for the back is mentioned. We are always to face our enemies.

15. And your feet shod with the preparation of the gospel - Let this be always ready to direct and confirm you in every step. This part of the armour, for the feet, is needful, considering what a journey we have to go; what a race to run. Our feet must be so shod, that our footsteps slip not. To order our life and conversation aright, we are prepared by the gospel blessing, the peace and love of God ruling in the heart, Colossians iii, 14, 15. By this only can we tread the rough ways, surmount our difficulties, and hold out to the end.

16. Above or over all - As a sort of universal covering to every other part of the armour itself, continually exercise a strong and lively faith. This you may use as a shield, which will quench all the fiery darts, the furious temptations, violent and sudden injections of the devil.

17. And take for an helmet the hope of salvation - 1 Thess. v, 8. The head is that part which is most carefully to be defended. One stroke here may prove fatal. The armour for this is the hope of salvation. The lowest degree of this hope is a confidence that God will work the whole work of faith in us; the highest is a full assurance of future glory, added to the experimental knowledge of pardoning love. Armed with this helmet, the hope of the joy set before him, Christ "endured the cross, and despised the shame," Heb. xii, 2. And the sword of the Spirit, the word of God - This Satan cannot withstand, when it is edged and wielded by faith. Till now our armour has been only defensive. But we are to attack Satan, as well as secure ourselves; the shield in one hand, and the sword in the other. Whoever fights with the powers of hell will need both. He that is covered with armour from head to foot, and neglects this, will be foiled after all. This whole description shows us how great a thing it is to be a Christian. The want of any one thing makes him incomplete. Though he has his loins girt with truth, righteousness for a breastplate, his feet shod with the preparation of the gospel, the shield of faith, the helmet of salvation, and the sword of the Spirit; yet one thing he wants after all. What is that? It follows,

18. Praying always - At all times, and on every occasion, in midst of all employments, inwardly praying without ceasing. By the Spirit - Through the influence of the Holy Spirit. With all prayer - With all sort of prayer, public, private, mental, vocal. Some are careful in respect of one kind of prayer, and negligent in others. If we would have the petitions we ask, let us use all. Some there are who use only mental prayer or ejaculations, and think they are in a state of grace, and use a way of worship, far superior to any other: but such only fancy themselves to be above what is really above them; it requiring far more grace to be enabled to pour out a fervent and continued prayer, than to offer up mental aspirations. And supplication - Repeating and urging our prayer, as Christ did in the garden. And watching - Inwardly attending on God, to know his will, to gain power to do it, and to attain to the blessings we desire. With all perseverance - Continuing to the end in this holy exercise. And supplication for all the saints - Wrestling in fervent, continued intercession for others, especially for the

faithful, that they may do all the will of God, and be steadfast to the end. Perhaps we receive few answers to prayer, because we do not intercede enough for others.

19. By the opening my mouth - Removing every inward and every outward hindrance.

20. An ambassador in bonds - The ambassadors of men usually appear in great pomp. How differently does the ambassador of Christ appear!

21. Ye also - As well as others.

22. That he might comfort your hearts - By relating the supports I find from God, and the success of the gospel.

23. Peace - This verse recapitulates the whole epistle.

24. In sincerity - Or in incorruption; without corrupting his genuine gospel, without any mixture of corrupt affections. And that with continuance, till grace issue in glory.

NOTES ON ST. PAUL'S EPISTLE TO THE PHILIPPIANS

PHILIPPI was so called from Philip, king of Macedonia, who much enlarged and beautified it. Afterwards it became a Roman colony, and the chief city of that part of Macedonia. Hither St. Paul was sent by a vision to preach and here, not long after his coming, he was shamefully entreated. Nevertheless many were converted by him, during the short time of his abode there; by whose liberality he was more assisted than by any other church of his planting. And they had now sent large assistance to him by Epaphroditus; by whom he returns them this epistle. It contains six parts:

I. The inscription, Chap. i. 1, 2

II. Thanksgiving and prayers for them, 3-11

III. He relates his present state and good hope: 12-24 Whence he exhorts them,
    1. While he remains with them to walk worthy of the gospel, 25- 30 ii. 1-16
    2. Though he should be killed, to rejoice with him, 17, 18 And promises,
    1. To certify them of all things by Timotheus, 19-24
    2. In the mean time to send Epaphroditus, 25-30

IV. He exhorts them to rejoice, iii. 1-3 admonishing them to beware of false teachers, and to imitate the true, 2-21 commending concord, iv. 1-3 He again exhorts them to joy and meekness 4-7 and to whatsoever things are excellent, 8-9

V. He accepts of their liberality, 10-20

VI. The conclusion, 21-23

PHILIPPIANS

I

1. Servants - St. Paul, writing familiarly to the Philippians, does not style himself an apostle. And under the common title of servants, he tenderly and modestly joins with himself his son Timotheus, who had come to Philippi not long after St. Paul had received him, Acts xvi, 3, 12. To all the saints - The apostolic epistles were sent more directly to the churches, than to the pastors of them. With the bishops and deacons - The former properly took care of the internal state, the latter, of the externals, of the church, 1 Tim. iii, 2-8; although these were not wholly confined to the one, neither those to the other. The word bishops here includes all the presbyters at Philippi, as well as the ruling presbyters: the names bishop and presbyter, or elder, being promiscuously used in the first ages.

4. With joy - After the epistle to the Ephesians, wherein love reigns, follows this, wherein there is perpetual mention of joy. "The fruit of the Spirit is love, joy." And joy peculiarly enlivens prayer. The sum of the whole epistle is, I rejoice. Rejoice ye.

5. The sense is, I thank God for your fellowship with us in all the blessings of the gospel, which I have done from the first day of your receiving it until now.

6. Being persuaded - The grounds of which persuasion are set down in the following verse. That he who hath begun a good work in you, will perfect it until the day of Christ - That he who having justified, hath begun to sanctify you, will carry on this work, till it issue in glory.

7. As it is right for me to think this of you all - Why? He does not say, "Because of an eternal decree;" or, "Because a saint must persevere;" but, because I have you in my heart, who were all partakers of my grace - That is, because ye were all (for which I have you in my heart, I bear you the most grateful and tender affection) partakers of my grace - That is, sharers in the afflictions which God

vouchsafed me as a grace or favour, ver. 29, 30; both in my bonds, and when I was called forth to answer for myself, and to confirm the gospel. It is not improbable that, after they had endured that great trial of affliction, God had sealed them unto full victory, of which the apostle had a prophetic sight.

8. I long for you with the bowels of Jesus Christ - In Paul, not Paul lives, but Jesus Christ. Therefore he longs for them with the bowels, the tenderness, not of Paul, but of Jesus Christ.

9. And this I pray, that your love - Which they had already shown. May abound yet more and more - The fire which burned in the apostle never says, It is enough. In knowledge and in all spiritual sense - Which is the ground of all spiritual knowledge. We must be inwardly sensible of divine peace, joy, love; otherwise, we cannot know what they are.

10. That ye may try - By that spiritual sense. The things that are excellent - Not only good, but the very best; the superior excellence of which is hardly discerned, but by the adult Christian. That ye may be inwardly sincere - Having a single eye to the very best things, and a pure heart. And outwardly without offense - Holy, unblamable in all things.

11. Being filled with the fruits of righteousness, which are through Jesus Christ, to the glory and praise of God - Here are three properties of that sincerity which is acceptable to God:

1. It must bear fruits, the fruits of righteousness, all inward and outward holiness, all good tempers, words, and works; and that so abundantly, that we may be filled with them.

2. The branch and the fruits must derive both their virtue and their very being from the all - supporting, all - supplying root, Jesus Christ.

3. As all these flow from the grace of Christ, so they must issue in the glory and praise of God.

12. The things concerning me - My sufferings. Have fallen out rather to the furtherance, than, as you feared, the hindrance, of the gospel.

13. My bonds in Christ - Endured for his sake. Have been made manifest - Much taken notice of. In the whole palace - Of the Roman emperor.

14. And many - Who were before afraid. Trusting in the Lord through my bonds - When they observed my constancy, and safety not withstanding, are more bold.

15, 16. Some indeed preach Christ out of contention - Envying St. Paul's success, and striving to hurt him thereby. Not sincerely - From a real desire to glorify God. But supposing - Though they were disappointed. To add more affliction to my bonds - By enraging the Roman against me.

17. But the others out of love - To Christ and me. Knowing - Not barely, supposing. That I am set - Literally, I lie; yet still going forward in his work. He remained at Rome as an ambassador in a place where he is employed on an important embassy.

18. In pretense - Under colour of propagating the gospel. In truth - With a real design so to do.

19. This shall turn to my salvation - Shall procure me an higher degree of glory. Through your prayer - Obtaining for me a larger supply of the Spirit.

20. As always - Since my call to the apostleship. In my body - however it may be disposed of. How that might be, he did not yet know. For the apostles did not know all things; particularly in things pertaining to themselves, they had room to exercise faith and patience.

21. To me to live is Christ - To know, to love, to follow Christ, is my life, my glory, my joy.

22. Here he begins to treat of the former clause of the preceding verse. Of the latter he treats, chap. ii, 17. But if I am to live is the flesh, this is the fruit of my labour - This is the fruit of my living longer, that I can labour more. Glorious labour! desirable fruit! in this view, long life is indeed a blessing. And what I should choose I know not - That is, if it were left to my choice.

23. To depart - Out of bonds, flesh, the world. And to be with Christ - In a nearer and fuller union. It is better to depart; it is far better to be with Christ.

25. I know - By a prophetic notice given him while he was writing this. That I shall continue some time longer with you - And doubtless he did see them after this confinement.

27. Only - Be careful for this, and nothing else. Stand fast in one spirit - With the most perfect unanimity. Striving together - With united strength and endeavours. For the faith of the gospel - For all the blessings revealed and promised therein.

28. Which - Namely, their being adversaries to the word of God, and to you the messengers of God. Is an evident token - That they are in the high road to perdition; and you, in the way of salvation.

29. For to you it is given - As a special token of God's love, and of your being in the way of salvation.

30. Having the same kind of conflict with your adversaries, which ye saw in me - When I was with you, Acts xvi, 12, 19, &c.

II

1. If there be therefore any consolation - In the grace of Christ. If any comfort - In the love of God. If any fellowship of the Holy Ghost; if any bowels of mercies - Resulting therefrom; any tender affection towards each other.

2. Think the same thing - Seeing Christ is your common Head. Having the same love - To God, your common Father. Being of one soul - Animated with the same affections and tempers, as ye have all drank ill to one spirit. Of one mind - Tenderly rejoicing and grieving together.

3. Do nothing through contention - Which is inconsistent with your thinking the same thing. Or vainglory - Desire of praise, which is directly opposite to the love of God. But esteem each the others better than themselves - (For every one knows more evil of himself than he can of another:) Which is a glorious fruit of the Spirit, and an admirable help to your continuing "of one soul."

4. Aim not every one at his own things - Only. If so, ye have not bowels of mercies.

6. Who being in the essential form - The incommunicable nature. Of God - From eternity, as he was afterward in the form of man; real God, as real man. Counted it no act of robbery - That is the precise meaning of the words, - no invasion of another's prerogative, but his own strict and unquestionable right. To be equal with God - the word here translated equal, occurs in the adjective form five or six times in the New Testament, Matt. xx, 12; Luke vi, 34; John v, 18; Acts xi, 17; Rev. xxi, 16. In all which places it expresses not a bare resemblance, but a real and proper equalitg. It here implies both the fulness and the supreme height of the Godhead; to which are opposed, he emptied and he humbled himself.

7. Yet - He was so far from tenaciously insisting upon, that he willingly relinquished, his claim. He was content to forego the glories of the Creator, and to appear in the form of a creature; nay, to be made in the likeness of the fallen creatures; and not only to share the disgrace, but to suffer the punishment, due to the meanest and vilest among them all. He emptied himself - Of that divine fulness, which he received again at his exaltation. Though he remained full, John i, 14, yet he appeared as if he had been empty; for he veiled his fulness from the sight of men and angels. Yea, he not only veiled, but, in some sense, renounced, the glory which he had before the world began. Taking - And by that very act emptying himself. The form of a servant - The form, the likeness, the fashion, though not exactly the same, are yet nearly related to each other. The form expresses something absolute; the likeness refers to other things of the same kind; the fashion respects what appears to sight and sense. Being made in the likeness of men - A real man, like other men. Hereby he took the form of a servant.

8. And being found in fashion as a man - A common man, without any peculiar excellence or comeliness. He humbled himself - To a still greater depth. Becoming obedient - To God, though equal with him. Even unto death - The greatest instance both of humiliation and obedience. Yea, the death of the cross - Inflicted on few but servants or slaves.

9. Wherefore - Because of his voluntary humiliation and obedience. He humbled himself; but God hath exalted him - So recompensing his humiliation. And hath given him - So recompensing his emptying himself. A name which is above every name - Dignity and majesty superior to every creature.

10. That every knee - That divine honour might be paid in every possible manner by every creature. Might bow - Either with love or trembling. Of those in heaven, earth, under the earth - That is, through the whole universe.

11. And every tongue - Even of his enemies. Confess that Jesus Christ is Lord - Jehovah; not now "in the form of a servant," but enthroned in the glory of God the Father.

12. Wherefore - Having proposed Christ's example, he exhorts them to secure the salvation which Christ has purchased. As ye have always - Hitherto. Obeyed - Both God, and me his minister. Now in my absence - When ye have not me to instruct, assist, and direct you. Work out your own salvation - Herein let every man aim at his own things. With fear and trembling - With the utmost care and diligence.

13. For it is God - God alone, who is with you, though I am not. That worketh in you according to his good pleasure - Not for any merit of yours. Yet his influences are not to supersede, but to encourage, our own efforts. Work out your own salvation - Here is our duty. For it is God that worketh in you - Here is our encouragement. And O, what a glorious encouragement, to have the arm of Omnipotence stretched out for our support and our succor!

14. Do all things - Not only without contention, ver. 3, but even without murmurings and disputings - Which are real, though smaller, hindrances of love.

15. That ye may be blameless - Before men. And simple - Before God, aiming at him alone. As the sons of God - The God of love; acting up to your high character. Unrebukable in the midst of a crooked - Guileful, serpentine, and perverse generation - Such as the bulk of mankind always were. Crooked - By a corrupt nature, and yet more perverse by custom and practice.

17. Here he begins to treat of the latter clause of chap. i, 22. Yea, and if I be offered - Literally, If I be poured out. Upon the sacrifice of your faith - The Philippians, as the other converted heathens, were

a sacrifice to God through St. Paul's ministry, Rom. xv, 16. And as in sacrificing, wine was poured at the foot of the altar, so he was willing that his blood should be poured out. The expression well agrees with that kind of martyrdom by which he was afterwards offered up to God.

18. Congratulate me - When I am offered up.

19. When I know - Upon my return, that ye stand steadfast.

20. I have none - Of those who are now with me.

21. For all - But Timotheus. Seek their own - Ease, safety, pleasure, or profit. Amazing! In that golden age of the church, could St. Paul throughly approve of one only, among all the labourers that were with him? chap. i, 14, 17. And how many do we think can now approve themselves to God? Not the things of Jesus Christ - They who seek these alone, will sadly experience this. They will find few helpers likeminded with themselves, willing naked to follow a naked Master.

22. As a son with his father - He uses an elegant peculiarity of phrase, speaking partly as of a son, partly as of a fellowlabourer.

25. To send Epaphroditus - Back immediately. Your messenger - The Philippians had sent him to St. Paul with their liberal contribution.

26. He was full of heaviness - Because he supposed you would be afflicted at hearing that he was sick.

27. God had compassion on him - Restoring him to health.

28. That I may be the less sorrowful - When I know you are rejoicing.

30. To supply your deficiency of service - To do what you could not do in person.

III

1. The same things - Which you have heard before.

2. Beware of dogs - Unclean, unholy, rapacious men. The title which the Jews usually gave the gentiles, he returns upon themselves. The concision - Circumcision being now ceased, the apostle will not call them the circumcision, but coins a term on purpose, taken from a Greek word used by the LXX, Lev. xxi, 5, for such a cutting as God had forbidden.

3. For we - Christians. Are the only true circumcision - The people now in covenant with God. Who worship God in spirit - Not barely in the letter, but with the spiritual worship of inward holiness. And glory in Christ Jesus - As the only cause of all our blessings. And have no confidence in the flesh - In any outward advantage or prerogative.

4. Though I - He subjoins this in the singular number, because the Philippians could not say thus.

5. Circumcised the eighth day - Not at ripe age, as a proselyte. Of the tribe of Benjamin - Sprung from the wife, not the handmaid. An Hebrew of Hebrews - By both my parents; in everything, nation, religion, language. Touching the law, a pharisee - One of that sect who most accurately observe it.

6. Having such a zeal for it as to persecute to the death those who did not observe it. Touching the righteousness which is described and enjoined by the Law - That is, external observances, blameless.

7. But all these things, which I then accounted gain, which were once my confidence, my glory, and joy, those, ever since I have believed, I have accounted loss, nothing worth in comparison of Christ.

8. Yea, I still account both all these and all things else to be mere loss, compared to the inward, experimental knowledge of Christ, as my Lord, as my prophet, priest, and king, as teaching me wisdom, atoning for my sins, and reigning in my heart. To refer this to justification only, is miserably to pervert the whole scope of the words. They manifestly relate to sanctification also; yea, to that chiefly. For whom I have actually suffered the loss of all things - Which the world loves, esteems, or admires; of which I am so far from repenting, that I still account them but dung - The discourse rises. Loss is sustained with patience, but dung is cast away with abhorrence. The Greek word signifies any, the vilest refuse of things, the dross of metals, the dregs of liquors, the excrements of animals, the most worthless scraps of meat, the basest offals, fit only for dogs. That I may gain Christ - He that loses all things, not excepting himself, gains Christ, and is gained by Christ. And still there is more; which even St. Paul speaks of his having not yet gained.

9. And be found by God ingrafted in him, not having my own righteousness, which is of the law - That merely outward righteousness prescribed by the law, and performed by my own strength. But that inward righteousness which is through faith - Which can flow from no other fountain. The righteousness which is from God - From his almighty Spirit, not by my own strength, but by faith alone. Here also the apostle is far from speaking of justification only.

10. The knowledge of Christ, mentioned in the eighth verse, is here more largely explained. That I may know him - As my complete saviour. And the power of his resurrection - Raising me from the death of sin, into all the life of love. And the fellowship of his sufferings - Being crucified with him. And made conformable to his death - So as to be dead to all things here below.

11. The resurrection of the dead - That is, the resurrection to glory.

12. Not that I have already attained - The prize. He here enters on a new set of metaphors, taken

from a race. But observe how, in the utmost fervour, he retains his sobriety of spirit. Or am already perfected - There is a difference between one that is perfect, and one that is perfected. The one is fitted for the race, ver. 15; the other, ready to receive the prize. But I pursue, if I may apprehend that - Perfect holiness, preparatory to glory. For, in order to which I was apprehended by Christ Jesus - Appearing to me in the way, Acts xxvi, 14. The speaking conditionally both here and in the preceding verse, implies no uncertainty, but only the difficulty of attaining.

13. I do not account myself to have apprehended this already; to be already possessed of perfect holiness.

14. Forgetting the things that are behind - Even that part of the race which is already run. And reaching forth unto - Literally, stretched out over the things that are before - Pursuing with the whole bent and vigour of my soul, perfect holiness and eternal glory. In Christ Jesus - The author and finisher of every good thing.

15. Let us, as many as are perfect - Fit for the race, strong in faith; so it means here. Be thus minded - Apply wholly to this one thing. And if in anything ye - Who are not perfect, who are weak in faith. Be otherwise minded - Pursuing other things. God, if ye desire it, shall reveal even this unto you - Will convince you of it.

16. But let us take care not to lose the ground we have already gained. Let us walk by the same rule we have done hitherto.

17. Mark them - For your imitation.

18. Weeping - As he wrote. Enemies of the cross of Christ - Such are all cowardly, all shamefaced, all delicate Christians.

19. Whose end is destruction - This is placed in the front, that what follows may be read with the greater horror. Whose God is their belly - Whose supreme happiness lies in gratifying their sensual appetites. Who mind - Relish, desire, seek, earthly things.

20. Our conversation - The Greek word is of a very extenslve meaning: our citizenship, our thoughts, our affections, are already in heaven.

21. Who will transform our vile body - Into the most perfect state, and the most beauteous form. It will then be purer than the unspotted firmament, brighter than the lustre of the stars and, which exceeds all parallel, which comprehends all perfection, like unto his glorious body - Like that wonderfully glorious body which he wears in his heavenly kingdom, and on his triumphant throne.

IV

1. So stand - As ye have done hitherto.

2. I beseech - He repeats this twice, as if speaking to each face to face, and that with the utmost tenderness.

3. And I entreat thee also, true yokefellow - St. Paul had many fellowlabourers, but not many yokefellows. In this number was Barnabas first, and then Silas, whom he probably addresses here; for Silas had been his yokefellow at the very place, Acts xvi, 19. Help those women who laboured together with me - Literally, who wrestled. The Greek word doth not imply preaching, or anything of that kind; but danger and toil endured for the sake of the gospel, which was also endured at the same time, probably at Philippi, by Clement and my other fellowlabourers - This is a different word from the former, and does properly imply fellowpreachers. Whose names, although not set down here, are in the book of life - As are those of all believers. An allusion to the wrestlers in the Olympic games, whose names were all enrolled in a book. Reader, is thy name there? Then walk circumspectly, lest the Lord blot thee out of his book!

5. Let your gentleness - Yieldingness, sweetness of temper, the result of joy in the Lord. Be known - By your whole behaviour. To all men - Good and bad, gentle and froward. Those of the roughest tempers are good natured to some, from natural sympathy and various motives; a Christian, to all. The Lord - The judge, the rewarder, the avenger. Is at hand - Standeth at the door.

6. Be anxiously careful for nothing - If men are not gentle towards you, yet neither on this, nor any other account, be careful, but pray. Carefulness and prayer cannot stand together. In every thing - Great and small. Let your requests be made known - They who by a preposterous shame or distrustful modesty, cover, stifle, or keep in their desires, as if they were either too small or too great, must be racked with care; from which they are entirely delivered, who pour them out with a free and filial confidence. To God - It is not always proper to disclose them to men. By supplication - Which is the enlarging upon and pressing our petition. With thanksgiving - The surest mark of a soul free from care, and of prayer joined with true resignation. This is always followed by peace. Peace and thanksgiving are both coupled together, Colossians iii, 15.

7. And the peace of God - That calm, heavenly repose, that tranquility of spirit, which God only can give. Which surpasseth all understanding - Which none can comprehend, save he that receiveth it. Shall keep - Shall guard, as a garrison does a city. Your hearts - Your affections. Your minds - Your

understandings, and all the various workings of them; through the Spirit and power of Christ Jesus, in the knowledge and love of God. Without a guard set on these likewise, the purity and vigour of our affections cannot long be preserved.

8. Finally - To sum up all. Whatsoever things are true - Here are eight particulars placed in two fourfold rows; the former containing their duty; the latter, the commendation of it. The first word in the former row answers the first in the latter; the second word, the second and so on. True - In speech. Honest - In action. Just - With regard to others. Pure - With regard to yourselves. Lovely - And what more lovely than truth? Of good report - As is honesty, even where it is not practiced. If there be any virtue - And all virtues are contained in justice. If there be any praise - In those things which relate rather to ourselves than to our neighbour. Think on these things - That ye may both practice them yourselves, and recommend them to others.

9. The things which ye have learned - As catechumens. And received - By continual instructions. And heard and seen - In my life and conversation. These do, and the God of peace shall be with you - Not only the peace of God, but God himself, the fountain of peace.

10. I rejoiced greatly - St. Paul was no Stoic: he had strong passions, but all devoted to God. That your care of me hath flourished again - As a tree blossoms after the winter. Ye wanted opportunity - Either ye had not plenty yourselves, or you wanted a proper messenger.

11. I have learned - From God. He only can teach this. In everything, therewith to be content - Joyfully and thankfully patient. Nothing less is Christian content. We may observe a beautiful gradation in the expressions, I have learned; I know; I am instructed; I can.

12. I know how to be abased - Having scarce what is needful for my body. And to abound - Having wherewith to relieve others also. Presently after, the order of the words is inverted, to intimate his frequent transition from scarcity to plenty, and from plenty to scarcity. I am instructed - Literally, I am initiated in that mystery, unknown to all but Christians. Both to be full and to be hungry - For one day. Both to abound and to want - For a longer season.

13. I can do all things - Even fulfil all the will of God.

15. In the beginning of the gospel - When it was first preached at Philippi. In respect of giving - On your part. And receiving - On mine.

17. Not that I desire - For my own sake, the very gift which I receive of you.

18. An odour of a sweet smell - More pleasing to God than the sweetest perfumes to men.

19. All your need - As ye have mine. According to his riches in glory - In his abundant, eternal glory.

NOTES ON ST. PAUL'S EPISTLE TO THE COLOSSIANS

COLOSSE was a city of the Greater Phrygia, not far from Laodicea and Hierapolis. Though St. Paul preached in many parts of Phrygia, yet he never had been at this city. It had received the gospel by the preaching of Epaphras, who was with St. Paul when he wrote this epistle. It seems the Colossians were now in danger of being seduced by those who strove to blend Judaism, or heathen superstitions, with Christianity; pretending that God, because of his great majesty, was not to be approached but by the mediation of angels; and that they were certain rites and observances, chiefly borrowed from the law, whereby these angels might be made our friends. In opposition to them, the apostle,

1. Commends the knowledge of Christ, as more excellent than all other, and so entire and perfect that no other knowledge was necessary for a Christian. He shows,
2. That Christ is above all angels, who are only his servants; and that, being reconciled to God through him, we have free access to him in all our necessities. This epistle contains,

I. The inscription, Chap. i. 1, 2

II. The doctrine, wherein the apostle pathetically explains the mystery of Christ, By thanksgiving for the Colossians, 3-8 By prayers for them, 9-23 With a declaration of his affection for them, 24-29 ii. 1-3

III. The exhortation,
   1. General, wherein he excites them to perseverance, and warns them not to be deceived, 4-8 Describes again the mystery of Christ in order, 9-15 And in the same order, draws his admonitions,
     1. From Christ the head, 16-19
     2. From his death, 20-23
     3. From his exaltation, iii. 1-4
   2. Particular, 5-9
     1. To avoid several vices,
     2. To practice several virtues, 10, 11 Especially to love one another, 12-15 And study the scriptures 16, 17
     3. To the relative duties of wives and husbands,. 18, 19 Children and parents, 20, 21 Servants and masters, 22-25 iv.1 Final, to prayer, 2-4 to spiritual wisdom 5, 6

V. The conclusion, 7-16

COLOSSIANS

I

   2. The saints-This word expresses their union with God. And brethren -- this, their union with their fellow-Christians.
   3. We give thanks - There is a near resemblance between this epistle, and those to the Ephesians and Philippians.
   5. Ye heard before - I wrote to you. In the word of truth, of the gospel - The true gospel preached to you.
   6. It bringeth forth fruit in all the world - That is, in every place where it is preached. Ye knew the grace of God in truth - Truly experienced the gracious power of God.
   7. The fellowservant - Of Paul and Timotheus.
   8. Your love in the Spirit - Your love wrought in you by the Spirit.
   9. We pray for you - This was mentioned in general, Colossians i, 3, but now more particularly. That ye may be filled with the knowledge of his will - Of his revealed will. In all wisdom - With all the

wisdom from above. And spiritual understanding - To discern by that light whatever agrees with, or differs from, his will.

10. That, knowing his whole will, ye may walk worthy of the Lord, unto all pleasing - So as actually to please him in all things; daily increasing in the living, experimental knowledge of God, our Father, saviour, Sanctifier.

11. Strengthened unto all patience and longsuffering with joyfulness - This is the highest point: not only to know, to do, to suffer, the whole will of God; but to suffer it to the end, not barely with patience, but with thankful joy.

12. Who, by justifying and sanctifying us, hath made us meet for glory.

13. Power detains reluctant captives, a kingdom cherishes willing subjects. His beloved Son - This is treated of in the fifteenth and following verses.

14. In whom we have redemption - This is treated of from the middle of Colossians i, 18. The voluntary passion of our Lord appeased the Father's wrath, obtained pardon and acceptance for us, and, consequently, dissolved the dominion and power which Satan had over us through our sins. So that forgiveness is the beginning of redemption, as the resurrection is the completion of it.

15. Who is - By describing the glory of Christ, and his preeminence over the highest angels, the apostle here lays a foundation for the reproof of all worshippers of angels. The image of the invisible God - Whom none can represent, but his only begotten Son; in his divine nature the invisible image, in his human the visible image, of the Father. The first begotten of every creature - That is, begotten before every creature; subsisting before all worlds, before all time, from all eternity.

16. For - This explains the latter part of the preceding verse. Through implies something prior to the particles by and for; so denoting the beginning, the progress, and the end. Him - This word, frequently repeated, signifies his supreme majesty, and excludes every creature. Were created all things that are in heaven - And heaven itself. But the inhabitants are named, because more noble than the house. Invisible - The several species of which are subjoined. Thrones are superior to dominions; principalities, to powers. Perhaps the two latter may express their office with regard to other creatures: the two former may refer to God, who maketh them his chariots, and, as it were, rideth upon their wings.

17. And he is before all things - It is not said, he was: he is from everlasting to everlasting. And by him all things consist - The original expression not only implies, that he sustains all things in being, but more directly, All things were and are compacted in him into one system. He is the cement, as well as support, of the universe. And is he less than the supreme God?

18. And - From the whole he now descends to the most eminent part, the church. He is the head of the church - Universal; the supreme and only head both of influence and of government to the whole body of believers. Who is - The repetition of the expression { Colossians i, 15} points out the entrance on a new paragraph. The beginning - Absolutely, the Eternal. The first begotten from the dead - From whose resurrection flows all the life, spiritual and eternal, of all his brethren. That in all things - Whether of nature or grace. He might have the preeminence - Who can sound this depth?

19. For it pleased the Father that all fulness - All the fulness of God. Should dwell in him - Constantly, as in a temple; and always ready for our approach to him.

20. Through the blood of the cross - The blood shed thereon. Whether things on earth - Here the enmity began: therefore this is mentioned first. Or things in heaven - Those who are now in paradise; the saints who died before Christ came.

21. And you that were alienated, and enemies - Actual alienation of affection makes habitual enmity. In your mind - Both your understanding and your affections. By wicked works - Which continually feed and increase inward alienation from, and enmity to, God. He hath now reconciled - From the moment ye believed.

22. By the body of his flesh - So distinguished from his body, the church. The body here denotes his entire manhood. Through death - Whereby he purchased the reconciliation which we receive by faith. To present you - The very end of that reconciliation. Holy - Toward God. Spotless - In yourselves. Unreprovable - As to your neighbour.

23. If ye continue in the faith - Otherwise, ye will lose all the blessings which ye have already begun to enjoy. And be not removed from the hope of the gospel - The glorious hope of perfect love. Which is preached - Is already begun to be preached to every creature under heaven.

24. Now I rejoice in my sufferings for you, and fill up - That is, whereby I fill up. That which is behind of the sufferings of Christ - That which remains to be suffered by his members. These are termed the sufferings of Christ,

1. Because the suffering of any member is the suffering of the whole; and of the head especially, which supplies strength, spirits, sense, and motion to all.

2. Because they are for his sake, for the testimony of his truth. And these also are necessary for the church; not to reconcile it to God, or satisfy for sin, (for that Christ did perfectly,) but for example to others, perfecting of the saints, and increasing their reward.

25. According to the dispensation of God which is given me - Or, the stewardship with which I am intrusted.

26. The mystery - Namely, Christ both justifying and sanctifying gentiles, as well as Jews. Which hath been comparatively hid from former ages and past generations of men.

27. Christ dwelling and reigning in you, The hope of glory - The ground of your hope.

28. We teach the ignorant, and admonish them that are already taught.

II

1. How great a conflict - Of care, desire, prayer. As many as have not seen my face - Therefore, in writing to the Colossians, he refrains from those familiar appellations, "Brethren," "Beloved."

2. Unto all riches of the full assurance of understanding, unto the acknowledgment of the mystery of God - That is, unto the fullest and clearest understanding and knowledge of the gospel.

6. So walk in him - In the same faith, love, holiness.

7. Rooted in him - As the vine. Built - On the sure foundation.

8. Through philosophy and empty deceit - That is, through the empty deceit of philosophy blended with Christianity. This the apostle condemns,

1. Because it was empty and deceitful, promising happiness, but giving none.

2. Because it was grounded, not on solid reason, but the traditions of men, Zeno, Epicurus, and the rest. And,

3. Because it was so shallow and superficial, not advancing beyond the knowledge of sensible things; no, not beyond the first rudiments of them.

9. For in him dwelleth - Inhabiteth, continually abideth, all the fulness of the Godhead. Believers are "filled with all the fulness of God," Eph. iii, 19. But in Christ dwelleth all the fulness of the Godhead; the most full Godhead; not only divine powers, but divine nature, Colossians i, 19. Bodily - Personally, really, substantially. The very substance of God, if one might so speak, dwells in Christ in the most full sense.

10. And ye - Who believe. Are filled with him - John i, 16. Christ is filled with God, and ye are filled with Christ. And ye are filled by him. The fulness of Christ overflows his church, Psalm cxxxiii, 3. He is originally full. We are filled by him with wisdom and holiness. Who is the head of all principality and power - Of angels as well as men Not from angels therefore, but from their head, are we to ask whatever we stand in need of.

11. By whom also ye have been circumcised - Ye have received the spiritual blessings typified of old by circumcision. With a circumcision not performed with hands - By an inward, spiritual operation. In putting off, not a little skin, but the whole body of the sins of the flesh - All the sins of your evil nature. By the circumcision of Christ - By that spiritual circumcision which Christ works in your heart.

12. Which he wrought in you, when ye were as it were buried with him in baptism - The ancient manner of baptizing by immersion is as manifestly alluded to here, as the other manner of baptizing by sprinkling or pouring of water is, Heb. x, 22. But no stress is laid on the age of the baptized, or the manner of performing it, in one or the other; but only on our being risen with Christ, through the powerful operation of God in the soul; which we cannot but know assuredly, if it really is so: and if we do not experience this, our baptism has not answered the end of its institution. By which ye are also risen with him - From the death of sin to the life of holiness. It does not appear, that in all this St. Paul speaks of justification at all, but of sanctification altogether.

13. And you who were dead - Doubly dead to God, not only wallowing in trespasses, outward sins, but also in the uncircumcision of your flesh - A beautiful expression for original sin, the inbred corruption of your nature, your uncircumcised heart and affections. Hath he - God the Father. Quickened together with him - Making you partakers of the power of his resurrection. It is evident the apostle thus far speaks, not of justification, but of sanctification only.

14. Having blotted out - in consequence of his gracious decrees, that Christ should come into the world to save sinners, and that whosoever believeth on him should have everlasting life. The handwriting against us - Where a debt is contracted, it is usually testified by some handwriting; and when the debt is forgiven, the handwriting is destroyed, either by blotting it out, by taking it away, or by tearing it. The apostle expresses in all these three ways, God's destroying the handwriting which was contrary to us, or at enmity with us. This was not properly our sins themselves, (they were the debt,) but their guilt and cry before God.

15. And having spoiled the principalities and powers - The evil angels, of their usurped dominion. He - God the Father. Exposed them openly - Before all the hosts of hell and heaven. Triumphing over them in or by him - By Christ. Thus the paragraph begins with Christ, goes on with him, and ends with him.

16. Therefore - Seeing these things are so. Let none judge you - That is, regard none who judge you. In meat or drink - For not observing the ceremonial law in these or any other particulars. Or in

respect of a yearly feast, the new moon, or the weekly Jewish sabbaths.

17. Which are but a lifeless shadow; but the body, the substance, is of Christ.

18. Out of pretended humility, they worshipped angels, as not daring to apply immediately to God. Yet this really sprung from their being puffed up: (the constant forerunner of a fall, (Prov. xvi, 18) so far was it from being an instance of true humility.

19. And not holding the head - He does not hold Christ, who does not trust in him alone. All the members are nourished by faith, and knit together by love and mutual sympathy.

20. Therefore - The inference begun, Colossians ii, 16; is continued. A new inference follows, Colossians iii, 1. If ye are dead with Christ from the rudiments of the world - That is, If ye are dead with Christ, and so freed from them, why receive ye ordinances - Which Christ hath not enjoined, from which he hath made you free.

21. Touch not - An unclean thing. Taste not - Any forbidden meat. Handle not - Any consecrated vessel.

22. Perish in the using - Have no farther use, no influence on the mind.

23. Not sparing the body - Denying it many gratifications, and putting it to many inconveniences. Yet they are not of any real value before God, nor do they, upon the whole, mortify, but satisfy, the flesh. They indulge our corrupt nature, our self-will, pride, and desire of being distinguished from others.

III

1. If ye are risen, seek the things above - As Christ being risen, immediately went to heaven.

3. For ye are dead - To the things on earth. And your real, spiritual life is hid from the world, and laid up in God, with Christ - Who hath merited, promised, prepared it for us, and gives us the earnest and foretaste of it in our hearts.

4. When Christ - The abruptness of the sentence surrounds us with sudden light. Our life - The fountain of holiness and glory. Shall appear - In the clouds of heaven.

5. Mortify therefore - Put to death, slay with a continued stroke. Your members - Which together make up the body of sin. Which are upon the earth - Where they find their nourishment. Uncleanness - In act, word, or thought. Inordinate affection - Every passion which does not flow from and lead to the love of God. Evil desire - The desire of the flesh, the desire of the eye, and the pride of life. Covetousness - According to the derivation of the word, means the desire of having more, or of any thing independent on God. Which is idolatry - Properly and directly; for it is giving the heart to a creature.

6. For which - Though the heathens lightly regarded them.

7. Living denotes the inward principle; walking, the outward acts.

8. Wrath - Is lasting anger. Filthy discourse - And was there need to warn even these saints of God against so gross and palpable a sin as this? O what is man, till perfect love casts out both fear and sin.

10. In knowledge - The knowledge of God, his will, his word.

11. Where - In which case, it matters not what a man is externally, whether Jew or gentile, circumcised, or uncircumcised, barbarian, void of all the advantages of education, yea, Scythian, of all barbarians most barbarous. But Christ is in all that are thus renewed, and is all things in them and to them.

12. All who are thus renewed are elected of God, holy, and therefore the more beloved of him. Holiness is the consequence of their election, and God's superior love, of their holiness.

13. Forbearing one another - If anything is now wrong. And forgiving one another - What is past.

14. The love of God contains the whole of Christian perfection, and connects all the parts of it together.

15. And then the peace of God shall rule in your hearts - Shall sway every temper, affection, thought, as the reward (so the Greek word implies) of your preceding love and obedience.

16. Let the word of Christ - So the apostle calls the whole scripture, and thereby asserts the divinity of his Master. Dwell - Not make a short stay, or an occasional visit, but take up its stated residence. Richly - In the largest measure, and with the greatest efficacy; so as to fill and govern the whole soul.

17. In the name - In the power and Spirit of the Lord Jesus. Giving thanks unto God - The Holy Ghost. And the Father through him - Christ.

18. Wives, submit - Or be subject to. It is properly a military term, alluding to that entire submission that soldiers pay to their general. Eph. v, 22, &c.

19. Be not bitter - (Which may be without any appearance of anger) either in word or spirit.

21. Lest they be discouraged - Which may occasion their turning either desperate or stupid.

22. Eyeservice - Being more diligent under their eye than at other times. Singleness of heart - A simple intention of doing right, without looking any further. Fearing God - That is, acting from this

principle.

23. Heartily - Cheerfully, diligently. Menpleasers are soon dejected and made angry: the single-hearted are never displeased or disappointed; because they have another aim, which the good or evil treatment of those they serve cannot disappoint.

IV

1. Just - According to your contract. Equitable - Even beyond the letter of your contract.

3. That God would open to us a door of utterance - That is, give us utterance, that we "may open our mouth boldly," Eph. vi, 19, and give us an opportunity of speaking, so that none may be able to hinder.

6. Let your speech be always with grace - Seasoned with the grace of God, as flesh is with salt.

10. Aristarchus my fellowprisoner - Such was Epaphras likewise for a time, Phil. i, 23. Ye have received directions - Namely, by Tychicus, bringing this letter. The ancients adapted their language to the time of reading the letter; not, as we do, to the time when it was written. It is not improbable, they might have scrupled to receive him, without this fresh direction, after he had left St. Paul, and "departed from the work."

11. These - Three, Aristarchus, Marcus, and Justus. Of all the circumcision - That is, of all my Jewish fellowlabourers. Are the only fellowworkers unto the kingdom of God - That is, in preaching the gospel. Who have been a comfort to me - What, then, can we expect? that all our fellowworkers should be a comfort to us?

12. Perfect - Endued with every Christian grace. Filled - As no longer being babes, but grown up to the measure of the stature of Christ; being full of his light, grace, wisdom, holiness.

14. Luke, the physician - Such he had been, at least, if he was not then.

15. Nymphas - Probably an eminent Christian at Laodicea.

16. The epistle from Laodicea - Not to Laodicea. Perhaps some letter had been written to St. Paul from thence.

17. And say to Archippus - One of the pastors of that church. Take heed - It is the duty of the flock to try them that say they are apostles to reject the false, and to warn, as well as to receive, the real. The ministry - Not a lordship, but a service; a labourious and painful work; an obligation to do and suffer all things; to be the least, and the servant, of all. In the Lord - Christ by whom, and for whose sake, we receive the various gifts of the Holy Spirit.

John Wesley

NOTES ON ST. PAUL'S FIRST EPISTLE TO THE THESSALONIANS

THIS is the first of all the epistles which St. Paul wrote. Thessalonica was one of the chief cities of Macedonia. Hither St. Paul went after the persecution at Philippi: but he had not preached here long before the unbelieving Jews raised a tumult against him and Silvanus and Timotheus. On this the brethren sent them away to Berea. Thence St. Paul went by sea to Athens, and sent for Silvanus and Timotheus to come speedily to him. But being in fear, lest the Thessalonian converts should be moved from their steadfastness, after a short time he sends Timotheus to them, to know the state of their church. Timotheus returning found the apostle at Corinth from whence he sent them this epistle, about a year after he had been at Thessalonica. The parts of it are these:

I. The inscription, Chap. i, 1

II. He celebrates the grace of God towards them,. 2-10 Mentions the sincerity of himself and his fellowlabourers, ii. 1-12 And the teachableness of the Thessalonians,. 13-16

III. He declares,
    1. His desire, 17-20
    2. His care, iii. 1-5
    3. His joy and prayer for them, 6-13

IV. He exhorts them to grow,
    1. In holiness, iv.1-8
    2. In brotherly love with industry, 9-12

V. He teaches and exhorts,
    1. Concerning them that sleep, 13-18
    2. Concerning the times, v.1-11

VI. He adds miscellaneous exhortations, 12-24

VII. The conclusion, 25-28

1 THESSALONIANS

I

1. Paul - In this epistle St. Paul neither uses the title of an apostle, nor any other, as writing to pious and simple-hearted men, with the utmost familiarity. There is a peculiar sweetness in this epistle, unmixed with any sharpness or reproof: those evils which the apostles afterward reproved having not yet crept into the church.

3. Remembering in the sight of God - That is, praising him for it. Your work of faith - Your active, ever-working faith. And labour of love - Love continually labouring for the bodies or souls of men. They who do not thus labour, do not love. Faith works, love labours, hope patiently suffers all things.

4. Knowing your election - Which is through faith, by these plain proofs.

5. With power - Piercing the very heart with a sense of sin and deeply convincing you of your want of a saviour from guilt, misery, and eternal ruin. With the Holy Ghost - Bearing an outward testimony, by miracles, to the truth of what we preached, and you felt: also by his descent through laying on of hands. With much assurance - Literally, with full assurance, and much of it: the Spirit bearing witness by shedding the love of God abroad in your hearts, which is the highest testimony that can be given. And these signs, if not the miraculous gifts, always attend the preaching of the gospel,

unless it be in vain: neither are the extraordinary operations of the Holy Ghost ever wholly withheld, where the gospel is preached with power, and men are alive to God. For your sake - Seeking your advantage, not our own.

6. Though in much affliction, yet with much joy.

8. For from you the word sounded forth - (Thessalonica being a city of great commerce.) Being echoed, as it were, from you. And your conversion was divulged far beyond Macedonia and Achaia. So that we need not speak anything - Concerning it.

9. For they themselves - The people wherever we come.

10. Whom he hath raised from the dead - In proof of his future coming to judgment. Who delivereth us - He redeemed us once; he delivers us continually; and will deliver all that believe from the wrath, the eternal vengeance, which will then come upon the ungodly.

II

1. What was proposed, chap. i, 5, 6, is now more largely treated of: concerning Paul and his fellowlabourers, ver. 1-12; concerning the Thessalonians, ver. 13-16.

2. We had suffered - In several places. We are bold - Notwithstanding. With much contention - Notwithstanding both inward and outward conflicts of all kinds.

3. For our exhortation - That is, our preaching. A part is put for the whole. Is not, at any time, of deceit - We preach not a lie, but the truth of God. Nor of uncleanness - With any unholy or selfish view. This expression is not always appropriated to lust, although it is sometimes emphatically applied thereto. Nor in guile - But with great plainness of speech.

5. Flattering words - This ye know. Nor a cloak of covetousness - Of this God is witness. He calls men to witness an open fact; God, the secret intentions of the heart. In a point of a mixed nature, ver. 10, he appeals both to God and man.

6. Nor from others - Who would have honoured us more, if we had been burdensome - That is, taken state upon ourselves.

7. But we were gentle - Mild, tender. In the midst of you - Like a hen surrounded with her young. Even as a nurse cherisheth her own children - The offspring of her own womb.

8. To impart our own souls - To lay down our lives for your sake.

10. Holily - In the things of God. Justly - With regard to men. Unblamable - In respect of ourselves. Among you that believe - Who were the constant observers of our behaviour.

11. By exhorting, we are moved to do a thing willingly; by comforting, to do it joyfully; by charging, to do it carefully.

12. To his kingdom here, and glory hereafter.

14. Ye suffered the same things - The same fruit, the same afflictions, and the same experience, at all times, and in all places, are an excellent criterion of evangelical truth. As they from the Jews - Their countrymen.

15. Us - Apostles and preachers of the gospel. They please not God - Nor are they even careful to please him, notwithstanding their fair professions. And are contrary to all men - Are common enemies of mankind; not only by their continual seditions and insurrections, and by their utter contempt of all other nations; but in particular, by their endeavouring to hinder their hearing or receiving the gospel.

16. To fill up - The measure of their sins always, as they have ever done. But the vengeance of God is come upon them - Hath overtaken them unawares, whilst they were seeking to destroy others, and will speedily complete their destruction.

17. In this verse we have a remarkable instance, not so much of the transient affections of holy grief, desire, or joy, as of that abiding tenderness, that loving temper, which is so apparent in all St. Paul's writings, towards those he styles his children in the faith. This is the more carefully to be observed, because the passions occasionally exercising themselves, and flowing like a torrent, in the apostle, are observable to every reader; whereas it requires a nicer attention to discern those calm standing tempers, that fixed posture of his soul, from whence the others only flow out, and which more peculiarly distinguish his character.

18. Satan - By those persecuting Jews, Acts xvii, 13.

19. Ye also - As well as our other children.

III

1. We - Paul and Silvanus. Could bear no longer - Our desire and fear for you.

3. We are appointed hereto - Are in every respect laid in a fit posture for it, by the very design and contrivance of God himself for the trial and increase of our faith and all other graces. He gives riches to the world; but stores up his treasure of wholesome afflictions for his children.

6. But now when Timotheus was come to us from you - Immediately after his return, St. Paul

wrote; while his joy was fresh, and his tenderness at the height.

8. Now we live - Indeed; we enjoy life: so great is our affection for you.

10. And perfect that which is wanting in your faith - So St. Paul did not know that "they who are once upon the rock no longer need to be taught by man."

11. Direct our way - This prayer is addressed to Christ, as well as to the Father.

13. With all his, Christ's, saints - Both angels and men.

IV

1. More and more - It is not enough to have faith, even so as to please God, unless we abound more and more therein.

3. Sanctification - Entire holiness of heart and life: particular branches of it are subjoined. That ye abstain from fornication - A beautiful transition from sanctification to a single branch of the contrary; and this shows that nothing is so seemingly distant, or below our thoughts, but we have need to guard against it.

4. That every one know - For this requires knowledge, as well as chastity. To possess his vessel - His wife. In sanctification and honour - So as neither to dishonour God or himself, nor to obstruct, but further, holiness; remembering, marriage is not designed to inflame, but to conquer, natural desires.

5. Not in passionate desire - Which had no place in man when in a state of innocence. Who know not God - And so may naturally seek happiness in a creature. What seemingly accidental words slide in; and yet how fine, and how vastly important!

6. In this matter - By violating his bed. The things forbidden, here are three: fornication, ver. 3; the passion of desire, or inordinate affection in the married state, ver. 5; and the breach of the marriage contract.

8. He that despiseth - The commandments we gave. Despiseth God - Himself. Who hath also given you his Holy Spirit - To convince you of the truth, and enable you to be holy. What naked majesty of words! How oratorical, and yet with what great simplicity!-a simplicity that does not impair, but improve, the understanding to the utmost; that, like the rays of heat through a glass, collects all the powers of reason into one orderly point, from being scattered abroad in utter confusion.

9. We need not write - Largely. For ye are taught of God - By his Spirit.

11. That ye study - Literally, that ye be ambitious: an ambition worthy a Christian. To work with your hands - Not a needless caution; for temporal concerns are often a cross to them who are newly filled with the love of God.

12. Decently - That they may have no pretense to say, (but they will say it still,) "This religion makes men idle, and brings them to beggary." And may want nothing - Needful for life and godliness. What Christian desires more?

13. Now - Herein the efficacy of Christianity greatly appears, - that it neither takes away nor embitters, but sweetly tempers, that most refined of all affections, our desire of or love to the dead.

14. So - As God raised him. With him - With their living head.

15. By the word of the Lord - By a particular Revelation. We who are left - This intimates the fewness of those who will be then alive, compared to the multitude of the dead. Believers of all ages and nations make up, as it were, one body; in consideration of which, the believers of that age might put themselves in the place, and speak in the person, of them who were to live till the coming of the Lord. Not that St. Paul hereby asserted (though some seem to have imagined so) that the day of the Lord was at hand.

16. With a shout - Properly, a proclamation made to a great multitude. Above this is, the voice of the archangel; above both, the trumpet of God; the voice of God, somewhat analogous to the sound of a trumpet.

17. Together - In the same moment. In the air - The wicked will remain beneath, while the righteous, being absolved, shall be assessors with their Lord in the judgment. With the Lord - In heaven.

V

1. But of the precise times when this shall be.
2. For this in general ye do know; and ye can and need know no more.
3. When they - The men of the world say.
4. Ye are not in darkness - Sleeping secure in sin.
6. Awake, and keep awake - Being awakened, let us have all our spiritual senses about us.
7. They usually sleep and are drunken in the night - These things do not love the light.
9. God hath not appointed us to wrath - As he hath the obstinately impenitent.
10. Whether we wake or sleep - Be alive or dead at his coming.
12. Know them that,

Wesley's Notes on the Bible - The New Testament

1. labour among you:

2. Are over you in the Lord:

3. Admonish you. Know - See, mark, take knowledge of them and their work. Sometimes the same person may both labour, that is, preach; be over, or govern; and admonish the flock by particular application to each: sometimes two or more different persons, according as God variously dispenses his gifts. But O, what a misery is it when a man undertakes this whole work without either gifts or graces for any part of it! Why, then, will he undertake it? for pay? What! will he sell both his own soul and all the souls of the flock? What words can describe such a wretch as this? And yet even this may be "an honourable man!"

13. Esteem them very highly - Literally, more than abundantly, in love - The inexpressible sympathy that is between true pastors and their flock is intimated, not only here, but also in divers other places of this epistle. See

chap. ii, 7, 8. For their work's sake - The principal ground of their vast regard for them. But how are we to esteem them who do not work at all?

14. Warn the disorderly - Them that stand, as it were, out of their rank in the spiritual warfare. Some such were even in that church. The feeble-minded - Literally, them of little soul; such as have no spiritual courage.

15. See that none - Watch over both yourselves and each other. Follow that which is good - Do it resolutely and perseveringly.

16. Rejoice evermore - In uninterrupted happiness in God. Pray without ceasing - Which is the fruit of always rejoicing in the Lord. In everything give thanks - Which is the fruit of both the former. This is Christian perfection. Further than this we cannot go; and we need not stop short of it. Our Lord has purchased joy, as well as righteousness, for us. It is the very design of the gospel that, being saved from guilt, we should be happy in the love of Christ. Prayer may be said to be the breath of our spiritual life. He that lives cannot possibly cease breathing. So much as we really enjoy of the presence of God, so much prayer and praise do we offer up without ceasing; else our rejoicing is but delusion. Thanksgiving is inseparable from true prayer: it is almost essentially connected with it. He that always prays is ever giving praise, whether in ease or pain, both for prosperity and for the greatest adversity. He blesses God for all things, looks on them as coming from him, and receives them only for his sake; not choosing nor refusing, liking nor disliking, anything, but only as it is agreeable or disagreeable to his perfect will.

18. For this - That you should thus rejoice, pray, give thanks. Is the will of God - Always good, always pointing at our salvation.

19. Quench not the Spirit - Wherever it is, it burns; it flames in holy love, in joy, prayer, thanksgiving. O quench it not, damp it not in yourself or others, either by neglecting to do good, or by doing evil!

20. Despise not prophesyings - That is, preaching; for the apostle is not here speaking of extraordinary gifts. It seems, one means of grace is put for all; and whoever despises any of these, under whatever pretense, will surely (though perhaps gradually and almost insensibly) quench the Spirit.

21. Meantime, prove all things - Which any preacher recommends. (He speaks of practice, not of doctrines.) Try every advice by the touchstone of scripture, and hold fast that which is good - Zealously, resolutely, diligently practice it, in spite of all opposition.

22. And be equally zealous and careful to abstain from all appearance of evil - Observe, those who "heap to themselves teachers, having itching ears," under pretense of proving all things, have no countenance or excuse from this scripture.

23. And may the God of peace sanctify you - By the peace he works in you, which is a great means of sanctification. Wholly - The word signifies wholly and perfectly; every part and all that concerns you; all that is of or about you. And may the whole of you, the spirit and the soul and the body - Just before he said you; now he denominates them from their spiritual state. The spirit - Gal. vi, 8; wishing that it may be preserved whole and entire: then from their natural state, the soul and the body; (for these two make up the whole nature of man, Matt. x, 28;) wishing it may be preserved blameless till the coming of Christ. To explain this a little further: of the three here mentioned, only the two last are the natural constituent parts of man. The first is adventitious, and the supernatural gift of God, to be found in Christians only. That man cannot possibly consist of three parts, appears hence: The soul is either matter or not matter: there is no medium. But if it is matter, it is part of the body: if not matter, it coincides with the Spirit.

24. Who also will do it - Unless you quench the Spirit.

27. I charge you by the Lord - Christ, to whom proper divine worship is here paid. That this epistle - The first he wrote. Be read to all the brethren -- that is, in all the churches. They might have concealed it out of modesty, had not this been so solemnly enjoined: but what Paul commands under so strong an adjuration, Rome forbids under pain of excommunication.

John Wesley

NOTES ON ST. PAUL'S SECOND EPISTLE TO THE THESSALONIANS

THIS epistle seems to have been written soon after the former, chiefly on occasion of some things therein which had been misunderstood. Herein he,
    1. Congratulates their constancy in the faith, and exhorts them to advance daily in grace and wisdom.
    2. Reforms their mistake concerning the coming of our Lord And,
    3. Recommends several Christian duties. The parts of it are five:

I. The inscription, Chap. i. 1, 2

II. Thanksgiving and prayer for them, 3-12

III. The doctrine concerning the man of sin,. ii. 1-12 Whence he comforts them against this trial, 13, 14 Adding exhortation and prayer, 15-17

IV. An exhortation to prayer, with a prayer for. iii. 1-5 them, to correct the disorderly, 6-16

V. The conclusion, 17, 18

2nd THESSALONIANS

I

    3. It is highly observable, that the apostle wraps up his praise of men in praise to God; giving him the glory. Your faith groweth - Probably he had heard from them since his sending the former letter. Aboundeth - Like water that overflows its banks, and yet increaseth still.
    4. Which ye endure - "That ye may be accounted worthy of the kingdom."
    5. A manifest token - This is treated of in the sixth and following verses.
    6. It is a righteous thing with God - (However men may judge) to transfer the pressure from you to them. And it is remarkable that about this time, at the passover, the Jews raising a tumult, a great number (some say thirty thousand) of them were slain. St. Paul seems to allude to this beginning of sorrows, 1 Thess. ii, 16, which did not end but with their destruction.
    8. Taking vengeance - Does God barely permit this, or (as "the Lord" once "rained brimstone and fire from the Lord out of heaven," Gen. xix, 24) does a fiery stream go forth from him forever? Who know not God - (The root of all wickedness and misery) who remain in heathen ignorance. And who obey not - This refers chiefly to the Jews, who had heard the gospel.
    9. From the glory of his power - Tremble, ye stout-hearted. Everlasting destruction - As there can be no end of their sins, (the same enmity against God continuing,) so neither of their punishment; sin and its punishment running parallel throughout eternity itself. They must of necessity, therefore, be cut off from all good, and all possibility of it. From the presence of the Lord - Wherein chiefly consists the salvation of the righteous. What unspeakable punishment is implied even in falling short of this, supposing that nothing more were implied in his taking vengeance!
    10. To be glorified in his saints - For the wonderful glory of Christ shall shine in them.
    11. All the good pleasure of his goodness - Which is no less than perfect holiness.
    12. That the name - The love and power of our Lord may be glorified - Gloriously displayed in you.

II

1. Our gathering together to him - In the clouds.
2. Be not shaken in mind - In judgment. Or terrified - As those easily are who are immoderately fond of knowing future things. Neither by any pretended Revelation from the Spirit, nor by pretense of any word spoken by me.
3. Unless the falling away - From the pure faith of the gospel, come first. This began even in the apostolic age. But the man of sin, the son of perdition - Eminently so called, is not come yet. However, in many respects, the Pope has an indisputable claim to those titles. He is, in an emphatical sense, the man of sin, as he increases all manner of sin above measure. And he is, too, properly styled, the son of perdition, as he has caused the death of numberless multitudes, both of his opposers and followers, destroyed innumerable souls, and will himself perish everlastingly. He it is that opposeth himself to the emperor, once his rightful sovereign; and that exalteth himself above all that is called God, or that is worshipped - Commanding angels, and putting kings under his feet, both of whom are called gods in scripture; claiming the highest power, the highest honour; suffering himself, not once only, to be styled God or vice-God. Indeed no less is implied in his ordinary title, "Most Holy Lord," or, "Most Holy Father." So that he sitteth - Enthroned. In the temple of God - Mentioned Rev. xi, 1. Declaring himself that he is God - Claiming the prerogatives which belong to God alone.
6. And now ye know - By what I told you when I was with you. That which restraineth - The power of the Roman emperors. When this is taken away, the wicked one will be revealed. In his time - His appointed season, and not before.
7. He will surely be revealed; for the mystery - The deep, secret power of iniquity, just opposite to the power of godliness, already worketh. It began with the love of honour, and the desire of power; and is completed in the entire subversion of the gospel of Christ. This mystery of iniquity is not wholly confined to the Romish church, but extends itself to others also. It seems to consist of,
   1. Human inventions added to the written word.
   2. Mere outside performances put in the room of faith and love.
   3. Other mediators besides the man Christ Jesus. The two last branches, together with idolatry and bloodshed, are the direct consequences of the former; namely, the adding to the word of God. Already worketh - In the church. Only he that restraineth - That is, the potentate who successively has Rome in his power. The emperors, heathen or Christian; the kings, Goths or Lombards; the Carolingian or German emperors.
8. And then - When every prince and power that restrains is taken away. Will that wicked one - Emphatically so called, be revealed. Whom the Lord will soon consume with the spirit of his mouth - His immediate power. And destroy - With the very first appearance of his glory.
10. Because they received not the love of the truth - Therefore God suffered them to fall into that "strong delusion."
11. Therefore God shall send them - That is, judicially permit to come upon them, strong delusion.
12. That they all may be condemned - That is, the consequence of which will be, that they all will be condemned who believed not the truth, but had pleasure in unrighteousness - That is, who believed not the truth, because they loved sin.
13. God hath from the beginning - Of your hearing the gospel. Chosen you to salvation - Taken you out of the world, and placed you in the way to glory.
14. To which - Faith and holiness. He hath called you by our gospel - That which we preached, accompanied with the power of his Spirit.
15. Hold - Without adding to, or diminishing from, the traditions which ye have been taught - The truths which I have delivered to you. Whether by word or by our epistle - He preached before he wrote. And he had written concerning this in his former epistle.

III

1. May run - Go on swiftly, without any interruption. And be glorified - Acknowledged as divine, and bring forth much fruit.
2. All men have not faith - And all men who have not are more or less unreasonable and wicked men.
3. Who will stablish you - That cleave to him by faith. And guard you from the evil one - And all his instruments.
4. We trust in the Lord concerning you - Thus only should we trust in any man.
5. Now the Lord - The Spirit, whose proper work this is. Direct - Lead you straight forward. Into the patience of Christ - Of which he set you a pattern.
6. That walketh disorderly - Particularly by not working. Not according to the tradition he received of us - The admonition we gave, both by word of mouth, and in our former epistle.

10. Neither let him eat - Do not maintain him in idleness.
11. Doing nothing, but being busybodies - To which idleness naturally disposes.
12. Work quietly - Letting the concerns of other people alone.

14. Have no company with him - No intimacy, no familiarity, no needless correspondence.
15. Admonish him as a brother - Tell him lovingly of the reason why you shun him.
16. The Lord of peace - Christ. Give you peace by all means - In every way and manner.

NOTES ON ST. PAUL'S FIRST EPISTLE TO TIMOTHY

THE mother of Timothy was a Jewess, but his father was a gentile. He was converted to Christianity very early; and while he was yet but a youth, was taken by St. Paul to assist him in the work of the gospel, chiefly in watering the churches which he had planted. He was therefore properly, as was Titus, an itinerant evangelist, a kind of secondary apostle, whose office was, to regulate all things in the churches to which he was sent; and to inspect and reform whatsoever was amiss either in the bishops, deacons, or people. St. Paul had doubtless largely instructed him in private conversation for the due execution of so weighty an office. Yet to fix things more upon his mind, and to give him an opportunity of having recourse to them afterward, and of communicating them to others, as there might be occasion, as also to leave divine directions in writing, for the use of the church and its ministers in all ages; he sent him this excellent pastoral letter, which contains a great variety of important sentiments for their regulation. Though St. Paul styles him his "own son in the faith," yet he does not appear to have been converted by the apostle; but only to have been exceeding dear to him, who had established him therein; and whom he had diligently and faithfully served, like a son with his father in the gospel. Phil. ii, 22. The epistle contains three parts:

I. The inscription, C.i.1, 2

II. The instruction of Timothy how to behave at Ephesus, wherein,
    1. In general, he gives him an injunction to deliver to them that taught the law in a wrong manner, and confirms at the same time the sum of the gospel as exemplified in himself, 3-20
    2. In particular,
        1. He prescribes to men, a method of prayer,. C.ii.1-8 To women, good works and modesty, 9-15
        2. He recounts the requisites of a bishop,. C.iii.1-7 The duties of deacons, 8-10 of women, 11-13
        3. He shows what Timothy should teach 14-C.iv.1-6 What he should avoid, 7-11 What follow after, 12-16 How he should treat men and women, C.v.1, 2 Widows, 3-16 Elders, 17-19 Offenders, 20, 21 Himself, 22, 23 Those he doubts of, 24, 25 Servants, C.vi.1, 2
        4. False teachers are reproved, 3-10 Timothy is admonished, quickened, 11, 12 and charged, 13-16 Precepts are prescribed to be enforced on the rich, 17-19

III. The conclusion, 20,

1st TIMOTHY

I

1. Paul an apostle - Familiarity is to be set aside where the things of God are concerned. According to the commandment of God - The authoritative appointment of God the Father. Our saviour - So styled in many other places likewise, as being the grand orderer of the whole scheme of our salvation. And Christ our hope - That is, the author, object, and ground, of all our hope.

2. Grace, mercy, peace - St. Paul wishes grace and peace in his epistles to the churches. To Timotheus he adds mercy, the most tender grace towards those who stand in need of it. The experience of this prepares a man to be a minister of the gospel.

3. Charge some to teach no other doctrine - Than I have taught. Let them put nothing in the place of it, add nothing to it.

4. Neither give heed - So as either to teach or regard them. To fables - Fabulous Jewish traditions. And endless genealogies - Nor those delivered in scripture, but the long intricate pedigrees whereby they strove to prove their descent from such or such a person. Which afford questions - Which lead only to useless and endless controversies.

5. Whereas the end of the commandment - of the whole Christian institution. Is love - And this

was particularly the end of the commandment which Timotheus was to enforce at Ephesus, ver. 3, 18. The foundation is faith; the end, love. But this can only subsist in an heart purified by faith, and is always attended with a good conscience.

6. From which - Love and a good conscience. Some are turned aside - An affectation of high and extensive knowledge sets a man at the greatest distance from faith, and all sense of divine things. To vain jangling - And of all vanities, none are more vain than dry, empty disputes on the things of God.

7. Understanding neither the very things they speak, nor the subject they speak of.

8. We grant the whole Mosaic law is good, answers excellent purposes, if a man use it in a proper manner. Even the ceremonial is good, as it points to Christ; and the moral law is holy, just, and good, on its own nature; and of admirable use both to convince unbelievers, and to guide believers in all holiness.

9. The law doth not lie against a righteous man - Doth not strike or condemn him. But against the lawless and disobedient - They who despise the authority of the lawgiver violate the first commandment, which is the foundation of the law, and the ground of all obedience. Against the ungodly and sinners - Who break the second commandment, worshipping idols, or not worshipping the true God. The unholy and profane - Who break the third commandment by taking his name in vain.

10. Manstealers - The worst of all thieves, in comparison of whom, highwaymen and housebreakers are innocent. What then are most traders in negroes, procurers of servants for America, and all who list soldiers by lies, tricks, or enticements?

11. According to the glorious gospel - Which, far from "making void," does effectually "establish, the law."

12. I thank Christ, who hath enabled me, in that he accounted me faithful, having put me into the ministry - The meaning is, I thank him for putting me into the ministry, and enabling me to be faithful therein.

13. A blasphemer - Of Christ. A persecutor - Of his church. A reviler - Of his doctrine and people. But I obtained mercy - He does not say, because I was unconditionally elected; but because I did it in ignorance. Not that his ignorance took away his sin; but it left him capable of mercy; which he would hardly have been, had he acted thus contrary to his own conviction.

14. And the grace - Whereby I obtained mercy. Was exceeding abundant with faith - Opposite to my preceding unbelief. And love - Opposite to my blasphemy, persecution, and oppression.

15. This is a faithful saying - A most solemn preface. And worthy of all acceptation - Well deserving to be accepted, received, embraced, with all the faculties of our whole soul. That Christ - Promised. Jesus - Exhibited. Came into the world to save sinners - All sinners, without exception.

16. For this cause God showed me mercy, that all his longsuffering might be shown, and that none might hereafter despair.

17. The King of eternity - A phrase frequent with the Hebrews. How unspeakably sweet is the thought of eternity to believers!

18. This charge I commit to thee - That thou mayest deliver it to the church. According to the prophecies concerning thee - Uttered when thou wast received as an evangelist, chap. iv, 14; probably by many persons, chap. vi, 12; that, being encouraged by them, thou mightest war the good warfare.

19. Holding fast faith - Which is as a most precious liquor. And a good conscience - Which is as a clean glass. Which - Namely, a good conscience. Some having thrust away - It goes away unwillingly it always says, "Do not hurt me." And they who retain this do not make shipwreck of their faith. Indeed, none can make shipwreck of faith who never had it. These, therefore, were once true believers: yet they fell not only foully, but finally; for ships once wrecked cannot be afterwards saved.

20. Whom - Though absent. I have delivered to Satan, that they may learn not to blaspheme - That by what they suffer they may be in some measure restrained, if they will not repent.

II

1. I exhort therefore - Seeing God is so gracious. In this chapter he gives directions,
    1. With regard to public prayers
    2. With regard to doctrine. Supplication is here the imploring help in time of need: prayer is any kind of offering up our desires to God. But true prayer is the vehemency of holy zeal, the ardour of divine love, arising from a calm, undisturbed soul, moved upon by the Spirit of God. Intercession is prayer for others. We may likewise give thanks for all men, in the full sense of the word, for that God "willeth all men to be saved," and Christ is the Mediator of all.

2. For all that are in authority - Seeing even the lowest country magistrates frequently do much good or much harm. God supports the power of magistracy for the sake of his own people, when, in the present state of men, it could not otherwise be kept up in any nation whatever. Godliness - Inward religion; the true worship of God. Honesty - A comprehensive word taking in the whole duty we owe to our neighbour.

3. For this - That we pray for all men. Do you ask, "Why are not more converted?" We do not pray

enough. Is acceptable in the sight of God our saviour - Who has actually saved us that believe, and willeth all men to be saved. It is strange that any whom he has actually saved should doubt the universality of his grace!

4. Who willeth seriously all men - Not a part only, much less the smallest part. To be saved - Eternally. This is treated of, ver. 5, 6. And, in order thereto, to come - They are not compelled. To the knowledge of the truth - Which brings salvation. This is treated of, ver. 6, 7.

5. For - The fourth verse is proved by the fifth; the first, by the fourth. There is one God - And they who have not him, through the one Mediator, have no God. One mediator also - We could not rejoice that there is a God, were there not a mediator also; one who stands between God and men, to reconcile man to God, and to transact the whole affair of our salvation. This excludes all other mediators, as saints and angels, whom the Papists set up and idolatrously worship as such: just as the heathens of old set up many mediators, to pacify their superior gods. The man - Therefore all men are to apply to this mediator, "who gave himself for all."

6. Who gave himself a ransom for all - Such a ransom, the word signifies, wherein a like or equal is given; as an eye for an eye, or life for life: and this ransom, from the dignity of the person redeeming, was more than equivalent to all mankind. To be testified of in due season - Literally, in his own seasons; those chosen by his own wisdom.

8. I will - A word strongly expressing his apostolical authority. Therefore - This particle connects the eighth with the first verse. That men pray in every place - Public and private. Wherever men are, there prayer should be. Lifting up holy hands - Pure from all known sin. Without wrath - In any kind, against any creature. And every temper or motion of our soul that is not according to love is wrath. And doubting - Which is contrary to faith. And wrath, or unholy actions, or want of faith in him we call upon, are the three grand hindrances of God's hearing our petitions. Christianity consists of faith and love, embracing truth and grace: therefore the sum of our wishes should be, to pray, and live, and die, without any wrath or doubt.

9. With sobriety - Which, in St. Paul's sense, is the virtue which governs our whole life according to true wisdom. Not with curled hair, not with gold - Worn by way of ornament. Not with pearls - Jewels of any kind: a part is put for the whole. Not with costly raiment - These four are expressly forbidden by name to all women (here is no exception) professing godliness, and no art of man can reconcile with the Christian profession the wilful violation of an express command.

12. To usurp authority over the man - By public teaching.

13. First - So that woman was originally the inferior.

14. And Adam was not deceived - The serpent deceived Eve: Eve did not deceive Adam, but persuaded him. "Thou hast hearkened unto the voice of thy wife," Gen. iii, 17. The preceding verse showed why a woman should not "usurp authority over the man." this shows why she ought not "to teach." She is more easily deceived, and more easily deceives. The woman being deceived transgressed - "The serpent deceived" her, Gen. iii, 13, and she transgressed.

15. Yet she - That is, women in general, who were all involved with Eve in the sentence pronounced, Gen. iii, 16. Shall be saved in childbearing - Carried safe through the pain and danger which that sentence entails upon them for the transgression; yea, and finally saved, if they continue in loving faith and holy wisdom.

III

1. He desireth a good work - An excellent, but labourious, employment.

2. Therefore - That he may be capable of it. A bishop - Or pastor of a congregation. Must be blameless - Without fault or just suspicion. The husband of one wife - This neither means that a bishop must be married, nor that he may not marry a second wife; which it is just as lawful for him to do as to marry a first, and may in some cases be his bounden duty. But whereas polygamy and divorce on slight occasions were common both among the Jews and heathens, it teaches us that ministers, of all others, ought to stand clear of those sins. Vigilant, prudent - Lively and zealous, yet calm and wise. Of good behaviour - Naturally flowing from that vigilance and prudence.

4. Having his children in subjection with all seriousness - For levity undermines all domestic authority; and this direction, by a parity of reason, belongs to all parents.

6. Lest being puffed up - With this new honour, or with the applause which frequently follows it. He fall into the condemnation of the devil - The same into which the devil fell.

7. He ought also to have a good report - To have had a fair character in time past. From them that are without - That are not Christians. Lest he fall into reproach - By their rehearsing his former life, which might discourage and prove a snare to him.

8. Likewise the deacons must be serious - Men of a grave, decent, venerable behaviour. But where are presbyters? Were this order essentially distinct from that of bishops, could the apostle have passed it over in silence? Not desirous of filthy gain - With what abhorrence does he everywhere speak of this!

All that is gained (above food and raiment) by ministering in holy things is filthy gain indeed; far more filthy than what is honestly gained by raking kennels, or emptying common sewers.

9. Holding fast the faith in a pure conscience - Steadfast in faith, holy in heart and life.

10. Let these be proved first - Let a trial be made how they believe. Then let them minister - Let them be fixed in that office.

11. Faithful in all things - Both to God, their husbands, and the poor.

13. They purchase a good degree - Or step, toward some higher office. And much boldness - From the testimony of a good conscience.

15. That thou mayest know how to behave - This is the scope of the epistle. In the house of God - Who is the master of the family. Which is - As if he had said, By the house of God, I mean the church.

16. The mystery of godliness - Afterwards specified in six articles, which sum up the whole economy of Christ upon earth. Is the pillar and ground - The foundation and support of all the truth taught in his church. God was manifest in the flesh - In the form of a servant, the fashion of a man, for three and thirty years. Justified by the Spirit - Publicly "declared to be the Son of God," by his resurrection from the dead. Seen - Chiefly after his resurrection. By angels - Both good and bad. Preached among the gentiles - This elegantly follows. The angels were the least, the gentiles the farthest, removed from him; and the foundation both of this preaching and of their faith was laid before his assumption. Was believed on in the world - Opposed to heaven, into which he was taken up. The first point is, He was manifested in the flesh; the last, He was taken up into glory.

IV

1. But the Spirit saith - By St. Paul himself to the Thessalonians, and probably by other contemporary prophets. Expressly - As concerning a thing of great moment, and soon to be fulfilled. That in the latter times - These extend from our Lord's ascension till his coming to judgment. Some - Yea, many, and by degrees the far greater part. Will depart from the faith - The doctrine once delivered to the saints. Giving heed to seducing spirits - Who inspire false prophets.

2. These will depart from the faith, by the hypocrisy of them that speak lies, having their own consciences as senseless and unfeeling as flesh that is seared with an hot iron.

3. Forbidding priests, monks, and nuns to marry, and commanding all men to abstain from such and such meats at such and such times. Which God hath created to be received by them that know the truth - That all meats are now clean. With thanksgiving - Which supposes a pure conscience.

5. It is sanctified by the word of God - Creating all, and giving it to man for food. And by prayer - The children of God are to pray for the sanctification of all the creatures which they use. And not only the Christians, but even the Jews, yea, the very heathens used to consecrate their table by prayer.

7. Like those who were to contend in the Grecian games, exercise thyself unto godliness - Train thyself up in holiness of heart and life, with the utmost labour, vigour, and diligence.

8. Bodily exercise profiteth a little - Increases the health and strength of the body.

10. Therefore - Animated by this promise. We both labour and suffer reproach - We regard neither pleasure, ease, nor honour. Because we trust - For this very thing the world will hate us. In the living God - Who will give us the life he has promised. Who is the saviour of all men - Preserving them in this life, and willing to save them eternally. But especially - In a more eminent manner. Of them that believe - And so are saved everlastingly.

12. Let no one have reason to despise thee for thy youth. To prevent this, Be a pattern in word - Public and private. In spirit - In your whole temper. In faith - When this is placed in the midst of several other Christian graces, it generally means a particular branch of it; fidelity or faithfulness.

13. Give thyself to reading - Both publicly and privately. Enthusiasts, observe this! Expect no end without the means.

14. Neglect not - They neglect it who do not exercise it to the full. The gift - Of feeding the flock, of power, and love, and sobriety. Which was given thee by prophecy - By immediate direction from God. By the laying on of my hands - 2 Tim. i, 6; while the elders joined also in the solemnity. This presbytery probably consisted of some others, together with Paul and Silas.

15. Meditate - The Bible makes no distinction between this and to contemplate, whatever others do. True meditation is no other than faith, hope, love, joy, melted down together, as it were, by the fire of God's Holy Spirit; and offered up to God in secret. He that is wholly in these, will be little in worldly company, in other studies, in collecting books, medals, or butterflies: wherein many pastors drone away so considerable a part of their lives.

16. Continue in them - In all the preceding advices.

V

1. Rebuke not - Considering your own youth, with such a severity as would otherwise be proper.

3. honour - That is, maintain out of the public stock.

4. Let these learn to requite their parents - For all their former care, trouble, and expense.

5. Widows indeed - Who have no near relations to provide for them; and who are wholly devoted to God. Desolate - Having neither children, nor grandchildren to relieve her.

6. She that liveth in pleasure - Delicately, voluptuously, in elegant, regular sensuality, though not in the use of any such pleasures as are unlawful in themselves.

7. That they - That is, the widows.

8. If any provide not - Food and raiment. For his own - Mother and grandmother, being desolate widows. He hath - Virtually. Denied the faith - Which does not destroy, but perfect, natural duties. What has this to do with heaping up money for our children, for which it is often so impertinently alleged? But all men have their reasons for laying up money. One will go to hell for fear of want; another acts like a heathen, lest he should be worse than an infidel.

9. Let not a widow be chosen - Into the number of deaconesses, who attended sick women or travelling preachers. Under threescore - Afterwards they were admitted at forty, if they were eminent for holiness. Having been the wife of one husband - That is, having lived in lawful marriage, whether with one or more persons successively.

10. If she hath washed the feet of the saints - Has been ready to do the meanest offices for them.

11. Refuse - Do not choose. For when they are waxed wanton against Christ - To whose more immediate service they had addicted themselves. They want to marry - And not with a single eye to the glory of God; and so withdraw themselves from that entire service of the church to which they were before engaged.

12. They have rejected their first faith - Have deserted their trust in God, and have acted contrary to the first conviction, namely, that wholly to devote themselves to his service was the most excellent way. When we first receive power to believe, does not the Spirit of God generally point out what are the most excellent things; and at the same time, give us an holy resolution to walk in the highest degree of Christian severity? And how unwise are we ever to sink into anything below it!

14. I counsel therefore the younger women - Widows or virgins, such as are not disposed to live single. To marry, to bear children, to guide the family - Then will they have sufficient employment of their own. And give no occasion of reproach to the adversary - Whether Jew or heathen.

15. Some - Widows. Have turned aside after Satan - Who has drawn them from Christ.

17. Let the elders that rule well - Who approve themselves faithful stewards of all that is committed to their charge. Be counted worthy of double honour - A more abundant provision, seeing that such will employ it all to the glory of God. As it was the most labourious and disinterested men who were put into these offices, so whatever any one had to bestow, in his life or death, was generally lodged in their hands for the poor. By this means the churchmen became very rich in after ages, but as the design of the donors was something else, there is the highest reason why it should be disposed of according to their pious intent. Especially those - Of them. Who labour - Diligently and painfully. In the word and teaching - In teaching the word.

18. Deut. xxv, 4

19. Against an elder - Or presbyter. Do not even receive an accusation, unless by two or three witnesses - By the Mosaic law, a private person might be cited (though not condemned) on the testimony of one witness; but St. Paul forbids an elder to be even cited on such evidence, his reputation being of more importance than that of others.

20. Those - Elders. That sin - Scandalously, and are duly convicted. Rebuke before all - The church.

21. I charge thee before God - Referring to the last judgment, in which we shall stand before God and Christ, with his elect, that is, holy, angels, who are the witnesses of our conversation. The apostle looks through his own labours, and even through time itself, and seems to stand as one already in eternity. That thou observe these things without prejudging - Passing no sentence till the cause is fully heard. Or partiality - For or against any one.

22. Lay hands suddenly on no man - That is, appoint no man to church offices without full trial and examination; else thou wilt be accessary to, and accountable for, his misbehaviour in his office. Keep thy self pure - From the blood of all men.

24. Some men's sins are manifest beforehand - Before any strict inquiry be made. Going before to judgment - So that you may immediately judge them unworthy of any spiritual office. And some they - Their sins. Follow after - More covertly.

25. They that are otherwise - Not so manifest. Cannot be long hid - From thy knowledge. On this account, also, be not hasty in laying on of hands.

John Wesley

VI

1. Let servants under the yoke - Of heathen masters. Account them worthy of all honour - All the honour due from a servant to a master. Lest the name of God and his doctrine be blasphemed - As it surely will, if they do otherwise.

2. Let them not despise them - Pay them the less honour or obedience. Because they are brethren -- and in that respect on a level with them. They that live in a religious community know the danger of this; and that greater grace is requisite to bear with the faults of a brother, than of an infidel, or man of the world. But rather do them service - Serve them so much the more diligently. Because they are joint partakers of the great benefit - Salvation. These things - Paul, the aged, gives young Timotheus a charge to dwell upon practical holiness. Less experienced teachers are apt to neglect the superstructure, whilst they lay the foundation; but of so great importance did St. Paul see it to enforce obedience to Christ, as well as to preach faith in his blood, that, after strongly urging the life of faith on professors, he even adds another charge for the strict observance of it.

3. If any teach otherwise - Than strict practical holiness in all Its branches. And consent not to sound words - Literally, healthful words; words that have no taint of falsehood, or tendency to encourage sin. And the doctrine which is after godliness - Exquisitely contrived to answer all the ends, and secure every interest, of real piety.

4. He is puffed up - Which is the cause of his not consenting to the doctrine which is after inward, practical religion. By this mark we may know them. Knowing nothing - As he ought to know. Sick of questions - Doatingly fond of dispute; an evil, but common, disease; especially where practice is forgotten. Such, indeed, contend earnestly for singular phrases, and favourite points of their own. Everything else, however, like the preaching of Christ and his apostles, is all "law," and "bondage," and "carnal reasoning." Strifes of words - Merely verbal controversies. Whereof cometh envy - Of the gifts and success of others. Contention - For the preeminence. Such disputants seldom like the prosperity of others, or to be less esteemed themselves. Evil surmisings - It not being their way to think well of those that differ from themselves in opinion.

5. Supposing that gain is godliness - Thinking the best religion is the getting of money: a far more common case than is usually supposed.

6. But godliness with content - The inseparable companion of true, vital religion. Is great gain - Brings unspeakable profit in time, as well as eternity.

7. Neither can we carry anything out - To what purpose, then, do we heap together so many things? O, give me one thing, - a safe and ready passage to my own country!

8. Covering - That is, raiment and an house to cover us. This is all that a Christian needs, and all that his religion allows him to desire.

9. They that desire to be rich - To have more than these; for then they would be so far rich; and the very desire banishes content, and exposes them to ruin. Fall-plunge - A sad gradation! Into temptation - Miserable food for the soul! And a snare - Or trap. Dreadful "covering!" And into many foolish and hurtful desires - Which are sown and fed by having more than we need. Then farewell all hope of content! What then remains, but destruction for the body, and perdition for the soul?

10. Love of money - Commonly called "prudent care" of what a man has. Is the root - The parent of all manner of evils. Which some coveting have erred - Literally, missed the mark. They aimed not at faith, but at something else. And pierced themselves with many sorrows - From a guilty conscience, tormenting passions, desires contrary to reason, religion, and one another. How cruel are worldly men to themselves!

11. But thou, O man of God - Whatever all the world else do. A man of God is either a prophet, a messenger of God, or a man devoted to God; a man of another world. Flee - As from a serpent, instead of coveting these things. Follow after righteousness - The whole image of God; though sometimes this word is used, not in the general, but in the particular, acceptation, meaning only that single branch of it which is termed justice. Faith - Which is also taken here in the general and full sense; namely, a divine, supernatural sight of God, chiefly in respect of his mercy in Christ. This faith is the foundation of righteousness, the support of godliness, the root of every grace of the Spirit. Love - This St. Paul intermixes with everything that is good: he, as it were, penetrates whatever he treats of with love, the glorious spring of all inward and outward holiness.

12. Fight the good fight of faith - Not about words. Lay hold on eternal life - Just before thee. Thou hast confessed the good confession - Perhaps at his baptism: so likewise, ver. 13; but with a remarkable variation of the expression. Thou hast confessed the good confession before many witnesses - To which they all assented. He witnessed the good confession; but Pilate did not assent to it.

13. I charge thee before God, who quickeneth all things - Who hath quickened thee, and will quicken thee at the great day.

15. Which - Appearing. In his own times - The power, the knowledge, and the Revelation of which, remain in his eternal mind.

16. Who only hath underived, independent immortality. Dwelling in light unapproachable - To the highest angel. Whom no man hath seen, or can see - With bodily eyes. Yet "we shall see him as he is."

17. What follows seems to be a kind of a postscript. Charge the rich in this world - Rich in such beggarly riches as this world affords. Not to be highminded - O who regards this! Not to think better of themselves for their money, or anything it can purchase. Neither to trust in uncertain riches - Which they may lose in an hour; either for happiness or defense. But in the living God - All the rest is dead clay. Who giveth us - As it were holding them out to us in his hand. All things - Which we have. Richly - Freely, abundantly. To enjoy - As his gift, in him and for him. When we use them thus, we do indeed enjoy all things. Where else is there any notice taken of the rich, in all the apostolic writings, save to denounce woes and vengeance upon them?

18. To do good - To make this their daily employ, that they may be rich - May abound in all good works. Ready to distribute - Singly to particular persons. Willing to communicate - To join in all public works of charity.

19. Treasuring up for themselves a good foundation - Of an abundant reward, by the free mercy of God. That they may lay hold on eternal life - This cannot be done by alms-deeds; yet they "come up for a memorial before God," Acts x, 4. And the lack even of this may be the cause why God will withhold grace and salvation from us.

20. Keep that which is committed to thy trust - The charge I have given thee, chap. i, 18. Avoid profane empty babblings - How weary of controversy was this acute disputant! And knowledge falsely so called - Most of the ancient heretics were great pretenders to knowledge.

John Wesley

NOTES ON ST. PAUL'S SECOND EPISTLE TO TIMOTHY

THIS epistle was probably wrote by St. Paul, during his second confinement at Rome, not long before his martyrdom. It is, as it were, the swan's dying song. But though it was wrote many years after the former, yet they are both of the same kind, and nearly resemble each other. It has three parts:

I. The inscription, Chap. i. 1, 2

II. An invitation, "Come to me," variously expressed,
    1. Having declared his love to Timothy, 3-5 he exhorts him, " Be not ashamed of me." 6-14 And subjoins various examples, 15-18
    2. He adds the twofold proposition,
        1. "Be strong,"
        2. "Commit the ministry" to faithful men,. ii. 1, 2 The former is treated of, 3-13 The latter, 14 With farther directions concerning his own behaviour, 15- iv.8
    3. "Come quickly." Here St. Paul, 9
        1. Mentions his being left alone, 10-12
        2. Directs to bring his books, 13
        3. Gives a caution concerning Alexander, 14, 15
        4. Observes the inconstancy of men, and the faithfulness of God, 16-18
    4. "Come before winter." Salutations, 19-21

III. The concluding blessing, 22

2nd TIMOTHY

I

3. Whom I serve from my forefathers - That is, whom both I and my ancestors served, with a pure conscience - He always worshipped God according to his conscience, both before and after his conversion One who stands on the verge of life is much refreshed by the remembrance of his predecessors, to whom he is going.
4. Being mindful of thy tears - Perhaps frequently shed, as well as at the apostle's last parting with him.
5. Which dwelt - A word not applied to a transient guest, but only to a settled inhabitant. First - Probably this was before Timothy was born, yet not beyond St. Paul's memory.
6. Wherefore - Because I remember this. I remind thee of stirring up - Literally, blowing up the coals into a flame. The gift of God - All the spiritual gifts, which the grace of God has given thee.
7. And let nothing discourage thee, for God hath not given us - That is, the spirit which God hath given us Christians, is not the spirit of fear - Or cowardice. But of power - Banishing fear. And love and sobriety - These animate us in our duties to God, our brethren, and ourselves. Power and sobriety are two good extremes. Love is between, the tie and temperament of both; preventing the two bad extremes of fearfulness and rashness. More is said concerning power, ver. 8; concerning love, chap. ii, 14, &c.; concerning sobriety, chap. iii, 1, &c.
8. Therefore be not thou ashamed - When fear is banished, evil shame also flees away. Of the testimony of our Lord - The gospel, and of testifying the truth of it to all men. Nor of me - The cause of the servants of God doing his work, cannot be separated from the cause of God himself. But be thou partaker of the afflictions - Which I endure for the gospel's sake. According to the power of God - This which overcomes all things is nervously described in the two next verses.
9. Who hath saved us - By faith. The love of the Father, the grace of our saviour, and the whole economy of salvation, are here admirably described. Having called us with an holy calling - Which is all

from God, and claims us all for God. According to his own purpose and grace - That is, his own gracious purpose. Which was given us - Fixed for our advantage, before the world began.

10. By the appearing of our saviour - This implies his whole abode upon earth. Who hath abolished death - Taken away its sting, and turned it into a blessing. And hath brought life and immortality to light - Hath clearly revealed by the gospel that immortal life which he hath purchased for us.

12. That which I have committed to him - My soul. Until that day - Of his final appearing.

13. The pattern of sound words - The model of pure, wholesome doctrine.

14. The good thing - This wholesome doctrine.

15. All who are in Asia - Who had attended me at Rome for a while. Are turned away from me - What, from Paul the aged, the faithful soldier, and now prisoner of Christ! This was a glorious trial, and wisely reserved for that time, when he was on the borders of immortality. Perhaps a little measure of the same spirit might remain with him under whose picture are those affecting words, "The true effigy of Francis Xavier, apostle of the Indies, forsaken of all men, dying in a cottage."

16. The family of Onesiphorus - As well as himself. Hath often refreshed me - Both at Ephesus and Rome.

II

2. The things - The wholesome doctrine, ver. 13. Commit - Before thou leavest Ephesus. To faithful men, who will be able, after thou art gone, to teach others.

4. No man that warreth entangleth himself - Any more than is unavoidable. In the affairs of this life - With worldly business or cares. That - Minding war only, he may please his captain. In this and the next verse there is a plain allusion to the Roman law of arms, and to that of the Grecian games. According to the former, no soldier was to engage in any civil employment; according to the latter, none could be crowned as conqueror, who did not keep strictly to the rules of the game.

6. Unless he labour first, he will reap no fruit.

8. Of the seed of David - This one genealogy attend to.

9. Is not bound - Not hindered in its course.

10. Therefore - Encouraged by this, that "the word of God be not bound." I endure all things - See the spirit of a real Christian? Who would not wish to be likeminded? Salvation is deliverance from all evil; glory, the enjoyment of all good.

11. Dead with him - Dead to sin, and ready to die for him.

12. If we deny him - To escape suffering for him.

13. If we believe not - That is, though some believe not, God will make good all his promises to them that do believe. He cannot deny himself - His word cannot fail.

14. Remind them - Who are under thy charge. O how many unnecessary things are thus unprofitably, nay hurtfully, contended for.

15. A workman that needeth not to be ashamed - Either of unfaithfulness or unskilfulness. Rightly dividing the word of truth - Duly explaining and applying the whole scripture, so as to give each hearer his due portion. But they that give one part of the gospel to all (the promises and comforts to unawakened, hardened, scoffing men) have real need to be ashamed.

16. They - Who babble thus will grow worse and worse.

17. And their word - If they go on, will be mischievous as well as vain, and will eat as a gangrene.

18. Saying the resurrection is already past - Perhaps asserting that it is only the spiritual passing from death unto life.

19. But the foundation of God - His truth and faithfulness. Standeth fast - Can never be overthrown; being as it were sealed with a seal, which has an inscription on each side: on the one, The Lord knoweth those that are his; on the other, Let every one who nameth the name of the Lord, as his Lord, depart from iniquity. Indeed, they only are his who depart from iniquity. To all others he will say, "I know you not." Matt. vii, 22, 23

20. But in a great house - Such as the church, it is not strange that there are not only vessels of gold and silver, designed for honourable uses, but also of wood and of earth - For less honourable purposes. Yet a vessel even of gold may be put to the vilest use, though it was not the design of him that made it.

21. If a man purge himself from these - Vessels of dishonour, so as to have no fellowship with them.

22. Flee youthful desires - Those peculiarly incident to youth. Follow peace with them - Unity with all true believers. Out of a pure heart-Youthful desires, destroy this purity: righteousness, faith, love, peace, accompany it.

24. A servant of the Lord must not - Eagerly or passionately. Strive - As do the vain wranglers spoken of, verse 23. But be apt to teach - Chiefly by patience and unwearied assiduity.

25. In meekness - He has often need of zeal, always of meekness. If haply God - For it is wholly his work. May give them repentance - The acknowledging of the truth would then quickly follow.

26. Who - At present are not only captives, but asleep; utterly insensible of their captivity.

III

1. In the last days - The time of the gospel dispensation, commencing at the time of our Lord's death, is peculiarly styled the last days. Grievous - Troublesome and dangerous.

2. For men - Even in the church. Will be - In great numbers, and to an higher degree than ever. Lovers of themselves - Only, not their neighbours, the first root of evil. Lovers of money - The second.

3. Without natural affection - To their own children. Intemperate, fierce - Both too soft, and too hard.

4. Lovers of sensual pleasure - Which naturally extinguishes all love and sense of God.

5. Having a form - An appearance of godliness, but not regarding, nay, even denying and blaspheming, the inward power and reality of it. Is not this eminently fulfilled at this day?

6. Of these - That is, mere formalists.

7. Ever learning - New things. But not the truth of God.

8. Several ancient writers speak of Jannes and Jambres, as the chief of the Egyptian magicians. Men of corrupt minds - Impure notions and wicked inclinations. Void of judgment - Quite ignorant, as well as careless, of true, spiritual religion.

9. They shall proceed no further--In gaining proselytes.

12. All that are resolved to live godly - Therefore count the cost. Art thou resolved? In Christ - Out of Christ there is no godliness. Shall suffer persecution - More or less. There is no exception. Either the truth of scripture fails, or those that think they are religious, and are not persecuted, in some shape or other, on that very account, deceive themselves.

13. Deceiving and being deceived - He who has once begun to deceive others is both the less likely to recover from his own error, and the more ready to embrace the errors of other men.

14. From whom - Even from me a teacher approved of God.

15. From an infant thou hast known the holy scriptures - Of the Old Testament. These only were extant when Timothy was an infant. Which are able to make thee wise unto salvation, through faith in the Messiah that was to come. How much more are the Old and New Testament together able, in God's hand, to make us more abundantly wise unto salvation! Even such a measure of present salvation as was not known before Jesus was glorified.

16. All scripture is inspired of God - The Spirit of God not only once inspired those who wrote it, but continually inspires, supernaturally assists, those that read it with earnest prayer. Hence it is so profitable for doctrine, for instruction of the ignorant, for the reproof or conviction of them that are in error or sin, for the correction or amendment of whatever is amiss, and for instructing or training up the children of God in all righteousness.

17. That the man of God - He that is united to and approved of God. May be perfect - Blameless himself, and throughly furnished - By the scripture, either to teach, reprove, correct, or train up others.

IV

1. I charge thee therefore - This is deduced from the whole preceding chapter. At his appearing and his kingdom - That is, at his appearing in the kingdom of glory.

2. Be instant - Insist on, urge these things in season, out of season - That is, continually, at all times and places. It might be translated, with and without opportunity - Not only when a fair occasion is given: even when there is none, one must be made.

3. For they will heap up teachers - Therefore thou hast need of "all longsuffering." According to their own desires - Smooth as they can wish. Having itching ears - Fond of novelty and variety, which the number of new teachers, as well as their empty, soft, or philosophical discourses, pleased. Such teachers, and such hearers, seldom are much concerned with what is strict or to the purpose. Heap to themselves - Not enduring sound doctrine, they will reject the sound preachers, and gather together all that suit their own taste. Probably they send out one another as teachers, and so are never at a loss for numbers.

5. Watch - An earnest, constant, persevering exercise. The scripture watching, or waiting, implies steadfast faith, patient hope, labouring love, unceasing prayer; yea, the mighty exertion of all the affections of the soul that a man is capable of. In all things - Whatever you are doing, yet in that, and in all things, watch. Do the work of an evangelist - Which was next to that of an apostle.

6. The time of my departure is at hand - So undoubtedly God had shown him. I am ready to be offered up - Literally, to be poured out, as the wine and oil were on the ancient sacrifices.

8. The crown of that righteousness - Which God has imputed to me and wrought in me. Will

render to all - This increases the joy of Paul, and encourages Timotheus. Many of these St. Paul himself had gained. That have loved his appearing - Which only a real Christian can do. I say a real Christian, to comply with the mode of the times: else they would not understand, although the word Christian necessarily implies whatsoever is holy, as God is holy. Strictly speaking, to join real or sincere to a word of so complete an import, is grievously to debase its noble signification, and is like adding long to eternity or wide to immensity.

9. Come to me - Both that he might comfort him, and be strengthened by him. Timotheus himself is said to have suffered at Ephesus.

10. Demas - Once my fellowlabourer, Phil. i, 24. Hath forsaken me. Crescens, probably a preacher also, is gone, with my consent, to Galatia, Titus to Dalmatia, having now left Crete. These either went with him to Rome, or visited him there.

11. Only Luke - Of my fellowlabourers, is with me - But God is with me; and it is enough. Take Mark - Who, though he once "departed from the work," is now again profitable to me.

13. The cloak - Either the toga, which belonged to him as a Roman citizen, or an upper garment, which might be needful as winter came on. Which I left at Troas with Carpus - Who was probably his host there. Especially the parchments - The books written on parchment.

14. The Lord will reward him - This he spoke prophetically.

16. All - My friends and companions. Forsook me - And do we expect to find such as will not forsake us? My first defense - Before the savage emperor Nero.

17. The preaching - The gospel which we preach.

18. And the Lord will deliver me from every evil work - Which is far more than delivering me from death. Yea, and, over and above, preserve me unto his heavenly kingdom - Far better than that of Nero.

20. When I came on, Erastus abode at Corinth - Being chamberlain of the city, Rom. xvi, 23. But Trophimus I have left sick - Not having power (as neither had any of the apostles) to work miracles when he pleased, but only when God pleased.

John Wesley

NOTES ON ST. PAUL'S EPISTLE TO TITUS

TITUS was converted from heathenism by St. Paul, and, as it seems, very early; since the apostle accounted him as his brother at his first going into Macedonia: and he managed and settled the churches there, when St. Paul thought not good to go thither himself. He had now left him at Crete, to regulate the churches; to assist him wherein, he wrote this epistle, as is generally believed, after the First, and before the Second, to Timothy. The tenor and style are much alike in this and in those; and they cast much light on each other, and are worthy the serious attention of all Christian ministers and churches in all ages. This epistle has four parts:

I. The inscription, Chap. i, 1-4

II. The instruction of Titus to this effect
    1. Ordain good presbyters, 5-9
    2. Such are especially needful at Crete, 10-12
    3. Reprove and admonish the Cretans, 13-16
    4. Teach aged men and women, ii. 1-5 And young men, being a pattern to them, 6-8 And servants, urging them by a glorious motive,. 9-15
    5. Press obedience to magistrates, and gentleness to all men, iii. 1-2
    Enforcing it by the same motive, 3-7
    6. Good works are to be done, foolish questions avoided. heretics shunned, 8-11

III. An invitation of Titus to Nicopolis, with some admonitions, 12-14

IV. The conclusion,

TITUS

I

    1. Paul, a servant of God, and an apostle of Jesus Christ - Titles suitable to the person of Paul, and the office he was assigning to Titus. According to the faith - The propagating of which is the proper business of an apostle. A servant of God - According to the faith of the elect. An apostle of Jesus Christ - According to the knowledge of the truth. We serve God according to the measure of our faith: we fulfil our public office according to the measure of our knowledge. The truth that is after godliness - Which in every point runs parallel with and supports the vital, spiritual worship of God; and, indeed, has no other end or scope. These two verses contain the sum of Christianity, which Titus was always to have in his eye. Of the elect of God - Of all real Christians
    2. In hope of eternal life - The grand motive and encouragement of every apostle and every servant of God. Which God promised before the world began - To Christ, our Head.
    3. And he hath in his own times - At sundry times; and his own times are fittest for his own work. What creature dares ask, "Why no sooner?" Manifested his word - Containing that promise, and the whole "truth which is after godliness." Through the preaching wherewith I am intrusted according to the commandment of God our saviour - And who dares exercise this office on any less authority?
    4. My own son - Begot in the same image of God, and repaying a paternal with a filial affection. The common faith - Common to me and all my spiritual children.
    5. The things which are wanting - Which I had not time to settle myself. Ordain elders - Appoint the most faithful, zealous men to watch over the rest. Their character follows, Tit i, 6-9. These were the elders, or bishops, that Paul approved of;-men that had living faith, a pure conscience, a blameless life.
    6. The husband of one wife - Surely the Holy Ghost, by repeating this so often, designed to leave the Romanists without excuse.
    7. As the steward of God - To whom he intrusts immortal souls. Not selfwilled - Literally, pleasing himself; but all men "for their good to edification." Not passionate - But mild, yielding, tender.
    9. As he hath been taught - Perhaps it might be more literally rendered, according to the teaching,

or doctrine, of the apostles; alluding to Acts ii, 42.

10. They of the circumcision - The Jewish converts.

11. Stopped - The word properly means, to put a bit into the mouth of an unruly horse.

12. A prophet - So all poets were anciently called; but, besides, Diogenes Laertius says that Epimenides, the Cretan poet, foretold many things. Evil wild beasts - Fierce and savage.

14. Commandments of men - The Jewish or other teachers, whoever they were that turned from the truth.

15. To the pure - Those whose hearts are purified by faith this we allow. All things are pure - All kinds of meat; the Mosaic distinction between clean and unclean meats being now taken away. But to the defiled and unbelieving nothing is pure - The apostle joins defiled and unbelieving, to intimate that nothing can be clean without a true faith: for both the understanding and conscience, those leading powers of the soul, are polluted; consequently, so is the man and all he does.

II

1. Wholesome - Restoring and preserving spiritual health.

2. Vigilant - As veteran soldiers, not easily to be surprised. Patience - A virtue particularly needful for and becoming them. Serious - Not drolling or diverting on the brink of eternity.

3. In behaviour - The particulars whereof follow. As becometh holiness - Literally, observing an holy decorum. Not slanderers - Or evil-speakers. Not given to much wine - If they use a little for their often infirmities. Teachers - Age and experience call them so to be. Let them teach good only.

4. That they instruct the young women - These Timothy was to instruct himself; Titus, by the elder women. To love their husbands, their children - With a tender, temperate, holy, wise affection. O how hard a lesson.

5. Discreet - Particularly in the love of their children. Chaste - Particularly in the love of their husbands. Keepers at home - Whenever they are not called out by works of necessity, piety, and mercy. Good - Well tempered, sweet, soft, obliging. Obedient to their husbands - Whose will, in all things lawful, is a rule to the wife. That the word of God be not blasphemed - Or evil spoken of; particularly by unbelieving husbands, who lay all the blame on the religion of their wives.

6. To be discreet - A virtue rarely found in youth.

7. Showing thyself a pattern - Titus himself was then young. In the doctrine which thou teachest in public: as to matter, uncorruptness; as to the manner of delivering it, seriousness - Weightiness, solemnity.

8. Wholesome speech - In private conversation.

9. Please them in all things - Wherein it can be done without sin. Not answering again - Though blamed unjustly. This honest servants are most apt to do. Not stealing - Not taking or giving any thing without their master's leave: this fair-spoken servants are apt to do.

10. Showing all good fidelity - Soft, obliging faithfulness That they may adorn the doctrine of God our saviour - More than St. Paul says of kings. How he raises the lowness of his subject! So may they, the lowness of their condition.

11. The saving grace of God - So it is in its nature, tendency, and design. Hath appeared to all men - High and low.

12. Instructing us - All who do not reject it. That, having renounced ungodliness - Whatever is contrary to the fear and love of God. And worldly desires - Which are opposite to sobriety and righteousness. We should live soberly - In all purity and holiness. Sobriety, in the scripture sense, is rather the whole temper of a man, than a single virtue in him. It comprehends all that is opposite to the drowsiness of sin, the folly of ignorance, the unholiness of disorderly passions. Sobriety is no less than all the powers of the soul being consistently and constantly awake, duly governed by heavenly prudence, and entirely conformable to holy affections. And righteously - Doing to all as we would they should do to us. And godly - As those who are consecrated to God both in heart and life.

13. Looking - With eager desire. For that glorious appearing - Which we hope for. Of the great God, even our saviour Jesus Christ - So that, if there be (according to the Arian scheme) a great God and a little God, Christ is not the little God, but the great one.

14. Who gave himself for us - To die in our stead. That he might redeem us - Miserable bondslaves, as well from the power and the very being, as from the guilt, of all our sins.

15. Let no man despise thee - That is, let none have any just cause to despise thee. Yet they surely will. Men who know not God will despise a true minister of his word.

III

1. Remind them - All the Cretan Christians. To be subject - Passively, not resisting. To principalities - Supreme. And powers - Subordinate governors. And to obey - Them actively, so far as conscience permits.

2. To speak evil - Neither of them nor any man. Not to be quarrelsome - To assault none. To be gentle - When assaulted. Toward all men - Even those who are such as we were.

3. For we - And as God hath dealt with us, so ought we to deal with our neighbour. Were without understanding - Wholly ignorant of God. And disobedient - When he was declared to us.

4. When the love of God appeared - By the light of his Spirit to our inmost soul.

5. Not by works - In this important passage the apostle presents us with a delightful view of our redemption. Herein we have,

1. The cause of it; not our works or righteousness, but "the kindness and love of God our saviour."
2. The effects; which are,

(1.) Justification; "being justified," pardoned and accepted through the alone merits of Christ, not from any desert in us, but according to his own mercy, "by his grace," his free, unmerited goodness.

(2.) Sanctification, expressed by the laver of regeneration, (that is, baptism, the thing signified, as well as the outward sign,) and the renewal of the Holy Ghost; which purifies the soul, as water cleanses the body, and renews it in the whole image of God.

3. The consummation of all; - that we might become heirs of eternal life, and live now in the joyful hope of it.

8. Be careful to excel in good works - Though the apostle does not lay these for the foundation, yet he brings them in at their proper place, and then mentions them, not slightly, but as affairs of great importance. He desires that all believers should be careful - Have their thoughts upon them: use their best contrivance, their utmost endeavours, not barely to practice, but to excel, to be eminent and distinguished in them: because, though they are not the ground of our reconciliation with God, yet they are amiable and honourable to the Christian profession. And profitable to men - Means of increasing the everlasting happiness both of ourselves and others.

10. An heretic (after a first and second admonition) reject - Avoid, leave to himself. This is the only place, in the whole scripture, where this word heretic occurs; and here it evidently means, a man that obstinately persists in contending about "foolish questions," and thereby occasions strife and animosities, schisms and parties in the church. This, and this alone, is an heretic in the scripture sense; and his punishment likewise is here fixed. Shun, avoid him, leave him to himself. As for the Popish sense, "A man that errs in fundamentals," although it crept, with many other things, early into the church, yet it has no shadow of foundation either in the Old or New Testament.

11. Such an one is perverted - In his heart, at least. And sinneth, being self-condemned - Being convinced in his own conscience that he acts wrong.

12. When I shall send Artemas or Tychicus - To succeed thee in thy office. Titus was properly an evangelist, who, according to the nature of that office, had no fixed residence; but presided over other elders, wherever he travelled from place to place, assisting each of the apostles according to the measure of his abilities. Come to me to Nicopolis - Very probably not the Nicopolis in Macedonia, as the vulgar subscription asserts: (indeed, none of those subscriptions at the end of St. Paul's epistles are of any authority:) rather it was a town of the same name which lay upon the sea-coast of Epirus. For I have determined to winter there - Hence it appears, he was not there yet; if so, he would have said, to winter here. Consequently, this letter was not written from thence.

13. Send forward Zenas the lawyer - Either a Roman lawyer or an expounder of the Jewish law.

14. And let ours - All our brethren at Crete. Learn - Both by thy admonition and example. Perhaps they had not before assisted Zenas and Apollos as they ought to have done.

NOTES ON ST. PAUL'S EPISTLE TO PHILEMON

ONESIMUS, a servant to Philemon, an eminent person in Colosse, ran away from his master to Rome. Here he was converted to Christianity by St. Paul, who sent him back to his master with this letter. It seems, Philemon not only pardoned, but gave him his liberty; seeing Ignatius makes mention of him, as succeeding Timotheus at Ephesus. The letter has three parts

I. The inscription, 1-3

II. After commending Philemon's faith and love,. 4-7 He desires him to receive Onesimus again,. 8-21 And to prepare a lodging for himself, 22

III. The conclusion, 23-23

PHILEMON

I

1. This single epistle infinitely transcends all the wisdom of the world. And it gives us a specimen how Christians ought to treat of secular affairs from higher principles. Paul a prisoner of Christ - To whom, as such, Philemon could deny nothing. And Timotheus - This was written before the second epistle to Timothy, ver. xxii.
2. To Apphia - His wife, to whom also the business in part belonged. And the church in thy house - The Christians who meet there.
5. Hearing - Probably from Onesimus.
6. I pray that the communication of thy faith may become effectual - That is, that thy faith may be effectually communicated to others, who see and acknowledge thy piety and charity.
7. The saints - To whom Philemon's house was open, verse ii.
8. I might be bold in Christ - Through the authority he hath given me.
9. Yet out of love I rather entreat thee - In how handsome a manner does the apostle just hint, and immediately drop, the consideration of his power to command, and tenderly entreat Philemon to hearken to his friend, his aged friend, and now prisoner for Christ! With what endearment, in the next verse, does he call Onesimus his son, before he names his name! And as soon as he had mentioned it, with what fine address does he just touch on his former faults, and instantly pass on to the happy change that was now made upon him! So disposing Philemon to attend to his request, and the motives wherewith he was going to enforce it.
10. Whom I have begotten in my bonds - The son of my age.
11. Now profitable - None should be expected to be a good servant before he is a good man. He manifestly alludes to his name, Onesimus, which signifies profitable.
12. Receive him, that is, my own bowels - Whom I love as my own soul. Such is the natural affection of a father in Christ toward his spiritual children.
13. To serve me in thy stead - To do those services for me which thou, if present, wouldest gladly have done thyself.
14. That thy benefit might not be by constraint - For Philemon could not have refused it.
15. God might permit him to be separated (a soft word) for a season, that thou mightest have him forever - Both on earth and in heaven.
16. In the flesh - As a dutiful servant. In the Lord - As a fellow-Christian.
17. If thou accountest me a partner - So that thy things are mine, and mine are thine.
19. I will repay it - If thou requirest it. Not to say, that then owest me thyself - It cannot be expressed, how great our obligation is to those who have gained our souls to Christ. Beside - Receiving Onesimus.
20. Refresh my bowels in Christ - Give me the most exquisite and Christian pleasure.
22. Given to you - Restored to liberty.

John Wesley

NOTES ON THE EPISTLE TO THE HEBREWS

IT is agreed by the general tenor of antiquity that this epistle was written by St. Paul, whose other epistles were sent to the gentile converts; this only to the Hebrews. But this improper inscription was added by some later hand. It was sent to the Jewish Hellenist Christians, dispersed through various countries. St. Paul's method and style are easily observed therein. He places, as usual, the proposition and division before the treatise, chap. ii, 17; he subjoins the exhortatory to the doctrinal part, quotes the same scriptures, chap. i, 6; ii, 8; x, 30, 38, 6; and uses the same expressions as elsewhere. But why does he not prefix his name, which, it is plain from chap. xiii, 19 was dear to them to whom he wrote? Because he prefixes no inscription, in which, if at all, the name would have been mentioned. The ardour of his spirit carries aim directly upon his subject, (just like St. John in his First Epistle,) and throws back his usual salutation and thanksgiving to the conclusion. This epistle of St. Paul, and both those of St. Peter, (one may add, that of St. James and of St. Jude also,) were written both to the same persons, dispersed through Pontus, Galatia, and other countries, and nearly at the same time. St. Paul suffered at Rome, three years before the destruction of Jerusalem. Therefore this epistle likewise, was written while the temple was standing. St. Peter wrote a little before his martyrdom, and refers to the epistles of St. Paul; this in particular. The scope of it is, to confirm their faith in Christ; and this he does by demonstrating his glory. All the parts of it are full of the most earnest and pointed admonitions and exhortations; and they go on in one tenor, the particle therefore everywhere connecting the doctrine and the use. The sum is, The glory of Christ appears,

I. From comparing with him the prophets and angels, i. 1-14 Therefore we ought to give heed to him, ii. 1-4

II. From his passion and consummation. Here we may observe,
    1. The proposition and sum, 5-9
    2. The treatise itself. We have a perfect author of salvation, who suffered for our sake, that he might be, (1.) a merciful, and (2.) a faithful, (3.) high priest,. 10-13 These three are particularly explained, his passion and consummation being continually interwoven
        1. He has the virtues of an high priest
            a. He is faithful, iii.1 Therefore be ye not unfaithful iv.13
            b. He is merciful, 15 Therefore come to him with confidence v.3
        2. He is called of God an high priest. Here,
            a. The sum is proposed, 4-10 With a summary exhortation 11- vi. 20
            b. The point is copiously,
    1. Explained. We have a great high priest,
    1. Such as is described in the hundred and tenth Psalm After the order of Melchisedec, vii. 1-19 Established by an oath, 20-22 For ever, 23-28
    2. Therefore peculiarly excellent-Heavenly, viii. 1-6 Of the new covenant, 7-13 By whom we have an entrance into the sanctuary ix. 1 x. 18
    2. Applied. Therefore,
    1. Believe, hope, love 19-25 These three are farther inculcated,
        a. Faith, with patience, 26-39 Which, after the example of the ancients,. xi.1 xii.1 And of Christ himself, 2, 3 Is to be exercised, 4-11 Cheerfully, peaceably, holily, 12-17
        b. Hope, 18-20
        c. Love, C.xiii. 1-6
    2. In order to grow in these graces, make use of The remembrance of your former, 7-16 The vigilance of your present, pastors, 17-19 To this period, and to the whole epistle, answers The prayer, the doxology, and the mild conclusion, 20-25 There are many comparisons in this epistle, which may be nearly reduced to two heads:
        1. The prophets, the angels, Moses, Joshua, Aaron, are great; but Jesus Christ is infinitely greater
        2. The ancient believers enjoyed high privileges; but Christian believers enjoy far higher. To illustrate this, examples both of happiness and misery are everywhere interspersed: so that in this epistle there is a kind of recapitulation of the whole Old Testament. In this also Judaism is abrogated, and

Christianity carried to its height.

HEBREWS

I

1. **God, who at sundry times** - The creation was revealed in the time of Adam; the last judgment, in the time of Enoch: and so at various times, and in various degrees, more explicit knowledge was given. **In divers manners** - In visions, in dreams, and by Revelations of various kinds. Both these are opposed to the one entire and perfect Revelation which he has made to us by Jesus Christ. The very number of the prophets showed that they prophesied only "in part." **Of old** - There were no prophets for a large tract of time before Christ came, that the great Prophet might be the more earnestly expected. **Spake** - A part is put for the whole; implying every kind of divine communication. **By the prophets** - The mention of whom is a virtual declaration that the apostle received the whole Old Testament, and was not about to advance any doctrine in contradiction to it. **Hath in these last times** - Intimating that no other Rev. is to be expected. **Spoken** - All things, and in the most perfect manner. **By his Son** - Alone. The Son spake by the apostles. The majesty of the Son of God is proposed,

1. Absolutely, by the very name of Son, verse 1, and by three glorious predicates, - "whom he hath appointed," "by whom he made," who "sat down;" whereby he is described from the beginning to the consummation of all things, ver. 2, 3

2. Comparatively to angels, ver. 4. The proof of this proposition immediately follows: the name of Son being proved, ver. 5; his being "heir of all things," ver. 6-9; his making the worlds, ver. 10- 12 his sitting at God's right hand, ver. 13, &c.

2. **Whom he hath appointed heir of all things** - After the name of Son, his inheritance is mentioned. God appointed him the heir long before he made the worlds, Eph. iii, 11; Prov. viii, 22, &c. The Son is the firstborn, born before all things: the heir is a term relating to the creation which followed, ver. 6. **By whom he also made the worlds** - Therefore the Son was before all worlds. His glory reaches from everlasting to everlasting, though God spake by him to us only "in these last days."

3. **Who sat down** - The third of these glorious predicates, with which three other particulars are interwoven, which are mentioned likewise, and in the same order, Colossians i, 15, 17, 20. **Who, being** - The glory which he received in his exaltation at the right hand of the Father no angel was capable of; but the Son alone, who likewise enjoyed it long before. **The brightness of his glory** - Glory is the nature of God revealed in its brightness. **The express image** - Or stamp. Whatever the Father is, is exhibited in the Son, as a seal in the stamp on wax. **Of his person** - Or substance. The word denotes the unchangeable perpetuity of divine life and power. **And sustaining all things** - Visible and invisible, in being. **By the word of his power** - That is, by his powerful word. **When he had by himself** - Without any Mosaic rites or ceremonies. **Purged our sins** - In order to which it was necessary he should for a time divest himself of his glory. In this chapter St. Paul describes his glory chiefly as he is the Son of God; afterwards, ver. 6, &c., the glory of the man Christ Jesus. He speaks, indeed, briefly of the former before his humiliation, but copiously after his exaltation; as from hence the glory he had from eternity began to be evidently seen. Both his purging our sins, and sitting on the right hand of God, are largely treated of in the seven following chapters. **Sat down** - The priests stood while they ministered: sitting, therefore, denotes the consummation of his sacrifice. This word, sat down, contains the scope, the theme, and the sum, of the epistle.

4. This verse has two clauses, the latter of which is treated of, ver. 5; the former, ver. 13. Such transpositions are also found in the other epistles of St. Paul, but in none so frequently as in this. The Jewish doctors were peculiarly fond of this figure, and used it much in all their writings. The apostle therefore, becoming all things to all men, here follows the same method. All the inspired writers were readier in all the figures of speech than the most experienced orators. **Being** - By his exaltation, after he had been lower than them, chap. ii, 9. **So much higher than the angels** - It was extremely proper to observe this, because the Jews gloried in their law, as it was delivered by the ministration of angels. How much more may we glory in the gospel, which was given, not by the ministry of angels, but of the very Son of God! **As he hath by inheritance a more excellent name** - Because he is the Son of God, he inherits that name, in right whereof he inherits all things His inheriting that name is more ancient than all worlds; his inheriting all things, as ancient as all things. **Than they** - This denotes an immense preeminence. The angels do not inherit all things, but are themselves a portion of the Son's inheritance, whom they worship as their Lord.

5. **Thou art my Son** - God of God, Light of Light. **This day have I begotten thee** - I have begotten thee from eternity, which, by its unalter able permanency of duration, is one continued, unsuccessive day. **I will be to him a Father, and he shall be to me a Son** - I will own myself to be his Father, and him to be my Son, by eminent tokens of my peculiar love The former clause relates to his natural Sonship, by an eternal, inconceivable generation; the other, to his Father's acknowledgment and treatment of him

as his incarnate Son. Indeed this promise related immediately to Solomon, but in a far higher sense to the Messiah. Psalm ii, 7; 2 Sam. vii, 14

6. And again - That is, in another scripture. He - God. Saith, when he bringeth in his first-begotten - This appellation includes that of Son, together with the rights of primogeniture, which the first-begotten Son of God enjoys, in a manner not communicable to any creature. Into the world - Namely, at his incarnation. He saith, Let all the angels of God worship him - So much higher was he, when in his lowest estate, than the highest angel. Psalm xcvii, 7.

7. Who maketh his angels - This implies, they are only creatures, whereas the Son is eternal, ver. 8; and the Creator himself, ver. 10. Spirits and a flame of fire - Which intimates not only their office, but also their nature; which is excellent indeed, the metaphor being taken from the most swift, subtle, and efficacious things on earth; but nevertheless infinitely below the majesty of the Son. Psalm civ, 4.

8. O God - God, in the singular number, is never in scripture used absolutely of any but the supreme God. Thy reign, of which the scepter is the ensign, is full of justice and equity. Psalm xlv, 6, 7.

9. Thou hast loved righteousness and hated iniquity - Thou art infinitely pure and holy. Therefore God - Who, as thou art Mediator, is thy God. Hath anointed thee with the oil of gladness - With the Holy Ghost, the fountain of joy. Above thy fellows - Above all the children of men.

10. Thou - The same to whom the discourse is addressed in the preceding verse. Psalm cii, 25, 26

12. As a mantle - With all ease. They shall be changed - Into new heavens and a new earth. But thou art eternally the same.

13. Psalm cx, 1.

14. Are they not all - Though of various orders. Ministering spirits, sent forth - Ministering before God, sent forth to men. To attend on them - In numerous offices of protection, care, and kindness. Who - Having patiently continued in welldoing, shall inherit everlasting salvation.

II

In this and the two following chapters the apostle subjoins an exhortation, answering each head of the preceding chapter.

1. Lest we should let them slip - As water out of a leaky vessel. So the Greek word properly signifies.

2. In giving the law, God spoke by angels; but in proclaiming the gospel, by his Son. Steadfast - Firm and valid. Every transgression - Commission of sin. Every disobedience - Omission of duty.

3. So great a salvation - A deliverance from so great wickedness and misery, into so great holiness and happiness. This was first spoken of (before he came it was not known) by Him who is the Lord - of angels as well as men. And was confirmed to us - Of this age, even every article of it. By them that had heard him - And had been themselves also both eye-witnesses and ministers of the word.

4. By signs and wonders - While he lived. And various miracles and distributions of the Holy Ghost - Miraculous gifts, distributed after his exaltation. According to his will - Not theirs who received them.

5. This verse contains a proof of the third; the greater the salvation is, and the more glorious the Lord whom we despise, the greater will be our punishment. God hath not subjected the world to come - That is, the dispensation of the Messiah; which being to succeed the Mosaic was usually styled by the Jews, the world to come, although it is still in great measure to come Whereof we now speak - Of which I am now speaking. In this last great dispensation the Son alone presides.

6. What is man - To the vast expanse of heaven, to the moon and the stars which thou hast ordained! This psalm seems to have been composed by David, in a clear, moonshiny, and starlight night, while he was contemplating the wonderful fabric of heaven; because in his magnificent description of its luminaries, he takes no notice of the sun, the most glorious of them all. The words here cited concerning dominion were doubtless in some sense applicable to Adam; although in their complete and highest sense, they belong to none but the second Adam. Or the son of man, that thou visitest him - The sense rises: we are mindful of him that is absent; but to visit, denotes the care of a present God. Psalm viii, 4.

7. Thou hast made him - Adam. A little lower than the angels - The Hebrew is, a little lower than (that is, next to) God. Such was man as he came out of the hands of his Creator: it seems, the highest of all created beings. But these words are also in a farther sense, as the apostle here shows, applicable to the Son of God. It should be remembered that the apostles constantly cited the Septuagint translation, very frequently without any variation. It was not their business, in writing to the Jews, who at that time had it in high esteem, to amend or alter this, which would of consequence have occasioned disputes without end.

8. Now this putting all things under him, implies that there is nothing that is not put under him. But it is plain, this is not done now, with regard to man in general.

9. It is done only with regard to Jesus, God-Man, who is now crowned with glory and honour - As

a reward for his having suffered death. He was made a little lower than the angels - Who cannot either suffer or die. That by the grace of God, he might taste death - An expression denoting both the reality of his death, and the shortness of its continuance. For every man - That ever was or will be born into the world.

10. In this verse the apostle expresses, in his own words, what he expressed before in those of the Psalmist. It became him - It was suitable to all his attributes, both to his justice, goodness, and wisdom. For whom - As their ultimate end. And by whom - As their first cause. Are all things, in bringing many adopted sons to glory - To this very thing, that they are sons, and are treated as such To perfect the captain - Prince, leader, and author of their salvation, by his atoning sufferings for them. To perfect or consummate implies the bringing him to a full and glorious end of all his troubles, chap. v, 9. This consummation by sufferings intimates,

    1. the glory of Christ, to whom, being consummated, all things are made subject.

    2. The preceding sufferings. Of these he treats expressly, ver. 11- 18; having before spoken of his glory, both to give an edge to his exhortation, and to remove the scandal of sufferings and death. A fuller consideration of both these points he interweaves with the following discourse on his priesthood. But what is here said of our Lord's being made perfect through sufferings, has no relation to our being saved or sanctified by sufferings. Even he himself was perfect, as God and as man, before ever be suffered. By his sufferings, in his life and death, he was made a perfect or complete sin-offering. But unless we were to be made the same sacrifice, and to atone for sin, what is said of him in this respect is as much out of our sphere as his ascension into heaven. It is his atonement, and his Spirit carrying on "the work of faith with power" in our hearts, that alone can sanctify us. Various afflictions indeed may be made subservient to this; and so far as they are blessed to the weaning us from sin, and causing our affections to be set on things above, so far they do indirectly help on our sanctification.

11. For - They are nearly related to each other. He that sanctifieth - Christ, chap. xiii, 12. And all they that are sanctified - That are brought to God; that draw near or come to him, which are synonymous terms. Are all of one - Partakers of one nature, from one parent, Adam.

12. I will declare thy name to my brethren -- Christ declares the name of God, gracious and merciful, plenteous in goodness and truth, to all who believe, that they also may praise him. In the midst of the church will I sing praise unto thee - As the precentor of the choir. This he did literally, in the midst of his apostles, on the night before his passion. And as it means, in a more general sense, setting forth the praise of God, he has done it in the church by his word and his Spirit; he still does, and will do it throughout all generations. Psalm xxii, 22.

13. And again - As one that has communion with his brethren in sufferings, as well as in nature, he says, I will put my trust in him - To carry me through them all. And again - With a like acknowledgment of his near relation to them, as younger brethren, who were yet but in their childhood, he presents all believers to God, saying, Behold I and the children whom thou hast given me. Isaiah viii, 17, 18

14. Since then these children partake of flesh and blood - Of human nature with all its infirmities. He also in like manner took part of the same; that through his own death he might destroy the tyranny of him that had, by God's permission, the power of death with regard to the ungodly. Death is the devil's servant and serjeant, delivering to him those whom he seizes in sin. That is, the devil - The power was manifest to all; but who exerted it, they saw not.

15. And deliver them, as many as through fear of death were all their lifetime, till then, subject to bondage - Every man who fears death is subject to bondage; is in a slavish, uncomfortable state. And every man fears death, more or less, who knows not Christ: death is unwelcome to him, if he knows what death is. But he delivers all true believers from this bondage.

16. For verily he taketh not hold of angels - He does not take their nature upon him. But he taketh hold of the seed of Abraham - He takes human nature upon him. St. Paul says the seed of Abraham, rather than the seed of Adam, because to Abraham was the promise made.

17. Wherefore it behoved him - It was highly fit and proper, yea, necessary, in order to his design of redeeming them. To be made in all things - That essentially pertain to human nature, and in all sufferings and temptations. Like his brethren -- this is a recapitulation of all that goes before: the sum of all that follows is added immediately. That he might be a merciful and faithful High Priest-Merciful toward sinners; faithful toward God. A priest or high priest is one who has a right of approaching God, and of bringing others to him. Faithful is treated of, chap. iii, 2, &c., with its use; merciful, chap. iv, 14, &c., with the use also; High Priest, chap. v, 4, &c., chap. vii, 1, &c. The use is added from chap. x, 19. In things pertaining to God, to expiate the sins of the people - Offering up their sacrifices and prayers to God; deriving God's grace, peace, and blessings upon them.

18. For in that he hath suffered being tempted himself he is able to succor them that are tempted - That is, he has given a manifest, demonstrative proof that he is able so to do.

III

1. The heavenly calling - God calls from heaven, and to heaven, by the gospel. Consider the Apostle - The messenger of God, who pleads the cause of God with us. And High Priest - Who pleads our cause with God. Both are contained in the one word Mediator. He compares Christ, as an Apostle, with Moses; as a Priest, with Aaron. Both these offices, which Moses and Aaron severally bore, he bears together, and far more eminently. Of our profession - The religion we profess.

2. His house - The church of Israel, then the peculiar family of God. Num. xii, 7.

3. He that hath builded it hath more glory than the house - Than the family itself, or any member of it.

4. Now Christ, he that built not only this house, but all things, is God - And so infinitely greater than Moses or any creature.

5. And Moses verily - Another proof of the preeminence of Christ above Moses. Was faithful in all his house, as a servant, for a testimony of the things which were afterwards to be spoken - That is, which was a full confirmation of the things which he afterward spake concerning Christ.

6. But Christ was faithful as a Son; whose house we are, while we hold fast, and shall be unto the end, if we hold fast our confidence in God, and glorying in his promises; our faith and hope.

7. Wherefore - Seeing he is faithful, be not ye unfaithful. Psalm xcv, 7, &c.

8. As in the provocation - When Israel provoked me by their strife and murmurings. In the day of temptation - When at the same time they tempted me, by distrusting my power and goodness. Exod. xvii, 7.

9. Where your fathers - That hard-hearted and stiff-necked generation. So little cause had their descendants to glory in them. Tempted me - Whether I could and would help them. Proved me - Put my patience to the proof, even while they saw my glorious works both of judgment and mercy, and that for forty years.

10. Wherefore - To speak after the manner of men. I was grieved - Displeased, offended with that generation, and said, They always err in their hearts - They are led astray by their stubborn will and vile affections. And - For this reason, because wickedness has blinded their understanding. They have not known my ways - By which I would have led them like a flock. Into my rest - In the promised land.

12. Take heed, lest there be in any of you - As there was in them. An evil heart of unbelief - Unbelief is the parent of all evil, and the very essence of unbelief lies in departing from God, as the living God - The fountain of all our life, holiness, happiness.

13. But, to prevent it, exhort one another, while it is called Today - This today will not last forever. The day of life will end soon, and perhaps the day of grace yet sooner.

14. For we are made partakers of Christ - And we shall still partake of him and all his benefits, if we hold fast our faith unto the end. If - But not else; and a supposition made by the Holy Ghost is equal to the, strongest assertion. Both the sentiment and the manner of expression are the same as ver. 6.

16. Were they not all that came out of Egypt - An awful consideration! The whole elect people of God (a very few excepted) provoked God presently after their great deliverance, continued to grieve his Spirit for forty years, and perished in their sin!

19. So we see they could not enter in - Though afterward they desired it.

IV

2. But the word which they heard did not profit them - So far from it, that it increased their damnation. It is then only when it is mixed with faith, that it exerts its saving power.

3. For we only that have believed enter into the rest - The proposition is, There remains a rest for us. This is proved, ver. 3- 11, thus: That Psalm mentions a rest: yet it does not mean,

1. God's rest from creating; for this was long before the time of Moses. Therefore in his time another rest was expected, of which they who then heard fell short Nor is it,

2. The rest which Israel obtained through Joshua; for the Psalmist wrote after him. Therefore it is,

3. The eternal rest in heaven. As he said - Clearly showing that there is a farther rest than that which followed the finishing of the creation. Though the works were finished - Before: whence it is plain, God did not speak of resting from them.

4. For, long after he had rested from his works, he speaks again. Gen. ii, 2.

5. In this psalm, of a rest yet to come.

7. After so long a time - It was above four hundred years from the time of Moses and Joshua to David. As it was said before - St. Paul here refers to the text he had just cited.

8. The rest - All the rest which God had promised.

9. Therefore - Since he still speaks of another day, there must remain a farther, even an eternal, rest for the people of God.

10. For they do not yet so rest. Therefore a fuller rest remains for them.

11. *Lest any one should fall* - Into perdition.

12. *For the word of God* - Preached, ver. 2, and armed with threatenings, ver. 3. *Is living and powerful* - Attended with the power of the living God, and conveying either life or death to the hearers. *Sharper than any two-edged sword* - Penetrating the heart more than this does the body. *Piercing* - Quite through, and laying open. *The soul and spirit, joints and marrow* - The inmost recesses of the mind, which the apostle beautifully and strongly expresses by this heap of figurative words. *And is a discerner* - Not only of the thoughts, but also of the intentions.

13. *In his sight* - It is God whose word is thus "powerful:" it is God in whose sight every creature is manifest; and of this his word, working on the conscience, gives the fullest conviction. *But all things are naked and opened* - Plainly alluding to the sacrifices under the law which were first flayed, and then (as the Greek word literally means) cleft asunder through the neck and backbone; so that everything both without and within was exposed to open view.

14. *Having therefore a great high priest* - Great indeed, being the eternal Son of God, *that is passed through the heavens* - As the Jewish high priest passed through the veil into the holy of holies, carrying with him the blood of the sacrifices, on the yearly day of atonement; so our great high priest went once for all through the visible heavens, with the virtue of his own blood, into the immediate presence God.

15. *He sympathizes with us* even in our innocent infirmities, wants, weaknesses, miseries, dangers. *Yet without sin* - And, therefore, is indisputably able to preserve us from it in all our temptations.

16. *Let us therefore come boldly* - Without any doubt or fear. *Unto the throne of God*, our reconciled Father, *even his throne of grace* - Grace erected it, and reigns there, and dispenses all blessings in a way of mere, unmerited favour.

V

1. *For every high priest being taken from among men* - Is, till he is taken, of the same rank with them. *And is appointed* - That is, is wont to be appointed. *In things pertaining to God* - To bring God near to men, and men to God. *That he may offer both gifts* - Out of things inanimate, and animal sacrifices.

2. *Who can have compassion* - In proportion to the offense: so the Greek word signifies. *On the ignorant* - Them that are in error. *And the wandering* - Them that are in sin. *Seeing himself also is compassed with infirmity* - Even with sinful infirmity; and so needs the compassion which he shows to others.

4. The apostle begins here to treat of the priesthood of Christ. The sum of what he observes concerning it is, Whatever is excellent in the Levitical priesthood is in Christ, and in a more eminent manner; and whatever is wanting in those priests is in him. *And no one taketh this honour* - The priesthood. *To himself, but he that is called of God, as was Aaron* - And his posterity, who were all of them called at one and the same time. But it is observable, Aaron did not preach at all; preaching being no part of the priestly office.

5. *So also Christ glorified not himself to be an high priest* - That is, did not take this honour to himself, but received it from him who said, *Thou art my Son, this day have I begotten thee* - Not, indeed, at the same time; for his generation was from eternity. Psalm ii, 7.

6. Psalm cx, 4.

7. The sum of the things treated of in the seventh and following chapters is contained, ver. 7-10; and in this sum is admirably comprised the process of his passion, with its inmost causes, in the very terms used by the evangelists. *Who in the days of his flesh* - Those two days, in particular, wherein his sufferings were at the height. *Having offered up prayers and supplications* - Thrice. *With strong crying and tears* - In the garden. *To him that was able to save him from death* - Which yet he endured, in obedience to the will of his Father. *And being heard in that which he particularly feared* - When the cup was offered him first, there was set before him that horrible image of a painful, shameful, accursed death, which moved him to pray conditionally against it: for, if he had desired it, his heavenly Father would have sent him more than twelve legions of angels to have delivered him. But what he most exceedingly feared was the weight of infinite justice; the being "bruised" and "put to grief" by the hand of God himself. Compared with this, everything else was a mere nothing; and yet, so greatly did he ever thirst to be obedient to the righteous will of his Father, and to "lay down" even "his life for the sheep," that he vehemently longed to be baptized with this baptism, Luke xii, 50. Indeed, his human nature needed the support of Omnipotence; and for this he sent up strong crying and tears: but, throughout his whole life, he showed that it was not the sufferings he was to undergo, but the dishonour that sin had done to so holy a God, that grieved his spotless soul. The consideration of its being the will of God tempered his fear, and afterwards swallowed it up; and he was heard not so that the cup should pass away, but so that he drank it without any fear.

8. *Though he were a Son* - This is interposed. lest any should be offended at all these instances of human weakness. In the garden, how frequently did he call God his Father! Matt. xxvi, 39, &c. And

hence it most evidently appears that his being the Son of God did not arise merely from his resurrection. Yet learned he - The word learned, premised to the word suffered, elegantly shows how willingly he learned. He learned obedience, when be began to suffer; when he applied himself to drink that cup: obedience in suffering and dying.

9. And being perfected - By sufferings, chap. ii, 10; brought through all to glory. He became the author - The procuring and efficient cause. Of eternal salvation to all that obey him - By doing and suffering his whole will.

10. Called - The Greek word here properly signifies surnamed. His name is, "the Son of God." The Holy Ghost seems to have concealed who Melchisedec was, on purpose that he might be the more eminent type of Christ. This only we know, - that he was a priest, and king of Salem, or Jerusalem.

11. Concerning whom - The apostle here begins an important digression, wherein he reproves, admonishes, and exhorts the Hebrews. We - Preachers of the gospel. Have many things to say, and hard to be explained - Though not so much from the subject- matter, as from your slothfulness in considering, and dulness in apprehending, the things of God.

12. Ye have need that one teach you again which are the first principles of religion. Accordingly these are enumerated in the first verse of the ensuing chapter. And have need of milk - The first and plainest doctrines.

13. Everyone that useth milk - That neither desires, nor can digest, anything else: otherwise strong men use milk; but not milk chiefly, and much less that only. Is unexperienced in the word of righteousness - The sublimer truths of the gospel. Such are all who desire and can digest nothing but the doctrine of justification and imputed righteousness.

14. But strong meat - These sublimer truths relating to "perfection," chap. vi, 1. Belong to them of full age, who by habit - Habit here signifies strength of spiritual understanding, arising from maturity of spiritual age. By, or in consequence of, this habit they exercise themselves in these things with ease, readiness, cheerfulness, and profit.

VI

1. Therefore leaving the principles of the doctrine of Christ - That is, saying no more of them for the present. Let us go on to perfection; not laying again the foundation of repentance from dead works - From open sins, the very first thing to be insisted on. And faith in God - The very next point. So St. Paul in his very first sermon at Lystra, Acts xiv, 15, "Turn from those vanities unto the living God." And when they believed, they were to be baptized with the baptism, not of the Jews, or of John, but of Christ. The next thing was, to lay hands upon them, that they might receive the Holy Ghost: after which they were more fully instructed, touching the resurrection, and the general judgment; called eternal, because the sentence then pronounced is irreversible, and the effects of it remain forever.

3. And this we will do - We will go on to perfection; and so much the more diligently, because,

4. It is impossible for those who were once enlightened - With the light of the glorious love of God in Christ. And have tasted the heavenly gift - Remission of sins, sweeter than honey and the honeycomb. And been made partakers of the Holy Ghost - Of the witness and the fruit of the Spirit.

5. And have tasted the good word of God - Have had a relish for, and a delight in it. And the powers of the world to come - Which every one tastes, who has an hope full of immortality. Every child that is naturally born, first sees the light, then receives and tastes proper nourishment, and partakes of the things of this world. In like manner, the apostle, comparing spiritual with natural things, speaks of one born of the Spirit, as seeing the light, tasting the sweetness, and partaking of the things "of the world to come."

6. And have fallen away - Here is not a supposition, but a plain relation of fact. The apostle here describes the case of those who have cast away both the power and the form of godliness; who have lost both their faith, hope, and love, ver. 10, &c., and that wilfully, chap. x, 26. Of these wilful total apostates he declares, it is impossible to renew them again to repentance. (though they were renewed once,) either to the foundation, or anything built thereon. Seeing they crucify the Son of God afresh - They use him with the utmost indignity. And put him to an open shame - Causing his glorious name to be blasphemed.

8. That which beareth thorns and briers - Only or chiefly. Is rejected - No more labour is bestowed upon it. Whose end is to be burned - As Jerusalem was shortly after.

9. But, beloved - in this one place he calls them so. he never uses this appellation, but in exhorting. We are persuaded of you things that accompany salvation - We are persuaded you are now saved from your sins; and that ye have that faith, love, and holiness, which lead to final salvation. Though we thus speak - To warn you, lest you should fall from your present steadfastness.

10. For - Ye give plain proof of your faith and love, which the righteous God will surely reward.

11. But we desire you may show the same diligence unto the end - And therefore we thus speak. To the full assurance of hope - Which you cannot expect, if you abate your diligence. The full assurance

of faith relates to present pardon; the full assurance of hope, to future glory. The former is the highest degree of divine evidence that God is reconciled to me in the Son of his love; the latter is the same degree of divine evidence (wrought in the soul by the same immediate inspiration of the Holy Ghost) of persevering grace, and of eternal glory. So much, and no more, as faith every moment "beholds with open face," so much does hope see to all eternity But this assurance of faith and hope is not an opinion, not a bare construction of scripture, but is given immediately by the power of the Holy Ghost; and what none can have for another, but for himself only.

12. Inherited the promises - The promised rest; paradise.

13. For - Ye have abundant encouragement, seeing no stronger promise could be made than that great promise which God made to Abraham, and in him to us.

14. Gen. xxii, 17.

15. After he had waited - Thirty years. He obtained the promise - Isaac, the pledge of all the promises.

16. Men generally swear by him who is infinitely greater than themselves, and an oath for confirmation, to confirm what is promised or asserted, usually puts an end to all contradiction. This shows that an oath taken in a religious manner is lawful even under the gospel: otherwise the apostle would never have mentioned it with so much honour, as a proper means to confirm the truth

17. God interposed by an oath - Amazing condescension! He who is greatest of all acts as if he were a middle person; as if while he swears, he were less than himself, by whom he swears! Thou that hearest the promise, dost thou not yet believe?

18. That by two unchangeable things - His promise and his oath, in either, much more in both of which, it was impossible for God to lie, we might have strong consolation - Swallowing up all doubt and fear. Who have fled - After having been tossed by many storms. To lay hold on the hope set before us - On Christ, the object of our hope, and the glory we hope for through him.

19. Which hope in Christ we have as an anchor of the soul - Entering into heaven itself, and fixed there. Within the veil - Thus he slides back to the priesthood of Christ.

20. A forerunner used to be less in dignity than those that are to follow him. But it is not so here; for Christ who is gone before us is infinitely superior to us. What an honour is it to believers, to have so glorious a forerunner, now appearing in the presence of God for them.

VII

1. The sum of this chapter is, Christ, as appears from his type, Melchisedec, who was greater than Abraham himself, from whom Levi descended, has a priesthood altogether excellent, new, firm, perpetual. Gen. xiv, 18, &c.

2. Being first - According to the meaning of his own name. King of righteousness, then - According to the name of his city. King of peace - So in him, as in Christ, righteousness and peace were joined. And so they are in all that believe in him.

3. Without father, without mother, without pedigree - Recorded, without any account of his descent from any ancestors of the priestly order. Having neither beginning of days, nor end of life - Mentioned by Moses. But being - In all these respects. Made like the Son of God - Who is really without father, as to his human nature; without mother, as to his divine; and in this also, without pedigree - Neither descended from any ancestors of the priestly order. Remaineth a priest continually - Nothing is recorded of the death or successor of Melchisedec. But Christ alone does really remain without death, and without successor.

4. The greatness of Melchisedec is described in all the preceding and following particulars. But the most manifest proof of it was, that Abraham gave him tithes as to a priest of God and a superior; though he was himself a patriarch, greater than a king, and a progenitor of many kings.

5. The sons of Levi take tithes of their brethren -- sprung from Abraham as well as themselves. The Levites therefore are greater than they; but the priests are greater than the Levites, the patriarch Abraham than the priests, and Melchisedec than him.

6. He who is not from them - The Levites Blessed - Another proof of his superiority. Even him that had the promises - That was so highly favoured of God. When St. Paul speaks of Christ, he says, "the promise;" promises refer to other blessings also.

7. The less is blessed - Authoritatively, of the greater.

8. And here - In the Levitical priesthood. But there - In the case of Melchisedec. He of whom it is testified that he liveth - Who is not spoken of as one that died for another to succeed him; but is represented only as living, no mention being made either of his birth or death.

9. And even Levi, who received tithes - Not in person, but in his successors, as it were, paid tithes - In the person of Abraham.

11. The apostle now demonstrates that the Levitical priesthood must yield to the priesthood of Christ, because Melchisedec, after whose order he is a priest,

1. Is opposed to Aaron, ver. 11-14.

2. Hath no end of life, ver. 15-19, but "remaineth a priest continually." If now perfection were by the Levitical priesthood - If this perfectly answered all God's designs and man's wants For under it the people received the law - Whence some might infer, that perfection was by that priesthood. What farther need was there, that another priest - Of a new order, should be set up? From this single consideration it is plain, that both the priesthood and the law, which were inseparably connected, were now to give way to a better priesthood and more excellent dispensation.

12. For - One of these cannot be changed without the other.

13. But the priesthood is manifestly changed from one order to another, and from one tribe to another. For he of whom these things are spoken - Namely, Jesus. Pertaineth to another tribe - That of Judah. Of which no man was suffered by the law to attend on, or minister at, the altar.

14. For it is evident that our Lord sprang out of Judah - Whatever difficulties have arisen since, during so long a tract of time, it was then clear beyond dispute.

15. And it is still far more evident, that - Both the priesthood and the law are changed, because the priest now raised up is not only of another tribe, but of a quite different order.

16. Who is made - A priest. Not after the law of a carnal commandment - Not according to the Mosaic law, which consisted chiefly of commandments that were carnal, compared to the spirituality of the gospel. But after the power of an endless life - Which he has in himself, as the eternal Son of God.

18. For there is implied in this new and everlasting priesthood, and in the new dispensation connected therewith, a disannulling of the preceding commandment - An abrogation of the Mosaic law. For the weakness and unprofitableness thereof - For its insufficiency either to justify or to sanctify.

19. For the law - Taken by itself, separate from the gospel. Made nothing perfect - Could not perfect its votaries, either in faith or love, in happiness or holiness. But the bringing in of a better hope - Of the gospel dispensation, which gives us a better ground of confidence, does. By which we draw nigh to God - Yea, so nigh as to be one spirit with him. And this is true perfection.

20. And - The greater solemnity wherewith he was made priest, farther proves the superior excellency of his priesthood.

21. The Lord swear and will not repent - Hence also it appears, that his is an unchangeable priesthood.

22. Of so much better a covenant - Unchangeable, eternal. Was Jesus made a surety - Or mediator. The word covenant frequently occurs in the remaining part of this epistle. The original word means either a covenant or a last will and testament. St. Paul takes it sometimes in the former, sometimes in the latter, sense; sometimes he includes both.

23. They were many priests - One after another.

24. He continueth forever - In life and in his priesthood. That passeth not away - To any successor.

25. Wherefore he is able to save to the uttermost - From all the guilt, power, root, and consequence of sin. Them who come - By faith. To God through him - As their priest. Seeing he ever liveth to make intercession - That is, he ever lives and intercedes. He died once; he intercedes perpetually.

26. For such an high priest suited us - Unholy, mischievous, defiled sinners: a blessed paradox! Holy - With respect to God. Harmless - With respect to men. Undefiled - With any sin in himself. Separated from sinners - As well as free from sin. And so he was when he left the world. And made - Even in his human nature. Higher than the heavens - And all their inhabitants.

27. Who needeth not to offer up sacrifices daily - That is, on every yearly day of expiation; for he offered once for all: not for his own sins, for he then offered up himself "without spot to God."

28. The law maketh men high priests that have infirmity - That are both weak, mortal, and sinful. But the oath which was since the law - Namely, in the time of David. Maketh the son, who is consecrated forever - Who being now free, both from sin and death, from natural and moral infirmity, remaineth a priest forever.

VIII

1. We have such an high priest - Having finished his description of the type in Melchisedec, the apostle begins to treat directly of the excellency of Christ's priesthood, beyond the Levitical. Who is set down - Having finished his oblation. At the right hand of the Majesty - Of God.

2. A minister - Who represents his own sacrifice, as the high priest did the blood of those sacrifices once a year. Of the sanctuary - Heaven, typified by the holy of holies. And of the true tabernacle - Perhaps his human nature, of which the old tabernacle was a type. Which the Lord hath fixed - Forever. Not man - As Moses fixed the tabernacle.

4. But if he were on earth - If his priesthood terminated here. He could not be a priest - At all, consistently with the Jewish institutions. There being other priests - To whom alone this office is allotted.

5. Who serve - The temple, which was not yet destroyed. After the pattern and shadow of heavenly

things - Of spiritual, evangelical worship, and of everlasting glory. The pattern - Somewhat like the strokes pencilled out upon a piece of fine linen, which exhibit the figures of leaves and flowers, but have not yet received their splendid colours and curious shades. And shadow - Or shadowy representation, which gives you some dim and imperfect idea of the body, but not the fine features, not the distinguishing air; none of those living graces which adorn the real person. Yet both the pattern and shadow lead our minds to something nobler than themselves: the pattern, to that holiness and glory which complete it; the shadow, to that which occasions it. Exod. xxv, 40.

6. And now he hath obtained a more excellent ministry - His priesthood as much excels theirs, as the promises of the gospel (whereof he is a surety) excels those of the law. These better promises are specified, ver. 10, xi, those in the law were mostly temporal promises.

7. For if the first had been faultless - If that dispensation had answered all God's designs and man's wants, if it had not been weak and unprofitable unable to make anything perfect, no place would have been for a second.

8. But there is; for finding fault with them - Who were under the old covenant he saith, I make a new covenant with the house of Israel - With all the Israel of God, in all ages and nations. It is new in many respects, though not as to the substance of it:
1. Being ratified by the death of Christ.
2. Freed from those burdensome rites and ceremonies.
3. Containing a more full and clear account of spiritual religion.
4. Attended with larger influences of the Spirit
5. Extended to all men. And,
6. Never to be abolished. Jer. xxxi, 31, &c.

9. When I took them by the hand - With the care and tenderness of a parent. And just while this was fresh in their memory, they obeyed; but presently after they shook off the yoke. They continued not in my covenant, and I regarded them not - So that covenant was soon broken in pieces.

10. This is the covenant I will make after those days - After the Mosaic dispensation is abolished. I will put my laws in their minds - I will open their eyes, and enlighten their understanding, to see the true, full, spiritual meaning thereof. And write them on their hearts - So that they shall inwardly experience whatever I have commanded. And I will be to them a God - Their all-sufficient portion, and exceeding great reward. And they shall be to me a people - My treasure, my beloved, loving, and obedient children.

11. And they who are under this covenant (though in other respects they will have need to teach each other to their lives' end, yet) shall not need to teach every one his brother, saying, Know the Lord; for they shall all know me - All real Christians. From the least to the greatest - In this order the saving knowledge of God ever did and ever will proceed; not first to the greatest, and then to the least. But "the Lord shall save the tents," the poorest, "of Judah first, that the glory of the house of David," the royal seed, "and the glory of the inhabitants of Jerusalem," the nobles and the rich citizens, "do not magnify themselves," Zech. xii, 7.

12. For I will justify them, which is the root of all true knowledge of God. This, therefore, is God's method. First, a sinner is pardoned: then he knows God, as gracious and merciful then God's laws are written on his heart: he is God's, and God is his.

13. In saying, A new covenant, he hath antiquated the first - Hath shown that it is disannulled, and out of date. Now that which is antiquated is ready to vanish away - As it did quickly after, when the temple was destroyed.

IX

1. The first covenant had ordinances of outward worship, and a worldly - a visible, material sanctuary, or tabernacle. Of this sanctuary he treats, ver. 2-5. Of those ordinances, ver. 6-10.

2. The first - The outward tabernacle. In which was the candlestick, and the table - The shewbread, shown continually before God and all the people, consisting of twelve loaves, according to the number of the tribes, was placed on this table in two rows, six upon one another in each row. This candlestick and bread seem to have typified the light and life which are more largely dispensed under the gospel by Him who is the Light of the world, and the Bread of life.

3. The second veil divided the holy place from the most holy, as the first veil did the holy place from the courts.

4. Having the golden censer - Used by the high priest only, on the great day of atonement. And the ark, or chest, of the covenant - So called from the tables of the covenant contained therein. Wherein was the manna - The monument of God's care over Israel. And Aaron's rod - The monument of the regular priesthood. And the tables of the covenant - The two tables of stone, on which the ten commandments were written by the finger of God the most venerable monument of all.

5. And over it were the cherubim of glory - Over which the glory of God used to appear. Some

suppose each of these had four faces, and so represented the Three-One God, with the manhood assumed by the Second Person. With out-spread wings shadowing the mercy-seat - Which was a lid or plate of gold, covering the ark.

6. Always - Every day. Accomplishing their services - Lighting the lamps, changing the shewbread, burning incense, and sprinkling the blood of the sin offerings.

7. Errors - That is, sins of ignorance, to which only those atonements extended.

8. The Holy Ghost evidently showing - By this token. That the way into the holiest - Into heaven. Was not made manifest - Not so clearly revealed. While the first tabernacle, and its service, were still subsisting - And remaining in force.

9. Which - Tabernacle, with all its furniture and services. Is a figure - Or type, of good things to come Which cannot perfect the worshipper - Neither the priest nor him who brought the offering. As to his conscience - So that he should be no longer conscious of the guilt or power of sin. Observe, the temple was as yet standing.

10. They could not so perfect him, with all their train of precepts relating to meats and drinks, and carnal, gross, external ordinances; and were therefore imposed only till the time of reformation - Till Christ came.

11. An high priest of good things to come - Described, ver. 15. Entered through a greater, that is, a more noble, and perfect tabernacle - Namely, his own body. Not of this creation - Not framed by man, as that tabernacle was.

12. The holy place - Heaven. For us - All that believe.

13. If the ashes of an heifer - Consumed by fire as a sin-offering, being sprinkled on them who were legally unclean. Purified the flesh - Removed that legal uncleanness, and re-admitted them to the temple and the congregation. Num. xix, 17, 18, 19.

14. How much more shall the blood of Christ. - The merit of all his sufferings. Who through the eternal Spirit - The work of redemption being the work of the whole Trinity. Neither is the Second Person alone concerned even in the amazing condescension that was needful to complete it. The Father delivers up the kingdom to the Son; and the Holy Ghost becomes the gift of the Messiah, being, as it were, sent according to his good pleasure. Offered himself - Infinitely more precious than any created victim, and that without spot to God. Purge our conscience - Our inmost soul. From dead works - From all the inward and outward works of the devil, which spring from spiritual death in the soul, and lead to death everlasting. To serve the living God - In the life of faith, in perfect love and spotless holiness.

15. And for this end he is the Mediator of a new covenant, that they who are called - To the engagements and benefits thereof. Might receive the eternal inheritance promised to Abraham: not by means of legal sacrifices, but of his meritorious death. For the redemption of the transgressions that were under the first covenant - That is, for the redemption of transgressors from the guilt and punishment of those sins which were committed in the time of the old covenant. The article of his death properly divides the old covenant from the new.

16. I say by means of death; for where such a covenant is, there must be the death of him by whom it is confirmed - Seeing it is by his death that the benefits of it are purchased. It seems beneath the dignity of the apostle to play upon the ambiguity of the Greek word, as the common translation supposes him to do.

17. After he is dead - Neither this, nor after men are dead is a literal translation of the words. It is a very perplexed passage.

18. Whence neither was the first - The Jewish covenant, originally transacted without the blood of an appointed sacrifice.

19. He took the blood of calves - Or heifers. And of goats, with water, and scarlet wool, and hyssop - All these circumstances are not particularly mentioned in that chapter of Exodus, but are supposed to be already known from other passages of Moses. And the book itself - Which contained all he had said. And sprinkled all the people - Who were near him. The blood was mixed with water to prevent its growing too stiff for sprinkling; perhaps also to typify that blood and water, John xix, 34. Exod. xxiv, 7, 8

20. Saying, This is the blood of the covenant which God hath enjoined me to deliver unto you - By this it is established. Exod. xxiv, 8.

21. And in like manner he ordered the tabernacle - When it was made, and all its vessels, to be sprinkled with blood once a year.

22. And almost all things - For some were purified by water or fire. Are according to the law purified with blood - Offered or sprinkled. And according to the law, there is no forgiveness of sins without shedding of blood - All this pointed to the blood of Christ effectually cleansing from all sin, and intimated, there can be no purification from it by any other means.

23. Therefore - That is, it plainly appears from what has been said. It was necessary - According to the appointment of God. That the tabernacle and all its utensils, which were patterns, shadowy representations, of things in heaven, should be purified by these - Sacrifices and sprinklings. But the

heavenly things themselves - Our heaven-born spirits: what more this may mean we know not yet. By better sacrifices than these - That is, by a better sacrifice, which is here opposed to all the legal sacrifices, and is expressed plurally, because it includes the signification of them all, and is of so much more eminent virtue.

24. For Christ did not enter into the holy place made with hands - He never went into the holy of holies at Jerusalem, the figure of the true tabernacle in heaven, chap. viii, 2. But into heaven itself, to appear in the presence of God for us - As our glorious high priest and powerful intercessor.

26. For then he must often have suffered from the foundation of the world - This supposes,

1. That by suffering once he atoned for all the sins which had been committed from the foundation of the world.

2. That he could not have atoned for them without suffering. At the consummation of the ages - The sacrifice of Christ divides the whole age or duration of the world into two parts, and extends its virtue backward and forward, from this middle point wherein they meet to abolish both the guilt and power of sin.

27. After this, the judgment - Of the great day. At the moment of death every man's final state is determined. But there is not a word in scripture of a particular judgment immediately after death.

28. Christ having once died to bear the sins - The punishment due to them. Of many - Even as many as are born into the world. Will appear the second time - When he comes to judgment. Without sin - Not as he did before, bearing on himself the sins of many, but to bestow everlasting salvation.

X

1. From all that has been said it appears, that the law, the Mosaic dispensation, being a bare, unsubstantial shadow of good things to come, of the gospel blessings, and not the substantial, solid image of them, can never with the same kind of sacrifices, though continually repeated, make the comers thereunto perfect, either as to justification or sanctification. How is it possible, that any who consider this should suppose the attainments of David, or any who were under that dispensation, to be the proper measure of gospel holiness; and that Christian experience is to rise no higher than Jewish?

2. They who had been once perfectly purged, would have been no longer conscious either of the guilt or power of their sins.

3. There is a public commemoration of the sins both of the last and of all the preceding years; a clear proof that the guilt thereof is not perfectly purged away.

4. It is impossible the blood of goats should take away sins - Either the guilt or the power of them.

5. When he cometh into the world - In the fortieth Psalm the Messiah's coming into the world is represented. It is said, into the world, not into the tabernacle, chap. ix, 1; because all the world is interested in his sacrifice. A body hast thou prepared for me - That I may offer up myself. Psalm xl, 6, &c.

7. In the volume of the book - In this very psalm it is written of me. Accordingly I come to do thy will - By the sacrifice of myself.

8. Above when he said, Sacrifice thou hast not chosen - That is, when the Psalmist pronounced those words in his name.

9. Then said he - in that very instant he subjoined. Lo, I come to do Thy will - To offer a more acceptable sacrifice; and by this very act he taketh away the legal, that he may establish the evangelical, dispensation.

10. By which will - Of God, done and suffered by Christ. We are sanctified - Cleansed from guilt, and consecrated to God.

11. Every priest standeth - As a servant in an humble posture.

12. But he - The virtue of whose one sacrifice remains for ever. Sat down - As a son, in majesty and honour.

13. Psalm cx, 1.

14. He hath perfected them forever - That is, has done all that was needful in order to their full reconciliation with God.

15. In this and the three following verses, the apostle winds up his argument concerning the excellency and perfection of the priesthood and sacrifice of Christ. He had proved this before by a quotation from Jeremiah; which he here repeats, describing the new covenant as now completely ratified, and all the blessings of it secured to us by the one offering of Christ, which renders all other expiatory sacrifices, and any repetition of his own, utterly needless.

16. Jer. xxxi, 33, &c.

19. Having finished the doctrinal part of his epistle, the apostle now proceeds to exhortation deduced from what has been treated of chap. v, 4, which he begins by a brief recapitulation. Having therefore liberty to enter,

20. By a living way - The way of faith, whereby we live indeed. Which he hath consecrated -

Prepared, dedicated, and established for us. Through the veil, that is, his flesh - As by rending the veil in the temple, the holy of holies became visible and accessible; so by wounding the body of Christ, the God of heaven was manifested, and the way to heaven opened.

22. Let us draw near - To God. With a true heart - In godly sincerity. Having our hearts sprinkled from an evil conscience - So as to condemn us no longer And our bodies washed with pure water - All our conversation spotless and holy, which is far more acceptable to God than all the legal sprinklings and washings.

23. The profession of our hope - The hope which we professed at our baptism.

25. Not forsaking the assembling ourselves - In public or private worship. As the manner of some is - Either through fear of persecution, or from a vain imagination that they were above external ordinances. But exhorting one another - To faith, love, and good works. And so much the more, as ye see the day approaching - The great day is ever in your eye.

26. For when we - Any of us Christians. Sin wilfully - By total apostasy from God, termed "drawing back," ver. 38. After having received the experimental knowledge of the gospel truth, there remaineth no more sacrifice for sins - None but that which we obstinately reject.

28. He that, in capital cases, despised (presumptuously transgressed) the law of Moses died without mercy - Without any delay or mitigation of his punishment.

29. Of how much sorer punishment is he worthy, who - By wilful, total apostasy. It does not appear that this passage refers to any other sin. Hath, as it were, trodden underfoot the Son of God - A lawgiver far more honourable than Moses. And counted the blood wherewith the better covenant was established, an unholy, a common, worthless thing. By which he hath been sanctified - Therefore Christ died for him also, and he was at least justified once. And done despite to the Spirit of grace - By rejecting all his motions.

30. The Lord will judge his people - Yea, far more rigorously than the heathens, if they rebel against him. Deut. xxxii, 35, &c.

31. To fall into the hands - Of his avenging justice.

32. Enlightened - With the knowledge of God and of his truth.

34. For ye sympathized with all your suffering brethren, and with me in particular; and received joyfully the loss of your own goods.

35. Cast not away therefore this your confidence - Your faith and hope; which none can deprive you of but yourselves.

36. The promise - Perfect love; eternal life.

37. He that cometh - To reward every man according to his works.

38. Now the just - The justified person. Shall live - In God's favour, a spiritual and holy life. By faith - As long as he retains that gift of God. But if he draw back - If he make shipwreck of his faith My soul hath no pleasure in him - That is, I abhor him; I cast him off. Hab. ii, 3, &c.

39. We are not of them who draw back to perdition - Like him mentioned ver. 38. But of them that believe - To the end, so as to attain eternal life.

XI

1. The definition of faith given in this verse, and exemplified in the various instances following, undoubtedly includes justifying faith, but not directly as justifying. For faith justifies only as it refers to, and depends on, Christ. But here is no mention of him as the object of faith; and in several of the instances that follow, no notice is taken of him or his salvation, but only of temporal blessings obtained by faith. And yet they may all be considered as evidences of the power of justifying faith in Christ, and of its extensive exercise in a course of steady obedience amidst difficulties and dangers of every kind. Now faith is the subsistence of things hoped for, the evidence or conviction of things not seen - Things hoped for are not so extensive as things not seen. The former are only things future and joyful to us; the latter are either future, past, or present, and those either good or evil, whether to us or others. The subsistence of things hoped for - Giving a kind of present subsistence to the good things which God has promised: the divine supernatural evidence exhibited to, the conviction hereby produced in, a believer of things not seen, whether past, future, or spiritual; particularly of God and the things of God.

2. By it the elders - Our forefathers. This chapter is a kind of summary of the Old Testament, in which the apostle comprises the designs, labours, sojournings, expectations, temptations, martyrdoms of the ancients. The former of them had a long exercise of their patience; the latter suffered shorter but sharper trials. Obtained a good testimony - A most comprehensive word. God gave a testimony, not only of them but to them: and they received his testimony as if it had been the things themselves of which he testified, ver. 4, 5, 39. Hence they also gave testimony to others, and others testified of them.

3. By faith we understand that the worlds - Heaven and earth and all things in them, visible and invisible. Where made - Formed, fashioned, and finished. By the word - The sole command of God, without any instrument or preceding matter. And as creation is the foundation and specimen of the

whole divine economy, so faith in the creation is the foundation and specimen of all faith. So that things which are seen - As the sun, earth, stars. Were made of things which do not appear - Out of the dark, unapparent chaos, Gen. i, 2. And this very chaos was created by the divine power; for before it was thus created it had no existence in nature.

4. By faith - In the future Redeemer. Abel offered a more excellent sacrifice - The firstlings of his flock, implying both a confession of what his own sins deserved, and a desire of sharing in the great atonement. Than Cain - Whose offering testified no such faith, but a bare acknowledgment of God the Creator. By which faith he obtained both righteousness and a testimony of it: God testifying - Visibly that his gifts were accepted; probably by sending fire from heaven to consume his sacrifice, a token that justice seized on the sacrifice instead of the sinner who offered it. And by it - By this faith. Being dead, he yet speaketh - That a sinner is accepted only through faith in the great sacrifice.

5. Enoch was not any longer found among men, though perhaps they sought for him as they did for Elijah, 2 Kings ii, 17. He had this testimony - From God in his own conscience.

6. But without faith - Even some divine faith in God, it is impossible to please him. For he that cometh to God - in prayer, or another act of worship, must believe that he is.

7. Noah being warned of things not seen as yet - Of the future deluge. Moved with fear, prepared an ark, by which open testimony he condemned the world - Who neither believed nor feared.

8. Gen. xii, 1-4

9. By faith he sojourned in the land of promise - The promise was made before, Gen. xii, 7. Dwelling in tents - As a sojourner With Isaac and Jacob - Who by the same manner of living showed the same faith Jacob was born fifteen years before the death of Abraham. The joint heirs of the same promise - Having all the same interest therein. Isaac did not receive this inheritance from Abraham, nor Jacob from Isaac, but all of them from God. Gen. xvii, 8

10. He looked for a city which hath foundations - Whereas a tent has none. Whose builder and former is God - Of which God is the sole contriver, former, and finisher.

11. Sarah also herself - Though at first she laughed at the promise, Gen. xviii, 12. Gen. xxi, 2.

12. As it were dead - Till his strength was supernaturally restored, which continued for many years after.

13. All these - Mentioned ver. 7-11. Died in faith - In death faith acts most vigorously. Not having received the promises - The promised blessings. Embraced - As one does a dear friend when he meets him.

14. They who speak thus show plainly that they seek their own country - That they keep in view, and long for, their native home.

15. If they had been mindful of - Their earthly country, Ur of the Chaldeans, they might have easily returned.

16. But they desire a better country, that is, an heavenly - This is a full convincing proof that the patriarchs had a Revelation and a promise of eternal glory in heaven. Therefore God is not ashamed to be called their God: seeing he hath prepared for them a city - Worthy of God to give.

17. By faith Abraham - When God made that glorious trial of him. Offered up Isaac - The will being accepted as if he had actually done it. Yea, he that had received the promises - Particularly that grand promise, "In Isaac shall thy seed be called." Offered up - This very son; the only one he had by Sarah. Gen. xxii, 1,&c.

18. In Isaac shall thy seed be called - From him shall the blessed seed spring. Gen. xxi, 12.

19. Accounting that God was able even to raise him from the dead - Though there had not been any instance of this in the world. From whence also - To speak in a figurative way. He did receive him - Afterwards, snatched from the jaws of death.

20. Blessed - Gen. xxvii, 27, 39; prophetically foretold the particular blessings they should partake of. Jacob and Esau - Preferring the elder before the younger.

21. Jacob when dying - That is, when near death. Bowing down on the top of his staff - As he sat on the side of his bed. Gen. xlviii, 16; Gen. xlvii, 31

22. Concerning his bones - To be carried into the land of promise.

23. They saw - Doubtless with a divine presage of things to come.

24. Refused to be called - Any longer.

26. The reproach of Christ - That which he bore for believing in the Messiah to come, and acting accordingly. For he looked off - From all those perishing treasures, and beyond all those temporal hardships Unto the recompence of reward - Not to an inheritance in Canaan; he had no warrant from God to look for this, nor did he ever attain it; but what his believing ancestors looked for, - a future state of happiness in heaven.

27. By faith he left Egypt - Taking all the Israelites with him. Not then fearing the wrath of the king - As he did many years before, Exod. ii, 14. Exod. xiv, 15, &c.

28. The pouring out of the blood - Of the paschal lamb, which was sprinkled on the door-posts, lest the destroying angel should touch the Israelites. Exod. xii, 12-18.

29. They - Moses, Aaron, and the Israelites. Passed the Red Sea - It washed the borders of Edom, which signifies red. Thus far the examples are cited from Genesis and Exodus; those that follow are from the former and the latter Prophets.

30. By the faith of Joshua.

31. Rahab - Though formerly one not of the fairest character.

32. After Samuel, the prophets are properly mentioned. David also was a prophet; but he was a king too. The prophets - Elijah, Elisha, &c., including likewise the believers who lived with them.

33, 34. David, in particular, subdued kingdoms. Samuel (not excluding the rest) wrought righteousness. The prophets, in general, obtained promises, both for themselves, and to deliver to others. Prophets also stopped the mouths of lions, as Daniel; and quenched the violence of fire, as Shadrach, Meshach, and Abednego. To these examples, whence the nature of faith clearly appears, those more ancient ones are subjoined, (by a transposition, and in an inverted order,) which receive light from these. Jephthah escaped the edge of the sword; Samson out of weakness was made strong; Barak became valiant in fight; Gideon put to flight armies of the aliens. Faith animates to the most heroic enterprises, both civil and military. Faith overcomes all impediments effects the greatest things; attains to the very best; and inverts, by its miraculous power the very course of nature. 2 Sam. viii, 1,&c.; 1 Sam. viii, 9,&c.; 1 Sam. xiii, 3,&c.; Dan. vi, 22; Dan. iii, 27; Jude xii, 3; Jude xv, 19,&c.; Jude xvi, 28,&c.; Jude iv, 14,&c.; Jude vii, 21.

35. Women - Naturally weak. Received their dead - Children. Others were tortured - From those who acted great things the apostle rises higher, to those who showed the power of faith by suffering. Not accepting deliverance - On sinful terms. That they might obtain a better resurrection - An higher reward, seeing the greater their sufferings the greater would be their glory. 1 Kings xvii, 22; 2 Kings iv, 35

36. And others - The apostle seems here to pass on to recent examples.

37. They were sawn asunder - As, according to the tradition of the Jews, Isaiah was by Manasseh. Were tempted - Torments and death are mentioned alternately. Every way; by threatenings, reproaches, tortures, the variety of which cannot be expressed; and again by promises and allurements.

38. Of whom the world was not worthy - It did not deserve so great a blessing. They wandered - Being driven out from men.

39. And all these - Though they obtained a good testimony, ver. 2, yet did not receive the great promise, the heavenly inheritance.

40. God having provided some better thing for us - Namely, everlasting glory. That they might not be perfected without us - That is, that we might all be perfected together in heaven.

XII

1. Wherefore, being encompassed with a cloud - A great multitude, tending upward with a holy swiftness. Of witnesses - Of the power of faith. Let us lay aside every weight - As all who run a race take care to do. Let us throw off whatever weighs us down, or damps the vigour of our Soul. And the sin which easily besetteth us - As doth the sin of our constitution, the sin of our education, the sin of our profession.

2. Looking - From all other things. To Jesus - As the wounded Israelites to the brazen serpent. Our crucified Lord was prefigured by the lifting up of this; our guilt, by the stings of the fiery serpents; and our faith, by their looking up to the miraculous remedy. The author and finisher of our faith - Who begins it in us, carries it on, and perfects it. Who for the joy that was set before him - Patiently and willingly endured the cross, with all the pains annexed thereto. And is set down - Where there is fulness of joy.

3. Consider - Draw the comparison and think. The Lord bore all this; and shall his servants bear nothing? Him that endured such contradiction from sinners - Such enmity and opposition of every kind Lest ye be weary - Dull and languid, and so actually faint in your course.

4. Unto blood - Unto wounds and death.

5. And yet ye seem already to have forgotten the exhortation - Wherein God speaketh to you with the utmost tenderness. Despise not thou the chastening of the Lord - Do not slight or make little of it; do not impute any affliction to chance or second causes but see and revere the hand of God in it. Neither faint when thou art rebuked of him - But endure it patiently and fruitfully. Pro iii, 11, &c.

6. For - All springs from love; therefore neither despise nor faint.

7. Whom his father chasteneth not - When he offends.

8. Of which all sons are partakers - More or less.

9. And we reverenced them - We neither despised nor fainted under their correction. Shall we not much rather - Submit with reverence and meekness To the Father of spirits - That we may live with him for ever. Perhaps these expressions, fathers of our flesh, and Father of spirits, intimate that our earthly fathers are only the parents of our bodies, our souls not being originally derived from them, but all

created by the immediate power of God; perhaps, at the beginning of the world.

10. *For they verily for a few days* - How few are even all our day on earth! *Chastened us as they thought good* - Though frequently they erred therein, by too much either of indulgence or severity. But he always, unquestionably, for our profit, that *we may be partakers of his holiness* - That is, of himself and his glorious image.

11. *Now all chastening* - Whether from our earthly or heavenly Father, *Is for the present grievous, yet it yieldeth the peaceable fruit of righteousness* - Holiness and happiness. *To them that are exercised thereby* - That receive this exercise as from God, and improve it according to his will.

12. *Wherefore lift up the hands* - Whether your own or your brethren's. *That hang down* - Unable to continue the combat. *And the feeble knees* - Unable to continue the race. Isaiah xxxv, 3.

13. *And make straight paths both for your own and for their feet* - Remove every hindrance, every offense. *That the lame* - They who are weak, scarce able to walk. *Be not turned out of the way* - Of faith and holiness.

14. *Follow peace with all men* - This second branch of the exhortation concerns our neighbours; the third, God. *And holiness* - The not following after all holiness, is the direct way to fall into sin of every kind.

15. *Looking diligently, lest any one* - If he do not lift up the hands that hang down. *Fall from the grace of God: lest any root of bitterness* - Of envy, anger, suspicion. *Springing up* - Destroy the sweet peace; lest any, not following after holiness, fall into fornication or profaneness. In general, any corruption, either in doctrine or practice, is a root of bitterness, and may pollute many.

16. Esau was profane for so slighting the blessing which went along with the birth-right.

17. *He was rejected* - He could not obtain it. *For he found no place for repentance* - There was no room for any such repentance as would regain what he had lost. *Though he sought it* - The blessing of the birth-right. *Diligently with tears* - He sought too late. Let us use the present time.

18. *For* - A strong reason this why they ought the more to regard the whole exhortation drawn from the priesthood of Christ: because both salvation and vengeance are now nearer at hand. *Ye are not come to the mountain that could be touched* - That was of an earthy, material nature.

19. *The sound of a trumpet* - Formed, without doubt, by the ministry of angels, and preparatory to the words, that is, the Ten Commandments, which were uttered with a loud voice, Deut. v, 22.

20. *For they could not bear* - The terror which seized them, when they heard those words proclaimed, If even a beast, &c. Exod. xix, 12, &c.

21. *Even Moses* - Though admitted to so near an intercourse with God, who "spake to him as a man speaketh to his friend." At other times he acted as a mediator between God and the people. But while the ten words were pronounced, he stood as one of the hearers, Exod. xix, 25; Exod. xx, 19.

22. *But ye* - Who believe in Christ. *Are come* - The apostle does not here speak of their coming to the church militant, but of that glorious privilege of New Testament believers, their communion with the church triumphant. But this is far more apparent to the eyes of celestial spirits than to ours which are yet veiled. St. Paul here shows an excellent knowledge of the heavenly economy, worthy of him who had been caught up into the third heaven. *To Mount Zion*--A spiritual mountain. *To the city of the living God, the heavenly Jerusalem* - All these glorious titles belong to the New Testament church. *And to an innumerable company* - Including all that are afterwards mentioned.

23. *To the general assembly* - The word properly signifies a stated convention on some festival occasion. *And church* - The whole body of true believers, whether on earth or in paradise. *Of the first-born*-The first-born of Israel were enrolled by Moses; but these are enrolled in heaven, as citizens there. It is observable, that in this beautiful gradation, these first-born are placed nearer to God than the angels. See Jam i, 18. *And to God the Judge of all* - Propitious to you, adverse to your enemies. *And to the spirits* - The separate souls. *Of just men* - It seems to mean, of New Testament believers. The number of these, being not yet large, is mentioned distinct from the innumerable company of just men whom their Judge hath acquitted. These are now made perfect in an higher sense than any who are still alive. Accordingly, St. Paul, while yet on earth, denies that he was thus made perfect, Phil. iii, 12.

24. *To Jesus, the mediator* - Through whom they had been perfected. *And to the blood of sprinkling* - To all the virtue of his precious blood shed for you, whereby ye are sprinkled from an evil conscience. This blood of sprinkling was the foundation of our Lord's mediatorial office. Here the gradation is at the highest point. *Which speaketh better things than that of Abel* - Which cried for vengeance.

25. *Refuse not* - By unbelief. *Him that speaketh* - And whose speaking even now is a prelude to the final scene. The same voice which spake both by the law and in the gospel, when heard from heaven, will shake heaven and earth. *For if they escaped not* - His vengeance. *Much more shall not we* - Those of us who turn from *him that speaketh from heaven* - That is, who came from heaven to speak to us.

26. *Whose voice then shook the earth* - When he spoke from Mount Sinai. *But now* - With regard to his next speaking. *He hath promised* - It is a joyful promise to the saints, though dreadful to the

wicked. Yet once more I will shake, not only the earth, but also the heaven - These words may refer in a lower sense to the dissolution of the Jewish church and state; but in their full sense they undoubtedly look much farther, even to the end of all things. This universal shaking began at the first coming of Christ. It will be consummated at his second coming. Haggai ii, 6.

27. The things which are shaken - Namely, heaven and earth. As being made - And consequently liable to change. That the things which are not shaken may remain - Even "the new heavens and the new earth," Rev. xxi, 1.

28. Therefore let us, receiving - By willing and joyful faith. A kingdom - More glorious than the present heaven and earth. Hold fast the grace, whereby we may serve God - In every thought, word, and work. With reverence - Literally, with shame. Arising from a deep consciousness of our own unworthiness. And godly fear - A tender, jealous fear of offending, arising from a sense of the gracious majesty of God.

29. For our God is a consuming fire - in the strictness of his justice, and purity of his holiness.

XIII

1. Brotherly love is explained in the following verses.

2. Some - Abraham and Lot. Have entertained angels unawares - So may an unknown guest, even now, be of more worth than he appears, and may have angels attending him, though unseen. Gen. xviii, 2; Gen. xix, 1.

3. Remember - In your prayers, and by your help. Them that are in bonds, as being bound with them - Seeing ye are members one of another. And them that suffer, as being yourselves in the body - And consequently liable to the same.

4. Marriage is honourable in, or for all sorts of men, clergy as well as laity: though the Romanists teach otherwise. And the bed undefiled - Consistent with the highest purity; though many spiritual writers, so called, say it is only licensed whoredom. But whoremongers and adulterers God will judge - Though they frequently escape the sentence of men.

5. He - God. Hath said - To all believers, in saying it to Jacob, Joshua, and Solomon. Gen. xxviii, 15; Josh. i, 5; 1 Chr xxviii, 20.

6. Psalm cxviii, 6.

7. Remember them - Who are now with God, considering the happy end of their conversation on earth.

8. Men may die; but Jesus Christ, yea, and his gospel, is the same from everlasting to everlasting.

9. Be not carried about with various doctrines - Which differ from that one faith in our one unchangeable Lord. Strange - To the ears and hearts of all that abide in him. For it is good - It is both honourable before God and pleasant and profitable That the heart be stablished with grace - Springing from faith in Christ. Not with meats - Jewish ceremonies, which indeed can never stablish the heart.

10. On the former part of this verse, the fifteenth and sixteenth depend; on the latter, the intermediate verses. We have an altar - The cross of Christ. Whereof they have no right to eat - To partake of the benefits which we receive therefrom. Who serve the tabernacle - Who adhere to the Mosaic law.

11. For - According to their own law, the sin-offerings were wholly consumed, and no Jew ever ate thereof. But Christ was a sin-offering. Therefore they cannot feed upon him, as we do, who are freed from the Mosaic law.

12. Wherefore Jesus also - Exactly answering those typical sin-offerings. Suffered without the gate - Of Jerusalem, which answered to the old camp of Israel. That he might sanctify - Reconcile and consecrate to God. The people - Who believe in him. By his own blood - Not those shadowy sacrifices, which are now of no further use.

13. Let us then go forth without the camp - Out of the Jewish dispensation. Bearing his reproach - All manner of shame, obloquy, and contempt for his sake.

14. For we have here - On earth No continuing city - All things here are but for a moment; and Jerusalem itself was just then on the point of being destroyed.

15. The sacrifice - The altar is mentioned, ver. 10; now the sacrifices:

1. Praise;

2. Beneficence; with both of which God is well pleased.

17. Obey them that have the rule over you - The word implies also, that lead or guide you; namely, in truth and holiness. And submit yourselves - Give up (not your conscience or judgment, but) your own will, in all things purely indifferent. For they watch over your souls - With all zeal and diligence, they guard and caution you against all danger. As they that must give account - To the great Shepherd, for every part of their behaviour toward you. How vigilant then ought every pastor to be! How careful of every soul committed to his charge! That they may do this - Watch over you. With joy and not with groans - He is not a good shepherd, who does not either rejoice over them, or groan for them. The

groans of other creatures are heard: how much more shall these come up in the ears of God! Whoever answers this character of a Christian pastor may undoubtedly demand this obedience.

20. The everlasting covenant - The Christian covenant, which is not temporary, like the Jewish, but designed to remain for ever. By the application of that blood, by which this covenant was established, may he make you, in every respect, inwardly and outwardly holy!

22. Suffer the word of exhortation - Addressed to you in this letter, which, though longer than my usual letters, is yet contained in few words, considering the copiousness of the subject.

23. If he come - To me.

25. - Grace be with you all - St. Paul's usual benediction. God apply it to our hearts!

John Wesley

NOTES ON THE GENERAL EPISTLE OF ST. JAMES

THIS is supposed to have been written by James the son of Alpheus the brother (or kinsman) of our Lord. It is called a General Epistle, because written not to a particular person or church, but to all the converted Israelites. Herein the apostle reproves that antinomian spirit, which had even then infected many, who had perverted the glorious doctrine of justification by faith into an occasion of licentiousness. He likewise comforts the true believers under their sufferings, and reminds them of the judgments that were approaching. It has three parts:

I. The inscription, Chap. i. 1

II. The exhortation,
    1. To patience, enduring outward, conquering inward, temptations, 2-15
    2. Considering the goodness of God, 16-18 to be swift to hear, slow to speak, slow to wrath And these three are,
    1. Proposed, 19-21
    2. Treated of at large.
        a. Let hearing be joined with practice, 22-26 Particularly with bridling the tongue, 26 With mercy and purity, 27 Without respect of persons, ii. 1-13 And so faith universally with works, 14-26
        b. Let the speech be modest, iii. 1-12
        c. Let anger, with all the other passions, be restrained, 13- iv.1- 17
    3. To patience again.
        a. Confirmed by the coming of the judge, in which draws near The calamity of the wicked, v.1-6 The deliverance of the righteous, 7-12
        b. Nourished by prayer, 13-18

III. The conclusion, 19

JAMES

I

1. *A servant of Jesus Christ* - Whose name the apostle mentions but once more in the whole epistle, chap. ii, 1. And not at all in his whole discourse, Acts xv, 14, &c.; or Acts xxi, 20-25. It might have seemed, if he mentioned him often, that he did it out of vanity, as being the brother of the Lord. *To the twelve tribes* - Of Israel; that is, those of them that believe. *Which are scattered abroad* - In various countries. Ten of the tribes were scattered ever since the reign of Hosea; and great part of the rest were now dispersed through the Roman empire: as was foretold, Deut. xxviii, 25, &c.xxx, 4. *Greeting* - That is, all blessings, temporal and eternal.

2. *My brethren, count it all joy* - Which is the highest degree of patience, and contains all the rest. *When ye fall into divers temptations* - That is, trials.

4. *Let patience have its perfect work* - Give it full scope, under whatever trials befall you. *That ye may be perfect and entire* - Adorned with every Christian grace. *And wanting nothing* - Which God requires in you.

5. *If any want* - The connection between the first and following verses, both here and in the fourth chapter, will be easily discerned by him who reads them, while he is suffering wrongfully. He will then readily perceive, why the apostle mentions all those various affections of the mind. *Wisdom* - To understand, whence and why temptations come, and how they are to be improved. Patience is in every pious man already. Let him exercise this, and ask for wisdom. The sum of wisdom, both in the temptation of poverty and of riches, is described in the ninth and tenth verses. *Who giveth to all* - That ask aright. *And upbraideth not* - Either with their past wickedness, or present unworthiness.

6. *But let him ask in faith* - A firm confidence in God. St. James also both begins and ends with faith, chap. v, 15; the hindrances of which he removes in the middle part of his epistle. *He that doubteth is like a wave of the sea* - Yea, such are all who have not asked and obtained wisdom. Driven with the

wind - From without. And tossed - From within, by his own unstableness.

8. A doubleminded man - Who has, as it were, two souls; whose heart is not simply given up to God. Is unstable - Being without the true wisdom; perpetually disagrees both with himself and others, chap. iii, 16.

9. Let the brother--St James does not give this appellation to the rich. Of low degree - Poor and tempted. Rejoice - The most effectual remedy against doublemindedness. In that he is exalted - To be a child of God, and an heir of glory.

10. But the rich, in that he is made low - Is humbled by a deep sense of his true condition. Because as the flower - Beautiful, but transient. He shall pass away - Into eternity.

11. For the sun arose and withered the grass - There is an unspeakable beauty and elegance, both in the comparison itself, and in the very manner of expressing it, intimating both the certainty and the suddenness of the event. So shall the rich fade away in his ways - In the midst of his various pleasures and employments.

12. Happy is the man that endureth temptation - Trials of various kinds. He shall receive the crown - That fadeth not away. Which the Lord hath promised to them that love him - And his enduring proves his love. For it is love only that "endureth all things."

13. But let no man who is tempted - To sin. Say, I am tempted of God - God thus tempteth no man.

14. Every man is tempted, when - In the beginning of the temptation. He is drawn away - Drawn out of God, his strong refuge. By his own desire - We are therefore to look for the cause of every sin, in, not out of ourselves. Even the injections of the devil cannot hurt before we make them our own. And every one has desires arising from his own constitution, tempers, habits, and way of life. And enticed - In the progress of the temptation, catching at the bait: so the original word signifies.

15. Then desire having conceived - By our own will joining therewith. Bringeth forth actual sin - It doth not follow that the desire itself is not sin. He that begets a man is himself a man. And sin being perfected - Grown up to maturity, which it quickly does. Bringeth forth death - Sin is born big with death.

16. Do not err - It is a grievous error to ascribe the evil and not the good which we receive to God.

17. No evil, but every good gift - Whatever tends to holiness. And every perfect gift - Whatever tends to glory. Descendeth from the Father of lights - The appellation of Father is here used with peculiar propriety. It follows, "he begat us." He is the Father of all light, material or spiritual, in the kingdom of grace and of glory. With whom is no variableness - No change in his understanding. Or shadow of turning - in his will. He infallibly discerns all good and evil; and invariably loves one, and hates the other. There is, in both the Greek words, a metaphor taken from the stars, particularly proper where the Father of lights is mentioned. Both are applicable to any celestial body, which has a daily vicissitude of day and night, and sometimes longer days, sometimes longer nights. In God is nothing of this kind. He is mere light. If there Is any such vicissitude, it is in ourselves, not in him.

18. Of his own will - Most loving, most free, most pure, just opposite to our evil desire, ver. 15. Begat he us - Who believe. By the word of truth - The true word, emphatically so termed; the gospel. That we might be a kind of first-fruits of his creatures - Christians are the chief and most excellent of his visible creatures; and sanctify the rest. Yet he says, A kind of - For Christ alone is absolutely the first-fruits.

19. Let every man be swift to hear - This is treated of from ver. 21 to the end of the next chapter. Slow to speak - Which is treated of in the third chapter. Slow to wrath - Neither murmuring at God, nor angry at his neighbour. This is treated of in the third, and throughout the fourth and fifth chapters.

20. The righteousness of God here includes all duties prescribed by him, and pleasing to him.

21. Therefore laying aside - As a dirty garment. All the filthiness and superfluity of wickedness - For however specious or necessary it may appear to worldly wisdom, all wickedness is both vile, hateful, contemptible, and really superfluous. Every reasonable end may be effectually answered without any kind or degree of it. Lay this, every known sin, aside, or all your hearing is vain. With meekness - Constant evenness and serenity of mind. Receive - Into your ears, your heart, your life. The word - Of the gospel. Ingrafted - In believers, by regeneration, ver. 18 and by habit, Heb. v, 14. Which is able to save your souls - The hope of salvation nourishes meekness.

23. Beholding his face in a glass - How exactly does the scripture glass show a man the face of his soul!

24. He beheld himself, and went away - To other business. And forgot - But such forgetting does not excuse.

25. But he that looketh diligently - Not with a transient glance, but bending down, fixing his eyes, and searching all to the bottom. Into the perfect law - Of love as established by faith. St. James here guards us against misunderstanding what St. Paul says concerning the "yoke and bondage of the law." He who keeps the law of love is free, John viii, 31, &c. He that does not, is not free, but a slave to sin, and a criminal before God, ver. 10. And continueth therein - Not like him who forgot it, and went away.

This man - There is a peculiar force in the repetition of the word. Shall be happy - Not barely in hearing, but doing the will of God.

26. If any one be ever so religious - Exact in the outward offices of religion. And bridleth not his tongue - From backbiting, talebearing, evilspeaking, he only deceiveth his own heart, if he fancies he has any true religion at all.

27. The only true religion in the sight of God, is this, to visit - With counsel, comfort, and relief. The fatherless and widows - Those who need it most. In their affliction - In their most helpless and hopeless state. And to keep himself unspotted from the world - From the maxims, tempers, and customs of it. But this cannot be done, till we have given our hearts to God, and love our neighbour as ourselves.

II

1. My brethren -- the equality of Christians, intimated by this name, is the ground of the admonition. Hold not the faith of our common Lord, the Lord of glory - Of which glory all who believe in him partake. With respect of persons - That is, honour none merely for being rich; despise none merely for being poor.

2. With gold rings - Which were not then so common as now.

3. Ye look upon him - With respect.

4. Ye distinguish not - To which the most respect is due, to the poor or to the rich. But are become evil-reasoning Judges - You reason ill, and so judge wrong: for fine apparel is no proof of worth in him that wears it.

5. Hearken - As if he had said, Stay, consider, ye that judge thus. Does not the presumption lie rather in favour of the poor man? Hath not God chosen the poor - That is, are not they whom God hath chosen, generally speaking, poor in this world? who yet are rich in faith, and heirs of the kingdom - Consequently, the most honourable of men: and those whom God so highly honours, ought not ye to honour likewise?

6. Do not the rich often oppress you - By open violence; often drag you - Under colour of law.

7. Do not they blaspheme that worthy name - Of God and of Christ. The apostle speaks chiefly of rich heathens: but are Christians, so called, a whit behind them?

8. If ye fulfil the royal law - The supreme law of the great King which is love; and that to every man, poor as well as rich, ye do well. Lev. xix, 18.

9. Being convicted - By that very law. Exod. xxiii, 3.

10. Whosoever keepeth the whole law, except in one point, he is guilty of all - Is as liable to condemnation as if he had offended in every point.

11. For it is the same authority which establishes every commandment.

12. So speak and act - In all things. As they that shall be judged - Without respect of persons. By the law of liberty - The gospel; the law of universal love, which alone is perfect freedom. For their transgressions of this, both in word and deed, the wicked shall be condemned; and according to their works, done in obedience to this, the righteous will be rewarded.

13. Judgment without mercy shall be to him - In that day. Who hath showed no mercy - To his poor brethren. But the mercy of God to believers, answering to that which they have shown, will then glory over judgment.

14. From chap. i, 22, the apostle has been enforcing Christian practice. He now applies to those who neglect this, under the pretense of faith. St. Paul had taught that "a man is justified by faith without the works of the law." This some began already to wrest to their own destruction. Wherefore St. James, purposely repeating (ver. 21, 23, 25) the same phrases, testimonies, and examples, which St. Paul had used, Rom. iv, 3, Heb. xi, 17, 31, refutes not the doctrine of St. Paul, but the error of those who abused it. There is, therefore, no contradiction between the apostles: they both delivered the truth of God, but in a different manner, as having to do with different kinds of men. On another occasion St. James himself pleaded the cause of faith, Acts xv, 13-21; and St. Paul himself strenuously pleads for works, particularly in his latter epistles. This verse is a summary of what follows. What profiteth it? is enlarged on, ver. 15-17; though a man say, ver. 18, 19 can that faith save him? ver. 20. It is not, though he have faith; but, though he say he have faith. Here, therefore, true, living faith is meant: but in other parts of the argument the apostle speaks of a dead, imaginary faith. He does not, therefore, teach that true faith can, but that it cannot, subsist without works: nor does he oppose faith to works; but that empty name of faith, to real faith working by love. Can that faith "which is without works" save him? No more than it can profit his neighbour.

17. So likewise that faith which hath not works is a mere dead, empty notion; of no more profit to him that hath it, than the bidding the naked be clothed is to him.

18. But one - Who Judges better. Will say - To such a vain talker. Show me, if thou canst, thy faith without thy works.

19. Thou believest there is one God - I allow this: but this proves only that thou hast the same faith

with the devils. Nay, they not only believe, but tremble - At the dreadful expectation of eternal torments. So far is that faith from either justifying or saving them that have it.

20. But art than willing to know - Indeed thou art not: thou wouldest fain be ignorant of it. O empty man - Empty of all goodness. That the faith which is without works is dead - And so is not properly faith, as a dead carcase is not a man.

21. Was not Abraham justified by works - St. Paul says he was justified by faith, Rom. iv, 2, &c.: yet St. James does not contradict him; for he does not speak of the same justification. St. Paul speaks of that which Abraham received many years before Isaac was born, Gen. xv, 6. St. James, of that which he did not receive till he had offered up Isaac on the altar. He was justified, therefore, in St. Paul's sense, (that is, accounted righteous,) by faith, antecedent to his works. He was justified in St. James's sense, (that is, made righteous,) by works, consequent to his faith. So that St. James's justification by works is the fruit of St. Paul's justification by faith.

22. Thou seest that faith - For by faith Abraham offered him, Heb. xi, 17. Wrought together with his works - Therefore faith has one energy and operation; works, another: and the energy and operation of faith are before works, and together with them. Works do not give life to faith, but faith begets works, and then is perfected by them. And by works was faith made perfect - Here St. James fixes the sense wherein he uses the word justified; so that no shadow of contradiction remains between his assertion and St. Paul's. Abraham returned from that sacrifice perfected in faith, and far higher in the favour of God. Faith hath not its being from works, (for it is before them,) but its perfection. That vigour of faith which begets works is then excited and increased thereby, as the natural heat of the body begets motion, whereby itself is then excited and increased. See 1 John iii, 22.

23. And the scripture - Which was afterwards written. Was hereby eminently fulfilled, Abraham believed God, and it was imputed to him for righteousness - This was twice fulfilled, - when Abraham first believed, and when he offered up Isaac. St. Paul speaks of the former fulfilling; St. James, of the latter. And he was called the Friend of God - Both by his posterity, 2 Chron. xx, 7; and by God himself, Isaiah xli, 8 so pleasing to God were the works be wrought in faith. Gen. xv, 6

24. Ye see then that a man is justified by works, and not by faith only - St. Paul, on the other hand, declares, "A man is justified by faith," and not by works, Rom. iii, 28. And yet there is no contradiction between the apostles: because,

1. They do not speak of the same faith: St. Paul speaking of living faith; St. James here, of dead faith.

2. They do not speak of the same works: St. Paul speaking of works antecedent to faith; St. James, of works subsequent to it.

25. After Abraham, the father of the Jews, the apostle cites Rahab, a woman, and a sinner of the gentiles; to show, that in every nation and sex true faith produces works, and is perfected by them; that is, by the grace of God working in the believer, while he is showing his faith by his works.

III

1. Be not many teachers - Let no more of you take this upon you than God thrusts out; seeing it is so hard not to offend in speaking much. Knowing that we - That all who thrust themselves into the office. Shall receive greater condemnation - For more offenses. St. James here, as in several of the following verses, by a common figure of speech, includes himself: we shall receive, - we offend, - we put bits, - we curse - None of which, as common sense shows, are to be interpreted either of him or of the other apostles.

2. The same is able to bridle the whole body - That is, the whole man. And doubtless some are able to do this, and so are in this sense perfect.

3. We - That is, men.

5. Boasteth great things - Hath great influence.

6. A world of iniquity - Containing an immense quantity of all manner of wickedness. It defileth - As fire by its smoke. The whole body - The whole man. And setteth on fire the course of nature - All the passions, every wheel of his soul.

7. Every kind - The expression perhaps is not to be taken strictly. Reptiles - That is, creeping things.

8. But no man can tame the tongue - Of another; no, nor his own, without peculiar help from God.

9. Men made after the likeness of God - Indeed we have now lost this likeness; yet there remains from thence an indelible nobleness, which we ought to reverence both in ourselves and others.

13. Let him show his wisdom as well as his faith by his works; not by words only.

14. If ye have bitter zeal - True Christian zeal is only the flame of love. Even in your hearts - Though it went no further. Do not lie against the truth - As if such zeal could consist with heavenly wisdom.

15. This wisdom - Which is consistent with such zeal. Is earthly - Not heavenly; not from the

Father of Lights. Animal - Not spiritual; not from the Spirit of God. Devilish - Not the gift of Christ, but such as Satan breathes into the soul.

17. But the wisdom from above is first pure - From all that is earthly, natural, devilish. Then peaceable - True peace attending purity, it is quiet, inoffensive. Gentle - Soft, mild, yielding, not rigid. Easy to be entreated - To be persuaded, or convinced; not stubborn, sour, or morose. Full of good fruits - Both in the heart and in the life, two of which are immediately specified. Without partiality - Loving all, without respect of persons; embracing all good things, rejecting all evil. And without dissimulation - Frank, open.

18. And the principle productive of this righteousness is sown, like good seed, in the peace of a believer's mind, and brings forth a plentiful harvest of happiness, (which is the proper fruit of righteousness,) for them that make peace - That labour to promote this pure and holy peace among all men.

IV

1. From whence come wars and fightings - Quarrels and wars among you, quite opposite to this peace? Is it not from your pleasures - Your desires of earthly pleasures. Which war - Against your souls. In your members - Here is the first seat of the war. Hence proceeds the war of man with man, king with king, nation with nation.

2. Ye kill - In your heart, for "he that hateth his brother is a murderer." Ye fight and war - That is, furiously strive and contend. Ye ask not - And no marvel; for a man full of evil desire, of envy or hatred, cannot pray.

3. But if ye do ask, ye receive not, because ye ask amiss - That is, from a wrong motive.

4. Ye adulterers and adulteresses - Who have broken your faith with God, your rightful spouse. Know ye not that the friendship or love of the world - The desire of the flesh, the desire of the eye, and the pride of life, or courting the favour of worldly men, is enmity against God? Whosoever desireth to be a friend of the world - Whosoever seeks either the happiness or favour of it, does thereby constitute himself an enemy of God; and can he expect to obtain anything of him?

5. Do you think that the scripture saith in vain - Without good ground. St. James seems to refer to many, not any one particular scripture. The spirit of love that dwelleth in all believers lusteth against envy - Gal. v, 17; is directly opposite to all those unloving tempers which necessarily flow from the friendship of the world.

6. But he giveth greater grace - To all who shun those tempers. Therefore it - The scripture. Saith, God resisteth the proud - And pride is the great root of all unkind affections. Prov. iii, 34

7. Therefore by humbly submitting yourselves to God, resist the devil - The father of pride and envy.

8. Then draw nigh to God in prayer, and he will draw nigh unto you, will hear you; which that nothing may hinder, cleanse your hands - Cease from doing evil. And purify your hearts - From all spiritual adultery. Be no more double minded, vainly endeavouring to serve both God and mammon.

9. Be afflicted - For your past unfaithfulness to God.

11. Speak not evil one of another - This is a grand hindrance of peace. O who is sufficiently aware of it! He that speaketh evil of another does in effect speak evil of the law, which so strongly prohibits it. Thou art not a doer of the law, but a judge - Of it; thou settest thyself above, and as it were condemnest, it.

12. There is one lawgiver that is able - To execute the sentence he denounces. But who art thou - A poor, weak, dying worm.

13. Come now, ye that say - As peremptorily as if your life were in your own hands.

15. Instead of your saying - That is, whereas ye ought to say.

17. Therefore to him that knoweth to do good and doeth it not - That knows what is right, and does not practice it. To him it is sin - This knowledge does not prevent, but increase, his condemnation.

V

1. Come now, ye rich - The apostle does not speak this so much for the sake of the rich themselves, as of the poor children of God, who were then groaning under their cruel oppression. Weep and howl for your miseries which are coming upon you - Quickly and unexpectedly. This was written not long before the siege of Jerusalem; during which, as well as after it, huge calamities came on the Jewish nation, not only in Judea, but through distant countries. And as these were an awful prelude of that wrath which was to fall upon them in the world to come, so this may likewise refer to the final vengeance which will then be executed on the impenitent.

2. The riches of the ancients consisted much in large stores of corn, and of costly apparel.

3. The canker of them - Your perishing stores and moth-eaten garments. Will be a testimony

against you - Of your having buried those talents in the earth, instead of improving them according to your Lord's will. And will eat your flesh as fire - Will occasion you as great torment as if fire were consuming your flesh. Ye have laid up treasure in the last days - When it is too late; when you have no time to enjoy them.

4. The hire of your labourers crieth - Those sins chiefly cry to God concerning which human laws are silent. Such are luxury, unchastity, and various kinds of injustice. The labourers themselves also cry to God, who is just coming to avenge their cause. Of sabaoth - Of hosts, or armies.

5. Ye have cherished your hearts - Have indulged yourselves to the uttermost. As in a day of sacrifice - Which were solemn feast-days among the Jews.

6. Ye have killed the just - Many just men; in particular, "that Just One," Acts iii, 14. They afterwards killed James, surnamed the Just, the writer of this epistle. He doth not resist you - And therefore you are secure. But the Lord cometh quickly, ver. 8.

7. The husbandman waiteth for the precious fruit - Which will recompense his labour and patience. Till he receives the former rain - Immediately after sowing. And the latter - Before the harvest.

8. Stablish your hearts - In faith and patience. For the coming of the Lord - To destroy Jerusalem. Is nigh - And so is his last coming to the eye of a believer.

9. Murmur not one against another - Have patience also with each other. The judge standeth before the door - Hearing every word, marking every thought.

10. Take the prophets for an example - Once persecuted like you, even for speaking in the name of the Lord. The very men that gloried in having prophets yet could not bear their message: nor did either their holiness or their high commission screen them from suffering.

11. We count them happy that endured - That suffered patiently. The more they once suffered, the greater is their present happiness. Ye have seen the end of the Lord - The end which the Lord gave him.

12. Swear not - However provoked. The Jews were notoriously guilty of common swearing, though not so much by God himself as by some of his creatures. The apostle here particularly forbids these oaths, as well as all swearing in common conversation. It is very observable, how solemnly the apostle introduces this command: above all things, swear not - As if he had said, Whatever you forget, do not forget this. This abundantly demonstrates the horrible iniquity of the crime. But he does not forbid the taking a solemn oath before a magistrate. Let your yea be yea; and your nay, nay - Use no higher asseverations in common discourse; and let your word stand firm. Whatever ye say, take care to make it good.

14. Having anointed him with oil - This single conspicuous gift, which Christ committed to his apostles, Mark vi, 13, remained in the church long after the other miraculous gifts were withdrawn. Indeed, it seems to have been designed to remain always; and St. James directs the elders, who were the most, if not the only, gifted men, to administer at. This was the whole process of physic in the Christian church, till it was lost through unbelief. That novel invention among the Romanists, extreme unction, practiced not for cure, but where life is despaired of, bears no manner of resemblance to this.

15. And the prayer offered in faith shall save the sick - From his sickness; and if any sin be the occasion of his sickness, it shall be forgiven him.

16. Confess your faults - Whether ye are sick or in health. To one another - He does not say, to the elders: this may, or may not, be done; for it is nowhere commanded. We may confess them to any who can pray in faith: he will then know how to pray for us, and be more stirred up so to do. And pray one for another, that ye may be healed - Of all your spiritual diseases.

17. Elijah was a man of like passions - Naturally as weak and sinful as we are. And he prayed - When idolatry covered the land.

18. He prayed again - When idolatry was abolished.

19. As if he had said, I have now warned you of those sins to which you are most liable; and, in all these respects, watch not only over yourselves, but every one over his brother also. labour, in particular, to recover those that are fallen. If any one err from the truth - Practically, by sin.

20. He shall save a soul - Of how much more value than the body! ver. 14. And hide a multitude of sins - Which shall no more, how many soever they are, be remembered to his condemnation.

NOTES ON THE FIRST EPISTLE GENERAL OF ST. PETER

THERE is a wonderful weightiness, and yet liveliness and sweetness, in the epistles of St. Peter. His design in both is, to stir up the minds of those to whom he writes, by way of remembrance, 2 Pet. iii, 1, and to guard them, not only against error, but also against doubting, chap. v, 12. This he does by reminding them of that glorious grace which God had vouchsafed them through the gospel, by which believers are inflamed to bring forth the fruits of faith, hope, love, and patience. The parts of this epistle are three: -

I. The inscription, Chap. i. 1, 2

II. The stirring up of them to whom he writes:
    1. As born of God. Here he recites and interweaves alternately both the benefits of God toward believers, and the duties of believers toward God:
        1. God hath regenerated us to a living hope, to an eternal inheritance, 3-12 Therefore hope to the end, 13
        2. As obedient children bring forth the fruit of faith to your heavenly Father, 14-21
        3. Being purified by the Spirit, love with a pure heart, 22, C.ii.10
    2. As strangers in the world, abstain from fleshly desires, 11 And show your faith by,
        1. A good conversation, 12
            a. In particular, Subjects, 13-17 Servants, after the example of Christ, 18-25 Wives, iii. 1-6 Husbands, 7
            b. In general, all, 8-15
        2. A good profession,
            a. By readiness to give an answer to every one, 15-22
            b. By shunning evil company, iv.1-6 (This part is enforced by what Christ both did and suffered, from his passion to his coming to judgment.)
            c. By the exercise of Christian virtues, and by a due use of miraculous gifts, 7-11
    3. As fellow-heirs of glory, sustain adversity, let each do this,
        1. In general, as a Christian, 12-19
        2. In his own particular state, v. 1-11 The title beloved divides the second part from the first, ii 11 and the third from the second, iv. 12

III. The conclusion, 12-14

1st PETER

I

1. To the sojourners - Upon earth, the Christians, chiefly those of Jewish extraction. Scattered - Long ago driven out of their own land. Those scattered by the persecution mentioned Acts viii, 1, were scattered only through Judea and Samaria, though afterwards some of them travelled to Phenice, Cyprus, and Antioch. Through Pontus, Galatia, Cappadocia, Asia, and Bithynia - He names these five provinces in the order wherein they occurred to him, writing from the east. All these countries lie in the Lesser Asia. The Asia here distinguished from the other provinces is that which was usually called the Proconsular Asia being a Roman province.

2. According to the foreknowledge of God - Speaking after the manner of men. Strictly speaking, there is no foreknowledge, no more than afterknowledge, with God: but all things are known to him as present from eternity to eternity. This is therefore no other than an instance of the divine condescension to our low capacities. Elect - By the free love and almighty power of God taken out of, separated from, the world. Election, in the scripture sense, is God's doing anything that our merit or power have no part

Wesley's Notes on the Bible - The New Testament

in. The true predestination, or fore-appointment of God is,

1. He that believeth shall be saved from the guilt and power of sin.
2. He that endureth to the end shall be saved eternally.
3. They who receive the precious gift of faith, thereby become the sons of God; and, being sons, they shall receive the Spirit of holiness to walk as Christ also walked. Throughout every part of this appointment of God, promise and duty go hand in hand. All is free gift; and yet such is the gift, that the final issue depends on our future obedience to the heavenly call. But other predestination than this, either to life or death eternal, the scripture knows not of. Moreover, it is.

1. Cruel respect of persons; an unjust regard of one, and an unjust disregard of another. It is mere creature partiality, and not infinite justice.
2. It is not plain scripture doctrine, if true; but rather, inconsistent with the express written word, that speaks of God's universal offers of grace; his invitations, promises, threatenings, being all general.
3. We are bid to choose life, and reprehended for not doing it.
4. It is inconsistent with a state of probation in those that must be saved or must be lost.
5. It is of fatal consequence; all men being ready, on very slight grounds, to fancy themselves of the elect number. But the doctrine of predestination is entirely changed from what it formerly was. Now it implies neither faith, peace, nor purity. It is something that will do without them all. Faith is no longer, according to the modern predestinarian scheme, a divine "evidence of things not seen," wrought in the soul by the immediate power of the Holy Ghost; not an evidence at all; but a mere notion. Neither is faith made any longer a means of holiness; but something that will do without it. Christ is no more a saviour from sin; but a defense, a countenancer of it. He is no more a fountain of spiritual life in the soul of believers, but leaves his elect inwardly dry, and outwardly unfruitful; and is made little more than a refuge from the image of the heavenly; even from righteousness, peace, and joy in the Holy Ghost. Through sanctification of the Spirit - Through the renewing and purifying influences of his Spirit on their souls. Unto obedience - To engage and enable them to yield themselves up to all holy obedience, the foundation of all which is, the sprinkling of the blood of Jesus Christ - The atoning blood of Christ, which was typified by the sprinkling of the blood of sacrifices under the law; in allusion to which it is called "the blood of sprinkling."

3. Blessed be the God and Father of our Lord Jesus Christ - His Father, with respect to his divine nature; his God, with respect to his human. Who hath regenerated us to a living hope - An hope which implies true spiritual life, which revives the heart, and makes the soul lively and vigourous. By the resurrection of Christ - Which is not only a pledge of ours, but a part of the purchase price. It has also a close connection with our rising from spiritual death, that as he liveth, so shall we live with him. He was acknowledged to be the Christ, but usually called Jesus till his resurrection; then he was also called Christ.

4. To an inheritance - For if we are sons, then heirs. Incorruptible - Not like earthly treasures. Undefiled - Pure and holy, incapable of being itself defiled, or of being enjoyed by any polluted soul. And that fadeth not away - That never decays in its value, sweetness, or beauty, like all the enjoyments of this world, like the garlands of leaves or flowers, with which the ancient conquerors were wont to be crowned. Reserved in heaven for you - Who "by patient continuance in welldoing, seek for glory and honour and immortality."

5. Who are kept - The inheritance is reserved; the heirs are kept for it. By the power of God - Which worketh all in all, which guards us against all our enemies. Through faith - Through which alone salvation is both received and retained. Ready to be revealed - That Rev. is made in the last day. It was more and more ready to be revealed, ever since Christ came.

6. Wherein - That is, in being so kept. Ye even now greatly rejoice, though now for a little while - Such is our whole life, compared to eternity. If need be - For it is not always needful. If God sees it to be the best means for your spiritual profit. Ye are in heaviness - Or sorrow; but not in darkness; for they still retained both faith, 1 Pe i, 5, hope, and love; yea, at this very time were rejoicing with joy unspeakable, 1 Pe i, 8.

7. That the trial of your faith - That is, your faith which is tried. Which is much more precious than gold - For gold, though it bear the fire, yet will perish with the world. May be found - Though it doth not yet appear. Unto praise - From God himself. And honour - From men and angels. And glory - Assigned by the great Judge.

8. Having not seen - In the flesh.
9. Receiving - Now already. Salvation - From all sin into all holiness, which is the qualification for, the forerunner and pledge of, eternal salvation.
10. Of which salvation - So far beyond all that was experienced under the Jewish dispensation. The very prophets who prophesied long ago of the grace of God toward you - Of his abundant, overflowing grace to be bestowed on believers under the Christian dispensation. Inquired - Were earnestly inquisitive. And searched diligently - Like miners searching after precious ore, after the meaning of the prophecies which they delivered.

John Wesley

11. Searching what time - What particular period. And what manner of time - By what marks to be distinguished. The glories that were to follow - His sufferings; namely, the glory of his resurrection, ascension, exaltation, and the effusion of his Spirit; the glory of the last judgment, and of his eternal kingdom; and also the glories of his grace in the hearts and lives of Christians.

12. To whom - So searching. It was revealed, that not for themselves, but for us they ministered - They did not so much by those predictions serve themselves, or that generation, as they did us, who now enjoy what they saw afar off. With the Holy Ghost sent down from heaven - Confirmed by the inward, powerful testimony of the Holy Ghost, as well as the mighty effusion of his miraculous gifts. Which things angels desire to look into - A beautiful gradation; prophets, righteous men, kings, desired to see and hear what Christ did and taught. What the Holy Ghost taught concerning Christ the very angels long to know.

13. Wherefore - Having such encouragement. Gird up the loins of your mind - As persons in the eastern countries were wont, in travelling or running, to gird up their long garments, so gather ye up all your thoughts and affections, and keep your mind always disencumbered and prepared to run the race which is set before you. Be watchful - As servants that wait for their Lord. And hope to the end - Maintain a full expectation of all the grace - The blessings flowing from the free favour of God. Which shall be brought to you at the final Revelation of Jesus Christ - And which are now brought to you by the Revelation of Christ in you.

14. Your desires - Which ye had while ye were ignorant of God.

16. Lev. xi, 44.

17. Who judgeth according to every man's work - According to the tenor of his life and conversation. Pass the time of your sojourning - Your short abode on earth. In humble, loving fear - The proper companion and guard of hope.

18. Your vain conversation - Your foolish, sinful way of life.

19. Without blemish - In himself. Without spot - From the world.

21. Who through him believe - For all our faith and hope proceed from the power of his resurrection. In God that raised Jesus, and gave him glory - At his ascension. Without Christ we should only dread God; whereas through him we believe, hope, and love.

22. Having purified your souls by obeying the truth through the Spirit, who bestows upon you freely, both obedience and purity of heart, and unfeigned love of the brethren, go on to still higher degrees of love. Love one another fervently - With the most strong and tender affection; and yet with a pure heart - Pure from any spot of unholy desire or inordinate passion.

23. Which liveth - Is full of divine virtue. And abideth the same forever.

24. All flesh - Every human creature is transient and withering as grass. And all the glory of it - His wisdom, strength, wealth, righteousness. As the flower - The most short-lived part of it. The grass - That is, man. The flower - That is, his glory. Is fallen off - As it were, while we are speaking. Isaiah xl, 6, &c.

II

1. Wherefore laying aside - As inconsistent with that pure love. All dissimulation - Which is the outward expression of guile in the heart.

2. Desire - Always, as earnestly as new born babes do, chap. i, 3. The milk of the word - That word of God which nourishes the soul as milk does the body, and which is sincere, pure from all guile, so that none are deceived who cleave to it. That you may grow thereby - In faith, love, holiness, unto the full stature of Christ.

3. Since ye have tasted - Sweetly and experimentally known.

4. To whom coming - By faith. As unto a living stone - Living from eternity; alive from the dead. There is a wonderful beauty and energy in these expressions, which describe Christ as a spiritual foundation, solid, firm, durable; and believers as a building erected upon it, in preference to that temple which the Jews accounted their highest glory. And St. Peter speaking of him thus, shows he did not judge himself, but Christ, to be the rock on which the church was built. Rejected indeed by men - Even at this day, not only by Jews, Turks, heathens, infidels; but by all Christians, so called, who live in sin, or who hope to be saved by their own works. But chosen of God - From all eternity, to be the foundation of his church. And precious - In himself, in the sight of God, and in the eyes of all believers.

5. Ye - Believers. As living stones - Alive to God through him. Are built up - In union with each other. A spiritual house - Being spiritual yourselves, and an habitation of God through the Spirit. An holy priesthood - Consecrated to God, and "holy as he is holy." To offer up - Your souls and bodies, with all your thoughts, words, and actions, as spiritual sacrifices to God.

6. He that believeth shall not be confounded - In time or in eternity. Isaiah xxviii, 16.

7. To them who believe, he is become the head of the corner - The chief corner stone, on which the whole building rests. Unbelievers too will at length find him such to their sorrow, Matt. xxi, 44.

Psalm cxviii, 22.

8. *Who stumble, whereunto also they were appointed* - They who believe not, stumble, and fall, and perish forever; God having appointed from all eternity, "he that believeth not shall be damned."

9. *But ye* - Who believe in Christ *Are* - In a higher sense than ever the Jews were. A chosen or elect race, a royal priesthood - "Kings and priests unto God," Rev. i, 6. As princes, ye have power with God, and victory over sin, the world, and the devil: as priests, ye are consecrated to God, for offering spiritual sacrifices. Ye Christians are as one holy nation, under Christ your King. A purchased people - Who are his peculiar property. *That ye may show forth* - By your whole behaviour, to all mankind. *The virtues* - The excellent glory, the mercy, wisdom, and power of him, Christ, who hath called you out of the darkness of ignorance, error, sin, and misery.

10. *Who in time past were not a people* - Much less the people of God; but scattered individuals of many nations. The former part of the verse particularly respects the gentiles; the latter, the Jews.

11. Here begins the exhortation drawn from the second motive. Sojourners: pilgrims - The first word properly means, those who are in a strange house; the second, those who are in a strange country. You sojourn in the body; you are pilgrims in this world. Abstain from desires of anything in this house, or in this country.

12. *Honest* - Not barely unblamable, but virtuous in every respect. But our language sinks under the force, beauty, and copiousness of the original expressions. *That they by your good works which they shall behold* - See with their own eyes. *May glorify God* - By owning his grace in you, and following your example. *In the day of visitation* - The time when he shall give them fresh offers of his mercy.

13. *Submit yourselves to every ordinance of man* - To every secular power. Instrumentally these are ordained by men; but originally all their power is from God.

14. Or to subordinate governors, or magistrates.

15. *The ignorance* - Of them who blame you, because they do not know you: a strong motive to pity them.

16. *As free* - Yet obeying governors, for God's sake.

17. *honour all men* - As being made in the image of God, bought by his Son, and designed for his kingdom. *honour the king* - Pay him all that regard both in affection and action which the laws of God and man require.

18. *Servants* - Literally, household servants. *With all fear* - Of offending them or God. Not only to the good - Tender, kind. *And gentle* - Mild, easily forgiving.

19. *For conscience toward God* - From a pure desire of pleasing him. *Grief* - Severe treatment.

21. *Hereunto are ye* - Christians. *Called* - To suffer wrongfully. *Leaving you an example* - When he went to God. *That ye might follow his steps* - Of innocence and patience.

22, 23. In all these instances the example of Christ is peculiarly adapted to the state of servants, who easily slide either into sin or guile, reviling their fellowservants, or threatening them, the natural result of anger without power. *He committed himself to him that judgeth righteously* - The only solid ground of patience in affliction. Isaiah liii, 4, 6, 7, 9.

22, 23. In all these instances the example of Christ is peculiarly adapted to the state of servants, who easily slide either into sin or guile, reviling their fellowservants, or threatening them, the natural result of anger without power. He committed himself to him that judgeth righteously - The only solid ground of patience in affliction.

24. *Who himself bore our sins* - That is, the punishment due to them. *In his afflicted, torn, dying body on the tree* - The cross, whereon chiefly slaves or servants were wont to suffer. *That we being dead to sin* - Wholly delivered both from the guilt and power of it: indeed, without an atonement first made for the guilt, we could never have been delivered from the power. *Might live to righteousness* - Which is one only. The sins we had committed, and he bore, were manifold.

25. *The bishop* - The kind observer, inspector, or overseer of your souls.

III

1. *If any* - He speaks tenderly. *Won* - Gained over to Christ.

2. Joined with a loving fear of displeasing them.

3. Three things are here expressly forbidden: curling the hair, wearing gold, (by way of ornament,) and putting on costly or gay apparel. These, therefore, ought never to be allowed, much less defended, by Christians.

4. *The hidden man of the heart* - Complete inward holiness, which implies a meek and quiet spirit. A meek spirit gives no trouble willingly to any: a quiet spirit bears all wrongs without being troubled. *In the sight of God* - Who looks at the heart. All superfluity of dress contributes more to pride and anger than is generally supposed. The apostle seems to have his eye to this by substituting meekness and quietness in the room of the ornaments he forbids. "I do not regard these things," is often said by those whose hearts are wrapped up in them: but offer to take them away, and you touch the very idol of their

soul. Some, indeed only dress elegantly that they may be looked on; that is, they squander away their Lord's talent to gain applause: thus making sin to beget sin, and then plead one in excuse of the other.

5. The adorning of those holy women, who trusted in God, and therefore did not act thus from servile fear, was,
 1. Their meek subjection to their husbands:
 2. Their quiet spirit, "not afraid," or amazed: and
 3. Their unblamable behaviour, "doing" all things "well."

6. Whose children ye are - In a spiritual as well as natural sense, and entitled to the same inheritance, while ye discharge your conjugal duties, not out of fear, but for conscience' sake. Gen. xviii, 12.

7. Dwell with the woman according to knowledge - Knowing they are weak, and therefore to be used with all tenderness. Yet do not despise them for this, but give them honour - Both in heart, in word, and in action; as those who are called to be joint-heirs of that eternal life which ye and they hope to receive by the free grace of God. That your prayers be not hindered - On the one part or the other. All sin hinders prayer; particularly anger. Anything at which we are angry is never more apt to come into our mind than when we are at prayer; and those who do not forgive will find no forgiveness from God.

8. Finally - This part of the epistle reaches to chap. iv, 11. The apostle seems to have added the rest afterwards. Sympathizing - Rejoicing and sorrowing together. Love all believers as brethren. Be pitiful - Toward the afflicted. Be courteous - To all men. Courtesy is such a behaviour toward equals and inferiors as shows respect mixed with love.

9. Ye are called to inherit a blessing - Therefore their railing cannot hurt you; and, by blessing them, you imitate God, who blesses you.

10. For he that desireth to love life, and to see good days - That would make life amiable and desirable. Psalm xxxiv, 12, &c.

11. Let him seek - To live peaceably with all men. And pursue it - Even when it seems to flee from him.

12. The eyes of the Lord are over the righteous - For good. Anger appears in the whole face; love, chiefly in the eyes.

13. Who is he that will harm you - None can.

14. But if ye should suffer - This is no harm to you, but a good. Fear ye not their fear - The very words of the Septuagint, Isaiah viii, 12, 13. Let not that fear be in you which the wicked feel.

15. But sanctify the Lord God in your hearts - Have an holy fear, and a full trust in his wise providence. The hope - Of eternal life. With meekness - For anger would hurt your cause as well as your soul. And fear - A filial fear of offending God, and a jealousy over yourselves, lest ye speak amiss.

16. Having a good conscience - So much the more beware of anger, to which the very consciousness of your innocence may betray you. Join with a good conscience meekness and fear, and you obtain a complete victory. Your good conversation in Christ - That is, which flows from faith in him.

17. It is infinitely better, if it be the will of God, ye should suffer. His permissive will appears from his providence.

18. For - This is undoubtedly best, whereby we are most conformed to Christ. Now Christ suffered once - To suffer no more. For sins - Not his own, but ours. The just for the unjust - The word signifies, not only them who have wronged their neighbours, but those who have transgressed any of the commands of God; as the preceding word, just, denotes a person who has fulfilled, not barely social duties, but all kind of righteousness. That he might bring us to God - Now to his gracious favour, hereafter to his blissful presence, by the same steps of suffering and of glory. Being put to death in the flesh - As man. But raised to life by the Spirit - Both by his own divine power, and by the power of the Holy Ghost.

19. By which Spirit he preached - Through the ministry of Noah. To the spirits in prison - The unholy men before the flood, who were then reserved by the justice of God, as in a prison, till he executed the sentence upon them all; and are now also reserved to the judgment of the great day.

20. When the longsuffering of God waited - For an hundred and twenty years; all the time the ark was preparing: during which Noah warned them all to flee from the wrath to come.

21. The antitype whereof - The thing typified by the ark, even baptism, now saveth us - That is, through the water of baptism we are saved from the sin which overwhelms the world as a flood: not, indeed, the bare outward sign, but the inward grace; a divine consciousness that both our persons and our actions are accepted through him who died and rose again for us.

22. Angels and authorities and powers - That is, all orders both of angels and men.

IV

1. Arm yourselves with the same mind - Which will be armour of proof against all your enemies. For he that hath suffered in the flesh - That hath so suffered as to be thereby made inwardly and truly conformable to the sufferings of Christ. Hath ceased from sin - Is delivered from it.

2. That ye may no longer live in the flesh - Even in this mortal body. To the desires of men - Either your own or those of others. These are various; but the will of God is one.

3. Revellings, banquetings - Have these words any meaning now? They had, seventeen hundred years ago. Then the former meant, meetings to eat; meetings, the direct end of which was, to please the taste: the latter, meetings to drink: both of which Christians then ranked with abominable idolatries.

4. The same - As ye did once. Speaking evil of you - As proud, singular, silly, wicked and the like.

5. Who shall give account - Of this, as well as all their other ways. To him who is ready - So faith represents him now.

6. For to this end was the gospel preached - Ever since it was given to Adam. To them that are now dead - In their several generations. That they might be judged - That though they were judged. In the flesh according to the manner of men - With rash, unrighteous judgment. They might live according to the will and word of God, in the Spirit; the soul renewed after his image.

7. But the end of all things - And so of their wrongs, and your sufferings. Is at hand: be ye therefore sober, and watch unto prayer - Temperance helps watchfulness, and both of them help prayer. Watch, that ye may pray; and pray, that ye may watch.

8. Love covereth a multitude of sins - Yea, "love covereth all things." He that loves another, covers his faults, how many soever they be. He turns away his own eyes from them; and, as far as is possible, hides them from others. And he continually prays that all the sinner's iniquities may be forgiven and his sins covered. Meantime the God of love measures to him with the same measure into his bosom.

9. One to another - Ye that are of different towns or countries. Without murmuring - With all cheerfulness. Prov. x, 12.

10. As every one hath received a gift - Spiritual or temporal, ordinary or extraordinary, although the latter seems primarily intended. So minister it one to another - Employ it for the common good. As good stewards of the manifold grace of God--The talents wherewith his free love has intrusted you.

11. If any man speak, let him - In his whole conversation, public and private. Speak as the oracles of God - Let all his words be according to this pattern, both as to matter and manner, more especially in public. By this mark we may always know who are, so far, the true or false prophets. The oracles of God teach that men should repent, believe, obey. He that treats of faith and leaves out repentance, or does not enjoin practical holiness to believers, does not speak as the oracles of God: he does not preach Christ, let him think as highly of himself as he will. If any man minister - Serve his brother in love, whether in spirituals or temporals. Let him minister as of the ability which God giveth - That is, humbly and diligently, ascribing all his power to God, and using it with his might. Whose is the glory - of his wisdom, which teaches us to speak. And the might - Which enables us to act.

12. Wonder not at the burning which is among you - This is the literal meaning of the expression. It seems to include both martyrdom itself, which so frequently was by fire, and all the other sufferings joined with, or previous to, it; which is permitted by the wisdom of God for your trial. Be not surprised at this.

13. But as ye partake of the sufferings of Christ - chap. 1, while ye suffer for his sake, rejoice in hope of more abundant glory. For the measure of glory answers the measure of suffering; and much more abundantly.

14. If ye are reproached for Christ - Reproaches and cruel mockings were always one part of their sufferings. The Spirit of glory and of God resteth upon you - The same Spirit which was upon Christ, Luke iv, 18. He is here termed, the Spirit of glory, conquering all reproach and shame, and the Spirit of God, whose Son, Jesus Christ is. On their part he is blasphemed, but on your part he is glorified - That is, while they are blaspheming Christ, you glorify him in the midst of your sufferings, chap. 16.

15. Let none of you deservedly suffer, as an evildoer - In any kind.

16. Let him glorify God - Who giveth him the honour so to suffer, and so great a reward for suffering.

17. The time is come for judgment to begin at the house of God - God first visits his church, and that both in justice and mercy. What shall the end be of them that obey not the gospel - How terribly will he visit them! The judgments which are milder at the beginning, grow more and more severe. But good men, having already sustained their part, are only spectators of the miseries of the wicked.

18. If the righteous scarcely be saved - Escape with the utmost difficulty. Where shall the ungodly - The man who knows not God. And the open sinner appear - In that day of vengeance. The salvation here primarily spoken of is of a temporal nature. But we may apply the words to eternal things, and then they are still more awful. Prov. xi, 31.

19. *Let them that suffer according to the will of God* - Both for a good cause, and in a right spirit. *Commit to him their souls* - (Whatever becomes of the body) as a sacred depositum. *In well doing* - Be this your care, to do and suffer well: He will take care of the rest. *As unto a faithful Creator* - In whose truth, love, and power, ye may safely trust.

V

1. *I who am a fellow-elder* - So the first though not the head of the apostles appositely and modestly styles himself. *And a witness of the sufferings of Christ* - Having seen him suffer, and now suffering for him.

2. *Feed the flock* - Both by doctrine and discipline. *Not by constraint* - Unwillingly, as a burden. *Not for filthy gain* - Which, if it be the motive of acting, is filthy beyond expression. O consider this, ye that leave one flock and go to another, merely because there is more gain, a large salary! Is it not astonishing that men can see no harm in this? that it is not only practiced, but avowed, all over the nation?

3. *Neither as lording over the heritage* - Behaving in a haughty, domineering manner, as though you had dominion over their conscience. The word translated heritage, is, literally, the portions. There is one flock under the one chief Shepherd; but many portions of this, under many pastors. But being examples to the flock - This procures the most ready and free obedience.

5. *Ye younger, be subject to the elder* - In years. *And be all* - Elder or younger. *Subject to each other* - Let every one be ready, upon all occasions, to give up his own will. *Be clothed with humility* - Bind it on, (so the word signifies,) so that no force may be able to tear it from you. James iv, 6; Prov. iii, 34

6. *The hand of God* - Is in all troubles.

7. *Casting all your care upon him* - In every want or pressure.

8. *But in the mean time watch*. There is a close connection between this, and the duly casting our care upon him. How deeply had St. Peter himself suffered for want of watching! *Be vigilant* - As if he had said, Awake, and keep awake. Sleep no more: be this your care. *As a roaring lion* - Full of rage. *Seeking* - With all subtilty likewise. *Whom he may devour or swallow up* - Both soul and body.

9. *Be the more steadfast, as ye know the same kind of afflictions are accomplished in* - That is, suffered by, your brethren, till the measure allotted them is filled up.

10. *Now the God of all grace* - By which alone the whole work is begun, continued, and finished in your soul. *After ye have suffered a while* - A very little while compared with eternity. *Himself* - Ye have only to watch and resist the devil: the rest God will perform. *Perfect* - That no defect may remain. *Stablish* - That nothing may overthrow you. *Strengthen* - That ye may conquer all adverse power. *And settle you* - As an house upon a rock. So the apostle, being converted, does now "strengthen his brethren."

12. *As I suppose* - As I judge, upon good grounds, though not by immediate inspiration. *I have written* - That is, sent my letter by him. *Adding my testimony* - To that which ye before heard from Paul, that this is the true gospel of the grace of God.

13. *The church that is at Babylon* - Near which St. Peter probably was, when he wrote this epistle. *Elected together with you* - Partaking of the same faith with you. *Mark* - It seems the evangelist. *My son* - Probably converted by St. Peter. And he had occasionally served him, "as a son in the gospel."

NOTES ON THE SECOND EPISTLE GENERAL OF ST. PETER

THE parts of this epistle, written not long before St. Peter's death, and the destruction of Jerusalem, with the same design as the former, are likewise three:

I. The inscription, Chap. i.1, 2

II. A further stirring up of the minds of true believers, in which,
    1. He exhorts them, having received the precious gift, to give all diligence to "grow in grace," 3-11
    2. To this he incites them,
        1. From the firmness of true teachers, 12-21
        2. From the wickedness of false teachers, ii.1-22
    3. He guards them against impostors,
        1. By confuting their error iii.1-9
        2. By describing the great day, adding suitable exhortations, 10-14

III. The conclusion, in which he,
    1. Declares his agreement with St. Paul, 15, 16
    2. Repeats the sum of the epistle, 17

2nd PETER

I

1. *To them that have obtained* - Not by their own works, but by the free grace of God. *Like precious faith with us* - The apostles. The faith of those who have not seen, being equally precious with that of those who saw our Lord in the flesh. *Through the righteousness* - Both active and passive. *Of our God and saviour* - It is this alone by which the justice of God is satisfied, and for the sake of which he gives this precious faith.

2. Through the divine, experimental knowledge of God and of Christ.

3. *As his divine power has given us all things* - There is a wonderful cheerfulness in this exordium, which begins with the exhortation itself. *That pertain to life and godliness* - To the present, natural life, and to the continuance and increase of spiritual life. *Through that divine knowledge of him* - Of Christ. *Who hath called us by* - His own glorious power, to eternal glory, as the end; by Christian virtue or fortitude, as the means.

4. *Through which* - Glory and fortitude. He hath given us exceeding great, and inconceivably precious promises - Both the promises and the things promised, which follow in their due season, that, sustained and encouraged by the promises, we may obtain all that he has promised. That, having escaped the manifold corruption which is in the world - From that fruitful fountain, evil desire. Ye may become partakers of the divine nature - Being renewed in the image of God, and having communion with them, so as to dwell in God and God in you.

5. *For this very reason* - Because God hath given you so great blessings. *Giving all diligence* - It is a very uncommon word which we render giving. It literally signifies, bringing in by the by, or over and above: implying, that good works the work; yet not unless we are diligent. Our diligence is to follow the gift of God, and is followed by an increase of all his gifts. *Add to* - And in all the other gifts of God. Superadd the latter, without losing the former. The Greek word properly means lead up, as in dance, one of these after the other, in a beautiful order. *Your faith,* that "evidence of things not seen," termed before "the knowledge of God and of Christ," the root of all Christian graces. *Courage* - Whereby ye may conquer all enemies and difficulties, and execute whatever faith dictates. In this most beautiful connection, each preceding grace leads to the following; each following, tempers and perfects the preceding. They are set down in the order of nature, rather than the order of time. For though every

grace bears a relation to every other, yet here they are so nicely ranged, that those which have the closest dependence on each other are placed together. And to your courage knowledge - Wisdom, teaching how to exercise it on all occasions.

6. And to your knowledge temperance; and to your temperance patience - Bear and forbear; sustain and abstain; deny yourself and take up your cross daily. The more knowledge you have, the more renounce your own will; indulge yourself the less. "Knowledge puffeth up," and the great boasters of knowledge (the Gnostics) were those that "turned the grace of God into wantonness." But see that your knowledge be attended with temperance. Christian temperance implies the voluntary abstaining from all pleasure which does not lead to God. It extends to all things inward and outward: the due government of every thought, as well as affection. "It is using the world," so to use all outward, and so to restrain all inward things, that they may become a means of what is spiritual; a scaling ladder to ascend to what is above. Intemperance is to abuse the world. He that uses anything below, looking no higher, and getting no further, is intemperate. He that uses the creature only so as to attain to more of the Creator, is alone temperate, and walks as Christ himself walked. And to patience godliness - Its proper support: a continual sense of God's presence and providence, and a filial fear of, and confidence in, him; otherwise your patience may be pride, surliness, stoicism; but not Christianity.

7. And to godliness brotherly kindness - No sullenness, sternness, moroseness: "sour godliness," so called, is of the devil. Of Christian godliness it may always be said, "Mild, sweet, serene, and tender is her mood, Nor grave with sternness, nor with lightness free: Against example resolutely good, Fervent in zeal, and warm in charity." And to brotherly kindness love - The pure and perfect love of God and of all mankind. The apostle here makes an advance upon the preceding article, brotherly kindness, which seems only to relate to the love of Christians toward one another.

8. For these being really in you - Added to your faith. And abounding - Increasing more and more, otherwise we fall short. Make you neither slothful nor unfruitful - Do not suffer you to be faint in your mind, or without fruit in your lives. If there is less faithfulness, less care and watchfulness, since we were pardoned, than there was before, and less diligence, less outward obedience, than when we were seeking remission of sin, we are both slothful and unfruitful in the knowledge of Christ, that is, in the faith, which then cannot work by love.

9. But he that wanteth these - That does not add them to his faith. Is blind - The eyes of his understanding are again closed. He cannot see God, or his pardoning love. He has lost the evidence of things not seen. Not able to see afar off - Literally, purblind. He has lost sight of the precious promises: perfect love and heaven are equally out of his sight. Nay, he cannot now see what himself once enjoyed. Having, as it were, forgot the purification from his former sins - Scarce knowing what he himself then felt, when his sins were forgiven.

10. Wherefore - Considering the miserable state of these apostates. Brethren - St. Peter nowhere uses this appellation in either of his epistles, but in this important exhortation. Be the more diligent - By courage, knowledge, temperance, &c. To make your calling and election firm - God hath called you by his word and his Spirit; he hath elected you, separated you from the world, through sanctification of the Spirit. O cast not away these inestimable benefits! If ye are thus diligent to make your election firm, ye shall never finally fall.

11. For if ye do so, an entrance shall be ministered to you abundantly into the everlasting kingdom - Ye shall go in full triumph to glory.

12. Wherefore - Since everlasting destruction attends your sloth, everlasting glory your diligence, I will not neglect always to remind you of these things - Therefore he wrote another, so soon after the former, epistle. Though ye are established in the present truth - That truth which I am now declaring.

13. In this tabernacle - Or tent. How short is our abode in the body! How easily does a believer pass out of it!

14. Even as the Lord Jesus showed me - In the manner which had foretold, John xxi, 18, &c. It is not improbable, he had also showed him that the time was now drawing nigh.

15. That ye may be able - By having this epistle among you.

16. These things are worthy to be always had in remembrance For they are not cunningly devised fables - Like those common among the heathens. While we made known to you the power and coming - That is, the powerful coming of Christ in glory. But if what they advanced of Christ was not true, if it was of their own invention, then to impose such a lie on the world as it was, in the very nature of things, above all human power to defend, and to do this at the expense of life and all things only to enrage the whole world, Jews and gentiles, against them, was no cunning, but was the greatest folly that men could have been guilty of. But were eyewitnesses of his majesty - At his transfiguration, which was a specimen of his glory at the last day.

17. For he received divine honour and inexpressible glory - Shining from heaven above the brightness of the sun. When there came such a voice from the excellent glory - That is, from God the Father. Matt. xvii, 5.

18. And we - Peter, James, and John. St. John was still alive. Being with him in the holy mount -

Made so by that glorious manifestation, as Mount Horeb was of old, Exod. iii, 4, 5.

19. And we - St. Peter here speaks in the name of all Christians. Have the word of prophecy - The words of Moses, Isaiah, and all the prophets, are one and the same word, every way consistent with itself. St. Peter does not cite any particular passage, but speaks of their entire testimony. More confirmed - By that display of his glorious majesty. To which word ye do well that ye take heed, as to a lamp which shone in a dark place - Wherein there was neither light nor window. Such anciently was the whole world, except that little spot where this lamp shone. Till the day should dawn - Till the full light of the gospel should break through the darkness. As is the difference between the light of a lamp and that of the day, such is that between the light of the Old Testament and of the New. And the morning star - Jesus Christ, Rev. xxii, 16. Arise in your hearts - Be revealed in you.

20. Ye do well, as knowing this, that no scripture prophecy is of private interpretation - It is not any man's own word. It is God, not the prophet himself, who thereby interprets things till then unknown.

21. For prophecy came not of old by the will of man - Of any mere man whatever. But the holy men of God - Devoted to him, and set apart by him for that purpose, spake and wrote. Being moved - Literally, carried. They were purely passive therein.

II

1. But there were false prophets also - As well as true. Among the people - Of Israel. Those that spake even the truth, when God had not sent them; and also those that were truly sent of him, and yet corrupted or softened their message, were false prophets. As there shall be false - As well as true. Teachers among you, who will privately briny in - Into the church. Destructive heresies - They first, by denying the Lord, introduced destructive heresies, that is, divisions; or they occasioned first these divisions, and then were given up to a reprobate mind, even to deny the Lord that bought them. Either the heresies are the effect of denying the Lord, or the denying the Lord was the consequence of the heresies. Even denying - Both by their doctrine and their works. The Lord that bought them - With his own blood. Yet these very men perish everlastingly. Therefore Christ bought even them that perish.

2. The way of truth will be evil spoken of - By those who blend all false and true Christians together.

3. They will make merchandise of you - Only use you to gain by you, as merchants do their wares. Whose judgment now of a long time lingereth not - Was long ago determined, and will be executed speedily. All sinners are adjudged to destruction; and God's punishing some proves he will punish the rest.

4. Cast them down to hell - The bottomless pit, a place of unknown misery. Delivered them - Like condemned criminals to safe custody, as if bound with the strongest chains in a dungeon of darkness, to be reserved unto the judgment of the great day. Though still those chains do not hinder their often walking up and down seeking whom they may devour.

5. And spared not the old, the antediluvian, world, but he preserved Noah the eighth person - that is, Noah and seven others, a preacher as well as practicer, of righteousness. Bringing a flood on the world of the ungodly - Whose numbers stood them in no stead.

9. It plainly appears, from these instances, that the Lord knoweth, hath both wisdom and power and will, to deliver the godly out of all temptations, and to punish the ungodly.

10. Chiefly them that walk after the flesh - Corrupt nature; particularly in the lust of uncleanness. And despise government - The authority of their governors. Dignities - Persons in authority.

11. Whereas angels - When they appear before the Lord, Job i, 6, Job ii, 1, to give an account of what they have seen and done on the earth.

12. Savage as brute beasts - Several of which in the present disordered state of the world, seem born to be taken and destroyed.

13. They count it pleasure to riot in the day time - They glory in doing it in the face of the sun. They are spots in themselves, blemishes to any church. Sporting themselves with their own deceivings - Making a jest of those whom they deceive and even jesting while they are deceiving their own souls.

15. The way of Balaam the son of Bosor - So the Chaldeans pronounced what the Jews termed Beor; namely, the way of covetousness. Who loved - Earnestly desired, though he did not dare to take, the reward of unrighteousness - The money which Balak would have given him for cursing Israel.

16. The beast - Though naturally dumb.

17. Fountains and clouds promise water: so do these promise, but do not perform.

18. They ensnare in the desires of the flesh - Allowing them to gratify some unholy desire. Those who were before entirely escaped from the spirit, custom, and company of them that live in error - In sin.

19. While they promise them liberty - From needless restraints and scruples; from the bondage of the law. Themselves are slaves of corruption - Even sin, the vilest of all bondage.

20. For if after they - Who are thus ensnared. Have escaped the pollutions of the world - The sins

which pollute all who know not God. Through the knowledge of Christ - That is, through faith in him, chap. i, 3. They are again entangled therein, and overcome, their last state is worse than the first - More inexcusable, and causing a greater damnation.

21. The commandment - The whole law of God, once not only delivered to their ears, but written in their hearts.

22. The dog, the sow - Such are all men in the sight of God before they receive his grace, and after they have made shipwreck of the faith. Prov. xxvi, 11.

III

2, 3. Be the more mindful thereof, because ye know scoffers will come first - Before the Lord comes. Walking after their own evil desires - Here is the origin of the error, the root of libertinism. Do we not see this eminently fulfilled?

4. Saying, Where is the promise of his coming - To judgment (They do not even deign to name him.) We see no sign of any such thing. For ever since the fathers - Our first ancestors. Fell asleep, all things - Heaven. water, earth. Continue as they were from the beginning of the creation - Without any such material change as might make us believe they will ever end.

5. For this they are willingly ignorant of - They do not care to know or consider. That by the almighty word of God - Which bounds the duration of all things, so that it cannot be either longer or shorter. Of old - Before the flood. The aerial heavens were, and the earth - Not as it is now, but standing out of the water and in the water - Perhaps the interior globe of earth was fixed in the midst of the great deep, the abyss of water; the shell or exterior globe standing out of the water, covering the great deep. This, or some other great and manifest difference between the original and present constitution of the terraqueous globe, seems then to have been so generally known, that St. Peter charges their ignorance of it totally upon their wilfulness.

6. Through which - Heaven and earth, the windows of heaven being opened, and the fountains of the great deep broken up. The world that then was - The whole antediluvian race. Being overflowed with water, perished - And the heavens and earth themselves, though they did not perish, yet underwent a great change. So little ground have these scoffers for saying that all things continue as they were from the creation.

7. But the heavens and the earth, that are now - Since the flood. Are reserved unto fire at the day wherein God will judge the world, and punish the ungodly with everlasting destruction.

8. But be not ye ignorant - Whatever they are. Of this one thing - Which casts much light on the point in hand. That one day is with the Lord as a thousand years, and a thousand years as one day - Moses had said, Psalm xc, 4, "A thousand years in thy sight are as one day;" which St. Peter applies with regard to the last day, so as to denote both his eternity, whereby he exceeds all measure of time in his essence and in his operation; his knowledge, to which all things past or to come are present every moment; his power, which needs no long delay, in order to bring its work to perfection; and his longsuffering, which excludes all impatience of expectation, and desire of making haste. One day is with the Lord as a thousand years - That is, in one day, in one moment he can do the work of a thousand years. Therefore he "is not slow:" he is always equally ready to fulfil his promise. And a thousand years are as one day - That is, no delay is long to God. A thousand years are as one day to the eternal God. Therefore "he is longsuffering:" he gives us space for repentance, without any inconvenience to himself. In a word, with God time passes neither slower nor swifter than is suitable to him and his economy; nor can there be any reason why it should be necessary for him either to delay or hasten the end of all things. How can we comprehend this? If we could comprehend it, St. Peter needed not to have added, with the Lord.

9. The Lord is not slow - As if the time fixed for it were past. Concerning his promise - Which shall surely be fulfilled in its season. But is longsuffering towards us - Children of men. Not willing that any soul, which he hath made should perish.

10. But the day of the Lord will come as a thief - Suddenly, unexpectedly. In which the heavens shall pass away with a great noise - Surprisingly expressed by the very sound of the original word. The elements shall melt with fervent heat - The elements seem to mean, the sun, moon, and stars; not the four, commonly so called; for air and water cannot melt, and the earth is mentioned immediately after. The earth and all the works - Whether of nature or art. That are therein shall be burned up - And has not God already abundantly provided for this?

1. By the stores of subterranean fire which are so frequently bursting out at Aetna, Vesuvius, Hecla, and many other burning mountains.

2. By the ethereal (vulgarly called electrical) fire, diffused through the whole globe; which, if the secret chain that now binds it up were loosed, would immediately dissolve the whole frame of nature.

3. By comets, one of which, if it touch the earth in its course toward the sun, must needs strike it into that abyss of fire; if in its return from the sun, when it is heated, as a great man computes, two

thousand times hotter than a red-hot cannonball, it must destroy all vegetables and animals long before their contact, and soon after burn it up.

11. Seeing then that all these things are dissolved - To the eye of faith it appears as done already. All these things - Mentioned before; all that are included in that scriptural expression, "the heavens and the earth;" that is, the universe. On the fourth day God made the stars, Gen. i, 16, which will be dissolved together with the earth. They are deceived, therefore, who restrain either the history of the creation, or this description of the destruction, of the world to the earth and lower heavens; imagining the stars to be more ancient than the earth, and to survive it. Both the dissolution and renovation are ascribed, not to the one heaven which surrounds the earth, but to the heavens in general, ver. 10, 13, without any restriction or limitation. What persons ought ye to be in all holy conversation - With men. And godliness - Toward your Creator.

12. Hastening on - As it were by your earnest desires and fervent prayers. The coming of the day of God - Many myriads of days he grants to men: one, the last, is the day of God himself.

13. We look for new heavens and a new earth - Raised as it were out of the ashes of the old; we look for an entire new state of things. Wherein dwelleth righteousness - Only righteous spirits. How great a mystery!

14. labour that whenever he cometh ye may be found in peace - May meet him without terror, being sprinkled with his blood, and sanctified by his Spirit, so as to be without spot and blameless. Isaiah lxv, 17; Isaiah lxvi, 22.

15. And account the longsuffering of the Lord salvation - Not only designed to lead men to repentance, but actually conducing thereto: a precious means of saving many more souls. As our beloved brother Paul also hath written to you - This refers not only to the single sentence preceding, but to all that went before. St. Paul had written to the same effect concerning the end of the world, in several parts of his epistles, and particularly in his Epistle to the Hebrews. Rom. ii, 4.

16. As also in all his epistles - St. Peter wrote this a little before his own and St. Paul's martyrdom. St. Paul therefore had now written all his epistles; and even from this expression we may learn that St. Peter had read them all, perhaps sent to him by St. Paul himself. Nor was he at all disgusted by what St. Paul had written concerning him in the Epistle to the Galatians. Speaking of these things - Namely, of the coming of our Lord, delayed through his longsuffering, and of the circumstances preceding and accompanying it. Which things the unlearned - They who are not taught of God. And the unstable - Wavering, double-minded, unsettled men. Wrest - As though Christ would not come. As they do also the other scriptures - Therefore St. Paul's writings were now part of the scriptures. To their own destruction - But that some use the scriptures ill, is no reason why others should not use them at all.

18. But grow in grace - That is, in every Christian temper. There may be, for a time, grace without growth; as there may be natural life without growth. But such sickly life, of soul or body, will end in death, and every day draw nigher to it. Health is the means of both natural and spiritual growth. If the remaining evil of our fallen nature be not daily mortified, it will, like an evil humour in the body, destroy the whole man. But "if ye through the Spirit do mortify the deeds of the body," (only so far as we do this,) "ye shall live" the life of faith, holiness, happiness. The end and design of grace being purchased and bestowed on us, is to destroy the image of the earthy, and restore us to that of the heavenly. And so far as it does this, it truly profits us; and also makes way for more of the heavenly gift, that we may at last be filled with all the fulness of God. The strength and well-being of a Christian depend on what his soul feeds on, as the health of the body depends on whatever we make our daily food. If we feed on what is according to our nature, we grow; if not, we pine away and die. The soul is of the nature of God, and nothing but what is according to his holiness can agree with it. Sin, of every kind, starves the soul, and makes it consume away. Let us not try to invert the order of God in his new creation: we shall only deceive ourselves. It is easy to forsake the will of God, and follow our own; but this will bring leanness into the soul. It is easy to satisfy ourselves without being possessed of the holiness and happiness of the gospel. It is easy to call these frames and feelings, and then to oppose faith to one and Christ to the other. Frames (allowing the expression) are no other than heavenly tempers, "the mind that was in Christ." Feelings are the divine consolations of the Holy Ghost shed abroad in the heart of him that truly believes. And wherever faith is, and wherever Christ is, there are these blessed frames and feelings. If they are not in us, it is a sure sign that though the wilderness became a pool, the pool is become a wilderness again. And in the knowledge of Christ - That is, in faith, the root of all. To him be the glory to the day of eternity - An expression naturally flowing from that sense which the apostle had felt in his soul throughout this whole chapter. Eternity is a day without night, without interruption, without end.

NOTES ON THE FIRST EPISTLE OF ST. JOHN

THE great similitude, or rather sameness, both of spirit and expression, which runs through St. John's Gospel and all his epistles, is a clear evidence of their being written by the same person. In this epistle he speaks not to any particular church, but to all the Christians of that age; and in them to the whole Christian church in all succeeding ages. Some have apprehended that it is not easy to discern the scope and method of this epistle. But if we examine it with simplicity, these may readily be discovered. St. John in this letter, or rather tract, (for he was present with part of those to whom he wrote,) has this apparent aim, to confirm the happy and holy communion of the faithful with God and Christ, by describing the marks of that blessed state. The parts of it are three:

I. The preface, Chap. i.1-4

II. The tract itself, 5- v.1-12

III. The conclusion, 13-21 In the preface he shows the authority of his own preaching and writing, and expressly points out, verse 3, the design of his present writing. To the preface exactly answers the conclusion, more largely explaining the same design, and recapitulating those marks, by we know thrice repeated, v. 18-20. The tract itself has two parts, treating,

I. Severally,
    1. Of communion with the Father, i. 5-10
    2. Of communion with the Son, ii. 1-12 With a distinct application to fathers, young men, and little children, 13-27 Whereto is annexed an exhortation to abide in him, 28- iii. 1-24 That the fruit of his manifestation in the flesh may extend to his manifestation in glory.
    3. Of the confirmation and fruit of this abiding through the Spirit, iv. 1-21

II. Conjointly, Of the testimony of the Father, and Son, and Spirit: on which faith in Christ, the being born of God, love to God and his children, the keeping his commandments and victory over the world, are founded, v. 1-12 The parts frequently begin and end alike. Sometimes there is an allusion in a preceding part, and a recapitulation in the subsequent. Each part treats of a benefit from God, and the duty of the faithful derived therefrom by the most natural inferences.

1st JOHN

I

    1. That which was - Here means, He which was the Word himself; afterwards it means, that which they had heard from him. Which was - Namely, with the Father, ver. 2, before he was manifested. From the beginning - This phrase is sometimes used in a limited sense; but here it properly means from eternity, being equivalent with, "in the beginning," John i, 1. That which we - The apostles. Have not only heard, but seen with our eyes, which we have beheld - Attentively considered on various occasions. Of the Word of life - He is termed the Word, John i, 1; the Life, John i, 4; as he is the living Word of God, who, with the Father and the Spirit, is the fountain of life to all creatures, particularly of spiritual and eternal life.
    2. For the life - The living Word. Was manifested - In the flesh, to our very senses. And we testify and declare - We testify by declaring, by preaching, and writing, 1 John i, 3, 4. Preaching lays the foundation, 1 John i, 5-x, writing builds there on. To you - Who have not seen. The eternal life - Which always was, and afterward appeared to us. This is mentioned in the beginning of the epistle. In the end of it is mentioned the same eternal life, which we shall always enjoy.
    3. That which we have seen and heard - Of him and from him. Declare we to you - For this end. That ye also may have fellowship with us - May enjoy the same fellowship which we enjoy. And truly our fellowship - Whereby he is in us and we in him. Is with the Father and with the son - Of the Holy Ghost he speaks afterwards.

4. **That your joy may be full** - So our Lord also, John xv, 11; xvi, 22. There is a joy of hope, a joy of faith, and a joy of love. Here the joy of faith is directly intended. It is a concise expression. **Your joy** - That is, your faith and the joy arising from it: but it likewise implies the joy of hope and love.

5. **And this is the sum of the message which we have heard of him** - The Son of God. That God is light - The light of wisdom, love, holiness, glory. What light is to the natural eye, that God is to the spiritual eye. And in him is no darkness at all - No contrary principle. He is pure, unmixed light.

6. **If we say** - Either with our tongue, or in our heart, if we endeavour to persuade either ourselves or others. We have fellowship with him, while we walk, either inwardly or outwardly, in darkness - In sin of any kind. We do not the truth - Our actions prove, that the truth is not in us.

7. **But if we walk in the light** - In all holiness. As God is (a deeper word than walk, and more worthy of God) in the light, then we may truly say, we have fellowship one with another - We who have seen, and you who have not seen, do alike enjoy that fellowship with God. The imitation of God being the only sure proof of our having fellowship with him. And the blood of Jesus Christ his Son - With the grace purchased thereby. Cleanseth us from all sin - Both original and actual, taking away all the guilt and all the power.

8. **If we say** - Any child of man, before his blood has cleansed us. We have no sin - To be cleansed from, instead of confessing our sins, 1 John i, 9, the truth is not in us - Neither in our mouth nor in our heart.

9. **But if with a penitent and believing heart, we confess our sins, he is faithful** - Because he had promised this blessing, by the unanimous voice of all his prophets. Just - Surely then he will punish: no; for this very reason he will pardon. This may seem strange; but upon the evangelical principle of atonement and redemption, it is undoubtedly true; because, when the debt is paid, or the purchase made, it is the part of equity to cancel the bond, and consign over the purchased possession. Both to forgive us our sins - To take away all the guilt of them. And to cleanse us from all unrighteousness - To purify our souls from every kind and every degree of it.

10. Yet still we are to retain, even to our lives' end, a deep sense of our past sins. Still if we say, we have not sinned, we make him a liar - Who saith, all have sinned. And his word is not in us - We do not receive it; we give it no place in our hearts.

II

1. **My beloved children** - So the apostle frequently addresses the whole body of Christians. It is a term of tenderness and endearment, used by our Lord himself to his disciples, John xiii, 33. And perhaps many to whom St. John now wrote were converted by his ministry. It is a different word from that which is translated "little children," in several parts of the epistle, to distinguish it from which, it is here rendered beloved children. I write these things to you, that ye may not sin - Thus he guards them beforehand against abusing the doctrine of reconciliation. All the words, institutions, and judgments of God are levelled against sin, either that it may not be committed, or that it may be abolished. But if any one sin - Let him not lie in sin, despairing of help. We have an advocate - We have for our advocate, not a mean person, but him of whom it was said, "This is my beloved son." Not a guilty person, who stands in need of pardon for himself; but Jesus Christ the righteous; not a mere petitioner, who relies purely upon liberality, but one that has merited, fully merited, whatever he asks.

2. **And he is the propitiation** - The atoning sacrifice by which the wrath of God is appeased. For our sins - Who believe. And not for ours only, but also for the sins of the whole world - Just as wide as sin extends, the propitiation extends also.

3. **And hereby we know that we truly and savingly know him** - As he is the advocate, the righteous, the propitiation. If we keep his commandments - Particularly those of faith and love.

5. **But whoso keepeth his word** - His commandments. Verily in him the love of God - Reconciled to us through Christ. Is perfected - Is perfectly known. Hereby - By our keeping his word. We know that we are in him - So is the tree known by its fruits. To "know him," to be "in him," to "abide in him," are nearly synonymous terms; only with a gradation, - knowledge, communion, constancy.

6. **He that saith he abideth in him** - which implies a durable state; a constant, lasting knowledge of, and communion with, him. Ought himself - Otherwise they are vain words. So to walk, even as he walked - In the world. As he, are words that frequently occur in this epistle. Believers having their hearts full of him, easily supply his name.

7. **When I speak of keeping his word, I write not a new commandment** - I do not speak of any new one. But the old commandment, which ye had - Even from your forefathers.

8. **Again, I do write a new commandment to you** - Namely, with regard to loving one another. A commandment which, though it also was given long ago, yet is truly new in him and in you. It was exemplified in him, and is now fulfilled by you, in such a manner as it never was before. For there is no comparison between the state of the Old Testament believers, and that which ye now enjoy: the darkness of that dispensation is passed away; and Christ the true light now shineth in your hearts.

9. He that saith he is in the light - In Christ, united to him. And hateth his brother - The very name shows the love due to him. Is in darkness until now - Void of Christ, and of all true light.

10. He that loveth his brother - For Christ's sake. Abideth in the light - Of God. And there is no occasion of stumbling in him - Whereas he that hates his brother is an occasion of stumbling to himself. He stumbles against himself, and against all things within and without; while he that loves his brother, has a free, disencumbered journey.

11. He that hateth his brother - And he must hate, if he does not love him: there is no medium. Is in darkness - In sin, perplexity, entanglement. He walketh in darkness, and knoweth not that he is in the high road to hell.

12. I have written to you, beloved children - Thus St. John bespeaks all to whom he writes. But from the thirteenth to 1 John ii, 13-27 the twenty-seventh verse, he divides them particularly into "fathers," "young men," and "little children." Because your sins are forgiven you - As if he had said, This is the sum of what I have now written. He then proceeds to other things, which are built upon this foundation.

13. The address to spiritual fathers, young men, and little children is first proposed in this verse, wherein he says, I write to you, fathers: I write to you, young men: I write to you, little children: and then enlarged upon; in doing which he says, "I have written to you, fathers," 1 John ii, 14. "I have written to you, young men," 1 John ii, 14-17. "I have written to you, little children," 1 John ii, 18-27. Having finished his address to each, he returns to all together, whom he again terms, (as 1 John ii, 12,) "beloved children." Fathers, ye have known him that is from the beginning - We have known the eternal God, in a manner wherein no other, even true believers, know him. Young men, ye have overcome the wicked one - In many battles, by the power of faith. Little children, ye have known the Father - As your Father, though ye have not yet overcome, by the Spirit witnessing with your Spirit, that ye are the children of God."

14. I have written to you, fathers - As if he had said, Observe well what I but now wrote. He speaks very briefly and modestly to these, who needed not much to be said to them, as having that deep acquaintance with God which comprises all necessary knowledge. Young men, ye are strong - In faith. And the word of God abideth in you - Deeply rooted in your hearts, whereby ye have often foiled your great adversary.

15. To you all, whether fathers, young men, or little children, I say, Love not the world - Pursue your victory by overcoming the world. If any man love the world - Seek happiness in visible things, he does not love God.

16. The desire of the flesh - Of the pleasure of the outward senses, whether of the taste, smell, or touch. The desire of the eye - Of the pleasures of imagination, to which the eye chiefly is subservient; of that internal sense whereby we relish whatever is grand, new, or beautiful. The pride of life - All that pomp in clothes, houses, furniture, equipage, manner of living, which generally procure honour from the bulk of mankind, and so gratify pride and vanity. It therefore directly includes the desire of praise, and, remotely, covetousness. All these desires are not from God, but from the prince of this world.

17. The world passeth away, and the desire thereof - That is, all that can gratify those desires passeth away with it. But he that doeth the will of God - That loves God, not the world. Abideth - In the enjoyment of what he loves, forever.

18. Little children, it is the last time - The last dispensation of grace, that which is to continue to the end of time, is begun. Ye have heard that antichrist cometh - Under the term antichrist, or the spirit of antichrist, he includes all false teachers and enemies to the truth; yea, whatever doctrines or men are contrary to Christ. It seems to have been long after this that the name of antichrist was appropriated to that grand adversary of Christ, the man of sin, 2 Thess. ii, 3 Antichrist, in St. John's sense, that is, antichristianism, has been spreading from his time till now; and will do so, till that great adversary arises, and is destroyed by Christ's coming.

19. They were not of us - When they went; their hearts were before departed from God, otherwise, they would have continued with us: but they went out, that they might be made manifest - That is, this was made manifest by their going out.

20. But ye have an anointing - A chrism; perhaps so termed in opposition to the name of antichrist; an inward teaching from the Holy Ghost, whereby ye know all things - Necessary for your preservation from these seducers, and for your eternal salvation. St. John here but just touches upon the Holy Ghost, of whom he speaks more largely, chap. iii, 24; iv, 13; v, 5.

21. I have written - Namely, 1 John ii, 13. To you because ye know the truth - That is, to confirm you in the knowledge ye have already. Ye know that no lie is of the truth - That all the doctrines of these antichrists are irreconcilable to it.

22. Who is that liar - Who is guilty of that lying, but he who denies that truth which is the sum of all Christianity? That Jesus is the Christ; that he is the Son of God; that he came in the flesh, is one undivided truth. and he that denies any part of this, in effect denies the whole. He is antichrist - And the spirit of antichrist, who in denying the Son denies the Father also.

23. Whosoever denieth the eternal Son of God, he hath not communion with the Father; but he that truly and believingly acknowledgeth the Son, hath communion with the Father also.

24. If that truth concerning the Father and the Son, which ye have heard from the beginning, abide fixed and rooted in you, ye also shall abide in that happy communion with the Son and the Father.

25. He - The Son. Hath promised us - If we abide in him.

26. These things - From 1 John ii, 21. I have written to you - St. John, according to his custom, begins and ends with the same form, and having finished a kind of parenthesis, 1 John ii, 20-26, continues, ii, 27, what he said in the twentieth verse, concerning them that would seduce you.

27. Ye need not that any should teach you, save as that anointing teacheth you - Which is always the same, always consistent with itself. But this does not exclude our need of being taught by them who partake of the same anointing. Of all things - Which it is necessary for you to know. And is no lie - Like that which antichrist teaches. Ye shall abide in him - This is added both by way of comfort and of exhortation. The whole discourse, from verse 18 to this, 1 John ii, 18-27 is peculiarly adapted to little children.

28. And now, beloved children - Having finished his address to each, he now returns to all in general. Abide in him, that we - A modest expression. May not be ashamed before him at his coming - O how will ye, Jews, Socinians, nominal Christians, be ashamed in that day!

29. Everyone - And none else. Who practiceth righteousness - From a believing, loving heart. Is born of him - For all his children are like himself.

III

1. That we should be called - That is, should be, the children of God. Therefore the world knoweth us not - They know not what to make of us. We are a mystery to them.

2. It doth not yet appear - Even to ourselves. What we shall be - It is something ineffable, which will raise the children of God to be, in a manner, as God himself. But we know, in general, that when he, the Son of God, shall appear, we shall be like him - The glory of God penetrating our inmost substance. For we shall see him as he is - Manifestly, without a veil. And that sight will transform us into the same likeness.

3. And every one that hath this hope in him - In God.

4. Whosoever committeth sin - Thereby transgresseth the holy, just, and good law of God, and so sets his authority at nought; for this is implied in the very nature of sin.

5. And ye know that he - Christ. Was manifested - That he came into the world for this very purpose. To take away our sins - To destroy them all, root and branch, and leave none remaining. And in him is no sin - So that he could not suffer on his own account, but to make us as himself.

6. Whosoever abideth in communion with him, by loving faith, sinneth not - While he so abideth. Whosoever sinneth certainly seeth him not - The loving eye of his soul is not then fixed upon God; neither doth he then experimentally know him - Whatever he did in time past.

7. Let no one deceive you - Let none persuade you that any man is righteous but he that uniformly practices righteousness; he alone is righteous, after the example of his Lord.

8. He that committeth sin is a child of the devil; for the devil sinneth from the beginning - That is, was the first sinner in the universe, and has continued to sin ever since. The Son of God was manifested to destroy the works of the devil - All sin. And will he not perform this in all that trust in him?

9. Whosoever is born of God - By living faith, whereby God is continually breathing spiritual life into his soul, and his soul is continually breathing out love and prayer to God, doth not commit sin. For the divine seed of loving faith abideth in him; and, so long as it doth, he cannot sin, because he is born of God - Is inwardly and universally changed.

10. Neither he that loveth not his brother - Here is the transition from the general proposition to one particular.

12. Who was of the wicked one - Who showed he was a child of the devil by killing his brother. And wherefore slew he him - For any fault? No, but just the reverse; for his goodness.

13. Marvel not if the world hate you - For the same cause.

14. We know - As if he had said, We ourselves could not love our brethren, unless we were passed from spiritual death to life, that is, born of God. He that loveth not his brother abideth in death - That is, is not born of God. And he that is not born of God, cannot love his brother.

15. He, I say, abideth in spiritual death, is void of the life of God. For whosoever hateth his brother, and there is no medium between loving and hating him, is, in God's account, a murderer: every degree of hatred being a degree of the same temper which moved Cain to murder his brother. And no murderer hath eternal life abiding in him - But every loving believer hath. For love is the beginning of eternal life. It is the same, in substance, with glory.

16. The word God is not in the original. It was omitted by the apostle just as the particular name is omitted by Mary, when she says to the gardener, "Sir, if thou hast born him hence;" and by the church,

when she says, "Let him kiss me with the kisses of his mouth," So i, 2; in both which places there is a language, a very emphatical language, even in silence. It declares how totally the thoughts were possessed by the blessed and glorious subject. It expresses also the superlative dignity and amiableness of the person meant, as though He, and He alone, was, or deserved to be, both known and admired by all. Because he laid down his life - Not merely for sinners, but for us in particular. From this truth believed, from this blessing enjoyed, the love of our brethren takes its rise, which may very justly be admitted as an evidence that our faith is no delusion.

17. But whoso hath this world's good - Worldly substance, far less valuable than life. And seeth his brother have need - The very sight of want knocks at the door of the spectator's heart. And shutteth up - Whether asked or not. His bowels of compassion from him, how dwelleth the love of God in him - Certainly not at all, however he may talk, 1 John iii, 18, of loving God.

18. Not in word - Only. But in deed - In action: not in tongue by empty professions, but in truth.

19. And hereby we know - We have a further proof by this real, operative love. That we are of the truth - That we have true faith, that we are true children of God. And shall assure our hearts before him - Shall enjoy the assurance of his favour, and the "testimony of a good conscience toward God." The heart, in St. John's language, is the conscience. The word conscience is not found in his writings.

20. For if we have not this testimony, if in anything our heart, our own conscience, condemn us, much more does God, who is greater than our heart - An infinitely holier and a more impartial Judge. And knoweth all things - So that there is no hope of hiding it from him.

21. If our heart condemn us not - If our conscience, duly enlightened by the word and Spirit of God, and comparing all our thoughts, words, and works with that word, pronounce that they agree therewith. Then have we confidence toward God - Not only our consciousness of his favour continues and increases, but we have a full persuasion, that whatsoever we ask we shall receive of him.

23. And this is his commandment - All his commandments in one word. That we should believe and love - in the manner and degree which he hath taught. This is the greatest and most important command that ever issued from the throne of glory. If this be neglected, no other can be kept: if this be observed, all others are easy.

24. And he that keepeth his commandments - That thus believes and loves. Abideth in him, and God in him: and hereby we know that he abideth in us, by the Spirit which he hath given us - Which witnesses with our spirits that we are his children, and brings forth his fruits of peace, love, holiness. This is the transition to the treating of the Holy Spirit which immediately follows.

IV

1. Believe not every spirit - Whereby any teacher is actuated. But try the spirits - By the rule which follows. We are to try all spirits by the written word: "To the law and to the testimony!" If any man speak not according to these, the spirit which actuates him is not of God.

2. Every spirit - Or teacher. Which confesseth - Both with heart and voice. Jesus Christ, who is come in the flesh, is of God - This his coming presupposes, contains, and draws after it, the whole doctrine of Christ.

3. Ye have heard - From our Lord and us, that it cometh.

4. Ye have overcome these seducers, because greater is the Spirit of Christ that is in you than the spirit of antichrist that is in the world.

5. They - Those false prophets. Are of the world - Of the number of those that know not God. Therefore speak they of the world - From the same principle, wisdom, spirit; and, of consequence, the world heareth them - With approbation.

6. We - Apostles. Are of God - Immediately taught, and sent by him. Hereby we know - From what is said, 1 John iv, 2-6.

7. Let us love one another - From the doctrine he has just been defending he draws this exhortation. It is by the Spirit that the love of God is shed abroad in our hearts. Everyone that truly loveth God and his neighbour is born of God.

8. God is love - This little sentence brought St. John more sweetness, even in the time he was writing it, than the whole world can bring. God is often styled holy, righteous, wise; but not holiness, righteousness, or wisdom in the abstract, as he is said to be love; intimating that this is his darling, his reigning attribute, the attribute that sheds an amiable glory on all his other perfections.

12. If we love one another, God abideth in us - This is treated of, 1 John iv, 13-16. And his love is perfected - Has its full effect. In us - This is treated of, 1 John iv, 17-19.

14. And in consequence of this we have seen and testify that the Father sent the Son - These are the foundation and the criteria of our abiding in God and God in us, the communion of the Spirit, and the confession of the Son.

15. Whosoever shall, from a principle of loving faith, openly confess in the face of all opposition and danger, that Jesus is the Son of God, God abideth in him.

16. And we know and believe - By the same Spirit, the love that God hath to us.

17. Hereby - That is, by this communion with God. Is our love made perfect; that we may - That is, so that we shall have boldness in the day of judgment - When all the stout-hearted shall tremble. Because as he - Christ. Is - All love. So are we - Who are fathers in Christ, even in this world.

18. There is no fear in love - No slavish fear can be where love reigns. But perfect, adult love casteth out slavish fear: because such fear hath torment - And so is inconsistent with the happiness of love. A natural man has neither fear nor love; one that is awakened, fear without love; a babe in Christ, love and fear; a father in Christ, love without fear.

19. We love him, because he first loved us - This is the sum of all religion, the genuine model of Christianity. None can say more: why should any one say less, or less intelligibly?

20. Whom he hath seen - Who is daily presented to his senses, to raise his esteem, and move his kindness or compassion toward him.

21. And this commandment have we from him - Both God and his opinions or mode of worship be, purely because he is the child, and bears the image, of God. Bigotry is properly the want of this pure and universal love. A bigot only loves those who embrace his opinions, and receives his way of worship; and he loves them for that, and not for Christ's sake.

V

1. The scope and sum of this whole paragraph appears from the conclusion of it, 1 John v, xiii, "These things have I written to you who believe, that ye may know that ye who believe have eternal life." So faith is the first and last point with St. John also. Every one who loveth - God that begat loveth him also that is begotten of him - Hath a natural affection to all his brethren.

2. Hereby we know - This is a plain proof. That we love the children of God - As his children.

3. For this is the love of God - The only sure proof of it. That we keep his commandments: and his commandments are not grievous - To any that are born of God.

4. For whatsoever - This expression implies the most unlimited universality. Is born of God overcometh the world - Conquers whatever it can lay in the way, either to allure or fright the children of God from keeping his commandments. And this is the victory - The grand means of overcoming. Even our faith - Seeing all things are possible to him that believeth.

5. Who is he that overcometh the world - That is superior to all worldly care, desire, fear? Every believer, and none else. The seventh verse (usually so reckoned) is a brief recapitulation of all which has been before advanced concerning the Father, the Son, and the Spirit. It is cited, in conjunction with the sixth and eighth, 1 John v, 6, 8 by Tertullian, Cyprian, and an uninterrupted train of Fathers. And, indeed, what the sun is in the world, what the heart is in a man, what the needle is in the mariner's compass, this verse is in the epistle. By this the sixth, eighth, and ninth verses 1 John v, 6, 8, 9 are indissolubly connected; as will be evident, beyond all contradiction, when they are accurately considered.

6. This is he - St. John here shows the immovable foundation of that faith that Jesus is the Son of God; not only the testimony of man, but the firm, indubitable testimony of God. Who came - Jesus is he of whom it was promised that he should come; and who accordingly, is come. And this the Spirit, and the water, and the blood testify. Even Jesus - Who, coming by water and blood, is by this very thing demonstrated to be the Christ. Not by the water only - Wherein he was baptized. But by the water and the blood - Which he shed when he had finished the work his Father had given him to do. He not only undertook at his baptism "to fulfil all righteousness," but on the cross accomplished what he had undertaken; in token whereof, when all was finished, blood and water came out of his side. And it is the Spirit who likewise testifieth - Of Jesus Christ, namely, by Moses and all the prophets, by John the Baptist, by all the apostles, and in all the writings of the New Testament. And against his testimony there can be no exception, because the Spirit is truth - The very God of truth.

7. What Bengelius has advanced, both concerning the transposition of these two verses, and the authority of the controverted verse, partly in his "Gnomon," and partly in his "Apparatus Criticus," will abundantly satisfy any impartial person. For there are three that testify - Literally, testifying, or bearing witness. The participle is put for the noun witnesses, to intimate that the act of testifying, and the effect of it, are continually present. Properly, persons only can testify; and that three are described testifying on earth, as if they were persons, is elegantly subservient to the three persons testifying in heaven. The Spirit - In the word, confirmed by miracles. The water - Of baptism, wherein we are dedicated to the Son, (with the Father and Spirit,) typifying his spotless purity, and the inward purifying of our nature. And the blood - Represented in the Lord's supper, and applied to the consciences of believer. And these three harmoniously agree in one - In bearing the same testimony, - that Jesus Christ is the divine, the complete, the only saviour of the world.

8. And there are three that testify in heaven - The testimony of the Spirit, the water, and the blood, is by an eminent gradation corroborated by three, who give a still greater testimony. The Father - Who

clearly testified of the Son, both at his baptism and at his transfiguration. The Word - Who testified of himself on many occasions, while he was on earth; and again, with still greater solemnity, after his ascension into heaven, Rev. i, 5; Rev. xix, 13. And the Spirit - Whose testimony was added chiefly after his glorification, chap. ii, 27; John xv, 26; Acts v, 32; Rom. viii, 16. And these three are one - Even as those two, the Father and the Son, are one, John x, 30. Nothing can separate the Spirit from the Father and the Son. If he were not one with the Father and the Son, the apostle ought to have said, The Father and the Word, who are one, and the Spirit, are two. But this is contrary to the whole tenor of Revelation. It remains that these three are one. They are one in essence, in knowledge, in will, and in their testimony. It is observable, the three in the one verse are opposed, not conjointly, but severally, to the three in the other: as if he had said, Not only the Spirit testifies, but also the Father, John v, 37; not only the water, but also the Word, John iii, 11, John x, 41; not only the blood, but also the Holy Ghost, John xv, 26, &c. It must now appear, to every reasonable man, how absolutely necessary the eighth verse is 1 John v, 8. St. John could not think of the testimony of the Spirit, and water, and blood, and subjoin, "The testimony of God is greater," without thinking also of the testimony of the Son and Holy Ghost; yea, and mentioning it in so solemn an enumeration. Nor can any possible reason be devised, why, without three testifying in heaven, he should enumerate three, and no more, who testify on earth. The testimony of all is given on earth, not in heaven; but they who testify are part on earth, part in heaven. The witnesses who are on earth testify chiefly concerning his abode on earth, though not excluding his state of exaltation: the witnesses who are in heaven testify chiefly concerning his glory at God's right hand, though not excluding his state of humiliation. The seventh verse, therefore, with the sixth, contains a recapitulation of the whole economy of Christ, from his baptism to pentecost; the eighth, the sum of the divine economy, from the time of his exaltation. Hence it further appears, that this position of the seventh 1 John v, 7, 8 and eighth verses, which places those who testify on earth before those who testify in heaven, is abundantly preferable to the other, and affords a gradation admirably suited to the subject.

9. If we receive the testimony of men - As we do continually, and must do in a thousand instances. The testimony of God is greater - Of higher authority, and much more worthy to be received; namely, this very testimony which God the Father, together with the Word and the Spirit, hath testified of the Son, as the saviour of the world.

10. He that believeth on the Son of God hath the testimony - The dear evidence of this, in himself: he that believeth not God, in this, hath made him a liar; because he supposes that to be false which God has expressly testified.

11. And this is the sum of that testimony, that God hath given us a title to, and the real beginning of, eternal life; and that this is purchased by, and treasured up in, his Son, who has all the springs and the fulness of it in himself, to communicate to his body, the church, first in grace and then in glory.

12. It plainly follows, he that hath the Son - Living and reigning in him by faith. Hath this life; he that hath not the Son of God hath not this life - Hath no part or lot therein. In the former clause, the apostle says simply, the Son; because believers know him: in the latter, the Son of God; that unbelievers may know how great a blessing they fall short of.

13. These things have I written - In the introduction, chap. i, 4, he said, I write: now, in the close, I have written. That ye may know - With a fuller and stronger assurance, that ye have eternal life.

14. And we - Who believe. Have this further confidence in him, that he heareth - That is, favourably regards, whatever prayer we offer in faith, according to his revealed will.

15. We have - Faith anticipates the blessings. The petitions which we asked of him - Even before the event. And when the event comes, we know it comes in answer to our prayer.

16. This extends to things of the greatest importance. If any one see his brother - That is. any man. Sin a sin which is not unto death - That is, any sin but total apostasy from both the power and form of godliness. Let him ask, and God will give him life - Pardon and spiritual life, for that sinner. There is a sin unto death: I do not say that he shall pray for that - That is, let him not pray for it. A sin unto death may likewise mean, one which God has determined to punish with death.

17. All deviation from perfect holiness is sin; but all sin is not unpardonable.

18. Yet this gives us no encouragement to sin: on the contrary, it is an indisputable truth, he that is born of God - That sees and loves God. Sinneth not - So long as that loving faith abides in him, he neither speaks nor does anything which God hath forbidden. He keepeth himself - Watching unto prayer. And, while he does this, the wicked one toucheth him not - So as to hurt him.

19. We know that we are children of God - By the witness and the fruit of his Spirit, chap. iii, 24. But the whole world - All who have not his Spirit, not only is "touched" by him, but by idolatry, fraud, violence lasciviousness, impiety, all manner of wickedness. Lieth in the wicked one - Void of life, void of sense. In this short expression the horrible state of the world is painted in the most lively colours; a comment on which we have in the actions, conversations, contracts, quarrels, and friendships of worldly men.

20. And we know - By all these infallible proofs. That the Son of God is come - Into the world.

And he hath given us a spiritual understanding, that we may know him, the true one -"The faithful and true witness." And we are in the true one - As branches in the vine, even in Jesus Christ, the eternal Son of God. This Jesus is the only living and true God, together with the father and the Spirit, and the original fountain of eternal life. So the beginning and the end of the epistle agree.

21. Keep yourselves from idols - From all worship of false gods, from all worship of images or of any creature, and from every inward idol; from loving, desiring, fearing anything more than God. Seek all help and defense from evil, all happiness in the true God alone.

NOTES ON THE SECOND EPISTLE OF ST. JOHN

THE parts of this epistle, written to some Christian matron, and her religious children, are three:

I. The inscription, v. 1-3

II. An exhortation to persevere in true faith and love,. 4-11

III. The conclusion, 12,13

2nd JOHN

I

    1. The elder - An appellation suited to a familiar letter, but upon a weighty subject. To the elect - That is, Christian. Kuria is undoubtedly a proper name, both here and in ver. 5; for it was not then usual to apply the title of lady to any but the Roman empress; neither would such a manner of speaking have been suitable to the simplicity and dignity of the apostle. Whom - Both her and her children. I love in the truth - With unfeigned and holy love.

    2. For the truth's sake, which abideth in us - As a living principle of faith and holiness.

    3. Grace takes away guilt; mercy, misery: peace implies the abiding in grace and mercy. It includes the testimony of God's Spirit, both that we are his children, and that all our ways are acceptable to him. This is the very foretaste of heaven itself, where it is perfected. In truth and love - Or, faith and love, as St. Paul speaks. Faith and truth are here synonymous terms.

    4. I found of thy children - Probably in their aunt's house, ver. 13. Walking in the truth - In faith and love.

    5. That which we had from the beginning - Of our Lord's ministry. Indeed it was, in some sense, from the beginning of the world. That we may love one another - More abundantly.

    6. And this is the proof of true love, universal obedience built on the love of God. This - Love. Is the great commandment which ye have heard from the beginning - Of our preaching.

    7. Carefully keep what ye have heard from the beginning, for many seducers are entered into the world, who confess not Jesus Christ that came in the flesh - Who disbelieve either his prophetic, or priestly, or kingly office. Whosoever does this is the seducer - From God. And the antichrist - Fighting against Christ.

    8. That we lose not the things which we have wrought - Which every apostate does. But receive a full reward - Having fully employed all our talents to the glory of him that gave them. Here again the apostle modestly transfers it to himself.

    9. Receive this as a certain rule: Whosoever transgresseth - Any law of God. Hath not God - For his Father and his God. He that abideth in the doctrine of Christ - Believing and obeying it. He hath both the Father and the Son - For his God.

    10. If any came to you - Either as a teacher or a brother. And bring not this doctrine - That is, advance anything contrary to it. Receive him not into your house - As either a teacher or a brother- Neither bid him God speed - Give him no encouragement therein.

    11. For he that biddeth him God speed - That gives him any encouragement, is accessory to his evil deeds.

    12. Having many things to write, I was not minded to write now - Only of these, which were then peculiarly needful.

    13. The children of thy elect or Christian sister - Absent, if not dead, when the apostle wrote this.

NOTES ON THE THIRD EPISTLE OF ST. JOHN

THE third epistle has likewise three parts:

I. The inscription, 1, 2

II. The commendation of Caius, 3-8 With a caution against Diotrephes 9-11 And a recommendation of Demetrius, 12

III. The conclusion, 13-15

3rd JOHN

I

1. Caius was probably that Caius of Corinth whom St. Paul mentions, Rom. xvi, 23. If so, either he was removed from Achaia into Asia, or St. John sent this letter to Corinth.

3. For - I know thou usest all thy talents to his glory. The truth that is in thee - The true faith and love.

4. I have no greater joy than this - Such is the spirit of every true Christian pastor. To hear that my children walk in the truth - Caius probably was converted by St. Paul. Therefore when St. John speaks of him. with other believers, as his children, it may be considered as the tender style of paternal love, whoever were the instruments of their conversion. And his using this appellation, when writing under the character of the elder, has its peculiar beauty.

5. Faithfully - Uprightly and sincerely.

6. Who have testified of thy love before the church - The congregation with whom I now reside. Whom if thou send forward on their journey - Supplied with what is needful. Thou shalt do well - How tenderly does the apostle enjoin this!

7. They went forth - To preach the gospel.

8. To receive - With all kindness. The truth - Which they preach.

9. I wrote to the church - Probably that to which they came. But Diotrephes - Perhaps the pastor of it. Who loveth to have the preeminence among them - To govern all things according to his own will. Receiveth us not - Neither them nor me. So did the mystery of iniquity already work!

10. He prateth against us - Both them and me, thereby endeavouring to excuse himself.

11. Follow not that which is evil - In Diotrephes. But that which is good - In Demetrius. He hath not seen God - Is a stranger to him.

12. And from the truth itself - That is, what they testify is the very truth. Yea, we also bear testimony - I and they that are with me.

14. Salute the friends by name - That is, in the same manner as if I had named them one by one. The word friend does not often occur in the New Testament, being swallowed up in the more endearing one of brother.

John Wesley

NOTES ON THE GENERAL EPISTLE OF ST. JUDE

THIS epistle has three parts:

I. The inscription, 1, 2

II. The treatise, in which,
    1. He exhorts them to contend for the faith, 3
    2. Describes the punishment and the manners of its adversaries, 4- 16
    3. Warns the believers, 17-19
    4. Confirms them, 20, 21
    5. Instructs them in their duty to others, 22, 23

III. The conclusion, 24,

JUDE

This epistle greatly resembles the second of St. Peter, which St. Jude seems to have had in view while he wrote. That was written but a very little before his death; and hence we may gather that St. Jude lived some time after it, and saw that grievous declension in the church which St. Peter had foretold. But he passes over some things mentioned by St. Peter, repeats some in different expressions and with a different view, and adds others; clearly evidencing thereby the wisdom of God which rested upon him. Thus St. Peter cites and confirms St. Paul's writings, and is himself cited and confirmed by St. Jude.

I

1. Jude, a servant of Jesus Christ - The highest glory which any, either angel or man, can aspire to. The word servant, under the old covenant, was adapted to the spirit of fear and bondage that clave to that dispensation. But when the time appointed of the Father was come, for the sending of his Son to redeem them that were under the law, the word servant (used by the apostles concerning themselves and all the children of God) signified one that, having the Spirit of adoption, is made free by the Son of God. His being a servant is the fruit and perfection of his being a son. And whenever the throne of God and of the Lamb shall be in the new Jerusalem, then will it be indeed that "his servants shall serve him," Rev. xxii, 3. The brother of James - St. James was the more eminent, usually styled, "the brother of the Lord." To them that are beloved - The conclusion, ver. 21, exactly answers the introduction. And preserved through Jesus Christ - So both the spring and the accomplishment of salvation are pointed out. This is premised, lest any of them should be discouraged by the terrible things which are afterwards mentioned. And called - To receive the whole blessing of God, in time and eternity.

3. When I gave all diligence to write to you of the common salvation - Designed for all, and enjoyed by all believers. Here the design of the epistle is expressed; the end of which exactly answers the beginning. It was needful to exhort you to contend earnestly - Yet humbly, meekly, and lovingly; otherwise your contention will only hurt your cause, if not destroy your soul. For the faith - All the fundamental truths. Once delivered - By God, to remain unvaried for ever.

4. There are certain men crept in, who were of old described before - Even as early as Enoch; of whom it was foretold, that by their wilful sins they would incur this condemnation. Turning the grace of God - Revealed in the gospel. Into lasciviousness - Into an occasion of more abandoned wickedness.

5. He afterwards destroyed - The far greater part of that very people whom he had once saved. Let none therefore presume upon past mercies, as if he was now out of danger.

6. And the angels, who kept not their first dignity - Once assigned them under the Son of God. But voluntarily left their own habitation - Then properly their own, by the free gift of God. He reserved - Delivered to be kept. In everlasting chains under darkness - O how unlike their own habitation! When these fallen angels came out of the hands of God, they were holy; else God made that which was evil: and being holy, they were beloved of God; else he hated the image of his own spotless purity. But now

he loves them no more; they are doomed to endless destruction. (for if he loved them still, he would love what is sinful:) and both his former love, and his present righteous and eternal displeasure towards the same work of his own hands, are because he changeth not; because he invariably loveth righteousness, and hateth iniquity. 2 Pet. ii, 4.

7. The cities which gave themselves over to fornication - The word here means, unnatural lusts. Are set forth as an example, suffering the vengeance of eternal fire - That is, the vengeance which they suffered is an example or a type of eternal fire.

8. In like manner these dreamers - Sleeping and dreaming all their lives. Despise authority - Those that are invested with it by Christ, and made by him the overseers of his flock. Rail at dignities - The apostle does not seem to speak of worldly dignities. These they had "in admiration for the sake of gain," ver. 16; but those holy men, who for the purity of their lives, the soundness of their doctrine, and the greatness of their labours in the work of the ministry, were truly honourable before God and all good men; and who were grossly vilified by those who turned the grace of God into lasciviousness. Probably they were the impure followers of Simon Magus, the same with the Gnostics and Nicolaitans, Rev. ii, 15. 2 Pet. ii, 10.

9. Yet Michael - It does not appear whether St. Jude learned this by any Revelation or from ancient tradition. It suffices, that these things were not only true, but acknowledged as such by them to whom he wrote. The archangel - This word occurs but once more in the sacred writings, 1 Thess. iv, 16. So that whether there be one archangel only, or more, it is not possible for us to determine. When he disputed with the devil - At what time we know not. Concerning the body of Moses - Possibly the devil would have discovered the place where it was buried, which God for wise reasons had concealed. Durst not bring even against him a railing accusation - Though so far beneath him in every respect. But simply said, (so great was his modesty!) The Lord rebuke thee - I leave thee to the Judge of all.

10. But these - Without all shame. Rail at the things of God which they know not - Neither can know, having no spiritual senses. And the natural things, which they know - By their natural senses, they abuse into occasions of sin.

11. Woe unto them - Of all the apostles St. Jude alone, and that in this single place, denounces a woe. St. Peter, to the same effect, pronounces them "cursed children." For they have gone in the way of Cain - The murderer. And ran greedily - Literally, have been poured out, like a torrent without banks. After the error of Balaam - The covetous false prophet. And perished in the gainsaying of Korah - Vengeance has overtaken them as it did Korah, rising up against those whom God had sent.

12. These are spots - Blemishes. In your feasts of love - Anciently observed in all the churches. Feeding themselves without fear - Without any fear of God, or jealousy over themselves. Twice dead - In sin, first by nature, and afterwards by apostasy. Plucked up by the roots - And so incapable of ever reviving.

13. Wandering stars - Literally, planets, which shine for a time, but have no light in themselves, and will be soon cast into utter darkness. Thus the apostle illustrates their desperate wickedness by comparisons drawn from the air, earth, sea, and heavens.

14. And of these also - As well as the antediluvian sinners Enoch - So early was the prophecy referred to, ver. 4. The seventh from Adam - There were only five of the fathers between Adam and Enoch, 1 Chron. i, 1-3. The first coming of Christ was revealed to Adam; his second, glorious coming, to Enoch; and the seventh from Adam foretold the things which will conclude the seventh age of the world. St. Jude might know this either from some ancient book, or tradition, or immediate Revelation. Behold - As if it were already done, the Lord cometh!

15. To execute judgment - Enoch herein looked beyond the flood. Upon all - Sinners, in general. And to convict all the ungodly, in particular, of all the grievous things which ungodly sinners (a sinner is bad; but the ungodly who sin without fear are worse) have spoken against him, ver. 8, 10, though they might not think, all those speeches were against him.

16. These are murmurers - Against men. Complainers - Literally, complainers of their fate, against God. Walking - With regard to themselves. After their own foolish and mischievous desires. Having men's persons in admiration for the sake of gain - Admiring and commending them only for what they can get.

17. By the apostles - He does not exempt himself from the number of apostles. For in the next verse he says, they told you, not us.

19. These are they who separate themselves, sensual, not having the Spirit - Having natural senses and understanding only, not the Spirit of God; otherwise they could not separate. For that it is a sin, and a very heinous one, "to separate from the church," is out of all question. But then it should be observed,

1. That by the church is meant a body of living Christians, who are "an habitation of God through the Spirit:"

2. That by separating is understood, renouncing all religious intercourse with them; no longer joining with them in solemn prayer, or the other public offices of religion: and,

3. That we have no more authority from scripture to call even this schism, than to call it murder.

John Wesley

20. But ye, beloved, not separating, but building yourselves up in your most holy faith - Than which none can be more holy in itself, or more conducive to the most refined and exalted holiness. Praying through the Holy Spirit - Who alone is able to build you up, as he alone laid the foundation. In this and the following verse St. Jude mentions the Father, Son, and Spirit, together with faith, love, and hope.

21. By these means, through his grace, keep yourselves in the love of God, and in the confident expectation of that eternal life which is purchased for you, and conferred upon you, through the mere mercy of our Lord Jesus Christ.

22. Meantime watch over others, as well as yourselves, and give them such help as their various needs require. For instance,

1. Some, that are wavering in judgment, staggered by others or by their own evil reasoning, endeavour more deeply to convince of the whole truth as it is in Jesus.

2. Some snatch, with a swift and strong hand, out of the fire of sin and temptation.

3. On others show compassion in a milder and gentler way; though still with a jealous fear, lest yourselves be infected with the disease you endeavour to cure. See, therefore, that while you love the sinners, ye retain the utmost abhorrence of their sins, and of any the least degree of, or approach to, them.

24. Now to him who alone is able to keep them from falling - Into any of these errors or sins. And to present them faultless in the presence of his glory - That is, in his own presence, when he shall be revealed in all his glory. Please see Notes at Matt. i, 1

NOTES ON THE REVELATION OF JOHN

IT is scarce possible for any that either love or fear God not to feel their hearts extremely affected in seriously reading either the beginning or the latter part of the Revelation. These, it is evident, we cannot consider too much; but the intermediate parts I did not study at all for many years; as utterly despairing of understanding them, after the fruitless attempts of so many wise and good men: and perhaps I should have lived and died in this sentiment, had I not seen the works of the great Bengelius. But these revived my hopes of understanding even the prophecies of this book; at least many of them in some good degree: for perhaps some will not be opened but in eternity. Let us, however, bless God for the measure of light we may enjoy, and improve it to his glory. The following notes are mostly those of that excellent man; a few of which are taken from his Gnornon Novi Testamenti, but far more from his Ekklarte Offenbarung, which is a full and regular comment on the Revelation. Every part of this I do not undertake to defend. But none should condemn him without reading his proofs at large. It did not suit my design to insert these: they are above the capacity of ordinary readers. Nor had I room to insert the entire translation of a book which contains near twelve hundred pages. All I can do is, partly to translate, partly abridge, the most necessary of his observations; allowing myself the liberty to alter some of them, and to add a few notes where he is not full. His text, it may be observed, I have taken almost throughout, which I apprehend he has abundantly defended both in the Gnomon itself, and in his Apparatus and Crisis in Apocalypsin. Yet I by no means pretend to understand or explain all that is contained in this mysterious book. I only offer what help I can to the serious inquirer, and shall rejoice if any be moved thereby more carefully to read and more deeply to consider the words of this prophecy. Blessed is he that does this with a single eye. His labour shall not be in vain.

I

1. The Revelation - Properly so called; for things covered before are here revealed, or unveiled. No prophecy in the Old Testament has this title; it was reserved for this alone in the New. It is, as it were, a manifesto, wherein the Heir of all things declares that all power is given him in heaven and earth, and that he will in the end gloriously exercise that power, maugre all the opposition of all his enemies. Of Jesus Christ - Not of "John the Divine," a title added in latter ages. Certain it is, that appellation, the Divine, was not brought into the church, much less was it affixed to John the apostle, till long after the apostolic age. It was St. John, indeed, who wrote this book, but the author of it is Jesus Christ. Which God gave unto him - According to his holy, glorified humanity, as the great Prophet of the church. God gave the Revelation to Jesus Christ; Jesus Christ made it known to his servants. To show - This word recurs, chap. xxii, 6; and in many places the parts of this book refer to each other. Indeed the whole structure of it breathes the art of God, comprising, in the most finished compendium, things to come, many, various; near, intermediate, remote; the greatest, the least; terrible, comfortable; old, new; long, short; and these interwoven together, opposite, composite; relative to each other at a small, at a great, distance; and therefore sometimes, as it were, disappearing, broken off, suspended, and afterwards unexpectedly and most seasonably appearing again. In all its parts it has an admirable variety, with the most exact harmony, beautifully illustrated by those very digressions which seem to interrupt it. In this manner does it display the manifold wisdom of God shining in the economy of the church through so many ages. His servants - Much is comprehended in this appellation. It is a great thing to be a servant of Jesus Christ. This book is dedicated particularly to the servants of Christ in the seven churches in Asia; but not exclusive of all his other servants, in all nations and ages. It is one single Revelation, and yet sufficient for them all, from the time it was written to the end of the world. Serve thou the Lord Jesus Christ in truth: so shalt thou learn his secret in this book; yea, and thou shalt feel in thy heart whether this book be divine, or not. The things which must shortly come to pass - The things contained in this prophecy did begin to be accomplished shortly after it was given; and the whole might be said to come to pass shortly, in the same sense as St. Peter says, "The end of all things is at hand;" and our Lord himself, "Behold, I come quickly." There is in this book a rich treasure of all the doctrines pertaining to faith and holiness. But these are also delivered in other parts of holy writ; so that the Revelation need not to have been given for the sake of these. The peculiar design of this is, to show the things which must come to pass. And this we are especially to have before our eyes whenever we

read or hear it. It is said afterward, "Write what thou seest;" and again, "Write what thou hast seen, and what is, and what shall be hereafter;" but here, where the scope of the book is shown, it is only said, the things which must come to pass. Accordingly, the showing things to come, is the great point in view throughout the whole. And St. John writes what he has seen, and what is, only as it has an influence on, or gives light to, what shall be. And he - Jesus Christ. Sent and signified them - Showed them by signs or emblems; so the Greek word properly means. By his angel - Peculiarly called, in the sequel, "the angel of God," and particularly mentioned, chap. xvii. 1; xxi, 9; xxii, 6, 16. To his servant John - A title given to no other single person throughout the book.

2. Who hath testified - In the following book. The word of God - Given directly by God. And the testimony of Jesus - Which he hath left us, as the faithful and true witness. Whatsoever things he saw - In such a manner as was a full confirmation of the divine original of this book.

3. Happy is he that readeth, and they that hear, the words of this prophecy - Some have miserably handled this book. Hence others are afraid to touch it; and, while they desire to know all things else, reject only the knowledge of those which God hath shown. They inquire after anything rather than this; as if it were written, "Happy is he that doth not read this prophecy." Nay, but happy is he that readeth, and they that hear, and keep the words thereof - Especially at this time, when so considerable a part of them is on the point of being fulfilled. Nor are helps wanting whereby any sincere and diligent inquirer may understand what he reads therein. The book itself is written in the most accurate manner possible. It distinguishes the several things whereof it treats by seven epistles, seven seals, seven trumpets, seven phials; each of which sevens is divided into four and three. Many things the book itself explains; as the seven stars; the seven candlesticks; the lamb, his seven horns and seven eyes; the incense; the dragon; the heads and horns of the beasts; the fine linen; the testimony of Jesus: and much light arises from comparing it with the ancient prophecies, and the predictions in the other books of the New Testament. In this book our Lord has comprised what was wanting in those prophecies touching the time which followed his ascension and the end of the Jewish polity. Accordingly, it reaches from the old Jerusalem to the new, reducing all things into one sum, in the exactest order, and with a near resemblance to the ancient prophets. The introduction and conclusion agree with Daniel; the description of the man child, and the promises to Zion, with Isaiah; the judgment of Babylon, with Jeremiah; again, the determination of times, with Daniel; the architecture of the holy city, with Ezekiel; the emblems of the horses, candlesticks, &c., with Zechariah. Many things largely described by the prophets are here summarily repeated; and frequently in the same words. To them we may then usefully have recourse. Yet the Revelation suffices for the explaining itself, even if we do not yet understand those prophecies; yea, it casts much light upon them. Frequently, likewise, where there is a resemblance between them, there is a difference also; the Revelation, as it were, taking a stock from one of the old prophets, and inserting a new graft into it. Thus Zechariah speaks of two olive trees; and so does St. John; but with a different meaning. Daniel has a beast with ten horns; so has St. John; but not with quite the same signification. And here the difference of words, emblems, things, times, ought studiously to be observed. Our Lord foretold many things before his passion; but not all things; for it was not yet seasonable. Many things, likewise, his Spirit foretold in the writings of the apostles, so far as the necessities of those times required: now he comprises them all in one short book; therein presupposing all the other prophecies, and at the same time explaining, continuing, and perfecting them in one thread. It is right therefore to compare them; but not to measure the fulness of these by the scantiness of those preceding. Christ, when on earth, foretold what would come to pass in a short time; adding a brief description of the last things. Here he foretells the intermediate things; so that both put together constitute one complete chain of prophecy. This book is therefore not only the sum and the key of all the prophecies which preceded, but likewise a supplement to all; the seals being closed before. Of consequence, it contains many particulars not revealed in any other part of scripture. They have therefore little gratitude to God for such a Revelation, reserved for the exaltation of Christ, who boldly reject whatever they find here which was not revealed, or not so clearly, in other parts of scripture. He that readeth and they that hear - St. John probably sent this book by a single person into Asia, who read it in the churches, while many heard. But this, likewise, in a secondary sense, refers to all that shall duly read or hear it in all ages. The words of this prophecy - It is a Revelation with regard to Christ who gives it; a prophecy, with regard to John who delivers it to the churches. And keep the things which are written therein - In such a manner as the nature of them requires; namely, with repentance, faith, patience, prayer, obedience, watchfulness, constancy. It behoves every Christian, at all opportunities, to read what is written in the oracles of God; and to read this precious book in particular, frequently, reverently, and attentively. For the time - Of its beginning to be accomplished. Is near - Even when St. John wrote. How much nearer to us is even the full accomplishment of this weighty prophecy!

4. John - The dedication of this book is contained in the fourth, fifth, and sixth verses; but the whole Revelation is a kind of letter. To the seven churches which are in Asia - That part of the Lesser Asia which was then a Roman province. There had been several other churches planted here; but it seems these were now the most eminent; and it was among these that St. John had laboured most during

his abode in Asia. In these cities there were many Jews. Such of them as believed in each were joined with the gentile believers in one church. Grace be unto you, and peace - The favour of God, with all temporal and eternal blessings. From him who is, and who was, and who cometh, or, who is to come - A wonderful translation of the great name JEHOVAH: he was of old, he is now, he cometh; that is, will be forever. And from the seven spirits which are before his throne - Christ is he who "hath the seven spirits of God." "The seven lamps which burn before the throne are the seven spirits of God." " The lamb hath seven horns and seven eyes, which are the seven spirits of God." Seven was a sacred number in the Jewish church: but it did not always imply a precise number. It sometimes is to be taken figuratively, to denote completeness or perfection. By these seven spirits, not seven created angels, but the Holy Ghost is to be understood. The angels are never termed spirits in this book; and when all the angels stand up, while the four living creatures and the four and twenty elders worship him that sitteth on the throne, and the Lamb, the seven spirits neither stand up nor worship. To these "seven spirits of God," the seven churches, to whom the Spirit speaks so many things, are subordinate; as are also their angels, yea, and "the seven angels which stand before God." He is called the seven spirits, not with regard to his essence, which is one, but with regard to his manifold operations.

5. And from Jesus Christ, the faithful witness, the first begotten from the dead, and the prince of the kings of the earth - Three glorious appellations are here given him, and in their proper order. He was the faithful witness of the whole will of God before his death, and in death, and remains such in glory. He rose from the dead, as "the first fruits of them that slept;" and now hath all power both in heaven and earth. He is here styled a prince: but by and by he hears his title of king; yea, King of kings, and Lord of lords." This phrase, the kings of the earth, signifies their power and multitude, and also the nature of their kingdom. It became the Divine Majesty to call them kings with a limitation; especially in this manifesto from his heavenly kingdom; for no creature, much less a sinful man, can bear the title of king in an absolute sense before the eyes of God.

6. To him that loveth us, and, out of that free, abundant love, hath washed us from the guilt and power of our sins with his own blood, and hath made us kings - Partakers of his present, and heirs of his eternal, kingdom. And priests unto his God and Father - To whom we continually offer ourselves, an holy, living sacrifice. To him be the glory - For his love and redemption. And the might - Whereby he governs all things.

7. Behold - In this and the next verse is the proposition, and the summary of the whole book. He cometh - Jesus Christ. Throughout this book, whenever it is said, He cometh, it means his glorious coming. The preparation for this began at the destruction of Jerusalem, and more particularly at the time of writing this book; and goes on, without any interruption, till that grand event is accomplished. Therefore it is never said in this book, He will come; but, He cometh. And yet it is not said, He cometh again: for when he came before, it was not like himself, but in "the form of a servant." But his appearing in glory is properly his coming; namely, in a manner worthy of the Son of God. And every eye - Of the Jews in particular. Shall see him - But with what different emotions, according as they had received or rejected him. And they who have pierced him - They, above all, who pierced his hands, or feet, or side. Thomas saw the print of these wounds even after his resurrection; and the same, undoubtedly, will be seen by all, when he cometh in the clouds of heaven. And all the tribes of the earth - The word tribes, in the Revelation, always means the Israelites: but where another word, such as nations or people, is joined with it, it implies likewise (as here) all the rest of mankind. Shall wail because of him - For terror and pain, if they did not wail before by true repentance. Yea, Amen - This refers to, every eye shall see him. He that cometh saith, Yea; he that testifies it, Amen. The word translated yea is Greek; Amen is Hebrew: for what is here spoken respects both Jew and gentile.

8. I am the Alpha and the Omega, saith the Lord God - Alpha is the first, Omega, the last, letter in the Greek alphabet. Let his enemies boast and rage ever so much in the intermediate time, yet the Lord God is both the Alpha, or beginning, and the Omega, or end, of all things. God is the beginning, as he is the Author and Creator of all things, and as he proposes, declares, and promises so great things: he is the end, as he brings all the things which are here revealed to a complete and glorious conclusion. Again, the beginning and end of a thing is in scripture styled the whole thing. Therefore God is the Alpha and the Omega, the beginning and the end; that is, one who is all things, and always the same.

9. I John - The instruction and preparation of the apostle for the work are described from the ninth to the twentieth verse. ver. 9- 20, Your brother - In the common faith. And companion in the affliction - For the same persecution which carried him to Patmos drove them into Asia. This book peculiarly belongs to those who are under the cross. It was given to a banished man; and men in affliction understand and relish it most. Accordingly, it was little esteemed by the Asiatic church, after the time of Constantine; but highly valued by all the African churches, as it has been since by all the persecuted children of God. In the affliction, and kingdom and patience of Jesus - The kingdom stands in the midst. It is chiefly under various afflictions that faith obtains its part in the kingdom; and whosoever is a partaker of this kingdom is not afraid to suffer for Jesus, 2 Tim. ii, 12. I was in the island Patmos - In the reign of Domitian and of Nerva. And there he saw and wrote all that follows. It was a place

peculiarly proper for these visions. He had over against him, at a small distance, Asia and the seven churches; going on eastward, Jerusalem and the land of Canaan; and beyond this, Antioch, yea, the whole continent of Asia. To the west, he had Romans, Italy, and all Europe, swimming, as it were, in the sea; to the south, Alexandria and the Nile with its outlets, Egypt, and all Africa; and to the north, what was afterwards called Constantinople, on the straits between Europe and Asia. So he had all the three parts of the world which were then known, with all Christendom, as it were, before his eyes; a large theatre for all the various scenes which were to pass before him: as if this island had been made principally for this end, to serve as an observatory for the apostle. For preaching the word of God he was banished thither, and for the testimony of Jesus - For testifying that he is the Christ.

10. I was in the Spirit - That is, in a trance, a prophetic vision; so overwhelmed with the power, and filled with the light, of the Holy Spirit, as to be insensible of outward things, and wholly taken up with spiritual and divine. What follows is one single, connected vision, which St. John saw in one day; and therefore he that would understand it should carry his thought straight on through the whole, without interruption. The other prophetic books are collections of distinct prophecies, given upon various occasions: but here is one single treatise, whereof all the parts exactly depend on each other. chap. iv, 1 is connected with ver. 19 and what is delivered in the fourth chapter goes on directly to the twenty- second. On the Lord's day - On this our Lord rose from the dead: on this the ancients believed he will come to judgment. It was, therefore, with the utmost propriety that St. John on this day both saw and described his coming. And I heard behind me - St. John had his face to the east: our Lord, likewise, in this appearance looked eastward toward Asia, whither the apostle was to write. A great voice, as of a trumpet - Which was peculiarly proper to proclaim the coming of the great King, and his victory over all his enemies.

11. Saying, What thou seest - And hearest. He both saw and heard. This command extends to the whole book. All the books of the New Testament were written by the will of God; but none were so expressly commanded to be written. In a book - So all the Revelation is but one book: nor did the letter to the angel of each church belong to him or his church only; but the whole book was sent to them all. To the churches - Hereafter named; and through them to all churches, in all ages and nations. To Ephesus - Mark. Thomas Smith, who in the year 1671 travelled through all these cities, observes, that from Ephesus to Smyrna is forty-six English miles; from Smyrna to Pergamos, sixty-four; from Pergamos to Thyatira, forty-eight; from Thyatira to Sardis, thirty-three; from Sardis to Philadelphia, twenty-seven; from Philadelphia to Laodicea, about forty-two miles.

12, 13. And I turned to see the voice - That is, to see him whose voice it was. And being turned, I saw - It seems, the vision presented itself gradually. First he heard a voice; and, upon looking behind, he saw the golden candlesticks, and then, in the midst of the candlesticks, which were placed in a circle, he saw one like a son of man - That is, in an human form. As a man likewise our Lord doubtless appears in heaven: though not exactly in this symbolical manner, wherein he presents himself as the head of his church. He next observed that our Lord was clothed with a garment down to the foot, and girt with a golden girdle - Such the Jewish high priests wore. But both of them are here marks of royal dignity likewise. Girt about at the breast - he that is on a journey girds his loins. Girding the breast was an emblem of solemn rest. It seems that the apostle having seen all this, looked up to behold the face of our Lord: but was beat back by the appearance of his flaming eyes, which occasioned his more particularly observing his feet. Receiving strength to raise his eyes again, he saw the stars in his right hand, and the sword coming out of his mouth: but upon beholding the brightness of his glorious countenance, which probably was much increased since the first glance the apostle had of it, he "fell at his feet as dead." During the time that St. John was discovering these several particulars, our Lord seems to have been speaking. And doubtless even his voice, at the very first, bespoke the God: though not so insupportably as his glorious appearance.

14. His head and his hair - That is, the hair of his head, not his whole head. Were white as white wool - Like the Ancient of Days, represented in Daniel's vision, Dan. vii, 9. Wool is commonly supposed to be an emblem of eternity. As snow - Betokening his spotless purity. And his eyes as a flame of fire - Piercing through all things; a token of his omniscience.

15. And his feet like fine brass - Denoting his stability and strength. As if they burned in a furnace - As if having been melted and refined, they were still red hot. And his voice - To the comfort of his friends, and the terror of his enemies. As the voice of many waters - Roaring aloud, and bearing down all before them.

16. And he had in his right hand seven stars - In token of his favour and powerful protection. And out of his mouth went a sharp two-edged sword - Signifying his justice and righteous anger, continually pointed against his enemies as a sword; sharp, to stab; two-edged, to hew. And his countenance was as the sun shineth in his strength - Without any mist or cloud.

17. And I fell at his feet as dead - Human nature not being able to sustain so glorious an appearance. Thus was he prepared (like Daniel of old, whom he peculiarly resembles) for receiving so weighty a prophecy. A great sinking of nature usually precedes a large communication of heavenly

things. St. John, before our Lord suffered, was so intimate with him, as to lean on his breast, to lie in his bosom. Yet now, near seventy years after, the aged apostle is by one glance struck to the ground. What a glory must this be! Ye sinners, be afraid cleanse your hands: purify your hearts. Ye saints, be humble, prepare: rejoice. But rejoice unto him with reverence: an increase of reverence towards this awful majesty can be no prejudice to your faith. Let all petulancy, with all vain curiosity, be far away, while you are thinking or reading of these things. And he laid his right hand upon me - The same wherein he held the seven stars. What did St. John then feel in himself? Saying, Fear not - His look terrifies, his speech strengthens. He does not call John by his name, (as the angels did Zechariah and others,) but speaks as his well known master. What follows is also spoken to strengthen and encourage him. I am - When in his state of humiliation he spoke of his glory, he frequently spoke in the third person, as Matt. xxvi, 64. But he now speaks of his own glory, without any veil, in plain and direct terms. The first and the last - That is, the one, eternal God, who is from everlasting to everlasting, Isaiah xli, 4.

18. And he that liveth - Another peculiar title of God. And I have the keys of death and of hades - That is, the invisible world. In the intermediate state, the body abides in death, the soul in hades. Christ hath the keys of, that is, the power over, both; killing or quickening of the body, and disposing of the soul, as it pleaseth him. He gave St. Peter the keys of the kingdom of heaven; but not the keys of death or of hades. How come then his supposed successor at Rome by the keys of purgatory? From the preceding description, mostly, are taken the titles given to Christ in the following letters, particularly the four first.

19. Write the things which thou hast seen - This day: which accordingly are written, ver. 11-18. And which are - The instructions relating to the present state of the seven churches. These are written, ver. 20-chap. iii, 22. And which shall be hereafter - To the end of the world; written, chap. iv, 1, &c.

20. Write first the mystery - The mysterious meaning of the seven stars - St. John knew better than we do, in how many respects these stars were a proper emblem of those angels: how nearly they resembled each other, and how far they differed in magnitude, brightness, and other circumstances. The seven stars are angels of the seven churches - Mentioned in the eleventh verse. In each church there was one pastor or ruling minister, to whom all the rest were subordinate. This pastor, bishop, or overseer, had the peculiar care over that flock: on him the prosperity of that congregation in a great measure depended, and he was to answer for all those souls at the judgment seat of Christ. And the seven candlesticks are seven churches - How significant an emblem is this! For a candlestick, though of gold, has no light of itself; neither has any church, or child of man. But they receive from Christ the light of truth, holiness, comfort, that it may shine to all around them. As soon as this was spoken St. John wrote it down, even all that is contained in this first chapter. Afterwards what was contained in the second and third chapters was dictated to him in like manner.

II

Of the following letters to the angels of the seven churches it may be necessary to speak first in general, and then particularly. In general we may observe, when the Israelites were to receive the law at Mount Sinai, they were first to be purified; and when the kingdom of God was at hand, John the Baptist prepared men for it by repentance. In like manner we are prepared by these letters for the worthy reception of this glorious Revelation. By following the directions given herein, by expelling incorrigibly wicked men, and putting away all wickedness, those churches were prepared to receive this precious depositum. And whoever in any age would profitably read or hear it, must observe the same admonitions. These letters are a kind of sevenfold preface to the book. Christ now appears in the form of a man, (not yet under the emblem of a lamb,) and speaks mostly in proper, not in figurative, words. It is not till chap. iv, 1, that St. John enters upon that grand vision which takes up the residue of the book. There is in each of these letters,

1. A command to write to the angel of the church;
2. A glorious title of Christ;
3. An address to the angel of that church, containing A testimony of his mixed, or good, or bad state; An exhortation to repentance or steadfastness; A declaration of what will be; generally, of the Lord's coming;
4. A promise to him that overcometh, together with the exhortation, "He that hath an ear to hear, let him hear" The address in each letter is expressed in plain words, the promise, in figurative. In the address our Lord speaks to the angel of each church which then was, and to the members thereof directly; whereas in the promise he speaks of all that should overcome, in whatever church or age, and deals out to them one of the precious promises, (by way of anticipation,) from the last chapters of the book.

1. Write - So Christ dictated to him every word. These things saith he who holdeth the seven stars in his right hand - Such is his mighty power! Such his favour to them and care over them, that they may indeed shine as stars, both by purity of doctrine and holiness of life! Who walketh - According to his

promise, "I am with you always, even to the end of the world." In the midst of the golden candlesticks - Beholding all their works and thoughts, and ready to "remove the candlestick out of its place," if any, being warned, will not repent. Perhaps here is likewise an allusion to the office of the priests in dressing the lamps, which was to keep them always burning before the Lord.

2. I know - Jesus knows all the good and all the evil, which his servants and his enemies suffer and do. Weighty word, "I know," how dreadful will it one day sound to the wicked, how sweet to the righteous! The churches and their angels must have been astonished, to find their several states so exactly described, even in the absence of the apostle, and could not but acknowledge the all-seeing eye of Christ and of his Spirit. With regard to us, to every one of us also he saith, "I know thy works." Happy is he that conceives less good of himself, than Christ knows concerning him. And thy labour - After the general, three particulars are named, and then more largely described in an inverted order,

1. Thy labour
6. Thou hast born for my name's sake and hast not fainted.
2. Thy patience:
5. Thou hast patience:
3. Thou canst not
4. Thou hast tried those who say they are bear evil men: apostles and are not, and hast found them liars. And thy patience - Notwithstanding which thou canst not bear that incorrigibly wicked men should remain in the flock of Christ. And thou hast tried those who say they are apostles, and are not - For the Lord hath not sent them.

4. But I have against thee, that thou hast left thy first love - That love for which all that church was so eminent when St. Paul wrote his epistle to them. He need not have left this. He might have retained it entire to the end. And he did retain it in part, or there could not have remained so much of what was commendable in him. But he had not kept, as he might have done, the first tender love in its vigour and warmth. Reader, hast thou?

5. It is not possible for any to recover the first love, but by taking these three steps,
1. Remember:
2. Repent:
3. Do the first works. Remember from whence thou art fallen - From what degree of faith, love, holiness, though perhaps insensibly. And repent - Which in the very lowest sense implies a deep and lively conviction of thy fall. Of the seven angels, two, at Ephesus and at Pergamos, were in a mixed state; two, at Sardis and at Laodicea, were greatly corrupted: all these are exhorted to repent; as are the followers of Jezebel at Thyatira: two, at Smyrna and Philadelphia, were in a flourishing state, and are therefore only exhorted to steadfastness. There can be no state, either of any pastor, church, or single person, which has not here suitable instructions. All, whether ministers or hearers, together with their secret or open enemies, in all places and all ages, may draw hence necessary self-knowledge, reproof, commendation, warning, or confirmation. Whether any be as dead as the angel at Sardis, or as much alive as the angel at Philadelphia, this book is sent to him, and the Lord Jesus hath something to say to him therein. For the seven churches with their angels represent the whole Christian church, dispersed throughout the whole world, as it subsists, not, as some have imagined, in one age after another, but in every age. This is a point of deep importance, and always necessary to be remembered: that these seven churches are, as it were, a sample of the whole church of Christ, as it was then, as it is now, and as it will be in all ages. Do the first works - Outwardly and inwardly, or thou canst never regain the first love. But if not - By this word is the warning sharpened to those five churches which are called to repent; for if Ephesus was threatened, how much more shall Sardis and Laodicea be afraid! And according as they obey the call or not, there is a promise or a threatening, ver. 5, 16, 22; chap. iii, 3, 20. But even in the threatening the promise is implied, in case of true repentance. I come to thee, and will remove thy candlestick out of its place - I will remove, unless thou repent, the flock now under thy care to another place, where they shall be better taken care of. But from the flourishing state of the church of Ephesus after this, there is reason to believe he did repent.

6. But thou hast this - Divine grace seeks whatever may help him that is fallen to recover his standing. That thou hatest the works of the Nicolaitans - Probably so called from Nicolas, one of the seven deacons, Acts vi, 5. Their doctrines and lives were equally corrupt. They allowed the most abominable lewdness and adulteries, as well as sacrificing to idols; all which they placed among things indifferent, and pleaded for as branches of Christian liberty.

7. He that hath an ear, let him hear - Every man, whoever can hear at all, ought carefully to hear this. What the Spirit saith - In these great and precious promises. To the churches - And in them to every one that overcometh; that goeth on from faith and by faith to full victory over the world, and the flesh, and the devil. In these seven letters twelve promises are contained, which are an extract of all the promises of God. Some of them are not expressly mentioned again in this book, as "the hidden manna," the inscription of "the name of the new Jerusalem," the "sitting upon the throne." Some resemble what is afterwards mentioned, as "the hidden name," chap. xix, 12; "the ruling the nations," chap. xix, 15; "the

morning star," chap. xxii, 16. And some are expressly mentioned, as "the tree of life," chap. xxii, 2; freedom from "the second death," chap. xx, 6; the name in "the book of life," chap. xx, 12; xxi, 27; the remaining "in the temple of God," chap. vii, 15; the inscription of "the name of God and of the Lamb," chap. xiv, 1; xxii, 4. In these promises sometimes the enjoyment of the highest goods, sometimes deliverance from the greatest evils, is mentioned. And each implies the other, so that where either part is expressed, the whole is to be understood. That part is expressed which has most resemblance to the virtues or works of him that was spoken to in the letter preceding. To eat of the tree of life - The first thing promised in these letters is the last and highest in the accomplishment, chap. xxii, 2, 14, 19. The tree of life and the water of life go together, chap. xxii, 1, 2; both implying the living with God eternally. In the paradise of my God - The word paradise means a garden of pleasure. In the earthly paradise there was one tree of life: there are no other trees in the paradise of God.

8. These things saith the first and the last, who was dead and is alive - How directly does this description tend to confirm him against the fear of death! verses 10, 11. ver. 10, 11 Even with the comfort wherewith St. John himself was comforted, chap. i, 17, 18, shall the angel of this church be comforted.

9. I know thy affliction and poverty - A poor prerogative in the eyes of the world! The angel at Philadelphia likewise had in their sight but "a little strength." And yet these two were the most honourable of all in the eyes of the Lord. But thou art rich - In faith and love, of more value than all the kingdoms of the earth. Who say they are Jews - God's own people. And are not - They are not Jews inwardly, not circumcised in heart. But a synagogue of Satan - Who, like them, was a liar and a murderer from the beginning.

10. The first and last words of this verse are particularly directed to the minister; whence we may gather, that his suffering and the affliction of the church were at the same time, and of the same continuance. Fear none of those things which thou art about to suffer - Probably by means of the false Jews. Behold - This intimates the nearness of the affliction. Perhaps the ten days began on the very day that the Revelation was read at Smyrna, or at least very soon after. The devil - Who sets all persecutors to work; and these more particularly. Is about to cast some of you - Christians at Smyrna; where, in the first ages, the blood of many martyrs was shed. Into prison, that ye may be tried - To your unspeakable advantage, chap. iv, 12, 14. And ye shall have affliction - Either in your own persons, or by sympathizing with your brethren. Ten days - (Literally taken) in the end of Domitian's persecution, which was stopped by the edict of the emperor Nerva. Be thou faithful - Our Lord does not say, "till I come," as in the other letters, but unto death - Signifying that the angel of this church should quickly after seal his testimony with his blood; fifty years before the martyrdom of Polycarp, for whom some have mistaken him. And I will give thee the crown of life - The peculiar reward of them who are faithful unto death.

11. The second death - The lake of fire, the portion of the fearful, who do not overcome, chap. xxi, 8.

12. The sword - With which I will cut off the impenitent, verse 16.

13. Where the throne of Satan is - Pergamos was above measure given to idolatry: so Satan had his throne and full residence there. Thou holdest fast my name - Openly and resolutely confessing me before men. Even in the days wherein Antipas - Martyred under Domitian. Was my faithful witness - Happy is he to whom Jesus, the faithful and true witness, giveth such a testimony!

14. But thou hast there - Whom thou oughtest to have immediately cast out from the flock. Them that hold the doctrine of Balaam - Doctrine nearly resembling his. Who taught Balak - And the rest of the Moabites. To cast a stumblingblock before the sons of Israel - They are generally termed, the children, but here, the sons, of Israel, in opposition to the daughters of Moab, by whom Balaam enticed them to fornication and idolatry. To eat things sacrificed to idols - Which, in so idolatrous a city as Pergamos, was in the highest degree hurtful to Christianity. And to commit fornication - Which was constantly joined with the idol-worship of the heathens.

15. In like manner thou also - As well as the angel at Ephesus. Hast them that hold the doctrine of the Nicolaitans - And thou sufferest them to remain in the flock.

16. If not, I come to thee - who wilt not wholly escape when I punish them. And will fight with them - Not with the Nicolaitans, who are mentioned only by the by, but the followers of Balaam. With the sword of my mouth - With my just and fierce displeasure. Balaam himself was first withstood by the angel of the Lord with "his sword drawn," Num. xxii, 23, and afterwards "slain with the sword," Num. xxxi, 8.

17. To him that overcometh - And eateth not of those sacrifices. Will I give of the hidden manna - Described, John vi. The new name answers to this: it is now "hid with Christ in God." The Jewish manna was kept in the ancient ark of the covenant. The heavenly ark of the covenant appears under the trumpet of the seventh angel, chap. xi, 19, where also the hidden manna is mentioned again. It seems properly to mean, the full, glorious, everlasting fruition of God. And I will give him a white stone - The ancients, on many occasions, gave their votes in judgment by small stones; by black, they condemned;

by white ones they acquitted. Sometimes also they wrote on small smooth stones. Here may be an allusion to both. And a new name - So Jacob, after his victory, gained the new name of Israel. Wouldest thou know what thy new name will be? The way to this is plain, - overcome. Till then all thy inquiries are vain. Thou wilt then read it on the white stone.

18. And to the angel of the church at Thyatira - Where the faithful were but a little flock. These things saith the Son of God - See how great he is, who appeared "like a son of man!" chap. i, 13. Who hath eyes as a flame of fire - "Searching the reins and the heart," verse 23. And feet like fine brass - Denoting his immense strength. Job comprises both these, his wisdom to discern whatever is amiss, and his power to avenge it, in one sentence, Job xlii, 2, "No thought is hidden from him, and he can do all things."

19. I know thy love - How different a character is this from that of the angel of the church at Ephesus! The latter could not bear the wicked, and hated the works of the Nicolaitans; but had left his first love and first works. The former retained his first love, and had more and more works, but did bear the wicked, did not withstand them with becoming vehemence. Mixed characters both; yet the latter, not the former, is reproved for his fall, and commanded to repent. And faith, and thy service, and patience - Love is shown, exercised, and improved by serving God and our neighbour; so is faith by patience and good works.

20. But thou sufferest that woman Jezebel - who ought not to teach at all, 1 Tim. ii, 12. To teach and seduce my servants - At Pergamos were many followers of Balaam; at Thyatira, one grand deceiver. Many of the ancients have delivered, that this was the wife of the pastor himself. Jezebel of old led the people of God to open idolatry. This Jezebel, fitly called by her name, from the resemblance between their works, led them to partake in the idolatry of the heathens. This she seems to have done by first enticing them to fornication, just as Balaam did: whereas at Pergamos they were first enticed to idolatry, and afterwards to fornication.

21. And I gave her time to repent - So great is the power of Christ! But she will not repent - So, though repentance is the gift of God, man may refuse it; God will not compel.

22. I will cast her into a bed-into great affliction-and them that commit either carnal or spiritual adultery with her, unless they repent - She had her time before. Of her works - Those to which she had enticed their and which she had committed with them. It is observable, the angel of the church at Thyatira was only blamed for suffering her. This fault ceased when God took vengeance on her. Therefore he is not expressly exhorted to repent, though it is implied.

23. And I will kill her children - Those which she hath born in adultery, and them whom she hath seduced. With death - This expression denotes death by the plague, or by some manifest stroke of God's hand. Probably the remarkable vengeance taken on her children was the token of the certainty of all the rest. And all the churches - To which thou now writest. Shall know that I search the reins - The desires. And hearts - Thoughts.

24. But I say to you who do not hold this doctrine - Of Jezebel. Who have not known the depths of Satan - O happy ignorance! As they speak - That were continually boasting of the deep things which they taught. Our Lord owns they were deep, even deep as hell: for they were the very depths of Satan. Were these the same of which Martin Luther speaks? It is well if there are not some of his countrymen now in England who know them too well! I will lay upon you no other burden - Than that you have already suffered from Jezebel and her adherents.

25. What ye - Both the angel and the church have.

26. By works - Those which I have commanded. To him will I give power over the nations - That is, I will give him to share with me in that glorious victory which the Father hath promised me over all the nations who as yet resist me, Psalm ii, 8, 9.

27. And he shall rule them - That is, shall share with me when I do this. With a rod of iron - With irresistible power, employed on those only who will not otherwise submit; who will hereby be dashed in pieces - Totally conquered.

28. I will give him the morning star - Thou, O Jesus, art the morning star! O give thyself to me! Then will I desire no sun, only thee, who art the sun also. He whom this star enlightens has always morning and no evening. The duties and promises here answer each other; the valiant conqueror has power over the stubborn nations. And he that, after having conquered his enemies, keeps the works of Christ to the end, shall have the morning star, - an unspeakable brightness and peaceable dominion in him.

Wesley's Notes on the Bible - The New Testament
III

1. The seven spirits of God - The Holy Spirit, from whom alone all spiritual life and strength proceed. And the seven stars - which are subordinate to him. Thou hast a name that thou livest - A fair reputation, a goodly outside appearance. But that Spirit seeth through all things, and every empty appearance vanishes before him.

2. The things which remain - In thy soul; knowledge of the truth, good desires, and convictions. Which were ready to die - Wherever pride, indolence, or levity revives, all the fruits of the Spirit are ready to die.

3. Remember how - Humbly, zealously, seriously. Thou didst receive the grace of God once, and hear - His word. And hold fast - The grace thou hast received. And repent - According to the word thou hast heard.

4. Yet thou hast a few names - That is, persons. But though few, they had not separated themselves from the rest; otherwise, the angel of Sardis would not have had them. Yet it was no virtue of his, that they were unspotted; whereas it was his fault that they were but few. Who have not defiled their garments - Either by spotting themselves, or by partaking of other men's sins. They shall walk with me in white - in joy; in perfect holiness; in glory. They are worthy - A few good among many bad are doubly acceptable to God. O how much happier is this worthiness than that mentioned, chap. xvi, 6.

5. He shall be clothed in white raiment - The colour of victory, joy, and triumph. And I will not blot his name out of the book of life - Like that of the angel of the church at Sardis: but he shall live forever. I will confess his name - As one of my faithful servants and soldiers.

7. The holy one, the true one - Two great and glorious names He that hath the key of David - A master of a family, or a prince, has one or more keys, wherewith he can open and shut all the doors of his house or palace. So had David a key, a token of right and sovereignty, which was afterward adjudged to Eliakim, Isaiah xxii, 22. Much more has Christ, the Son of David, the key of the spiritual city of David, the New Jerusalem; the supreme right, power, and authority, as in his own house. He openeth this to all that overcome, and none shutteth: he shutteth it against all the fearful, and none openeth. Likewise when he openeth a door on earth for his works or his servants, none can shut; and when he shutteth against whatever would hurt or defile, none can open.

8. I have given before thee an opened door - To enter into the joy of thy Lord; and, meantime, to go on unhindered in every good work. Thou hast a little strength - But little outward human strength; a little, poor, mean, despicable company. Yet thou hast kept my word - Both in judgment and practice.

9. Behold, I - who have all power; and they must then comply. I will make them come and bow down before thy feet - Pay the thee the lowest homage. And know - At length, that all depends on my love, and that thou hast a place therein. O how often does the judgment of the people turn quite round, when the Lord looketh upon them! Job xlii, 7, &c.

10. Because thou hast kept the word of my patience - The word of Christ is indeed a word of patience. I also will keep thee - O happy exemption from that spreading calamity! From the hour of temptation - So that thou shalt not enter into temptation; but it shall pass over thee. The hour denotes the short time of its continuance; that is, at any one place. At every one it was very sharp, though short; wherein the great tempter was not idle, chap. ii, 10. Which hour shall come upon the whole earth - The whole Roman empire. It went over the Christians, and over the Jews and heathens; though in a very different manner. This was the time of the persecution under the seemingly virtuous emperor Trajan. The two preceding persecutions were under those monsters, Nero and Domitian; but Trajan was so admired for his goodness, and his persecution was of such a nature, that it was a temptation indeed, and did throughly try them that dwelt upon the earth.

11. Thy crown - Which is ready for thee, if thou endure to the end.

12. I will make him a pillar in the temple of my God - I will fix him as beautiful, as useful, and as immovable as a pillar in the church of God. And he shall go out no more - But shall be holy and happy forever. And I will write upon him the name of my God - So that the nature and image of God shall appear visibly upon him. And the name of the city of my God - Giving him a title to dwell in the New Jerusalem. And my new name - A share in that joy which I entered into, after overcoming all my enemies.

14. To the angel of the church at Laodicea - For these St. Paul had had a great concern, Colossians ii, 1. These things saith the Amen - That is, the True One, the God of truth. The beginning - The Author, Prince, and Ruler. Of the creation of God - Of all creatures; the beginning, or Author, by whom God made them all.

15. I know thy works - Thy disposition and behaviour, though thou knowest it not thyself. That thou art neither cold - An utter stranger to the things of God, having no care or thought about them. Nor hot - As boiling water: so ought we to be penetrated and heated by the fire of love. O that thou wert - This wish of our Lord plainly implies that he does not work on us irresistibly, as the fire does on the water which it heats. Cold or hot - Even if thou wert cold, without any thought or profession of religion,

there would be more hope of thy recovery.

16. So because thou art lukewarm - The effect of lukewarm water is well known. I am about to spue thee out of my mouth - I will utterly cast thee from me; that is, unless thou repent.

17. Because thou sayest - Therefore "I counsel thee," &c. I am rich - In gifts and grace, as well as worldly goods. And knowest not that thou art - In God's account, wretched and pitiable.

18. I counsel thee - who art poor, and blind, and naked. To buy of me - Without money or price. Gold purified in the fire - True, living faith, which is purified in the furnace of affliction. And white raiment - True holiness. And eyesalve - Spiritual illumination; the "unction of the Holy One," which teacheth all things.

19. Whomsoever I love - Even thee, thou poor Laodicean! O how much has his unwearied love to do! I rebuke - For what is past. And chasten - That they may amend for the time to come.

20. I stand at the door, and knock - Even at this instant; while he is speaking this word. If any man open - Willingly receive me. I will sup with him - Refreshing him with my graces and gifts, and delighting myself in what I have given. And he with me - In life everlasting.

21. I will give him to sit with me on my throne - In unspeakable happiness and glory. Elsewhere, heaven itself is termed the throne of God: but this throne is in heaven.

22. He that hath an ear, let him hear, &c. - This stands in the three former letters before the promise; in the four latter, after it; clearly dividing the seven into two parts; the first containing three, the last, four letters. The titles given our Lord in the three former letters peculiarly respect his power after his resurrection and ascension, particularly over his church; those in the four latter, his divine glory, and unity with the Father and the Holy Spirit. Again, this word being placed before the promises in the three former letters, excludes the false apostles at Ephesus, the false Jews at Smyrna, and the partakers with the heathens at Pergamos, from having any share therein. In the four latter, being placed after them, it leaves the promises immediately joined with Christ's address to the angel of the church, to show that the fulfilling of these was near; whereas the others reach beyond the end of the world. It should be observed, that the overcoming, or victory, (to which alone these peculiar promises are annexed,) is not the ordinary victory obtained by every believer; but a special victory over great and peculiar temptations, by those that are strong in faith.

IV

We are now entering upon the main prophecy. The whole Revelation may be divided thus:- The first, second, and third chapters contain the introduction; The fourth and fifth, the proposition; The sixth, seventh, eighth, and ninth describe things which are already fulfilled; The tenth to the fourteenth, things which are now fulfilling; The fifteenth to the nineteenth, things which will be fulfilled shortly; The twentieth, twenty-first, and twenty-second, things at a greater distance.

1. After these things - As if he had said, After I had written these letters from the mouth of the Lord. By the particle and, the several parts of this prophecy are usually connected: by the expression, after these things, they are distinguished from each other, chap. vii, 9; xix, 1. By that expression, and after these things, they are distinguished, and yet connected, chap. vii, 1; xv, 5; xviii, 1. St. John always saw and heard, and then immediately wrote down one part after another: and one part is constantly divided from another by some one of these expressions. I saw - Here begins the relation of the main vision, which is connected throughout; as it appears from "the throne, and him that sitteth thereon;" "the Lamb;" (who hitherto has appeared in the form of a man;) " the four living creatures;" and " the four and twenty elders," represented from this place to the end. From this place, it is absolutely necessary to keep in mind the genuine order of the texts, as it stands in the preceding table. A door opened in heaven - Several of these openings are successively mentioned. Here a door is opened; afterward, "the temple of God in heaven," chap. xi, 19; xv, 5; and, at last, "heaven" itself, xix, 11. By each of these St. John gains a new and more extended prospect. And the first voice which I had heard - Namely, that of Christ: afterward, he heard the voices of many others. Said, Come up hither - Not in body, but in spirit; which was immediately done.

2. And immediately I was in the spirit - Even in an higher degree than before, chap. i, 10. And, behold, a throne was set in heaven - St. John is to write "things which shall be;" and, in order thereto, he is here shown, after an heavenly manner, how whatever "shall be," whether good or bad, flows out of invisible fountains; and how, after it is done on the visible theatre of the world and the church, it flows back again into the invisible world, as its proper and final scope. Here commentators divide: some proceed theologically; others, historically; whereas the right way is, to join both together. The court of heaven is here laid open; and the throne of God is, as it were, the center from which everything in the visible world goes forth, and to which everything returns. Here, also, the kingdom of Satan is disclosed; and hence we may extract the most important things out of the most comprehensive and, at the same time, most secret history of the kingdom of hell and heaven. But herein we must be content to know only what is expressly revealed in this book. This describes, not barely what good or evil is successively

transacted on earth, but how each springs from the kingdom of light or darkness, and continually tends to the source whence it sprung: So that no man can explain all that is contained therein, from the history of the church militant only. And yet the histories of past ages have their use, as this book is properly prophetical. The more, therefore, we observe the accomplishment of it, so much the more may we praise God, in his truth, wisdom, justice, and almighty power, and learn to suit ourselves to the time, according to the remarkable directions contained in the prophecy. And one sat on the throne - As a king, governor, and judge. Here is described God, the Almighty, the Father of heaven, in his majesty, glory, and dominion.

3. And he that sat was in appearance - Shone with a visible lustre, like that of sparkling precious stones, such as those which were of old on the high priest's breastplate, and those placed as the foundations of the new Jerusalem, chap. xxi, 19, 20. If there is anything emblematical in the colours of these stones, possibly the jasper, which is transparent and of a glittering white, with an intermixture of beautiful colours, may be a symbol of God's purity, with various other perfections, which shine in all his dispensations. The sardine stone, of a blood-red colour, may be an emblem of his justice, and the vengeance he was about to execute on his enemies. An emerald, being green, may betoken favour to the good; a rainbow, the everlasting covenant. See Gen. ix, 9. And this being round about the whole breadth of the throne, fixed the distance of those who stood or sat round it.

4. And round about the throne - In a circle, are four and twenty thrones, and on the thrones four and twenty elders - The most holy of all the former ages, Isaiah xxiv, 23; Heb. xii, 1; representing the whole body of the saints. Sitting - In general; but falling down when they worship. Clothed in white raiment - This and their golden crowns show, that they had already finished their course and taken their place among the citizens of heaven. They are never termed souls, and hence it is probable that they had glorified bodies already. Compare Matt. xxvii, 52.

5. And out of the throne go forth lightnings - Which affect the sight. Voices - Which affect the hearing. Thunderings - Which cause the whole body to tremble. Weak men account all this terrible; but to the inhabitants of heaven it is a mere source of joy and pleasure, mixed with reverence to the Divine Majesty. Even to the saints on earth these convey light and protection; but to their enemies, terror and destruction.

6. And before the throne is a sea as of glass, like crystal - Wide and deep, pure and clear, transparent and still. Both the "seven lamps of fire" and this sea are before the throne; and both may mean "the seven spirits of God," the Holy Ghost; whose powers and operations are frequently represented both under the emblem of fire and of water. We read again, chap. xv, 2, of "a sea as of glass," where there is no mention of "the seven lamps of fire;" but, on the contrary, the sea itself is "mingled with fire." We read also, chap. xxii, 1, of "a stream of water of life, clear as crystal." Now, the sea which is before the throne, and the stream which goes out of the throne, may both mean the same; namely, the Spirit of God. And in the midst of the throne - With respect to its height. Round about the throne - That is, toward the four quarters, east, west, north, and south. Were four living creatures - Not beasts, no more than birds. These seem to be taken from the cherubim in the visions of Isaiah and Ezekiel, and in the holy of holies. They are doubtless some of the principal powers of heaven; but of what order, it is not easy to determine. It is very probable that the twenty-four elders may represent the Jewish church: their harps seem to intimate their having belonged to the ancient tabernacle service, where they were wont to be used. If so, the living creatures may represent the Christian church. Their number, also, is symbolical of universality, and agrees with the dispensation of the gospel, which extended to all nations under heaven. And the "new song" which they all sing, saying, "Thou hast redeemed us out of every kindred, and tongue, and people, and nation," chap. v, 9, could not possibly suit the Jewish without the Christian church. The first living creature was like a lion - To signify undaunted courage. The second, like a calf - Or ox, Ezek. i, 10, to signify unwearied patience. The third, with the face of a man - To signify prudence and compassion. The fourth, like an eagle - To signify activity and vigour. Full of eyes - To betoken wisdom and knowledge. Before - To see the face of him that sitteth on the throne. And behind - To see what is done among the creatures.

7. And the first - Just such were the four cherubim in Ezekiel, who supported the moving throne of God; whereas each of those that overshadowed the mercy-seat in the holy of holies had all these four faces: whence a late great man supposes them to have been emblematical of the Trinity, and the incarnation of the second Person. A flying eagle - That is, with wings expanded.

8. Each of them hath six wings - As had each of the seraphim in Isaiah's vision. "Two covered his face," in token of humility and reverence: "two his feet," perhaps in token of readiness and diligence for executing divine commissions. Round about and within they are full of eyes. Round about - To see everything which is farther off from the throne than they are themselves. And within - On the inner part of the circle which they make with one another. First, they look from the center to the circumference, then from the circumference to the center. And they rest not - O happy unrest! Day and night - As we speak on earth. But there is no night in heaven. And say, Holy, holy, holy - Is the Three-One God. There are two words in the original, very different from each other; both which we translate holy. The one

means properly merciful; but the other, which occurs here, implies much more. This holiness is the sum of all praise, which is given to the almighty Creator, for all that he does and reveals concerning himself, till the new song brings with it new matter of glory. This word properly signifies separated, both in Hebrew and other languages. And when God is termed holy, it denotes that excellence which is altogether peculiar to himself; and the glory flowing from all his attributes conjoined, shining forth from all his works, and darkening all things besides itself, whereby he is, and eternally remains, in an incomprehensible manner separate and at a distance, not only from all that is impure, but likewise from all that is created. God is separate from all things. He is, and works from himself, out of himself, in himself, through himself, for himself. Therefore, he is the first and the last, the only one and the Eternal, living and happy, endless and unchangeable, almighty, omniscient, wise and true, just and faithful, gracious and merciful. Hence it is, that holy and holiness mean the same as God and Godhead: and as we say of a king, "His Majesty;" so the scripture says of God, "His Holiness," Heb. xii, 10. The Holy Spirit is the Spirit of God. When God is spoken of, he is often named "the Holy One:" and as God swears by his name, so he does also by his holiness; that is, by himself. This holiness is often styled glory: often his holiness and glory are celebrated together, Lev. x, 3; Isaiah vi, 3. For holiness is covered glory, and glory is uncovered holiness. The scripture speaks abundantly of the holiness and glory of the Father, the Son, and the Holy Ghost. And hereby is the mystery of the Holy Trinity eminently confirmed. That is also termed holy which is consecrated to him, and for that end separated from other things: and so is that wherein we may be like God, or united to him. In the hymn resembling this, recorded by Isaiah, Isaiah vi, 3, is added, "The whole earth is full of his glory." But this is deferred in the Revelation, till the glory of the Lord (his enemies being destroyed) fills the earth.

9, 10. And when the living creatures give glory-the elders fall down - That is, as often as the living creatures give glory, immediately the elders fall down. The expression implies, that they did so at the same instant, and that they both did this frequently. The living creatures do not say directly, "Holy, holy, holy art thou;" but only bend a little, out of deep reverence, and say, "Holy, holy, holy is the Lord." But the elders, when they are fallen down, may say, "Worthy art thou, O Lord our God."

11. Worthy art thou to receive - This he receives not only when he is thus praised, but also when he destroys his enemies and glorifies himself anew. The glory and the honour and the power - Answering the thrice-holy of the living creatures, verse 9. ver. 9, For thou hast created all things - Creation is the ground of all the works of God: therefore, for this, as well as for his other works, will he be praised to all eternity. And through thy will they were - They began to be. It is to the free, gracious and powerfully- working will of Him who cannot possibly need anything that all things owe their first existence. And are created - That is, continue in being ever since they were created.

V

1. And I saw - This is a continuation of the same narrative. In the right hand - The emblem of his all-ruling power. He held it openly, in order to give it to him that was worthy. It is scarce needful to observe, that there is not in heaven any real book of parchment or paper or that Christ does not really stand there, in the shape of a lion or of a lamb. Neither is there on earth any monstrous beast with seven heads and ten horns. But as there is upon earth something which, in its kind, answers such a representation; so there are in heaven divine counsels and transactions answerable to these figurative expressions. All this was represented to St. John at Patmos, in one day, by way of vision. But the accomplishment of it extends from that time throughout all ages. Writings serve to inform us of distant and of future things. And hence things which are yet to come are figuratively said to be "written in God's book;" so were at that time the contents of this weighty prophecy. But the book was sealed. Now comes the opening and accomplishing also of the great things that are, as it were, the letters of it. A book written within and without - That is, no part of it blank, full of matter. Sealed with seven seals - According to the seven principal parts contained in it, one on the outside of each. The usual books of the ancients were not like ours, but were volumes or long pieces of parchment, rolled upon a long stick, as we frequently roll silks. Such was this represented, which was sealed with seven seals. Not as if the apostle saw all the seals at once; for there were seven volumes wrapped up one within another, each of which was sealed: so that upon opening and unrolling the first, the second appeared to be sealed up till that was opened, and so on to the seventh. The book and its seals represent all power in heaven and earth given to Christ. A copy of this book is contained in the following chapters. By "the trumpets," contained under the seventh seal, the kingdom of the world is shaken, that it may at length become the kingdom of Christ. By "the vials," under the seventh trumpet, the power of the beast, and whatsoever is connected with it, is broken. This sum of all we should have continually before our eyes: so the whole Revelation flows in its natural order.

2. And I saw a strong angel - This proclamation to every creature was too great for a man to make, and yet not becoming the Lamb himself. It was therefore made by an angel, and one of uncommon eminence.

3. *And none* - No creature; no, not Mary herself. *In heaven, or in earth, neither under the earth* - That is, none in the universe. For these are the three great regions into which the whole creation is divided. *Was able to open the book* - To declare the counsels of God. *Nor to look thereon* - So as to understand any part of it.

4. *And I wept much* - A weeping which sprung from greatness of mind. The tenderness of heart which he always had appeared more clearly now he was out of his own power. The Revelation was not written without tears; neither without tears will it be understood. How far are they from the temper of St. John who inquire after anything rather than the contents of this book! yea, who applaud their own clemency if they excuse those that do inquire into them!

5. *And one of the elders* - Probably one of those who rose with Christ, and afterwards ascended into heaven. Perhaps one of the patriarchs. Some think it was Jacob, from whose prophecy the name of Lion is given him, Gen. xlix, 9. *The Lion of the tribe of Judah* - The victorious prince who is, like a lion, able to tear all his enemies in pieces. *The root of David* - As God, the root and source of David's family, Isaiah xi, 1, 10. *Hath prevailed to open the book* - Hath overcome all obstructions, and obtained the honour to disclose the divine counsels.

6. *And I saw* - First, Christ in or on the midst of the throne; secondly, the four living creatures making the inner circle round him; and, thirdly, the four and twenty elders making a larger circle round him and them. *Standing* - He lieth no more; he no more falls on his face; the days of his weakness and mourning are ended. He is now in a posture of readiness to execute all his offices of prophet, priest, and king. *As if he had been slain* - Doubtless with the prints of the wounds which he once received. And because he was slain, he is worthy to open the book, verse 9, to the joy of his own people, and the terror of his enemies. *Having seven horns* - As a king, the emblem of perfect strength. *And seven eyes* - The emblem of perfect knowledge and wisdom. By these he accomplishes what is contained in the book, namely, by his almighty and all-wise Spirit. To these seven horns and seven eyes answer the seven seals and the sevenfold song of praise, verse 12. In Zechariah, likewise, iii, 9; iv, 10. Zech. iii, 9, Zech. iv, 10 mention is made of "the seven eyes of the Lord, which go forth over all the earth." *Which* - Both the horns and the eyes. *Are the seven spirits of God sent forth into all the earth* - For the effectual working of the Spirit of God goes through the whole creation; and that in the natural, as well as spiritual, world. For could mere matter act or move? Could it gravitate or attract? Just as much as it can think or speak.

7. *And he came* - Here was "Ask of me," Psalm ii, 8, fulfilled in the most glorious manner. *And took* - it is one state of exaltation that reaches from our Lord's ascension to his coming in glory. Yet this state admits of various degrees. At his ascension, "angels, and principalities, and powers were subjected to him." Ten days after, he received from the Father and sent the Holy Ghost. And now he took the book out of the right hand of him that sat upon the throne - who gave it him as a signal of his delivering to him all power in heaven and earth. He received it, in token of his being both able and willing to fulfil all that was written therein.

8. *And when he took the book, the four living creatures fell down* - Now is homage done to the Lamb by every creature. These, together with the elders, make the beginning; and afterward, chap. v, 14, the conclusion. They are together surrounded with a multitude of angels, chap. v, 11, and together sing the new song, as they had before praised God together, chap. iv, 8, &c. *Having every one* - The elders, not the living creatures. *An harp* - Which was one of the chief instruments used for thanksgiving in the temple service: a fit emblem of the melody of their hearts. *And golden phials* - Cups or censers. *Full of incense, which are the prayers of the saints* - Not of the elders themselves, but of the other saints still upon earth, whose prayers were thus emblematically represented in heaven.

9. *And they sing a new song* - One which neither they nor any other had sung before. *Thou hast redeemed us* - So the living creatures also were of the number of the redeemed. This does not so much refer to the act of redemption, which was long before, as to the fruit of it; and so more directly to those who had finished their course, "who were redeemed from the earth," ver. 1, *out of every tribe, and tongue, and people, and nation* - That is, out of all mankind.

10. *And hast made them* - The redeemed. So they speak of themselves also in the third person, out of deep self-abasement. *They shall reign over the earth* - The new earth: herewith agree the golden crowns of the elders. The reign of the saints in general follows, under the trumpet of the seventh angel; particularly after the first resurrection, as also in eternity, chap. xi, 18; xv, 7; xx, 4; xxii, 5;Dan. vii, 27;Psalm xlix, 14.

11. *And I saw* - The many angels. *And heard* - The voice and the number of them. *Round about the elders* - So forming the third circle. It is remarkable, that men are represented through this whole vision as nearer to God than any of the angels. *And the number of them was* - At least two hundred millions, and two millions over. And yet these were but a part of the holy angels. Afterward, chap. vii, 11, St. John heard them all.

12. *Worthy is the Lamb* - The elders said, ver. 9, "Worthy art thou." They were more nearly allied to him than the angels. *To receive the power, &c.* - This sevenfold applause answers the seven seals, of which the four former describe all visible, the latter all invisible, things, made subject to the Lamb. And

every one of these seven words bears a resemblance to the seal which it answers.

13. *And every creature* - In the whole universe, good or bad. *In the heaven, on the earth, under the earth, on the sea* - With these four regions of the world, agrees the fourfold word of praise. What is in heaven, says blessing; what is on earth, honour; what is under the earth, glory: what is on the sea, strength; *is unto him.* This praise from all creatures begins before the opening of the first seal; but it continues from that time to eternity, according to the capacity of each. His enemies must acknowledge his glory; but those in heaven say, Blessed be God and the Lamb. This royal manifesto is, as it were, a proclamation, showing how Christ fulfils all things, and "every knee bows to him," not only on earth, but also in heaven, and under the earth. This book exhausts all things, 1 Cor. xv, 27, 28, and is suitable to an heart enlarged as the sand of the sea. It inspires the attentive and intelligent reader with such a magnanimity, that he accounts nothing in this world great; no, not the whole frame of visible nature, compared to the immense greatness of what he is here called to behold, yea, and in part, to inherit. St. John has in view, through the whole following vision, what he has been now describing, namely, the four living creatures, the elders, the angels, and all creatures, looking together at the opening of the seven seals.

VI

The seven seals are not distinguished from each other by specifying the time of them. They swiftly follow the letters to the seven churches, and all begin almost at the same time. By the four former is shown, that all the public occurrences of all ages and nations, as empire, war, provision, calamities, are made subject to Christ. And instances are intimated of the first in the east, the second in the west, the third in the south, the fourth in the north and the whole world. The contents, as of the phials and trumpets, so of the seals, are shown by the songs of praise and thanksgiving annexed to them. They contain therefore "the power, and riches, and wisdom, and strength, and honour, and glory, and blessing," which the Lamb received. The four former have a peculiar connection with each other; and so have the three latter seals. The former relate to visible things, toward the four quarters to which the four living creatures look. Before we proceed, it may be observed,

1. No man should constrain either himself or another to explain everything in this book. It is sufficient for every one to speak just so far as he understands.

2. We should remember that, although the ancient prophets wrote the occurrences of those kingdoms only with which Israel had to do, yet the Revelation contains what relates to the whole world, through which the Christian church is extended. Yet,

3. We should not prescribe to this prophecy, as if it must needs admit or exclude this or that history, according as we judge one or the other to be of great or small importance. "God seeth not as a man seeth;" therefore what we think great is often omitted, what we think little inserted, in scripture history or prophecy.

4. We must take care not to overlook what is already fulfilled; and not to describe as fulfilled what is still to come. We are to look in history for the fulfilling of the four first seals, quickly after the date of the prophecy. In each of these appears a different horseman. In each we are to consider, first, the horseman himself; secondly, what he does. The horseman himself, by an emblematical prosopopoeia, represents a swift power, bringing with it either,

1. A flourishing state; or,
2. Bloodshed; or,
3. Scarcity of provisions; or,
4. Public calamities. With the quality of each of these riders the colour of his horse agrees. The fourth horseman is expressly termed "death;" the first, with his bow and crown, "a conqueror;" the second, with his great sword, is a warrior, or, as the Roman termed him, Mars; the third, with the scales, has power over the produce of the land. Particular incidents under this or that Roman emperor are not extensive enough to answer any of these horsemen. The action of every horseman intimates farther,

1. Toward the east, wide spread empire, and victory upon victory:
2. Toward the west, much bloodshed:
3. Toward the south, scarcity of provisions:
4. Toward the north, the plague and various calamities.

1. *I heard one*-That is, the first. *Of the living creatures* - Who looks forward toward the east.

2. *And I saw, and behold a white horse, and he that sat on him had a bow* - This colour, and the bow shooting arrows afar off, betoken victory, triumph, prosperity, enlargement of empire, and dominion over many people. Another horseman, indeed, and of quite another kind, appears on a white horse, chap. xix, 11. But he that is spoken of under the first seal must be so understood as to bear a proportion to the horsemen in the second, third, and fourth seal. Nerva succeeded the emperor Domitian at the very time when the Revelation was written, in the year of our Lord 96. He reigned scarce a year alone; and three months before his death he named Trajan for his colleague and successor, and died in

Wesley's Notes on the Bible - The New Testament

the year 98. Trajan's accession to the empire seems to be the dawning of the seven seals. And a crown was given him - This, considering his descent, Trajan could have no hope of attaining. But God gave it him by the hand of Nerva; and then the east soon felt his power. And he went forth conquering and to conquer - That is, from one victory to another. In the year 108 the already victorious Trajan went forth toward the east, to conquer not only Armenia, Assyria, and Mesopotamia, but also the countries beyond the Tigris, carrying the bounds of the Roman empire to a far greater extent than ever. We find no emperor like him for making conquests. He aimed at nothing else; he lived only to conquer. Meantime, in him was eminently fulfilled what had been prophesied of the fourth empire, Dan. ii, 40, vii, 23, that he should "devour, tread down, and break in pieces the whole earth."

3. And when he had opened the second seal, I heard the second living creature - Who looked toward the west. Saying, Come - At each seal it was necessary to turn toward that quarter of the world which it more immediately concerned.

4. There went forth another horse that was red - A colour suitable to bloodshed. And to him that sat thereon it was given to take peace from the earth - Vespasian, in the year 75, had dedicated a temple to Peace; but after a time we hear little more of peace. All is full of war and bloodshed, chiefly in the western world, where the main business of men seemed to be, to kill one another. To this horseman there was given a great sword; and he had much to do with it; for as soon as Trajan ascended the throne, peace was taken from the earth. Decebalus, king of Dacia, which lies westward from Patmos, put the Roman to no small trouble. The war lasted five years, and consumed abundance of men on both sides; yet was only a prelude to much other bloodshed, which followed for a long season. All this was signified by the great sword, which strikes those who are near, as the bow does those who are at a distance.

5. And when he had opened the third seal, I heard the third living creature - Toward the south. Saying, Come. And behold a black horse - A fit emblem of mourning and distress; particularly of black famine, as the ancient poets term it. And he that sat on him had a pair of scales in his hand - When there is great plenty, men scarce think it worth their while to weigh and measure everything, Gen. xli, 49. But when there is scarcity, they are obliged to deliver them out by measure and weight, Ezek. iv, 16. Accordingly, these scales signify scarcity. They serve also for a token, that all the fruits of the earth, and consequently the whole heavens, with their courses and influences; that all the seasons of the year, with whatsoever they produce, in nature or states, are subject to Christ. Accordingly his hand is wonderful, not only in wars and victories, but likewise in the whole course of nature.

6. And I heard a voice - It seems, from God himself. Saying - To the horseman, "Hitherto shalt thou come, and no farther." Let there be a measure of wheat for a penny - The word translated measure, was a Grecian measure, nearly equal to our quart. This was the daily allowance of a slave. The Roman penny, as much as a labourer then earned in a day, was about sevenpence halfpenny English. According to this, wheat would be near twenty shillings per bushel. This must have been fulfilled while the Grecian measure and the Roman money were still in use; as also where that measure was the common measure, and this money the current coin. It was so in Egypt under Trajan. And three measures of barley for a penny - Either barley was, in common, far cheaper among the ancients than wheat, or the prophecy mentions this as something peculiar. And hurt not the oil and the wine - Let there not be a scarcity of everything. Let there be some provision left to supply the want of the rest This was also fulfilled in the reign of Trajan, especially in Egypt, which lay southward from Patmos. In this country, which used to be the granary of the empire, there was an uncommon dearth at the very beginning of his reign; so that he was obliged to supply Egypt itself with corn from other countries. The same scarcity there was in the thirteenth year of his reign, the harvest failing for want of the rising of the Nile: and that not only in Egypt, but in all those other parts of Afric, where the Nile uses to overflow.

7. I heard the voice of the fourth living creature - Toward the north.

8. And I saw, and behold a pale horse - Suitable to pale death, his rider. And hades - The representative of the state of separate souls. Followeth even with him - The four first seals concern living men. Death therefore is properly introduced. Hades is only occasionally mentioned as a companion of death. So the fourth seal reaches to the borders of things invisible, which are comprised in the three last seals. And power was given to him over the fourth part of the earth - What came single and in a lower degree before, comes now together, and much more severely. The first seal brought victory with it: in the second was "a great sword;" but here a scimitar. In the third was moderate dearth; here famine, and plague, and wild beasts beside. And it may well be, that from the time of Trajan downwards, the fourth part of men upon the earth, that is, within the Roman empire, died by sword, famine, pestilence, and wild beasts. "At that time," says Aurelius Victor, "the Tyber overflowed much more fatally than under Nerva, with a great destruction of houses and there was a dreadful earthquake through many provinces, and a terrible plague and famine, and many places consumed by fire." By death - That is, by pestilence wild beasts have, at several times, destroyed abundance of men; and undoubtedly there was given them, at this time, an uncommon fierceness and strength. It is observable that war brings on scarcity, and scarcity pestilence, through want of wholesome sustenance; and

pestilence, by depopulating the country, leaves the few survivors an easier prey to the wild beasts. And thus these judgments make way for one another in the order wherein they are here represented. What has been already observed may be a fourfold proof that the four horsemen, as with their first entrance in the reign of Trajan, (which does by no means exhaust the contents of the four first seals,) so with all their entrances in succeeding ages, and with the whole course of the world and of visible nature, are in all ages subject to Christ, subsisting by his power, and serving his will, against the wicked, and in defense of the righteous. Herewith, likewise, a way is paved for the trumpets which regularly succeed each other; and the whole prophecy, as to what is future, is confirmed by the clear accomplishment of this part of it.

9. And when he opened the fifth seal - As the four former seals, so the three latter, have a close connection with each other. These all refer to the invisible world; the fifth, to the happy dead, particularly the martyrs; the sixth, to the unhappy; the seventh, to the angels, especially those to whom the trumpets are given. And I saw - Not only the church warring under Christ, and the world warring under Satan; but also the invisible hosts, both of heaven and hell, are described in this book. And it not only describes the actions of both these armies upon earth; but their respective removals from earth, into a more happy or more miserable state, succeeding each other at several times, distinguished by various degrees, celebrated by various thanksgivings; and also the gradual increase of expectation and triumph in heaven, and of terror and misery in hell. Under the altar - That is, at the foot of it. Two altars are mentioned in the Revelation, "the golden altar" of incense, chap. ix, 13; and the altar of burnt-offerings, mentioned here, and chap. viii, 5, xiv, 18, xvi, 7. At this the souls of the martyrs now prostrate themselves. By and by their blood shall be avenged upon Babylon; but not yet, whence it appears that the plagues in the fourth seal do not concern Rome in particular.

10. And they cried - This cry did not begin now, but under the first Roman persecution. The Roman themselves had already avenged the martyrs slain by the Jews on that whole nation. How long - They knew their blood would be avenged; but not immediately, as is now shown them. O Lord - The Greek word properly signifies the master of a family: it is therefore beautifully used by these, who are peculiarly of the household of God. Thou Holy One and true - Both the holiness and truth of God require him to execute judgment and vengeance. Dost thou not judge and avenge our blood? - There is no impure affection in heaven: therefore, this desire of theirs is pure and suitable to the will of God. The martyrs are concerned for the praise of their Master, of his holiness and truth: and the praise is given him, chap. xix, 2, where the prayer of the martyrs is changed into a thanksgiving:- Thou holy One and true: "True and right are thy judgments." How long dost thou not judge "He hath judged the great whore, and avenge our blood? and hath avenged the blood of his servants."

11. And there was given to every one a white robe - An emblem of innocence, joy, and victory, in token of honour and favourable acceptance. And it was said to them - They were told how long. They were not left in that uncertainty. That they should rest - Should cease from crying. They rested from pain before. A time - This word has a peculiar meaning in this book, to denote which, we may retain the original word chronos. Here are two classes of martyrs specified, the former killed under heathen Rome, the latter, under papal Rome. The former are commanded to rest till the latter are added to them. There were many of the former in the days of John: the first fruits of the latter died in the thirteenth century. Now, a time, or chronos, is 1111 years. This chronos began A. 98, and continued to the year 1209; or from Trajan's persecution, to the first crusade against the Waldenses. Till - It is not said, Immediately after this time is expired, vengeance shall be executed; but only, that immediately after this time their brethren and fellowservants will come to them. This event will precede the other; and there will be some space between.

12. And I saw - This sixth seal seems particularly to point out God's judgment on the wicked departed. St. John saw how the end of the world was even then set before those unhappy spirits. This representation might be made to them, without anything of it being perceived upon earth. The like representation is made in heaven, chap. xi, 18. And there was a great earthquake - Or shaking, not of the earth only, but the heavens. This is a farther description of the representation made to those unhappy souls.

13. And the stars fell to, or towards, the earth - Yea, and so they surely will, let astronomers fix their magnitude as they please. As a fig tree casteth its untimely figs, when it is shaken by a mighty wind - How sublimely is the violence of that shaking expressed by this comparison!

14. And the heavens departed as a book that is rolled together - When the scripture compares some very great with a little thing, the majesty and omnipotence of God, before whom great things are little, is highly exalted. Every mountain and island - What a mountain is to the land, that an island is to the sea.

15. And the kings of the earth - They who had been so in their day. And the great men and chief captains - The generals and nobles. Hid themselves - So far as in them lay. In the rocks of the mountains - There are also rocks on the plains; but they were rocks on high, which they besought to fall upon them.

16. To the mountains and the rocks - Which were tottering already, verse

1. And after these things - What follows is a preparation for the seventh seal, which is the weightiest of all. It is connected with the sixth by the particle and; whereas what is added, verse 9, stands free and unconnected. I saw four angels - Probably evil ones. They have their employ with the four first trumpets, as have other evil angels with the three last; namely, the angel of the abyss, the four bound in the Euphrates, and Satan himself. These four angels would willingly have brought on all the calamities that follow without delay. But they were restrained till the servants of God were sealed, and till the seven angels were ready to sound: even as the angel of the abyss was not let loose, nor the angels in the Euphrates unbound, neither Satan cast to the earth, till the fifth, sixth, and seventh angels severally sounded. Standing on the four corners of the earth - East, west, south, north. In this order proceed the four first trumpets. Holding the four winds - Which else might have softened the fiery heat, under the first, second, and third trumpet. That the wind should not blow upon the earth, nor on the sea, nor on any tree - It seems, that these expressions betoken the several quarters of the world; that the earth signifies that to the east of Patmos, Asia, which was nearest to St. John, and where the trumpet of the first angel had its accomplishment. Europe swims in the sea over against this; and is accordingly termed by the prophets, "the islands." The third part, Africa, seems to be meant, chap. viii, 7, 8, 10, by "the streams of water," or "the trees," which grow plentifully by them.

2. And I saw another (a good) angel ascending from the east - The plagues begin in the east; so does the sealing. Having the seal of the only living and true God: and he cried with a loud voice to the four angels - Who were hasting to execute their charge. To whom it was given to hurt the earth and the sea - First, and afterwards "the trees."

3. Hurt not the earth, till we - Other angels were joined in commission with him. Have sealed the servants of our God on their foreheads - Secured the servants of God of the twelve tribes from the impending calamities; whereby they shall be as clearly distinguished from the rest, as if they were visibly marked on their foreheads.

4. Of the children of Israel - To these will afterwards be joined a multitude out of all nations. But it may be observed, this is not the number of all the Israelites who are saved from Abraham or Moses to the end of all things; but only of those who were secured from the plagues which were then ready to fall on the earth. It seems as if this book had, in many places, a special view to the people of Israel.

5. Judah is mentioned first, in respect of the kingdom, and of the Messiah sprung therefrom.

7. After the Levitical ceremonies were abolished, Levi was again on a level with his brethren.

8. Of the tribe of Joseph - Or Ephraim; perhaps not mentioned by name, as having been, with Daniel, the most idolatrous of all the tribes. It is farther observable of Daniel, that it was very early reduced to a single family; which family itself seems to have been cut off in war, before the time of Ezra; for in the Chronicles, where the posterity of the patriarchs is recited, Dan. is wholly omitted.

9. A great multitude - Of those who had happily finished their course. Such multitudes are afterwards described, and still higher degrees of glory which they attain after a sharp fight and magnificent victory, chap. xiv, 1; xv, 2; xix, 1; xx, 4. There is an inconceivable variety in the degrees of reward in the other world. Let not any slothful one say, "If I get to heaven at all, I will be content:" such an one may let heaven go altogether. In worldly things, men are ambitious to get as high as they can. Christians have a far more noble ambition. The difference between the very highest and the lowest state in the world is nothing to the smallest difference between the degrees of glory. But who has time to think of this? Who is at all concerned about it? Standing before the throne - In the full vision of God. And palms in their hands - Tokens of joy and victory.

10. Salvation to our God - Who hath saved us from all evil into all the happiness of heaven. The salvation for which they praise God is described, verse 15; that for which they praise the Lamb, verse 14; and both, in the sixteenth and seventeenth verses. ver. 16, 17

11. And all the angels stood - In waiting. Round about the throne, and the elders and the four living creatures - That is, the living creatures, next the throne; the elders, round these; and the angels, round them both. And they fell on their faces - So do the elders, once only, chap. xi, 16. The heavenly ceremonial has its fixed order and measure.

12. Amen - With this word all the angels confirm the words of the "great multitude;" but they likewise carry the praise much higher. The blessing, and the glory, and the wisdom, and the thanksgiving, and the honour, and the power, and the strength, be unto our God forever and ever - Before the Lamb began to open the seven seals, a sevenfold hymn of praise was brought him by many angels, chap. v, 12. Now he is upon opening the last seal, and the seven angels are going to receive seven trumpets, in order to make the kingdoms of the world subject to God. All the angels give sevenfold praise to God.

13. And one of the elders - What stands, verses 13-17, ver. 13-17 might have immediately followed the tenth verse; but that the praise of the angels, which was at the same time with that of the "great multitude," came in between. Answered - He answered St. John's desire to know, not any words

that he spoke.

14. My Lord - Or, my master; a common term of respect. So Zechariah, likewise, bespeaks the angel, Zech. i, 9; iv, 4; vi, 4. Thou knowest - That is, I know not; but thou dost. These are they - Not martyrs; for these are not such a multitude as no man can number. But as all the angels appear here, so do all the souls of the righteous who had lived from the beginning of the world. Who come - He does not say, who did come; but, who come now also: to whom, likewise, pertain all who will come hereafter. Out of great affliction - Of various kinds, wisely and graciously allotted by God to all his children. And have washed their robes - From all guilt. And made them white - In all holiness. By the blood of the Lamb - Which not only cleanses, but adorns us also.

15. Therefore - Because they came out of great affliction, and have washed their robes in his blood. Are they before the throne - It seems, even nearer than the angels. And serve him day and night - Speaking after the manner of men; that is, continually. In his temple - Which is in heaven. And he shall have his tent over them - Shall spread his glory over them as a covering.

16. Neither shall the sun light on them - For God is there their sun. Nor any painful heat, or inclemency of seasons.

17. For the Lamb will feed them - With eternal peace and joy; so that they shall hunger no more. And will lead them to living fountains of water - The comforts of the Holy Ghost; so that they shall thirst no more. Neither shall they suffer or grieve any more; for God "will wipe away all tears from their eyes."

VIII

1. And when he had opened the seventh seal, there was silence in heaven - Such a silence is mentioned but in this one place. It was uncommon, and highly observable: for praise is sounding in heaven day and night. In particular, immediately before this silence, all the angels, and before them the innumerable multitude, had been crying with a loud voice; and now all is still at once: there is an universal pause. Hereby the seventh seal is very remarkably distinguished from the six preceding. This silence before God shows that those who were round about him were expecting, with the deepest reverence, the great things which the Divine Majesty would farther open and order. Immediately after, the seven trumpets are heard, and a sound more august than ever. Silence is only a preparation: the grand point is, the sounding the trumpets to the praise of God. About half an hour - To St. John, in the vision, it might seem a common half hour.

2. And I saw - The seven trumpets belong to the seventh seal, as do the seven phials to the seventh trumpet. This should be carefully remembered, that we may not confound together the times which follow each other. And yet it may be observed, in general, concerning the times of the incidents mentioned in this book, it is not a certain rule, that every part of the text is fully accomplished before the completion of the following part begins. All things mentioned in the epistles are not full accomplished before the seals are opened; neither are all things mentioned under the seals fulfilled before the trumpets begin; nor yet is the seventh trumpet wholly past before the phials are poured out. Only the beginning of each part goes before the beginning of the following. Thus the epistles begin before the seals, the seals before the trumpets, the trumpets before the phials. One epistle begins before another, one seal before another, one trumpet especially before another, one phial before another. Yet, sometimes, what begins later than another thing ends sooner; and what begins earlier than another thing ends later: so the seventh trumpet begins earlier than the phials, and yet extends beyond them all. The seven angels which stood before God - A character of the highest eminence. And seven trumpets were given them. - When men desire to make known openly a thing of public concern, they give a token that may be seen or heard far and wide; and, among such, none are more ancient than trumpets, Lev. xxv, 9; Num. x, 2; Amos iii, 6. The Israelites, in particular, used them, both in the worship of God and in war; therewith openly praising the power of God before, after, and in, the battle, Josh. vi, 4; 2 Chron. xiii, 14, &c. And the angels here made known by these trumpets the wonderful works of God, whereby all opposing powers are successively shaken, till the kingdom of the world becomes the kingdom of God and his Anointed. These trumpets reach nearly from the time of St. John to the end of the world; and they are distinguished by manifest tokens. The place of the four first is specified; namely, east, west, south, and north successively: in the three last, immediately after the time of each, the place likewise is pointed out. The seventh angel did not begin to sound, till after the going forth of the second woe: but the trumpets were given to him and the other six together; (as were afterward the phials to the seven angels;) and it is accordingly said of all the seven together, that "they prepared themselves to sound." These, therefore, were not men, as some have thought, but angels, properly so called.

3. And - In the second verse, the "trumpets were given" to the seven angels; and in the sixth, they "prepared to sound." But between these, the incense of this angel and the prayers of the saints are mentioned; the interposing of which shows, that the prayers of the saints and the trumpets of the angels go together: and these prayers, with the effects of them, may well be supposed to extend through all the

Wesley's Notes on the Bible - The New Testament

seven. Another angel - Another created angel. Such are all that are here spoken of. In this part of the Revelation, Christ is never termed an angel; but, "the Lamb." Came and stood at the altar - Of burnt-offerings. And there was given him a golden censer - A censer was a cup on a plate or saucer. This was the token and the business of the office. And much incense was given-Incense generally signifies prayer: here it signifies the longing desires of the angels, that the holy counsel of God might be fulfilled. And there was much incense; for as the prayers of all the saints in heaven and earth are here joined together: so are the desires of all the angels which are brought by this angel. That he might place it - It is not said, offer it; for he was discharging the office of an angel, not a priest. With the prayers of all the saints - At the same time; but not for the saints. The angels are fellowservants with the saints, not mediators for them.

4. And the smoke of the incense came up before God, with the prayers of the saints - A token that both were accepted.

5. And there were thunderings, and lightnings, and voices, and an earthquake - These, especially when attended with fire, are emblems of God's dreadful judgments, which are immediately to follow.

6. And the seven angels prepared themselves to sound - That each, when it should come to his turn, might sound without delay. But while they do sound, they still stand before God.

7. And the first sounded - And every angel continued to sound, till all which his trumpet brought was fulfilled and till the next began. There are intervals between the three woes, but not between the four first trumpets. And there was hail and fire mingled with blood, and there were cast upon the earth - The earth seems to mean Asia; Palestine, in particular. Quickly after the Revelation was given, the Jewish calamities under Adrian began: yea, before the reign of Trajan was ended. And here the trumpets begin. Even under Trajan, in the year 114, the Jews made an insurrection with a most dreadful fury; and in the parts about Cyrene, in Egypt, and in Cyprus, destroyed four hundred and sixty thousand persons. But they were repressed by the victorious power of Trajan, and afterward slaughtered themselves in vast multitudes. The alarm spread itself also into Mesopotamia, where Lucius Quintius slew a great number of them. They rose in Judea again in the second year of Adrian; but were presently quelled. Yet in 133 they broke out more violently than ever, under their false messiah Barcochab; and the war continued till the year 135, when almost all Judea was desolated. In the Egyptian plague also hail and fire were together. But here hail is to be taken figuratively, as also blood, for a vehement, sudden, powerful, hurtful invasion; and fire betokens the revenge of an enraged enemy, with the desolation therefrom. And they were cast upon the earth - That is, the fire and hail and blood. But they existed before they were cast upon the earth. The storm fell, the blood flowed, and the flames raged round Cyrene, and in Egypt, and Cyprus, before they reached Mesopotamia and Judea. And the third part of the earth was burnt up - Fifty well-fortified cities, and nine hundred and eighty-five well-inhabited towns of the Jews, were wholly destroyed in this war. Vast tracts of land were likewise left desolate and without inhabitant. And the third part of the trees was burned up, and all the green grass was burned up - Some understand by the trees, men of eminence among the Jews; by the grass, the common people. The Roman spared many of the former: the latter were almost all destroyed. Thus vengeance began at the Jewish enemies of Christ's kingdom; though even then the Roman did not quite escape. But afterwards it came upon them more and more violently: the second trumpet affects the Roman heathens in particular; the third, the dead, unholy Christians; the fourth, the empire itself.

8. And the second angel sounded, and as it were a great mountain burning with fire was cast into the sea - By the sea, particularly as it is here opposed to the earth, we may understand the west, or Europe; and chiefly the middle parts of it, the vast Roman empire. A mountain here seems to signify a great force and multitude of people. Jer. li, 25; so this may point at the irruption of the barbarous nations into the Roman empire. The warlike Goths broke in upon it about the year 21, and from that time the irruption of one nation after another never ceased till the very form of the Roman empire, and all but the name, was lost. The fire may mean the fire of war, and the rage of those savage nations. And the third part of the sea became blood - This need not imply, that just a third part of the Roman was slain; but it is certain an inconceivable deal of blood was shed in all these invasions.

9. And the third part of the creatures that were in the sea - That is, of all sorts of men, of every station and degree. Died - By those merciless invaders. And the third part of the ships were destroyed - It is a frequent thing to resemble a state or republic to a ship, wherein many people are embarked together, and share in the same dangers. And how many states were utterly destroyed by those inhuman conquerors! Much likewise of this was literally fulfilled. How often was the sea tinged with blood! How many of those who dwelt mostly upon it were killed! And what number of ships destroyed!

10. And the third angel sounded, and there fell from heaven a great star, and it fell on the third part of the rivers - It seems Africa is meant by the rivers; (with which this burning part of the world abounds in an especial manner;) Egypt in particular, which the Nile overflows every year far and wide. In the whole African history, between the irruption of the barbarous nations into the Roman empire, and the ruin of the western empire, after the death of Valentinian the Third, there is nothing more momentous than the Arian calamity, which sprung up in the year 315. It is not possible to tell how many persons,

particularly at Alexandria, in all Egypt, and in the neighbouring countries, were destroyed by the rage of the Arians. Yet Africa fared better than other parts of the empire, with regard to the barbarous nations, till the governor of it, whose wife was a zealous Arian, and aunt to Genseric, king of the Vandals, was, under that pretense, unjustly accused before the empress Placidia. He was then prevailed upon to invite the Vandals into Afric; who under Genseric, in the year 428, founded there a kingdom of their own, which continued till the year 533. Under these Vandal kings the true believers endured all manner of afflictions and persecutions. And thus Arianism was the inlet to all heresies and calamities, and at length to Mahometanism itself. This great star was not an angel, (angels are not the agents in the two preceding or the following trumpet,) but a teacher of the church, one of the stars in the right hand of Christ. Such was Arius. He fell from on high, as it were from heaven, into the most pernicious doctrines, and made in his fall a gazing on all sides, being great, and now burning as a torch. He fell on the third part of the rivers - His doctrine spread far and wide, particularly in Egypt. And on the fountains of water - wherewith Afric abounds.

11. And the name of the star is called Wormwood - The unparalleled bitterness both of Arius himself and of his followers show the exact propriety of his title. And the third part of the waters became wormwood - A very considerable part of Afric was infected with the same bitter doctrine and Spirit. And many men (though not a third part of them) died - By the cruelty of the Arians.

12. And the fourth angel sounded, and the third part of the sun was smitten - Or struck. After the emperor Theodosius died, and the empire was divided into the eastern and the western, the barbarous nations poured in as a flood. The Goths and Hunns in the years 403 and 405 fell upon Italy itself with an impetuous force; and the former, in the year 410, took Rome by storm, and plundered it without mercy. In the year 452 Attila treated the upper part of Italy in the same manner. In 455 Valentinian the Third was killed, and Genseric invited from Afric. He plundered Rome for fourteen days together. Recimer plundered it again in 472. During all these commotions, one province was lost after another, till, in the year 476, Odoacer seized upon Rome, deposed the emperor, and put an end to the empire itself. An eclipse of the sun or moon is termed by the Hebrews, a stroke. Now, as such a darkness does not come all at once, but by degrees, so likewise did the darkness which fell on the Roman, particularly the western empire; for the stroke began long before Odoacer, namely, when the barbarians first conquered the capital city. And the third part of the moon, and the third part of the stars; so that the third part of them was darkened - As under the first, second, and third trumpets by "the earth," "sea, " and "rivers," are to be understood the men that inhabit them; so here by the sun, moon, and stars, may be understood the men that live under them, who are so overwhelmed with calamities in those days of darkness, that they can no longer enjoy the light of heaven: unless it may be thought to imply their being killed; so that the sun, moon, and stars shine to them no longer. The very same expression we find in Ezek. xxxii, 8. "I will darken all the lights of heaven over them." As then the fourth seal transcends the three preceding seals, so does the fourth trumpet the three preceding trumpets. For in this not the third part of the earth, or sea, or rivers only, but of all who are under the sun, are affected. And the day shone not for a third part thereof - That is, shone with only a third part of its usual brightness. And the night likewise - The moon and stars having lost a third part of their lustre, either with regard to those who, being dead, saw them no longer, or those who saw them with no satisfaction. The three last trumpets have the time of their continuance fixed, and between each of them there is a remarkable pause: whereas between the four former there is no pause, nor is the time of their continuance mentioned; but all together these four seem to take up a little less than four hundred years.

13. And I saw, and heard an angel flying - Between the trumpets of the fourth and fifth angel. In the midst of heaven - The three woes, as we shall see, stretch themselves over the earth from Persia eastward, beyond Italy, westward; all which space had been filled with the gospel by the apostles. In the midst of this lies Patmos, where St. John saw this angel, saying, Woe, woe, woe - Toward the end of the fifth century, there were many presages of approaching calamities. To the inhabitants of the earth - All without exception. Heavy trials were coming on them all. Even while the angel was proclaiming this, the preludes of these three woes were already in motion. These fell more especially on the Jews. As to the prelude of the first woe in Persia, Isdegard II., in 454, was resolved to abolish the sabbath, till he was, by Rabbi Mar, diverted from his purpose. Likewise in the year 474, Phiruz afflicted the Jews much, and compelled many of them to apostatize. A prelude of the second woe was the rise of the Saracens, who, in 510, fell into Arabia and Palestine. To prepare for the third woe, Innocent I., and his successors, not only endeavoured to enlarge their episcopal jurisdiction beyond all bounds, but also their worldly power, by taking every opportunity of encroaching upon the empire, which as yet stood in the way of their unlimited monarchy.

IX

1. And the fifth angel sounded, and I saw a star - Far different from that mentioned, chap. viii, 11. This star belongs to the invisible world. The third woe is occasioned by the dragon cast out of heaven; the second takes place at the loosing of the four angels who were bound in the Euphrates. The first is here brought by the angel of the abyss, which is opened by this star, or holy angel. Falling to the earth - Coming swiftly and with great force. And to him was given - when he was come. The key of the bottomless pit - A deep and hideous prison; but different from "the lake of fire."

2. And there arose a smoke out of the pit - The locusts, who afterwards rise out of it, seem to be, as we shall afterwards see, the Persians; agreeable to which, this smoke is their detestable idolatrous doctrine, and false zeal for it, which now broke out in an uncommon paroxysm. As the smoke of a great furnace - where the clouds of it rise thicker and thicker, spread far and wide, and press one upon another, so that the darkness increases continually. And the sun and the air were darkened - A figurative expression, denoting heavy affliction. This smoke occasioned more and more such darkness over the Jews in Persia.

3. And out of the smoke - Not out of the bottomless pit, but from the smoke which issued thence. There went forth locusts - A known emblem of a numerous, hostile, hurtful people. Such were the Persians, from whom the Jews, in the sixth century, suffered beyond expression. In the year 540 their academies were stopped, nor were they permitted to have a president for near fifty years. In 589 this affliction ended; but it began long before 540. The prelude of it was about the year 455 and 47iv, the main storm came on in the reign of Cabades, and lasted from 483 to 532. Toward the beginning of the sixth century, Mar Rab Isaac, president of the academy, was put to death. Hereon followed an insurrection of the Jews, which lasted seven years before they were conquered by the Persians. Some of them were then put to death, but not many; the rest were closely imprisoned. And from this time the nation of the Jews were hated and persecuted by the Persians, till they had well nigh rooted them out. The scorpions of the earth - The most hurtful kind. The scorpions of the air have wings.

4. And it was commanded them - By the secret power of God. Not to hurt the grass, neither any green thing, nor any tree - Neither those of low, middling, or high degree, but only such of them as were not sealed - Principally the unbelieving Israelites. But many who were called Christians suffered with them.

5. Not to kill them - Very few of them were killed: in general, they were imprisoned and variously tormented.

6. The men - That is, the men who are so tormented.

7. And the appearances - This description suits a people neither throughly civilized, nor entirely savage; and such were the Persians of that age. Of the locusts are like horses - With their riders. The Persians excelled in horsemanship. And on their heads are as it were crowns - Turbans. And their faces are as the faces of men - Friendly and agreeable.

8. And they had hair as the hair of women - All the Persians of old gloried in long hair. And their teeth were as the teeth of lions - Breaking and tearing all things in pieces.

9. And the noise of their wings was as the noise of chariots of many horses - With their war-chariots, drawn by many horses, they, as it were, flew to and fro.

10. And they have tails like scorpions - That is, each tail is like a scorpion, not like the tail of a scorpion. To hurt the unsealed men five months - Five prophetic months; that is, seventy-nine common years So long did these calamities last.

11. And they have over them a king - One by whom they are peculiarly directed and governed. His name is Abaddon - Both this and Apollyon signify a destroyer. By this he is distinguished from the dragon, whose proper name is Satan.

12. One woe is past; behold, there come yet two woes after these things - The Persian power, under which was the first woe, was now broken by the Saracens: from this time the first pause made a wide way for the two succeeding woes. In 589, when the first woe ended, Mahomet was twenty years old, and the contentions of the Christians with each other were exceeding great. In 591 Chosroes II. reigned in Persia, who, after the death of the emperor, made dreadful disturbances in the east, Hence Mahomet found an open door for his new religion and empire. And when the usurper Phocas had, in the year 606, not only declared the Bishop of Rome, Boniface III., universal bishop, but also the church of Rome the head of all churches, this was a sure step to advance the Papacy to its utmost height. Thus, after the passing away of the first woe, the second, yea, and the third, quickly followed; as indeed they were both on the way together with it before the first effectually began.

13. And the sixth angel sounded - Under this angel goes forth the second woe. And I heard a voice from the four corners of the golden altar - This golden altar is the heavenly pattern of the Levitical altar of incense. This voice signified that the execution of the wrath of God, mentioned verses 20, 21, ver. 20, 21 should, at no intercession, be delayed any longer.

14. Loose the four angels - To go every way; to the four quarters. These were evil angels, or they

would not have been bound. Why, or how long, they were bound we know not.

15. And the four angels were loosed, who were prepared - By loosing them, as well as by their strength and rage. To kill the third part of men - That is, an immense number of them. For the hour, and day, and month, and year - All this agrees with the slaughter which the Saracens made for a long time after Mahomet's death. And with the number of angels let loose agrees the number of their first and most eminent caliphs. These were Ali, Abubeker, Omar, and Osman. Mahomet named Ali, his cousin and son-in-law, for his successor; but he was soon worked out by the rest, till they severally died, and so made room for him. They succeeded each other, and each destroyed innumerable multitudes of men. There are in a prophetic Com. Years. Com. Days. Hour 8 \ Day 196 \ in all 212 years. Month 15 318 / Year 196 117 / Now, the second woe, as also the beginning of the third, has its place between the ceasing of the locusts and the rising of the beast out of the sea, even at the time that the Saracens, who were chiefly cavalry, were in the height of their carnage; from their, first caliph, Abubeker, till they were repulsed from Rome under Leo IV. These 212 years may therefore be reckoned from the year 634 to 847. The gradation in reckoning the time, beginning with the hour and ending with a year, corresponds with their small beginning and vast increase. Before and after Mahomet's death, they had enough to do to settle their affairs at home. Afterwards Abubeker went farther, and in the year 634 gained great advantage over the Persians and Rom. in Syria. Under Omar was the conquest of Mesopotamia, Palestine, and Egypt made. Under Osman, that of Afric, (with the total suppression of the Roman government in the year 647,) of Cyprus, and of all Persia in 651. After Ali was dead, his son Ali Hasen, a peaceable prince, was driven out by Muavia; under whom, and his successors, the power of the Saracens so increased, that within fourscore years after Mahomet's death they had extended their conquests farther than the warlike Roman did in four hundred years.

16. And the number of the horsemen was two hundred millions - Not that so many were ever brought into the field at once, but (if we understand the expression literally) in the course of "the hour, and day, and month, and year." So neither were "the third part of men killed" at once, but during that course of years.

17. And thus I saw the horses and them that sat on them in the vision - St. John seems to add these words, in the vision, to intimate that we are not to take this description just according to the letter. Having breastplates of fire - Fiery red. And hyacinth - Dun blue. And brimstone - A faint yellow. Of the same colour with the fire and smoke and brimstone, which go out of the mouths of their horses. And the heads of their horses are as the heads of lions - That is, fierce and terrible. And out of their mouth goeth fire and smoke and brimstone - This figurative expression may denote the consuming, blinding, all-piercing rage, fierceness, and force of these horsemen.

18. By these three - Which were inseparably joined. Were the third part of men - In the countries they over-ran. Killed - Omar alone, in eleven years and a half, took thirty-six thousand cities or forts. How many men must be killed therein!

19. For the power of these horses is in their mouths, and in their tails - Their riders fight retreating as well as advancing: so that their rear is as terrible as their front. For their tails are like serpents, having heads - Not like the tails of serpents only. They may be fitly compared to the amphisbena, a kind of serpent, which has a short tail, not unlike a head from which it throws out its poison as if it had two heads.

20. And the rest of the men who were not killed - Whom the Saracens did not destroy. It is observable, the countries they over-ran were mostly those where the gospel had been planted. By these plagues - Here the description of the second woe ends. Yet repented not - Though they were called Christians. Of the works of their hands - Presently specified. That they should not worship devils - The invocation of departed saints, whether true, or false, or doubtful, or forged, crept early into the Christian church, and was carried farther and farther; and who knows how many who are invoked as saints are among evil, not good, angels; or how far devils have mingled with such blind worship, and with the wonders wrought on those occasions? And idols - About the year 590, men began to venerate images; and though upright men zealously opposed it, yet, by little and little, images grew into manifest idols. For after much contention, both in the east and west, in the year 787, the worship of images was established by the second Council of Nice. Yet was image worship sharply opposed some time after, by the emperor Theophilus. But when he died, in 842, his widow, Theodoura, established it again; as did the Council at Constantinople in the year 863, and again in 871.

21. Neither repented of their murders, nor of their sorceries - Whoever reads the histories of the seventh, eighth, and ninth centuries, will find numberless instances of all these in every part of the Christian world. But though God cut off so many of these scandals to the Christian name, yet the rest went on in the same course. Some of them, however, might repent under the plagues which follow.

From the first verse of this chapter to chap. xi. 13, preparation is made for the important trumpet of the seventh angel. It consists of two parts, which run parallel to each other: the former reaches from the first to the seventh verse of this chapter; the latter, from the eighth of this to the thirteenth verse of the eleventh chapter: whence, also, the sixth verse of this chapter is parallel to the eleventh verse. The period to which both these refer begins during the second woe, as appears, chap. xi. 14; but, being once begun, it extends in a continued course far into the trumpet of the seventh angel. Hence many things are represented here which are not fulfilled till long after. So the joyful "consummation of the mystery of God" is spoken of in the seventh verse of this chapter, which yet is not till after "the consummation of the wrath of God," chap. xv, 1. So the ascent of the beast "out of the bottomless pit" is mentioned, chap. xi, 7, which nevertheless is still to come, chap. xvii, 8; and so "the earthquake," by which a tenth part of the great city falls, and the rest are converted, chap. xi, 13, is really later than that by which the same city is "split into three parts," chap. xvi, 19. This is a most necessary observation, whereby we may escape many and great mistakes.

1. And I saw another mighty angel - Another from that "mighty angel," mentioned, chap. v, 2; yet he was a created angel; for he did not swear by himself, verse 6. Clothed with a cloud - In token of his high dignity. And a rainbow upon his head - A lovely token of the divine favour. And yet it is not too glorious for a creature: the woman, chap. xii, 1, is described more glorious still. And his face as the sun - Nor is this too much for a creature: for all the righteous "shall shine forth as the sun," Matt. xiii, 43. And his feet as pillars of fire - Bright as flame.

2. And he had in his hand - His left hand: he swore with his right. He stood with his right foot on the sea, toward the west; his left, on the land, toward the east: so that he looked southward. And so St. John (as Patmos lies near Asia) could conveniently take the book out of his left hand. This sealed book was first in the right hand of him that sat on the throne: thence the Lamb took it, and opened the seals. And now this little book, containing the remainder of the other, is given opened, as it was, to St. John. From this place the Revelation speaks more clearly and less figuratively than before. And he set his right foot upon the sea - Out of which the first beast was to come. And his left foot upon the earth - Out of which was to come the second. The sea may betoken Europe; the earth, Asia; the chief theatres of these great things.

3. And he cried - Uttering the words set down, verse 6. And while he cried, or was crying - At the same instant. Seven thunders uttered their voices - In distinct words, each after the other. Those who spoke these words were glorious, heavenly powers, whose voice was as the loudest thunder.

4. And I heard a voice from heaven - Doubtless from him who had at first commanded him to write, and who presently commands him to take the book; namely, Jesus Christ. Seal up those things which the seven thunders have uttered, and write them not - These are the only things of all which he heard that he is commanded to keep secret: so something peculiarly secret was revealed to the beloved John, besides all the secrets that are written in this book. At the same time we are prevented from inquiring what it was which these thunders uttered: suffice that we may know all the contents of the opened book, and of the oath of the angel.

5. And the angel - This manifestation of things to come under the trumpet of the seventh angel hath a twofold introduction: first, the angel speaks for God, verse 7; then Christ speaks for himself, chap. xi, 3. The angel appeals to the prophets of former times; Christ, to his own two witnesses. Whom I saw standing upon the earth and upon the sea, lifted up his right hand toward heaven - As yet the dragon was in heaven. When he is cast thence he brings the third and most dreadful woe on the earth and sea: so that it seems as if there would be no end of calamities. Therefore the angel comprises, in his posture and in his oath, both heaven, sea, and earth, and makes on the part of the eternal God and almighty Creator, a solemn protestation, that he will assert his kingly authority against all his enemies. He lifted up his right hand toward heaven - The angel in Daniel, Dan. xii, 7, (not improbably the same angel,) lifted up both his hands.

6. And swear - The six preceding trumpets pass without any such solemnity. It is the trumpet of the seventh angel alone which is confirmed by so high an oath. By him that liveth forever and ever - Before whom a thousand years are but a day. Who created the heaven, the earth, the sea, and the things that are therein - And, consequently, has the sovereign power over all: therefore, all his enemies, though they rage a while in heaven, on the sea, and on the earth, yet must give place to him. That there shall be no more a time - "But in the days of the voice of the seventh angel, the mystery of God shall be fulfilled:" that is, a time, a chronos, shall not expire before that mystery is fulfilled. A chronos (1111 years) will nearly pass before then, but not quite. The period, then, which we may term a non-chronos (not a whole time) must be a little, and not much, shorter than this. The non-chronos here mentioned seems to begin in the year 800, (when Charles the Great instituted in the west a new line of emperors, or of "many kings,") to end in the year 1836; and to contain, among other things, the "short time" of the third woe, the "three times and a half" of the woman in the wilderness, and the "duration" of the beast.

7. **But in the days of the voice of the seventh angel** - Who sounded not only at the beginning of those days, but from the beginning to the end. **The mystery of God shall be fulfilled** - It is said, chap. xvii, 17, "The word of God shall be fulfilled." The word of God is fulfilled by the destruction of the beast; the mystery, by the removal of the dragon. But these great events are so near together, that they are here mentioned as one. The beginning of them is in heaven, as soon as the seventh trumpet sounds; the end is on the earth and the sea. So long as the third woe remains on the earth and the sea, the mystery of God is not fulfilled. And the angel's swearing is peculiarly for the comfort of holy men, who are afflicted under that woe. Indeed the wrath of God must be first fulfilled, by the pouring out of the phials: and then comes the joyful fulfilling of the mystery of God. **As he hath declared to his servants the prophets** - The accomplishment exactly answering the prediction. The ancient prophecies relate partly to that grand period, from the birth of Christ to the destruction of Jerusalem; partly to the time of the seventh angel, wherein they will be fully accomplished. To the seventh trumpet belongs all that occurs from chap. xi, 15 - chap. xxii, 5. And the third woe, which takes place under the same, properly stands, chap. xii, 12, xiii, 1-18.

8. **And** - what follows from this verse to chap. xi, 13, runs parallel with the oath of the angel, and with "the fulfilling of the mystery of God," as it follows under the trumpet of the seventh angel; what is said, verse 11, concerning St. John's "prophesying again," is unfolded immediately after; what is said, verse 7, concerning "the fulfilling the mystery of God," is unfolded, chap. xi, 15-19 and in the following chapters.

9. **Eat it up** - The like was commanded to Ezekiel. This was an emblem of thoroughly considering and digesting it. **And it will make thy belly bitter, but it will be sweet as honey in thy mouth** - The sweetness betokens the many good things which follow, chap. xi, 1, 15, &c.; the bitterness, the evils which succeed under the third woe.

11. **Thou must prophesy again** - Of the mystery of God; of which the ancient prophets had prophesied before. And he did prophesy, by "measuring the temple," chap. xi, 1; as a prophecy may be delivered either by words or actions. **Concerning people, and nations, and tongues, and many kings** - The people, nations, and tongues are contemporary; but the kings, being many, succeed one another. These kings are not mentioned for their own sake, but with a view to the "holy city," chap. xi, 2. Here is a reference to the great kingdoms in Spain, England, Italy, &c., which arose from the eighth century; or at least underwent a considerable change, as France and Germany in particular; to the Christian, afterward Turkish, empire in the east; and especially to the various potentates, who have successively reigned at or over Jerusalem, and do now, at least titularly, reign over it.

XI

In this chapter is shown how it will fare with "the holy city," till the mystery of God is fulfilled; in the twelfth, what will befall the woman, who is delivered of the man-child; in the thirteenth, how it will be with the kingdom of Christ, while the "two beasts" are in the height of their power. **And there was given me** - By Christ, as appears from the third verse. **And he said, Arise** - Probably he was sitting to write. **And measure the temple of God** - At Jerusalem, where he was placed in the vision. Of this we have a large description by Ezekiel, Ezek. xl - xlviii; concerning which we may observe,

1. Ezekiel's prophecy was not fulfilled at the return from the Babylonish captivity.
2. Yet it does not refer to the "New Jerusalem," which is far more gloriously described.
3. It must infallibly be fulfilled even then "when they are ashamed of all that they have done," Ezek. xliii, 11.
4. Ezekiel speaks of the same temple which is treated of here.
5. As all things are there so largely described, St. John is shorter and refers thereto.

2. **But the court which is without the temple** - The old temple had a court in the open air, for the heathens who worshipped the God of Israel. **Cast out** - Of thy account. **And measure it not** - As not being holy In so high a degree. **And they shall tread** - Inhabit. **The holy city** - Jerusalem, Matt. iv, 5. So they began to do, before St. John wrote. And it has been trodden almost ever since by the Romans, Persians, Saracens, and Turks. But that severe kind of treading which is here peculiarly spoken of, will not be till under the trumpet of the seventh angel, and toward the end of the troublous times. This will continue but forty-two common months, or twelve hundred and sixty common days; being but a small part of the non-chronos.

3. **And I** - Christ. **Will give to my two witnesses** - These seem to be two prophets; two select, eminent instruments. Some have supposed (though without foundation) that they are Moses and Elijah, whom they resemble in several respects. **To prophesy twelve hundred and sixty days** - Common days, that is, an hundred and eighty weeks. So long will they prophesy, (even while that last and sharp treading of the holy city continues,) both by word and deed, witnessing that Jesus is the Son of God, the heir of all things, and exhorting all men to repent, and fear, and glorify God. **Clothed in sackcloth** - The habit of the deepest mourners, out of sorrow and concern for the people.

4. *These are the two olive trees* - That is, as Zerubbabel and Joshua, the two olive trees spoken of by Zechariah, Zech. iii, 9, iv, 10, were then the two chosen instruments in God's hand, even so shall these, be in their season. Being themselves full of the unction of the Holy One, they shall continually transmit the same to others also. *And the two candlesticks* - Burning and shining lights. *Standing before the Lord of the earth* - Always waiting on God, without the help of man, and asserting his right over the earth and all things therein.

5. *If any would kill them* - As the Israelites would have done Moses and Aaron, Num. xvi, 41. *He must be killed thus* - By that devouring fire.

6. *These have power* - And they use that power. See verse 10. *To shut heaven, that it rain not in the days of their prophesying* - During those "twelve hundred and sixty days." *And have power over the waters* - In and near Jerusalem. *To turn them into blood* - As Moses did those in Egypt. *And to smite the earth with all plagues, as often as they will* - This is not said of Moses or Elijah, or any mere man besides. And how is it possible to understand this otherwise than of two individual persons?

7. *And when they shall have finished their testimony* - Till then they are invincible. *The wild beast* - Hereafter to be described. *That ascendeth* - First out of the sea, chap. xiii, 1, and then out of the bottomless pit, chap. xvii, 8. *Shall make war with them* - It is at his last ascent, not out of the sea, but the bottomless pit, that the beast makes war upon the two witnesses. And even hereby is fixed the time of "treading the holy city," and of the "two witnesses." That time ends after the ascent of the beast out of the abyss, and yet before the fulfilling of the mystery. *And shall conquer them* - The fire no longer proceeding out of their mouth when they have finished their work. *And kill them* - These will be among the last martyrs, though not the last of all.

8. *And their bodies shall be* - Perhaps hanging on a cross. *In the street of the great city* - Of Jerusalem, a far greater city, than any other in those parts. This is described both spiritually and historically: spiritually, as it is called Sodom Isaiah i, and Egypt; on account of the same abominations abounding there, at the time of the witnesses, as did once in Egypt and Sodom. Historically: *Where also their Lord was crucified* - This possibly refers to the very ground where his cross stood. Constantine the Great inclosed this within the walls of the city. Perhaps on that very spot will their bodies be exposed.

9. *Three days and a half* - So exactly are the times set down in this prophecy. If we suppose this time began in the evening, and ended in the morning, and included (which is no way impossible) Friday, Saturday, and Sunday, the weekly festival of the Turkish people, the Jewish tribes, and the Christian tongues; then all these together, with the heathen nations, would have full leisure to gaze upon and rejoice over them.

10. *And they that dwell upon the earth* - Perhaps this expression may peculiarly denote earthly-minded men. *Shall make merry* - As did the Philistines over Samson. *And send gifts to one another* - Both Turks, and Jews, and heathens, and false Christians.

11. *And great fear fell upon them that saw them* - And now knew that God was on their side.

12. *And I heard a great voice* - Designed for all to hear. *And they went up to heaven, and their enemies beheld them* - who had not taken notice of their rising again; by which some had been convinced before.

13. *And there was a great earthquake and the tenth part of the city fell* - We have here an unanswerable proof that this city is not Babylon or Rome, but Jerusalem. For Babylon shall be wholly burned before the fulfilling of the mystery of God. But this city is not burned at all; on the contrary, at the fulfilling of that mystery, a tenth part of it is destroyed by an earthquake, and the other nine parts converted. *And there were slain in the earthquake seven thousand men* - Being a tenth part of the inhabitants, who therefore were seventy thousand in all. *And the rest* - The remaining sixty-three thousand were converted: a grand step toward the fulfilling of the mystery of God. Such a conversion we no where else read of. So there shall be a larger as well as holier church at Jerusalem than ever was yet. *Were terrified* - Blessed terror! *And gave glory* - The character of true conversion, Jer. xiii, 16. *To the God of heaven* - He is styled, "The Lord of the earth," verse 4, when he declares his right over the earth by the two witnesses; but the God of heaven, when he not only gives rain from heaven after the most afflicting drought, but also declares his majesty from heaven, by taking his witnesses up into it. When the whole multitude gives glory to the God of heaven, then that "treading of the holy city" ceases. This is the point so long aimed at, the desired "fulfilling of the mystery of God," when the divine promises are so richly fulfilled on those who have gone through so great afflictions. All this is here related together, that whereas the first and second woe went forth in the east, the rest of the eastern affairs being added at once, the description of the western might afterwards remain unbroken. It may be useful here to see how the things here spoken of, and those hereafter described, follow each other in their order.

1. The angel swears; the non-chronos begins; John eats the book; the many kings arise.

2. The non-chronos and the "many kings" being on the decline, that treading" begins, and the "two witnesses" appear.

3. The beast, after he has with the ten kings destroyed Babylon, wars with them and kills them.

After three days and an half they revive and ascend to heaven. There is a great earthquake in the holy city: seven thousand perish, and the rest are converted. The "treading" of the city by the gentiles ends.

4. The beast, and the kings of the earth, and their armies are assembled to fight against the Great King.

5. Multitudes of his enemies are killed, and the beast and the false prophet cast alive into the lake of fire.

6. while John measures the temple of God and the altar with the worshippers, the true worship of God is set up. The nations who had trodden the holy city are converted. Hereby the mystery of God is fulfilled.

7. Satan is imprisoned. Being released for a time, he, with Gog and Magog, makes his last assault upon Jerusalem.

14. The second woe is past - The butchery made by the Saracens ceased about the year 847, when their power was so broken by Charles the Great that they never recovered it. Behold, the third woe cometh quickly - Its prelude came while the Roman see took all opportunities of laying claim to its beloved universality, and enlarging its power and grandeur. And in the year 755 the bishop of Rome became a secular prince, by king Pepin's giving him the exarchate of Lombardy. The beginning of the third woe itself stands, chap. xii, 12.

15. And the seventh angel sounded - This trumpet contains the most important and joyful events, and renders all the former trumpets matter of joy to all the inhabitants of heaven. The allusion therefore in this and all the trumpets is to those used in festal solemnities. All these seven trumpets were heard in heaven: perhaps the seventh shall once be heard on earth also, 1 Thess. iv, 16. And there were great voices - From the several citizens of heaven. At the opening of the seventh seal "there was silence in heaven;" at the sounding of the seventh trumpet, great voices. This alone is sufficient to show that the seven seals and seven trumpets do not run parallel to each other. As soon as the seventh angel sounds, the kingdom falls to God and his Christ. This immediately appears in heaven, and is there celebrated with joyful praise. But on earth several dreadful occurrences are to appear first. This trumpet comprises all that follows from these voices to chap. xxii, 5. The kingdom of the world - That is, the royal government over the whole world, and all its kingdoms, Zech. xiv, 9. Is become the kingdom of the Lord - This province has been in the enemy's hands: it now returns to its rightful Master. In the Old Testament, from Moses to Samuel, God himself was the King of his own people. And the same will be in the New Testament: he will himself reign over the Israel of God. And of his Christ - This appellation is now first given him, since the introduction of the book, on the mention of the kingdom devolving upon him, under the seventh trumpet. Prophets and priests were anointed, but more especially kings: whence that term, the anointed, is applied only to a king. Accordingly, whenever the Messiah is mentioned in scripture, his kingdom is implied. Is become - In reality, all things (and so the kingdom of the world) are God's in all ages: yet Satan and the present world, with its kings and lords, are risen against the Lord and against his Anointed. God now puts an end to this monstrous rebellion, and maintains his right to all things. And this appears in an entirely new manner, as soon as the seventh angel sounds.

16. And the four and twenty elders - These shall reign over the earth, chap. v, 10. Who sit before God on their thrones - which we do not read of any angel.

17. The Almighty - He who hath all things in his power as the only Governor of them. Who is, and who was - God is frequently styled, "He who is, and who was, and who is to come." but now he is actually come, the words, "who is to come," are, as it were, swallowed up. When it is said, We thank thee that thou hast taken thy great power, it is all one as, "We thank thee that thou art come." This whole thanksgiving is partly an enlargement on the two great points mentioned in the fifteenth verse; partly a summary of what is hereafter more distinctly related. Here it is mentioned, how the kingdom is the Lord's; afterwards, how it is the kingdom of his Christ. Thou hast taken thy great power - This is the beginning of what is done under the trumpet of the seventh angel. God has never ceased to use his power; but he has suffered his enemies to oppose it, which he will now suffer no more.

18. And the heathen nations were wroth - At the breaking out of the power and kingdom of God. This wrath of the heathens now rises to the highest pitch; but it meets the wrath of the Almighty, and melts away. In this verse is described both the going forth and the end of God's wrath, which together take up several ages. And the time of the dead is come - Both of the quick and dead, of whom those already dead are far the more numerous part. That they be judged - This, being infallibly certain, they speak of as already present. And to give a reward - At the coming of Christ, chap. xxii, 12; but of free grace, not of debt,

1. To his servants the prophets:

2. To his saints: to them who were eminently holy:

3. To them that fear his name: these are the lowest class. Those who do not even fear God will have no reward from him. Small and great - All universally, young and old, high and low, rich and poor. And to destroy them that destroyed the earth - The earth was destroyed by the "great whore" in

particular, chap. xix, 2; xvii, 2, 5; but likewise in general, by the open rage and hate of wicked men against all that is good; by wars, and the various destruction and desolation naturally flowing therefrom; by such laws and constitutions as hinder much good, and occasion many offenses and calamities; by public scandals, whereby a door is opened for all dissoluteness and unrighteousness; by abuse of secular and spiritual powers; by evil doctrines, maxims, and counsels; by open violence and persecution; and by sins crying to God to send plagues upon the earth. This great work of God, destroying the destroyers, under the trumpet of the seventh angel, is not the third woe, but matter of joy, for which the elders solemnly give thanks. All the woes, and particularly the third, go forth over those "who dwell upon the earth;" but this destruction, over those "who destroy the earth," and were also instruments of that woe.

19. And the temple of God-The inmost part of it. Was opened in heaven - And hereby is opened a new scene of the most momentous things, that we may see how the contents of the seventh trumpet are executed; and, notwithstanding the greatest opposition, (particularly by the third woe,) brought to a glorious conclusion. And the ark of the covenant was seen in his temple - The ark of the covenant which was made by Moses was not in the second temple, being probably burnt with the first temple by the Chaldeans. But here is the heavenly ark of the everlasting covenant, the shadow of which was under the Old Testament, Heb. ix, 4. The inhabitants of heaven saw the ark before: St. John also saw it now; for a testimony, that what God had promised, should be fulfilled to the uttermost. And there were lightnings, and voices, and thunders, and an earthquake, and great hail - The very same there are, and in the same order, when the seventh angel has poured out his phial; chap. xvi, 17-xxi, one place answers the other. What the trumpet here denounces in heaven, is there executed by the phial upon earth. First it is shown what will be done; and afterwards it is done.

XII

The great vision of this book goes straight forward, from the fourth to the twenty-second chapter. Only the tenth, with part of the eleventh chapter, was a kind of introduction to the trumpet of the seventh angel; after which it is said, "The second woe is past: behold, the third woe cometh quickly." Immediately the seventh angel sounds, under whom the third woe goes forth. And to this trumpet belongs all that is related to the end of the book. Verse

1. And a great sign was seen in heaven - Not only by St. John, but many heavenly spectators represented in the vision. A sign means something that has an uncommon appearance, and from which we infer that some unusual thing will follow. A woman - The emblem of the church of Christ, as she is originally of Israel, though built and enlarged on all sides by the addition of heathen converts; and as she will hereafter appear, when all her "natural branches are again "grafted in." She is at present on earth; and yet, with regard to her union with Christ, may be said to be in heaven, Eph. ii, 6. Accordingly, she is described as both assaulted and defended in heaven, verses 4, 7. chap. xii, 4, 7 Clothed with the sun, and the moon under her feet, and on her head a crown of twelve stars - These figurative expressions must he so interpreted as to preserve a due proportion between them. So, in Joseph's dream, the sun betokened his father; the moon, his mother; the stars, their children. There may be some such resemblance here; and as the prophecy points out the "power over all nations," perhaps the sun may betoken the Christian world; the moon, the Mahometans, who also carry the moon in their ensigns; and the crown of twelve stars, the twelve tribes of Israel; which are smaller than the sun and moon. The whole of this chapter answers the state of the church from the ninth century to this time.

2. And being with child she crieth, travailing in birth - The very pain, without any outward opposition, would constrain a woman in travail to cry out. These cries, throes, and pains to be delivered, were the painful longings, the sighs, and prayers of the saints for the coming of the kingdom of God. The woman groaned and travailed in spirit, that Christ might appear, as the Shepherd and King of all nations.

3. And behold a great red dragon - His fiery-red colour denoting his disposition. Having seven heads - Implying vast wisdom. And ten horns - Perhaps on the seventh head; emblems of mighty power and strength, which he still retained. And seven diadems on his heads - Not properly crowns, but costly bindings, such as kings anciently wore; for, though fallen, he was a great potentate still, even "the prince of this world."

4. And his tail - His falsehood and subtilty. Draweth - As a train. The third part - A very large number. Of the stars of heaven - The Christians and their teachers, who before sat in heavenly places with Christ Jesus. And casteth them to the earth - Utterly deprives them of all those heavenly blessings. This is properly a part of the description of the dragon, who was not yet himself on earth, but in heaven: consequently, this casting them down was between the beginning of the seventh trumpet and the beginning of the third woe; or between the year 847 and the year 947; at which time pestilent doctrines, particularly that of the Manichees in the east, drew abundance of people from the truth. And the dragon stood before the woman, that when she had brought forth, he might devour the child - That he might hinder the kingdom of Christ from spreading abroad, as it does under this trumpet.

5. And she brought forth a man child - Even Christ, considered not in his person, but in his kingdom. In the ninth age, many nations with their princes were added to the Christian church. Who was to rule all nations - When his time is come. And her child - Which was already in heaven, as were the woman and the dragon. Was caught up to God - Taken utterly out of his reach.

6. And the woman fled into the wilderness - This wilderness is undoubtedly on earth, where the woman also herself is now supposed to be. It betokens that part of the earth where, after having brought forth, she found a new abode. And this must be in Europe; as Asia and Afric were wholly in the hands of the Turks and Saracens; and in a part of it where the woman had not been before. In this wilderness, God had already prepared a place; that is, made it safe and convenient for her. The wilderness is, those countries of Europe which lie on this side the Danube; for the countries which lie beyond it had received Christianity before. That they may feed her - That the people of that place may provide all things needful for her. Twelve hundred and sixty days - So many prophetic days, which are not, as some have supposed, twelve hundred and sixty, but seven hundred and seventy-seven, common years. This Bengelius has shown at large in his German Introduction. These we may compute from the year 847 to 1524. So long the woman enjoyed a safe and convenient place in Europe, which was chiefly Bohemia; where she was fed, till God provided for her more plentifully at the Reformation.

7. And there was war in heaven - Here Satan makes his grand opposition to the kingdom of God; but an end is now put to his accusing the saints before God. The cause goes against him, verses 10, 11, chap. xii, 10, 11 and Michael executes the sentence. That Michael is a created angel, appears from his not daring, in disputing with Satan, Jude 9, to bring a railing accusation; but only saying, "The Lord rebuke thee." And this modesty is implied in his very name; for Michael signifies, "Who is like God?" which implies also his deep reverence toward God, and distance from all self-exaltation. Satan would be like God: the very name of Michael asks, "Who is like God?" Not Satan; not the highest archangel. It is he likewise that is afterward employed to seize, bind, and imprison that proud spirit.

8. And he prevailed not - The dragon himself is principally mentioned; but his angels, likewise, are to be understood. Neither was this place found any more in heaven - So till now he had a place in heaven. How deep a mystery is this! One may compare this with Luke x, 18; Eph. ii, 2; iv, 8; vi, 12.

9. And the great dragon was cast out - It is not yet said, unto the earth - He was cast out of heaven; and at this the inhabitants of heaven rejoice. He is termed the great dragon, as appearing here in that shape, to intimate his poisonous and cruel disposition. The ancient serpent - In allusion to his deceiving Eve in that form. Dragons are a kind of large serpent. Who is called the Devil and Satan - These are words of exactly the same meaning; only the former is Greek; the latter, Hebrew; denoting the grand adversary of all the saints, whether Jews or gentiles. He has deceived the whole world - Not only in their first parents, but through all ages, and in all countries, into unbelief and all wickedness; into the hating and persecuting faith and all goodness. He was cast out unto the earth - He was cast out of heaven; and being cast out thence, himself came to the earth. Nor had he been unemployed on the earth before, although his ordinary abode was in heaven.

10. Now is come - Hence it is evident that all this chapter belongs to the trumpet of the seventh angel. In the eleventh chapter, from the fifteenth to the eighteenth verse, are proposed the contents of this extensive trumpet; the execution of which is copiously described in this and the following chapters. The salvation - Of the saints. The might - Whereby the enemy is cast out. The kingdom - Here the majesty of God is shown. And the power of his Christ - Which he will exert against the beast; and when he also is taken away, then will the kingdom be ascribed to Christ himself, chap. xix, 16; xx, 4. The accuser of our brethren -- so long as they remained on earth. This great voice, therefore, was the voice of men only. Who accused them before our God day and night - Amazing malice of Satan, and patience of God!

11. And they have overcome him - Carried the cause against him. By the blood of the Lamb - Which cleanses the soul from all sin, and so leaves no room for accusing. And by the word of their testimony - The word of God, which they believed and testified, even unto death. So, for instance, died Olam, king of Sweden, in the year 900, whom his own subjects would have compelled to idolatry; and, upon his refusal, slew as a sacrifice to the idol which he would not worship. So did multitudes of Bohemian Christians, in the year 916, when queen Drahomire raised a severe persecution, wherein many "loved not their lives unto the death."

12. Woe to the earth and the sea - This is the fourth and last denunciation of the third woe, the most grievous of all. The first was only, the second chiefly, on the earth, Asia; the third, both on the earth and the sea, Europe. The earth is mentioned first, because it began in Asia, before the beast brought it on Europe. He knoweth he hath but a little time - Which extends from his casting out of heaven to his being cast into the abyss. We are now come to a most important period of time. The non-chronos hastens to an end. We live in the little time wherein Satan hath great wrath; and this little time is now upon the decline. We are in the "time, times, and half a time," wherein the woman is "fed in the wilderness;" yea, the last part of it, "the half time," is begun. We are, as will be shown, towards the close of the "forty-two months" of the beast; and when his number is fulfilled, grievous things will be.

Let him who does not regard the being seized by the wrath of the devil; the falling unawares into the general temptation; the being born away, by the most dreadful violence, into the worship of the beast and his image, and, consequently, drinking the unmixed wine of the wrath of God, and being tormented day and night forever and ever in the lake of fire and brimstone; let him also who is confident that he can make his way through all these by his own wisdom and strength, without need of any such peculiar preservative as the word of this prophecy affords; let him, I say, go hence. But let him who does not take these warnings for senseless outcries, and blind alarms, beg of God, with all possible earnestness, to give him his heavenly light herein. God has not given this prophecy, in so solemn a manner, only to show his providence over his church, but also that his servants may know at all times in what particular period they are. And the more dangerous any period of time is, the greater is the help which it affords. But where may we fix the beginning and end of the little time? which is probably four-fifths of a chronos, or somewhat above 888 years. This, which is the time of the third woe, may reach from 947, to the year 1836. For,

    1. The short interval of the second woe, (which woe ended in the year 840,) and the 777 years of the woman, which began about the year 847, quickly after which followed the war in heaven, fix the beginning not long after 8lxiv, and thus the third woe falls in the tenth century, extending from 900 to 1000; called the dark, the iron, the unhappy age.

    2. If we compare the length of the third woe with the period of time which succeeds it in the twentieth chapter, it is but a little time to that vast space which reaches from the beginning of the non-chronos to the end of the world.

    13. *And when the dragon saw* - That he could no longer accuse the saints in heaven, he turned his wrath to do all possible mischief on earth. *He persecuted the woman* - The ancient persecutions of the church were mentioned, chap. i, 9, ii, 10, vii, 14; but this persecution came after her flight, verse 6, just at the beginning of the third woe. Accordingly, in the tenth and eleventh centuries, the church was furiously persecuted by several heathen powers. In Prussia, king Adelbert was killed in the year 997, king Brunus in 1008; and when king Stephen encouraged Christianity in Hungary, he met with violent opposition. After his death, the heathens in Hungary set themselves to root it out, and prevailed for several years. About the same time, the army of the emperor, Henry the Third, was totally overthrown by the Vandals. These, and all the accounts of those times, show with what fury the dragon then persecuted the woman.

    14. *And there were given to the woman the two wings of the great eagle, that she might fly into the wilderness to her place* - Eagles are the usual symbols of great potentates. So Ezek. xvii, 3, by "a great eagle', means the king of Babylon. Here the great eagle is the Roman empire; the two wings, the eastern and western branches of it. A place in the wilderness was mentioned in the sixth verse also; but it is not the same which is mentioned here. In the text there follow one after the other,

    1. The dragon's waiting to devour the child.
    2. The birth of the child, which is caught up to God.
    3. The fleeing of the woman into the wilderness.
    4. The war in heaven, and the casting out of the dragon.
    5. The beginning of the third woe.
    6. The persecution raised by the dragon against the woman.
    7. The woman's flying away upon the eagle's wings. In like manner there follow one after the other,

    1. The beginning of the twelve hundred and sixty days.
    2. The beginning of the little time.
    3. The beginning of the time, times, and half a time. This third period partly coincides both with the first and the second. After the beginning of the twelve hundred and sixty days, or rather of the third woe, Christianity was exceedingly propagated, in the midst of various persecutions. About the year 948 it was again settled in Denmark; in 965, in Poland and Silesia; in 980, through all Russia. In 997 it was brought into Hungary; into Sweden and Norway, both before and after. Transylvania received it about 1000; and, soon after, other parts of Dacia. Now, all the countries in which Christianity was settled between the beginning of the twelve hundred and sixty days, and the imprisonment of the dragon, may be understood by the wilderness, and by her place in particular. This place contained many countries; so that Christianity now reached, in an uninterrupted tract, from the eastern to the western empire; and both the emperors now lent their wings to the woman, and provided a safe abode for her. *Where she is fed* - By God rather than man; having little human help. *For a time, and times, and half a time* - The length of the several periods here mentioned seems to be nearly this: - YEARS

    1. The non-chronos contains less than 1111
    2. The little time 888
    3. The time, times, and half a time 777
    4. The time of the beast 666 And comparing the prophecy and history together, they seem to begin and end nearly thus:

1. The non-chronos extends from about 800 to 1836
2. The 1260 days of the woman from 847-1524
3. The little time 947-1836
4. The time, time, and half 1058-1836

5. The time of the beast is between the beginning and end of the three times and a half. In the year 1058 the empires had a good understanding with each other, and both protected the woman. The bishops of Rome, likewise, particularly Victor II., were duly subordinate to the emperor. We may observe, the twelve hundred and sixty days of the woman, from 847 to 1524, and the three times and a half, refer to the same wilderness. But in the former part of the twelve hundred and sixty days, before the three times and an half began, namely, from the year 847 to 1058, she was fed by others, being little able to help herself; whereas, from 1058 to 1524, she is both fed by others, and has food herself. To this the sciences transplanted into the west from the eastern countries much contributed; the scriptures, in the original tongues, brought into the west of Europe by the Jews and Greeks, much more; and most of all, the Reformation, grounded on those scriptures.

15. Water is an emblem of a great people; this water, of the Turks in particular. About the year 1060 they overran the Christian part of Asia. Afterward, they poured into Europe, and spread farther and farther, till they had overflowed many nations.

16. But the earth helped the woman - The powers of the earth; and indeed she needed help through this whole period. "The time" was from 1058 to 1280; during which the Turkish flood ran higher and higher, though frequently repressed by the emperors, or their generals, helping the woman. "The" two "times" were from 1280 to 1725. During these likewise the Turkish power flowed far and wide; but still from time to time the princes of the earth helped the woman, that she was not carried away by it. "The half time" is from 1725 to 1836. In the beginning of this period the Turks began to meddle with the affairs of Persia: wherein they have so entangled themselves, as to be the less able to prevail against the two remaining Christian empires. Yet this flood still reaches the woman "in her place;" and will, till near the end of the "half time," itself be swallowed up, perhaps by means of Russia, which is risen in the room of the eastern empire.

17. And the dragon was wroth - Anew, because he could not cause her to be carried away by the stream. And he went forth - Into other lands. To make war with the rest of her seed - Real Christians, living under heathen or Turkish governors.

XIII

1. And I stood on the sand of the sea - This also was in the vision. And I saw - Soon after the woman flew away. A wild beast coming up - He comes up twice; first from the sea, then from the abyss. He comes from the sea before the seven phials; "the great whore" comes after them. O reader, this is a subject wherein we also are deeply concerned, and which must be treated, not as a point of curiosity, but as a solemn warning from God! The danger is near. Be armed both against force and fraud, even with the whole armour of God. Out of the sea - That is, Europe. So the three woes (the first being in Persia, the second about the Euphrates) move in a line from east to west. This beast is the Romish Papacy, as it came to a point six hundred years since, stands now, and will for some time longer. To this, and no other power on earth, agrees the whole text, and every part of it in every point; as we may see, with the utmost evidence, from the propositions following: - PROP. 1. It is one and the same beast, having seven heads, and ten horns, which is described in this and in the seventeenth chapter. Of consequence, his heads are the same, and his horns also. PROP. 2. This beast is a spiritually secular power, opposite to the kingdom of Christ. A power not merely spiritual or ecclesiastical, nor merely secular or political but a mixture of both. He is a secular prince; for a crown, yea, and a kingdom are ascribed to him. And yet he is not merely secular; for he is also a false prophet. PROP. 3. The beast has a strict connection with the city of Rome. This clearly appears from the seventeenth chapter. PROP. 4. The beast is now existing. He is not past. for Rome is now existing; and it is not till after the destruction of Rome that the beast is thrown into the lake. He is not altogether to come: for the second woe is long since past, after which the third came quickly; and presently after it began, the beast rose out of the sea. Therefore, whatever he is, he is now existing. PROP. 5. The beast is the Romish Papacy. This manifestly follows from the third and fourth propositions; the beast has a strict connection with the city of Rome; and the beast is now existing: therefore, either there is some other power more strictly connected with that city, or the Pope is the beast. PROP. 6. The Papacy, or papal kingdom, began long ago. The most remarkable particulars relating to this are here subjoined; taken so high as abundantly to show the rise of the beast, and brought down as low as our own time, in order to throw a light on the following part of the prophecy: A.D. 1033. Benedict the Ninth, a child of eleven years old, is bishop of Rome, and occasions grievous disorders for above twenty years. A.D. 1048. Damasus II. introduces the use of the triple crown. A.D. 1058. The church of Milan is, after long opposition, subjected to the Roman. A.D. 1073. Hildebrand, or Gregory VII., comes to the throne. A.D. 1076. He deposes and excommunicates the

emperor. A.D. 1077. He uses him shamefully and absolves him. A.D. 1080. He excommunicates him again, and sends a crown to Rodulph, his competitor. A.D. 1083. Rome is taken. Gregory flees. Clement is made Pope, and crowns the emperor. A.D. 1085. Gregory VII. dies at Salerno. A.D. 1095. Urban II. holds the first Popish council, at Clermont and gives rise to the crusades. A.D. 1111. Paschal II. quarrels furiously with the emperor. A.D. 1123. The first western general council in the Lateran. The marriage of priests is forbidden. A.D. 1132. Innocent II declares the emperor to be the Pope's liege-man, or vassal. A.D. 1143. The Roman set up a governor of their own, independent on Innocent II. He excommunicates them, and dies. Celestine II. is, by an important innovation, chosen to the Popedom without the suffrage of the people; the right of choosing the Pope is taken from the people, and afterward from the clergy, and lodged in the Cardinals alone. A.D. 1152. Eugene II. assumes the power of canonizing saints. A.D. 1155. Adrian IV. puts Arnold of Brixia to death for speaking against the secular power of the Papacy. A.D. 1159. Victor IV. is elected and crowned. But Alexander III. conquers him and his successor. A.D. 1168. Alexander III. excommunicates the emperor, and brings him so low, that, A.D. 1177. he submits to the Pope's setting his foot on his neck. A.D. 1204. Innocent III. sets up the Inquisition against the Vaudois. A.D. 1208. He proclaims a crusade against them. A.D. 1300. Boniface VIII. introduces the year of jubilee. A.D. 1305. The Pope's residence is removed to Avignon. A.D. 1377. It is removed back to Rome. A.D. 1378. The fifty years' schism begins. A.D. 1449. Felix V., the last Antipope, submits to Nicholas V. A.D. 1517. The Reformation begins. A.D. 1527. Rome is taken and plundered. A.D. 1557. Charles V. resigns the empire; Ferdinand I. thinks the being crowned by the Pope superfluous. A.D. 1564. Pius IV. confirms the Council of Trent. A.D. 1682. Doctrines highly derogatory to the Papal authority are openly taught in France. A.D. 1713. The constitution Unigenitus. A.D. 1721. Pope Gregory VII. canonized anew. He who compares this short table with what will be observed, verse 3, and chap. xvii, 10, will see that the ascent of the beast out of the sea must needs be fixed toward the beginning of it, and not higher than Gregory VII., nor lower than Alexander III. The secular princes now favoured the kingdom of Christ; but the bishops of Rome vehemently opposed it. These at first were plain ministers or pastors of the Christian congregation at Rome, but by degrees they rose to an eminence of honour and power over all their brethren till, about the time of Gregory VII. (and so ever since) they assumed all the ensigns of royal majesty; yea, of a majesty and power far superior to that of all other potentates on earth. We are not here considering their false doctrines, but their unbounded power. When we think of those, we are to look at the false prophet, who is also termed a wild beast at his ascent out of the earth. But the first beast then properly arose, when, after several preludes thereto, the Pope raised himself above the emperor. PROP. 7. Hildebrand, or Gregory VII., is the proper founder of the papal kingdom. All the patrons of the Papacy allow that he made many considerable additions to it; and this very thing constituted the beast, by completing the spiritual kingdom: the new maxims and the new actions of Gregory all proclaim this. Some of his maxims are,

1. That the bishop of Rome alone is universal bishop.
2. That he alone can depose bishops, or receive them again.
3. That he alone has power to make new laws in the church.
4. That he alone ought to use the ensigns of royalty.
5. That all princes ought to kiss his foot.
6. That the name of Pope is the only name under heaven; and that his name alone should be recited in the churches.
7. That he has a power to depose emperors.
8. That no general synod can be convened but by him.
9. That no book is canonical without his authority.
10. That none upon earth can repeal his sentence, but he alone can repeal any sentence.
11. That he is subject to no human judgment.
12. That no power dare to pass sentence on one who appeals to the Pope.
13. That all weighty causes everywhere ought to be referred to him.
14. That the Roman church never did, nor ever can, err.
15. That the Roman bishop, canonically ordained, is immediately made holy, by the merits of St. Peter.
16. That he can absolve subjects from their allegiance. These the most eminent Romish writers own to be his genuine sayings. And his actions agree with his words. Hitherto the Popes had been subject to the emperors, though often unwillingly; but now the Pope began himself, under a spiritual pretext, to act the emperor of the whole Christian world: the immediate dispute was, about the investiture of bishops, the right of which each claimed to himself. And now was the time for the Pope either to give up, or establish his empire forever: to decide which, Gregory excommunicated the emperor Henry IV.; "having first," says Platina, "deprived him of all his dignities." The sentence ran in these terms: "Blessed Peter, prince of the apostles, incline, I beseech thee, thine ears, and hear me thy servant. In the name of the omnipotent God, Father, Son, and Holy Ghost, I cast down the emperor Henry from all imperial and regal authority, and absolve all Christians, that were his subjects, from the

oath whereby they used to swear allegiance to true kings. And moreover, because he had despised mine, yea, thy admonitions, I bind him with the bond of an anathema." The same sentence he repeated at Rome in these terms: "Blessed Peter, prince of the apostles, and thou Paul, teacher of the gentiles, incline, I beseech you, your ears to me, and graciously hear me. Henry, whom they call emperor, hath proudly lifted up his horns and his head against the church of God, - who came to me, humbly imploring to be absolved from his excommunication, - I restored him to communion, but not to his kingdom, - neither did I allow his subjects to return to their allegiance. Several bishops and princes of Germany, taking this opportunity, in the room of Henry, justly deposed, chose Rodulph emperor, who immediately sent ambassadors to me, informing me that he would rather obey me than accept of a kingdom, and that he should always remain at the disposal of God and us. Henry then began to be angry, and at first intreated us to hinder Rodulph from seizing his kingdom. I said I would see to whom the right belonged, and give sentence which should be preferred. Henry forbad this. Therefore I bind Henry and all his favourers with the bond of an anathema, and again take from him all regal power. I absolve all Christians from their oath of allegiance, forbid them to obey Henry in anything, and command them to receive Rodulph as their king. Confirm this, therefore, by your authority, ye most holy princes of the apostles, that all may now at length know, as ye have power to bind and loose in heaven, so we have power to give and take away on earth, empires, kingdoms, principalities, and whatsoever men can have." When Henry submitted, then Gregory began to reign without control. In the same year, 1077, on September 1, he fixed a new era of time, called the Indiction, used at Rome to this day. Thus did the Pope claim to himself the whole authority over all Christian princes. Thus did he take away or confer kingdoms and empires, as a king of kings. Neither did his successors fail to tread in his steps. It is well known, the following Popes have not been wanting to exercise the same power, both over kings and emperors. And this the later Popes have been so far from disclaiming, that three of them have sainted this very Gregory, namely, Clement VIII., Paul V., and Benedict XIII. Here is then the beast, that is, the king: in fact such, though not in name: according to that remarkable observation of Cardinal Bellarmine, "Antichrist will govern the Roman empire, yet without the name of Roman emperor." His spiritual title prevented his taking the name, while he exerciseth all the power. Now Gregory was at the head of this novelty. So Aventine himself, "Gregory VII was the first founder of the pontifical empire." Thus the time of the ascent of the beast is clear. The apostasy and mystery of iniquity gradually increased till he arose, "who opposeth and exalteth himself above all." 2 Thess. ii, 4. Before the seventh trumpet the adversary wrought more secretly; but soon after the beginning of this, the beast openly opposes his kingdom to the kingdom of Christ. PROP 8. The empire of Hildebrand properly began in the year 1077. Then it was, that upon the emperor's leaving Italy, Gregory exercised his power to the full. And on the first of September, in this year, he began his famous epocha. This may be farther established and explained by the following observations:-

OBS. 1. The beast is the Romish Papacy, which has now reigned for some ages. OBS. 2. The beast has seven heads and ten horns. OBS. 3. The seven heads are seven hills, and also seven kings. One of the heads could not have been, "as it were, mortally wounded," had it been only a hill. OBS. 4. The ascent of the beast out of the sea is different from his ascent out of the abyss; the Revelation often mentions both the sea and the abyss but never uses the terms promiscuously. OBS. 5. The heads of the beast do not begin before his rise out of the sea, but with it. OBS. 6. These heads, as kings, succeed each other. OBS. 7. The time which they take up in this succession is divided into three parts. "Five" of the kings signified thereby "are fallen: one is, the other is not yet come." OBS. 8. "One is:" namely, while the angel was speaking this. He places himself and St. John in the middlemost time, that he might the more commodiously point out the first time as past, the second as present, the third as future. OBS. 9. The continuance of the beast is divided in the same manner. The beast "was, is not, will ascend out of the abyss," chap. xvii, 8, 11. Between these two verses, that is interposed as parallel with them, "Five are fallen, one is, the other is not yet come." OBS. 10. Babylon is Rome. All things which the Revelation says of Babylon, agree to Romans, and Roman only. It commenced "Babylon," when it commenced "the great." When Babylon sunk in the east, it arose in the west; and it existed in the time of the apostles, whose judgment is said to be "avenged on her." OBS. 11. The beast reigns both before and after the reign of Babylon. First, the beast reigns, chap. xiii, 1, &c.; then Babylon, chap. xvii, 1, &c.; and then the beast again, chap. xvii, 8, &c. OBS. 12. The heads are of the substance of the beast; the horns are not. The wound of one of the heads is called "the wound of the beast" itself, verse 3; but the horns, or kings, receive the kingdom "with the beast," chap. xvii, 12. That word alone, "the horns and the beast," chap. xvii, 16, sufficiently shows them to be something added to him. OBS. 13. The forty-two months of the beast fall within the first of the three periods. The beast rose out of the sea in the year 1077. A little after, power was given him for forty-two months. This power is still in being. OBS. 14. The time when the beast "is not," and the reign of "Babylon," are together. The beast, when risen out of the sea, raged violently, till "his kingdom was darkened" by the fifth phial. But it was a kingdom still; and the beast having a kingdom, though darkened, was the beast still. But it was afterwards said, "the beast was," (was the beast, that is, reigned,) "and is not;" is not the beast; does not reign, having lost his kingdom. Why? because "the woman sits upon the beast," who "sits a queen," reigning over the kings of the earth: till the beast, rising out of the abyss, and taking with him the ten kings, suddenly destroys her. OBS. 15. The difference there is between Rome and the Pope, which has always subsisted, will then be most apparent. Rome, distinct from the Pope, bears three meanings; the city itself, the Roman church, and the people of Rome. In the last sense of the word, Rome with its dutchy, which contained part of Tuscany and Campania, revolted from the Greek emperor in 726, and became a free state, governed by its senate. From this time the senate, and not the Pope, enjoyed the supreme civil power. But in 796, Leo III., being chosen Pope, sent to Charles the Great, desiring him to come and subdue the senate and people of Rome, and constrain them to swear allegiance to him. Hence arose a sharp contention between the Pope and the Roman people, who seized and thrust him into a monastery. He escaped and fled to the emperor, who quickly sent him back in great state. In the year 800 the emperor came to Rome, and shortly after, the Roman people, who had hitherto chosen their own bishops, and looked upon themselves and their senate as having the same rights with the ancient senate and people of Rome, chose Charles for their emperor, and subjected themselves to him, in the same manner as the ancient Roman did to their emperors. The Pope crowned him, and paid him homage on his knees, as was formerly done to the Roman emperors: and the emperor took an oath "to defend the holy Roman church in all its emoluments." He was also created consul, and styled himself thenceforward Augustus, Emperor of the Romans. Afterwards he gave the government of the city and dutchy of Rome to the Pope, yet still subject to himself. What the Roman church is, as distinct from the Pope, appears,

1. When a council is held before the Pope's confirmation;
2. When upon a competition, judgment is given which is the true Pope;
3. When the See is vacant;
4. When the Pope himself is suspected by the Inquisition.

How Rome, as it is a city, differs from the Pope, there is no need to show. OBS. 16. In the first and second period of his duration, the beast is a body of men; in the third, an individual. The beast with seven heads is the Papacy of many ages: the seventh head is the man of sin, antichrist. He is a body of men from chap. xiii, 1 - chap. xvii, 7; he is a body of men and an individual, chap. xvii, 8 - chap. xvii, 11; he is an individual, chap. xvii, 12 - chap. xix, 20. OBS. 17. That individual is the seventh head of the beast, or, the other king after the five and one, himself being the eighth, though one of the seven. As he is a Pope, he is one of the seven heads. But he is the eighth, or not a head, but the beast himself, not, as he is a Pope, but as he bears a new and singular character at his coming from the abyss. To illustrate this by a comparison: suppose a tree of seven branches, one of which is much larger than the rest; if those six are cut away, and the seventh remain, that is the tree. OBS. 18. "He is the wicked one, the man of sin, the son of perdition" usually termed antichrist. OBS. 19. The ten horns, or kings, "receive power as kings with the wild beast one hour," chap. xvii, 12; with the individual beast, "who was not." But he receives his power again, and the kings with it, who quickly give their new power to him. OBS. 20. The whole power of the Roman monarchy, divided into ten kingdoms, will be conferred on the beast, chap. xvii, 13, 16, 17.

OBS. 21. The ten horns and the beast will destroy the whore, chap. xvii, 16. OBS. 22. At length the beast, the ten horns, and the other kings of the earth, will fall in that great slaughter, chap. xix, 19. OBS. 23. Daniel's fourth beast is the Roman monarchy, from the beginning of it, till the thrones are set. This, therefore, comprises both the apocalyptic beast, and the woman, and many other things. This monarchy is like a river which runs from its fountain in one channel, but in its course sometimes takes in other rivers, sometimes is itself parted into several streams, yet is still one continued river. The Roman power was at first undivided; but it was afterwards divided into various channels, till the grand division into the eastern and western empires, which likewise underwent various changes. Afterward the kings of the Heruli, Goths, Lombards, the exarchs of Ravenna, the Roman themselves the emperors, French and German, besides other kings, seized several parts of the Roman power. Now whatever power the Roman had before Gregory VII., that Daniel's beast contains; whatever power the Papacy has had from Gregory VII., this the apocalyptic beast represents, but this very beast (and so Rome with its last authority) is comprehended under that of Daniel. And upon his heads a name of blasphemy - To ascribe to a man what belongs to God alone is blasphemy. Such a name the beast has, not on his horns, nor on one head, but on all. The beast himself bears that name, and indeed through his whole duration. This is the name of Papa or Pope; not in the innocent sense wherein it was formerly given to all bishops, but in that high and peculiar sense wherein it is now given to the bishop of Rome by himself, and his followers: a name which comprises the whole pre-eminence of the highest and most holy father upon earth. Accordingly among the above cited sayings of Gregory, those two stand together, that his "name alone should be recited in the churches;" and that it is "the only name in the world." So both the church and the world were to name no other father on the face of the earth.

2. The three first beasts in Daniel are like "a leopard," "a bear," and "a lion." In all parts, except his feet and mouth, this beast was like a leopard or female panther; which is fierce as a lion or bear, but is also swift and subtle. Such is the Papacy, which has partly by subtilty, partly by force, gained power

over so many nations. The extremely various usages, manners, and ways of the Pope, may likewise be compared to the spots of the leopard. And his feet were as the feet of a bear - Which are very strong, and armed with sharp claws. And, as clumsy as they seem, he can therewith walk, stand upright, climb, or seize anything. So does this beast seize and take for his prey whatever comes within the reach of his claws. And his mouth was as the mouth of a lion - To roar, and to devour. And the dragon - Whose vassal and vicegerent he is. Gave him his power - His own strength and innumerable forces. And his throne - So that he might command whatever he would, having great, absolute authority. The dragon had his throne in heathen Rome, so long as idolatry and persecution reigned there. And after he was disturbed in his possession, yet would he never wholly resign, till he gave it to the beast in Christian Rome, so called.

3. And I saw one - Or the first. Of his heads as it were wounded - So it appeared as soon as ever it rose. The beast is first described more generally, then more particularly, both in this and in the seventeenth chapter. The particular description here respects the former parts; there, the latter parts of his duration: only that some circumstances relating to the former are repeated in the seventeenth chapter. chap. xvii, 1-18 This deadly wound was given him on his first head by the sword, verse 14; chap. xiii, 14 that is, by the bloody resistance of the secular potentates, particularly the German emperors. These had for a long season had the city of Rome, with her bishop, under their jurisdiction. Gregory determined to cast off this yoke from his own, and to lay it on the emperor's shoulders. He broke loose, and excommunicated the emperor, who maintained his right by force, and gave the Pope such a blow, that one would have thought the beast must have been killed thereby, immediately after his coming up. But he recovered, and grew stronger than before. The first head of the beast extends from Gregory VII., at least to Innocent III. In that tract of time the beast was much wounded by the emperors. But, notwithstanding, the wound was healed. Two deadly symptoms attended this wound:

1. Schisms and open ruptures in the church. For while the emperors asserted their right, there were from the year 1080 to the year 1176 only, five open divisions, and at least as many antipopes, some of whom were, indeed, the rightful Popes. This was highly dangerous to the papal kingdoms. But a still more dangerous symptom was,

2. The rising of the nobility at Rome, who would not suffer their bishop to be a secular prince, particularly over themselves. Under Innocent II. they carried their point, re-established the ancient commonwealth, took away from the Pope the government of the city, and left him only his episcopal authority. "At this," says the historian, "Innocent II. and Celestine II. fretted themselves to death: Lucius II., as he attacked the capitol, wherein the senate was, sword in hand, was struck with a stone, and died in a few days: Eugene III., Alexander III., and Lucius III., were driven out of the city: Urban III. and Gregory VIII. spent their days in banishment At length they came to an agreement with Clement III., who was himself a Roman." And the whole earth - The whole western world. Wondered after the wild beast - That is, followed him with wonder, in his councils, his crusades, and his jubilees. This refers not only to the first head, but also to the four following.

4. And they worshipped the dragon - Even in worshipping the beast, although they knew it not. And worshipped the wild beast - Paying him such honour as was not paid to any merely secular potentate. That very title, "Our most holy Lord," was never given to any other monarch on earth. Saying, Who is like the wild beast - "Who is like him?" is a peculiar attribute of God; but that this is constantly attributed to the beast, the books of all his adherents show.

5. And there was given him - By the dragon, through the permission of God. A mouth speaking great things and blasphemy - The same is said of the little horn on the fourth beast in Daniel. Nothing greater, nothing more blasphemous, can be conceived, than what the Popes have said of themselves, especially before the Reformation. And authority was given him forty-two months - The beginning of these is not to be dated immediately from his ascent out of the sea, but at some distance from it.

6. To blaspheme his name - Which many of the Popes have done explicitly, and in the most dreadful manner. And his tabernacle, even them that dwell in heaven - (For God himself dwelleth in the inhabitance of heaven.) Digging up the bones of many of them, and cursing them with the deepest execrations.

7. And it was given him - That is, God permitted him. To make war with his saints - With the Waldenses and Albigenses. It is a vulgar mistake, that the Waldenses were so called from Peter Waldo of Lyons. They were much more ancient than him; and their true name was Vallenses or Vaudois from their inhabiting the valleys of Lucerne and Agrogne. This name, Vallenses, after Waldo appeared about the year 1160, was changed by the Papists into Waldenses, on purpose to represent them as of modern original. The Albigenses were originally people of Albigeois, part of Upper Languedoc, where they considerably prevailed, and possessed several towns in the year 1200. Against these many of the Popes made open war. Till now the blood of Christians had been shed only by the heathens or Arians; from this time by scarce any but the Papacy. In the year 1208 Innocent III. proclaimed a crusade against them. In June, 1209, the army assembled at Toulouse; from which time abundance of blood was shed, and the second army of martyrs began to be added to the first, who had cried "from beneath the altar."

And ever since, the beast has been warring against the saints, and shedding their blood like water. And authority was given him over every tribe and people - Particularly in Europe. And when a way was found by sea into the East Indies, and the West, these also were brought under his authority.

8. And all that dwell upon the earth will worship him - All will be carried away by the torrent, but the little flock of true believers. The name of these only is written in the Lamb's book of life. And if any even of these "make shipwreck of the faith," he will blot them "out of his book;" although they were written therein from (that is, before) the foundation of the world, chap. xvii, 8.

9. If any one have an ear, let him hear - It was said before, "He that hath an ear, let him hear." This expression, if any, seems to imply, that scarce will any that hath an ear be found. Let him hear - With all attention the following warning, and the whole description of the beast,

10. If any man leadeth into captivity - God will in due time repay the followers of the beast in their own kind. Meanwhile, here is the patience and faithfulness of the saints exercised: their patience, by enduring captivity or imprisonment; their faithfulness, by resisting unto blood.

11. And I saw another wild beast - So he is once termed to show his fierceness and strength, but in all other places, "the false prophet." He comes to confirm the kingdom of the first beast. Coming up - After the other had long exercised his authority. Out of the earth - Out of Asia. But he is not yet come, though he cannot be far off for he is to appear at the end of the forty-two months of the first beast. And he had two horns like a lamb - A mild, innocent appearance. But he spake like a dragon - Venomous, fiery, dreadful. So do those who are zealous for the beast.

12. And he exerciseth all the authority of the first wild beast - Described in the second, fourth, fifth, and seventh verses. chap. xiii, 2, 3, 5, 7 Before him - For they are both together. Whose deadly wound was healed - More throughly healed by means of the second beast.

13. He maketh fire - Real fire. To come down - By the power of the devil.

14. Before the wild beast - Whose usurped majesty is confirmed by these wonders. Saying to them - As if it were from God. To make an image to the wild beast - Like that of Nebuchadnezzar, whether of gold, silver, or stone. The original image will be set up where the beast himself shall appoint. But abundance of copies will be taken, which may be carried into all parts, like those of Diana of Ephesus.

15. So that the image of the wild beast should speak - Many instances of this kind have been already among the Papists, as well as the heathens. And as many as will not worship - When it is required of them; as it will be of all that buy or sell. Shall be killed - By this the Pope manifests that he is antichrist, directly contrary to Christ. It is Christ who shed his own blood; it is antichrist who sheds the blood of others. And yet, it seems, his last and most cruel persecution is to come. This persecution, the reverse of all that preceded, will, as we may gather from many scriptures, fall chiefly on the outward court worshippers, the formal Christians. It is probable that few real, inward Christians shall perish by it: on the contrary, those who "watch and pray always" shall be "accounted worthy to escape all these things, and to stand before the Son of man," Luke xxi, 36.

16. On their forehead - The most zealous of his followers will probably choose this. Others may receive it on their hand.

17. That no man might buy or sell - Such edicts have been published long since against the poor Vaudois. But he that had the mark, namely, the name of the first beast, or the number of his name - The name of the beast is that which he bears through his whole duration; namely, that of Papa or Pope: the number of his name is the whole time during which he bears this name. Whosoever, therefore, receives the mark of the beast does as much as if he said expressly, "I acknowledge the present Papacy, as proceeding from God;" or, "I acknowledge that what St. Gregory VII. has done, according to his legend, (authorized by Benedict XIII.,) and what has been maintained in virtue thereof, by his successors to this day, is from God." By the former, a man hath the name of the beast as a mark; by the latter, the number of his name. In a word, to have the name of the beast is, to acknowledge His papal Holiness; to have the number of his name is, to acknowledge the papal succession. The second beast will enforce the receiving this mark under the severest penalties.

18. Here is the wisdom - To be exercised. "The patience of the saints" availed against the power of the first beast: the wisdom God giveth them will avail against the subtilty of the second. Let him that hath understanding - Which is a gift of God, subservient to that wisdom. Count the number of the wild beast - Surely none can be blamed for attempting to obey this command. For it is the number of a man - A number of such years as are common among men. And his number is six hundred and sixty-six years - So long shall he endure from his first appearing.

XIV

1. And I saw on Mount Zion - The heavenly Zion. An hundred forty-four thousand - Either those out of all mankind who had been the most eminently holy, or the most holy out of the twelve tribes of Israel the same that were mentioned, chap. vii, 4, and perhaps also, chap. xvi, 2. But they were then in the world, and were sealed in their foreheads, to preserve them from the plagues that were to follow. They are now in safety, and have the name of the Lamb and of his Father written on their foreheads, as being the redeemed of God and of the Lamb, his now unalienable property. This prophecy often introduces the inhabitants of heaven as a kind of chorus with great propriety and elegance. The church above, making suitable reflections on the grand events which are foretold in this book, greatly serves to raise the attention of real Christians, and to teach the high concern they have in them. Thus is the church on earth instructed, animated, and encouraged, by the sentiments temper, and devotion of the church in heaven.

2. And I heard a sound out of heaven - Sounding clearer and clearer: first, at a distance, as the sound of many waters or thunders; and afterwards, being nearer, it was as of harpers harping on their harps. It sounded vocally and instrumentally at once.

3. And they - The hundred forty-four thousand-Sing a new song - and none could learn that song - To sing and play it in the same manner. But the hundred forty-four thousand who were redeemed from the earth - From among men; from all sin.

4. These are they who had not been defiled with women - It seems that the deepest defilement, and the most alluring temptation, is put for every other. They are virgins - Unspotted souls; such as have preserved universal purity. These are they who follow the Lamb - Who are nearest to him. This is not their character, but their reward Firstfruits - Of the glorified spirits. Who is ambitious to be of this number?

5. And in their mouth there was found no guile - Part for the whole. Nothing untrue, unkind, unholy. They are without fault - Having preserved inviolate a virgin purity both of soul and body.

6. And I saw another angel - A second is mentioned, verse 8; a third, verse 9. chap. xiv, 8, 9 These three denote great messengers of God with their assistants; three men who bring messages from God to men. The first exhorts to the fear and worship of God; the second proclaims the fall of Babylon; the third gives warning concerning the beast. Happy are they who make the right use of these divine messages! Flying - Going on swiftly. In the midst of heaven - Breadthways. Having an everlasting gospel - Not the gospel, properly so called; but a gospel, or joyful message, which was to have an influence on all ages. To preach to every nation, and tribe, and tongue, and people - Both to Jew and gentile, even as far as the authority of the beast had extended.

7. Fear God and give glory to him; for the hour of his judgment is come - The joyful message is properly this, that the hour of God's judgment is come. And hence is that admonition drawn, Fear God and give glory to him. They who do this will not worship the beast, neither any image or idol whatsoever. And worship him that made - Whereby he is absolutely distinguished from idols of every kind. The heaven, and the earth, and the sea, and fountains of water - And they who worship him shall be delivered when the angels pour out their phials on the earth, sea, fountains of water, on the sun, and in the air.

8. And another angel followed, saying, Babylon is fallen - With the overthrow of Babylon, that of all the enemies of Christ, and, consequently, happier times, are connected. Babylon the great - So the city of Rome is called upon many accounts. Babylon was magnificent, strong, proud, powerful. So is Rome also. Babylon was first, Rome afterwards, the residence of the emperors of the world. What Babylon was to Israel of old, Roman hath been both to the literal and spiritual "Israel of God." Hence the liberty of the ancient Jews was connected with the overthrow of the Babylonish empire. And when Rome is finally overthrown, then the people of God will be at liberty. Whenever Babylon is mentioned in this book, the great is added, to teach us that Rome then commenced Babylon, when it commenced the great city; when it swallowed up the Grecian monarchy and its fragments, Syria in particular; and, in consequence of this, obtained dominion over Jerusalem about sixty years before the birth of Christ. Then it began, but it will not cease to be Babylon till it is finally destroyed. Its spiritual greatness began in the fifth century, and increased from age to age. It seems it will come to its utmost height just before its final overthrow. Her fornication is her idolatry; invocation of saints and angels; worship of images; human traditions; with all that outward pomp, yea, and that fierce and bloody zeal, wherewith she pretends to serve God. But with spiritual fornication, as elsewhere, so in Rome, fleshly fornication is joined abundantly. Witness the stews there, licensed by the Pope, which are no inconsiderable branch of his revenue. This is fitly compared, to wine, because of its intoxicating nature. Of this wine she hath, indeed, made all nations drink - More especially by her later missions. We may observe, this making them drink is not ascribed to the beast, but to Babylon. For Rome itself, the Roman inquisitions, congregations, and Jesuits, continually propagate the idolatrous doctrines and practices, with or without the consent of this or that Pope, who himself is not secure from their censure.

9. **And a third angel followed** - At no great distance of time. Saying, If any one worship the wild beast - This worship consists, partly in an inward submission, a persuasion that all who are subject to Christ must be subject to the beast or they cannot receive the influences of divine grace, or, as their expression is, there is no salvation out of their church; partly in a suitable outward reverence to the beast himself, and consequently to his image.

10. **He shall drink** - With Babylon, chap. xvi, 19. And shall be tormented - With the beast, chap. xx, 10. In all the scripture there is not another so terrible threatening as this. And God by this greater fear arms his servants against the fear of the beast. The wrath of God, which is poured unmixed - Without any mixture of mercy; without hope. Into the cup of his indignation - And is no real anger implied in all this? O what will not even wise men assert, to serve an hypothesis!

11. **And the smoke** - From the fire and brimstone wherein they are tormented. Ascendeth forever and ever - God grant thou and I may never try the strict, literal eternity of this torment!

12. **Here is the patience of the saints** - Seen, in suffering all things rather than receive this mark. Who keep the commandments of God - The character of all true saints; and particularly the great command to believe in Jesus.

13. **And I heard a voice** - This is most seasonably heard when the beast is in his highest power and fury. Out of heaven - Probably from a departed saint. Write - He was at first commanded to write the whole book. Whenever this is repeated it denotes something peculiarly observable. Happy are the dead - From henceforth particularly:

1. Because they escape the approaching calamities:

2. Because they already enjoy so near an approach to glory. Who die in the Lord - In the faith of the Lord Jesus. For they rest - No pain, no purgatory follows; but pure, unmixed happiness. From their labours - And the more labourious their life was, the sweeter is their rest. How different this state from that of those, verse 11, chap. xiv, 11 who "have no rest day or night!" Reader, which wilt thou choose? Their works - Each one's peculiar works. Follow - or accompany them; that is, the fruit of their works. Their works do not go before to procure them admittance into the mansions of joy; but they follow them when admitted.

14. In the following verses, under the emblem of an harvest and a vintage, are signified two general visitations; first, many good men are taken from the earth by the harvest; then many sinners during the vintage. The latter is altogether a penal visitation; the former seems to be altogether gracious. Here is no reference in either to the day of judgment, but to a season which cannot be far off. And I saw a white cloud - An emblem of mercy. And on the cloud sat one like a son of man - An angel in an human shape, sent by Christ, the Lord both of the vintage and of the harvest. Having a golden crown on his head - In token of his high dignity. And a sharp sickle in his hand - The sharper the welcomer to the righteous.

15. **And another angel came out of the temple** - "Which is in heaven," verse 17. chap. xiv, 17 Out of which came the judgments of God in the appointed seasons.

16. **Crying** - By the command of God. Thrust in thy sickle, for the harvest is ripe - This implies an high degree of holiness in those good men, and an earnest desire to be with God.

18. **And another angel from the altar** - Of burnt offering; from whence the martyrs had cried for vengeance. Who had power over fire - As "the angel of the waters," chap. xvi, 5, had over water. Cried, saying, Lop off the clusters of the vine of the earth - All the wicked are considered as constituting one body.

20. **And the winepress was trodden** - By the Son of God, chap. xix, 15. Without the city - Jerusalem. They to whom St. John writes, when a man said, "The city," immediately understood this. And blood came out of the winepress, even to the horses' bridles - So deep at its first flowing from the winepress! One thousand six hundred furlongs - So far! at least two hundred miles, through the whole land of Palestine.

XV

1. **And I saw seven holy angels having the seven last plagues** - Before they had the phials, which were as instruments whereby those plagues were to be conveyed. They are termed the last, because by them the wrath of God is fulfilled - Hitherto. God had born his enemies with much longsuffering; but now his wrath goes forth to the uttermost, pouring plagues on the earth from one end to the other, and round its whole circumference. But, even after these plagues, the holy wrath of God against his other enemies does not cease, chap. xx, 15.

2. **The song was sung** while the angels were coming out, with their plagues, who are therefore mentioned both before and after it, verses 1-6. chap. xv, 1-6, And I saw as it were a sea of glass mingled with fire - It was before "clear as crystal," chap. iv, 6, but now mingled with fire, which devours the adversaries. And them that gained, or were gaining, the victory over the wild beast - More of whom were yet to come. The mark of the beast, the mark of his name, and the number of his name, seem to

mean here nearly the same thing. Standing at the sea of glass - Which was before the throne. Having the harps of God - Given by him, and appropriated to his praise.

3. And they sing the song of Moses - So called, partly from its near agreement, with the words of that song which he sung after passing the Red Sea, Exod. xv, 11, and of that which he taught the children of Israel a little before his death, Deut. xxxii, 3, 4. But chiefly because Moses was the minister and representative of the Jewish church, as Christ is of the church universal. Therefore it is also termed the sons of the Lamb. It consists of six parts, which answer each other: 1. Great and wonderful are thy. 2. For thou only art gracious. works, Lord God Almighty. 3. Just and true are thy ways, O. 4. For all the nations shall come King of the nations and worship before thee. 5. Who would not fear thee, O. 6. For thy judgments are made Lord, and glorify thy name? manifest. We know and acknowledge that all thy works in and toward all the creatures are great and wonderful; that thy ways with all the children of men, good and evil, are just and true. For thou only art gracious - And this grace is the spring of all those wonderful works, even of his destroying the enemies of his people. Accordingly in Psalm cxxxvi, 1-26., that clause, "For his mercy endureth forever," is subjoined to the thanksgiving for his works of vengeance as well as for his delivering the righteous. For all the nations shall come and worship before thee - They shall serve thee as their king with joyful reverence. This is a glorious testimony of the future conversion of all the heathens. The Christians are now a little flock: they who do not worship God, an immense multitude. But all the nations shall come, from all parts of the earth, to worship him and glorify his name. For thy judgments are made manifest - And then the inhabitants of the earth will at length learn to fear him.

5. After these things the temple of the tabernacle of the testimony - The holiest of all. Was opened - Disclosing a new theatre for the coming forth of the judgments of God now made manifest.

6. And the seven angels came out of the temple - As having received their instructions from the oracle of God himself. St. John saw them in heaven, verse 1, chap. xv, 1 before they went into the temple. They appeared in habits like those the high priest wore when he went into the most holy place to consult the oracle. In this was the visible testimony of God's presence. Clothed in pure white linen - Linen is the habit of service and attendance. Pure - unspotted, unsullied. White - Or bright and shining, which implies much more than bare innocence. And having their breasts girt with golden girdles - In token of their high dignity and glorious rest.

7. And one of the four living creatures gave the seven angels - After they were come out of the temple. Seven golden phials - Or bowls. The Greek word signifies vessels broader at the top than at the bottom. Full of the wrath of God, who liveth forever and ever - A circumstance which adds greatly to the dreadfulness of his wrath.

8. And the temple was filled with smoke - The cloud of glory was the visible manifestation of God's presence in the tabernacle and temple. It was a sign of protection at erecting the tabernacle and at the dedication of the temple. But in the judgment of Korah the glory of the Lord appeared, when he and his companions were swallowed up by the earth. So proper is the emblem of smoke from the glory of God, or from the cloud of glory, to express the execution of judgment, as well as to be a sign of favour. Both proceed from the power of God, and in both he is glorified. And none - Not even of those who ordinarily stood before God. Could go into the temple - That is, into the inmost part of it. Till the seven plagues of the seven angels were fulfilled - Which did not take up a long time, like the seven trumpets, but swiftly followed each other.

XVI

1. Pour out the seven phials - The epistles to the seven churches are divided into three and four: the seven seals, and so the trumpets and phials, into four and three. The trumpets gradually, and in a long tract of time, overthrow the kingdom of the world: the phials destroy chiefly the beast and his followers, with a swift and impetuous force. The four first affect the earth, the sea, the rivers, the sun; the rest fall elsewhere, and are much more terrible.

2. And the first went - So the second, third, &c., without adding angel, to denote the utmost swiftness; of which this also is a token, that there is no period of time mentioned in the pouring out of each phial. They have a great resemblance to the plagues of Egypt, which the Hebrews generally suppose to have been a month distant from each other. Perhaps so may the phials; but they are all yet to come. And poured out his phial upon the earth - Literally taken. And there came a grievous ulcer - As in Egypt, Exod. ix, 10, 11. On the men who had the mark of the wild beast - All of them, and them only. All those plagues seem to be described in proper, not figurative, words.

3. The second poured out his phial upon the sea - As opposed to the dry land. And it become blood, as of a dead man - Thick, congealed, and putrid. And every living soul - Men, beasts, and fishes, whether on or in the sea, died.

4. The third poured out his phial on the rivers and fountains of water - Which were over all the earth. And they became blood - So that none could drink thereof.

Wesley's Notes on the Bible - The New Testament

5. **The Gracious one** - So he is styled when his judgments are abroad, and that with a peculiar propriety. In the beginning of the book he is termed "The Almighty." In the time of his patience, he is praised for his power, which otherwise might then be less regarded. In the time of his taking vengeance, for his mercy. Of his power there could then be no doubt.

6. **Thou hast given then, blood to drink** - Men do not drink out of the sea, but out of fountains and rivers. Therefore this is fitly added here. **They are worthy** - Is subjoined with a beautiful abruptness.

7. **Yea** - Answering the angel of the waters, and affirming of God's judgments in general, what he had said of one particular judgment.

8. **The fourth poured out his phial upon the sun** - Which was likewise affected by the fourth trumpet. There is also a plain resemblance between the first, second, and third phials, and the first, second, and third trumpet. **And it was given him** - The angel. **To scorch the men** - Who had the mark of the beast. **With fire** - As well as with the beams of the sun. So these four phials affected earth, water, fire, and air.

9. **And the men blasphemed God, who had power over these plagues** - They could not but acknowledge the hand of God, yet did they harden themselves against him.

10. The four first phials are closely connected together; the fifth concerns the throne of the beast, the sixth the Mahometans, the seventh chiefly the heathens. The four first phials and the four first trumpets go round the whole earth; the three last phials and the three last trumpets go lengthways over the earth in a straight line. **The fifth poured out his phial upon the throne of the wild beast** - It is not said, "on the beast and his throne." Perhaps the sea will then be vacant. **And his kingdom was darkened** - With a lasting, not a transient, darkness. However the beast as yet has his kingdom. Afterward the woman sits upon the beast. and then it is said, "The wild beast is not," chap. xvii, 3, 7, 8.

11. **And they** - His followers. **Gnawed their tongues** - Out of furious impatience. **Because of their pains and because of their ulcers** - Now mentioned together, and in the plural number, to signify that they were greatly heightened and multiplied.

12. **And the sixth poured out his phial upon the great river Euphrates** - Affected also by the sixth trumpet. **And the water of it** - And of all the rivers that flow into it. **Was dried up** - The far greater part of the Turkish empire lies on this side the Euphrates. The Romish and Mahometan affairs ran nearly parallel to each other for several ages. In the seventh century was Mahomet himself; and, a little before him, Boniface III., with his universal bishopric. In the eleventh, both the Turks and Gregory VII. carried all before them. In the year 1300, Boniface appeared with his two swords at the newly-erected jubilee. In the self-same year arose the Ottoman Porte; yea, and on the same day. And here the phial, poured out on the throne of the beast, is immediately followed by that poured out on the Euphrates; **that the way of the kings from the east might be prepared** - Those who lie east from the Euphrates, in Persia, India, &c., who will rush blindfold upon the plagues which are ready for them, toward the Holy Land, which lies west of the Euphrates.

13. **Out of the mouth of the dragon, the wild beast, and the false prophet** - It seems, the dragon fights chiefly against God; the beast, against Christ; the false prophet, against the Spirit of truth; and that the three unclean spirits which come from them, and exactly resemble them, endeavour to blacken the works of creation, of redemption, and of sanctification. **The false prophet** - So is the second beast frequently named, after the kingdom of the first is darkened; for he can then no longer prevail by main strength, and so works by lies and deceit. Mahomet was first a false prophet, and afterwards a powerful prince: but this beast was first powerful as a prince; afterwards a false prophet, a teacher of lies. **Like frogs** - Whose abode is in fens, marshes, and other unclean places. **To the kings of the whole world** - Both Mahometan and pagan. **To gather them** - To the assistance of their three principals.

15. **Behold, I come as a thief** - Suddenly, unexpectedly. Observe the beautiful abruptness. **I** - Jesus Christ. Hear him. Happy is he that watcheth. - Looking continually for him that "cometh quickly." **And keepeth on his garments** - Which men use to put off when they sleep. **Lest he walk naked, and they see his shame** - Lest he lose the graces which he takes no care to keep, and others see his sin and punishment.

16. **And they gathered them together to Armageddon** - Mageddon, or Megiddo, is frequently mentioned in the Old Testament. Armageddon signifies the city or the mountain of Megiddo; to which the valley of Megiddo adjoined. This was a place well known in ancient times for many memorable occurrences; in particular, the slaughter of the kings of Canaan, related, Judg. v, 19. Here the narrative breaks off. It is resumed, chap. xix, 19.

17. **And the seventh poured out his phial upon the air** - Which encompasses the whole earth. This is the most weighty phial of all, and seems to take up more time than any of the preceding. **It is done** - What was commanded, verse 1. chap. xvi, 1 The phials are poured out.

18. **A great earthquake, such as had not been since men were upon the earth** - It was therefore a literal, not figurative, earthquake.

19. **And the great city** - Namely, Jerusalem, here opposed to the heathen cities in general, and in particular to Rome. **And the cities of the nations fell** - Were utterly overthrown. **And Babylon was**

remembered before God - He did not forget the vengeance which was due to her, though the execution of it was delayed.

20. Every island and mountain was "moved out of its place," chap. vi, 14; but here they all flee away. What a change must this make in the face of the terraqueous globe! And yet the end of the world is not come.

21. And a great hail falleth out of heaven - From which there was no defense. From the earthquake men would fly into the fields; but here also they are met by the hail: nor were they secure if they returned into the houses, when each hail-stone weighed sixty pounds.

XVII

1. And there came one of the seven angels, saying, Come hither - This relation concerning the great whore, and that concerning the wife of the Lamb, chap. xxi, 9, 10, have the same introduction, in token of the exact opposition between them. I will show thee the judgment of the great whore - Which is now circumstantially described. That sitteth as a queen - In pomp, power, ease, and luxury. Upon many waters - Many people and nations, verse 15. chap. xvii, 15

2. With whom the kings of the earth - Both ancient and modern, for many ages. Have committed fornication - By partaking of her idolatry and various wickedness. And the inhabitants of the earth - The common people. Have been made drunk with the wine of her fornication - No wine can more thoroughly intoxicate those who drink it, than false zeal does the followers of the great whore.

3. And he carried me away - In the vision. Into a wilderness - The campagna di Romansa, the country round about Rome, is now a wilderness, compared to what it was once. And I saw a woman - Both the scripture and other writers frequently represent a city under this emblem. Sitting upon a scarlet wild beast - The same which is described in the thirteenth chapter. chap. xiii, 1-18 But he was there described as he carried on his own designs only: here, as he is connected with the whore. There is, indeed, a very close connection between them; the seven heads of the beast being "seven hills on which the woman sitteth." And yet there is a very remarkable difference between them, - between the papal power and the city of Rome. This woman is the city of Rome, with its buildings and inhabitants; especially the nobles. The beast, which is now scarlet-coloured, (bearing the bloody livery, as well as the person, of the woman,) appears very different from before. Therefore St. John says at first sight, I saw a beast, not the beast, full of names of blasphemy - He had before "a name of blasphemy upon his head," chap. xiii, i, now he has many. From the time of Hildebrand, the blasphemous titles of the Pope have been abundantly multiplied. Having seven heads - Which reach in a succession from his ascent out of the sea to his being cast into the lake of fire. And ten horns - Which are contemporary with each other, and belong to his last period.

4. And the woman was arrayed - With the utmost pomp and magnificence. In purple and scarlet - These were the colours of the imperial habit: the purple, in times of peace; and the scarlet, in times of war. Having in her hand a golden cup - Like the ancient Babylon, Jer. li, 7. Full of abominations - The most abominable doctrines as well as practices.

5. And on her forehead a name written - Whereas the saints have the name of God and the Lamb on their foreheads. Mystery - This very word was inscribed on the front of the Pope's mitre, till some of the Reformers took public notice of it. Babylon the great - Benedict XIII., in his proclamation of the jubilee, A.D. 1725, explains this sufficiently. His words are, "To this holy city, famous for the memory of so many holy martyrs, run with religious alacrity. Hasten to the place which the Lord hath chose. Ascend to this new Jerusalem, whence the law of the Lord and the light of evangelical truth hath flowed forth into all nations, from the very first beginning of the church: the city most rightfully called 'The Palace,' placed for the pride of all ages, the city of the Lord, the Sion of the Holy One of Israel. This catholic and apostolical Roman church is the head of the world, the mother of all believers, the faithful interpreter of God and mistress of all churches." But God somewhat varies the style. The mother of harlots - The parent, ringleader, patroness, and nourisher of many daughters, that losely copy after her. And abominations - Of every kind, spiritual and fleshly. Of the earth - In all lands. In this respect she is indeed catholic or universal.

6. And I saw the woman drunk with the blood of the saints - So that Rome may well be called, "The slaughter-house of the martyrs." She hath shed much Christian blood in every age; but at length she is even drunk with it, at the time to which this vision refers. The witnesses of Jesus - The preachers of his word. And I wondered exceedingly - At her cruelty and the patience of God.

7. I will tell thee the mystery - The hidden meaning of this.

8. The beast which thou sawest (namely, verse 3) chap. xvii, 3 was, &c. This is a very observable and punctual description of the beast, verses 8, 10, 11. chap. xvii, 8, 10, 11 His whole duration is here divided into three periods, which are expressed in a fourfold manner.

I. He,

1. Was; 2 And is not;

Wesley's Notes on the Bible - The New Testament

3. And will ascend out of the bottomless pit, and go into perdition.

II. He,

1. Was;
2. And is not;
3. And will be again.

III. The seven heads are seven hills and seven kings:

1. Five are fallen;
2. One is;
3. The other is not come; and when he cometh, he must continue a short space.

IV. He,

1. Was;
2. And is not; 3 Even he is the eighth, and is one of the seven, and goeth into perdition. The first of these three is described in the thirteenth chapter. chap. xiii, 1-18 This was past when the angel spoke to St. John. The second was then in its course; the third woe to come. And is not - The fifth phial brought darkness upon his kingdom: the woman took this advantage to seat herself upon him. Then it might be said, He is not. Yet shall he afterwards ascend out of the bottomless pit - Arise again with diabolical strength and fury. But he will not reign long: soon after his ascent he goeth into perdition forever.

9. Here is the mind that hath wisdom - Only those who are wise will understand this. The seven heads are seven hills.

10. And they are seven kings - Anciently there were royal palaces on all the seven Roman hills. These were the Palatine, Capitoline, Coelian, Exquiline, Viminal, Quirinal, Aventine hills. But the prophecy respects the seven hills at the time of the beast, when the Palatine was deserted and the Vatican in use. Not that the seven heads mean hills distinct from kings; but they have a compound meaning, implying both together. Perhaps the first head of the beast is the Coelian hill, and on it the Lateran, with Gregory VII. and his successors; the second, the Vatican with the church of St. Peter, chosen by Boniface VIII. the third, the Quirinal, with the church of St. Mark, and the Quirinal palace built by Paul II. and the fourth, the Exquiline hill, with the temple of St. Maria Maggiore, where Paul V. reigned. The fifth will be added hereafter. Accordingly, in the papal register, four periods are observable since Gregory VII. In the first almost all the bulls made in the city are dated in the Lateran; in the second, at St. Peter's; in the third, at St. Mark's, or in the Quirinal; in the fourth, at St. Maria Maggiore. But no fifth, sixth, or seventh hill has yet been the residence of any Pope. Not that the hill was deserted, when another was made the papal residence; but a new one was added to the other sacred palaces. Perhaps the times hitherto mentioned might be fixed thus:- 1058. Wings are given to the woman. 1077. The beast ascends out of the sea. 1143. The forty-two months begin. 1810. The forty-two months end. 1832. The beast ascends out of the bottomless pit. 1836. The beast finally overthrown. The fall of those five kings seems to imply, not only the death of the Popes who reigned on those hills, but also such a disannulling of all they had done there, that it will be said, The beast is not; the royal power, which had so long been lodged in the Pope, being then transferred to the city. One is, the other is not yet come - These two are remarkably distinguished from the five preceding, whom they succeed in their turns. The former of them will continue not a short space, as may be gathered from what is said of the latter: the former is under the government of Babylon; the latter is with the beast. In this second period, one is, at the same time that the beast is not. Even then there will be a Pope, though not with the power which his predecessors had. And he will reside on one of the remaining hills, leaving the seventh for his successor.

11. And the wild beast that was, and is not, even he is the eighth - When the time of his not being is over. The beast consists, as it were, of eight parts. The seven heads are seven of them; and the eighth is his whole body, or the beast himself. Yet the beast himself, though he is in a sense termed the eighth, is of the seven, yea, contains them all. The whole succession of Popes from Gregory VII. are undoubtedly antichrist. Yet this hinders not, but that the last Pope in this succession will be more eminently the antichrist, the man of sin, adding to that of his predecessors a peculiar degree of wickedness from the bottomless pit. This individual person, as Pope, is the seventh head of the beast; as the man of sin, he is the eighth, or the beast himself.

12. The ten horns are ten kings - It is nowhere said that these horns are on the beast, or on his heads. And he is said to have them, not as he is one of the seven, but as he is the eighth. They are ten secular potentates, contemporary with, not succeeding, each other, who receive authority as kings with the beast, probably in some convention, which, after a very short space, they will deliver up to the beast. Because of their short continuance, only authority as kings, not a kingdom, is ascribed to them. While they retain this authority together with the beast, he will be stronger than ever before; but far stronger still, when their power is also transferred to him.

13. In the thirteenth and fourteenth verses chap. xvii, 13, 14 is summed up what is afterwards mentioned, concerning the horns and the beast, in this and the two following chapters. These have one mind, and give - They all, with one consent, give their warlike power and royal authority to the wild beast.

14. These - Kings with the beast. He is Lord of lords - Rightful sovereign of all, and ruling all things well. And King of kings - As a king he fights with and conquers all his enemies. And they that are with him - Beholding his victory, are such as were, while in the body, called, by his word and Spirit. And chosen - Taken out of the world, when they were enabled to believe in him. And faithful - Unto death.

15. People, and multitudes, and nations, and tongues - It is not said tribes: for Israel hath nothing to do with Rome in particular.

16. And shall eat her flesh - Devour her immense riches.

17. For God hath put it into their heart - Which indeed no less than almighty power could have effected. To execute his sentence - till the words of God - Touching the overthrow of all his enemies, should be fulfilled.

18. The woman is the great city, which reigneth - Namely, while the beast "is not," and the woman "sitteth upon him."

XVIII

1. And I saw another angel coming down out of heaven - Termed another, with respect to him who "came down out of heaven," chap. x, 1. And the earth was enlightened with his glory - To make his coming more conspicuous. If such be the lustre of the servant, what images can display the majesty of the Lord, who has "thousand thousands" of those glorious attendants "ministering to him, and ten thousand times ten thousand standing before him?"

2. And he cried, Babylon is fallen - This fall was mentioned before, chap. xiv, 8; but is now declared at large. And is become an habitation - A free abode. Of devils, and an hold - A prison. Of every unclean spirit - Perhaps confined there where they had once practiced all uncleanness, till the judgment of the great day. How many horrid inhabitants hath desolate Babylon! of invisible beings, devils, and unclean spirits; of visible, every unclean beast, every filthy and hateful bird. Suppose, then, Babylon to mean heathen Rome; what have the Romanists gained, seeing from the time of that destruction, which they say is past, these are to be its only inhabitants forever.

4. And I heard another voice - Of Christ, whose people, secretly scattered even there, are warned of her approaching destruction. That ye be not partakers of her sins - That is, of the fruits of them. What a remarkable providence it was that the Revelation was printed in the midst of Spain, in the great Polyglot Bible, before the Reformation! Else how much easier had it been for the Papists to reject the whole book, than it is to evade these striking parts of it.

5. Even to heaven - An expression which implies the highest guilt.

6. Reward her - This God speaks to the executioners of his vengeance. Even as she hath rewarded - Others; in particular, the saints of God. And give her double - This, according to the Hebrew idiom, implies only a full retaliation.

7. As much as she hath glorified herself - By pride, and pomp, and arrogant boasting. And lived deliciously - In all kinds of elegance, luxury, and wantonness. So much torment give her - Proportioning the punishment to the sin. Because she saith in her heart - As did ancient Babylon, Isai xlvii, 8, 9. I sit - Her usual style. Hence those expressions, "The chair, the seat of Rome: he sat so many years." As a queen - Over many kings, "mistress of all churches; the supreme; the infallible; the only spouse of Christ; out of which there is no salvation." And am no widow - But the spouse of Christ. And shall see no sorrow - From the death of my children, or any other calamity; for God himself will defend "the church."

8. Therefore - as both the natural and judicial consequence of this proud security Shall her plagues come - The death of her children, with an incapacity of bearing more. Sorrow - of every kind. And famine - In the room of luxurious plenty: the very things from which she imagined herself to be most safe. For strong is the Lord God who judgeth her - Against whom therefore all her strength, great as it is, will not avail.

10. Thou strong city - Rome was anciently termed by its inhabitants, Valentia, that is, strong. And the word Rome itself, in Greek, signifies strength. This name was given it by the Greek strangers.

12. Merchandise of gold, &c. - Almost all these are still in use at Rome, both in their idolatrous service, and in common life. Fine linen - The sort of it mentioned in the original is exceeding costly. Thyine wood - A sweet-smelling wood not unlike citron, used in adorning magnificent palaces. Vessels of most precious wood - Ebony, in particular, which is often mentioned with ivory: the one excelling in whiteness, the other in blackness; and both in uncommon smoothness.

13. Amomum - A shrub whose wood is a fine perfume. And beasts - Cows and oxen. And of chariots - a purely Latin word is here inserted in the Greek. This St. John undoubtedly used on purpose, in describing the luxury of Rome. And of bodies - A common term for slaves. And souls of men - For these also are continually bought and sold at Rome. And this of all others is the most gainful merchandise to the Roman traffickers.

14. *And the fruits* - From what was imported they proceed to the domestic delicates of Rome; none of which is in greater request there, than the particular sort which is here mentioned. The word properly signifies, pears, peaches, nectarines, and all of the apple and plum kinds. *And all things that are dainty* - To the taste. *And splendid* - To the sight; as clothes, buildings, furniture.

19. *And they cast dust on their heads* - As mourners. Most of the expressions here used in describing the downfall of Babylon are taken from Ezekiel's description of the downfall of Tyre, Ezek. xxvi, 1 - Ezek. xxviii, 19.

20. *Rejoice over her, thou heaven* - That is, all the inhabitants of it; and more especially, ye saints; and among the saints still more eminently, ye apostles and prophets.

21. *And a mighty angel took up a stone, and threw it into the sea* - By a like emblem Jeremiah fore-showed the fall of the Chaldean Babylon, Jer. li, 63, 64.

22. *And the voice of harpers* - Players on stringed instruments. *And musicians* - Skilful singers in particular. *And pipers* - Who played on flutes, chiefly on mournful, whereas trumpeters played on joyful, occasions. *Shall be heard no more in thee; and no artificer* - Arts of every kind, particularly music, sculpture, painting, and statuary, were there carried to their greatest height. *No, nor even the sound of a mill-stone shall be heard any more in thee* - Not only the arts that adorn life, but even those employments without which it cannot subsist, will cease from thee forever. All these expressions denote absolute and eternal desolation. *The voice of harpers* - Music was the entertainment of the rich and great; trade, the business of men of middle rank; preparing bread and the necessaries of life, the employment of the lowest people: marriages, in which lamps and songs were known ceremonies, are the means of peopling cities, as new births supply the place of those that die. The desolation of Rome is therefore described in such a manner, as to show that neither rich nor poor, neither persons of middle rank, nor those of the lowest condition, should be able to live there any more. Neither shall it be repeopled by new marriages, but remain desolate and uninhabited forever.

23. *For thy merchants were the great men of the earth* - A circumstance which was in itself indifferent, and yet led them into pride, luxury, and numberless other sins.

24. *And in her was found the blood of the prophets and saints* - The same angel speaks still, yet he does not say "in thee," but in her, now so sunk as not to hear these last words. *And of all that had been slain* - Even before she was built. See Matt. xxiii, 35. There is no city under the sun which has so clear a title to catholic blood-guiltiness as Rome. The guilt of the blood shed under the heathen emperors has not been removed under the Popes, but hugely multiplied. Nor is Rome accountable only for that which hath been shed in the city, but for that shed in all the earth. For at Rome under the Pope, as well as under the heathen emperors, were the bloody orders and edicts given: and wherever the blood of holy men was shed, there were the grand rejoicings for it. And what immense quantities of blood have been shed by her agents! Charles IX., of France, in his letter to Gregory XIII., boasts, that in and not long after the massacre of Paris, he had destroyed seventy thousand Hugonots. Some have computed, that, from the year 1518, to 1548, fifteen millions of Protestants have perished by the Inquisition. This may be overcharged; but certainly the number of them in those thirty years, as well as since, is almost incredible. To these we may add innumerable martyrs, in ancient, middle, and late ages, in Bohemia, Germany, Holland, France, England, Ireland, and many other parts of Europe, Afric, and Asia.

XIX

1. *I heard a loud voice of a great multitude* - Whose blood the great whore had shed. *Saying, Hallelujah* - This Hebrew word signifies, Praise ye Jah, or Him that is. God named himself to Moses, EHEIEH, that is, I will be, Exod. iii, 14; and at the same time, "Jehovah," that is, "He that is, and was, and is to come:" during the trumpet of the seventh angel, he is styled, "He that is and was," chap. xvi, 5; and not "He that is to come;" because his long-expected coming is under this trumpet actually present. At length he is styled, "Jah," "He that is;" the past together with the future being swallowed up in the present, the former things being no more mentioned, for the greatness of those that now are. This title is of all others the most peculiar to the everlasting God. *The salvation* - Is opposed to the destruction which the great whore had brought upon the earth. *His power and glory* - Appear from the judgment executed on her, and from the setting up his kingdom to endure through all ages.

2. *For true and righteous are his judgments* - Thus is the cry of the souls under the altar changed into a song of praise.

4. *And the four and twenty elders, and the four living creatures felt down* - The living creatures are nearer the throne than the elders. Accordingly they are mentioned before them, with the praise they render to God, chap. iv, 9, 10; v, 8, 14; inasmuch as there the praise moves from the center to the circumference. But here, when God's judgments are fulfilled, it moves back from the circumference to the center. Here, therefore, the four and twenty elders are named before the living creatures.

5. *And a voice came forth from the throne* - Probably from the four living creatures, saying, *Praise our God* - The occasion and matter of this song of praise follow immediately after, verses 6, &c.; God

was praised before, for his judgment of the great whore, verses 1-4. chap. xix, 1-4 Now for that which follows it: for that the Lord God, the Almighty, takes the kingdom to himself, and avenges himself on the rest of his enemies. Were all these inhabitants of heaven mistaken? If not, there is real, yea, and terrible anger in God.

6. And I heard the voice of a great multitude. So all his servants did praise him. The Almighty reigneth - More eminently and gloriously than ever before.

7. The marriage of the Lamb is come - Is near at hand, to be solemnized speedily. What this implies, none of "the spirits of just men," even in paradise, yet know. O what things are those which are yet behind! And what purity of heart should there be, to meditate upon them! And his wife hath made herself ready - Even upon earth; but in a far higher sense, in that world. After a time allowed for this, the new Jerusalem comes down, both made ready and adorned, chap. xxi, 2.

8. And it is given to her - By God. The bride is all holy men, the whole invisible church. To be arrayed in fine linen, white and clean - This is an emblem of the righteousness of the saints - Both of their justification and sanctification.

9. And he - The angel, saith to me, Write - St. John seems to have been so amazed at these glorious sights, that he needeth to be reminded of this. Happy are they who are invited to the marriage supper of the Lamb - Called to glory. And he saith - After a little pause.

10. And I fell before his feet to worship him - It seems, mistaking him for the angel of the covenant. But he saith, See thou do it not - In the original, it is only, See not, with a beautiful abruptness. To pray to or worship the highest creature is flat idolatry. I am thy fellowservant and of thy brethren that have the testimony of Jesus - I am now employed as your fellowservant, to testify of the Lord Jesus, by the same Spirit which inspired the prophets of old.

11. And I saw the heaven opened - This is a new and peculiar opening of it, in order to show the magnificent expedition of Christ and his attendants, against his great adversary. And behold a white horse - Many little regarded Christ, when he came meek, "riding upon an ass;" but what will they say, when he goes forth upon his white horse, with the sword of his mouth? White - Such as generals use in solemn triumph. And he that sitteth on him, called Faithful - In performing all his promises. And True - In executing all his threatenings. And in righteousness - With the utmost justice. He judgeth and maketh war - Often the sentence and execution go together.

12. And his eyes are a flame of fire - They were said to be as or like a flame of fire, before, chap. i, 14; an emblem of his omniscience. And upon his head are many diadems - For he is king of all nations. And he hath a name written, which none knoweth but himself - As God he is incomprehensible to every creature.

13. And he is clothed in a vesture dipped in blood - The blood of the enemies he hath already conquered. Isaiah lxiii, 1, &c.

15. And he shall rule them - Who are not slain by his sword. With a rod of iron - That is, if they will not submit to his golden scepter. And he treadeth the wine press of the wrath of God - That is, he executes his judgments on the ungodly. This ruler of the nations was born (or appeared as such) immediately after the seventh angel began to sound. He now appears, not as a child, but as a victorious warrior. The nations have long ago felt his "iron rod," partly while the heathen Romans, after their savage persecution of the Christians, themselves groaned under numberless plagues and calamities, by his righteous vengeance; partly, while other heathens have been broken in pieces by those who bore the Christian name. For although the cruelty, for example, of the Spaniards in America, was unrighteous and detestable, yet did God therein execute his righteous judgment on the unbelieving nations; but they shall experience his iron rod as they never did yet, and then will they all return to their rightful Lord.

16. And he hath on his vesture and on his thigh - That is, on the part of his vesture which is upon his thigh. A name written - It was usual of old, for great personages in the eastern countries, to have magnificent titles affixed to their garments.

17. Gather yourselves together to the great supper of God - As to a great feast, which the vengeance of God will soon provide; a strongly figurative expression, (taken from Ezek. xxxix, 17,) denoting the vastness of the ensuing slaughter.

19. And I saw the kings of the earth - The ten kings mentioned chap. xvii, 12; who had now drawn the other kings of the earth to them, whether Popish, Mahometan, or pagan. Gathered together to make war with him that sat upon the horse - All beings, good and evil, visible and invisible, will be concerned in this grand contest. See Zech. xiv, 1, &c.

20. The false prophet, who had wrought the miracles before him - And therefore shared in his punishment; these two ungodly men were cast alive - Without undergoing bodily death. Into the lake of fire - And that before the devil himself, chap. xx, 10. Here is the last of the beast. After several repeated strokes of omnipotence, he is gone alive into hell. There were two that went alive into heaven; perhaps there are two that go alive into hell. It may be, Enoch and Elijah entered at once into glory, without first waiting in paradise; the beast and the false prophet plunge at once into the extremest degree of torment, without being reserved in chains of darkness till the judgment of the great day. Surely, none but the

beast of Rome would have hardened himself thus against the God he pretended to adore, or refused to have repented under such dreadful, repeated visitations! Well is he styled a beast, from his carnal and vile affections; a wild beast, from his savage and cruel spirit! The rest were slain - A like difference is afterwards made between the devil, and Gog and Magog, chap. xx, 9, 10.

21. Here is a most magnificent description of the overthrow of the beast and his adherents. It has, in particular, one exquisite beauty; that, after exhibiting the two opposite armies, and all the apparatus for a battle, verses 11-19; chap. xix, 11-19 then follows immediately, verse 20, xix, 20 the account of the victory, without one word of an engagement or fighting. Here is the most exact propriety; for what struggle can there be between omnipotence, and the power of all the creation united against it! Every description must have fallen short of this admirable silence.

XX

1. And I saw an angel decending out of heaven - Coming down with a commission from God. Jesus Christ himself overthrew the beast: the proud dragon shall be bound by an angel; even as he and his angels were cast out of heaven by Michael and his angels. Having the key of the bottomless pit - Mentioned before, chap. ix, 1. And a great chain in his hand - The angel of the bottomless pit was shut up therein before the beginning of the first woe. But it is now first that Satan, after he had occasioned the third woe, is both chained and shut up.

2. And he laid hold on the dragon - With whom undoubtedly his angels were now cast into the bottomless pit, as well as finally "into everlasting fire," Matt. xxv, 41. And bound him a thousand years - That these thousand do not precede, or run parallel with, but wholly follow, the times of the beast, may manifestly appear,

1. From the series of the whole book, representing one continued chain of events.

2. From the circumstances which precede. The woman's bringing forth is followed by the casting of the dragon out of heaven to the earth. With this is connected the third woe, whereby the dragon through, and with, the beast, rages horribly. At the conclusion of the third woe the beast is overthrown and cast into "the lake of fire." At the same time the other grand enemy, the dragon, shall be bound and shut up.

3. These thousand years bring a new, full, and lasting immunity from all outward and inward evils, the authors of which are now removed, and an affluence of all blessings. But such time the church has never yet seen. Therefore it is still to come.

4. These thousand years are followed by the last times of the world, the letting loose of Satan, who gathers together Gog and Magog, and is thrown to the beast and false prophet "in the lake of fire." Now Satan's accusing the saints in heaven, his rage on earth, his imprisonment in the abyss, his seducing Gog and Magog, and being cast into the lake of fire, evidently succeed each other.

5. What occurs from chap. xx, 11 - chap. xxii, 5, manifestly follows the things related in the nineteenth chapter. The thousand years came between; whereas if they were past, neither the beginning nor the end of them would fall within this period. In a short time those who assert that they are now at hand will appear to have spoken the truth. Meantime let every man consider what kind of happiness he expects therein. The danger does not lie in maintaining that the thousand years are yet to come; but in interpreting them, whether past or to come, in a gross and carnal sense. The doctrine of the Son of God is a mystery. So is his cross; and so is his glory. In all these he is a sign that is spoken against. Happy they who believe and confess him in all!

3. And set a seal upon him - How far these expressions are to be taken literally, how far figuratively only, who can tell? That he might deceive the nations no more - One benefit only is here expressed, as resulting from the confinement of Satan. But how many and great blessings are implied! For the grand enemy being removed, the kingdom of God holds on its uninterrupted course among the nations; and the great mystery of God, so long foretold, is at length fulfilled; namely, when the beast is destroyed and Satan bound. This fulfilment approaches nearer and nearer; and contains things of the utmost importance, the knowledge of which becomes every day more distinct and easy. In the mean time it is highly necessary to guard against the present rage and subtilty of the devil. Quickly he will be bound: when he is loosed again, the martyrs will live and reign with Christ. Then follow his coming in glory, the new heaven, new earth, and new Jerusalem. The bottomless pit is properly the devil's prison; afterwards he is cast into the lake of fire. He can deceive the nations no more till the "thousand years," mentioned before, verse 2, chap. xx, 2 are fulfilled. Then he must be loosed - So does the mysterious wisdom of God permit. For a small time - Small comparatively: though upon the whole it cannot be very short, because the things to be transacted therein, verses 8, 9, chap. xx, 8, 9 must take up a considerable space. We are very shortly to expect, one after another, the calamities occasioned by the second beast, the harvest and the vintage, the pouring out of the phials, the judgment of Babylon, the last raging of the beast and his destruction, the imprisonment of Satan. How great things these! and how short the time! What is needful for us? Wisdom, patience, faithfulness, watchfulness. It is no time to

settle upon our lees. This is not, if it be rightly understood, an acceptable message to the wise, the mighty, the honourable, of this world. Yet that which is to be done, shall be done: there is no counsel against the Lord.

4. And I saw thrones - Such as are promised the apostles, Matt. xix, 28; Luke xxii, 30. And they - Namely, the saints, whom St. John saw at the same time, Dan. vii, 22, sat upon them; and Judgment was given to them. 1 Cor. vi, 2. Who, and how many, these are, is not said. But they are distinguished from the souls, or persons, mentioned immediately after; and from the saints already raised. And I saw the souls of those who had been beheaded - With the axe: so the original word signifies. One kind of death, which was particularly inflicted at Rome, is mentioned for all. For the testimony of Jesus, and for the word of God - The martyrs were sometimes killed for the word of God in general; sometimes particularly for the testimony of Jesus: the one, while they refused to worship idols; the other, while they confessed the name of Christ. And those who had not worshipped the wild beast, nor his image - These seem to be a company distinct from those who appeared, chap. xv, 2. Those overcame, probably, in such contests as these had not. Before the number of the beast was expired, the people were compelled to worship him, by the most dreadful violence. But when the beast "was not," they were only seduced into it by the craft of the false prophet. And they lived - Their souls and bodies being re-united. And reigned with Christ - Not on earth, but in heaven. The "reigning on earth" mentioned, chap. xi, 15, is quite different from this. A thousand years - It must be observed, that two distinct thousand years are mentioned throughout this whole passage. Each is mentioned thrice; the thousand wherein Satan is bound, verses 2, 3, 7; chap. xx, 2, 3, 7, the thousand wherein the saints shall reign, verses 4-6. chap. xx, 4-6 The former end before the end of the world; the latter reach to the general resurrection. So that the beginning and end of the former thousand is before the beginning and end of the latter. Therefore as in the second verse, chap. xx, 2 at the first mention of the former; so in the fourth verse, chap. xx, 2 at the first mention of the latter, it is only said, a thousand years; in the other places, "the thousand," verses 3, 5, 7, chap. xx, 3, 5, 7 that is, the thousand mentioned before. During the former, the promises concerning the flourishing state of the church, chap. x, 7, shall be fulfilled; during the latter, while the saints reign with Christ in heaven, men on earth will be careless and secure.

5. The rest of the dead lived not till the thousand years - Mentioned, verse 4. Were ended - The thousand years during which Satan is bound both begin and end much sooner. The small time, and the second thousand years, begin at the same point, immediately after the first thousand. But neither the beginning of the first nor of the second thousand will be known to the men upon earth, as both the imprisonment of Satan and his loosing are transacted in the invisible world. By observing these two distinct thousand years, many difficulties are avoided. There is room enough for the fulfilling of all the prophecies, and those which before seemed to clash are reconciled; particularly those which speak, on the one hand, of a most flourishing state of the church as yet to come; and, on the other, of the fatal security of men in the last days of the world.

6. They shall be priests of God and of Christ - Therefore Christ is God. And shall reign with him - With Christ, a thousand years.

7. And when the former thousand years are fulfilled, Satan shall be loosed out of his prison - At the same time that the first resurrection begins. There is a great resemblance between this passage and chap. xii, 12. At the casting out of the dragon, there was joy in heaven, but there was woe upon earth: so at the loosing of Satan, the saints begin to reign with Christ; but the nations on earth are deceived.

8. And shall go forth to deceive the nations in the four corners of the earth - (That is, in all the earth)-the more diligently, as he hath been so long restrained, and knoweth he hath but a small time. Gog and Magog - Magog, the second son of Japhet, is the father of the innumerable northern nations toward the east. The prince of these nations, of which the bulk of that army will consist, is termed Gog by Ezekiel also, Ezek. xxxviii, 2. Both Gog and Magog signify high or lifted up; a name well suiting both the prince and people. When that fierce leader of many nations shall appear, then will his own name be known. To gather them - Both Gog and his armies. Of Gog, little more is said, as being soon mingled with the rest in the common slaughter. The Revelation speaks of this the more briefly, because it had been so particularly described by Ezekiel. Whose number is as the sand of the sea - Immensely numerous: a proverbial expression.

9. And they went up on the breadth of the earth, or the land - Filling the whole breadth of it. And surrounded the camp of the saints - Perhaps the gentile church, dwelling round about Jerusalem. And the beloved city - So termed, likewise, Ecclesiasticus xxiv. 11.

10. And they - All these. Shall be tormented day and night - That is, without any intermission. Strictly speaking, there is only night there: no day, no sun, no hope!

11. And I saw - A representation of that great day of the Lord. A great white throne - How great, who can say? White with the glory of God, of him that sat upon it, - Jesus Christ. The apostle does not attempt to describe him here; only adds that circumstance, far above all description, From whose face the earth and the heaven fled away - Probably both the aerial and the starry heaven; which "shall pass away with a great noise." And there was found no place for them - But they were wholly dissolved, the

very "elements melting with fervent heat." It is not said, they were thrown into great commotions, but they fled entirely away; not, they started from their foundations, but they " fell into dissolution;" not, they removed to a distant place, but there was found no place for them; they ceased to exist; they were no more. And all this, not at the strict command of the Lord Jesus; not at his awful presence, or before his fiery indignation; but at the bare presence of his Majesty, sitting with severe but adorable dignity on his throne.

12. And I saw the dead, great and small - Of every age and condition. This includes, also, those who undergo a change equivalent to death, 1 Cor. xv, 51. And the books - Human Judges have their books written with pen and ink: how different is the nature of these books! Were opened - O how many hidden things will then come to light; and how many will have quite another appearance than they had before in the sight of men! With the book of God's omniscience, that of conscience will then exactly tally. The book of natural law, as well as of revealed, will then also be displayed. It is not said, The books will be read: the light of that day will make them visible to all. Then, particularly, shall every man know himself, and that with the last exactness This will be the first true, full, impartial, universal history. And another book - Wherein are enrolled all that are accepted through the Beloved; all who lived and died in the faith that worketh by love. Which is the book of life, was opened - What manner of expectation will then be, with regard to the issue of the whole! Mal. iii, 16, &c.

13. Death and hades gave up the dead that were in them - Death gave up all the bodies of men; and hades, the receptacle of separate souls, gave them up, to be re-united to their bodies.

14. And death and hades were cast into the lake of fire - That is, were abolished forever; for neither the righteous nor the wicked were to die any more: their souls and bodies were no more to be separated. Consequently, neither death nor hades could any more have a being.

XXI

1. And I saw - So it runs, chap. xix, 11, xx, 1, 4, 11, in a succession. All these several representations follow one another in order: so the vision reaches into eternity. A new heaven and a new earth - After the resurrection and general judgment. St. John is not now describing a flourishing state of the church, but a new and eternal state of all things. For the first heaven and the first earth - Not only the lowest part of heaven, not only the solar system, but the whole ethereal heaven, with all its host, whether of planets or fixed stars, Isai xxxiv, 4 Matt. xxiv, 29. All the former things will be done away, that all may become new, verses 4, 5, 2 Pet. iii, 10, 12. Are passed away - But in the fourth verse it is said, "are gone away." There the stronger word is used; for death, mourning, and sorrow go away all together: the former heaven and earth only pass away, giving place to the new heaven and the new earth.

2. And I saw the holy city - The new heaven, the new earth, and the new Jerusalem, are closely connected. This city is wholly new, belonging not to this world, not to the millennium, but to eternity. This appears from the series of the vision, the magnificence of the description, and the opposition of this city to the second death, chap. xx, 11, 12; xxi, 1, 2, 5, 8, 9; xxii, 5. Coming down - In the very act of descending.

3. They shall be his people, and God himself shall be with them, and be their God - So shall the covenant between God and his people be executed in the most glorious manner.

4. And death shall be no more - This is a full proof that this whole description belongs not to time, but eternity. Neither shall sorrow, or crying, or pain, be any more: for the former things are gone away - Under the former heaven, and upon the former earth, there was death and sorrow, crying and pain; all which occasioned many tears: but now pain and sorrow are fled away, and the saints have everlasting life and joy.

5. And he that sat upon the throne said - Not to St. John only. From the first mention of "him that sat upon the throne," chap. iv, 2, this is the first speech which is expressly ascribed to him. And he - The angel. Saith to me Write - As follows. These sayings are faithful and true - This includes all that went before. The apostle seems again to have ceased writing, being overcome with ecstasy at the voice of him that spake.

6. And he - That sat upon the throne. Said to me, It is done - All that the prophets had spoken; all that was spoken, chap. iv, 1. We read this expression twice in this prophecy: first, chap. xvi, 17, at the fulfilling of the wrath of God; and here, at the making all things new. I am the Alpha and the Omega, the beginning and the end - The latter explains the former: the Everlasting. I will give to him that thirsteth - The Lamb saith the same, chap. xxii, 17.

7. He that overcometh - Which is more than, "he that thirsteth." Shall inherit these things - Which I have made new. I will be his God, and he shall be my son - Both in the Hebrew and Greek language, in which the scriptures were written, what we translate shall and will are one and the same word. The only difference consists in an English translation, or in the want of knowledge in him that interprets

what he does not understand.

8. But the fearful and unbelieving - Who, through want of courage and faith, do not overcome. And abominable - That is, sodomites. And whoremongers, and sorcerers, and idolaters - These three sins generally went together; their part is in the lake.

9. And there came one of the seven angels that had the seven phials - Whereby room had been made for the kingdom of God. Saying, Come, I will show thee the bride - The same angel had before showed him Babylon, chap. xvii, 1, which is directly opposed to the new Jerusalem.

10. And he carried me away in the spirit - The same expression as before, chap. xvii, 3. And showed me the holy city Jerusalem - The old city is now forgotten, so that this is no longer termed the new, but absolutely Jerusalem. O how did St. John long to enter in! but the time was not yet come. Ezekiel also describes "the holy city," and what pertains thereto, xl.-xlviii. Ezek. xl, 1-Ezek. xlviii, 35 but a city quite different from the old Jerusalem, as it was either before or after the Babylonish captivity. The descriptions of the prophet and of the apostle agree in many particulars; but in many more they differ. Ezekiel expressly describes the temple, and the worship of God therein, closely alluding to the Levitical service. But St. John saw no temple, and describes the city far more large, glorious, and heavenly than the prophet. Yet that which he describes is the same city; but as it subsisted soon after the destruction of the beast. This being observed, both the prophecies agree together and one may explain the other.

11. Having the glory of God - For her light, verse 23, ver. 23, Isaiah xl, 1, 2, Zech. ii, 5. Her window - There was only one, which ran all round the city. The light did not come in from without through this for the glory of God is within the city. But it shines out from within to a great distance, verses 23, 24. chap. xxi, 23, 24

12. Twelve angels - Still waiting upon the heirs of salvation.

14. And the wall of the city had twelve foundations, and on them the names of the twelve apostles of the Lamb - Figuratively showing that the inhabitants of the city had built only on that faith which the apostles once delivered to the saints.

15. And he measured the city, twelve thousand furlongs - Not in circumference, but on each of the four sides. Jerusalem was thirtythree furlongs in circumference; Alexandria thirty in length, ten in breadth. Nineveh is reported to have been four hundred furlongs round; Babylon four hundred and eighty. But what inconsiderable villages were all these compared to the new Jerusalem! By this measure is understood the greatness of the city, with the exact order and just proportion of every part of it; to show, figuratively, that this city was prepared for a great number of inhabitants, how small soever the number of real Christians may sometimes appear to be; and that everything relating to the happiness of that state was prepared with the greatest order and exactness. The city is twelve thousand furlongs high; the wall, an hundred and forty-four reeds. This is exactly the same height, only expressed in a different manner. The twelve thousand furlongs, being spoken absolutely, without any explanation, are common, human furlongs: the hundred forty-four reeds are not of common human length, but of angelic, abundantly larger than human. It is said, the measure of a man that is, of an angel because St. John saw the measuring angel in an human shape. The reed therefore was as great as was the stature of that human form in which the angel appeared. In treating of all these things a deep reverence is necessary; and so is a measure of spiritual wisdom; that we may neither understand them too literally and grossly, nor go too far from the natural force of the words. The gold, the pearls, the precious stones, the walls, foundations, gates, are undoubtedly figurative expressions; seeing the city itself is in glory, and the inhabitants of it have spiritual bodies: yet these spiritual bodies are also real bodies, and the city is an abode distinct from its inhabitants, and proportioned to them who take up a finite and a determinate space. The measures, therefore, above mentioned are real and determinate.

18. And the building of the wall was jasper - That is, the wall was built of jasper. And the city - The houses, was of pure gold.

19. And the foundations were adorned with precious stones - That is, beautifully made of them. The precious stones on the high priest's breastplate of judgment were a proper emblem to express the happiness of God's church in his presence with them, and in the blessing of his protection. The like ornaments on the foundations of the walls of this city may express the perfect glory and happiness of all the inhabitants of it from the most glorious presence and protection of God. Each precious stone was not the ornament of the foundation, but the foundation itself. The colours of these are remarkably mixed. A jasper is of the colour of white marble, with a light shade of green and of red; a sapphire is of a sky-blue, speckled with gold; a chalcedony, or carbuncle, of the colour of red-hot iron; an emerald, of a grass green.

20. A sardonyx is red streaked with white; a sardius, of a deep red; a chrysolite, of a deep yellow; a beryl, sea-green; a topaz, pale yellow; a chrysoprase is greenish and transparent, with gold specks; a jacinth, of a red purple; an amethyst, violet purple.

22. The Lord God and the Lamb are the temple of it - He fills the new heaven and the new earth. He surrounds the city and sanctifies it, and all that are therein. He is "all in all."

23. The glory of God - Infinitely brighter than the shining of the sun.

24. And the nations - The whole verse is taken from Isaiah lx, 3. Shall walk by the light thereof - Which throws itself outward from the city far and near. And the kings of the earth - Those of them who have a part there. Bring their glory into it - Not their old glory, which is now abolished; but such as becomes the new earth, and receives an immense addition by their entrance into the city.

26. And they shall bring the glory of the nations into it - It seems, a select part of each nation; that is, all which can contribute to make this city honourable and glorious shall be found in it; as if all that was rich and precious throughout the world was brought into one city.

27. Common - That is. unholy. But those who are written in the Lamb's book of life - True, holy, persevering believers. This blessedness is enjoyed by those only; and, as such, they are registered among them who are to inherit eternal life.

XXII

1. And he showed me a river of the water of life - The ever fresh and fruitful effluence of the Holy Ghost. See Ezek. xlvii, 1-12; where also the trees are mentioned which "bear fruit every month," that is, perpetually. Proceeding out of the throne of God, and of the Lamb - "All that the Father hath," saith the Son of God, "is mine;" even the throne of his glory.

2. In the midst of the street - Here is the paradise of God, mentioned, chap. ii, 7. Is the tree of life - Not one tree only, but many. Every month - That is, in inexpressible abundance. The variety, likewise, as well as the abundance of the fruits of the Spirit, may be intimated thereby. And the leaves are for the healing of the nations - For the continuing their health, not the restoring it; for no sickness is there.

3. And there shall be no more curse - But pure life and blessing; every effect of the displeasure of God for sin being now totally removed. But the throne of God and the Lamb shall be in it - That is, the glorious presence and reign of God. And his servants - The highest honour in the universe. Shalt worship him - The noblest employment.

4. And shall see his face - Which was not granted to Moses. They shall have the nearest access to, and thence the highest resemblance of, him. This is the highest expression in the language of scripture to denote the most perfect happiness of the heavenly state, 1 John iii, 2. And his name shall be on their foreheads - Each of them shall be openly acknowledged as God's own property, and his glorious nature most visibly shine forth in them. And they shall reign - But who are the subjects of these kings? The other inhabitants of the new earth. For there must needs be an everlasting difference between those who when on earth excelled in virtue, and those comparatively slothful and unprofitable servants, who were just saved as by fire. The kingdom of God is taken by force; but the prize is worth all the labour. Whatever of high, lovely, or excellent is in all the monarchies of the earth is all together not a grain of dust, compared to the glory of the children of God. God "is not ashamed to be called their God, for whom he hath prepared this city." But who shall come up into his holy place? "They who keep his commandments," verse 14. ver. 14

5. And they shall reign forever and ever - What encouragement is this to the patience and faithfulness of the saints, that, whatever their sufferings are, they will work out for them "an eternal weight of glory!" Thus ends the doctrine of this Revelation, in the everlasting happiness of all the faithful. The mysterious ways of Providence are cleared up, and all things issue in an eternal Sabbath, an everlasting state of perfect peace and happiness, reserved for all who endure to the end.

6. And he said to me - Here begins the conclusion of the book, exactly agreeing with the introduction, (particularly verses 6, 7, 10, ver. 6, 7, 10 with chap. i, 1, 3,) chap. i, 1, 3 and giving light to the whole book, as this book does to the whole scripture. These sayings are faithful and true - All the things which you have heard and seen shall be faithfully accomplished in their order, and are infallibly true. The Lord, the God of the holy prophets - Who inspired and authorised them of old. Hath now sent me his angel, to show his servants - By thee. The things which must be done shortly - Which will begin to be performed immediately.

7. Behold, I come quickly - Saith our Lord himself, to accomplish these things. Happy is he that keepeth - Without adding or diminishing, verses 18, 19, ver. 18, 19 the words of this book.

8. I fell down to worship at the feet of the angel - The very same words which occur, chap. xix, 10. The reproof of the angel, likewise, See thou do it not, for I am thy fellowservant, is expressed in the very same terms as before. May it not be the very same incident which is here related again? Is not this far more probable, than that the apostle would commit a fault again, of which he had been so solemnly warned before?

9. See thou do it not - The expression in the original is short and elliptical, as is usual in showing vehement aversion.

10. And he saith to me - After a little pause. Seal not the sayings of this book - Conceal them not, like the things that are sealed up. The time is nigh - Wherein they shall begin to take place.

11. He that is unrighteous - As if he had said, The final judgment is at hand; after which the

condition of all mankind will admit of no change forever. Unrighteous - Unjustified. Filthy - Unsanctified, unholy.

12. I - Jesus Christ. Come quickly - To judge the world. And my reward is with me - The rewards which I assign both to the righteous and the wicked are given at my coming. To give to every man according as his work - His whole inward and outward behaviour shall be.

13. I am the Alpha and the Omega, the first and the last - Who exist from everlasting to everlasting. How clear, incontestable a proof, does our Lord here give of his divine glory!

14. Happy are they that do his commandments - His, who saith, I come - He speaks of himself. That they may have right - Through his gracious covenant. To the tree of life - To all the blessings signified by it. When Adam broke his commandment, he was driven from the tree of life. They who keep his commandments "shall eat thereof."

15. Without are dogs - The sentence in the original is abrupt, as expressing abhorrence. The gates are ever open; but not for dogs; fierce and rapacious men.

16. I Jesus have sent my angel to testify these things - Primarily. To you - The seven angels of the churches; then to those churches - and afterwards to all other churches in succeeding ages. I - as God. Am the root - And source of David's family and kingdom; as man, an descended from his loins. "I am the star out of Jacob," Num. xxiv, 17; like the bright morning star, who put an end to the night of ignorance, sin, and sorrow, and usher in an eternal day of light, purity, and joy.

17. The Spirit and the bride - The Spirit of adoption in the bride, in the heart of every true believer. Say - With earnest desire and expectation. Come - And accomplish all the words of this prophecy. And let him that thirsteth, come - Here they also who are farther off are invited. And whosoever will, let him take the water of life - He may partake of my spiritual and unspeakable blessings, as freely as he makes use of the most common refreshments; as freely as he drinks of the running stream.

18, 19. I testify to every one, &c. - From the fulness of his heart, the apostle utters this testimony, this weighty admonition, not only to the churches of Asia, but to all who should ever hear this book. He that adds, all the plagues shall be added to him; he that takes from it, all the blessings shall be taken from him; and, doubtless, this guilt is incurred by all those who lay hindrances in the way of the faithful, which prevent them from hearing their Lord's "I come," and answering, "Come, Lord Jesus." This may likewise be considered as an awful sanction, given to the whole New Testament; in like manner as Moses guarded the law, Deut. iv, 2, and Deut. xii, 32; and as God himself did, Mal. iv, 4, in closing the canon of the Old Testament.

20. He that testifieth these things - Even all that is contained in this book. Saith - For the encouragement of the church in all her afflictions. Yea - Answering the call of the Spirit and the bride. I come quickly - To destroy all her enemies, and establish her in a state of perfect and everlasting happiness. The apostle expresses his earnest desire and hope of this, by answering, Amen. Come, Lord Jesus!

21. The grace - The free love. Of the Lord Jesus - And all its fruits. Be with all - Who thus long for his appearing! It may be proper to subjoin here a short view of the whole contents of this book. In the year of the world, 3940. Jesus Christ is born, three years before the common computation. In that which is vulgarly called, the thirtieth year of our Lord, Jesus Christ dies; rises; ascends. Year (A.D.) Event As Described In Revelation Chapter/Verse 96 The Revelation is given; the coming of our Lord is declared to the seven churches in Asia, and their angels, Rev i., ii., iii. 97, 98 The seven seals are opened, and under the fifth the chronos is declared, iv.-vi. Seven trumpets are given to the seven angels, vii. viii. Century, 2d, 3d, 4th, 5th, the trumpet of the 1st, 2d, 3d, 4th angel, viii.

    510-589 The first woe, \...............

    589-634 The interval after the first woe} ix......

    634-840 The second woe, /...............

    800 The beginning of the non-chronos \............... many kings, } ix., x.

    840-947 The interval after the second woe, /...............

    847-1521 The twelve hundred and sixty days of the woman, after she hath brought forth the man child, C xii. 6

    947-1836 The third woe, 12

    1058-1836 The time, times, and half a time, and \.................. within that period, the beast, his forty}to xiii. 5 two months, his number 666, /...................

    1209 War with the saints: the end of the chronos, 7

    1614 An everlasting gospel promulged, xiv. 6

    1810 The end of the forty-two months of the beast; after which, and the pouring out of the phials, he is not, and Babylon reigns queen, xv., xvi.

    1832 The beast ascends from the bottomless pit, xvii., xviii.

    1836 The end of the non-chronos, and of the many kings; the fulfilling of the word, and of the mystery of God; the repentance of the survivors in the great city; the end of the "little time," and of the three times and a half; the destruction of the east; the imprisonment of Satan, xix., xx. Afterward The loosing of Satan for a small time; the beginning of the thousand years' reign of the saints; the end of the small time, xx. The end of the world; all things new, xx., xxii. The several ages, from the time of St. John's being in Patmos, down to the present time, may, according to the chief incidents mentioned in the Revelation, be distinguished thus: Age Event As Described In Revelation Chapter/Verse

II. The destruction of the Jews by Adrian, C viii. 7
III. The inroads of the barbarous nations, 8
IV. The Arian bitterness, 10
V. The end of the western empire. 12
VI. The Jews tormented in Persia, ix. 1
VII. The Saracen cavalry. 13
VIII. Many kings, x. 11
IX. The ruler of the nations born, xii. 5
X. The third woe, 12
XI. The ascent of the beast out of the pen, xiii. 1
XII. Power given to the beast, 5
XIII. War with the saints, 7
XIV. The middle of the third woe,
XV. The beast in the midst of his strength,
XVI. The Reformation; the woman better fed, 9
XVII. An everlasting gospel promulged, xiv. 6
XVIII. The worship of the beast and of his image, 9

O God, whatsoever stands or falls, stands or falls by thy judgment. Defend thy own truth! Have mercy on me and my readers! To thee be glory forever!

www.ingramcontent.com/pod-product-compliance
Lightning Source LLC
Chambersburg PA
CBHW020635230426
43665CB00008B/180